THE Intext SERIES IN FINANCE

E. Bruce Fredrikson
Syracuse University

FRONTIERS OF
INVESTMENT ANALYSIS

FRONTIERS OF
INVESTMENT ANALYSIS

revised edition

edited by

E. Bruce Fredrikson
Syracuse University

Scranton
Toronto
London

Intext Educational Publishers

14006

LIBRARY OF CONGRESS CATALOG CARD NUMBER 75–143625

ISBN 0–7002–2337–1

to Peggie

Preface

The content of this book reflects a single objective: the stimulation of students to creative thought, discussion, and research on the nature of investment values. The selections are unified principally by their usefulness to the serious student of economics and investments, whether an advanced undergraduate, a graduate student, or a member of the financial community. Consequently, the reader may expect only partial attainment of other measures of homogeneity. For example, the level of academic sophistication—statistical, mathematical, economical—required for full comprehension by the reader varies markedly. A useful investments text can hardly ignore significant theoretical and empirical advances, yet neither can it prove uniformly difficult to all but the most brilliant students. For this reason, when screening essays which employ advanced mathematical and statistical reasoning, the editor required also careful and straightforward verbal exposition of the argument.

Perhaps a brief description of the editor's standard of usefulness will assist the reader in understanding the scope and content of the present volume. Useful contributions to the field of investments are not limited to the fruits of quantitative analysis. And, conversely, several areas of the field have yet to emerge from a pretheoretic state. Indeed, perhaps the most fascinating aspect of investment management is the opportunity it presents for the exercise of individual judgment. Yet judgment in investments is a product of accumulated wisdom. A useful article, then, should increment the individual's accumulated wisdom by furthering his understanding of the factors that influence investment values. While many of the selections which meet this standard draw upon analytical tools to develop normative or positive theory, several others are simply outstanding qualitative contributions, valuable for the guidance and perspective they offer investment managers. Undergraduates may find several selections excessively arduous, while graduate students may complain of the absence of rigorous analytical method in others. In any event, the editor is confident that a majority of the selections will prove rewarding at either level of instruction. Needless to say, a great number of worthwhile and useful essays were omitted because of spatial and budgetary constraints.

One further refinement of the criterion of usefulness warrants mention. The analytical selections are indeed useful for the empirical and theoretical conclusions they present; but perhaps more significant is the intellectual stimulus provided by the exciting variety of original approaches to the resolution of problem areas in investments. Had the readings been limited to impervious theoretical models or definitive empirical results, a scanty volume would have emerged. Thus it is the tentative nature of the conclusions reached in the analytical contributions which recommends them to this study. Definitive guidelines for investment decisions are not to be expected, for there are few if any unalterable truths in the field of investments. This will become apparent to the student who traces the chronological development of theory in this text. Yet empirical and normative research holds the key to successively higher degrees of certainty. Students in search of appropriate subjects for research projects will be richly rewarded; and, hopefully, investment knowledge will be furthered by the labors of those students who rise to the many challenges they encounter here.

Perhaps nothing is more indicative of the widespread interest in developing an analytical structure for investment analysis than the gratifyingly favorable response which the first edition of this book received. I am most grateful to the many persons who have encouraged this revision and suggested pieces for inclusion. Finally, I thank the authors and publishers of the articles for generously allowing me permission to reprint.

E. Bruce Fredrikson

Syracuse, New York
February, 1971

Contents

FRONTIERS OF
INVESTMENT ANALYSIS

Introduction

Various authorities may differ in their appraisals of the current boundaries of the state of investments knowledge, but most agree that the frontiers have been advanced significantly during the past several decades. The articles reprinted here are generally representative of the pioneering works responsible for these advances.

The many-faceted nature of investment analysis precludes precise delineation of the frontiers to which we refer. In fact, it may be argued that the fields of progress are more properly seen as segments of a single great frontier which circumvents the area encompassed by investment analysis and management. This is the frontier of risk evaluation and control. Perhaps the most exciting recent development in investment analysis has been the explicit integration of considerations of risk and uncertainty into the framework of investment analysis, and those responsible for this development are well represented here. Yet broad expanses of conceptual and empirical territory remain unexplored or uncharted. This despite the great increase in relevant research since the first edition of this book appeared in 1965. A brief review of the problem areas will serve to acquaint the reader with the questions at issue in this volume.

Four general areas of concern are discernible in those essays which deal explicitly with risk. Although two or more aspects are often discussed concurrently, it is convenient to distinguish problems of definition, measurement, rational response, and observed response.

The term "risk" is employed in many contexts and is, therefore, subject to numerous definitions. It may be defined negatively as the absence of certainty, and thus may be, and often is, used synonymously with "uncertainty." Uncertainty is not, however, a workable concept because, strictly interpreted, it implies complete ignorance of possible outcomes; and one can question whether many actual investment decision problems are in fact encountered under conditions of complete ignorance. Additionally, and more important, uncertainty analysis is presently limited chiefly to the choice of one from a number of unsatisfactory, or at least often unsatisfying, game strategies.

1

In many contemporary economic studies "risk" as an environmental characteristic is distinguished not only from certainty but also from uncertainty. Under conditions of risk, the possible outcomes of each alternative course of action, as well as the likelihood of occurrence of each outcome, are known; or more correctly, each possible outcome is assigned a subjective probability of occurrence. The relevant parameters of the subjective probability distribution are generally derived from historical data; but the consistent assumption is that the relevant estimates of these parameters are those which appear most valid at the time the decision is made, whether or not they find statistical support in past data.

Unfortunately, the definition of risk as a condition involving a probability distribution with known or assumed parameters does not avoid the multiplicity of meanings intended or implied by those authors who employ the term "risk." One useful concept of risk, a concept which is certainly central to the objectives of most investors, is the chance that a desired or expected future wealth position will not be attained. That is, given an estimate of future wealth position (the mean of the probability distribution of possible values), risk is represented by that portion of the distribution which lies below the mean. Alternatively, if a minimum expected future wealth position is determined by compounding the value of assets presently held at the rate of return available upon nominally safe securities (such as insured savings deposits or government obligations), the risk associated with less secure investments (such as common stocks) can be defined as the chance that the yield eventually realized will be lower than that offered by safe media. It seems only fair to warn the reader that rather than these specific concepts of risk, characteristics of the distribution on both sides of the mean are generally considered.

Measurement is a second aspect of the risk problem, closely related to that of definition. For example, if risk is defined as unfavorable chance, it can be measured, in a simple, nonrepetitive situation, by the probability of failure. Or, if several possible outcomes are involved, we might assign subjective probabilities to each and feel satisfied that risk had been adequately measured. More likely, however, we would require a statistical measure of variability. A number of different measures are used by the authors represented here. For example, Hirshleifer [2] employs the standard deviation of the probability distribution of outcomes as a measure of "variability risk," but allows the possibility that other moments of the distribution may be equally useful or superior measures of risk. Whitbeck and Kisor [32] utilize the standard deviation of earnings around a trend line determined by regression analysis. Several empirical studies included within employ the standard deviation of past rates of return as an estimator of risk class. Markowitz [4] develops a normative theory of portfolio selection using variance of expected return as a measure of risk. In predicting risk premiums on corporate bonds, Fisher [14] employs a regression equation composed of four independent variables as measures of risk. In reporting frequency distributions of wealth ratios, Fisher and Lorie [16] discuss two relatively obscure measures of variability, Gini's mean difference and Gini's coefficient of concentration.

The remaining aspects of risk analysis, rational and observed response, represent normative and positive sides of the same question. Normatively, we are concerned with three queries: given an expected return from a specific investment situation, how should the individual evaluate the values of the moments (or related parameters) about the arithmetic mean; what is the best policy for long-run investment in securities characterized by risky returns; and, given rational investment decisions by participants in the securities markets, how will equilibrium prices of capital assets be determined? Positively, we wish to learn whether risk premiums arise in operative capital markets and, if so, of what relative magnitude. More generally, we wonder how investment decisions are affected by risk.

Consider first the normative aspect. Investment advisers typically counsel that different securities and security classes are characterized by varying degrees of risk, and that safety and profitability are ordinarily contradictory investment objectives. Most simply, we learn in Finance I that bonds are safer than stocks, but offer lower returns. These general observations offer little guidance, however, for the investment decision maker. Indeed, one suspects that the typical investor finds the dilemma frustrating if not irresolvable. Consider the case of a healthy, young or middle-aged individual investor interested, presumably, in maximizing his wealth at some undefined but distant date. When faced with the brokerage house query, "Are you primarily seeking safety of principal or capital appreciation?" he finds neither alternative completely satisfactory. He would, in fact, like to be offered investments characterized by both attributes.

One may question the relevance of the articles included here to this typical investor's problem, for none resolves what we have termed the investor's dilemma. Aggregately, however, they establish a framework of reasoning within which logical and consistent responses to individual and institutional problems are attainable. They alert the student to the possibility of a rational, analytical approach to risky decisions and to a scheme for *ex post* evaluation of performance.

If we begin with the generally (but not universally) accepted premise that an investor who wishes to earn a return above the level prevailing for "riskless" investments must accept some degree of risk, it is apparent that an objective criterion for risk preference is necessary. This is the first part of the normative aspect. The first two articles are directed toward the question of rational response to risk. The Friedman and Savage essay [1] is nominally positive, since it is presented as an empirical test based upon the authors' observations of individual reaction to choices involving risk. It has, however, strong normative undertones and is a classic illustration of the application of utility theory to choices between risky alternatives.

Hirshleifer [2] employs indifference curves representing individual risk preferences in building a framework for analysis. He proposes that certain future income be measured against the expected value of expected (uncertain) future income. The decision criteria advanced for risky situations is maximization of certainty-equivalent value, analogous to maximization of present value under certainty conditions. Hirshleifer's assumption of perfectly-correlated investment returns prevents the intrusion of the law of large numbers. Next Robichek [3] considers the broad question of risk and the value of securities. His essay serves as an introduction to the important section on portfolio selection and capital theory, probably the most challenging and exciting section of the text.

In Section B of Part I the focus shifts from a conceptual framework for risk analysis to the effect of diversification on the riskiness of portfolio returns. Diversification is certainly not a new discovery; indeed, it is the standard answer provided by stockbrokers to prospective investors made hesitant by the prospect of loss of principal. By purchasing a number of stocks representing different industry groups the investor reduces the chance of a large loss in two ways: adverse business and market conditions are bound to affect different industries in varying degrees, and a loss on any one security will represent only a small percentage of the total portfolio value. Despite its general acceptance, diversification as an investment principle was long limited in usefulness by the absence of a theoretical framework within which a given investment objective could be consistently optimized.

The pioneering essay by Markowitz [4] establishes the theoretical foundation for analytical approaches to portfolio selection. Beginning with the assumption that the investor does, or should, consider high expected returns desirable and high variance of expected returns undesirable, Markowitz provides a format for maximizing expected return (or minimizing variance) given an acceptable degree of variance (or a desired level of expected return). Markowitz's model is justified by the covariance of investment returns; a significant implication is that the suitability of a particular security for a particular portfolio can only be determined with reference to the other securities to be held. A security with a high variance of returns may in fact reduce the variance of the overall portfolio.

Sharpe [5] extends Markowitz's work on portfolio analysis. After summarizing the earlier work, Sharpe develops the concept of a diagonal model, which assumes that the returns from individual securities are related through common relationships with an underlying factor. The task of applying practically the portfolio selection technique is greatly simplified. Fama [6] generalizes upon the Markowitz-Sharpe diagonal model. He develops conditions under which diversification reduces dispersion of the distribution of portfolio returns, even if the variance of the distribution is infinite. Fama's piece also links the portfolio theory area with the speculative prices discussion in Part V.

Sharpe's second contribution [7] is considered a major theoretical step toward the construction of a market equilibrium theory for pricing capital assets under conditions of risk. It builds upon the earlier studies of optimal individual investment behavior and examines their implications for capital market equilibrium and asset prices. Sharpe's paper was written without knowledge of a similar model being developed by Lintner.[1] Fama [8] discusses both papers and shows that both models lead to the same conclusion regarding the risk of an asset, and the relationship between risk and rate of return.

Financial management and investment finance are closely related, perhaps indistinguishable, as Mossin [9] indicates. Here, by modifying an earlier extension of Sharpe's model, he indicates its implications for the analysis of optimal investment and financing decisions by the firm.

Lifetime planning of consumption and investment decisions is the focus of Professor Paul Samuelson [10]. A prime conclusion is that the popular concept of businessman's risk is invalid; that is, investing for many periods does not by itself allow extra risk tolerance beyond that acceptable at later stages of life.

Selections [11] and [12] are concerned with the evaluation of investment performance. Jensen's [11] is the more general paper, presenting a method for determining both efficiency and performance of portfolios of risky assets. Jensen provides a review of the theory of rational choice under uncertainty, the normative theory of portfolio selection, and the pricing of capital assets under uncertainty. Unfortunately, space did not permit the reprinting of Jensen's empirical results; for these, the reader is referred to the original source. Treynor's approach [12] to the same problem is similar but less general; it offers the opportunity of a graphical technique for appraising investment performance. Both Jensen's and Treynor's methods allow specific integration of investment risk in the appraisal of performance. In the final article in this section, Renshaw [13] provides a simplified restatement of basic portfolio theory and describes methods for constructing reasonably efficient portfolios with relatively little effort. Renshaw also considers the question of selecting an optimal point along an efficient risk-return frontier.

The underlying assumption of these approaches to risky investment

[1] John Lintner, "Security Prices, Risk, and Maximal Gains from Diversification," *Journal of Finance* (December, 1965), pp. 587–615.

decisions is in accord with the traditional feeling of the investment community that risk premiums should exist. The greater the risk, the greater should be the expected return. Implicit, and often explicit, in the normative models is the positive assumption that risk premiums do indeed arise in financial markets. By risk premiums, we mean the difference between the rate of return available on riskless investments and that expected to be realized on securities involving higher orders of risk.[2] The expectational yield on this latter class will ordinarily be lower than the nominal yield because of the losses anticipated. Thus the positive question is whether premiums over and above the amount required to compensate for anticipated losses arise in capital markets; that is, premiums for accepting variability of return.

Among the major obstacles to resolution is the measurement of investor expectations. As the Malkiel [20] essay makes clear, it is difficult to gauge or assess expectations even when conditions approach the ideal as, for example, in the corporate bond market where returns are limited on the upside and a plethora of data regarding the current and historical structure of rates is readily available.

One convenient approach is simply to measure realized yields (*ex post*) on various risk classes of securities and assume that investors exhibited perfect foresight. If realized yields converge, risk premiums are nonexistent; if they diverge, risk premiums of known magnitude exist. This is the approach taken by several of our authors.

Section C of Part I includes five of the many empirical studies concerned with risk and rate of return. Fisher [14] finds that risk premiums in corporate bond yields vary according to coefficient of variation in earnings, period of solvency, equity/debt ratio, and market value of outstanding, publicly-traded bonds; and that the relationships are generally stable over time. Data computed by Luigi Tambini and included here indicate these conclusions to be valid for more recent benchmark years than those reported in the original article. Risk premiums are also the focus of Soldofsky and Miller [15]. They use *ex post* realized yields to develop risk-premium curves for government and corporate bonds and preferred and common stocks for the period 1950–66. The curves represent the trade off between return, as measured by the geometric mean of the annual rates of return and risk, as measured by the standard deviations of these annual rates.

Articles [16] and [17] are both concerned with variability of returns on investments in common stocks. Article [16] presents the abridged results of three studies of variability of returns on investments in common

---

[2] A number of authors represented here, particularly Fisher [6], use the term "risk premium" in the more conventional way; that is, in reference to the differential between the pure rate of interest and the current market yield.

stocks, for periods of as long as 40 years. These studies, carried out by Professors Fisher & Lorie at the Center for Research in Security Prices at the University of Chicago, provide detailed information on frequency distributions of returns, and also provide some guidelines as to the efficiency of diversification in reducing variability.

Pratt's paper [17], published here for the first time, explores the relationship between *ex post* variability of returns and subsequent levels of rate of return, for the period 1926–60. He finds that, by accepting stocks characterized by relatively high degrees of variability (but not the highest variability) in the past, a portfolio manager would have been able to increase his subsequent realized returns.

The final empirical study in this section, by Latané and Young [18], also employs *ex post* returns to evaluate investment strategies. The authors test alternate rules for building portfolios by using past holding-period returns to represent probability beliefs of investors. Their findings provide empirical verification for the maxim that diversification pays and point to the advantages of leverage in increasing annual return and terminal wealth.

II. STOCK PRICE MOVEMENTS

Few phenomena are more obviously characterized by risk than speculative markets, among which our particular concern is with the market for common stocks. Along the frontier representing the nature of stock price fluctuations, recent investigations are responsible for exciting and significant advances. Speculators have long studied recorded price movements in search of clues to future movements, and the speculative activities of a substantial number of professionals are apparently guided by such technical methods as point-and-figure charting and the Dow theory. Until recently, however, academicians remained generally aloof to market techniques and the possibility of "beating the market" on other than fundamental grounds. Consequently, with the exception of a pioneering and comprehensive study by the French mathematician Bachelier in 1900, and several publications by Alfred Cowles during the thirties, empirical investigations into the nature of stock price fluctuations remained the exclusive province of the speculator until the mid-1950's. During the past two decades, however, the statistical and mathematical tools of modern time series analysis have been applied to stock price series with sustained vigor.

The arguments and investigations center upon what is generally termed the random-walk hypothesis. Briefly, the theory postulates that, since all information bearing upon security values is reflected in the current price and the appearance of new information or revised expectations is a matter of chance, successive price changes must be statistically independent. Consequently, flipping a coin or spinning a wheel to represent the stochastic process implied by independence of successive price changes will prove at least as effective a forecasting tool as the analysis of historical price changes. By formulating a successful nonrandom model based upon recorded price changes, or by finding evidence of dependence between successive changes in a time series, it is possible, as Cootner [38] has done, to seriously question the positive validity of the random-walk theory.

Smidt [37] also questions the theory, by deduction rather than by empirical evidence. He concentrates on evaluation of kinds of behavior likely to produce systematic tendencies in sequences of price changes. Included are demand for liquidity, lags in response to new information, and inappropriate investor response to new information. In contrast, Godfrey, Granger, and Morgenstern [39], after applying spectral analysis to weekly, daily, and individual-transaction data, conclude that the random-walk model provides a good explanation of the valuation of stock market prices.

The random-walk controversy is not a shallow one. It touches upon much of what Wall Street holds sacred. If, indeed, stock prices follow a random walk, there is no market strategy which will make money in the long run. (It should be noted that most researchers take account of an upward drift in stock prices, allowing thereby for the long-run profitability of common stock investments.) If sufficient dependence of successive changes does exist, a profitable strategy is possible. Yet as Cootner indicates, the market imperfections are so slight that commission costs encountered in repeated purchases and sales are likely to eliminate any gross profits.

The literature, both theoretical and empirical, relating to the random-walk hypothesis is far too extensive to be treated comprehensively here. Fortunately, Cootner has recently compiled all significant studies available by mid-1963 within a single volume.[3] In addition to the contributions cited, two additional studies touch upon the issues. Clarkson [40] provides keen insight into the market-making functions of securities brokers and analyzes the relationship between brokers and traders. He thus provides a behavioral framework for evaluating price changes in the securities markets. The study by Cowles [41] analyzes the effectiveness and foresight of a number of forecasting services. Because it finds little or no evidence of predictive ability on the part of professional services, it may, by implication, be counted as sustaining the random-walk theory, which denies the possibility of consistently successful predictions. (The

[3] Paul H. Cootner, ed., *The Random Character of Stock Market Prices* (Cambridge, Mass.: M.I.T. Press, 1964).

experience of the one consistently successful forecasting service, which based its predictions on the pattern of sequences and reversals, is not directly relevant here because the theory was based upon the assumption of cycles of several years duration, and no attempt was made to anticipate cyclical turning points.)

The selections concerned explicitly with risk analysis are largely accounted for. Yet, in a larger sense, as mentioned previously, risk considerations arise in practically every selection. The reason is elementary: were it not for the uncertainty of the economic environment, few problems would remain for investment analysis. Yet the eager student need not worry. Unlike its terrestrial analogue, the uncertainty frontier will not soon, if ever, disappear.

part One

RISK AND INVESTMENT ANALYSIS

*Milton Friedman**
Leonard J. Savage†

1. The Utility Analysis of Choices Involving Risk[1]

Reprinted from **The Journal of Political Economy,** Vol. LVI, No. 4 (August, 1948), pp. 279–304, by permission of the University of Chicago Press. Copyright, 1948, by the University of Chicago.

I. THE PROBLEM AND ITS BACKGROUND

The purpose of this paper is to suggest that an important class of reactions of individuals to risk can be rationalized by a rather simple extension of orthodox utility analysis.

Individuals frequently must, or can, choose among alternatives that differ, among other things, in the degree of risk to which the individual will be subject. The clearest examples are provided by insurance and gambling. An individual who buys fire insurance on a house he owns is accepting the certain loss of a small sum (the insurance premium) in preference to the combination of a small chance of a much larger loss (the value of the house) and a large chance of no loss. That is, he is choosing certainty in preference to uncertainty. An individual who buys a lottery ticket is subjecting himself to a large chance of losing a small amount (the price of the lottery ticket) plus a small chance of winning a large amount (a prize) in preference to avoiding both risks. He is choosing uncertainty in preference to certainty.

This choice among different degrees of risk so prominent in insurance and gambling, is clearly present and important in a much broader range of economic choices. Occupations differ greatly in the variability of the income they promise: in some, for example, civil service employment, the prospective income is rather clearly defined and is almost certain to be within rather narrow limits; in others, for example, salaried employment as an accountant, there is somewhat more variability yet almost no chance

---

* Professor of Economics, University of Chicago.
† Professor of Statistics, Yale University.
[1] The fundamental ideas of this paper were worked out jointly by the two authors. The paper was written primarily by the senior author.

of either an extremely high or an extremely low income; in still others, for example, motion-picture acting, there is extreme variability, with a small chance of an extremely high income and a larger chance of an extremely low income. Securities vary similarly, from government bonds and industrial "blue chips" to "blue-sky" common stocks; and so do business enterprises or lines of business activity. Whether or not they realize it and whether or not they take explicit account of the varying degree of risk involved, individuals choosing among occupations, securities, or lines of business activity are making choices analogous to those that they make when they decide whether to buy insurance or to gamble. Is there any consistency among the choices of this kind that individuals make? Do they neglect the element of risk? Or does it play a central role? If so, what is that role?

These problems have, of course, been considered by economic theorists, particularly in their discussions of earnings in different occupations and of profits in different lines of business.[2] Their treatment of these problems has, however, never been integrated with their explanation of choices among riskless alternatives. Choices among riskless alternatives are explained in terms of maximization of utility: individuals are supposed to choose as they would if they attributed some common quantitative characteristic—designated utility—to various goods and then selected the combination of goods that yielded the largest total amount of this common characteristic. Choices among alternatives involving different degrees of risk, for example, among different occupations, are explained in utterly different terms—by ignorance of the odds or by the fact that "young men of an adventurous disposition are more attracted by the prospects of a great success than they are deterred by the fear of failure," by "the overweening conceit which the greater part of men have of their own abilities," by "their absurd presumption in their own good fortune," or by some similar *deus ex machina*.[3]

The rejection of utility maximization as an explanation of choices among different degrees of risk was a direct consequence of the belief in diminishing marginal utility. If the marginal utility of money diminishes, an individual seeking to maximize utility will never participate in a "fair" game of chance, for example, a game in which he has an equal chance of winning or losing a dollar. The gain in utility from winning a dollar will be less than the loss in utility from losing a dollar, so that the expected utility from participation in the game is negative. Diminishing marginal

[2] E.g., see Adam Smith, *The Wealth of Nations*, Book I, Ch. x (Modern Library reprint of Cannan ed.), pp. 106–11; Alfred Marshall, *Principles of Economics*, 8th ed. (London, England: Macmillan & Co., Ltd., 1920), pp. 398–400, 554–55, 613.

[3] Marshall, *op cit.*, p. 554 (first quotation); Smith, *op cit.*, p. 107 (last two quotations).

utility plus maximization of expected utility would thus imply that individuals would always have to be paid to induce them to bear risk.[4] But this implication is clearly contradicted by actual behavior. People not only engage in fair games of chance, they engage freely and often eagerly in such unfair games as lotteries. Not only do risky occupations and risky investments not always yield a higher average return than relatively safe occupations or investments, they frequently yield a much lower average return.

Marshall resolved this contradiction by rejecting utility maximization as an explanation of choices involving risk. He need not have done so, since he did not need diminishing marginal utility—or, indeed, any quantitative concept of utility—for the analysis of riskless choices. The shift from the kind of utility analysis employed by Marshall to the indifference-curve analysis of F. Y. Edgeworth, Irving Fisher, and Vilfredo Pareto revealed that to rationalize riskless choices, it is sufficient to suppose that individuals can rank baskets of goods by total utility. It is unnecessary to suppose that they can compare differences between utilities. But diminishing, or increasing, marginal utility implies a comparison of differences between utilities and hence is an entirely gratuitous assumption in interpreting riskless choices.

The idea that choices among alternatives involving risk can be explained by the maximization of expected utility is ancient, dating back at least to D. Bernoulli's celebrated analysis of the St. Petersburg paradox.[5]

---

[4] See Marshall, op. cit., p. 135 n.; Mathematical Appendix, n. ix (p. 843). "Gambling involves an economic loss, even when conducted on perfectly fair and even terms.... A theoretically fair insurance against risks is always an economic gain" (p. 135). "The argument that fair gambling is an economic blunder...requires no further assumption than that, firstly the pleasures of gambling may be neglected; and, secondly $\phi''(x)$ is negative for all values of x, where $\phi(x)$ is the pleasure derived from wealth equal to x.... It is true that this loss of probable happiness need not be greater than the pleasure derived from the excitement of gambling, and we are then thrown back upon the induction that pleasures of gambling are in Bentham's phrase 'impure'; since experience shows that they are likely to engender a restless, feverish character, unsuited for steady work as well as for the higher and more solid pleasures of life" (p. 843).

[5] See Daniel Bernoulli, Versuch einer neuen Theorie der Wertbestimmung von Glücksfällen (Leipzig, 1896), translated by A. Pringsheim from "Specimen theoriae novae de mensura sortis," Commentarii academiae scientiarum imperialis Petropolitanae, Vol. V, for the years 1730 and 1731, published in 1738.

In an interesting note appended to his paper Bernoulli points out that Cramer [presumably Gabriel Cramer (1704–52)], a famous mathematician of the time, had anticipated some of his own views by a few years. The passages that he quotes from a letter in French by Cramer contain what, to us, is the truly essential point in Bernoulli's paper, namely, the idea of using the mathematical expectation of utility (the "moral expectation") instead of the mathematical expection of income to compare alternatives involving risk. Cramer has not in general been attributed this much credit, apparently because the essential point in Bernoulli's paper has been taken to be the suggestion that the logarithm of income is an appropriate utility function.

It has been repeatedly referred to since then but almost invariably rejected as the correct explanation—commonly because the prevailing belief in diminishing marginal utility made it appear that the existence of gambling could not be so explained. Even since the widespread recognition that the assumption of diminishing marginal utility is unnecessary to explain riskless choices, writers have continued to reject maximization of expected utility as "unrealistic."[6] This rejection of maximization of expected utility has been challenged by John Von Neumann and Oskar Morgenstern in their recent book, *Theory of Games and Economic Behavior.*[7] They argue that "under the conditions on which the indifference curve analysis is based very little extra effort is needed to reach a numerical utility," the expected value of which is maximized in choosing among alternatives involving risk.[8] The present paper is based on their treatment but has been made self-contained by the paraphrasing of essential parts of their argument.

If an individual shows by his market behavior that he prefers A to B and B to C, it is traditional to rationalize this behavior by supposing that he attaches more utility to A than to B and more utility to B than to C. All utility functions that give the same ranking to possible alternatives will provide equally good rationalizations of such choices, and it will make no difference which particular one is used. If, in addition, the individual should show by his market behavior that he prefers a 50-50 chance of A or C to the certainty of B, it seems natural to rationalize this behavior by supposing that the *difference* between the utilities he attaches to A and B is greater than the *difference* between the utilities he attaches to B and C, so that the *expected* utility of the preferred combination is greater than

---

[6] "It has been the assumption in the classical literature on this subject that the individual in question will always try to maximize the mathematical expectation of his gain or utility. . . . This may appear plausible, but it is certainly not an assumption which must hold true in all cases. It has been pointed out that the individual may also be interested in, and influenced by, the range or the standard deviation of the different possible utilities derived or some other measure of dispersion. It appears pretty evident from the behavior of people in lotteries or football pools that they are not a little influenced by the skewness of the probability distribution" [Gerhard Tintner, "A Contribution to the Non-Static Theory of Choice," *Quarterly Journal of Economics*, Vol. LVI (February, 1942), p. 278].

"It would be definitely unrealistic. . .to confine ourselves to the mathematical expectation only, which is the usual but not justifiable practice of the traditional calculus of 'moral probabilities' " [J. Marschak, "Money and the Theory of Assets," *Econometrica*, Vol. VI (1938), p. 320].

Tintner's inference, apparently also shared by Marschak, that the facts he cites are necessarily inconsistent with maximization of expected utility is erroneous (see Secs. III and IV below). He is led to consider a formally more general solution because of his failure to appreciate the real generality of the kinds of behavior explicable by the maximization of expected utility.

[7] Princeton University Press, 1st ed., 1944; 2d ed., 1947; pp. 15–31 (both eds.), pp. 617–32 (2d ed. only); succeeding references are to 2d ed.

[8] *Ibid.*, p. 17.

the utility of B. The class of utility functions, if there be any, that can provide the same ranking of alternatives that involve risk is much more restricted than the class that can provide the same ranking of alternatives that are certain. It consists of utility functions that differ only in origin and unit of measure (i.e., the utility functions in the class are linear functions of one another).[9] Thus, in effect, the ordinal properties of utility functions can be used to rationalize riskless choices, the numerical properties to rationalize choices involving risk.

It does not, of course, follow that there will exist a utility function that will rationalize in this way the reactions of individuals to risk. It may be that individuals behave inconsistently—sometimes choosing a 50-50 chance of A or C instead of B and sometimes the reverse; or sometimes choosing A instead of B, B instead of C, and C instead of A—or that in some other way their behavior is different from what it would be if they were seeking rationally to maximize expected utility in accordance with a given utility function. Or it may be that some types of reactions to risk can be rationalized in this way while others cannot. Whether a numerical utility function will in fact serve to rationalize any particular class of reactions to risk is an empirical question to be tested; there is no obvious contradiction such as was once thought to exist.

This paper attempts to provide a crude empirical test by bringing together a few broad observations about the behavior of individuals in choosing among alternatives involving risk (Section II) and investigating whether these observations are consistent with the hypothesis revived by Von Neumann and Morgenstern (Sections III and IV). It turns out that these empirical observations are entirely consistent with the hypothesis if a rather special shape is given to the total utility curve of money (Section IV). This special shape, which can be given a tolerably satisfactory interpretation (Section V), not only brings under the aegis of rational utility maximization much behavior that is ordinarily explained in other terms but also has implications about observable behavior not used in deriving it (Section VI). Further empirical work should make it possible to determine whether or not these implications conform to reality.

It is a testimony to the strength of the belief in diminishing marginal utility that it has taken so long for the possibility of interpreting gambling and similar phenomena as a contradiction of universal diminishing marginal utility, rather than of utility maximization, to be recognized. The initial mistake must have been at least partly a product of a strong introspective belief in diminishing marginal utility: a dollar must mean less to a rich man than to a poor man; see how much more a man will spend when he is rich than when he is poor to avoid any given amount of pain or discom-

[9] *Ibid.*, pp. 15–31, esp. p. 25.

fort.[10] Some of the comments that have been published by competent economists on the utility analysis of Von Neumann and Morgenstern are even more remarkable testimony to the hold that diminishing marginal utility has on economists. Vickrey remarks: "There is abundant evidence that individual decisions in situations involving risk are not always made in ways that are compatible with the assumption that the decisions are made rationally with a view to maximizing the mathematical expectation of a utility function. The purchase of tickets in lotteries, sweepstakes, and 'numbers' pools would imply, on such a basis, that the marginal utility of money is an increasing rather than a decreasing function of income. Such a conclusion is obviously unacceptable as a guide to social policy."[11] Kaysen remarks, "Unfortunately, these postulates [underlying the Von Neumann and Morgenstern discussion of utility measurement] involve an assumption about economic behavior which is contrary to experience. . . . That this assumption is contradicted by experience can easily be shown by hundreds of examples [including] the participation of individuals in lotteries in which their mathematical expectation of gain (utility) is negative."[12]

II. OBSERVABLE BEHAVIOR TO BE RATIONALIZED

The economic phenomena to which the hypothesis revived by Von Neumann and Morgenstern is relevant can be divided into, first, the phenomena ordinarily regarded as gambling and insurance; second, other economic phenomena involving risk. The latter are clearly the more important, and the ultimate significance of the hypothesis will depend primarily on the contribution it makes to an understanding of them. At the same time, the influence of risk is revealed most markedly in gambling and insurance, so that these phenomena have a significance for testing and elaborating the hypothesis out of proportion to their importance in actual economic behavior.

At the outset it should be confessed that we have conducted no exten-

---

[10] This elemental argument seems so clearly to justify diminishing marginal utility that it may be desirable even now to state explicitly how this phenomenon can be rationalized equally well on the assumption of increasing marginal utility of money. It is only necessary to suppose that the avoidance of pain and the other goods that can be bought with money are related goods and that, while the marginal utility of money increases as the amount of money increases, the marginal utility of avoiding pain increases even faster.

[11] William Vickrey, "Measuring Marginal Utility by Reactions to Risk," *Econometrica*, Vol. XIII (1945), pp. 319–33. The quotation is from pp. 327 and 328. "The purchase of tickets in lotteries, sweepstakes, and 'numbers' pools" does not imply that marginal utility of money increases with income everywhere (See Sec. IV below). Moreover, it is entirely unnecessary to identify the quantity that individuals are to be interpreted as maximizing with a quantity that should be given special importance in public policy.

[12] C. Kaysen, "A Revolution in Economic Theory?" *Review of Economic Studies*, Vol. XIV, No. 35 (1946–47), pp. 1–15; quotation is from p. 13.

sive empirical investigation of either class of phenomena. For the present, we are content to use what is already available in the literature, or obvious from casual observation, to provide a first test of the hypothesis and to impose significant substantive restrictions on it.

The major economic decisions of an individual in which risk plays an important role concern the employment of the resources he controls: what occupation to follow, what entrepreneurial activity to engage in, how to invest (nonhuman) capital. Alternative possible uses of resources can be classified into three broad groups according to the degree of risk involved: (a) those involving little or no risk about the money return to be received—occupations like schoolteaching, other civil service employment, clerical work; business undertakings of a standard, predictable type like many public utilities; securities like government bonds, high-grade industrial bonds; some real property, particularly owner-occupied housing; (b) those involving a moderate degree of risk but unlikely to lead to either extreme gains or extreme losses—occupations like dentistry, accountancy, some kinds of managerial work; business undertakings of fairly standard kinds in which, however, there is sufficient competition to make the outcome fairly uncertain; securities like lower-grade bonds, preferred stocks, higher-grade common stocks; (c) those involving much risk, with some possibility of extremely large gains and some of extremely large losses—occupations involving physical risks, like piloting aircraft, automobile racing, or professions like medicine and law; business undertakings in untried fields; securities like highly speculative stocks; some types of real property.

The most significant generalization in the literature about choices among these three uses of resources is that, other things the same, uses a or c tend in general to be preferred to use b; that is, people must in general be paid a premium to induce them to undertake moderate risks instead of subjecting themselves to either small or large risks. Thus Marshall says:

> There are many people of a sober steady-going temper, who like to know what is before them, and who would far rather have an appointment which offered a certain income of say £400 a year than one which was not unlikely to yield £600, but had an equal chance of affording only £200. Uncertainty, therefore, which does not appeal to great ambitions and lofty aspirations, has special attractions for very few; while it acts as a deterrent to many of those who are making their choice of a career. And as a rule the certainty of moderate success attracts more than an expectation of an uncertain success that has an equal actuarial value.
>
> But on the other hand, if an occupation offers a few extremely high prizes, its attractiveness is increased out of all proportion to their aggregate value.[13]

[13] Marshall, *op. cit.*, pp. 554–55.

Adam Smith comments similarly about occupational choices and, in addition, says of entrepreneurial undertakings:

> The ordinary rate of profits always rises more or less with the risk. It does not, however, seem to rise in proportion to it, or so as to compensate it completely.... The presumptuous hope of success seems to act here as upon all other occasions, and to entice so many adventurers into those hazardous trades, that their competition reduces the profit below what is sufficient to compensate the risk.[14]

Edwin Cannan, in discussing the rate of return on investments, concludes that "the probability is that the classes of investments which on the average return most to the investor are neither the very safest of all nor the very riskiest, but the intermediate classes which do not appeal either to timidity or to the gambling instinct."[15]

This asserted preference for extremely safe or extremely risky investments over investments with an intermediate degree of risk has its direct counterpart in the willingness of persons to buy insurance and also to buy lottery tickets or engage in other forms of gambling involving a small chance of a large gain. The extensive market for highly speculative stocks— the kind of stocks that "blue-sky" laws are intended to control—is a borderline case that could equally well be designated as investment or gambling.

The empirical evidence for the willingness of persons of all income classes to buy insurance is extensive.[16] Since insurance companies have

[14] Smith, *op. cit.*, p. 111.

[15] Article on "Profit," in *Dictionary of Political Economy*, ed. R. H. Inglis Palgrave (new edition, ed. Henry Higgs; London, 1926); see also the summary of the views of different writers on risk-taking in F. H. Knight, *Risk, Uncertainty, and Profit* (New York, 1921; reprint London School of Economics and Political Science, 1933), pp. 362–67.

[16] E.g., see U.S. Bureau of Labor Statistics, *Bulletin 648: Family Expenditures in Selected Cities, 1935–36*; Vol. I: *Family Expenditures for Housing, 1935–36*; Vol. VI: *Family Expenditures for Transportation, 1935–36*; and Vol. VIII: *Changes in Assets and Liabilities, 1935–36*.

Table 6 of the Tabular Summary of Vol. I gives the percentage of home-owning families reporting the payment of premiums for insurance on the house. These percentages are given separately for each income class in each of a number of cities or groups of cities. Since premiums are often paid less frequently than once a year, the percentages given definitely understate the percentage of families carrying insurance. Yet the bulk of the percentages are well over 40.

Table 5 of the Tabular Summary of Vol. VI gives the percentage of families (again by income classes and cities or groups of cities) reporting expenditures for automobile insurance. These figures show a very rapid increase in the percentage of automobile operators that had insurance (this figure is derived by dividing the percentage of families reporting automobile insurance by the percentage of families operating cars) as income increases. In the bottom income classes, where operation of a car is infrequent, only a minority of those who operate cars carry insurance. In the upper income classes, where most families operate cars, the majority of operators carry insurance. A convenient summary of these percentages for selected income classes in six large cities, given in text Table 10 (p. 26), has 42 entries. These vary from 4% to 98%, and 23 are over 50%.

costs of operation that are covered by their premium receipts, the purchaser is obviously paying a larger premium than the average compensation he can expect to receive for the losses against which he carries insurance. That is, he is paying something to escape risk.

The empirical evidence for the willingness of individuals to purchase lottery tickets, or engage in similar forms of gambling, is also extensive. Many governments find, and more governments have found, lotteries an

---

Table 3 of the Tabular Summary of Vol. VIII gives the percentage of families in each income class in various cities or groups of cities reporting the payment of life, endowment, or annuity insurance premiums. The percentages are uniformly high. For example, for New York City the percentage of white families reporting the payment of insurance premiums is 75% or higher for every income class listed and varies from 75% in the income class $500–$749 to over 95% in the upper-income classes; the percentage of Negro families purchasing insurance was 38% for the $1,000–$1,249 class but 60% or higher for every other class. This story is repeated for city after city, the bulk of the entries in the table for the percentage of families purchasing insurance being above 80%.

These figures cannot be regarded as direct estimates of the percentage of families willing to pay something—that is, to accept a smaller actuarial value—in order to escape risk, the technical meaning of the purchase of insurance that is relevant for our purpose. (1) The purchase of automobile and housing insurance may not be a matter of choice. Most owned homes have mortgages (see Vol. I, p. 361, Table L) and the mortgage may require that insurance be carried. The relevant figure for mortgaged homes would be the fraction of owners carrying a larger amount of insurance than is required by the mortgage. Similarly, finance companies generally require that insurance be carried on automobiles purchased on the instalment plan and not fully paid for, and the purchase of automobile insurance is compulsory in some states. (2) For automobile property damage and liability insurance (but not collision insurance) the risks to the operator and to the insurance company may not be the same, particularly to persons in the lower-income classes. The loss to the uninsured operator is limited by his wealth and borrowing power, and the maximum amount that he can lose may be well below the face value of the policy that he would purchase. The excess of the premium over the expected loss is thus greater for him than for a person with more wealth or borrowing power. The rise in the percentage of persons carrying automobile insurance as income rises may therefore reflect not an increased willingness to carry insurance but a reduction in the effective price that must be paid for insurance. (3) This tendency may be reversed for the relatively high-income classes for both automobile and housing insurance by the operation of the income tax. Uninsured losses are in many instances deductible from income before computation of income tax under the United States federal income tax, while insurance premiums are not. This tends to make the net expected loss less for the individual than for the insurance company. This effect is almost certainly negligible for the figures cited above, both because they do not effectively cover very high incomes and because the federal income tax was relatively low in 1935–36. (4) Life insurance at times comes closer to gambling (the choice of an uncertain alternative in preference to a certain alternative with a higher expected value) than to the payment of a premium to escape risk. For example, special life insurance policies purchased to cover a single railroad or airplane trip are probably more nearly comparable to a lottery ticket than a means of achieving certainty. (5) Even aside from these qualifications, actual purchase of insurance would give at best a lower limit to the number willing to buy insurance, since there will always be some who will regard the price asked as too high.

These qualifications offset one another to some extent. It seems highly unlikely that their net effect could be sufficient to reverse the conclusion suggested by the evidence cited that a large fraction of people in all income classes are willing to buy insurance.

effective means of raising revenue.[17] Though illegal, the "numbers" game and similar forms of gambling are reported to flourish in the United States,[18] particularly among the lower-income classes.

It seems highly unlikely that there is a sharp dichotomy between the individuals who purchase insurance and those who gamble. It seems much more likely that many do both or, at any rate, would be willing to. We can cite no direct evidence for this asserted fact, though indirect evidence and casual observation give us considerable confidence that it is correct. Its validity is suggested by the extensiveness of both gambling and the purchase of insurance. It is also suggested by some of the available evidence on how people invest their funds. The widespread legislation against "bucket shops" suggests that relatively poor people must have been willing to buy extremely speculative stocks of a "blue-sky" variety. Yet the bulk of the property income of the lower-income classes consists of interest and rents and relatively little of dividends, whereas the reverse is true for the upper-income classes.[19] Rents and interest are types of receipts that tend to be derived from investments with relatively little risk, and so correspond to the purchase of insurance, whereas investment in speculative stocks corresponds to the purchase of lottery tickets.

Offhand it appears inconsistent for the same person both to buy insurance and to gamble: he is willing to pay a premium, in the one case, to avoid risk, in the other, to bear risk. And indeed it would be inconsistent for a person to be willing to pay something (no matter how little) in excess of actuarial value to avoid every possible risk and also something in excess of actuarial value to assume every possible risk. One must distinguish among different kinds of insurance and different kinds of gambling, since

[17] France, Spain, and Mexico, to name but three examples, currently conduct lotteries for revenue. Russia attaches a lottery feature to bonds sold to the public. Great Britain conducted lotteries from 1694 to 1826. In the United States lotteries were used extensively before the Revolution and for some time thereafter, both directly by state governments and under state charters granted to further specific projects deemed to have a state interest. For the history of lotteries in Great Britain see C. L'Estrange Ewen, *Lotteries and Sweepstakes* (London, 1932); in New York State, A. F. Ross, "History of Lotteries in New York," *Magazine of History*, Vol. V (New York, 1907). There seem to be no direct estimates of the fraction of the people who purchase tickets in state or other legal lotteries, and it is clear that such figures would be difficult to get from data obtained in connection with running the lotteries. The receipts from legal lotteries, and casual impressions of observers, suggest that a substantial fraction of the relevant units (families or, alternatively, individual income recipients) purchase tickets.

[18] Evidence from wagering on horse races, where this has been legalized, is too ambiguous to be of much value. Since most legal wagering is at the track, gambling is available only to those who go to watch the races and is combined with participation in the mechanics of the game of chance.

[19] *Delaware Income Statistics*, Vol. I (Bureau of Economic and Business Research, University of Delaware, 1941), Table 1; *Minnesota Incomes, 1938–39*, Vol. II (Minnesota Resources Commission, 1942), Table 27; F. A. Hanna, J. A. Pechman, S. M. Lerner, *Analysis of Wisconsin Income* ["Studies in Income and Wealth," Vol. IX (National Bureau of Economic Research, 1948)], Part II, Table 1.

a willingness to pay something for only some kinds of insurance would not necessarily be inconsistent with a willingness to engage in only some kinds of gambling. Unfortunately, very little empirical evidence is readily available on the kinds of insurance that people are willing to buy and the kinds of gambling that they are willing to engage in. About the only clear indication is that people are willing to enter into gambles that offer a small chance of a large gain—as in lotteries and "blue-sky" securities.

Lotteries seem to be an extremely fruitful, and much neglected, source of information about reactions of individuals to risk. They present risk in relatively pure form, with little admixture of other factors; they have been conducted in many countries and for many centuries, so that a great deal of evidence is available about them; there has been extensive experimentation with the terms and conditions that would make them attractive, and much competition in conducting them, so that any regularities they may show would have to be interpreted as reflecting corresponding regularities in human behavior.[20] It is, of course, not certain that inferences from lotteries would carry over to other choices involving risk. There would, however, seem to be some presumption that they would do so, though of course the validity of this presumption would have to be tested.[21]

The one general feature of lotteries that is worth noting in this preliminary survey, in addition to the general willingness of people to participate in them, is the structure of prizes that seems to have developed. Lotteries rarely have just a single prize equal to the total sum to be paid out as prizes. Instead, they tend to have several or many prizes. The largest prize is ordinarily not very much larger than the next largest, and often there is not one largest prize but several of the same size.[22] This tendency is so general that one would expect it to reflect some consistent feature of individual reactions, and any hypothesis designed to explain reactions to uncertainty should explain it.

III. THE FORMAL HYPOTHESIS

The hypothesis that is proposed for rationalizing the behavior just summarized can be stated compactly as follows: In choosing among alternatives open to it, whether or not these alternatives involve risk, a consumer

---

[20] Aside from their value in providing information about reactions to risk, data from lotteries may be of broader interest in providing evidence about the stability of tastes and preferences over time and their similarity in different parts of the world. Here is a "commodity" which has remained unchanged over centuries, which is the same all over the globe, and which has been dealt in widely for the entire period and over much of the globe. It is hard to conceive of any other commodity for which this is true.

[21] See Smith, *op. cit.*, p. 108, for a precedent.

[22] See Ewen, *op. cit.*, *passim*, but esp. descriptions of state lotteries in Ch. VII, pp. 199–244; see also the large numbers of bills advertising lotteries in John Ashton, *A History of English Lotteries* (London: Leadenhall Press, 1893).

unit (generally a family, sometimes an individual) behaves as if (*a*) it had a consistent set of preferences; (*b*) these preferences could be completely described by a function attaching a numerical value—to be designated "utility"—to alternatives each of which is regarded as certain; (*c*) its objective were to make its expected utility as large as possible. It is the contribution of Von Neumann and Morgenstern to have shown that an alternative statement of the same hypothesis is: An individual chooses in accordance with a system of preferences which has the following properties:

1. The system is complete and consistent; that is, an individual can tell which of two objects he prefers or whether he is indifferent between them, and if he does not prefer C to B and does not prefer B to A, then he does not prefer C to A.[23] (In this context, the word "object" includes combinations of objects with stated probabilities; for example, if A and B are objects, a 40-60 chance of A or B is also an object.)
2. Any object which is a combination of other objects with stated probabilities is never preferred to every one of these other objects, nor is every one of them ever preferred to the combination.
3. If the object A is preferred to the object B and B to the object C, there will be some probability combination of A and C such that the individual is indifferent between it and B.[24]

This form of statement is designed to show that there is little difference between the plausibility of this hypothesis and the usual indifference-curve explanation of riskless choices.

These statements of the hypothesis conceal by their very compactness most of its implications. It will pay us, therefore, to elaborate them. It simplifies matters, and involves no loss in generality, to regard the alternatives open to the consumer unit as capable of being expressed entirely in terms of money or money income. Actual alternatives are not, of course, capable of being so expressed: the same money income may be valued

---

[23] The transitivity of the relation of indifference assumed in this postulate is, of course, an idealization. It is clearly possible that the difference between successive pairs of alternatives in a series might be imperceptible to an individual, yet the first of the series definitely preferable to the last. This idealization, which is but a special case of the idealization involved in the geometric concept of a dimensionless point, seems to us unobjectionable. However, the use of this idealization in indifference-curve analysis is the major criticism offered by W. E. Armstrong in an attack on indifference-curve analysis in his article "The Determinateness of the Utility Function," *Economic Journal*, Vol. XLIX (September, 1939), pp. 453–67. In a more recent article ["Uncertainty and the Utility Function," *Economic Journal*, Vol. LVIII (March, 1948), pp. 1–10] Armstrong repeats this criticism and adds to it the criticism that choices involving risk cannot be rationalized by the ordinal properties of utility functions.

[24] For a rigorous presentation of the second statement and a rigorous proof that the statements are equivalent see Von Neumann and Morgenstern, *op. cit.*, pp. 26–27, 617–32.

very differently according to the terms under which it is to be received, the nonpecuniary advantages or disadvantages associated with it, and so on. We can abstract from these factors, which play no role in the present problem, by supposing either that they are the same for different incomes compared or that they can be converted into equivalent sums of money income.[25] This permits us to consider total utility a function of money income alone.

Let I represent the income of a consumer unit per unit time, and $U(I)$ the utility attached to that income if it is regarded as certain. Measure I along the horizontal axis of a graph and U along the vertical. In general, $U(I)$ will not be defined for all values of I, since there will be a lower limit to the income a consumer unit can receive, namely, a negative income equal (in absolute value) to the maximum amount that the consumer unit can lose per unit time for the period to which the utility curve refers.

Alternatives open to the consumer unit that involve no risk consist of possible incomes, say I', I'', ... The hypothesis then implies simply that the consumer unit will choose the income to which it attaches the most utility. Other things the same, we know from even casual observation that the consumer unit will in general choose the largest income: put differently, we consider it pathological for an individual literally to throw money away, yet this means of choosing a smaller income is always available. It follows that the hypothesis can rationalize riskless choices of the limited kind considered here if, and only if, the utility of money income is larger, the higher the income. Consideration of riskless choices imposes no further requirements on the utility function.

Alternatives involving risk consist of probability distributions of possible incomes. Fortunately, it will suffice for our purpose to consider only a particularly simple kind of alternative involving risk, namely (A) a chance $a(0 < a < 1)$ of an income I_1, and a chance $(1 - a)$ of an income I_2, where for simplicity I_2 is supposed always greater than I_1. This simplification is possible because, as we shall see later, the original hypothesis implies that choices of consumer units among more complicated alternatives can be predicted from complete knowledge of their preferences among alternatives like A and a riskless alternative (B) consisting of a certain income I_0.

Since "other things" are supposed the same for alternatives A and

---

[25] The other factors abstracted from must not, of course, include any that cannot in fact be held constant while money income varies. For example, a higher income is desired because it enables a consumer unit to purchase a wider variety of commodities. The consumption pattern of the consumer unit must not therefore be supposed to be the same at different incomes. As another example, a higher income may mean that a consumer unit must pay a higher price for a particular commodity (e.g., medical service). Such variation in price should not be impounded in *ceteris paribus*, though price changes not necessarily associated with changes in the consumer unit's income should be.

B, the utility of the two alternatives may be taken to be functions solely of the incomes and probabilities involved and not also of attendant circumstances. The utility of alternative B is $U(I_0)$. The expected utility of A is given by

$$\bar{U}(A) = aU(I_1) + (1 - a)U(I_2)$$

According to the hypothesis, a consumer unit will choose A if $\bar{U} > U(I_0)$, will choose B if $\bar{U} < U(I_0)$, and will be indifferent between A and B if $\bar{U} = U(I_0)$.

Let $\bar{I}(A)$ be the actuarial value of A, i.e., $\bar{I}(A) = aI_1 + (1 - a)I_2$. If I_0 is equal to $\bar{I}$, the "gamble" or "insurance" is said to be "fair" since the consumer unit gets the same actuarial value whichever alternative it chooses. If, under these circumstances, the consumer unit chooses A, it shows a preference for this risk. This is to be interpreted as meaning that $\bar{U} > U(\bar{I})$ and indeed $\bar{U} - U(\bar{I})$ may be taken to measure the utility it attaches to this particular risk.[26] If the consumer unit chooses B, it shows a preference for certainty. This is to be interpreted as meaning that $\bar{U} < U(\bar{I})$. Indifference between A and B is to be interpreted as meaning that $\bar{U} = U(\bar{I})$.

Let I^* be the certain income that has the same utility as A, that is, $U(I^*) = \bar{U}$.[27] Call I^* the income equivalent to A. The requirement, derived from consideration of riskless choices, that utility increase with income means that

$$\bar{U} \gtrless U(\bar{I})$$

implies

$$I^* \gtrless \bar{I}$$

If I^* is greater than $\bar{I}$, the consumer unit prefers this particular risk to a certain income of the same actuarial value and would be willing to pay a maximum of $I^* - \bar{I}$ for the privilege of "gambling." If I^* is less than $\bar{I}$, the consumer unit prefers certainty and is willing to pay a maximum of $\bar{I} - I^*$ for "insurance" against this risk.

These concepts are illustrated for a consumer unit who is willing to pay for insurance ($\bar{I} > I^*$) in Figure 1a, and for a consumer unit who is

---

[26] This interpretation of $\bar{U} - U(\bar{I})$ as the utility attached to a particular risk is directly relevant to a point to which von Neumann and Morgenstern and commentators on their work have given a good deal of attention, namely, whether there may "not exist in an individual a (positive or negative) utility of the mere act of 'taking a chance,' of gambling, which the use of the mathematical expectation obliterates" (von Neumann and Morgenstern, *op. cit.*, p. 28). In our view the hypothesis is better interpreted as a rather special explanation why gambling has utility or disutility to a consumer unit, and as providing a particular measure of the utility or disutility, than as a denial that gambling has utility (see *ibid.*, pp. 28, 629–32).

[27] Since U has been assumed strictly monotonic to rationalize riskless choices, there will be only one income, if any, that has the same utility as A. There will be one if U is continuous which, for simplicity, we assume to be the case throughout this paper.

FIGURE 1

ILLUSTRATION OF UTILITY ANALYSIS OF CHOICES INVOLVING RISK: a) PREFERENCE FOR
CERTAINTY; b) PREFERENCE FOR RISK

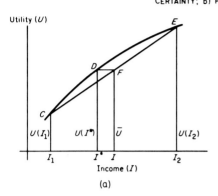

(a)

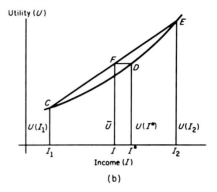

(b)

willing to pay for the privilege of gambling $(\bar{I} < I^*)$ in Figure 1b. In both figures, money income is measured along the horizontal axis, and utility along the vertical. On the horizontal axis, designate I_1 and I_2. $\bar{I}$, the actuarial value of I_1 and I_2, is then represented by a point that divides the interval I_1 to I_2 in the proportion

$$\frac{1-a}{a} \left(\text{i.e., } \frac{\bar{I} - I_1}{I_2 - \bar{I}} = \frac{1-a}{a}\right)$$

Draw the utility curve $(CDE$ in both figures). Connect the points $[I_1, U(I_1)]$, $[I_2, U(I_2)]$ by a straight line (CFE). The vertical distance of this line from the horizontal axis at $\bar{I}$ is then equal to $\bar{U}$. [Since $\bar{I}$ divides the distance between I_1 and I_2 in the proportion $(1 - a)/a$, F divides the vertical distance between C and E in the same proportion, so the vertical distance from F to the horizontal axis is the expected value of $U(I_1)$ and $U(I_2)$]. Draw a horizontal line through F and find the income corresponding to its intersection with the utility curve (point D). This is the income the utility of which is the same as the expected utility of A, hence by definition is I^*.

In Figure 1a, the utility curve is so drawn as to make I^* less than $\bar{I}$. If the consumer unit is offered a choice between A and a certain income I_0 greater than I^*, it will choose the certain income. If this certain income I_0 were less than $\bar{I}$, the consumer unit would be paying $\bar{I} - I_0$ for certainty—in ordinary parlance it would be "buying insurance"; if the certain income were greater than $\bar{I}$, it would be being paid $I_0 - \bar{I}$ for accepting certainty, even though it is willing to pay for certainty—we might say that it is "selling a gamble" rather than "buying insurance." If the consumer unit were offered a choice between A and a certain income I_0 less than I^*, it would choose A because, while it is willing to pay a price for certainty, it is being asked to pay more than the maximum amount $(\bar{I} - I^*)$ that it is willing to pay. The price of insurance has become so high that it has, as it were, been converted into a seller rather than a buyer of insurance.

In Figure 1b, the utility curve is so drawn as to make I^* greater than $\bar{I}$. If the consumer unit is offered a choice between A and a certain income I_0 less than I^*, it will choose A. If this certain income I_0 were greater than $\bar{I}$, the consumer unit would be paying $I_0 - \bar{I}$ for this risk—in ordinary parlance, it would be choosing to gamble or, one might say, "to buy a gamble"; if the certain income were less than $\bar{I}$, it would be being paid $\bar{I} - I_0$ for accepting this risk even though it is willing to pay for the risk—we might say that it is "selling insurance" rather than "buying a gamble." If the consumer unit is offered a choice between A and a certain income I_0 greater than I^*, it will choose the certain income because, while it is willing to pay something for a gamble, it is not willing to pay more than $I^* - \bar{I}$. The price of the gamble has become so high that it is converted into a seller, rather than a buyer, of gambles.

It is clear that the graphical condition for a consumer unit to be willing to pay something for certainty is that the utility function be above its chord at $\bar{I}$. This is simply a direct translation of the condition that $U(\bar{I}) > \bar{U}$. Similarly, a consumer unit will be willing to pay something for a risk if the utility function is below its chord at $\bar{I}$.

The relationship between these formalized "insurance" and "gambling" situations and what are ordinarily called insurance and gambling is fairly straight-forward. A consumer unit contemplating buying insurance is to be regarded as having a current income of I_2 and as being subject to a chance of losing a sum equal to $I_2 - I_1$, so that if this loss should occur its income would be reduced to I_1. It can insure against this loss by paying a premium equal to $I_2 - I_0$. The premium, in general, will be larger than $I_2 - \bar{I}$, the "loading" being equal to $\bar{I} - I_0$. Purchase of insurance therefore means accepting the certainty of an income equal to I_0 instead of a pair of alternative incomes having a higher expected value. Similarly, a consumer unit deciding whether to gamble (e.g., to purchase a lottery ticket) can be interpreted as having a current income equal to I_0. It can have a chance $(1 - a)$ of a gain equal to $I_2 - I_0$ by subjecting itself to a chance a of losing a sum equal to $I_0 - I_1$. If it gambles, the actuarial value of its income is $\bar{I}$, which in general is less than I_0. $I_0 - \bar{I}$ is the premium it is paying for the chance to gamble (the "take" of the house, or the "banker's cut").

It should be emphasized that this analysis is all an elaboration of a particular hypothesis about the way consumer units choose among alternatives involving risk. This hypothesis describes the reactions of consumer units in terms of a utility function, unique except for origin and unit of measure, which gives the utility assigned to certain incomes and which has so far been taken for granted. Yet for choices among certain incomes only a trivial characteristic of this function is relevant, namely, that it rises with income. The remaining characteristics of the function are relevant only to choices among alternatives involving risk and can therefore be inferred only from observation of such choices. The precise manner in which these characteristics are implicit in the consumer unit's preferences among alternatives involving risk can be indicated most easily by describing a conceptual experiment for determining the utility function.

Select any two incomes, say $500 and $1,000. Assign any arbitrary utilities to these incomes, say 0 utiles and 1 utile, respectively. This corresponds to an arbitrary choice of origin and unit of measure. Select any intermediate income, say $600. Offer the consumer unit the choice between (A) a chance a of $500 and $(1 - a)$ of $1,000 or (B) a certainty of $600, varying a until the consumer unit is indifferent between the two (i.e., until $I^* = \$600$). Suppose this indifference value of a is $\frac{2}{5}$. If the hypothesis is correct, it follows that

$$U(600) = \tfrac{2}{5}U(500) + \tfrac{3}{5}U(1000) = \tfrac{2}{5}\,0 + \tfrac{3}{5}\cdot 1 = \tfrac{3}{5} = .60$$

In this way the utility attached to every income between $500 and $1,000 can be determined. To get the utility attached to any income outside the interval $500 to $1,000, say $10,000, offer the consumer unit a choice between (A) a chance a of $500 and $(1 - a)$ of $10,000 or (B) a certainty of $1,000, varying a until the consumer unit is indifferent between the two (i.e., until $I^* = \$1,000$). Suppose this indifference value of a is $\frac{4}{5}$. If the hypothesis is correct, it follows that

$$\tfrac{4}{5}U(500) + \tfrac{1}{5}U(10,000) = U(1000)$$

or

$$\tfrac{4}{5}\cdot 0 + \tfrac{1}{5}U(10,000) = 1$$

or

$$U(10,000) = 5$$

In principle, the possibility of carrying out this experiment, and the reproducibility of the results, would provide a test of the hypothesis. For example, the consistency of behavior assumed by the hypothesis would be contradicted if a repetition of the experiment using two initial incomes other than $500 and $1,000 yielded a utility function differing in more than origin and unit of measure from the one initially obtained.

Given a utility function obtained in this way, it is possible, if the hypothesis is correct, to compute the utility attached to (that is, the expected utility of) any set or sets of possible incomes and associated probabilities and thereby to predict which of a number of such sets will be chosen. This is the precise meaning of the statement made toward the beginning of this section that, if the hypothesis were correct, complete knowledge of the preferences of consumer units among alternatives like A and B would make it possible to predict their reactions to any other choices involving risk.

The choices a consumer unit makes that involve risk are typically far more complicated than the simple choice between A and B that we have used to elaborate the hypothesis. There are two chief sources of complication: Any particular alternative typically offers an indefinitely large number of possible incomes, and "other things" are generally not the same.

The multiplicity of possible incomes is very general: losses insured against ordinarily have more than one possible value; lotteries ordinarily have more than one prize; the possible income from a particular occupation, investment, or business enterprise may be equal to any of an indefinitely large number of values. A hypothesis that the essence of choices among the degrees of risk involved in such complex alternatives is contained in such simple choices as the choice between A and B is by no means tautological.

The hypothesis does not, of course, pretend to say anything about how consumer choices will be affected by differences in things other than degree of risk. The significance for our purposes of such differences is rather that they greatly increase the difficulty of getting evidence about reactions to differences in risk alone. Much casual experience, particularly experience bearing on what is ordinarily regarded as gambling, is likely to be misinterpreted, and erroneously regarded as contradictory to the hypothesis, if this difficulty is not explicitly recognized. In much so-called gambling the individual chooses not only to bear risk but also to participate in the mechanics of a game of chance; he buys, that is, a gamble, in our technical sense, and entertainment. We can conceive of separating these two commodities: he could buy entertainment alone by paying admission to participate in a game using valueless chips; he could buy the gamble alone by having an agent play the game of chance for him according to detailed instructions.[28] Further, insurance and gambles are often purchased in almost pure form. This is notably true of insurance. It is true also of gambling by the purchase of lottery tickets when the purchaser is not a spectator to the drawing of the winners (e.g., Irish sweepstakes tickets bought in this country or the "numbers" game), and of much stock-market speculation.

An example of behavior that would definitely contradict the assertion, contained in the hypothesis, that the same utility function can be used to

----

[28] It does not, of course, follow that the price an individual is willing to pay for the joint commodity is simply the sum of the prices he is willing to pay for them separately. Indeed, it may well be the possible existence of such a difference that people have in mind when they speak of a "specific utility of gambling."

explain choices that do and do not involve risk would be willingness by an individual to pay more for a gamble than the maximum amount he could win. In order to explain riskless choices it is necessary to suppose that utility increases with income. It follows that the average utility of two incomes can never exceed the utility of the larger income and hence that an individual will never be willing to pay, for example, a dollar for a chance of winning, at most, 99 cents.

More subtle observation would be required to contradict the assertion that the reactions of persons to complicated gambles can be inferred from their reactions to simple gambles. For example, suppose an individual refuses an opportunity to toss a coin for a dollar and also to toss a coin for two dollars but then accepts an opportunity to toss two coins in succession, the first to determine whether the second toss is to be for one dollar or for two dollars. This behavior would definitely contradict the hypothesis. On the hypothesis, the utility of the third gamble is an average of the utility of the first two. His refusal of the first two indicates that each of them has a lower utility than the alternative of not gambling; hence, if the hypothesis were correct, the third should have a lower utility than the same alternative, and he should refuse it.

IV. RESTRICTIONS ON UTILITY FUNCTION REQUIRED TO RATIONALIZE OBSERVABLE BEHAVIOR

The one restriction imposed on the utility function in the preceding section is that total utility increase with the size of money income. This restriction was imposed to rationalize the first of the facts listed below. We are now ready to see whether the behavior described in Section II can be rationalized by the hypothesis, and, if so, what additional restrictions this behavior imposes on the utility function. To simplify the task, we shall take as a summary of the essential features of the behavior described in Section II the following five statements, alleged to be facts: (1) consumer units prefer larger to smaller certain incomes; (2) low-income consumer units buy, or are willing to buy, insurance; (3) low-income consumer units buy, or are willing to buy, lottery tickets; (4) many low-income consumer units buy, or are willing to buy, both insurance and lottery tickets; (5) lotteries typically have more than one prize.

These particular statements are selected not because they are the most important in and of themselves but because they are convenient to handle and the restrictions imposed to rationalize them turn out to be sufficient to rationalize all the behavior described in Section II.

It is obvious from Figure 1 and our discussion of it that if the utility function were everywhere convex from above (for utility functions with a continuous derivative, if the marginal utility of money does not increase for any income), the consumer unit, on our hypothesis, would be willing to enter into any fair insurance plan but would be unwilling to pay anything in excess of the actuarial value for any gamble. If the utility function were everywhere concave from above (for functions with a continuous derivative, if the marginal utility of money does not diminish for any income), the consumer unit would be willing to enter into any fair gamble but would be unwilling to pay anything in excess of the actuarial value for insurance against any risk.

It follows that our hypothesis can rationalize statement 2, the purchase of insurance by low-income consumer units, only if the utility functions of the corresponding units are not everywhere concave from above; that it can rationalize statement 3, the purchase of lottery tickets by low-income consumer units, only if the utility functions of the corresponding units are not everywhere convex from above; and that it can rationalize statement 4, the purchase of both insurance and lottery tickets by low-income consumer units, only if the utility functions of the corresponding units are neither everywhere concave from above nor everywhere convex from above.

The simplest utility function (with a continuous derivative) that can rationalize all three statements simultaneously is one that has a segment convex from above followed by a segment concave from above and no other segments.[29] The convex segment must precede the concave segment because of the kind of insurance and of gambling the low-income consumer units are said to engage in: a chord from the existing income to a lower income must be below the utility function to rationalize the purchase of insurance against the risk of loss; a chord from the immediate neighborhood of the existing income to a higher income must be above the utility function at the existing income to rationalize the purchase for a small sum of a small chance of a large gain.[30]

Figure 2 illustrates a utility function satisfying these requirements. Let this utility function be for a low-income consumer unit whose current income is in the initial convex segment, say at the point designated $I*$. If some risk should arise of incurring a loss, the consumer unit would clearly (on our hypothesis) be willing to insure against the loss (if it did not have to pay too much "loading") since a chord from the utility curve at $I*$ to the utility curve at the lower income that would be the consequence of the actual occurrence of the loss would everywhere be below the utility func-

---

[29] A kink or a jump in the utility function could rationalize either the gambling or the insurance. For example, the utility function could be composed of two convex or two concave segments joined in a kink. There is no essential loss in generality in neglecting such cases, as we shall do from here on, since one can always think of rounding the kink ever so slightly.

[30] If there are more than two segments and a continuous derivative, a convex segment necessarily precedes a concave segment.

FIGURE 2

ILLUSTRATION OF UTILITY FUNCTION CONSISTENT
WITH WILLINGNESS OF A LOW-INCOME CONSUMER
UNIT BOTH TO PURCHASE INSURANCE AND TO GAMBLE

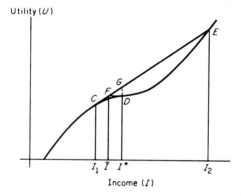

tion. The consumer unit would not be willing to engage in small gambling. But suppose it is offered a fair gamble of the kind represented by a lottery involving a small chance of winning a relatively large sum equal to $I_2 - I^*$ and a large chance of losing a relatively small sum equal to $I^* - I_1$. The consumer unit would clearly prefer the gamble, since the expected utility (I^*G) is greater than the utility of I^*. Indeed it would be willing to pay any premium up to $I^* - \bar{I}$ for the privilege of gambling; that is, even if the expected value of the gamble were almost as low as $\bar{I}$, it would accept the gamble in preference to a certainty of receiving I^*. The utility curve in Figure 2 is therefore clearly consistent with statements 2, 3, and 4.

These statements refer solely to the behavior of relatively low-income consumer units. It is tempting to seek to restrict further the shape of the utility function, and to test the restrictions so far imposed, by appealing to casual observation of the behavior of relatively high-income consumer units.[31] It does not seem desirable to do so, however, for two major reasons: (1) it is far more difficult to accumulate reliable information about the behavior of relatively high-income consumer units than about the behavior of the more numerous low-income units; (2) perhaps even more important, the progressive income tax so affects the terms under which the relatively high-income consumer units purchase insurance or gamble as to make

---

[31] For example, a high-income consumer unit that had a utility function like that in Fig. 2 and a current income of I_2 would be willing to participate in a wide variety of gambling, including the purchase of lottery tickets; it would be unwilling to insure against losses that had a small expected value (i.e., involved payment of a small premium) though it might be willing to insure against losses that had a large expected value. Consequently, unwillingness of relatively high-income consumer units to purchase lottery tickets, or willingness to purchase low-premium insurance, would contradict the utility function of Fig. 2 and require the imposition of further restrictions.

evidence on their behavior hard to interpret for our purposes.[32] Therefore, instead of using observations about the behavior of relatively high-income consumer units, we shall seek to learn more about the upper end of the curve by using statement 5, the tendency for lotteries to have more than one prize.

In order to determine the implications of this statement for the utility function, we must investigate briefly the economics of lotteries. Consider an entrepreneur conducting a lottery and seeking to maximize his income from it. For simplicity, suppose that he conducts the lottery by deciding in advance the number of tickets to offer and then auctioning them off at the highest price he can get.[33] Aside from advertising and the like, the variables at his disposal are the terms of the lottery: the number of tickets to sell, the total amount to offer as prizes (which together, of course, determine the actuarial value of a ticket), and the structure of prizes to offer. For any given values of the first two, the optimum structure of prizes is clearly that which maximizes the price he can get per ticket or, what is the same thing, the excess of the price of a ticket over its actuarial value—the "loading" per ticket.

In the discussion of Figure 2, it was noted that $I^* - \bar{I}$ was the maximum amount in excess of the actuarial value that the corresponding con-

---

[32] The effect of the income tax, already referred to in footnote 16 above, depends greatly on the specific provisions of the tax law and of the insurance or gambling plan. For example, if an uninsured loss is deductible in computing taxable income (as is loss of an owned home by fire under the federal income tax) while the premium for insuring against the loss is not (as a fire insurance premium on an owned home is not), the expected value of the loss is less to the consumer unit than to the firm selling insurance. A premium equal to the actuarial value of the loss to the insurance company then exceeds the actuarial value of the loss to the consumer unit. That is, the government in effect pays part of the loss but none of the premium. On the other hand, if the premium is deductible (as a health insurance premium may be), while an uninsured loss is not (as the excess of medical bills over $2,500 for a family is not), the net premium to the consumer unit is less than the premium received by the insurance company. Similarly, gambling gains in excess of gambling losses are taxable under the federal income tax, while gambling losses in excess of gambling gains are not deductible. The special treatment of capital gains and losses under the existing United States federal income tax adds still further complications.

Even if both the premium and the uninsured loss are deductible, or a gain taxable and the corresponding loss deductible, the income tax may change the terms because of the progressive rates. The tax saving from a large loss may be a smaller fraction of the loss than the tax payable on the gain is of the gain.

These comments clearly apply not only to insurance and gambling proper but also to other economic decisions involving risk—the purchase of securities, choice of occupation or business, etc. The neglect of these considerations has frequently led to the erroneous belief that a progressive income tax does not affect the allocation of resources and is in this way fundamentally different from excise taxes.

[33] This was, in fact, the way in which the British government conducted many of its official lotteries. It frequently auctioned off the tickets to lottery dealers, who served as the means of distributing the tickets to the public (see Ewen, *op. cit.*, pp. 234–40).

sumer unit would pay for a gamble involving a chance $(1 - a)$ of winning $I_2 - I^*$ and a chance a of losing $I^* - I_1$. This gamble is equivalent to a lottery offering a chance $(1 - a)$ of a prize $I_2 - I_1$ in return for the purchase of a ticket at a price of $I^* - I_1$, the chance of winning the prize being such that $\bar{I} - I_1$ is the actuarial worth of a ticket [i.e., is equal to $(1 - a) \times (I_2 - I_1)$]. If the consumer unit won the prize, its net winnings would be $I_2 - I^*$, since it would have to subtract the cost of the ticket from the gross prize. The problem of the entrepreneur, then, is to choose the structure of prizes that will maximize $I^* - \bar{I}$ for a given actuarial value of a ticket, that is, for a given value of $\bar{I} - I_1$. Changes in the structure of prizes involve changes in $I_2 - I_1$. If there is a single prize, $I_2 - I_1$ is equal to the total amount to be distributed [$(1 - a)$ is equal to the reciprocal of the number of tickets]. If there are two equal prizes, $I_2 - I_1$ is cut in half [$(1 - a)$ is then equal to twice the reciprocal of the number of tickets]. Suppose Figure 2 referred to this latter situation in which there were two equal prizes, I^* on the diagram designating both the current income of the consumer unit and the income equivalent to the lottery. If the price and actuarial worth of the ticket were kept unchanged, but a single prize was substituted for the two prizes [and $(1 - a)$ correspondingly reduced], the gamble would clearly become more attractive to the consumer unit. I_2 would move to the right, the chord connecting $U(I_1)$ and $U(I_2)$ would rotate upward, $\bar{U}$ would increase, and the consumer unit would be paying less than the maximum amount it was willing to pay. The price of the ticket could accordingly be increased; that is, I_2, $\bar{I}$, and I_1 could be moved to the left until the I^* for the new gamble were equal to the consumer unit's current income (the I^* for the old gamble). The optimum structure of prizes clearly consists therefore of a single prize, since this makes $I_2 - I_1$ as large as possible.

Statement 5, that lotteries typically have more than one prize, is

FIGURE 3

ILLUSTRATION OF TYPICAL SHAPE OF UTILITY CURVE

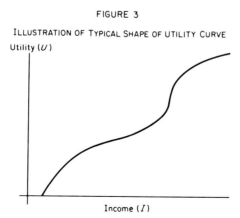

Utility (U)

Income (I)

therefore inconsistent with the utility function of Figure 2. This additional fact can be rationalized by terminating the utility curve with a suitable convex segment. This yields a utility curve like that drawn in Figure 3. With such a utility curve, $I^* - \bar{I}$ would be a maximum at the point at which a chord from $U(I_1)$ was tangent to the utility curve, and a larger prize would yield a smaller value of $I^* - \bar{I}$.[34]

A utility curve like that drawn in Figure 3 is the simplest one consistent with the five statements listed at the outset of this section.

V. A DIGRESSION

It seems well to digress at this point to consider two questions that, while not strictly relevant to our main theme, are likely to occur to many readers: first, is not the hypothesis patently unrealistic; second, can any plausible interpretation be given to the rather peculiar utility function of Figure 3?

The descriptive "realism" of the hypothesis

An objection to the hypothesis just presented that is likely to be raised by many, if not most, readers is that it conflicts with the way human beings actually behave and choose. Is it not patently unrealistic to suppose that individuals consult a wiggly utility curve before gambling or buying insurance, that they know the odds involved in the gambles or insurance plans open to them, that they can compute the expected utility of a gamble or insurance plan, and that they base their decision on the size of the expected utility?

While entirely natural and understandable, this objection is not strictly relevant. The hypothesis does not assert that individuals explicitly or consciously calculate and compare expected utilities. Indeed, it is not at all clear what such an assertion would mean or how it could be tested. The hypothesis asserts rather that, in making a particular class of decisions, individuals behave *as if* they calculated and compared expected utility and *as if* they knew the odds. The validity of this assertion does not depend on whether individuals know the precise odds, much less on whether they

[34] An additional convex segment guarantees that there will always exist current incomes of the consumer unit for which (a) attractive gambles exist and (b) the optimum prize for attractive gambles has a maximum. It does not guarantee that b will be true for every income for which attractive gambles exist. The condition on the current income that attractive gambles exist is that the tangent to the utility curve at the current income be below the utility curve for some income (this argument, like many in later technical footnotes, holds not only for the utility function of Fig. 3 but for any differentiable utility function). A single prize will be the optimum, no matter what the amount distributed in prizes or the fixed actuarial worth of the prize if, and only if, every chord from the utility curve at the current income to the utility of a higher income is everywhere above the utility curve. A particular, and somewhat interesting, class of utility functions for which b will be true for every income for which a is true is the class for which utility approaches a finite limit as income increases.

say that they calculate and compare expected utilities or think that they do, or whether it appears to others that they do, or whether psychologists can uncover any evidence that they do, but solely on whether it yields sufficiently accurate predictions about the class of decisions with which the hypothesis deals. Stated differently, the test by results is the only possible method of determining whether the *as if* statement is or is not a sufficiently good approximation to reality for the purpose at hand.

A simple example may help to clarify the point at issue. Consider the problem of predicting, before each shot, the direction of travel of a billiard ball hit by an expert billiard player. It would be possible to construct one or more mathematical formulas that would give the directions of travel that would score points and, among these, would indicate the one (or more) that would leave the balls in the best positions. The formulas might, of course, be extremely complicated, since they would necessarily take account of the location of the balls in relation to one another and to the cushions and of the complicated phenomena introduced by "English." Nonetheless, it seems not at all unreasonable that excellent predictions would be yielded by the hypothesis that the billiard player made his shots *as if* he knew the formulas, could estimate accurately by eye the angles, etc., describing the location of the balls, could make lightning calculations from the formulas, and could then make the ball travel in the direction indicated by the formulas. It would in no way disprove or contradict the hypothesis, or weaken our confidence in it, if it should turn out that the billiard player had never studied any branch of mathematics and was utterly incapable of making the necessary calculations: unless he was capable in some way of reaching approximately the same result as that obtained from the formulas, he would not in fact be likely to be an expert billiard player.

The same considerations are relevant to our utility hypothesis. Whatever the psychological mechanism whereby individuals make choices, these choices appear to display some consistency, which can apparently be described by our utility hypothesis. This hypothesis enables predictions to be made about phenomena on which there is not yet reliable evidence. The hypothesis cannot be declared invalid for a particular class of behavior until a prediction about that class proves false. No other test of its validity is decisive.

A possible interpretation of the utility function

A possible interpretation of the utility function of Figure 3 is to regard the two convex segments as corresponding to qualitatively different socio-economic levels, and the concave segment to the transition between the two levels. On this interpretation, increases in income that raise the relative position of the consumer unit in its own class but do not shift the unit out of its class yield diminishing marginal utility, while increases that shift it into a new class, that give it a new social and economic status, yield increasing marginal utility. An unskilled worker may prefer the certainty of an income about the same as that of the majority of unskilled workers to an actuarially fair gamble that at best would make him one of the most prosperous unskilled workers and at worst one of the least prosperous. Yet he may jump at an actuarially fair gamble that offers a small chance of lifting him out of the class of unskilled workers and into the "middle" or "upper" class, even though it is far more likely than the preceding gamble to make him one of the least prosperous unskilled workers. Men will and do take great risks to distinguish themselves, even when they know what the risks are. May not the concave segment of the utility curve of Figure 3 translate the economic counterpart of this phenomenon appropriately?

A number of additions to the hypothesis are suggested by this interpretation. In the first place, may there not be more than two qualitatively distinguishable socioeconomic classes? If so, might not each be reflected by a convex segment in the utility function? At the moment, there seems to be no observed behavior that requires the introduction of additional convex segments, so it seems undesirable and unnecessary to complicate the hypothesis further. It may well be, however, that it will be necessary to add such segments to account for behavior revealed by further empirical evidence. In the second place, if different segments of the curve correspond to different socioeconomic classes, should not the dividing points between the segments occur at roughly the same income for different consumer units in the same community? If they did, the fruitfulness of the hypothesis would be greatly extended. Not only could the general shape of the utility function be supposed typical; so also could the actual income separating the various segments. The initial convex segment could be described as applicable to "relatively low-income consumer units" and the terminal convex segment as applicable to "relatively high-income consumer units"; and the groups so designated could be identified by the actual income or wealth of different consumer units.

Interpreting the different segments of the curve as corresponding to different socioeconomic classes would, of course, still permit wide variation among consumer units in the exact shape and height of the curve. In addition, it would not be necessary to suppose anything more than rough similarity in the location of the incomes separating the various segments. Different socioeconomic classes are not sharply demarcated from one another; each merges into the next by imperceptible gradations (which, of course, accounts for the income range encompassed by the concave segment); and the generally accepted dividing line between classes will vary from time to time, place to place, and consumer unit to consumer unit. Finally, it is not necessary that every consumer unit have a utility curve like that in Figure 3. Some may be inveterate gamblers; others, inveterately cautious. It is enough that many consumer units have such a utility curve.

VI. FURTHER IMPLICATIONS OF THE HYPOTHESIS

To return to our main theme, we have two tasks yet to perform; first, to show that the utility function of Figure 3 is consistent with those features of the behavior described in Section II not used in deriving it; second, to suggest additional implications of the hypothesis capable of providing a test of it.

The chief generalization of Section II not so far used is that people must in general be paid a premium to induce them to bear moderate risks instead of either small or large risks. Is this generalization consistent with the utility function of Figure 3?

It clearly is for a consumer unit whose income places it in the initial convex segment. Such a relatively low-income consumer unit will be willing to pay something more than the actuarial value for insurance against any kind of risk that may arise; it will be averse to small fair gambles; it may be averse to all fair gambles; if not, it will be attracted by fair gambles that offer a small chance of a large gain; the attractiveness of such gambles, with a given possible loss and actuarial value, will initially increase as the size of the possible gain increases and will eventually decrease.[35] Such con-consumer units therefore prefer either certainty or a risk that offers a small chance of a large gain to a risk that offers the possibility of moderate gains

---

[35] The willingness of a consumer unit in the initial convex segment to pay something more than the actuarial value for insurance against any kind of risk follows from the fact that a chord connecting the utility of its current income with the utility of any lower income to which it might be reduced by the risk in question will everywhere be below the utility curve. The expected utility is therefore less than the utility of the expected income.

To analyze the reaction of such a consumer unit to different gambles, consider the limiting case in which the gamble is fair, i.e., $\bar{I} = I_0$. $\bar{I}$ then is both the expected income of the consumer unit if it takes the gamble and its actual income if it does not (i.e., its current income). The possible gains (and associated probabilities) that will be attractive to the unit for a given value of I_1 (i.e., a given possible loss) can be determined by drawing a straight line through $U(I_1)$ and $U(\bar{I})$. All values of $I_2 > \bar{I}$ for which $U(I_2)$ is greater than the ordinate of the extended straight line will be attractive; no others will be.

Since $\bar{I}$ is assumed to be in the first convex segment, there will always exist some values of $I_2 > \bar{I}$ for which $U(I_2)$ is less than the ordinate of the extended straight line. This is the basis for the statement that the consumer unit will be averse to small gambles.

Consider the line that touches the curve at only two points and is nowhere below the utility curve. Call the income at the first of the points at which it touches the curve, which may be the lowest possible income, I', and the income at the second point, I''. The consumer unit will be averse to all gambles if its income ($I_0 = \bar{I}$) is equal to or less than I'. This follows from the fact that a tangent to the curve at $\bar{I}$ will then be steeper than the "double tangent" and will intersect the latter prior to I'; a chord from $\bar{I}$ to a lower income will be even steeper. This is the basis for the statement that the consumer unit may be averse to all gambles.

If the income is above I', there will always be some attractive gambles. These will offer a small chance of a large gain. The statement about the changing attractiveness of the gamble as the size of the possible gain changes follows from the analysis in Sec. IV of the conditions under which it would be advantageous to have a single prize in a lottery.

or losses. They will therefore have to be paid a premium to induce them to undertake such moderate risks.

The generalization is clearly false for a consumer unit whose income places it in the concave segment. Such an "intermediate-income" consumer unit will be attracted by every small fair gamble; it may be attracted by every fair gamble; it may be averse to all fair insurance; if not, it will be attracted by insurance against relatively large losses.[36] Such consumer units will therefore be willing to pay a premium in order to assume moderate risks.

The generalization is partly true, partly false, for a consumer unit whose income places it in the terminal convex segment. Such a relatively high-income consumer unit will be willing to insure against any small possible loss and may be attracted to every fair insurance plan; the only insurance plans it may be averse to are plans involving rather large losses; it may be averse to all fair gambles; if not, it will be attracted by gambles that involve a reasonably sure, though fairly small, gain, with a small possibility of a sizable loss; it will be averse to gambles of the lottery variety.[37] These consumer units therefore prefer certainty to moderate risks; in this respect they conform to the generalization. However, they may prefer moderate risks to extreme risks, though these adjectives hardly suffice to characterize the rather complex pattern of risk preferences implied for high-income consumer units by a utility curve like that of Figure 3. Nonetheless, in this respect the implied behavior of the high-income consumer units is either neutral or contrary to the generalization.

Our hypothesis does not therefore lead inevitably to a rate of return higher to uses of resources involving moderate risk than to uses involving little or much risk. It leads to a rate of return higher for uses involving moderate risk than for uses involving little risk only if consumer units in the two convex segments outweigh in importance, for the resource use in question, consumer units in the concave segment.[38] Similarly, it leads to a rate of return higher for uses involving moderate risk than for uses involving much risk only if consumer units in the initial convex segment outweigh

[36] Consider the tangent to the utility curve at the income the consumer unit would have if it did not take the gamble ($\bar{I} = I_0$). If this income is in the concave section, the tangent will be below the utility curve at least for an interval of incomes surrounding $\bar{I}$. A chord connecting any two points of the utility curve on opposite sides of $\bar{I}$ and within this interval will always be above the utility curve at $\bar{I}$ (i.e., the expected utility will be above the utility of the expected income), so these gambles will be attractive. The tangent may lie below the utility curve for all incomes. In this case, every fair gamble will be attractive. The unit will be averse to insuring against a loss, whatever the chance of its occurring, if a chord from the current income to the lower income to which it would be reduced by the loss is everywhere above the utility curve. This will surely be true for small losses and may be true for all possible losses.

[37] These statements follow directly from considerations like those in the two preceding footnotes.

[38] This statement is deliberately vague. The actual relative rates of return will depend not only on the conditions of demand for risks of different kinds but also on the conditions of supply, and both would have to be taken into account in a comprehensive statement.

in importance consumer units in both the concave and the terminal convex segments—though this may be a more stringent condition than is necessary in view of the uncertainty about the exact role of consumer units in the terminal convex segment.

This relative distribution of consumer units among the various segments could be considered an additional restriction that would have to be imposed to rationalize the alleged higher rate of return to moderately risky uses of resources. It is not clear, however, that it need be so considered, since there are two independent lines of reasoning that, taken together, establish something of a presumption that relatively few consumer units are in the concave segment.

One line of reasoning is based on the interpretation of the utility function suggested in Section V. If the concave segment is a border line between two qualitatively different social classes, one would expect relatively few consumer units to be between the two classes.

The other line of reasoning is based on the implications of the hypothesis for the relative stability of the economic status of consumer units in the different segments. Units in the intermediate segment are tempted by every small gamble and at least some large ones. If opportunities are available, they will be continually subjecting themselves to risk. In consequence, they are likely to move out of the segment; upwards, if they are lucky; downwards, if they are not. Consumer units in the two convex segments, on the other hand, are less likely to move into the intermediate segment. The gambles that units in the initial segment accept will rarely pay off and, when they do, are likely to shift them all the way into the terminal convex segment. The gambles that units in the terminal segment accept will rarely involve losses and, when they do, may shift them all the way into the lower segment. Under these conditions, maintenance of a stable distribution of the population among the three segments would require that the two convex segments contain many more individuals than the concave segment. These considerations, while persuasive, are not, of course, conclusive. Opportunities to assume risks may not exist. More important, the status of consumer units is determined not alone by the outcome of risks deliberately assumed but also by random events over which they cannot choose and have no control; and it is conceivable that these random events might be distributed in such a way that their main effect was to multiply the number in the concave segment.

The absolute number of persons in the various segments will count most for choices among the uses of human resources; wealth will count most for choices among uses of nonhuman resources.[39] In consequence,

[39] This distinction requires qualification because of the need for capital to enter some types of occupations and the consequent existence of "noncompeting groups"; see Milton Friedman and Simon Kuznets, *Income from Independent Professional Practice* (New York: National Bureau of Economic Research, 1945), Ch. III, Sec. 3; Ch. IV, Sec. 2.

one might expect that the premium for bearing moderate risks instead of large risks would be greater for occupations than for investments. Indeed, for investments, the differential might in some cases be reversed, since the relatively high-income consumer units (those in the terminal segment) count for more in wealth than in numbers and they may prefer moderate to extreme risks.

In judging the implications of our hypothesis for the market as a whole, we have found it necessary to consider separately its implications for different income groups. These offer additional possibilities of empirical test. Perhaps the most fruitful source of data would be the investment policies of different income groups.

It was noted in Section II that, although many persons with low incomes are apparently willing to buy extremely speculative stocks, the low-income group receives the bulk of its property income in the form of interest and rents. These observations are clearly consistent with our hypothesis. Relatively high-income groups might be expected, on our hypothesis, to prefer bonds and relatively safe stocks. They might be expected to avoid the more speculative common stocks but to be attracted to higher-grade preferred stocks, which pay a higher nominal rate of return than high-grade bonds to compensate for a small risk of capital loss. Intermediate income groups might be expected to hold relatively large shares of their assets in moderately speculative common stocks and to furnish a disproportionate fraction of entrepreneurs.

Of course, any empirical study along these lines will have to take into account, as noted above, the effect of the progressive income tax in modifying the terms of investment. The current United States federal income tax has conflicting effects: the progressive rates discourage risky investments; the favored treatment of capital gains encourages them. In addition, such a study will have to consider the risk of investments as a group, rather than of individual investments, since the rich may be in a position to "average" risks.

Another implication referred to above that may be susceptible of empirical test, and the last one we shall cite, is the implied difference in the stability of the relative income status of various economic groups. The unattractiveness of small risks to both high- and low-income consumer units would tend to give them a relatively stable status. By contrast, suppose the utility curve had no terminal convex segment but was like the curve of Figure 2. Low-income consumer units would still have a relatively stable status: their willingness to take gambles at long odds would pay off too seldom to shift many from one class to another. High-income consumer units would not. They would then take almost any gamble, and those who had high incomes today almost certainly would not have high incomes tomorrow. The average period from "shirt sleeves to shirt sleeves" would be far shorter than "three generations."[40] Unlike the other two groups, the middle-income class might be expected to display considerable instability of relative income status.[41]

VII. CONCLUSION

A plausible generalization of the available empirical evidence on the behavior of consumer units in choosing among alternatives open to them is provided by the hypothesis that a consumer unit (generally a family, sometimes an individual) behaves as if

1. It had a consistent set of preferences;
2. These preferences could be completely described by attaching a numerical value—to be designated "utility"—to alternatives each of which is regarded as certain;
3. The consumer unit chose among alternatives not involving risk that one which has the largest utility;
4. It chose among alternatives involving risk that one for which the expected utility (as contrasted with the utility of the expected income) is largest;
5. The function describing the utility of money income had in general the following properties:
    (a) Utility rises with income, i.e., marginal utility of money income everywhere positive;
    (b) It is convex from above below some income, concave between that income and some larger income, and convex for all higher incomes, i.e., diminishing marginal utility of money income for incomes below some income, increasing marginal utility of money income for incomes between that income and some larger income, and diminishing marginal utility of money income for all higher incomes;
6. Most consumer units tend to have incomes that place them in the segments of the utility function for which marginal utility of money income diminishes.

[40] We did not use the absence of such instability to derive the upper convex segment because of the difficulty of allowing for the effect of the income tax.

[41] The existing data on stability of relative income status are too meager to contradict or to confirm this implication. In their study of professional incomes Friedman and Kuznets found that relative status was about equally stable at all income levels. However, this study is hardly relevant, since it was for homogeneous occupational groups that would tend to fall in a single one of the classes considered here. Mendershausen's analysis along similar lines for family incomes in 1929 and 1933 is inconclusive. See Friedman and Kuznets, *op. cit.*, Chap. VII; Horst Mendershausen, *Changes in Income Distribution during the Great Depression* (New York: National Bureau of Economic Research, 1946), Chap. III.

Points 1, 2, 3, and 5a of this hypothesis are implicit in the orthodox theory of choice; point 4 is an ancient idea recently revived and given new content by Von Neumann and Morgenstern; and points 5b and 6 are the consequence of the attempt in this paper to use this idea to rationalize existing knowledge about the choices people make among alternatives involving risk.

Point 5b is inferred from the following phenomena: (a) low-income consumer units buy, or are willing to buy, insurance; (b) low-income consumer units buy, or are willing to buy, lottery tickets; (c) many consumer units buy, or are willing to buy, both insurance and lottery tickets; (d) lotteries typically have more than one prize. These statements are taken as a summary of the essential features of observed behavior not because they are the most important features in and of themselves but because they are convenient to handle and the restrictions imposed to rationalize them turn out to be sufficient to rationalize all the behavior described in Section II of this paper.

A possible interpretation of the various segments of the utility curve specified in 5b is that the segments of diminishing marginal utility correspond to socioeconomic classes, the segment of increasing marginal utility to a transitional stage between a lower and a higher socioeconomic class. On this interpretation the boundaries of the segments should be roughly similar for different people in the same community; and this is one of several independent lines of reasoning leading to point 6.

This hypothesis has implications for behavior, in addition to those used in deriving it, that are capable of being contradicted by observable data. In particular, the fundamental supposition that a single utility curve can generalize both riskless choices and choices involving risk would be contradicted if (a) individuals were observed to choose the larger of two certain incomes offered to them but (b) individuals were willing to pay more than the largest possible gain for the privilege of bearing risk. The supposition that individuals seek to maximize expected utility would be contradicted if individuals' reactions to complicated gambles could not be inferred from their reactions to simple ones. The particular shape of the utility curve specified in 5b would be contradicted by any of a large number of observations, for example, (a) general willingness of individuals, whatever their income, who buy insurance against small risks to enter into small fair gambles under circumstances under which they are not also buying "entertainment," (b) the converse of a, namely an unwillingness to engage in small fair gambles by individuals who are not willing to buy fair insurance against small risks, (c) a higher average rate of return to uses of resources involving little risk than to uses involving a moderate amount of risk when other things are the same, (d) a concentration of investment portfolios of relatively low-income groups on speculative (but not highly speculative) investments or of relatively high-income groups on either moderately or highly speculative investments, (e) great instability in the relative income status of high-income groups or of low-income groups as a consequence of a propensity to engage in speculative activities.

Jack Hirshleifer[*]

2. Risk, the Discount Rate, and Investment Decisions

Reprinted from the **American Economic Review**, Vol. LI, No. 2 (May, 1961), pp. 112–120, by permission of the author and the publisher.

The problem of risky investment decision has both normative and positive aspects. Looked at normatively, the question is: What is the appropriate technique of analysis—for individuals, firms, or government agencies—to use in evaluating risky investment alternatives? Looking at the problem positively, we ask: Why do the mean experienced yields in different risk classes of securities diverge, even when average yields for the different risk classes are calculated over many individual securities and over long time periods to eliminate random effects? If we first examine the positive aspect, the major explanations that have been offered for the yield divergences mentioned above (e.g., the divergences between stock and bond yields, or between earnings on industrial and utility shares) attribute them either to imperfections of capital markets or to market premiums for risk bearing. I will be adopting the latter approach. What I will be presenting is quite a simple market theory of risk, modeled upon Fisher's treatment of time preference and interest (but definitely not modeled upon Fisher's treatment of risk). On the normative side, I attempt to show how the criterion of maximizing present value—now generally accepted, despite some recent heresies, as the guiding principle of evaluation of riskless investment alternatives[1]—must be modified or generalized when risky investments are considered. In brief, I try to indicate the appropriate rate of discount to use, in the present-value formula, to allow for uncertainty of return as well as futurity of return.

I. THE MEANING OF "RISK"

First, however, it is absolutely necessary to clarify an elementary point that has been the source of much confusion. There are at least two quite

[*] Professor of Economics, University of California, Los Angeles.

[1] For a discussion of the present-value criterion and a qualified vindication of it against proposed alternative investment criteria, see my paper, "On the Theory of Optimal Investment Decision," *Journal of Political Economy* (August, 1958).

preferences, initial endowment, and productive opportunities.
ential point is the concavity of the productive opportunity locus,
ential point is the concavity of the productive opportunity locus,
ing diminishing marginal (expected) productivity of risk. The idea
, by shifting his investments from the secure to the risky medium,
dividual can first obtain a very favorable rate of exchange, but as he
s the process further it will become less and less favorable. The tan-
y slope will indicate the equality of the marginal rate of risk-aversion
the marginal productivity of risk-bearing.

Finally, if we bring a market into our two-media world and assume
ect competition, there will be a governing rate of exchange between
ain income and expected income, which will be determined in such a
y as to equate the sums of individuals' desired holdings in the two
edia with the actual quantities socially available in terms of original
dowments and productive transformations between the two forms. As
the familiar Fisherian solution for time-preference decisions, the inser-
ion of the market exchange line permits attainment of a higher indifference
curve than would otherwise be possible. In Figure 2 the "Robinson Crusoe"
solution is at R, while the market for risk-bearing permits attainment of
the point W. With the introduction of the market, we may speak of the
individual's decision criterion as maximization of certainty-equivalent value
(V_c in the diagram), in analogy with the maximization of present value in
the theory of time-preference.

I do not feel it necessary to describe how these indifference curves
can be made consistent with Friedman-Savage utility-of-wealth functions

FIGURE 2

"ROBINSON CRUSOE" SOLUTION (R) AND MARKET SOLUTION
(W) FOR RISKY INVESTMENT

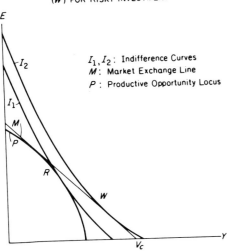

I_1, I_2 : Indifference Curves
M : Market Exchange Line
P : Productive Opportunity Locus

different senses in which investments may be said to be risky. First of all,
an investment with a certain nominal or quoted yield (e.g., a corporate
bond) is often said to involve a risk of partial or total default. Here risk
means only "unfavorable chance." Its measure is the difference between
the nominal return and the true mathematical expectation of return. I shall
call this difference or bias "expected-value risk," but the concept will not
play any important role because I will henceforth ordinarily be speaking
of investment yield in the expected-value sense. It is worth remarking,
however, that expected-value risk does not occur solely in dealing with
investments of fixed nominal yield, like bonds. It has been convincingly
demonstrated, for example, that the predicted benefit-cost yields of federal
water-resource investment projects are not, on the average, realized. Here
also predicted yields are biased estimates of the mathematical expectation
of yields.

The concept of risk I will use herein, however, concerns not the
expected value but the variability of the probability distribution of outcomes. For concreteness, we may think of the standard deviation, the
most common measure of variability, as a quantifier of "variability risk"—
or, as we shall say henceforth, simply risk. However, I do not want to
commit myself to saying that the standard deviation is *the* measure of risk.
It may well be that other moments of the distribution are also involved in
determining what we ordinarily call risk premiums on security yields.[2]

II. A MARKET THEORY OF THE RISK PREMIUM

In this section I propose to present only some elements of a theory of the
market process by which risk premiums on investments are determined,
in the belief that even a partial theory may serve to bring some order to
the subject and settle a few debated points. My basic contention will be
that the market risk premium can be understood as the interaction of
individuals' willingness to bear variability risks and of the technical
fact of the productivity of risk, given individual endowments of more
and less risky income opportunities. I have quite deliberately stated these
determinants of the risk premium to suggest an analogy with the theory
of determination of interest—that is, of the time premium—that we associate primarily with the names of Böhm-Bawerk and Fisher. In what
follows I will attempt to develop various aspects of this analogy.

First of all, we can distinguish between widening and deepening of
risk in a sense quite parallel to the familiar widening and deepening in
time. We widen investments in time when, given the period of the invest-

[2] Markowitz discusses the question of the appropriate measure of risk in his
valuable work, *Portfolio Selection* (Wiley, 1959), pp. 180–201, 287–97. See also James
Tobin, "Liquidity Preference as Behavior Towards Risk," *Review of Economic Studies*
(February, 1958).

ment, we increase the aggregate of current sacrifice on behalf of the future; we widen investments in risk when, given the degrees of riskiness of differing securities (for concreteness, we may think in terms of investments with specified standard deviations σ of yield per dollar invested), we shift more of our current sacrifice from a relatively low-σ to a relatively high-σ medium. We deepen investments in time when, holding the aggregate of current sacrifice constant, we shift from quick-yielding to slow-yielding investments; we deepen investments in risk when, given the amount of resources held out of secure media, we shift from lower to higher variability commitments of these resources. As a practical example of the distinction in terms of risk, consider a dry farmer in an arid region where returns are highly uncertain. For a particular set of lands subject to essentially identical conditions, he can widen his risk by cultivating more acres. Or he can deepen his risk by shifting all or part of his operations to lands with still higher variability of outcomes.

In the theory of risk, as in the theory of interest, it is simpler to analyze widening than deepening. This is especially so in the former case, as the standard deviation is a less perfect quantifier for depth of risk than its analogue—the period of production—is for depth in time. However, the main point is that, so long as we stick to the simple widening case, troubles about a perfect measure of depth of risk need not unduly concern us. Once we have made the vital distinction between widening and deepening, I believe it may be possible to grasp intuitively the general consequences of shifts in the depth dimension, even though a theory of the latter will have to wait for another occasion.

Limiting ourselves, then, to the pure widening case, we may start by asking ourselves what we can reasonably assert about the nature of individuals' preferences between, to take the simplest situation, only two investment media—on the assumption that in any case the investor sacrifices current consumption which is certain. One of these media may be taken to be a perfectly secure investment, with a known certain future yield. The other offers a known expected value of yield, subject to a specified type of variability. For concreteness, we may think of the unit of certain yield as, simply, a dollar—and of the unit of risky yield as a lottery ticket representing equal chances of winning $2.00 or nothing. It is necessary, to keep to the simplest possible situation, to assume that the returns from the risky units are perfectly correlated. In other words, if we have 1,000 lottery tickets, we must win either $2,000 or nothing. The correlation assumption prevents the intrusion of the law of large numbers. It is reasonably close to the true situation in our acreage cultivation example, where if the crop fails on any acre it is very likely to fail on all.

With this situation in mind, we can draw indifference curves, between certain yield and uncertain expected yield, that express individuals' risk

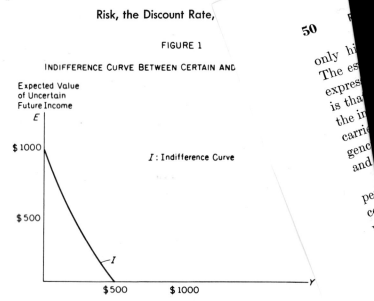

FIGURE 1

INDIFFERENCE CURVE BETWEEN CERTAIN AND

preferences. Indifference curve I in Figure 1 indicates that the in question is indifferent between $500 certain and an expected $1,000 representing equal chances of $2,000 or nothing. I feel very asserting convexity of the indifference curves (diminishing margin of substitution between certain income and expected uncertain in Consider an individual whose initial endowment consists of a risk pected value of $1,000, with no sure income at all. It seems natur assume that he would be willing initially to sacrifice expected value certainty at a rate far better than 1:1—perhaps as high as 10:1. But his certain wealth or income comes to attain a more balanced relation his uncertain prospects, the rate of exchange he is prepared to offer fo more certainty would become much more moderate. Indeed, it is conceivable that, given an initial endowment consisting solely of $500 certain, the same individual might be willing to sacrifice more than $1.00 of certain income for an expected value of $1.00. If so, then in this range he would be demonstrating risk-preference rather than risk-aversion. However, for convexity it is not necessary to assert that the individual is ever a risk-preferrer (that is, that the slope of his indifference curve will ever be less than 1 in absolute value)—all that is required is that the rate of exchange he is willing to offer change steadily from one reflecting strong risk-aversion at the upper left to one representing much more moderate risk-aversion or even risk-preference at the lower right.

Having introduced the risk-preference function and the initial endowments, we may now bring in the productive opportunity locus and the market opportunity locus. In a "Robinson Crusoe" situation no market opportunities exist, and the individual must find his optimum in terms of based upon the Von Neumann-Morgenstern postulates. The indifference curves, to use a horrible metaphor, stand on their own feet as descriptive of what seems to me obviously reasonable and typical patterns of behavior. Other analysts have not, so far as I am aware, arrived at the simple results outlined above. I believe the reason is that they unconsciously started with the more difficult deepening case—leading most frequently to the construction of indifference curves between expected value of return and standard deviation of return.[3] Unfortunately, assertions about the shape of these indifference curves carry little immediate conviction, and the situation is not improved by appeal to an underlying Friedman-Savage utility-of-wealth function.

III. SOME IMPLICATIONS

Without attempting strict proof, I believe a number of refutable statements can be derived as implications of the foregoing approach. First and foremost, there will ordinarily be a positive market premium on risk. That is, expected risky yields will be higher than sure yields. This is due to the general tilt of the preference functions illustrated in Figure 1 (expressing reluctance to bear risk) interacting with the fact that risk-bearing is ordinarily productive. That the market does pay positive risk premiums is a statement so refutable that many people (in particular, Knight) claim it has in fact been refuted. However, I believe that the weight of the evidence indicates that risky media of investment do in fact have higher expected yields than secure media (or, in other words, uncertain expected values are discounted relative to certain values). Over any reasonably long period of measurement, stocks yield more than bonds, and risky bonds more than secure bonds.[4] Of course, this theory does not allow for acceptance of "unfair" gambles. Alternative explanations would have to be sought for the phenomenon of Las Vegas.

A second implication is that individuals will typically diversify. The relationships among the curves are such that interior optima are normal, and corner optima exceptional. A third implication is that—so long as we are dealing with interior rather than corner optima and the assumption of perfect markets applies—on the margin everyone has the same degree of risk-aversion. We should, therefore, exercise care before labeling some individuals "risk-preferrers" and others "risk-avoiders." What is true is

[3] See Tobin, *op. cit.*, pp. 71–82; F. A. and V. Lutz, *The Theory of Investment of the Firm*, pp. 179–92.

[4] That stocks yield more in the long run than bonds is a notorious fact not requiring demonstration here. The recent study by W. Braddock Hickman, *Corporate Bond Quality and Investor Experience*, supports my contention about bonds—that investors demand an extra premium, over and above the expected loss by default, to hold risky bonds.

that, in the process of attaining marginal equality, some individuals will have shifted away from relatively secure initial endowments and so in a sense sought out risk, while others will have moved in the opposite direction; but this shift will reflect not merely preferences as to risk-bearing but also initial endowments and access to risky productive opportunities.

Translating the third implication above into normative language, we may say that all investors should discount risks at the rate of exchange between certain and risky prospects established by the market for the risk-class within which the investment in question falls. This contradicts a traditional view that, in evaluating risky investment opportunities, the investor ought to specify the expected values involved and then discount them by some kind of "caution coefficient" expressing his own preferences toward risk-bearing.[5] The error here has an analogy in the domain of time preference, where theorists have sometimes advised investors to use their personal time-discount rates rather than the market rate in discounting future income prospects. In the latter case, it is not difficult to show that, given a perfect market for exchange of present and future funds, highest levels of satisfaction are attained by maximizing present value calculated at the market rate of discount. Similarly in the case of risk, the optimization rule is to maximize certainty-equivalent value, discounting uncertain expected yields at the market rate of exchange between such yields and certain ones (always assuming that perfect markets exist). In the one case, this implies adjustment of all personal marginal time preferences, by appropriate shifts between present and future funds, to the market time-discount rate; in the other, adjustment of personal risk-preferences, by appropriate shifts between secure and risky media, to the market risk premium rate.

IV. CORPORATE FINANCE AND INVESTMENT DECISIONS

The analysis presented above suffices to provide the answer to the simplest problem of corporate finance. If the investment in question involves only widening in time and in risk (i.e., shifting from secure and current funds to future and uncertain ones of a given degree of risk), if it is a new venture so that there are no interactions with returns on past investments, and if only equity financing is involved, the market time-and-risk discount rate should be used in deciding how far to carry the investment. While the list of simplifying conditions sounds formidable, I should comment that the market discount rate in question—the "impure" (inclusive of risk-premium) rate of interest—is at least more of an observable magnitude than the abstract riskless rate of interest. It is assumed that the entrepreneur and the potential investors are both aware of the mathe-

[5] Irving Fisher, *The Nature of Capital and Income*, p. 277.

matical expectations of returns at different dates and the appropriate market capitalization rate, $1/\rho$ (where ρ is the "impure" interest rate) for expected yields in that risk class. The investment in question should, of course, be widened until its marginal expected yield per current certain dollar sacrificed falls to ρ.

The listener may possibly have detected by this time a certain resemblance to the line of thought put forward in the recent provocative article by Modigliani and Miller.[6] Modigliani and Miller go beyond the analysis presented here in centering attention upon the market yields of debt-equity combinations and the implications thereof for investment decisions. However, I believe that the theoretical analysis of risk-bearing presented here is that implicitly underlying the Modigliani-Miller paper. The most essential parallel is that Modigliani and Miller select market-value maximization as their criterion (page 264), which in the context is essentially maximization of the certainty-equivalent value described above. The Modigliani-Miller "equivalent-return classes" (pages 266 ff.) seem to be essentially what I have called "risk classes"; in addition, Modigliani and Miller assume a positive market premium for risk-bearing (page 271).

Limitations of time, unfortunately, prevent my presenting a fuller analysis here of what I regard as the major normative conclusion of the Modigliani-Miller analysis: that, setting aside consideration of corporate income tax, even firms with complex debt-equity capital structures should use, in evaluating investment alternatives, the discount rate determined by the market in capitalizing pure equity streams of comparable risk (page 288). I believe that this conclusion is basically sound. It is, with some qualifications, quite consistent with the theory of risk-bearing presented above, provided one accepts in addition the famous "Proposition I" of Modigliani and Miller: that the "value of the firm," the sum of the market value of its debt and equity, is a constant—determined by capitalizing its expected asset return at the appropriate risky discount rate (page 268). Without getting into tortured debates about what constitutes "arbitrage," I would agree that a divergence between a firm's net asset value and the sum of its debt and equity cannot be expected to persist—unless market imperfections are brought in.

There is one qualification I would like to make here, however, arising out of the theory presented above. Modigliani and Miller describe the discount rate recommended for investment decision as the pure-equity capitalization rate for the asset-earnings of the firm as a whole. Their risk-class concept is a characteristic of the firm rather than of the individual investment. Evidently they are thinking of marginal investments as being

[6] Franco Modigliani and Merton H. Miller, "The Cost of Capital, Corporation Finance, and the Theory of Investment," *American Economic Review* (June, 1958), pp. 261–97.

equally risky with those previously adopted—what I have called risk-widening rather than risk-deepening. This is justifiable as simplifying the analysis, though the problem remains of evaluating risk-deepening investments. Another problem is created by imperfect correlation of investment returns. While the theoretical analysis above assumed perfect correlation to avoid the operation of the law of large numbers, in the real world the advantages of risk-pooling are very important. In fact, a marginal investment that is individually very risky may substantially reduce the overall variability risk of the firm's total portfolio of investments. I am inclined to think that the best way of rescuing the analysis is to take note of the fact that, where large numbers of individual investments are involved, the variability of the overall investment return approaches the value of the average covariance among the individual investments.[7] The risk classes into which firms are divided, then, would depend very importantly upon the diversity of returns of their portfolios as a whole, and the variability of individual investments can be correspondingly neglected. The established all-equity discount rate for the firm can then be used without great error in evaluating marginal investments whose individual variability and intercorrelation with other investments are not too divergent from the overall pattern.

[7] See Markowitz, *op. cit.*, p. 111.

*Alexander A. Robichek**

3.   Risk and the Value of Securities

Reprinted from the **Journal of Financial and Quantitative Analysis,** Vol. IV, No. 4 (December, 1969), pp. 513–538, by permission of the author and the publisher.

In retrospect, writing about "risk and valuation" is somewhat akin to killing Hydra, the mythical, many-headed creature which would grow two heads whenever one was cut off. It is only fair to admit at the outset that I cannot lay claim to have slain the beast. As a matter of fact, by the time the reader finishes the article, he may have concluded that the beast has more heads than ever!

Keeping the above warning in mind, the reader will find that the paper is addressed to two broad objectives. The principal one is an attempt to place the problem of risk and security valuation into perspective. The secondary purpose is to provide brief syntheses of the state-of-the-art in the various subareas under review and to propose directions for future research.[1] Rarely shall I be able to claim satisfactory resolution of thorny issues. Rather the analysis and conclusions should be viewed as exploratory and suggestive. They are merely steps on the long yellow brick road.

THE MEANING OF RISK IN THE CONTEXT OF SECURITY VALUATION

Few topics have received the attention given to "risk" in general and "risk and valuation" in particular. Still, the problem of defining "risk" as

* Professor of Finance, Stanford University. The analysis in this paper deals with the relationship between risk, however defined, and the value of securities. When the editor of this journal issued a call for articles concerning this general topic, I offered to revise a previously written paper on the subject [41]. The assignment appeared to offer excellent opportunities for tieing together a number of loose ends.

[1] In providing "brief syntheses of the state-of-the-art" it became necessary to limit the number of specific citations in the body of the paper. These limitations were necessary because of the enormous body of literature in the various subject areas under review. However, a great many contributions are grouped under major subject headings in the bibliography. The reader should be aware that the contributions included in the bibliography are far from uniform, either in terms of difficulty or quality; the selection was based on the desire to obtain breadth of coverage rather than uniformity of approach.

applied to investment decisions in a meaningful way needs consideration. By "in a meaningful way" I mean in a manner that will permit the formulation of theoretically valid hypotheses and ways of empirically testing these hypotheses. Finally, such a definition of risk should apply to the whole range of investments; i.e., to stocks, bonds, real estate, and even insurance.

The most common definition of risk in the context of valuation is as follows: risk relates to the possibility that actual returns may vary from expected returns. The origin of this definition lies in statistics: a random variable is one for which actual outcomes may differ from the mean. On the surface, the definition seems satisfactory. But, consider the following example. Is an investment in a long-term government bond riskless because actual returns should equal expected (promised) returns? One might say that the investment has no risk *if* the investor plans to hold the bond to maturity. On the other hand, if sale prior to maturity is a possibility, then an element of risk is introduced because bonds fluctuate in market value over time. But is it not true that even if the investor does not contemplate the sale of the bond, his "wealth" over time may be affected? Or, he may have to forego possibilities of more attractive future investments?

In general, the assumption is made (implicitly or explicitly) that investors as a group tend to be "risk averse," in the sense that, given equal expected returns, they prefer a security with no risk (or less risk) to one with more risk. Also, as noted in a previous paper [40], the assumption is often made that the manner in which risk affects value can be defined independently of the valuation process itself. The contention of this paper is that risk and valuation are inseparable; they are two sides of the same coin. If risk and valuation are inseparable, then can any real meaning be attached to the role of risk in the valuation process? The answer to the last question is a qualified "Yes." So, let us now turn to a specific analysis of that question.

THE VALUATION PROCESS

General

Under the assumption of perfect markets and certainty, traditional theory tells us that equilibrium conditions in the capital markets will lead to a unique term structure of interest rates. More precisely, if i_τ denotes the short-term interest rate at a future time τ, an investor can either invest or borrow at this rate for that particular time period. The various i_τ's constitute opportunity costs for the time value of money and thus serve as a basis for determining the present value of any stream of future benefits. Under these conditions, the present value of an investment V_o

is given by

$$V_o = \sum_{t=1}^{\infty} \frac{F_t}{\prod_{\tau=1}^{t} (1 + i_\tau)} \tag{1}$$

where F_t = return in time t and

$$\prod_{\tau=1}^{t} (1 + i_\tau) = (1 + i_1)(1 + i_2) \cdots (1 + i_t)$$

Frequently, Eq. (1) is simplified by making the further assumption that $i_\tau = i$ for all τ. In that case, the value of an investment is given by the well-known formula,

$$V_o = \sum_{t=1}^{\infty} \frac{F_t}{(1 + i)^t} \tag{2}$$

Without loss of generality and for ease of exposition Eq. (2) shall serve as a take-off point for our analysis of the role of risk in the valuation process.

The risk-premium approach

In the absence of certainty, the simplest approach to the manner in which risk affects value is to restate Eq. (2) as

$$V_o = \sum_{t=1}^{\infty} \frac{\bar{F}_t}{(1 + k)^t} \tag{3}$$

where $\bar{F}_t$ = expected value of future benefits;
$\quad k$ = the discount rate required on "risky" investments.

This risk-adjusted discount rate k is presumed to adjust for two factors simultaneously: time and risk. In general, the assumption is made that $k > i$, i.e., the discount rate for a risky security exceeds the rate on a "riskless" security.

It has been demonstrated by Sharpe [43] and Robichek and Myers [40] that if returns from the various investments are uncorrelated, a necessary condition for market equilibrium is for $k_j = i$ for all securities, where k_j is the risk-adjusted discount rate for the jth investment. Only if returns on the investments are correlated in some manner can the k_j's vary from i. Moreover, the degree to which the k_j's will vary from i cannot be estimated by analyzing a single investment's distribution of returns, but will depend directly on the co-variation of jth security's returns with the returns of other securities.

The expectation-variance portfolio approach

Markowitz [38], Sharpe [43], Lintner [37], and others have pointed out that investors invest in portfolios and that the "risk" of any individual security depends on how the addition of the security to a portfolio affects the risk of the portfolio. Specifically, under the assumption that investors use the expectations-variance criterion for making investment decisions, one arrives at the condition ([40], p. 219)

$$k_j = \frac{r_j \cdot \sigma_j}{\sigma_p} (k_p - i) + i \tag{4}$$

where r_j = correlation coefficient between the returns of security j and a portfolio p;

σ_j = standard deviation of expected returns on security j;

σ_p = standard deviation of expected returns on portfolio p;

k_p = required expected rate of return on portfolio p.

Equation (4) tells us that an investment, which by itself may be quite risky, may command a "discount rate" less than a riskless investment if the addition of the investment to a portfolio tends to reduce the risk (as measured by σ_p) of the overall portfolio.

While this type of analysis has broadened our understanding of financial theory, it has serious limitations. The assumptions in this analysis are:

1. The market is concerned only with the expected rate of return and the variance of portfolios.
2. Investment decisions are made using a one-period model.
3. The adjustment for risk and time can be made in the form of a "rate per period."

The adjustment for risk vs. time

As noted above, in the absence of uncertainty the interest rate reflects the adjustment of value for the dimension of time. But, the adjustment for time *and* risk by adding a constant factor to the "riskless" interest rate assumes a particular relationship between time and risk. Specifically, a constant k greater than a constant i presumes that uncertainty is expected to be resolved at a constant rate over time (see [70]). Additional problems arise if a constant risk-adjusted discount rate is assumed for a "risky" stream of benefits while the underlying term structure of interest rates on "riskless" investments varies as a function of time.

While the problem of adjusting for time and risk by means of a rate tends to compromise the theoretical foundations for the use of risk-adjusted rates, conditions may exist where a constant risk-adjusted discount rate can be justified within the limited dimensions of the framework of analysis discussed thus far. However, more serious conceptual and practical problems will be raised in the next section.

THE STATE-PREFERENCE APPROACH

A number of writers[2] have approached the problem of valuation in a "state-preference" framework. Basically, this approach assumes that the present values of uncertain future returns depend on the pattern of returns across various states-of-nature, the utility for money in the various states, and the likelihood of occurrence of the particular states. The framework lends itself admirably to the task at hand: placing risk and valuation into perspective.

State-preference and the valuation of "riskless" securities

In order to illustrate the basic concepts of the state-preference framework, let us initially make the following assumptions:

1. A one-period model.
2. Three states of nature.
3. The customary assumption of perfect markets and no taxes.

Let s = a particular state of nature;
$F_{s.1}$ = return in state s for Security 1;
P_s = probability of state s;
Y_s = value at $t=0$ per \$1 of returns promised in state s.

Consider a security (Security 1) that offers a return of \$100 in each of the three assumed states of nature in period 1 and other factors as shown in Table 1.

TABLE 1. VALUATION OF A "RISKLESS" SECURITY

State	P_s	F_s	Y_s	$P_s \cdot F_{s.1}$	$P_s \cdot F_{s.1} \cdot Y_s$
1	.30	100	.80	30	24.00
2	.60	100	.96	60	57.60
3	.10	100	1.20	10	12.00
				100	93.60

The Y_s's are similar in concept to Arrow's [3] "primitive securities." Their value is determined in a general equilibrium framework by the forces of supply and demand. The concept is discussed in some depth by Myers [39]. In essence, the approach assumes that present values (or utilities) of future returns are contingent on the states of nature. In Table 1, for

---

[2] See, for example, Arrow [3], Hirschleifer [17], and Myers [39].

example, state 1 might be associated with inflation, state 2 with normal economic conditions, and state 3 with a recession.

The differences in present values per \$1 of return in the various states of nature may be attributed to differences in expected purchasing power and to the fact that the utility of "real" money varies with the different states for reasons to be discussed later.

Given the assumptions, the present value of the "riskless" security is shown in the last column of the table:

$$V_{0.1} = \sum_{s=1}^{3} P_s \cdot F_{s.1} \cdot Y_s = \$93.60 \tag{5}$$

where $V_{0.1}$ = value at time 0 for Security 1.

Several other observations appear in order. The expected value of returns in period 1 for Security 1, $\bar{F}_{1.1}$, is computed in the next-to-last column of Table 1:

$$\bar{F}_{1.1} = \sum_{s=1}^{3} P_s \cdot F_{s.1} = \$100.00 \tag{6}$$

In this example, $\bar{F}_{1.1}$ is not a random variable because its returns are invariant across the various states of nature. Using the common definition, the security is "riskless." Given $V_{0.1}$ from Eq. (5) and $F_{1.1}$ from Eq. (6), we can now derive the one-period "riskless" interest rate. Specifically,

$$i_1 = \frac{F_{1.1}}{V_{0.1}} - 1 = \frac{100.00}{93.60} - 1 = .068 \text{ or } 6.8\% \tag{7}$$

The important thing to note is that the interest rate was the dependent variable in this analysis, $F_{1.1}$ and $V_{0.1}$ were independently determined and then used to compute i_1.

Valuation of risky securities

Table 2 illustrates the returns and the valuation process for a "risky" security (Security 2). The security is "risky" in the sense that its returns are not identical in each state of nature.

TABLE 2.   VALUATION OF A "RISKY" SECURITY

State	P_s	F_s	Y_s	$P_s \cdot F_{s.2}$	$P_s \cdot F_{s.2} \cdot Y_s$
1	.30	110	.80	33	26.40
2	.60	100	.96	60	57.60
3	.10	70	1.20	7	8.40
				$\bar{F}_{1.2} = 100$	92.60

Note that the expected return on the "risky" security, $\bar{F}_{1.2}$ is equal to the expected return for the "riskless" security. However, the value of the risky security is only \$92.60. We can now compute the "discount rate" for the risky security in a manner analogous to the computation of the riskless rate i_1 in Eq. (7). Thus,

$$k_1 = \frac{\bar{F}_{1.2}}{V_{0.2}} - 1 = \frac{100.00}{92.60} - 1 = .080 \text{ or } 8.0\% \tag{8}$$

Traditional theory would attribute the difference in yields between the risky and the riskless security (i.e., .08 − .068) to the presence of risk aversion in the market. *This conclusion is incorrect for the examples used above and, moreover, it is unwarranted when considering valuation in general.*

Let us examine the reasons for the observed difference in yields. From a purely mathematical standpoint, the difference in yields is a direct result of different market values for the two securities, since the expected returns are identical. And the reason for the difference in market values of the two securities is easily identified—compared to the "riskless" security, the "risky" security is expected to provide relatively high monetary returns in a state where the "present value" of these returns is low (state 1) and low returns when the value is high (state 3).

In order to understand fully the nature of the problem it will be useful to separate the valuation process into: (1) the effects of purchasing power, and (2) the effects of other factors.

Valuation, purchasing power, and other factors

As a first step, let us assume that the utility of monetary returns is a direct reflection of purchasing power. Table 3 provides an example for the riskless (Security 1) and the risky (Security 2) securities previously described and using assumed purchasing power indices for the three states of nature.

TABLE 3. PURCHASING POWER OF RETURNS ON SECURITIES 1 AND 2

State	P_s	I_s	Security 1: $P_s \cdot F_{s.1} \cdot I_s$	Security 2: $P_s \cdot F_{s.2} \cdot I_s$
1	.3	.95	28.50	31.35
2	.6	1.00	60.00	60.00
3	.1	1.15	11.50	8.05
			$\bar{Z}_{1.1} = 100.00$	$\bar{Z}_{1.2} = 99.40$

I_s = purchasing power index in state s.
$\bar{Z}_{1.j}$ = expected purchasing power in period 1 for security j.

The last two columns in Table 3 give us the "expected purchasing power" of the returns from the two securities. Note that $\bar{Z}_{1.1} = \bar{F}_{1.1}$, i.e., the expected purchasing power of the "riskless" security is equal to its expected return. This implies that no loss of general purchasing power is expected in period 1. However, for the "risky" security $\bar{Z}_{1.2} = \$99.40$ which is less than $\bar{F}_{1.2}$ the expected return. *Without any risk aversion* in the market the price of Security 2 $V_{0.2}$ would be less than $V_{0.1}$ the price of Security 1. Specifically,

$$V_{0.2} = \frac{\bar{Z}_{1.2}}{\bar{Z}_{1.1}} \cdot V_{0.1} \qquad (9)$$

And, of course, given a lower price for Security 2, $k_1 > i_1$ even though we specified valuation without risk aversion. Since, in general, "risky investments" such as common stocks are expected to have higher returns in periods when purchasing power is less (and vice versa), one might hypothesize that this factor alone would cause $k_j > i$.

As mentioned earlier, it is possible that factors other than purchasing power influence the utility of money in the various states. For example, if one expects to lose his job in a recession, his utility for money in that state may be quite a bit higher than what the purchasing power index may indicate. Also, the holdings of such investments as fire and life insurance may be explained in this context. These "investments" generally have a negative expected return and bear little or no correlation to returns from other securities in the market. The inclusion of "insurance" in a portfolio cannot be theoretically explained in the expectations-variance framework. But, the rationale for "investing" in insurance is quite straightforward in a state-preference framework—the large returns from an insurance policy would fall in a state where these returns have extremely high utility.

"Risk" and the state preference framework

Given the preceding discussion, what can be said about the meaning of risk in the context of security valuation? Even within the simplified framework assumed in the preceding analysis, certain conclusions appear in order. Risk, and its impact on valuation, must be considered in relation to the attainment of investment goals. In a state preference context, investors seek to achieve a preferred pattern of returns across various states-of-nature which will maximize their utility. Quite likely, this pattern is subject to a variety of constraints. For example, the constraints might take the following form: The returns from investments in period 1 must be at least (1) \$3,000 should there be a recession; (2) \$4,000 should there be a mild inflation; (3) \$25,000 should my house burn down; (4) \$10,000 should I become disabled; (5) \$100,000 should I die; etc. Obviously, as stated, several of the constraints may not be mutually exclusive, but they were merely used to illustrate the idea.

In setting the above constraints, an investor presumably takes into account his consumption needs, his returns from sources other than investments, the investment alternatives open to him, his available resources, and any other factors relevant to him.

If the preceding comments are a reasonably accurate description of the investment decision process (and I believe that the description is not far off the mark), then *"investment risk" must refer to the possibility of not attaining the required (or desired) pattern of returns.* Viewed in this manner, the common distinction between a "riskless" and a "risky" security loses meaning. A so-called "riskless" security is extremely risky from the standpoint of providing required returns in inflation or in the case of a family disaster such as fire or death. Conversely, a "risky" security, such as a common stock, may well serve to reduce the overall investment risk by providing a desired "inflation hedge." And, to complicate matters further, what may be "risky" to one investor may be "riskless" or at least reduce risk to other investors.

The example of the long-term government bond near the beginning of the paper is a case in point. Investment in such a bond may be of low risk to a pension fund which faces fixed future monetary obligations; on the other hand, this investment may be quite "risky" to a private investor who seeks inflation protection.

The actual "market," in turn, is populated by literally millions of investors, each of whom may differ as to:

1. Investment goals, constraints, current incomes, and consumption patterns.
2. Assessments of the relevant probabilities of states, returns, future purchasing power, and utilities toward monetary returns.
3. Knowledge of the universe of opportunities and available information.
4. Personal tax rates.
5. Analytical capability, and possibly other factors.

The interactions of this heterogeneous group of investors lead to a system of market prices which, by definition, is in equilibrium. Faced with continuously changing goals, prices, etc., individual investors must be prepared to alter their investment holdings as conditions and needs change. The decision to change the composition of a portfolio rests, in part, on the "going prices" for the various investment alternatives. And, individual actions may well affect prices and, thus, induce other investors to act, and so on.

In summary, more questions have been raised than have been answered. In a sense, it is like opening Pandora's Box. But, hopefully not all the items in the box are "evil." A few preliminary conclusions and their theoretical and practical implications appear in order.

1. The term "risk" as applied to investments in general has no clearly defined meaning. In particular, serious doubt is cast on the value of such risk-measuring surrogates as variance of returns, covariance of returns, and the coefficient of variation.
2. The "risk" of an investment refers to the possibility that an investment will not provide a desired or required pattern of returns. "Investment risk" is unique to the individual investor; what may be "risky" to one investor need not be risky to another.
3. There is no theoretical justification for any generalized statement as to how risk affects the value of securities. The common presumption that risky investments are expected to yield more than riskless investments is unwarranted. Several exceptions to this generalization were noted in the preceding comments.
4. It may be possible to segregate securities into broad classes and then study the impact on value of changes in particular decision variables, such as the use of debt. Presumably, changes in these variables would affect the perceived pattern of returns to the investors. After adjusting for the dimensions of time and purchasing power, the investor's "risk attitude" will lead to a residual adjustment in the "present utilities" of returns. At the margin, it is this residual adjustment that reflects the influence of risk on value; it is difficult to say, however, whether this element can in fact be isolated.
5. Introduction of the multiperiod investment problem and differential personal taxes complicates the analysis but does not compromise the principal conclusions. Additional theoretical work needs to be done to integrate these factors into a logical conceptual framework.

INVESTMENT "RISK" AND PRACTICE

The preceding analysis raised some questions about basic issues concerning risk and investments. At best, the state of knowledge on the subject can be said to be in a state of flux. A more radical view would be to say that the problem is a "can of worms."

A great deal of useful work has been done and can be done to provide grounds for a better understanding of the practical problems. The remainder of the paper will take a more pragmatic view of the issues involved.

Despite the theoretical difficulties, the investment community is concerned with "investment risk" and even appears to agree broadly in its reference to it. In general, the "risk" of an investment tends to be associated with the possibility that the returns, particularly as reflected in the market value of the investment, may decline over time—commonly referred to as "downside risk." Most investors do not think of "upside potential" as "risk." Also, a substantial number of investors, particularly institutions, limit their universe of investments to securities, such as common stocks and bonds, and thus may be concerned only with a part of the overall investment problem discussed here.

From a practical standpoint, it may be useful to separate the securities valuation process into the following segments:

1. Identify a set of "general states of nature" that influence returns on investments.
2. Given the set of general states, estimate the "specific states of returns" on particular securities.
3. Assign probabilities to the occurrence of the various "general-specific" state combinations.
4. Estimate "present value" factors for the returns in the various states, using whatever goals or constraints may be relevant.

Figure 1 illustrates a hypothetical set of general states of nature for a one-period environment and assumed probabilities pertaining to these states. The figure is not intended to be representative of a real-life situation but indicative of the general approach that may be followed.

Given this "general set," a considerably more difficult task is to identify the "specific states of returns" on the various securities. In the first place, should the returns reflect only actual cash flows or should the end-of-period market value of a longer-term security also be included? The answer depends on the investments goals of the individual investor. An investor, such as a life insurance company, may be primarily concerned with the pattern of actual cash flows over many time periods and have little interest in short-run fluctuations in market value. In that case, market value may be properly excluded from periodic "returns."

However, many investors make decisions using short-term investment horizons (say one year). In that case, the end-of-period market value would be a significant part of the "returns" and should be so considered. This market value, of course, would depend on expectations and valuation methods employed by the "market" at the end of the period. And therein lies one of the principal difficulties: what factors do investors consider in arriving at the market value of a long-term security? Much of the theoretical and empirical research (see bibliography) has attempted to find

FIGURE 1

HYPOTHETICAL SET OF GENERAL STATES OF NATURE

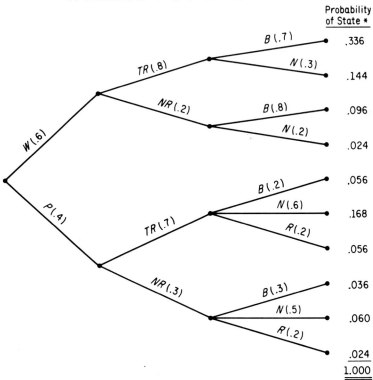

Probability
of State *

.336

.144

.096

.024

.056

.168

.056

.036

.060

.024
1.000

W = War or P = Peace
TR = Tax Reform or NR = No Tax Reform
B = Boom
N = Normal
R = Recession

* The probability of occurrence is shown inside the parentheses.

answers to the above question. The results of all this research have stimulated a great deal of useful dialogue and additional research. But, the
problem is that frequently research findings tend to be in direct conflict.
For example, one researcher may find that past variability in earnings per
share has an adverse effect on the market multiplier of common stocks,
whereas another researcher may offer equally convincing evidence showing
no discernible effect. Or, a statistical model is reported able to "explain"
90 percent or more of the market prices for the period tested, but the same

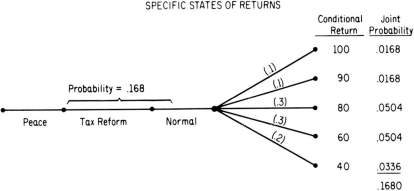

FIGURE 2

SPECIFIC STATES OF RETURNS

valuation model is almost useless a year later when applied to the same set of securities. The availability of more and better financial information to researchers in computer readable form should help us gain more insight into the actual valuation process. But much work remains to be done. Still, assume that by some process the investor arrives at his estimates of future market prices, and thus at the value of returns for purposes of our example. Figure 2 shows how these values and their associated probabilities may be combined with one "branch" from Figure 1.

The probabilities shown in Figures 1 and 2 are subjective in nature and reflect the individual investor's opinions. Little empirical work has been done which offers promise in this area.

The final stumbling block is the last of the four "segments" of the valuation process—the estimation of the "present value" factors. At this stage, not much can be added to what has been said in the preceding section of this paper. A number of areas offer potential for fruitful research, such as:

1. Identify the influence of various "general states of nature" on the returns from broad classes of securities, such as bonds and stocks of particular industries.
2. Study the manner in which various economic developments influence operating results of firms issuing securities.
3. Continue studies attempting to identify the valuation processes actually used by the investors. These studies may get at the problem indirectly by analyzing and testing a variety of hypotheses using available data. Or, perhaps meaningful information can be obtained by direct surveys of investors.

The comments in this section dealt with the general problem of investing in an uncertain environment. A few specific comments related to particular security groups will conclude the paper.

VALUATION AND SECURITY GROUPS

Up to this point, the comments in this paper dealt with "valuation and risk" in general. In real life, select security groups tend to share some of the basic characteristics that influence valuation. A brief review of the common features for government bonds, corporate bonds, and common stocks follows.

Government bonds

The valuation of government bonds and related studies of the term structure of interest rates have been favorite subjects of researchers for years. But, much of the research has been directed at the analysis and interpretation of the "term structure of interest rates." Only recently have researchers studied the problem of "risk" in holding government bonds by measuring the price variability of these bonds over time (see Michaelson [56], and Van Horne and Bowers [57]).

As noted in a preceding section, government bonds (particularly long-term) may well have considerable "investment risk" because their market value fluctuates over time. In the context of a one-period, state-preference framework, the portion of the end-of-period return represented by the market value of the bond may be variable across the various states of nature. This variability is not caused by uncertainties as to "future" returns; rather, it is due to possible shifts in the structure of interest rates on government securities. And, since interest rates merely reflect the market's utilities for future returns Eq. (7), one can say that the variability in the market price of government bonds over time is caused by changes in the utility of returns across the various states of nature.

Additional research should be directed to the study of:

1. Variability of government bond prices over time.
2. Forecasting models for future interest rates.
3. The effect of various provisions of the tax laws on observed market yields.
4. The manner in which the potential variability of bond prices affects the value of the bonds.

Corporate bonds

The principal difference between corporate (nonconvertible) and government bonds lies in the fact that actual periodic returns on corporate bonds may not equal promised returns. In other words, the returns across the various states of nature may be unequal. For example, actual returns may be below promised returns due to a default on the part of the issuer. Or, in some instances, the returns may be higher than indicated by the promised coupon rate because the bond is called before maturity at a premium. As a general rule, the investor in a straight corporate bond accepts a high probability (say 90 percent or more) of actually receiving the promised return and a small probability of receiving considerably less than the promised return. Except for the fact that the periodic returns and the final maturity payment may be random variables, the valuation problem for corporate bonds is similar to the one for government bonds. In either case, the length of time over which the returns are to be received is generally fixed and the actual returns tend to equal (with the exception noted) promised returns.

A number of researchers have attempted to measure the "risk of default" in corporate bonds. Hickman [60] amassed large quantities of data subsequently used by Fraine and Mills [59] and Johnson [62]. Fisher [58] attempted to identify the determinants of yields on corporate bonds by using multiple regression analysis.

Several studies appear indicated:

1. Examination of the yield differentials between corporate and government bonds as functions of (a) the rate level on government bonds, and (b) time to maturity.
2. Development of a complete theory of valuation as applied to "risky" bonds.
3. Analysis of investor attitudes toward possible variability in returns on corporate bonds.
4. A study of the degree of covariance between prices of the various grades of corporate bonds and government bonds.

Common stocks

Common stocks present an entirely different valuation problem from the one encountered in the analysis of fixed-income, limited horizon securities. Although dividends of many companies tend to follow fairly regular patterns, there are no promised payments to serve as the basis for estimating future dividends. Also, the security itself has an unlimited life. Despite these differences, the basic concepts of valuation discussed in this paper are applicable to common stocks. The main difference, as a rule, is that an investor in common stocks is faced with a far larger set of return-state combinations than one who limits his investments to fixed-income securities. In particular, the set of "specific states of returns" shown in Figure 2 may need to reflect the many possible alternative values for the end-of-period market price.

The development of financial data banks in computer-readable form has enabled researchers to use a great deal of data and to test empirically a wide range of hypotheses in attempts to identify the factors that determine the market values of common stocks. All this empirical work is necessary and useful. But, great care needs to be exercised in correctly formulating the hypotheses before doing any empirical testing. Not infrequently one finds *ex post* data used in testing *ex ante* hypotheses or models tested that may not be valid either in theory or in practice.

Most of the empirical work dealing with common stocks involves the use of multivariate regression analysis and generally includes one or more variables designed to measure "risk." The most common surrogates for "risk" are the standard deviation of earnings per share from a trend line, the variability of the rate of return on shareholder capital, and the debt/equity ratio. In general, the empirical tests are of two kinds: those that hold "risk" constant and those that attempt to explain the influence of some specific "risk" variable on the market price. The first category would include much of the work by Miller and Modigliani [69] and [85]. In the second category we find tests of: leverage on value (Barges [76], Wippern [89]); standard deviation of earnings around a trend on value (Ahlers [74]); standard deviation of holding period returns on the realized rates of return (Pratt [86]); and variability of returns on stockholder capital on the average rates of return on capital (Fisher and Hall [81]).

A common impediment to researchers is the disparity between the theory of valuation and practice. Theoretical models may or may not be appropriate representations of real life. As noted, we must attempt to become more familiar with the manner in which investors approach the stock valuation problem in practice and then relate these approaches to theoretical models. It might, however, be a difficult task to formulate a "model" which adequately describes a ouija board or a "hot tip."

Useful hypotheses to be investigated include:

1. The effect of variability in rates of return on capital and earnings on price/earnings ratios, prices, and the holding period returns to shareholders.
2. Do investors apply a "yield" notion to their investments in common stocks? How can this "required yield" be estimated?
3. How do investors adjust for perceived "risk" in evaluating stocks?
4. Develop and test theoretically consistent models relating to the effects of "growth" on value and whether "growth" creates risks in the minds of investors.
5. Attempt to gather *ex ante* data for comparison with *ex post* results.
6. Study the differences in the factors that affect prices for stocks in different industries.

SUMMARY

At the outset, I stated that this report should be considered exploratory and suggestive. A great many questions were raised, a few answers were offered, and a limited number of topics were listed as deserving further study.

I hope to have at least stimulated some thinking in the area of risk and the value of securities. It looks like we have a long way to go, but the future appears bright.

REFERENCES

I. Risk and Value in General

[1] Angell, J. W., "Uncertainty, Likelihoods and Investment Decisions," *Quarterly Journal of Economics* (February 1960), pp. 1–28.

[2] Armstrong, W. E., "Uncertainty and the Utility Function," *Economics Journal* (March 1948), pp. 1–10.

[3] Arrow, Kenneth J., "Alternative Approaches to the Theory of Choice in Risk Taking Situations," *Econometrica* (October 1951), pp. 404–37.

[4] ——, *Aspects of the Theory of Risk Bearing.* Yrjö Jahnssonin Säätiö, Helsinki, Finland: The Academic Book Store, 1965.

[5] Borch, Karl, "A Note on Utility and Attitudes to Risk," *Management Science* (July 1963), pp. 697–700.

[6] Edwards, Ward, "The Theory of Decision Making," *Psychological Bulletin* (July 1954), pp. 380–441. Look at bibliography.

[7] Egerton, R. A. D., *Investment Decisions Under Uncertainty.* Liverpool, England: Liverpool U. P., 1960.

[8] ——, "Investment, Uncertainty, and Expectations," *Review of Economic Studies* (No. 2, 1955), pp. 143–50.

[9] Ellsberg, Daniel, "Risk, Ambiguity, and the Savage Axions," *Quarterly Journal of Economics* (November 1961), pp. 643–69; "Reply," *Quarterly Journal of Economics* (May 1963), pp. 336–42.

[10] Fellner, William, "Distortion of Subjective Probabilities as a Reaction to Uncertainty," *Quarterly Journal of Economics* (November 1961), pp. 670–89; "Reply," *Quarterly Journal of Economics* (November 1963), pp. 676–90.

[11] ——, *Probability and Profit.* Homewood, Illinois: Irwin, 1965.

[12] Friedman, Milton, and L. Savage, "The Utility Analysis of Choices Involving Risk," *Journal of Political Economy* (August 1948), pp. 279–304.

[13] ——, "The Expected Utility Hypothesis and the Measurability of Utility," *Journal of Political Economy* (December 1952), pp. 463–75.

[14] Gray, Roger W., "The Search for a Risk Premium," *Journal of Political Economy* (June 1961), pp. 250–60.

[15] Haynes, John, "Risk as an Economic Factor," *Quarterly Journal of Economics* (July 1895), pp. 409–49.

[16] Hirshleifer, Jack, "On the Theory of Optimal Investment Decision," *Journal of Political Economy* (August 1958), pp. 329–52.

[17] ——, "Risk, the Discount Rate, and Investment Decisions," *American Economic Review* (May 1961), pp. 112–20.

[18] Knight, F. H., *Risk, Uncertainty and Profit*. Boston, Mass.: Houghton Mifflin, 1921.

[19] Latané, Henry Allen, "Criteria for Choice Among Risky Ventures," *Journal of Political Economy* (April 1959), pp. 144–55.

[20] Pratt, J. W., "Risk Aversion in the Small and in the Large," *Econometrica* (April 1964), pp. 122–36.

[21] ——, Howard Raiffa, and Robert Schlaifer, "The Foundations of Decision Under Uncertainty," *Journal of the American Statistical Association* (June 1964), pp. 353–75.

[22] Smith, Vernon L., "Time Preference and Risk in Investment Theory," *American Economic Review* (May 1961), pp. 124–27.

[23] Stigler, George J., "The Development of Utility Theory," *Journal of Political Economy* (October 1950), pp. 373–96.

[24] Tintner, Gerhard, "The Theory of Choice Under Subjective Risk and Uncertainty," *Econometrica* (July–October 1941), pp. 298–304.

II. Risk and Security Markets in General

[25] Alchian, Armen A., and K. Arrow, "The Role of Securities in the Optimal Allocation of Risk-Bearing," *Review of Economic Studies* (April 1964), pp. 91–96.

[26] Archer, Stephen H., "Diversification and Risk Reduction," *University of Washington Business Review* (April–June 1964), pp. 19–25.

[27] Baumol, William J., "An Expected Gain-Confidence Limit Criterion for Portfolio Selection," *Management Science* (October 1963), pp. 174–82.

[28] ——, "Mathematical Analysis of Portfolio Selection," *Financial Analysts Journal* (September–October 1966), pp. 95–99.

[29] Clarkson, Geoffrey P. E., and Allen Meltzer, "Portfolio Selection: A Heuristic Approach," *Journal of Finance* (December 1960), pp. 465–80.

[30] Cohen, Kalman, and Edwin Elton, "Inter-temporal Portfolio Analysis Based on Simulation of Joint Returns," *Management Science* (September 1967), pp. 5–18.

[31] Cootner, Paul H., and Daniel M. Holland, *Risk and Rate of Return*. DSR Project No. 9565 (February 1964).

[32] Fanning, James E., and M. Steglitz, "A Risk Measure for Common Stock Portfolios," Paper at Chicago Seminar (November 4, 1966).

[33] Freund, Rudolf J., "The Introduction of Risk Into a Programming Model," *Econometrica* (July 1956), pp. 253–63.

[34] Haney, Lewis, "Different Values of Income from Short Loans, Bonds and Stocks," *Analysts Journal* (February 1954), pp. 9–13.

[35] Hirshleifer, Jack, "Efficient Allocation of Capital in an Uncertain World," *American Economic Review* (May 1964), pp. 77–85.

[36] Latané, Henry Allen, "Investment Criteria—A Three Asset Portfolio Balance Model," *Review of Economics and Statistics* (November 1963), pp. 427–30.

[37] Lintner, John, "Security Prices, Risk and Maximal Gains from Diversification," *Journal of Finance* (December 1965), pp. 587–615.

[38] Markowitz, Harry M., "Portfolio Selection," *Journal of Finance* (March 1952), pp. 77–91.

[39] Myers, Stewart C., "A Time-State-Preference Model of Security Valuation," *Journal of Financial and Quantitative Analysis.* (March 1968), pp. 1–34.

[40] Robichek, Alexander A., and Stewart C. Myers, "Valuation of the Firm: Effects of Uncertainty in the Market Context," *Journal of Finance* (May 1966), pp. 215–27.

[41] ——, "The Impact of Risk on the Value of Securities," paper presented before the Institute for Quantitative Research in Finance, October 1968.

[42] Roy, A. D., "Safety First and the Holding of Assets," *Econometrica* (July 1952), pp. 431–49.

[43] Sharpe, William F., "Capital Asset Prices: A Theory of Market Equilibrium Under Conditions of Risk," *Journal of Finance* (September 1964), pp. 425–42.

[44] ——, "Risk Aversion in the Stock Market: Some Empirical Evidence," *Journal of Finance* (September 1965), pp. 416–22.

[45] ——, "A Simplified Model for Portfolio Analysis," *Management Science* (January 1963), pp. 277–93.

III. The Term Structure of Interest Rates

[46] Conard, Joseph, *Introduction to the Theory of Interest.* (Berkeley, Calif.: U. of Calif. P., 1959).

[47] Culbertson, J. M., "The Term Structure of Interest Rates," *Quarterly Journal of Economics* (November 1957), pp. 485–517.

[48] Durand, David, *Basic Yields of Corporate Bonds, 1900–1942.* (New York, N. Y.: National Bureau of Economic Research, 1942).

[49] Fisher, Irving, *The Theory of Interest.* (New York, N. Y.: Macmillan, 1930).

[50] Grossman, Herschel I., "Risk Aversion, Financial Intermediation, and the Term Structure of Interest Rates," *Journal of Finance* (December 1967), pp. 611–22.

[51] Hicks, J. R., *Value and Capital.* 2d ed. (London, England: Oxford U. P., 1946).

[52] Kessel, Reuben, *The Cyclical Behavior of the Term Structure of Interest Rates.* (New York: National Bureau of Economic Research, 1965).

[53] Lutz, F. A., "The Structure of Interest Rates," *Quarterly Journal of Economics* (November 1940), pp. 36–63.

[54] Malkiel, B. G., *The Term Structure of Interest Rates* (Princeton, N. J.: Princeton U. P., 1966).

[55] Meiselman, David, *The Term Structure of Interest Rates* (Englewood Cliffs, N. J.: Prentice-Hall, 1962).

[56] Michaelson, Jacob B., "The Term Structure of Interest Rates and Holding Period Yields on Government Securities," *Journal of Finance* (September 1965), pp. 444–63.

[57] Van Horne, James, and David Bowers, "The Liquidity Impact of Debt Management," *Southern Economic Journal* (April 1968), pp. 526–37.

IV. The Risk Structure of Interest Rate

[58] Fisher, Lawrence, "Determinants of Risk Premiums on Corporate Bonds," *Journal of Political Economy* (June 1959), pp. 217–37.

[59] Fraine, Harold G., and Robert Mills, "Effect of Defaults and Credit Deterioration on Yields of Corporate Bonds," *Journal of Finance* (September 1961), pp. 423–34.

[60] Hickman, W. B., *Corporate Bond Quality and Investor Experience* (Princeton, N. J.: Princeton U. P., 1958).

[61] Jen, Frank C., and James E. Wert, "The Effects of Call Risk on Corporate Bond Yields," *Journal of Finance* (December 1967), pp. 637–51.

[62] Johnson, Ramon E., "Term Structure of Corporate Bond Yields as a Function of Risk of Default," *Journal of Finance* (May 1967), pp. 313–50 + disc.

[63] Sloane, Peter E., "Determinants of Bond Yield Differentials," *Yale Economic Essays* (Spring 1963), pp. 3–55.

V. General Stock Valuation Models

[64] Brigham, Eugene, and James Pappas, "Duration of Growth, Changes in Growth Rates and Corporate Share Prices," *Financial Analysts Journal* (May–June 1966), pp. 157–62.

[65] Gordon, Myron J., *The Investment, Financing and Valuation of the Corporation* (Homewood, Ill.: Irwin, 1962).

[66] Holt, C. C., "The Influence of Growth Duration on Share Prices," *Journal of Finance* (September 1962), pp. 465–75.

[67] Lerner, Eugene, and Willard T. Carleton, *A Theory of Financial Analysis* (New York, N. Y.: Harcourt, Brace & World, 1966)

[68] Malkiel, Burton G., "Equity Yields, Growth and the Structure of Share Prices," *American Economic Review* (December 1963), pp. 1004–31.

[69] Miller, Merton H., and Franco Modigliani, "Dividend Policy, Growth, and the Valuation of Shares," *Journal of Business* (October 1961), pp. 411–33.

[70] Robichek, Alexander A., and Stewart C. Myers, *Optimal Financing Decisions* (Englewood Cliffs, N. J.: Prentice-Hall, 1965).

[71] Solomon, Ezra, *The Theory of Financial Management* (New York, N. Y.: Columbia U. P., 1963).

[72] Williams, J. B., *Theory of Investment Value* (Amsterdam, Holland: North-Holland Publishing Company, 1956).

[73] Walter, J. E., "Dividend Policies and Common Stock Prices," *Journal of Finance* (March 1956).

VI. Empirical Tests of Stock Valuation Models

[74] Ahlers, D. M., "SEM: A Security Evaluation Mode," in Cohen, K., and F. Hammer. *Analytical Methods in Banking* (Homewood, Ill.: Irwin, 1966), pp. 300–36.

[75] Arditti, Fred D., "Risk and the Required Return on Equity," *Journal of Finance* (March 1967), pp. 19–36.

[76] Barges, A., *The Effect of Capital Structure on the Cost of Capital* (Englewood Cliffs, N. J.: Prentice-Hall, 1963).

[77] Benishay, Haskell, "Variability in Earnings-Price Ratios," *American Economic Review* (March 1961), pp. 61–94. "Reply," *American Economic Review* (March 1962), pp. 209–16.

[78] Clendenin, John C., "Quality vs. Price as Factors Influencing Common Stock Fluctuations," *Journal of Finance* (December 1951), pp. 398–405.

[79] Conrad, Gordon R., and I. H. Plotkin, "Risk/Return: U.S. Industry Pattern," *Harvard Business Review* (March–April 1968), pp. 90–99.

[80] Fama, E. F., "The Behavior of Stock Market Prices," *Journal of Business* (January 1966).

[81] Fisher, Irving, and George Hall, "Risk and the Aerospace Rate of Return," RAND memo RM-5440-PR (December 1967).

[82] Friend, I., and M. Puckett, "Dividends and Stock Prices," *American Economic Review* (September 1964), pp. 656–82.

[83] Gordon, M. J., *The Investment, Financing, and Valuation of the Corporation* (Homewood, Ill.: Irwin, 1962).

[84] Heins, A. James, and S. Allison, "Some Factors Affecting Stock Price Variability," *Journal of Business* (January 1966), pp. 19–23.

[85] Miller, M., and F. Modigliani, "Some Estimates of the Cost of Capital to the Electric Utility Industry, 1954–57," *American Economic Review* (June 1966), pp. 333–91.

[86] Pratt, S. P., "The Relationship Between Risk and Rate of Return," paper presented at the annual meeting of the Western Finance Association (Corvallis, Oregon, August 22, 1968).

[87] Robichek, A., J. McDonald, and R. Higgins, "Some Estimates of the Cost of Capital to the Electric Utility Industry, 1954–57: Comment," *American Economic Review* (December 1967), pp. 1278–88.

[88] Stigler, G. J., *Capital and Rates of Return in Manufacturing Industries* (Princeton, N. J.: National Bureau of Economic Research, 1963).

[89] Wippern, R. F., "Financial Structure and the Value of the Firm," *Journal of Finance* (December 1966), pp. 615–33.

Harry Markowitz[*]

4.　Portfolio Selection[1]

Reprinted from **The Journal of Finance,** Vol. VII, No. 1 (March, 1952), pp. 77–91, by permission of the publisher.

The process of selecting a portfolio may be divided into two stages. The first stage starts with observation and experience and ends with beliefs about the future performances of available securities. The second stage starts with the relevant beliefs about future performances and ends with the choice of portfolio. This paper is concerned with the second stage. We first consider the rule that the investor does (or should) maximize discounted expected, or anticipated, returns. This rule is rejected both as a hypothesis to explain, and as a maxim to guide investment behavior. We next consider the rule that the investor does (or should) consider expected return a desirable thing *and* variance of return an undesirable thing. This rule has many sound points, both as a maxim for, and hypothesis about, investment behavior. We illustrate geometrically relations between beliefs and choice of portfolio according to the "expected returns—variance of returns" rule.

One type of rule concerning choice of portfolio is that the investor does (or should) maximize the discounted (or capitalized) value of future returns.[2] Since the future is not known with certainty, it must be "expected" or "anticipated" returns which we discount. Variations of this type of rule can be suggested. Following Hicks, we could let "anticipated" returns include an allowance for risk.[3] Or, we could let the rate at which we capitalize the returns from particular securities vary with risk.

The hypothesis (or maxim) that the investor does (or should) maximize discounted return must be rejected. If we ignore market imperfections the foregoing rule never implies that there is a diversified portfolio which

[*] Dr. Markowitz is associated with the Rand Corporation.

[1] This paper is based on work done by the author while at the Cowles Commission for Research in Economics and with the financial assistance of the Social Science Research Council. It will be reprinted as Cowles Commission Paper, New Series, No. 60.

[2] See, for example, J. B. Williams, *The Theory of Investment Value* (Cambridge, Mass.: Harvard University Press, 1938), pp. 55–75.

[3] J. R. Hicks, *Value and Capital* (New York, N.Y.: Oxford University Press, 1939), p. 126. Hicks applies the rule to a firm rather than a portfolio.

is preferable to all nondiversified portfolios. Diversification is both observed and sensible; a rule of behavior which does not imply the superiority of diversification must be rejected both as a hypothesis and as a maxim.

The foregoing rule fails to imply diversification no matter how the anticipated returns are formed; whether the same or different discount rates are used for different securities; no matter how these discount rates are decided upon or how they vary over time.[4] The hypothesis implies that the investor places all his funds in the security with the greatest discounted value. If two or more securities have the same value, then any of these or any combination of these is as good as any other.

We can see this analytically: suppose there are N securities; let r_{it} be the anticipated return (however decided upon) at time t per dollar invested in security i; let d_{it} be the rate at which the return on the ith security at time t is discounted back to the present; let X_i be the relative amount invested in security i. We exclude short sales, thus $X_i \geq 0$ for all i. Then the discounted anticipated return of the portfolio is

$$R = \sum_{t=1}^{\infty} \sum_{i=1}^{N} d_{it} r_{it} X$$

$$= \sum_{i=1}^{N} X_i (\sum_{t=1}^{\infty} d_{it} r_{it})$$

$R_i = \sum_{t=1}^{\infty} d_{it} r_{it}$ is the discounted return of the ith security, therefore

$R = \Sigma X_i R_i$ where R_i is independent of X_i. Since $X_i \geq 0$ for all i and $\Sigma X_i = 1$, R is a weighted average of R_i with the X_i as nonnegative weights. To maximize R, we let $X_i = 1$ for i with maximum R_i. If several Ra_a, $a = 1, \ldots, K$ are maximum then any allocation with

$$\sum_{a=1}^{K} Xa_a = 1$$

maximizes R. In no case is a diversified portfolio preferred to all non-diversified portfolios.[5]

It will be convenient at this point to consider a static model. Instead of speaking of the time series of returns from the ith security $(r_{i1}, r_{i2}, \ldots, r_{it}, \ldots)$ we will speak of "the flow of returns" (r_i) from the ith security. The flow of returns from the portfolio as a whole is $R = \Sigma X_i r_i$. As in the dynamic case if the investor wished to maximize

---

[4] The results depend on the assumption that the anticipated returns and discount rates are independent of the particular investor's portfolio.

[5] If short sales were allowed, an infinite amount of money would be placed in the security with highest r.

"anticipated" return from the portfolio he would place all his funds in that security with maximum anticipated returns.

There is a rule which implies both that the investor should diversify and that he should maximize expected return. The rule states that the investor does (or should) diversify his funds among all those securities which give maximum expected return. The law of large numbers will insure that the actual yield of the portfolio will be almost the same as the expected yield.[6] This rule is a special case of the expected returns—variance of returns rule (to be presented below). It assumes that there is a portfolio which gives both maximum expected return and minimum variance, and it commends this portfolio to the investor.

This presumption, that the law of large numbers applies to a portfolio of securities, cannot be accepted. The returns from securities are too intercorrelated. Diversification cannot eliminate all variance.

The portfolio with maximum expected return is not necessarily the one with minimum variance. There is a rate at which the investor can gain expected return by taking on variance, or reduce variance by giving up expected return.

We saw that the expected returns or anticipated returns rule is inadequate. Let us now consider the expected returns—variance of returns (E-V) rule. It will be necessary to first present a few elementary concepts and results of mathematical statistics. We will then show some implications of the E-V rule. After this we will discuss its plausibility.

In our presentation we try to avoid complicated mathematical statements and proofs. As a consequence a price is paid in terms of rigor and generality. The chief limitations from this source are (1) we do not derive our results analytically for the n-security case; instead, we present them geometrically for the 3- and 4-security cases; (2) we assume static probability beliefs. In a general presentation we must recognize that the probability distribution of yields of the various securities is a function of time. The writer intends to present, in the future, the general, mathematical treatment which removes this limitation.

We will need the following elementary concepts and results of mathematical statistics:

Let Y be a random variable, i.e., a variable whose value is decided by chance. Suppose, for simplicity of exposition, that Y can take on a finite number of values $y_1, y_2, \ldots, y_N$. Let the probability that $Y = y_1$, be p_1; that $Y = y_2$ be p_2; etc. The expected value (or mean) of Y is defined to be

$$E = p_1 y_1 + p_2 y_2 + \cdots + p_N y_N$$

[6] Williams, *op. cit.*, pp. 68, 69.

The variance of Y is defined to be

$$V = p_1(y_1 - E)^2 + p_2(y_2 - E)^2 + \cdots + p_N(y_N - E)^2$$

V is the average squared deviation of Y from its expected value. V is a commonly used measure of dispersion. Other measures of dispersion, closely related to V are the standard deviation, $\sigma = \sqrt{V}$, and the coefficient of variation, σ/E.

Suppose we have a number of random variables: $R_1, \ldots, R_n$. If R is a weighted sum (linear combination) of the R_i

$$R = a_1 R_1 + a_2 R_2 + \cdots + a_n R_n$$

then R is also a random variable. (For example, R_1 may be the number which turns up on one die; R_2, that of another die; and R the sum of these numbers. In this case $n = 2$, $a_1 = a_2 = 1$).

It will be important for us to know how the expected value and variance of the weighted sum (R) are related to the probability distribution of the $R_1, \ldots, R_n$. We state these relations below; we refer the reader to any standard text for proof.[7]

The expected value of a weighted sum is the weighted sum of the expected values, i.e., $E(R) = a_1 E(R_1) + a_2 E(R_2) + \cdots + a_n E(R_n)$. The variance of a weighted sum is not as simple. To express it we must define "covariance." The covariance of R_1 and R_2 is

$$\sigma_{12} = E\{[R_1 - E(R_1)][R_2 - E(R_2)]\}$$

i.e., the expected value of [(the deviation of R_1 from its mean) times (the deviation of R_2 from its mean)]. In general we define the covariance between R_i and R_j as

$$\sigma_{ij} = E\{[R_i - E(R_i)][R_j - E(R_j)]\}$$

σ_{ij} may be expressed in terms of the familiar correlation coefficient (ρ_{ij}). The covariance between R_i and R_j is equal to [(their correlation) times (the standard deviation of R_i) times (the standard deviation of R_j)]:

$$\sigma_{ij} = \rho_{ij}\sigma_i\sigma_j$$

The variance of a weighted sum is

$$V(R) = \sum_{i=1}^{N} a_i^2 V(X_i) + 2 \sum_{i=1}^{N} \sum_{j>1}^{N} a_i a_j \sigma_{ij}$$

[7] For example, J. V. Uspensky, *Introduction to Mathematical Probability* (New York, N.Y.: McGraw-Hill, 1937), Ch. 9, pp. 161–81.

If we use the fact that the variance of R_i is σ_{ii} then

$$V(R) = \sum_{i=1}^{N} \sum_{j=1}^{N} a_i a_j \sigma_{ij}$$

Let R_i be the return on the ith security. Let μ_i be the expected value of R_i; σ_{ij}, be the covariance between R_i and R_j (thus σ_{ii} is the variance of R_i). Let X_i be the percentage of the investor's assets which are allocated to the ith security. The yield (R) on the portfolio as a whole is

$$R = \sum R_i X_i$$

The R_i (and consequently R) are considered to be random variables.[8] The X_i are not random variables, but are fixed by the investor. Since the X_i are percentages we have $\Sigma X_i = 1$. In our analysis we will exclude negative values of the X_i (i.e., short sales); therefore $X_i \geq 0$ for all i.

The return (R) on the portfolio as a whole is a weighted sum of random variables (where the investor can choose the weights). From our discussion of such weighted sums we see that the expected return E from the portfolio as a whole is

$$E = \sum_{i=1}^{N} X_i \mu_i$$

and the variance is

$$V = \sum_{i=1}^{N} \sum_{j=1}^{N} \sigma_{ij} X_i X_j$$

For fixed probability beliefs (μ_i, σ_{ij}) the investor has a choice of various combinations of E and V depending on his choice of portfolio $X_1, \ldots, X_N$. Suppose that the set of all obtainable (E, V) combinations were as in Figure 1. The E-V rule states that the investor would (or should) want to select one of those portfolios which give rise to the (E, V) combinations indicated as efficient in the figure; i.e., those with minimum V for given E or more and maximum E for given V or less.

There are techniques by which we can compute the set of efficient portfolios and efficient (E, V) combinations associated with given μ_i and

[8] That is, we assume that the investor does (and should) act as if he had probability beliefs concerning these variables. In general we would expect that the investor could tell us, for any two events (A and B), whether he personally considered A more likely than B, B more likely than A, or both equally likely. If the investor were consistent in his opinions on such matters, he would possess a system of probability beliefs. We cannot expect the investor to be consistent in every detail. We can, however, expect his probability beliefs to be roughly consistent on important matters that have been carefully considered. We should also expect that he will base his actions upon these probability beliefs—even though they be in part subjective.

This paper does not consider the difficult question of how investors do (or should) form their probability beliefs.

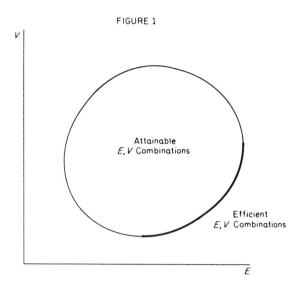

FIGURE 1

σ_{ij}. We will not present these techniques here. We will, however, illustrate geometrically the nature of the efficient surfaces for cases in which N (the number of available securities) is small.

The calculation of efficient surfaces might possibly be of practical use. Perhaps there are ways, by combining statistical techniques and the judgment of experts, to form reasonable probability beliefs (μ_i, σ_{ij}). We could use these beliefs to compute the attainable efficient combinations of (E, V). The investor, being informed of what (E, V) combinations were attainable, could state which he desired. We could then find the portfolio which gave this desired combination.

Two conditions—at least—must be satisfied before it would be practical to use efficient surfaces in the manner described above. First, the investor must desire to act according to the E-V maxim. Second, we must be able to arrive at reasonable μ_i and σ_{ij}. We will return to these matters later.

Let us consider the case of three securities. In the three-security case our model reduces to

$$E = \sum_{i=1}^{3} X_i \mu_i \tag{1}$$

$$V = \sum_{i=1}^{3} \sum_{j=1}^{3} X_i X_j \sigma_{ij} \tag{2}$$

$$\sum_{i=1}^{3} X_i = 1 \tag{3}$$

$$X_i \geq 0 \quad \text{for} \quad i = 1, 2, 3. \tag{4}$$

From (3) we get

$$X_3 = 1 - X_1 - X_2 \tag{3a}$$

If we substitute (3a) in (1) and (2), we get E and V as functions of X_1 and X_2. For example we find

$$E = \mu_3 + X_1(\mu_1 - \mu_3) + X_2(\mu_2 - \mu_3) \tag{1a}$$

The exact formulas are not too important here (that of V is given below).[9] We can simply write

$$E = E(X_1, X_2) \tag{a}$$

$$V = V(X_1, X_2) \tag{b}$$

$$X_1 \geq 0, \qquad X_2 \geq 0, \qquad 1 - X_1 - X_2 \geq 0 \tag{c}$$

By using relations (a), (b), (c), we can work with two-dimensional geometry.

The attainable set of portfolios consists of all portfolios which satisfy constraints (c) and (3a) (or equivalently 3 and 4). The attainable combinations of X_1, X_2 are represented by the triangle abc in Figure 2. Any point to the left of the X_2 axis is not attainable because it violates the condition that $X_1 \geq 0$. Any point below the X_1 axis is not attainable because it violates the condition that $X_2 \geq 0$. Any point above the line $(1 - X_1 - X_2 = 0)$ is not attainable because it violates the condition that $X_3 = 1 - X_1 - X_2 \geq 0$.

We define an *isomean* curve to be the set of all points (portfolios) with a given expected return. Similarly an *isovariance* line is defined to be the set of all points (portfolios) with a given variance of return.

An examination of the formulae for E and V tells us the shapes of the isomean and isovariance curves. Specifically, they tell us that typically[10] the isomean curves are a system of parallel straight lines; the isovariance curves are a system of concentric ellipses (see Figure 2). For example, if $\mu_2 \neq \mu_3$ Eq. (1a) can be written in the familiar form $X_2 = a + bX_1$; specifically

$$X_2 = \frac{E - \mu_3}{\mu_2 - \mu_3} - \frac{\mu_1 - \mu_3}{\mu_2 - \mu_3} X_1$$

Thus the slope of the isomean line associated with $E = E_0$ is $-(\mu_1 - \mu_3)/(\mu_2 - \mu_3)$; its intercept is $(E_0 - \mu_3)/(\mu_2 - \mu_3)$. If we change E we change

[9] $V = X_1^2(\sigma_{11} - 2\sigma_{13} + \sigma_{33}) + X_2^2(\sigma_{22} - 2\sigma_{23} + \sigma_{33}) + 2X_1X_2(\sigma_{12} - \sigma_{13} - \sigma_{23} + \sigma_{33}) + 2X_1(\sigma_{13} - \sigma_{33}) + 2X_2(\sigma_{23} - \sigma_{33}) + \sigma_{33}$.

[10] The isomean "curves" are as described above except when $\mu_1 = \mu_2 = \mu_3$. In the latter case all portfolios have the same expected return and the investor chooses the one with minimum variance.

As to the assumptions implicit in our description of the isovariance curves see footnote 13.

FIGURE 2

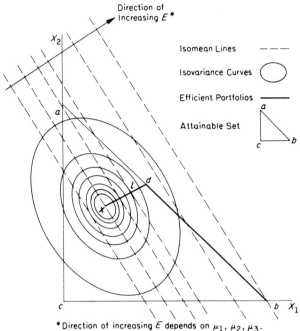

*Direction of increasing E depends on μ_1, μ_2, μ_3.

the intercept but not the slope of the isomean line. This confirms the contention that the isomean lines form a system of parallel lines.

Similarly, by a somewhat less simple application of analytic geometry, we can confirm the contention that the isovariance lines form a family of concentric ellipses. The "center" of the system is the point which minimizes V. We will label this point X. Its expected return and variance we will label E and V. Variance increases as you move away from X. More precisely, if one isovariance curve, C_1, lies closer to X than another, C_2, then C_1 is associated with a smaller variance than C_2.

With the aid of the foregoing geometric apparatus let us seek the efficient sets.

X, the center of the system of isovariance ellipses, may fall either inside or outside the attainable set. Figure 2 illustrates a case in which X falls inside the attainable set. In this case: X is efficient. For no other portfolio has a V as low as X; therefore no portfolio can have either smaller V (with the same or greater E) or greater E with the same or smaller V. No point (portfolio) with expected return E less than E is efficient. For we have $E > E$ and $V < V$.

Consider all points with a given expected return E; i.e., all points on the isomean line associated with E. The point of the isomean line at which

FIGURE 3

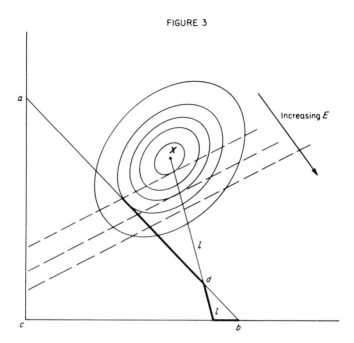

V takes on its least value is the point at which the isomean line is tangent to an isovariance curve. We call this point $\hat{X}(E)$. If we let E vary, $\hat{X}(E)$ traces out a curve.

Algebraic considerations (which we omit here) show us that this curve is a straight line. We will call it the critical line l. The critical line passes through X for this point minimizes V for all points with $E(X_1, X_2) = \boldsymbol{E}$. As we go along l in either direction from X, V increases. The segment of the critical line from X to the point where the critical line crosses the boundary of the attainable set is part of the efficient set. The rest of the efficient set is (in the case illustrated) the segment of the $\overline{ab}$ line from d to b. b is the point of maximum attainable E. In Figure 3, X lies outside the admissible area but the critical line cuts the admissible area. The efficient line begins at the attainable point with minimum variance (in this case on the $\overline{ab}$ line). It moves toward b until it intersects the critical line, moves along the critical line until it intersects a boundary and finally moves along the boundary to b. The reader may wish to construct and examine the following other cases: (1) X lies outside the attainable set and the critical line does not cut the attainable set. In this case there is a security which does not enter into any efficient portfolio. (2) Two securities have the same μ_i. In this case the isomean lines are parallel to a boundary line. It may happen that the efficient portfolio with maximum E is a diversified portfolio. (3) A case wherein only one portfolio is efficient.

FIGURE 4

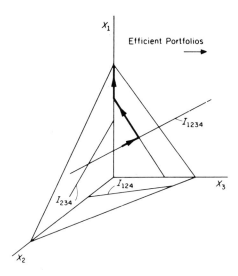

The efficient set in the 4-security case is, as in the 3-security and also the N-security case, a series of connected line segments. At one end of the efficient set is the point of minimum variance; at the other end is a point of maximum expected return[11] (see Figure 4).

Now that we have seen the nature of the set of efficient portfolios, it is not difficult to see the nature of the set of efficient (E, V) combinations. In the 3-security case $E = a_0 + a_1X_1 + a_2X_2$ is a plane; $V = b_0 + b_1X_1 + b_2X_2 + b_{12}X_1X_2 + b_{11}X_1^2 + b_{22}X_2^2$ is a paraboloid.[12] As shown

[11] Just as we used the equation $\sum\limits_{i=1}^{4} X_i = 1$ to reduce the dimensionality in the 3-security case, we can use it to represent the 4-security case in 3-dimensional space. Eliminating X_4 we get $E = E(X_1, X_2, X_3)$, $V = V(X_1, X_2, X_3)$. The attainable set is represented, in 3-space, by the tetrahedron with vertices $(0, 0, 0)$, $(0, 0, 1)$, $(0, 1, 0)$, $(1, 0, 0)$, representing portfolios with, respectively, $X_4 = 1$, $X_3 = 1$, $X_2 = 1$, $X_1 = 1$.

Let s_{123} be the subspace consisting of all points with $X_4 = 0$. Similarly we can define $s_{a1}, \ldots, a\alpha$ to be the subspace consisting of all points with $X_i = 0$, $i \neq a_1, \ldots, a\alpha$. For each subspace $s_{a1}, \ldots, a\alpha$ we can define a *critical line* $la_1, \ldots a\alpha$. This line is the locus of points P where P minimizes V for all points in $s_{a1}, \ldots, a\alpha$ with the same E as P. If a point is in $s_{a1}, \ldots, a\alpha$ and is efficient it must be on $la_1, \ldots, a\alpha$. The efficient set may be traced out by starting at the point of minimum available variance, moving continuously along various $la_1, \ldots, a\alpha$ according to definite rules, ending in a point which gives maximum E. As in the 2-dimensional case the point with minimum available variance may be in the interior of the available set or on one of its boundaries. Typically we proceed along a given critical line until either this line intersects one of a larger subspace or meets a boundary (and simultaneously the critical line of a lower dimensional subspace). In either of these cases the efficient line turns and continues along the new line. The efficient line terminates when a point with maximum E is reached.

[12] See footnote 9.

FIGURE 5

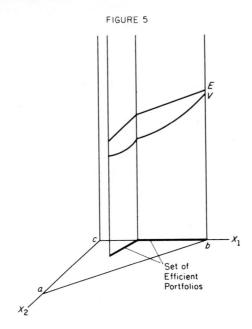

in Figure 5, the section of the E-plane over the efficient portfolio set is a series of connected line segments. The section of the V-paraboloid over the efficient portfolio set is a series of connected parabola segments. If we plotted V against E for efficient portfolios we would again get a series of connected parabola segments (see Figure 6). This result obtains for any number of securities.

FIGURE 6

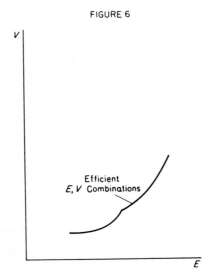

Various reasons recommend the use of the expected return-variance of return rule, both as a hypothesis to explain well-established investment behavior and as a maxim to guide one's own action. The rule serves better, we will see, as an explanation of, and guide to, "investment" as distinguished from "speculative" behavior.

Earlier we rejected the expected returns rule on the grounds that it never implied the superiority of diversification. The expected return-variance of return rule, on the other hand, implies diversification for a wide range of μ_i, σ_{ij}. This does not mean that the E-V rule never implies the superiority of an undiversified portfolio. It is conceivable that one security might have an extremely higher yield and lower variance than all other securities; so much so that one particular undiversified portfolio would give maximum E and minimum V. But for a large, presumably representative range of μ_i, σ_{ij} the E-V rule leads to efficient portfolios almost all of which are diversified.

Not only does the E-V hypothesis imply diversification, it implies the "right kind" of diversification for the "right reason." The adequacy of diversification is not thought by investors to depend solely on the number of different securities held. A portfolio with 60 different railway securities, for example, would not be as well diversified as the same size portfolio with some railroad, some public utility, mining, various sort of manufacturing, etc. The reason is that it is generally more likely for firms within the same industry to do poorly at the same time than for firms in dissimilar industries.

Similarly in trying to make variance small it is not enough to invest in many securities. It is necessary to avoid investing in securities with high covariances among themselves. We should diversify across industries because firms in different industries, expecially industries with different economic characteristics, have lower covariances than firms within an industry.

The concepts "yield" and "risk" appear frequently in financial writings. Usually if the term "yield" were replaced by "expected yield" or "expected return," and "risk" by "variance of return," little change of apparent meaning would result.

Variance is a well-known measure of dispersion about the expected. If instead of variance the investor was concerned with standard error, $\sigma = \sqrt{V}$, or with the coefficient of dispersion, σ/E, his choice would still lie in the set of efficient portfolios.

Suppose an investor diversifies between two portfolios (i.e., if he puts some of his money in one portfolio, the rest of his money in the other. An example of diversifying among portfolios is the buying of the shares of two different investment companies). If the two original portfolios have *equal* variance then typically[13] the variance of the resulting (compound) portfolio will be less than the variance of either original portfolio. This is illustrated by Figure 7. To interpret Figure 7 we note that a portfolio P

FIGURE 7

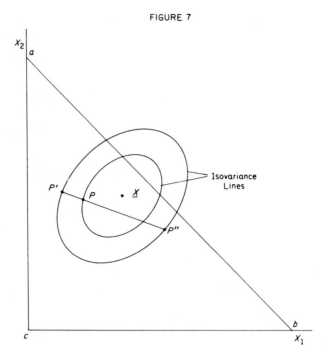

which is built out of two portfolios $P' = (X_1', X_2')$ and $P'' = (X_1'', X_2'')$ is of the form $P = \lambda P' + (1 - \lambda)P'' = [\lambda X_1' + (1 - \lambda)X_1'', \lambda X_2' + (1 - \lambda)X_2'']$. P is on the straight line connecting P' and P''.

The E-V principle is more plausible as a rule for investment behavior as distinguished from speculative behavior. The third moment[14] M_3 of the probability distribution of returns from the portfolio may be connected with a propensity to gamble. For example if the investor maximizes utility U which depends on E and V $[U = U(E, V), \partial U/\partial E > 0, \partial U/\partial E < 0]$, he will never accept an actuarially fair bet.[15] But if $U = U(E, V, M_3)$ and if $\partial U/\partial M_3 \neq 0$ then there are some fair bets which would be accepted.

Perhaps—for a great variety of investing institutions which consider yield to be a good thing; risk, a bad thing; gambling, to be avoided—E, V efficiency is reasonable as a working hypothesis and a working maxim.

[13] In no case will variance be increased. The only case in which variance will not be decreased is if the returns from both portfolios are perfectly correlated. To draw the isovariance curves as ellipses it is both necessary and sufficient to assume that no two distinct portfolios have perfectly correlated returns.

[14] If R is a random variable that takes on a finite number of values $r_1, \ldots, r_n$ with probabilities $p_1, \ldots, p_n$ respectively, and expected value E, then $M_3 = \sum_{i=1}^{n} p_i(r_i - E)^3$.

[15] One in which the amount gained by winning the bet times the probability of winning is equal to the amount lost by losing the bet, times the probability of losing.

Two uses of the *E-V* principle suggest themselves. We might use it in theoretical analyses, or we might use it in the actual selection of portfolios.

In theoretical analyses we might inquire, for example, about the various effects of a change in the beliefs generally held about a firm, or a general change in preference as to expected return versus variance of return, or a change in the supply of a security. In our analyses the X_i might represent individual securities or they might represent aggregates such as, say, bonds, stocks, and real estate.[16]

To use the *E-V* rule in the selection of securities we must have procedures for finding reasonable μ_i and σ_{ij}. These procedures, I believe, should combine statistical techniques and the judgment of practical men. My feeling is that the statistical computations should be used to arrive at a tentative set of μ_i and σ_{ij}. Judgment should then be used in increasing or decreasing some of these μ_i and σ_{ij} on the basis of factors or nuances not taken into account by the formal computations. Using this revised set of μ_i and σ_{ij}, the set of efficient E, V combinations could be computed, the investor could select the combination he preferred, and the portfolio which gave rise to this E, V combination could be found.

One suggestion as to tentative μ_i, σ_{ij} is to use the observed μ_i, σ_{ij} for some period of the past. I believe that better methods, which take into account more information, can be found. I believe that what is needed is essentially a "probabilistic" reformulation of security analysis. I will not pursue this subject here, for this is "another story." It is a story of which I have read only the first page of the first chapter.

In this paper we have considered the second stage in the process of selecting a portfolio. This stage starts with the relevant beliefs about the securities involved and ends with the selection of a portfolio. We have not considered the first stage: the formation of the relevant beliefs on the basis of observation.

---

[16] Care must be used in using and interpreting relations among aggregates. We cannot deal here with the problems and pitfalls of aggregation.

*William F. Sharpe**

5. A Simplified Model for Portfolio Analysis

Reprinted from **Management Science**, Vol. 9, No. 2 (January, 1963), pp. 277–293, by permission of the author and the publisher.

I. INTRODUCTION

Markowitz has suggested that the process of portfolio selection be approached by (1) making probabilistic estimates of the future performances of securities, (2) analyzing those estimates to determine an *efficient set* of portfolios and (3) selecting from that set the portfolios best suited to the investor's preferences [1, 2, 3]. This paper extends Markowitz' work on the second of these three stages—*portfolio analysis*. The preliminary sections state the problem in its general form and describe Markowitz' solution technique. The remainder of the paper presents a simplified model of the relationships among securities, indicates the manner in which it allows the portfolio analysis problem to be simplified, and provides evidence on the costs as well as the desirability of using the model for practical applications of the Markowitz technique.

II. THE PORTFOLIO ANALYSIS PROBLEM

A security analyst has provided the following predictions concerning the future returns from each of N securities:

$E_i \equiv$ the expected value of R_i (the return from security i)
C_{i1} through C_{in}; C_{ij} represents the covariance between R_i and R_j (as usual, when $i = j$ the figure is the variance of R_i)

* Professor of Economics, University of California, Irvine. The author wishes to express his appreciation for the cooperation of the staffs of both the Western Data Processing Center at UCLA and the Pacific Northwest Research Computer Laboratory at the University of Washington where the program was tested. His greatest debt, however, is to Dr. Harry M. Markowitz of the RAND Corporation, with whom he was privileged to have a number of stimulating conversations during the past year. It is no longer possible to segregate the ideas in this paper into those which were his, those which were the author's, and those which were developed jointly. Suffice it to say that the only accomplishments which are unquestionably the property of the author are those of authorship—first of the computer program and then of this article.

The portfolio analysis problem is as follows. Given such a set of predictions, determine the set of *efficient portfolios*; a portfolio is efficient if none other gives either (*a*) a higher expected return and the same variance of return or (*b*) a lower variance of return and the same expected return.

Let X_i represent the proportion of a portfolio invested in security i. Then the expected return (E) and variance of return (V) of any portfolio can be expressed in terms of (*a*) the basic data (E_i-values and C_{ij}-values) and (*b*) the amounts invested in various securities:

$$E = \sum_i X_i E_i$$

$$V = \sum_i \sum_j X_i X_j C_{ij}$$

Consider an objective function of the form:

$$\phi = \lambda E - V$$
$$= \lambda \sum_i X_i E_i - \sum_i \sum_j X_i X_j C_{ij}$$

Given a set of values for the parameters (λ, E_i's and C_{ij}'s), the value of ϕ can be changed by varying the X_i values as desired, as long as two basic restrictions are observed:

1. The entire portfolio must be invested:[1]

$$\sum_i X_i = 1$$

2. No security may be held in negative quantities:[2]

$$X_i \geq 0 \qquad \text{for all } i$$

A portfolio is described by the proportions invested in various securities—in our notation by the values of X_i. For each set of admissable values of the X_i variables there is a corresponding predicted combination of E and V and thus of ϕ. Figure 1 illustrates this relationship for a particular value of λ. The line ϕ_1 shows the combinations of E and V which give $\phi = \phi_1$, where $\phi = \lambda_k E - V$; the other lines refer to larger values of $\phi (\phi_3 > \phi_2 > \phi_1)$. Of all possible portfolios, one will maximize the value of ϕ;[3] in Figure 1 it is portfolio C. The relationship between this solution and the portfolio analysis problem is obvious. The E, V combination ob-

---

[1] Since cash can be included as one of the securities (explicitly or implicitly) this assumption need cause no lack of realism.

[2] This is the standard formulation. Cases in which short sales are allowed require a different approach.

[3] This fact is crucial to the critical line computing procedure described in the next section.

FIGURE 1

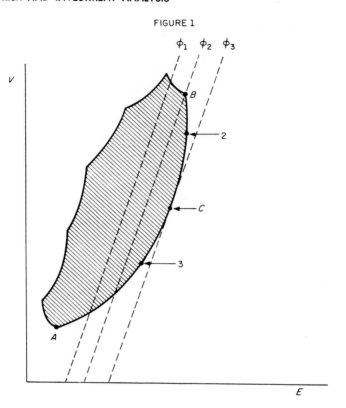

tained will be on the boundary of the set of attainable combinations; more-over, the objective function will be tangent to the set at that point. Since this function is of the form

$$\phi = \lambda E - V$$

the slope of the boundary at the point must be λ; thus, by varying λ from $+\infty$ to 0, every solution of the portfolio analysis problem can be obtained.

For any given value of λ the problem described in this section requires the maximization of a quadratic function, ϕ (which is a function of X_i, X_i^2, and X_iX_j terms) subject to a linear constraint ($\sum_i X_i = 1$), with the variables restricted to nonnegative values. A number of techniques have been developed to solve such *quadratic programming problems*. The critical line method, developed by Markowitz in conjunction with his work on portfolio analysis, is particularly suited to this problem and was used in the program described in this paper.

III. THE CRITICAL LINE METHOD

Two important characteristics of the set of efficient portfolios make system-atic solution of the portfolio analysis problem relatively straightforward.

The first concerns the relationships among portfolios. Any set of efficient portfolios can be described in terms of a smaller set of *corner portfolios*. Any point on the E, V curve (other than the points associated with corner portfolios) can be obtained with a portfolio constructed by dividing the total investment between the two adjacent corner portfolios. For example, the portfolio which gives E, V combination C in Figure 1 might be some linear combination of the two corner portfolios with E, V combinations shown by points 2 and 3. This characteristic allows the analyst to restrict his attention to corner portfolios rather than the complete set of efficient portfolios; the latter can be readily derived from the former.

The second characteristic of the solution concerns the relationships among corner portfolios. Two corner portfolios which are adjacent on the E, V curve are related in the following manner: one portfolio will contain either (1) all the securities which appear in the other, plus one additional security or (2) all but one of the securities which appear in the other. Thus in moving down the E, V curve from one corner portfolio to the next, the quantities of the securities in efficient portfolios will vary until either one drops out of the portfolio or another enters. The point at which a change takes place marks a new corner portfolio.

The major steps in the critical line method for solving the portfolio analysis problem are:

1. The corner portfolio with $\lambda = \infty$ is determined. It is composed entirely of the one security with the highest expected return.[4]
2. Relationships between (a) the amounts of the various securities contained in efficient portfolios and (b) the value of λ are computed. It is possible to derive such relationships for any section of the E, V curve between adjacent corner portfolios. The relationships which apply to one section of the curve will not, however, apply to any other section.
3. Using the relationships computed in (2), each security is examined to determine the value of λ at which a change in the securities included in the portfolio would come about:
   (a) securities presently in the portfolio are examined to determine the value of λ at which they would drop out, and
   (b) securities not presently in the portfolio are examined to determine the value of λ at which they would enter the portfolio.
4. The next largest value of λ at which a security either enters or drops out of the portfolio is determined. This indicates the location of the next corner portfolio.

[4] In the event that two or more of the securities have the same (highest) expected return, the first efficient portfolio is the combination of such securities with the lowest variance.

5. The composition of the new corner portfolio is computed, using the relationships derived in (2). However, since these relationships held only for the section of the curve between this corner portfolio and the preceding one, the solution process can only continue if new relationships are derived. The method thus returns to step (2) unless $\lambda = 0$, in which case the analysis is complete.

The amount of computation required to complete a portfolio analysis using this method is related to the following factors:

1. The number of securities analyzed. This will affect the extent of the computation in step (2) and the number of computations in step (3).
2. The number of corner portfolios. Steps (2) through (5) must be repeated once to find each corner portfolio.
3. The complexity of the variance-covariance matrix. Step (2) requires a matrix be inverted and must be repeated once for each corner portfolio.

The amount of computer memory space required to perform a portfolio analysis will depend primarily on the size of the variance-covariance matrix. In the standard case, if N securities are analyzed this matrix will have $\frac{1}{2}(N^2 + N)$ elements.

IV. THE DIAGONAL MODEL

Portfolio analysis requires a large number of comparisons; obviously the practical application of the technique can be greatly facilitated by a set of assumptions which reduces the computational task involved in such comparisons. One such set of assumptions (to be called the diagonal model) is described in this article. This model has two virtues: it is one of the simplest which can be constructed without assuming away the existence of interrelationships among securities, and there is considerable evidence that it can capture a large part of such interrelationships.

The major characteristic of the diagonal model is the assumption that the returns of various securities are related only through common relationships with some basic underlying factor. The return from any security is determined solely by random factors and this single outside element; more explicitly:

$$R_i = A_i + B_iI + C_i$$

where A_i and B_i are parameters, C_i is a random variable with an expected value of zero and variance Q_i, and I is the level of some index. The index, I, may be the level of the stock market as a whole, the Gross National

Product, some price index or any other factor thought to be the most important single influence on the returns from securities. The future level of I is determined in part by random factors:

$$I = A_{n+1} + C_{n+1}$$

where A_{n+1} is a parameter and C_{n+1} is a random variable with an expected value of zero and a variance of Q_{n+1}. It is assumed that the covariance between C_i and C_j is zero for all values of i and $j (i \neq j)$.

Figure 2 provides a graphical representation of the model. A_i and B_i serve to locate the line which relates the expected value of R_i to the level of I. Q_i indicates the variance of R_i around the expected relationship (this variance is assumed to be the same at each point along the line). Finally, A_{n+1} indicates the expected value of I and Q_{n+1} the variance around that expected value.

FIGURE 2

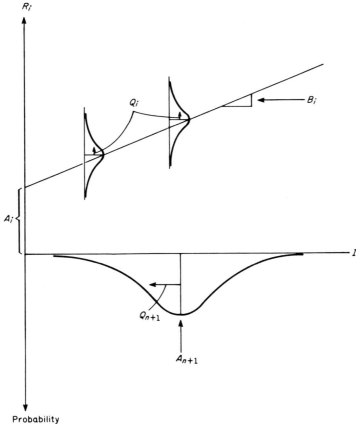

The diagonal model requires the following predictions from a security analyst:

1. values of A_i, B_i and Q_i for each of N securities;
2. values of A_{n+1} and Q_{n+1} for the index I.

The number of estimates required from the analyst is thus greatly reduced from 5,150 to 302 for an analysis of 100 securities and from 2,003,000 to 6,002 for an analysis of 2,000 securities.

Once the parameters of the diagonal model have been specified all the inputs required for the standard portfolio analysis problem can be derived. The relationships are:

$$E_i = A_i + B_i(A_{n+1})$$

$$V_i = (B_i)^2(Q_{n+1}) + Q_i$$

$$C = (B_i)(B_j)(Q_{n+1})$$

A portfolio analysis could be performed by obtaining the values required by the diagonal model, calculating from them the full set of data required for the standard portfolio analysis problem and then performing the analysis with the derived values. However, additional advantages can be obtained if the portfolio analysis problem is restated directly in terms of the parameters of the diagonal model. The following section describes the manner in which such a restatement can be performed.

V. THE ANALOGUE

The return from a portfolio is the weighted average of the returns from its component securities:

$$R_p = \sum_{i=1}^{N} X_i R_i$$

The contribution of each security to the total return of a portfolio is simply $X_i R_i$ or, under the assumptions of the diagonal model:

$$X_i(A_i + B_i I + C_i)$$

The total contribution of a security to the return of the portfolio can be broken into two components: (1) an investment in the "basic characteristics" of the security in question and (2) an "investment" in the index:

$$X_i(A_i + B_i I + C_i) = X_i(A_i + C_i) \tag{1}$$

$$+ X_i B_i I \tag{2}$$

The return of a portfolio can be considered to be the result of (1) a series of investments in N "basic securities" and (2) an investment in the index:

$$R_p = \sum_{i=1}^{N} X_i(A_i + C_i) + [\sum_{i=1}^{N} X_i B_i]I$$

Defining X_{n+1} as the weighted average responsiveness of R_p to the level of I:

$$X_{n+1} \equiv \sum_{i=1}^{N} X_i B_i$$

and substituting this variable and the formula for the determinants of I, we obtain:

$$R_p = \sum_{i=1}^{N} X_i(A_i + C_i) + X_{n+1}(A_{n+1} + C_{n+1})$$

$$= \sum_{i=1}^{N+1} X_i(A_i + C_i)$$

The expected return of a portfolio is thus:

$$E = \sum_{i=1}^{N+1} X_i A_i$$

while the variance is:[5]

$$V = \sum_{i=1}^{N+1} X_i^2 Q_i$$

This formulation indicates the reason for the use of the parameters A_{n+1} and Q_{n+1} to describe the expected value and variance of the future value of I. It also indicates the reason for calling this the "diagonal model." The variance-covariance matrix, which is full when N securities are considered, can be expressed as a matrix with non-zero elements only along the diagonal by including an $(n + 1)$st security defined as indicated. This vastly reduces the number of computations required to solve the portfolio analysis problem (primarily in step 2 of the critical line method, when the variance-covariance matrix must be inverted) and allows the problem to be stated directly in terms of the basic parameters of the diagonal model:

Maximize

$$\lambda E - V$$

[5] Recall that the diagonal model assumes $\text{cov}(C_i, C_j) = 0$ for all i and j $(i \neq j)$.

where

$$E = \sum_{i=1}^{N+1} X_i A_i$$

$$V = \sum_{i=1}^{N+1} X_i^2 Q_i$$

subject to $X_i \geq 0$ for all i from 1 to N

$$\sum_{i=1}^{N} X_i = 1$$

$$\sum_{i=1}^{N} X_i B_i = X_{n+1}$$

VI. THE DIAGONAL MODEL PORTFOLIO ANALYSIS CODE

As indicated in the previous section, if the portfolio analysis problem is expressed in terms of the basic parameters of the diagonal model, computing time and memory space required for solution can be greatly reduced. This section describes a machine code, written in the FØRTRAN language, which takes full advantage of the characteristics of the diagonal model. It uses the critical line method to solve the problem stated in the previous section.

The computing time required by the diagonal code is considerably smaller than that required by standard quadratic programming codes. The RAND QP code[6] required 33 minutes to solve a 100-security example on an IBM 7090 computer; the same problem was solved in 30 seconds with the diagonal code. Moreover, the reduced storage requirements allow many more securities to be analyzed: with the IBM 709 or 7090 the RAND QP code can be used for no more than 249 securities, while the diagonal code can analyze up to 2,000 securities.

Although the diagonal code allows the total computing time to be greatly reduced, the cost of a large analysis is still far from insignificant. Thus there is every incentive to limit the computations to those essential for the final selection of a portfolio. By taking into account the possibilities of borrowing and lending money, the diagonal code restricts the computations to those absolutely necessary for determination of the final set of

---

[6] The program is described in [4]. Several alternative quadratic programming codes are available. A recent code, developed by IBM, which uses the critical line method is likely to prove considerably more efficient for the portfolio analysis problem. The RAND code is used for comparison since it is the only standard program with which the author has had experience.

efficient portfolios. The importance of these alternatives, their effect on the portfolio analysis problem, and the manner in which they are taken into account in the diagonal code are described in the remainder of this section.

A. The "lending portfolio"

There is some interest rate (r_l) at which money can be lent with virtual assurance that both principal and interest will be returned; at the least, money can be buried in the ground $(r_l = 0)$. Such an alternative could be included as one possible security $(A_i = 1 + r_l, B_i = 0, Q_i = 0)$ but this would necessitate some needless computation.[7] In order to minimize computing time, lending at some pure interest rate is taken into account explicitly in the diagonal code.

FIGURE 3

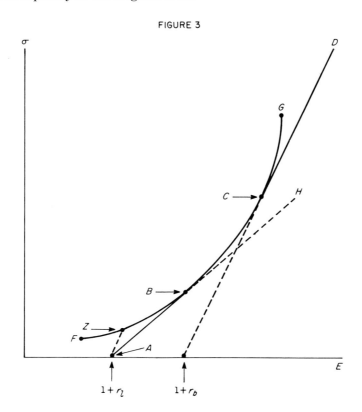

[7] Actually, the diagonal code cannot accept nonpositive values of Q_i; thus if the lending alternative is to be included as simply another security, it must be assigned a very small value of Q_i. This procedure will give virtually the correct solution but is inefficient.

The relationship between lending and efficient portfolios can best be seen in terms of an E, σ curve showing the combinations of expected return and standard deviation of return $(=\sqrt{V})$ associated with efficient portfolios. Such a curve is shown in Figure 3 (FBCG); point A indicates the E, σ combination attained if all funds are lent. The relationship between lending money and purchasing portfolios can be illustrated with the portfolio which has the E, σ combination shown by point Z. Consider a portfolio with X_z invested in portfolio Z and the remainder $(1 - X_z)$ lent at the rate r_l. The expected return from such a portfolio would be:

$$E = X_z E_z + (1 - X_z)(1 + r_l)$$

and the variance of return would be:

$$V = X_z^2 V_z + (1 - X_z)^2 V_l + 2X_z(1 - X_z)(\text{cov}_{zl})$$

But, since V_l and cov_{zl} are both zero:

$$V = X_z^2 V_z$$

and the standard deviation of return is:

$$\sigma = X_z \sigma_z$$

Since both E and σ are linear functions of X_z, the E, σ combinations of all portfolios made up of portfolio Z plus lending must lie on a straight line connecting points Z and A. In general, by splitting his investment between a portfolio and lending, an investor can attain any E, σ combination on the line connecting the E, σ combinations of the two components.

Many portfolios which are efficient in the absence of the lending alternative become inefficient when it is introduced. In Figure 3, for example, the possibility of attaining E, σ combinations along the line AB makes all portfolios along the original E, σ curve from point F to point B inefficient. For any desired level of E below that associated with portfolio B, the most efficient portfolio will be some combination of portfolio B and lending. Portfolio B can be termed the "lending portfolio" since it is the appropriate portfolio whenever some of the investor's funds are to be lent at the rate r_l. This portfolio can be found readily once the E, σ curve is known. It lies at the point on the curve at which a ray from $(E = 1 + r_l$, $\sigma = 0)$ is tangent to the curve. If the E, σ curve is not known in its entirety it is still possible to determine whether or not a particular portfolio is the lending portfolio by computing the rate of interest which *would* make the portfolio in question the lending portfolio. For example, the rate of interest associated in this manner with portfolio C is r_b, found by extending a tangent to the curve down to the E-axis. The diagonal code computes such a rate of interest for each corner portfolio as the analysis proceeds; when it falls below the previously stated lending rate the code computes the composition of the lending portfolio and terminates the analysis.

B. The "borrowing portfolio"

In some cases an investor may be able to borrow funds in order to purchase even greater amounts of a portfolio than his own funds will allow. If the appropriate rate for such borrowing were r_b, illustrated in Figure 3, the E, σ combinations attainable by purchasing portfolio C with both the investor's funds and with borrowed funds would lie along the line CD, depending on the amount borrowed. Inclusion of the borrowing alternative makes certain portfolios inefficient which are efficient in the absence of the alternative; in this case the affected portfolios are those with E, σ combinations along the segment of the original E, σ curve from C to G. Just as there is a single appropriate portfolio if any lending is contemplated, there is a single appropriate portfolio if borrowing is contemplated. This "borrowing portfolio" is related to the rate of interest at which funds can be borrowed in exactly the same manner as the "lending portfolio" is related to the rate at which funds can be lent.

The diagonal code does not take account of the borrowing alternative in the manner used for the lending alternative since it is necessary to compute all previous corner portfolios in order to derive the portion of the E, σ curve below the borrowing portfolio. For this reason all computations required to derive the full E, σ curve above the lending portfolio must be made. However, the code does allow the user to specify the rate of interest at which funds can be borrowed. If this alternative is chosen, none of the corner portfolios which will be inefficient when borrowing is considered will be printed. Since as much as 65 percent of the total computer time can be spent recording (on tape) the results of the analysis this is not an insignificant saving.

VII. THE COST OF PORTFOLIO ANALYSIS WITH THE DIAGONAL CODE

The total time (and thus cost) required to perform a portfolio analysis with the diagonal code will depend upon the number of securities analyzed, the number of corner portfolios and, to some extent, the composition of the corner portfolios. A formula which gives quite an accurate estimate of the time required to perform an analysis on an IBM 709 computer was obtained by analyzing a series of runs during which the time required to complete each major segment of the program was recorded. The approximate time required for the analysis will be:[8]

Number of seconds = .6
+ .114 × number of securities analyzed
+ .54 × number of corner portfolios
+ .0024 × number of securities analyzed
× number of corner portfolios

Unfortunately only the number of securities analyzed is known before the analysis is begun. In order to estimate the cost of portfolio analysis before it is performed, some relationship between the number of corner portfolios and the number of securities analyzed must be assumed. Since no theoretical relationship can be derived and since the total number of corner portfolios could be several times the number of securities analyzed, it seemed desirable to obtain some crude notion of the typical relationship when "reasonable" inputs are used. To accomplish this, a series of portfolio analyses was performed using inputs generated by a Monte Carlo model.

Data were gathered on the annual returns during the period 1940–1951 for 96 industrial common stocks chosen randomly from the New York Stock Exchange. The returns of each security were then related to the level of a stock market index and estimates of the parameters of the diagonal model obtained. These parameters were assumed to be samples from a population of A_i, B_i and Q_i triplets related as follows:

$$A_i = \bar{A} + r_1$$

$$B_i = \bar{B} + \psi A_i + r_2$$

$$Q_i = \bar{Q} + \theta A_i + \gamma B_i + r_3$$

where r_1, r_2 and r_3 are random variables with zero means. Estimates for the parameters of these three equations were obtained by regression analysis and estimates of the variances of the random variables determined.[9] With this information the characteristics of any desired number of securities could be generated. A random number generator was used to select a value for A_i; this value, together with an additional random number determined the value of B_i; the value of Q_i was then determined with a third random number and the previously obtained values of A_i and B_i.

Figure 4 shows the relationship between the number of securities

[8] The computations in this section are based on the assumption that no corner portfolios prior to the lending portfolio are printed. If the analyst chooses to print all preceding portfolios, the estimates given in this section should be multiplied by 2.9; intermediate cases can be estimated by interpolation.

[9] The random variables were considered normally distributed; in one case, to better approximate the data, two variances were used for the distribution—one for the portion above the mean and another for the portion below the mean.

FIGURE 4

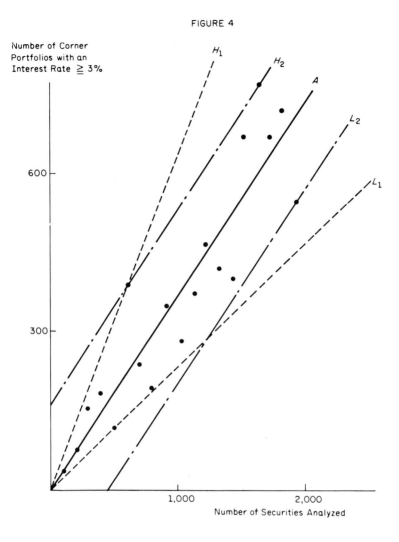

Number of Corner
Portfolios with an
Interest Rate $\geq 3\%$

H_1

H_2

A

L_2

600

L_1

300

1,000

2,000

Number of Securities Analyzed

analyzed and the number of corner portfolios with interest rates greater
than 3 percent (an approximation to the "lending rate"). Rather than
perform a sophisticated analysis of these data, several lines have been used
to bracket the results in various ways. These will be used subsequently
as extreme cases, on the presumption that most practical cases will lie
within these extremes (but with no presumption that these limits will
never be exceeded). Curve A indicates the average relationship between
the number of portfolios and the number of securities: average $(N_p/N_s) =$
.37. Curve H_1 indicates the highest such relationship: maximum $(N_p/N_s) =$

.63; the line L_1 indicates the lowest: minimum (N_p/N_s) = .24. The other two curves, H_2 and L_2, indicate respectively the maximum deviation above (155) and below (173) the number of corner portfolios indicated by the average relationship $N_p = .37N_s$.

In Figure 5 the total time required for a portfolio analysis is related to the number of securities analyzed under various assumptions about the relationship between the number of corner portfolios and the number of securities analyzed. Each of the curves shown in Figure 5 is based on the corresponding curve in Figure 4; for example, curve A in Figure 5 indicates

FIGURE 5

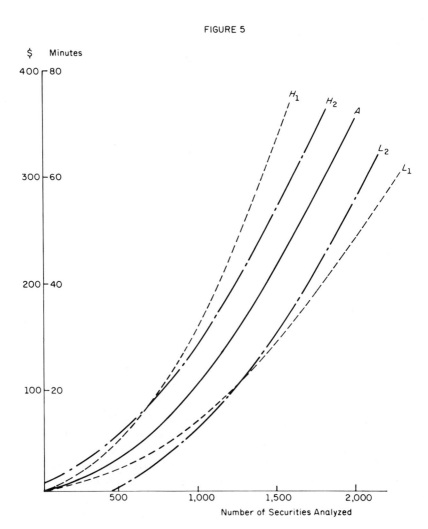

Number of Securities Analyzed

the relationship between total time and number of securities analyzed on the assumption that the relationship between the number of corner portfolios and the number of securities is that shown by curve A in Figure 4. For convenience a second scale has been provided in Figure 5, showing the total cost of the analysis on the assumption that an IBM 709 computer can be obtained at a cost of $300 per hour.

VIII. THE VALUE OF PORTFOLIO ANALYSIS BASED ON THE DIAGONAL MODEL

The assumptions of the diagonal model lie near one end of the spectrum of possible assumptions about the relationships among securities. The model's extreme simplicity enables the investigator to perform a portfolio analysis at a very small cost, as we have shown. However, it is entirely possible that this simplicity so restricts the security analyst in making his predictions that the value of the resulting portfolio analysis is also very small.

In order to estimate the ability of the diagonal model to summarize information concerning the performance of securities a simple test was performed. Twenty securities were chosen randomly from the New York Stock Exchange and their performance during the period 1940–51 used to obtain two sets of data: (1) the actual mean returns, variances of returns and covariances of returns during the period and (2) the parameters of the diagonal model, estimated by regression techniques from the performance of the securities during the period. A portfolio analysis was then performed on each set of data. The results are summarized in Figures 6a and 6b. Each security which entered any of the efficient portfolios in significant amounts is represented by a particular type of line; the height of each line above any given value of E indicates the percentage of the efficient portfolio with that particular E composed of the security in question. The two figures thus indicate the compositions of all the efficient portfolios chosen from the analysis of the historical data (Figure 6b) and the compositions of all the portfolios chosen from the analysis of the parameters of the diagonal model (Figure 6a). The similarity of the two figures indicates that the 62 parameters of the diagonal model were able to capture a great deal of the information contained in the complete set of 230 historical relationships. An additional test, using a second set of 20 securities, gave similar results.

These results are, of course, far too fragmentary to be considered conclusive but they do suggest that the diagonal model may be able to represent the relationships among securities rather well and thus that the value of portfolio analyses based on the model will exceed their rather

FIGURE 6

COMPOSITION OF EFFICIENT PORTFOLIOS DERIVED FROM THE
ANALYSIS OF a) THE PARAMETERS OF THE DIAGONAL MODEL, b) HISTORICAL DATA

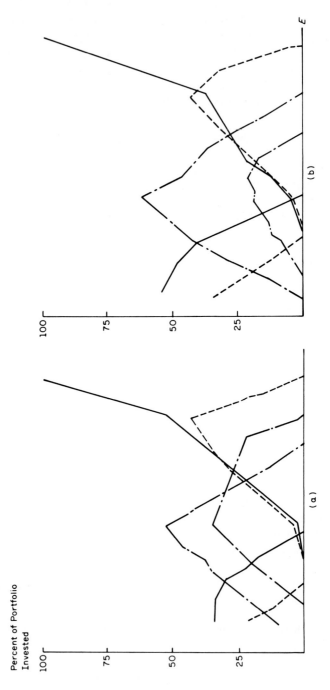

nominal cost. For these reasons it appears to be an excellent choice for the initial practical applications of the Markowitz technique.

REFERENCES

[1] Markowitz, Harry M., *Portfolio Selection, Efficient Diversification of Investments* (New York, N. Y.: Wiley, 1959).

[2] Markowitz, Harry M., "Portfolio Selection," *The Journal of Finance*, Vol. 12 (March 1952), pp. 77–91.

[3] Markowitz, Harry M., "The Optimization of a Quadratic Function Subject to Linear Constraints," *Naval Research Logistics Quarterly*, Vol. 3 (March and June, 1956), pp. 111–33.

[4] Wolfe, Philip, "The Simplex Method for Quadratic Programming," *Econometrica*, Vol. 27 (July, 1959), pp. 382–98.

*Eugene F. Fama**

6. Portfolio Analysis in a Stable Paretian Market

Reprinted from **Management Science,** Vol. II, No. 3 (January, 1965),
pp. 404–419, by permission of the author and publisher.

Recently evidence has come forth which suggests that empirical probability distributions of returns on securities conform better to stable Paretian distributions with infinite variances than to the normal distribution. Using a generalized form of a technique proposed by Sharpe [17] in a recent issue of this journal, this article develops a portfolio analysis model for a stable Paretian market. The article also shows the range of conditions under which diversification is a meaningful economic activity, even though probability distributions of returns on individual securities have infinite variances.

I. INTRODUCTION

In recent years there has been a vigorous rebirth of interest in the theory of random walks in stock prices. The theory states that successive, percentage price changes for a given differencing interval are independent, identically distributed, random variables.[1] Until the last few years it was generally believed that the relevant distribution for the price changes was probably the normal or Gaussian. Most recently, however, Mandelbrot [12] and others [6], [7], have put forth theoretical arguments and em-

* Professor of Finance, University of Chicago. This study was partially supported by funds from a grant by the Ford Foundation to the Graduate School of Business, University of Chicago. I am also indebted to my colleagues Merton H. Miller and Harry V. Roberts for their more than helpful comments.
    [1] The appropriate scale of measurement for the price changes is not rigidly specified by the theory. The earliest work just used the simple price changes, but, for various reasons, modern writers have tended to argue in favor of either percentage price changes or changes in log price.

pirical evidence which strongly suggest that the price changes conform more closely to stable Paretian distributions with characteristic exponents less than two. For the purposes of portfolio analysis the most important feature of these distributions is that their variances are infinite.[2]

In the well-known Markowitz [13] portfolio model the set of efficient portfolios is defined as those portfolios which have maximum expected returns for given variances of expected return. The one period return on a security is defined as

$$R_{jt} = d_{jt}/p_{jt} + (p_{j,t+1} - p_{jt})/p_{jt} \qquad (1)$$

where R_{jt} is the return on security j during time period t, d_{jt} is the dividend payment during time period t, $p_{j,t+1}$ is the price of security j at the end of time t, and p_{jt} is its price at the beginning of time t. From (1) it is clear that if the distribution of the percentage price changes has infinite variance, the distribution of the return on the security must also have infinite variance. In this case the Markowitz definition of an efficient portfolio loses its meaning and must be replaced so as not to depend on the variance as a measure of dispersion.

The purpose of this paper is to develop a general model for portfolio analysis in a market where returns follow stable Paretian distributions. Our main goal is to demonstrate that in certain very general circumstances the concept of diversification has economic meaning in a stable Paretian market, even though its effects on the dispersion of the distribution of the return on the portfolio can no longer be described by the variance. In essence, we shall see that a statistical interpretation of the effects of diversification can be developed as long as the model is defined in terms of a scale parameter more natural to stable Paretian distributions than the variance.

The model we shall use is a generalization of the "diagonal" model suggested by Markowitz[3] and discussed more extensively by Sharpe [17] in a recent issue of this journal. In fact we shall see later that the Markowitz-Sharpe diagonal model is the special case of the model to be presented here for the situation where all probability distributions of returns are Gaussian or normal.

---

[2] Various aspects of the random walk theory have been discussed by Bachelier [2], Kendall [9], Osborne [15], Roberts [16], Alexander [1], Cootner [5], Moore [14], Mandelbrot [11], [12], and Fama [6], [7]. Bachelier is the pioneer in the field. Evidence concerning the independence of price changes is discussed by Kendall, Roberts, Alexander, Cootner, Moore, and Fama. Osborne and Moore argue specifically in favor of the normal distribution, whereas Mandelbrot and Fama give theoretical support and empirical evidence in favor of the stable Paretian hypothesis.

[3] Markowitz [13], pp. 96–101.

II. THE STABLE PARETIAN DISTRIBUTIONS

The statistical theory of stable Paretian distributions has been discussed extensively elsewhere.[4] Therefore in this paper we limit ourselves to a discussion of those statistical properties which are most important for the portfolio model to be presented later.

The general form of the logarithm of the characteristic function for the stable Paretian family of distributions is

$$\log f(t) = \log E(e^{i\tilde{x}t})$$
$$= i\delta t - \gamma \mid t \mid^{\alpha}[1 + i\beta(t/\mid t \mid)w(t, \alpha)] \qquad (2)$$

where $\tilde{x}$ is the random variable, t is any real number, i is $\sqrt{-1}$, and

$$w(t, \alpha) = \begin{cases} \tan \dfrac{\pi\alpha}{2}, & \alpha \neq 1 \\ \\ \dfrac{2}{\pi} \log \mid t \mid, & \alpha = 1 \end{cases}$$

Stable Paretian distributions have four parameters, α, β, δ, and γ. The parameter α is called the characteristic exponent of the distribution. It determines the height of, or total probability contained in, the extreme tails of the distribution. It can take any value in the interval $0 < \alpha \leq 2$. When $\alpha = 2$, the relevant stable Paretian distribution is the normal distribution.[5] When α is in the interval $0 < \alpha < 2$, the extreme tails of the stable Paretian distributions are higher than those of the normal distribution, with the total probability in the extreme tails larger the smaller the value of α. The most important consequence of this is that the variance exists (i.e., is finite) only in the limiting case $\alpha = 2$. The mean, however, exists[6] as long as $\alpha > 1$.

The parameter β is an index of skewness which can take any value in the interval $-1 \leq \beta \leq 1$. When $\beta = 0$, the distribution is symmetric.

---

[4] The derivation of most of the important properties of stable Paretian distributions is due to Paul Lévy [10]. A rigorous and compact mathematical treatment of the statistical theory can be found in Gnedenko and Kolmogorov [8]. A more comprehensive mathematical treatment can be found in Mandelbrot [12], while Fama [6], [7] provides a descriptive-intuitive approach.

[5] The logarithm of the characteristic function of a normal distribution is

$$\log f(t) = i\mu t - (\sigma^2/2)t^2$$

This is the log characteristic function of a stable Paretian distribution with parameters $\alpha = 2$, $\delta = \mu$, and $\gamma = \sigma^2/2$.

It is probably also well to note that when $\alpha = 1$ and $\beta = 0$, the relevant stable Paretian distribution is the Cauchy. Thus the Gaussian and the Cauchy are the two most familiar members of the stable Paretian family.

[6] For a proof of these statements see [8], pp. 179–183.

When $\beta > 0$, the distribution is skewed right (i.e., has a long tail to the right), and the degree of right skewness is larger the larger the value of β. Similarly when $\beta < 0$ the distribution is skewed left, with the degree of left skewness larger the smaller the value of β.

The parameter δ is the location parameter of the stable Paretian distribution. When α is greater than 1, δ is the expected value or mean of the distribution. When $\alpha \leq 1$, however, the mean of the distribution is infinite. In this case δ will be some other parameter (e.g., the median when $\beta = 0$), which will define the location of the distribution.

In our development of a portfolio model for a stable Paretian market our attention will be concentrated primarily on the parameter γ. The value of this parameter defines the scale of a stable Paretian distribution. For example, when $\alpha = 2$ (the normal distribution), γ is one-half the variance. When $\alpha < 2$, however, the variance of the stable Paretian distribution is infinite. In this case there will be a finite parameter γ which defines the scale of the distribution, but it will not be the variance. For example, when $\alpha = 1, \beta = 0$, (which is the Cauchy distribution), γ is the semiinterquartile range (i.e., one-half of the .75 fractile minus the .25 fractile).

For the purposes of portfolio analysis a key property of stable Paretian distributions is stability. By definition, a stable Paretian distribution is any distribution that is stable or invariant under addition. That is, the distribution of sums of independent, identically distributed, stable Paretian variables is itself stable Paretian and has the same form as the distribution of the individual summands. The phrase "has the same form" is, of course, an imprecise verbal expression for a precise mathematical property. A more rigorous definition of stability is given by the logarithm of the characteristic function of sums of independent, identically distributed, stable Paretian variables. The expression for this function is

$$n \log f(t) = i(n\delta)t - (n\gamma) \mid t \mid^{\alpha}[1 + i\beta(t/\mid t \mid)w(t, \alpha)] \qquad (3)$$

where n is the number of variables in the sum and $\log f(t)$ is the log characteristic function for the distribution of the individual summands. Expression (3) is the same as (2), the expression for $\log f(t)$, except that the parameters δ (location) and γ (scale) are multiplied by n. That is, the distribution of the sums is, except for origin and scale, exactly the same as the distribution of the individual summands. More simply, stability means that the values of the parameters α and β remain constant under addition.

So far we have assumed that the individual, stable Paretian variables in the sum are identically distributed. That is, the distribution of each individual summand has the same values of the four parameters, α, β, δ, and γ. It will now be shown that the property of stability continues to hold when the values of the location and scale parameters, δ and γ, are not the same for each variable in the sum. The logarithm of the characteristic function of sums of n such variables, each with different location and scale parameters, δ_j and γ_j, is

$$\sum_{j=1}^{n} \log f_j(t) = i(\sum_{j=1}^{n} \delta_j)t - (\sum_{j=1}^{n} \gamma_j) \mid t \mid^\alpha [1 + i\beta(t/\mid t \mid)w(t, \alpha)] \quad (4)$$

where $\log f_j(t)$ is the log characteristic function of the jth variable in the sum.

Expression (4) is the characteristic function of a stable Paretian distribution with parameters α and β, and with location and scale parameters equal, respectively, to the sums of the location and scale parameters of the distributions of the individual summands. That is, the sum of stable Paretian variables, where each variable in the sum has the same values of the parameters α and β but different location and scale parameters, is also stable Paretian with the same values of α and β.

Stable Paretian distributions have two other properties which we mention briefly. First they are the only possible limiting distributions for sums of independent identically distributed random variables.[7] It is well-known, of course, that when the distribution of the individual variables in the sum has finite variance, the limiting distribution of the sum will be the normal distribution (i.e., $\alpha = 2$). When the distribution of the variables in the sum has infinite variance, however, and if the sums have a limiting distribution, the limiting distribution must be stable Paretian with characteristic exponent $\alpha < 2$. Second, Paul Lévy [10] has shown that the tails of stable Paretian distributions with characteristic exponents $\alpha < 2$ follow an asymptotic form of the law of Pareto.[8] Thus we see that the name stable Paretian arises from the property of stability and the asymptotically Paretian nature of the extreme tail areas.

Finally, we shall henceforth assume that we are dealing only with symmetric, stable Paretian variables (i.e., $\beta = 0$). This is done partly for expositional simplicity but also because it does not seem to be a bad representation of reality. The portfolio model to be developed is completely general in the sense that it will apply equally well to cases where the distributions of returns on securities are asymmetric. Most empirical evidence, however, (cf. [6], [9], [14], [15], and [16]) seems to indicate that the actual distributions are symmetric. This is important for *practical* purposes since it means that the number of parameters to be estimated can be reduced by one.

[7] For a proof see [8], pp. 162–3.
[8] That is,

$$\Pr(\tilde{x} > x) \rightarrow (x/U_1)^{-\alpha} \quad \text{as} \quad x \rightarrow \infty$$

and
$$\Pr(\tilde{x} < x) \rightarrow (\mid x \mid/U_2)^{-\alpha} \quad \text{as} \quad x \rightarrow -\infty$$

where U_1 and U_2 are constants.

III. THE PORTFOLIO ANALYSIS MODEL

In attempting to construct a general portfolio model for a stable Paretian market, we are faced immediately with two conceptual problems. First, if the characteristic exponent α of the distributions of returns is less than 2, then the variances of these distributions will be infinite, and it will be necessary to use some other parameter as a measure of dispersion. We shall see that the scale parameter γ is the most natural candidate. Second, when $\alpha < 2$ it can be shown that the covariance is not a well-defined statistical concept.[9] Thus in constructing a stable Paretian portfolio model we must avoid the concept of covariance in describing relationships between securities. Let us now see how this can be done.

Begin with a market composed of N securities. The return on security j is $\tilde{R}_j$, $j = 1, \ldots, N$, where the tilde denotes the fact that the return on each security is a random variable with its own probability distribution. Assume that the returns $\tilde{R}_j$ on the different securities are related to each other only by the fact that each is related to a common underlying factor, say the market as represented by the index number $\tilde{I}$ which is itself subject to a probability distribution. That is,

$$\tilde{R}_j = A_j + b_j \tilde{I} + \tilde{C}_j \qquad j = 1, \ldots, N \tag{5}$$

The coefficient b_j in (5) is a measure of the relationship between the return $\tilde{R}_j$ and the index number $\tilde{I}$. This relationship is subject to random error or noise, expressed by the random variable $\tilde{C}_j$. It is assumed that $E(\tilde{C}_j) = 0$, $j = 1, \ldots, N$, and that the $\tilde{C}_j$ for the different securities are unrelated.

When the distributions of all the various random variables are normal, or at least have finite variances, expression (5) and the assumptions above define the Markowitz-Sharpe diagonal model discussed extensively by Sharpe in [17]. The diagonal method was developed by Markowitz and Sharpe for the purpose of simplifying practical applications of portfolio analysis. The simplification, of course, is achieved by not explicitly introducing the concept of covariance in discussing relationships between securities. Because it does not require the notion of covariance, we shall now see that the diagonal model provides a natural framework for portfolio analysis in a stable Paretian market.

Let us assume that $\tilde{I}$ and $\tilde{C}_j$, $j = 1, \ldots, N$, are symmetric, stable Paretian, random variables, independent of one another but with the same characteristic exponent $\alpha < 2$. It is convenient to form new random variables

$$\tilde{D}_j = A_j + \tilde{C}_j \qquad j = 1, \ldots, N \tag{6}$$

which, of course, will be symmetric, stable Paretian with expected values A_j, $j = 1, \ldots, N$. If we think of the term $b_j \tilde{I}$ in (5) as the market com-

---

[9] Cf., Mandelbrot [12], p. 411.

ponent of the return on security j, then $\tilde{D}_j$ can be thought of as the individualistic component, i.e., that portion of the return which is due to factors affecting company j alone. Expression (5) can now be rewritten as

$$\tilde{R}_j = \tilde{D}_j + b_j \tilde{I} \tag{7}$$

Since the return on a security, $\tilde{R}_j$, is expressed as a linear combination of symmetric, stable Paretian variables, it will also be symmetric stable Paretian. The logarithm of its characteristic function will be of the general form

$$\log f_{R_i}(t) = i\delta_j t - \gamma_j \,|\, t \,|^\alpha \tag{8}$$

where δ_j is the location parameter of the distribution of $\tilde{R}_j$, and γ_j is its scale parameter. Similarly, the logarithms of the characteristic functions of the random variables $\tilde{D}_j$ and $\tilde{I}$ are of the form

$$\log f_{D_j}(t) = iA_j t - \eta_j \,|\, t \,|^\alpha \qquad j = 1, \ldots, N \tag{9}$$

$$\log f_I(t) = i\mu t - \gamma_I \,|\, t \,|^\alpha \tag{10}$$

where A_j and μ are the location parameters, while η_j and γ_I are the scale parameters for the distributions of $\tilde{D}_j$ and $\tilde{I}$. Since $\tilde{R}_j$ is a linear combination of the stable variables $\tilde{D}_j$ and $\tilde{I}$, the logarithm of its characteristic function can be expressed in terms of (9) and (10) as

$$
\begin{aligned}
\log f_{R_j}(t) &= \log f_{D_j}(t) + \log f_I(b_j t) \\
&= (iA_j t - \eta_j \,|\, t \,|^\alpha) + (ib_j\mu t - \gamma_I \,|\, b_j \,|^\alpha \,|\, t \,|^\alpha) \\
&= i(A_j + b_j\mu)t - (\eta_j + \gamma_I \,|\, b_j \,|^\alpha) \,|\, t \,|^\alpha
\end{aligned}
\tag{11}
$$

Thus the location and scale parameters of the distribution of $\tilde{R}_j$ are related to those of the distributions of $\tilde{D}_j$ and $\tilde{I}$ by

$$\delta_j = A_j + b_j\mu, \tag{12}$$

$$\gamma_j = \eta_j + \gamma_I \,|\, b_j \,|^\alpha \tag{13}$$

Now the return $\tilde{R}_p$ on a portfolio of securities can be expressed as

$$
\begin{aligned}
\tilde{R}_p &= \sum_{j=1}^{n} X_j \tilde{R}_j \\
&= \sum_{j=1}^{n} X_j (\tilde{D}_j + b_j \tilde{I}) \\
&= \sum_{j=1}^{n} X_j \tilde{D}_j + \bar{b}_n \tilde{I}
\end{aligned}
\tag{14}
$$

where n is the number of securities in the portfolio ($n \leq N$), $\bar{b}_n$ is the weighted average of the b_j over the n securities in the portfolio, X_j is the proportion of the total value of the portfolio accounted for by security j, and $\sum X_j = 1$. Since the random variable $\tilde{R}_p$ is a weighted sum of stable Paretian variables, it will also be stable Paretian. The logarithm of its characteristic function will be

$$\log f_{R_p}(t) = \sum_{j=1}^{n} \log f_{Rj}(X_j t)$$

$$= \sum_{j=1}^{n} \log f_{Dj}(X_j t) + \log f_I(\bar{b}_n t)$$

$$= i \sum_{j=1}^{n} X_j(A_j + b_j\mu)t - [\sum_{j=1}^{n} |X_j|^\alpha \eta_j + \gamma_I |\bar{b}_n|^\alpha] |t|^\alpha \quad (15)$$

The location and scale parameters of the distribution of $\tilde{R}_p$ are thus

$$\delta_p = \sum_{j=1}^{n} X_j(A_j + b_j\mu) = \sum_{j=1}^{n} X_j A_j + \bar{b}_n\mu \quad (16)$$

and

$$\gamma_p = \sum_{j=1}^{n} |X_j|^\alpha \eta_j + \gamma_I |\bar{b}_n|^\alpha \quad (17)$$

It is clear from (16) that the location parameter of the distribution of the return on the portfolio is a sum of two components: (1) a weighted average of the location parameters for the distributions of the individualistic components of the returns on the individual securities (the $\tilde{D}_j$), and (2) a weighted average of the coefficients b_j times the location parameter of the distribution of the market index $\tilde{I}$. Similar statements can be made concerning (17) and the scale parameter γ_p. Thus in this type model a portfolio is most naturally thought of as a series of investments in individual securities *plus* an investment in the market.[10]

[10] The model presented in the text is actually more general than it first appears. For example, the return on a security may be a function of industry factors as well as of market and individualistic factors. If the industry factors enter linearly into the model, we have

$$\tilde{R}_j = \tilde{D}_j + b_j\tilde{I} + \sum_{k=1}^{m} a_{kj}\tilde{F}_k \qquad j = 1, \ldots, N \quad (5a)$$

where $\tilde{F}_k$ is an index for industry k, and a_{kj} indicates the relationship between the return on security j and the industry index $\tilde{F}_k$. For a given firm (j) one or more of the a_{kj} may be non-zero, depending on the number of industries in which the firm participates.
    As long as the F_k are stable Paretian random variables, independent of each other and of $\tilde{I}$ and the $\tilde{D}_j$, then $\tilde{R}_j$ will be a linear combination of stable Paretian variables. Thus by the property of stability $\tilde{R}_j$ will itself be stable Paretian. Similarly, $\tilde{R}_p$ is a linear combination of the $\tilde{R}_j$, and thus it will also be stable Paretian. The derivation of the relationships between the parameters of the distributions of $\tilde{R}_p$, $\tilde{R}_j$, $\tilde{D}_j$, $\tilde{I}$, and the $\tilde{F}_k$ is identical to the corresponding derivation for the simple diagonal model in the text, and so it is omitted.

This completes the analysis of the formal structure of a portfolio model in a stable Paretian market. As a check on the derivations the reader will note that in the Gaussian case ($\alpha = 2$) expressions (16) and (17) are identical to the corresponding formulas given by the Markowitz-Sharpe diagonal model [17]. The model outlined in expressions (1)–(13), however, is formally correct for any value of α in the interval $0 < \alpha \leq 2$ and in fact can very easily be extended to cover cases where the distributions of returns follow asymmetric stable laws.

This should not, however, be interpreted to mean that diversification is always a meaningful *economic* concept. We shall see in the next section that diversification only makes economic sense for a narrower range of values of α.

IV. THE PRINCIPLE OF DIVERSIFICATION

The purpose of diversification is to reduce the dispersion of the distribution of the return on a portfolio. In this section we shall discuss the conditions under which diversification will achieve this result in a stable Paretian market.

The scale parameter (γ_p) of the distribution of the return on a portfolio is given by (17). Let us simplify this expression by assuming that

$$X_j = 1/n \qquad j = 1, \ldots, n \tag{18}$$

where n is the number of securities in the portfolio. That is, we assume that the same proportion of the total value of the portfolio is invested in each security. Expression (17) now becomes

$$\gamma_p = (1/n)^\alpha \sum_{j=1}^{n} \eta_j + \gamma_I \mid \bar{b}_n \mid^\alpha \tag{19}$$

In (19) as n is increased the behavior of γ_p depends very definitely on the value of α. In particular, when $\alpha = 1$,

$$\gamma_p = \bar{\eta}_n + \gamma_I \mid \bar{b}_n \mid \tag{20}$$

where $\bar{\eta}_n$ and $\bar{b}_n$ are the averages of the η_j and b_j over the n securities in the portfolio. Thus if we can assume for purposes of illustration that there are an infinite number of different securities in the market, we have

$$\lim_{n \to \infty} \gamma_p = \bar{\eta} + \gamma_I \mid \bar{b} \mid \tag{21}$$

where $\bar{\eta}$ and $\bar{b}$ are the averages of the η_j and b_j over all existing securities. In this case diversification makes no obvious sense unless there is very substantial uncertainty about the values of η_j and b_j for the different securities.

When $\alpha > 1$, however,

$$\gamma_p < \bar{\eta}_n + \gamma_I \, | \, \bar{b}_n \, |^\alpha \tag{22}$$

since

$$(1/n)^\alpha \sum_{j=1}^n \eta_j < \bar{\eta}_n \tag{23}$$

In the limit (22) becomes

$$\lim_{n \to \infty} \gamma_p = \gamma_I \, | \, \bar{b} \, |^\alpha \tag{24}$$

Finally, when $\alpha < 1$,

$$\gamma_p > \bar{\eta}_n + \gamma_I \, | \, \bar{b}_n \, |^\alpha \tag{25}$$

since

$$(1/n)^\alpha \sum_{j=1}^n \eta_j > \bar{\eta}_n \tag{26}$$

In this case (25) becomes in the limit

$$\lim_{n \to \infty} \gamma_p = \infty \tag{27}$$

Thus from expressions (20)–(27) we see that in general increased diversification is effective in reducing the dispersion or scale of the distribution of the return on a portfolio only when the characteristic exponent $\alpha > 1$. Moreover, a given amount of diversification will be more effective the higher the value of α. That is, other things equal, when $\alpha > 1$ the rate of approach of γ_p to $\gamma_I \, | \, \bar{b} \, |^\alpha$ will be greater the higher the value of α. When $\alpha = 1$ diversification is in general ineffective in reducing the dispersion of the distribution of the return of the portfolio, and when $\alpha < 1$, increasing diversification actually causes the dispersion of the return to increase.

These statements can be explained in more intuitive terms. We saw earlier (expressions 17 and 19) that the dispersion parameter γ_p is actually made up of two separate terms, one of which depends on the scale parameters of the distributions of the individualistic components of security returns (i.e., the η_j), while the other depends on the scale parameter of the market index (i.e., γ_I). Our previous discussion shows that the market component of γ_p is, for given α, more or less independent of the number of securities in the portfolio. Thus the effect of diversification on γ_p must work through the term which represents the individualistic components. In (19) this term is

$$(1/n)^\alpha \sum_{j=1}^n \eta_j \tag{28}$$

Now (28) can be regarded as sort of an average of the η_j over the n securities in the portfolio. When $\alpha = 1$, (28) is just a simple average of the η_j which, in general, will neither increase nor decrease consistently with n. When $\alpha > 1$, however, we are "averaging" the η_j by a power of $1/n$, so that in general the average will decrease with increasing n. In fact provided that each η_j has some finite upper bound, the value of (28) will approach zero as n approaches infinity. Moreover, the rate of approach will be an increasing function of α.

By contrast when $\alpha < 1$ in (28), we are "averaging" the η_j but with a term that is less than $1/n$. Thus as n is increased $\sum_{j=1}^{n} \eta_j$ will usually increase faster than $(1/n)^{\alpha}$ decreases, so that the value of (28) actually increases with increasing n. For this reason diversification is not an effective procedure for reducing the dispersion of the distribution of the return on a portfolio when the characteristic exponent $\alpha < 1$.

In statistical terms all this means is that for $\alpha > 1$ there is a law of large numbers at work which makes the return on a portfolio more certain as the number of securities in the portfolio is increased. The law becomes weaker as α moves away from 2 in the direction of 1; and when $\alpha = 1$, there is no law of large numbers at work. Finally, when $\alpha < 1$, the law of large numbers actually works in reverse so that the return on the portfolio becomes less certain as the number of securities in the portfolio is increased.

A simple numerical example will make the above discussion more concrete. Table 1 shows the behavior of the scale parameter γ_p of the distribution of $\tilde{R}_p$ for various values of α and n under the following simplified conditions:[11]

$$b_j = 1 \qquad j = 1, \ldots, n$$

$$\eta_j = 1 \qquad j = 1, \ldots, n$$

$$X_j = 1/n \qquad j = 1, \ldots, n$$

$$\gamma_I = 1$$

---

[11] Although the illustration represents an extremely oversimplified situation, certain of its features are quite realistic. First, we have thus far neglected to discuss the type of market index that should be used for I in the model. In principle this is an easy problem. If the model given by (5) correctly describes the process generating returns on securities, then the ideal market index would be a weighted average of the returns on each individual security in the market, with the proportions of the total market value of all outstanding shares accounted for by each individual security as weights. In other words, the ideal market index would be the return on the "market's portfolio," i.e., a portfolio consisting of all the outstanding shares of all existing securities in the market. With such an index, of course, $\bar{b}$, the average of the b_j in (5) over all existing securities, would be equal to 1 as in the illustration of Table 1.

Second, recent empirical work suggests that on the average the market seems to account for about 50 percent of the variability of the returns on individual securities. Thus an average value of 1 for the ratio of η_j to γ_I is not unreasonable.

TABLE 1. VALUES OF γ_p FOR DIFFERENT α AND n

		n		
α	*1*	*10*	*100*	*1,000*
2.00	2	1.100	1.010	1.0010
1.75	2	1.178	1.0316	1.0056
1.50	2	1.316	1.100	1.0316
1.25	2	1.562	1.316	1.1780
1.00	2	2	2	2
.50	2	4.162	11.000	32.6228

It is clear from the table that when $\alpha = 1$ diversification is ineffective in reducing the dispersion of the distribution of the return on the portfolio. When $\alpha = 1$, under the simple conditions we have assumed for this example the scale parameter γ_p is equal to 2, regardless of the number of securities in the portfolio. When $\alpha < 1$, the table demonstrates that the return on a more diversified portfolio is actually subject to a higher degree of dispersion than the return on a less diversified portfolio. When $\alpha = .5$, the distribution of the return on a portfolio of ten securities has a scale parameter γ_p over twice as large as the scale parameter of the distribution of the return on a portfolio of one security, whereas the distribution of the return on a portfolio of one hundred securities has a scale parameter over five times as large as that of the distribution of the return on a portfolio of a single security.

When $\alpha > 1$ diversification will reduce the dispersion of the distribution of the return on the portfolio. In addition, Table 1 demonstrates that diversification is more effective the higher the value of α. When $\alpha > 1$, the scale parameter γ_p of the distribution of $\tilde{R}_p$ approaches the value $\gamma_I = 1$ as the number of securities in the portfolio is allowed to increase without bound. As n is increased, however, γ_p will fall toward the value $\gamma_I = 1$ at different rates depending on the value of α. For example, when $\alpha = 2.0$ a portfolio of ten securities will have a scale parameter $\gamma_p = 1.1$, whereas when $\alpha = 1.5$ it will require a portfolio of 100 securities to attain this level of dispersion.

These results can be explained more simply. Under the conditions assumed for Table 1, the expression for the scale parameter γ_p reduces to

$$\gamma_p = (1/n)^\alpha \sum_{j=1}^{n} \eta_j + \gamma_I \mid \bar{b}_n \mid^\alpha$$

$$= (1/n)^\alpha n + 1 \tag{19a}$$

When $\alpha = 1$, the first term in (19a) becomes $n/n = 1$, and $\gamma_p = 2$ for all values of n. When $\alpha > 1$, however, $(1/n)^\alpha$ decreases faster than n increases

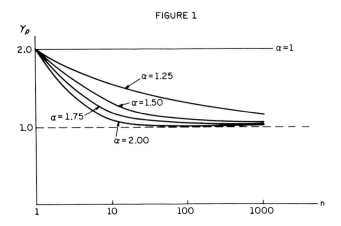

FIGURE 1

so that the first term in (19a) approaches 0, and the value of γ_p approaches the value of $\gamma_I = 1$. Moreover, it is clear from (19a) that for $\alpha > 1$ the rate of approach of γ_p to 1 is an increasing function of the value of α. When $\alpha < 1$, however, n increases faster than $(1/n)^\alpha$ decreases so that the first term in (19a) becomes very large as n becomes very large. Thus when $\alpha < 1$, γ_p actually increases with increasing n.

An encouraging feature of Table 1 is the fact that for values of $\alpha \geq 1.5$, γ_p moves relatively quickly towards its asymptotic value as the number of securities in the portfolio is increased. This is illustrated graphically in Fig. 1 which shows γ_p plotted against n. Each curve in the figure is for a different value of α. In order to include a large range of n in the graph, the horizontal axis is expressed in logarithmic units. The dashed line at the level $\gamma_p = 1$ is the asymptote of γ_p when $\alpha > 1$.

Since the empirical work to date[12] seems to indicate that for the stocks of large American companies the value of α is most probably between 1.7 and 1.9, the investor should be considerably heartened by the discussion of the previous paragraphs. When α is in this range, both Table 1 and Figure 1 indicate that diversification is still an effective tool for decreasing the dispersion of the distribution of the return on the portfolio, even though it is not as effective as in the Gaussian case, $\alpha = 2$.

V. APPLICATION OF THE STABLE PARETIAN PORTFOLIOS MODEL

At this point the major goal of the paper has been accomplished. Using a measure of variability (γ_p) more natural to stable Paretian distributions than the variance, a model has been developed which, at least in theory,

[12] Cf., Fama [6].

fully describes the effect of diversification on the distribution of the return on a portfolio. With this model it was possible to define the range of values of the characteristic exponent α for which diversification has the effect of reducing the dispersion of the distribution of the return on the portfolio.

However, although the model discussed in the previous sections provides a complete theoretical structure for a portfolio model in a stable Paretian market, there are several difficulties involved in applying the model in practical situations. It is to a discussion of these difficulties that we now turn.

A. Estimation of the relationships between the $\tilde{R}_j$ and $\tilde{I}$

In order to apply our model in a practical situation it is necessary to estimate the relationships between returns on individual securities and the market. That is, it is necessary to estimate A_j and b_j in

$$\tilde{R}_j = A_j + b_j\tilde{I} + \tilde{C}_j \qquad j = 1, \ldots, N \qquad [5]$$

If we have historical data on $\tilde{R}_j$ and $\tilde{I}$, we may be willing to use statistical techniques to estimate (5). The question is, which technique do we use? If $\alpha < 2$, least squares is not very appealing since it involves the variances of $\tilde{R}_j$, $\tilde{I}$, and $\tilde{C}_j$, and these may be infinite.

One possible alternative estimation procedure is absolute value regression.[13] This involves estimating the coefficients of a regression equation by minimizing the sum of the absolute values of deviations between actual and predicted values of the dependent variable. For the portfolio problem this means finding values of A_j and b_j which

$$\min \sum_{t=1}^{T} | R_{jt} - (A_j + b_jI_t) | \qquad (29)$$

where R_{jt} and I_t are the tth observations on $\tilde{R}_j$ and $\tilde{I}$ out of a total sample of T observations. Minimization of (29) is equivalent to minimizing $\sum_{t=1}^{T} | C_{jt} |$.

The absolute value regression problem can be put into the form of a linear programming problem. First express C_{jt} as the differences between two nonnegative variables, ϵ_{jt}' and ϵ_{jt}''.

$$C_{jt} = \epsilon_{jt}' - \epsilon_{jt}'' \qquad t = 1, \ldots, T \qquad (30)$$

The problem then becomes

$$\min \sum_{t=1}^{T} (\epsilon_{jt}' + \epsilon_{jt}'')$$

---

[13] For discussions of absolute value regression techniques see Charnes, Cooper and Ferguson [4] or Wagner [18], [19].

subject to

$$A_j + b_j I_t + \epsilon_{jt}' - \epsilon_{jt}'' = R_{jt} \qquad t = 1, \ldots, T$$

$$A_j, b_j \text{ unrestricted;} \qquad \epsilon_{jt}', \epsilon_{jt}'' \geq 0 \qquad t = 1, \ldots, T \qquad (31)$$

Of course it is true that we know very little about the sampling properties of parameters estimated by absolute value regression. The same is true of least squares estimates, however, when the underlying normality assumption is badly violated.

B. The problem with γ

Expressions (16) and (17) define the location parameter δ_p and the scale parameter γ_p of the distribution of the return on a portfolio. In theory for given values of the b_j coefficients and the characteristic exponent α these expressions are sufficient to describe the effects of diversification on the distribution of the return on the portfolio. The difficulty at this stage is that the scale parameter γ of a stable Paretian distribution is, for most values of α, a theoretical concept. That is, the mathematical statistics of stable Paretian distributions has not yet been well enough developed to give operational or computational meaning to γ in all cases. In the Gaussian case ($\alpha = 2$) γ corresponds to $\sigma^2/2$, whereas in the Cauchy case ($\alpha = 1$, $\beta = 0$) γ is equal to the semi-interquartile range. For all other values of α, however, a computational definition of the parameter is not yet available.

This does *not* mean, however, that we are powerless in measuring the effectiveness of diversification in reducing the dispersion of the distribution of the return on a portfolio. In fact it is possible to define, both conceptually and operationally, the effects of diversification on the *scale* of the distribution of the return even though the *scale parameter* γ_p is not an operational concept.

For example, consider the distribution of sums of n independent, identically distributed, symmetric, stable Paretian variables. The logarithm of the characteristic function of this distribution will have the general form

$$n \log f(t) = in\delta t - n\gamma \mid t \mid^\alpha \qquad (32)$$

where $\log f(t)$ is the log characteristic function of the distribution of the individual summands.

Let us now pose the problem of finding a change of scale for the distribution of sums which will make its scale the same as that of the distribution of the individual summands. That is, we wish to find a transformation $(a\,t)$ such that

$$n\gamma \mid a\,t \mid^\alpha = \gamma \mid t \mid^\alpha \qquad (33)$$

Solving (33) for a we get

$$a = n^{-1/\alpha} \qquad (34)$$

which implies that the scale of the distribution of sums is $n^{1/\alpha}$ times the scale of the distribution of the individual summands (a well-known fact for the Gaussian and Cauchy cases). Thus we can make statements concerning the scale of the distribution of sums relative to the *scale* of the distribution of the individual summands even though the *scale parameter* γ cannot be operationally defined for either distribution. For example, we can make the operational statement that the intersextile range of the distribution of sums is $n^{1/\alpha}$ times the intersextile range of the distribution of the individual summands, even though we cannot operationally define the scale parameter γ of either distribution.

Using arguments similar to those in the preceding paragraphs we shall now discuss the effects of diversification on the scale of the distribution of the return on a portfolio. When a new security is added to a portfolio, the log characteristic function of $\tilde{R}_p$ becomes

$$\log f_{R_p}(t) = i \sum_{j=1}^{n+1} X_j'(A_j + b_j\mu)t - \left[\sum_{j=1}^{n+1} |X_j'|^\alpha \eta_j + \gamma_I |\bar{b}_{n+1}|^\alpha\right] |t|^\alpha \quad (35)$$

Expression (35) is identical to (15) except that one new term is added to each summation, and the X_j must be adjusted so that

$$\sum_{j=1}^{n} X_j = \sum_{j=1}^{n+1} X_j' = 1 \quad (36)$$

Given that $\alpha > 1$, if the purpose of the increase in diversification is to reduce the scale or dispersion of the distribution of $\tilde{R}_p$, a set of X_j', $j = 1, \ldots, n+1$, must be found such that

$$\left[\sum_{j=1}^{n+1} |X_j'|^\alpha \eta_j + \gamma_I |\bar{b}_{n+1}|^\alpha\right] |t|^\alpha < \left[\sum_{j=1}^{n} |X_j|^\alpha \eta_j + \gamma_I |\bar{b}_n|^\alpha\right] |t|^\alpha \quad (37)$$

This implies that the $(n+1)$st security and the rearrangement of the X_j must be chosen such that

$$|X'_{n+1}|^\alpha \eta_{n+1} < \sum_{j=1}^{n} (|X_j|^\alpha - |X_j'|^\alpha)\eta_j + (|\bar{b}_n|^\alpha - |\bar{b}_{n+1}|^\alpha)\gamma_I \quad (38)$$

Thus when a new security is added to a portfolio, the change in the scale of the distribution of the return on the portfolio will depend on the size of η_{n+1} relative to the η_j, $j = 1, \ldots, n$, on the size of b_{n+1} relative to the b_j, $j = 1, \ldots, n$, and also on the changes in the X_j caused by introducing X'_{n+1} into the new portfolio. Given the n securities that are already in the portfolio, the dispersion of the return on the portfolio will in general decrease when the $(n+1)$st security is one which has a low value of b_{n+1}, (i.e., one that is not strongly related to the market), and also one which has low dispersion (η_{n+1}) in the distribution of the individualistic component $(\tilde{D}_{n+1})$ of its return. Moreover, if we are concerned with minimizing dispersion, the X_j, $j = 1, \ldots, n$, should be rearranged so that securities whose distributions of returns have low values of η_j and b_j receive higher weight relative to securities whose distributions of returns have higher values of η_j and b_j.

Now η_j, $j = 1, \ldots, N$, and γ_I are the "formal" scale parameters of stable Paretian distributions. That is, they are the scale parameters that appear in the characteristic functions of the distributions of the $\tilde{D}_j$ and $\tilde{I}$. We saw in the beginning of this section that for most values of the characteristic exponent α, statistical theory has not yet been well enough developed to give computational meaning to these parameters. However, we saw in our earlier discussion that statements in terms of the "formal" scale parameters of stable Paretian distributions can be translated into statements in terms of other scale parameters (e.g., the intersextile range) which do have operational meaning. Thus statements in terms of the scale parameters η_j and γ_I of the distributions of $\tilde{D}_j$ and $\tilde{I}$ can be translated into statements in terms of the intersextile ranges of these distributions. These comments are admittedly somewhat vague, but they at least indicate that it is possible to speak in a practical as well as conceptual fashion about portfolio analysis in a stable Paretian market.

VI. SUMMARY

The main purpose of this paper was to present a formal portfolio model for the case where returns on securities follow stable Paretian distributions with characteristic exponents less than 2. The model shows conditions under which diversification leads to a reduction in the dispersion of the distribution of the return on a portfolio, even though the variance of this distribution is infinite.

Although the model presented is sufficient to accomplish these theoretical goals, there are admittedly difficult problems involved in applying it to practical situations. Most of these difficulties are due to the fact that economic models involving stable Paretian generating processes have developed more rapidly than the statistical theory of stable Paretian distributions. It is our hope that papers like this will arouse the interest of statisticians in exploring more fully the properties of these distributions.

REFERENCES

[1] Alexander, S. S., "Price Movements in Speculative Markets; Trends or Random Walks," *Industrial Management Review*, Vol. 2 (1961), pp. 7–26.

[2] Bachelier, L. J. B. A., *Théorie de la Speculation* (Paris, France: Gauthier-Villars, 1900).

[3] Baumol, W. J., "An Expected Gain-Confidence Limit Criterion for Portfolio Selection," *Management Science*, Vol. 10-1 (1963), pp. 174–82.

[4] Charnes, A., Cooper, W. W. and Ferguson, R. O., "Optimal Estimation of Executive Compensation by Linear Programming," *Management Science*, Vol. 2-2, pp. 138–52.

[5] Cootner, Paul H., "Stock Prices: Random vs. Systematic Changes," *Industrial Management Review*, Vol. 3 (1962), pp. 25–45.

[6] Fama, Eugene F., "The Behavior of Stock Prices," *Journal of Business*, Vol. 38-1 (1965).

[7] ——, "Mandelbrot and the Stable Paretian Hypothesis," *Journal of Business*, Vol. 36-4 (1963), pp. 420–29.

[8] Gnedenko, B. V. and Kolmogorov, A. N., *Limit Distributions for Sums of Independent Random Variables*, trans. by K. L. Chung. (Reading, Mass.: Addison-Wesley, 1954), Chap. 7.

[9] Kendall, M. G., "The Analysis of Economic Time Series, I: Prices," *Journal of the Royal Statistical Society*, Ser. A (1953), pp. 11–25.

[10] Lévy, Paul, *Calcul des Probabilities* (Paris, France: Gauthier-Villars, 1925), part II, Chap. 6.

[11] Mandelbrot, Benoit, "New Methods in Statistical Economics," *Journal of Political Economy*, Vol. 61 (1963).

[12] ——, "The Variation of Certain Speculative Prices," *Journal of Business*, Vol. 36-4 (1963), pp. 394–419.

[13] Markowitz, Harry, *Portfolio Selection: Efficient Diversification of Investments* (New York, N. Y.: Wiley, 1959).

[14] Moore, Arnold, "A Statistical Analysis of Common Stock Prices," unpublished doctoral dissertation (Graduate School of Business, U. of Chicago, 1962).

[15] Osborne, M. F. M., "Brownian Motion in the Stock Market," *Operations Research*, Vol. VII (1959), pp. 145–173.

[16] Roberts, Harry V., "Stock Market 'Patterns' and Financial Analysis: Methodological Suggestions," *Journal of Finance*, Vol. 14 (1959), pp. 1–10.

[17] Sharpe, W. F., "A Simplified Model for Portfolio Analysis," *Management Science*, Vol. 9-2 (1963), pp. 277–93.

[18] Wagner, H. M., "Linear Programming Techniques for Regression Analysis," *Journal of the American Statistical Association*, Vol. 54 (1959), pp. 206–12.

[19] ——, "Nonlinear Regression with Minimal Assumptions," *Journal of the · American Statistical Association*, Vol. 57 (1962), pp. 572–78.

*William F. Sharpe**

7. Capital Asset Prices: A Theory of Market Equilibrium Under Conditions of Risk[†]

Reprinted from **The Journal of Finance,** Vol. XIX, No. 3 (September, 1964), pp. 425–442, by permission of the author and publisher.

I. INTRODUCTION

One of the problems which has plagued those attempting to predict the behavior of capital markets is the absence of a body of positive micro-economic theory dealing with conditions of risk. Although many useful insights can be obtained from the traditional models of investment under conditions of certainty, the pervasive influence of risk in financial trans-actions has forced those working in this area to adopt models of price behavior which are little more than assertions. A typical classroom expla-nation of the determination of capital asset prices, for example, usually begins with a careful and relatively rigorous description of the process through which individual preferences and physical relationships interact to determine an equilibrium pure interest rate. This is generally followed by the assertion that somehow a market risk-premium is also determined, with the prices of assets adjusting accordingly to account for differences in their risk.

A useful representation of the view of the capital market implied in such discussions is illustrated in Figure 1. In equilibrium, capital asset prices have adjusted so that the investor, if he follows rational procedures (primarily diversification), is able to attain any desired point along a

* Professor of Economics, University of California.

† A great many people provided comments on early versions of this paper which led to major improvements in the exposition. In addition to the referees, who were most helpful, the author wishes to express his appreciation to Dr. Harry Markowitz of the RAND Corporation, Professor Jack Hirshleifer of the University of California at Los Angeles, and to Professors Yoram Barzel, George Brabb, Bruce Johnson, Walter Oi and R. Haney Scott of the University of Washington.

FIGURE 1

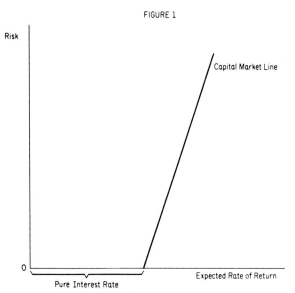

capital market line.[1] He may obtain a higher expected rate of return on his holdings only by incurring additional risk. In effect, the market presents him with two prices: the *price of time*, or the pure interest rate (shown by the intersection of the line with the horizontal axis) and the *price of risk*, the additional expected return per unit of risk borne (the reciprocal of the slope of the line).

At present there is no theory describing the manner in which the price of risk results from the basic influences of investor preferences, the physical attributes of capital assets, etc. Moreover, lacking such a theory, it is difficult to give any real meaning to the relationship between the price of a single asset and its risk. Through diversification, some of the risk inherent in an asset can be avoided so that its total risk is obviously not the relevant influence on its price; unfortunately little has been said concerning the particular risk component which is relevant.

In the last ten years a number of economists have developed *normative* models dealing with asset choice under conditions of risk. Markowitz,[2] following Von Neumann and Morgenstern, developed an analysis based on the expected utility maxim and proposed a general solution for the portfolio selection problem. Tobin[3] showed that under certain conditions

---

[1] Although some discussions are also consistent with a nonlinear (but monotonic) curve.

[2] Harry M. Markowitz, *Portfolio Selection, Efficient Diversification of Investments* (New York, N.Y.: John Wiley and Sons, Inc., 1959). The major elements of the theory first appeared in his article "Portfolio Selection," *The Journal of Finance*, XII (March 1952), 77–91.

[3] James Tobin, "Liquidity Preference as Behavior Towards Risk," *The Review of Economic Studies*, XXV (February, 1958), 65–86.

Markowitz's model implies that the process of investment choice can be broken down into two phases: first, the choice of a unique optimum combination of risky assets; and second, a separate choice concerning the allocation of funds between such a combination and a single riskless asset. Recently, Hicks[4] has used a model similar to that proposed by Tobin to derive corresponding conclusions about individual investor behavior, dealing somewhat more explicitly with the nature of the conditions under which the process of investment choice can be dichotomized. An even more detailed discussion of this process, including a rigorous proof in the context of a choice among lotteries has been presented by Gordon and Gangolli.[5]

Although all the authors cited use virtually the same model of investor behavior,[6] none has yet attempted to extend it to construct a *market* equilibrium theory of asset prices under conditions of risk.[7] We will show that such an extension provides a theory with implications consistent with the assertions of traditional financial theory described above. Moreover, it sheds considerable light on the relationship between the price of an asset and the various components of its overall risk. For these reasons it warrants consideration as a model of the determination of capital asset prices.

Part II provides the model of individual investor behavior under conditions of risk. In part III the equilibrium conditions for the capital market are considered and the capital market line derived. The implications for the relationship between the prices of individual capital assets and the various components of risk are described in Part IV.

II. OPTIMAL INVESTMENT POLICY FOR THE INDIVIDUAL

The investor's preference function

Assume that an individual views the outcome of any investment in probabilistic terms; that is, he thinks of the possible results in terms of

[4] John R. Hicks, "Liquidity," *The Economic Journal*, LXXII (December, 1962), 787–802.

[5] M. J. Gordon and Ramesh Gangolli, "Choice Among and Scale of Play on Lottery Type Alternatives," College of Business Administration, University of Rochester, 1962. For another discussion of this relationship see W. F. Sharpe, "A Simplified Model for Portfolio Analysis," *Management Science*, Vol. 9, No. 2 (January, 1963), 277–293. A related discussion can be found in F. Modigliani and M. H. Miller, "The Cost of Capital, Corporation Finance, and the Theory of Investment," *The American Economic Review*, XLVIII (June, 1958), 261–297.

[6] Recently Hirshleifer has suggested that the mean-variance approach used in the articles cited is best regarded as a special case of a more general formulation due to Arrow. See Hirshleifer's "Investment Decision Under Uncertainty," *Papers and Proceedings of the Seventy-Sixth Annual Meeting of the American Economic Association*, Dec. 1963, or Arrow's "Le Role des Valeurs Boursieres pour la Repartition la Meilleure des Risques," *International Colloquium on Econometrics*, 1952.

[7] After preparing this paper the author learned that Mr. Jack L. Treynor, of Arthur D. Little, Inc., had independently developed a model similar in many respects to the one described here. Unfortunately Mr. Treynor's excellent work on this subject is, at present, unpublished.

FIGURE 2

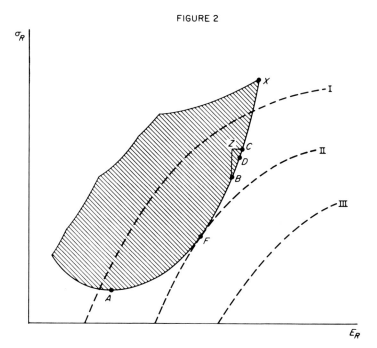

some probability distribution. In assessing the desirability of a particular investment, however, he is willing to act on the basis of only two parameters of this distribution—its expected value and standard deviation.[8] This can be represented by a total utility function of the form:

$$U = f(E_w, \sigma_w)$$

where E_w indicates expected future wealth and σ_w the predicted standard deviation of the possible divergence of actual future wealth from E_w.

Investors are assumed to prefer a higher expected future wealth to a lower value, ceteris paribus $(dU/dE_w > 0)$. Moreover, they exhibit risk-aversion, choosing an investment offering a lower value of σ_w to one with a greater level, given the level of E_w $(dU/d\sigma_w < 0)$. These assumptions imply that indifference curves relating E_w and σ_w will be upward-sloping.[9]

To simplify the analysis, we assume that an investor has decided to commit a given amount (W_i) of his present wealth to investment. Letting

---

[8] Under certain conditions the mean-variance approach can be shown to lead to unsatisfactory predictions of behavior. Markowitz suggests that a model based on the semi-variance (the average of the squared deviations below the mean) would be preferable; in light of the formidable computational problems, however, he bases his analysis on the variance and standard deviation.

[9] While only these characteristics are required for the analysis, it is generally assumed that the curves have the property of diminishing marginal rates of substitution between E_w and σ_w, as do those in our diagrams.

W_t be his terminal wealth and R the rate of return on his investment:

$$R \equiv \frac{W_t - W_i}{W_i}$$

we have

$$W_t = RW_i + W_i$$

This relationship makes it possible to express the investor's utility in terms of R, since terminal wealth is directly related to the rate of return:

$$U = g(E_R, \sigma_R)$$

Figure 2 summarizes the model of investor preferences in a family of indifference curves; successive curves indicate higher levels of utility as one moves down and/or to the right.[10]

The investment opportunity curve

The model of investor behavior considers the investor as choosing from a set of investment opportunities that one which maximizes his utility. Every investment plan available to him may be represented by a point in the E_R, σ_R plane. If all such plans involve some risk, the area composed of such points will have an appearance similar to that shown in Figure 2. The investor will choose from among all possible plans the one placing him on the indifference curve representing the highest level of utility (point F). The decision can be made in two stages: first, find the set of efficient investment plans and, second choose one from among this set. A plan is said to be efficient if (and only if) there is no alternative with either (1) the same E_R and a lower σ_R, (2) the same σ_R and a higher E_R or (3) a higher E_R and a lower σ_R. Thus investment Z is inefficient since investments B, C, and D (among others) dominate it. The only plans

[10] Such indifference curves can also be derived by assuming that the investor wishes to maximize expected utility and that his total utility can be represented by a quadratic function of R with decreasing marginal utility. Both Markowitz and Tobin present such a derivation. A similar approach is used by Donald E. Farrar in *The Investment Decision Under Uncertainty* (Prentice-Hall, 1962). Unfortunately Farrar makes an error in his derivation; he appeals to the Von Neumann-Morgenstern cardinal utility axioms to transform a function of the form:

$$E(U) = a + bE_R - cE_R{}^2 - c\sigma_R{}^2$$

into one of the form:

$$E(U) = k_1 E_R - k_2 \sigma_R{}^2$$

That such a transformation is not consistent with the axioms can readily be seen in this form, since the first equation implies non-linear indifference curves in the E_R, $\sigma_R{}^2$ plane while the second implies a linear relationship. Obviously no three (different) points can lie on both a line and a non-linear curve (with a monotonic derivative). Thus the two functions must imply different orderings among alternative choices in at least some instance.

which would be chosen must lie along the lower right-hand boundary
($AFBDCX$)—the *investment opportunity curve.*

To understand the nature of this curve, consider two investment
plans—A and B, each including one or more assets. Their predicted expected values and standard deviations of rate of return are shown in
Figure 3. If the proportion α of the individual's wealth is placed in plan A
and the remainder $(1 - \alpha)$ in B, the expected rate of return of the combination will lie between the expected returns of the two plans:

$$E_{Rc} = \alpha E_{Ra} + (1 - \alpha) E_{Rb}$$

The predicted standard deviation of return of the combination is:

$$\sigma_{Rc} = \sqrt{\alpha^2 \sigma_{Ra}{}^2 + (1 - \alpha)^2 \sigma_{Rb}{}^2 + 2r_{ab}\alpha(1 - \alpha)\sigma_{Ra}\sigma_{Rb}}$$

Note that this relationship includes r_{ab}, the correlation coefficient between
the predicted rates of return of the two investment plans. A value of $+1$
would indicate an investor's belief that there is a precise positive relationship between the outcomes of the two investments. A zero value would
indicate a belief that the outcomes of the two investments are completely
independent, and -1 that the investor feels that there is a precise inverse

FIGURE 3

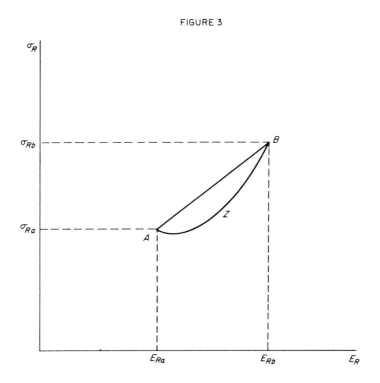

relationship between them. In the usual case r_{ab} will have a value between 0 and $+1$.

Figure 3 shows the possible values of E_{Rc} and σ_{Rc} obtainable with different combinations of A and B under two different assumptions about the value of r_{ab}. If the two investments are perfectly correlated, the combinations will lie along a straight line between the two points, since in this case both E_{Rc} and σ_{Rc} will be linearly related to the proportions invested in the two plans.[11] If they are less than perfectly positively correlated, the standard deviation of any combination must be less than that obtained with perfect correlation (since r_{ab} will be less); thus the combinations must lie along a curve below the line AB.[12] AZB shows such a curve for the case of complete independence $(r_{ab} = 0)$; with negative correlation the locus is even more U-shaped.[13]

The manner in which the investment opportunity curve is formed is relatively simple conceptually, although exact solutions are usually quite difficult.[14] One first traces curves indicating E_R, σ_R values available with simple combinations of individual assets, then considers combinations of combinations of assets. The lower right-hand boundary must be either linear or increasing at an increasing rate $(d^2\sigma_R/dE_R{}^2 > 0)$. As suggested earlier, the complexity of the relationship between the characteristics of individual assets and the location of the investment opportunity curve makes it difficult to provide a simple rule for assessing the desirability of individual assets, since the effect of an asset on an investor's over-all investment opportunity curve depends not only on its expected rate of return (E_{Ri}) and risk (σ_{Ri}), but also on its correlations with the other avail-

[11]
$$E_{Rc} = \alpha E_{Ra} + (1 - \alpha)E_{Rb} = E_{Rb} + (E_{Ra} - E_{Rb})\alpha$$

$$\sigma_{Rc} = \sqrt{\alpha^2\sigma_{Ra}{}^2 + (1 - \alpha)^2\sigma_{Rb}{}^2 + 2r_{ab}\alpha(1 - \alpha)\sigma_{Ra}\sigma_{Rb}}$$

but $r_{ab} = 1$, therefore the expression under the square root sign can be factored:

$$\sigma_{Rc} = \sqrt{[\alpha\sigma_{Ra} + (1 - \alpha)\sigma_{Rb}]^2}$$

$$= \alpha\sigma_{Ra} + (1 - \alpha)\sigma_{Rb}$$

$$= \sigma_{Rb} + (\sigma_{Ra} - \sigma_{Rb})\alpha$$

[12] This curvature is, in essence, the rationale for diversification.

[13] When $r_{ab} = 0$, the slope of the curve at point A is $-\dfrac{\sigma_{Ra}}{E_{Rb} - E_{Ra}}$, at point B it is

$\dfrac{\sigma_{Rb}}{E_{Rb} - E_{Ra}}$. When $r_{ab} = -1$, the curve degenerates to two straight lines to a point on the horizontal axis.

[14] Markowitz has shown that this is a problem in parametric quadratic programming. An efficient solution technique is described in his article, "The Optimization of a Quadratic Function Subject to Linear Constraints," *Naval Research Logistics Quarterly*, Vol. 3 (March and June, 1956), 111–133. A solution method for a special case is given in the author's "A Simplified Model for Portfolio Analysis," *op. cit.*

able opportunities $(r_{i1}, r_{i2}, \ldots, r_{in})$. However, such a rule is implied by the equilibrium conditions for the model, as we will show in part IV.

The pure rate of interest

We have not yet dealt with riskless assets. Let P be such an asset; its risk is zero $(\sigma_{Rp} = 0)$ and its expected rate of return, E_{Rp}, is equal (by definition) to the pure interest rate. If an investor places α of his wealth in P and the remainder in some risky asset A, he would obtain an expected rate of return:

$$E_{Rc} = \alpha E_{Rp} + (1 - \alpha) E_{Ra}$$

The standard deviation of such a combination would be:

$$\sigma_{Rc} = \sqrt{\alpha^2 \sigma_{Rp}^2 + (1 - \alpha)^2 \sigma_{Ra}^2 + 2r_{pa}\alpha(1 - \alpha)\sigma_{Rp}\sigma_{Ra}}$$

but since $\sigma_{Rp} = 0$, this reduces to:

$$\sigma_{Rc} = (1 - \alpha)\sigma_{Ra}$$

This implies that all combinations involving any risky asset or combination of assets plus the riskless asset must have values of E_{Rc} and σ_{Rc} which lie along a straight line between the points representing the two components. Thus in Figure 4 all combinations of E_R and σ_R lying along the line PA are attainable if some money is loaned at the pure rate and some placed in A. Similarly, by lending at the pure rate and investing in B, combinations along PB can be attained. Of all such possibilities, however, one will dominate: that investment plan lying at the point of the original investment opportunity curve where a ray from point P is tangent to the curve. In Figure 4 all investments lying along the original curve from X to ϕ are dominated by some combination of investment in ϕ and lending at the pure interest rate.

Consider next the possibility of borrowing. If the investor can borrow at the pure rate of interest, this is equivalent to disinvesting in P. The effect of borrowing to purchase more of any given investment than is possible with the given amount of wealth can be found simply by letting α take on negative values in the equations derived for the case of lending. This will obviously give points lying along the extension of line PA if borrowing is used to purchase more of A; points lying along the extension of PB if the funds are used to purchase B, etc.

As in the case of lending, however, one investment plan will dominate all others when borrowing is possible. When the rate at which funds can be borrowed equals the lending rate, this plan will be the same one which is dominant if lending is to take place. Under these conditions, the investment opportunity curve becomes a line ($P\phi Z$ in Figure 4). Moreover, if the original investment opportunity curve is not linear at point ϕ, the

FIGURE 4

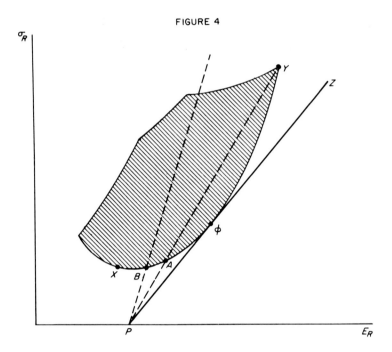

process of investment choice can be dichotomized as follows: first select the (unique) optimum combination of risky assets (point ϕ), and second borrow or lend to obtain the particular point on PZ at which an indifference curve is tangent to the line.[15]

Before proceeding with the analysis, it may be useful to consider alternative assumptions under which only a combination of assets lying at the point of tangency between the original investment opportunity curve and a ray from P can be efficient. Even if borrowing is impossible, the investor will choose ϕ (and lending) if his risk-aversion leads him to a point below ϕ on the line $P\phi$. Since a large number of investors choose to place some of their funds in relatively risk-free investments, this is not an unlikely possibility. Alternatively, if borrowing is possible but only up to some limit, the choice of ϕ would be made by all but those investors willing

[15] This proof was first presented by Tobin for the case in which the pure rate of interest is zero (cash). Hicks considers the lending situation under comparable conditions but does not allow borrowing. Both authors present their analysis using maximization subject to constraints expressed as equalities. Hicks' analysis assumes independence and thus insures that the solution will include no negative holdings of risky assets; Tobin's covers the general case, thus his solution would generally include negative holdings of some assets. The discussion in this paper is based on Markowitz's formulation, which includes nonnegativity constraints on the holdings of all assets.

to undertake considerable risk. These alternative paths lead to the main conclusion, thus making the assumption of borrowing or lending at the pure interest rate less onerous than it might initially appear to be.

III. EQUILIBRIUM IN THE CAPITAL MARKET

In order to derive conditions for equilibrium in the capital market we invoke two assumptions. First, we assume a common pure rate of interest, with all investors able to borrow or lend funds on equal terms. Second, we assume homogeneity of investor expectations:[16] investors are assumed to agree on the prospects of various investments—the expected values, standard deviations and correlation coefficients described in Part II. Needless to say, these are highly restrictive and undoubtedly unrealistic assumptions. However, since the proper test of a theory is not the realism of its assumptions but the acceptability of its implications, and since these assumptions imply equilibrium conditions which form a major part of classical financial doctrine, it is far from clear that this formulation should be rejected—especially in view of the dearth of alternative models leading to similar results.

Under these assumptions, given some set of capital asset prices, each investor will view his alternatives in the same manner. For one set of prices the alternatives might appear as shown in Figure 5. In this situation, an investor with the preferences indicated by indifference curves A_1 through A_4 would seek to lend some of his funds at the pure interest rate and to invest the remainder in the combination of assets shown by point ϕ, since this would give him the preferred overall position A^*. An investor with the preferences indicated by curves B_1 through B_4 would seek to invest all his funds in combination ϕ, while an investor with indifference curves C_1 through C_4 would invest all his funds plus additional (borrowed) funds in combination ϕ in order to reach his preferred position (C^*). In any event, all would attempt to purchase only those risky assets which enter combination ϕ.

The attempts by investors to purchase the assets in combination ϕ and their lack of interest in holding assets not in combination ϕ would, of course, lead to a revision of prices. The prices of assets in ϕ will rise and, since an asset's expected return relates future income to present price, their expected returns will fall. This will reduce the attractiveness of combinations which include such assets; thus point ϕ (among others) will move to the left of its initial position.[17] On the other hand, the prices of

---

[16] A term suggested by one of the referees.

[17] If investors consider the variability of future dollar returns unrelated to present price, both E_R and σ_R will fall; under these conditions the point representing an asset would move along a ray through the origin as its price changes.

FIGURE 5

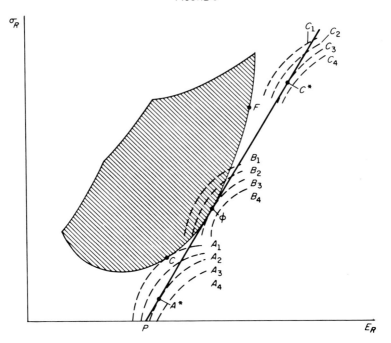

assets not in ϕ will fall, causing an increase in their expected returns and a rightward movement of points representing combinations which include them. Such price changes will lead to a revision of investors' actions; some new combination or combinations will become attractive, leading to different demands and thus to further revisions in prices. As the process continues, the investment opportunity curve will tend to become more linear, with points such as ϕ moving to the left and formerly inefficient points (such as F and G) moving to the right.

Capital asset prices must, of course, continue to change until a set of prices is attained for which every asset enters at least one combination lying on the capital market line. Figure 6 illustrates such an equilibrium condition.[18] All possibilities in the shaded area can be attained with combinations of risky assets, while points lying along the line PZ can be attained by borrowing or lending at the pure rate plus an investment in some combination of risky assets. Certain possibilities (those lying along PZ from point A to point B) can be obtained in either manner. For example, the E_R, σ_R values shown by point A can be obtained solely by some

[18] The area in Figure 6 representing E_R, σ_R values attained with only risky assets has been drawn at some distance from the horizontal axis for emphasis. It is likely that a more accurate representation would place it very close to the axis.

FIGURE 6

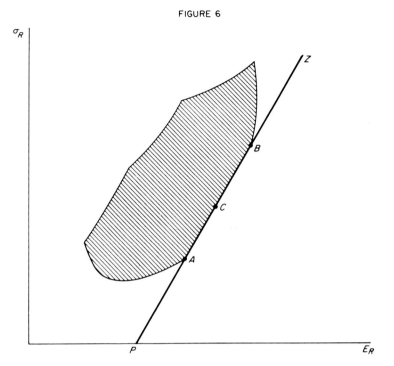

combination of risky assets; alternatively, the point can be reached by a combination of lending and investing in combination C of risky assets.

It is important to recognize that in the situation shown in Figure 6 many alternative combinations of risky assets are efficient (i.e., lie along line PZ), and thus the theory does not imply that all investors will hold the same combination.[19] On the other hand, all such combinations must be perfectly (positively) correlated, since they lie along a linear border of the E_R, σ_R region.[20] This provides a key to the relationship between the prices of capital assets and different types of risk.

[19] This statement contradicts Tobin's conclusion that there will be a unique optimal combination of risky assets. Tobin's proof of a unique optimum can be shown to be incorrect for the case of perfect correlation of efficient risky investment plans if the line connecting their E_R, σ_R points would pass through point P. In the graph on page 83 of this article (*op. cit.*) the constant-risk locus would, in this case, degenerate from a family of ellipses into one of straight lines parallel to the constant-return loci, thus giving multiple optima.

[20] E_R, σ_R values given by combinations of any two combinations must lie within the region and cannot plot above a straight line joining the points. In this case they cannot plot below such a straight line. But since only in the case of perfect correlation will they plot along a straight line, the two combinations must be perfectly correlated. As shown in Part IV, this does not necessarily imply that the individual securities they contain are perfectly correlated.

IV. THE PRICES OF CAPITAL ASSETS

We have argued that in equilibrium there will be a simple linear relationship between the expected return and standard deviation of return for efficient combinations of risky assets. Thus far nothing has been said about such a relationship for individual assets. Typically the E_R, σ_R values associated with single assets will lie above the capital market line, reflecting the inefficiency of undiversified holdings. Moreover, such points may be scattered throughout the feasible region, with no consistent relationship between their expected return and total risk (σ_R). However, there will be a consistent relationship between their expected returns and what might best be called *systematic risk*, as we will now show.

FIGURE 7

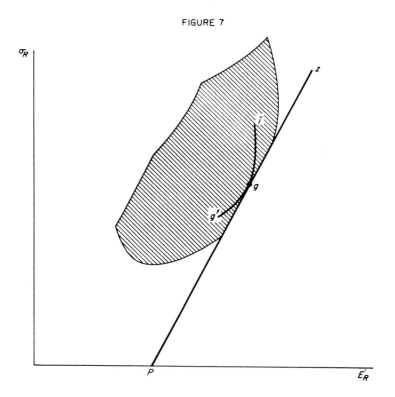

Figure 7 illustrates the typical relationship between a single capital asset (point i) and an efficient combination of assets (point g) of which it is a part. The curve igg' indicates all E_R, σ_R values which can be obtained with feasible combinations of asset i and combination g. As before, we denote such a combination in terms of a proportion α of asset i and

$(1 - \alpha)$ of combination g. A value of $\alpha = 1$ would indicate pure investment in asset i while $\alpha = 0$ would imply investment in combination g.
Note, however, that $\alpha = .5$ implies a total investment of more than half
the funds in asset i, since half would be invested in i itself and the other
half used to purchase combination g, which also includes some of asset i.
This means that a combination in which asset i does not appear at all
must be represented by some negative value of α. Point g' indicates such
a combination.

In Figure 7 the curve igg' has been drawn tangent to the capital
market line (PZ) at point g. This is no accident. All such curves must be
tangent to the capital market line in equilibrium, since (1) they must
touch it at the point representing the efficient combination and (2) they
are continuous at that point.[21] Under these conditions a lack of tangency
would imply that the curve intersects PZ. But then some feasible combination of assets would lie to the right of the capital market line, an obvious
impossibility since the capital market line represents the efficient boundary
of feasible values of E_R and σ_R.

The requirement that curves such as igg' be tangent to the capital
market line can be shown to lead to a relatively simple formula which

FIGURE 8

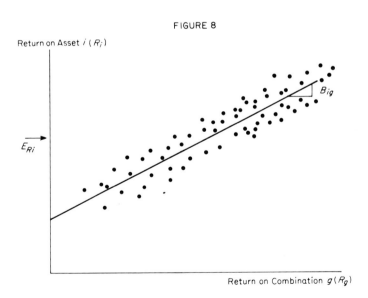

Return on Asset i (R_i)

B_{ig}

E_{Ri}

Return on Combination g (R_g)

[21] Only if $r_{ig} = -1$ will the curve be discontinuous over the range in question.

relates the expected rate of return to various elements of risk for all assets which are included in combination g.[22] Its economic meaning can best be seen if the relationship between the return of asset i and that of combination g is viewed in a manner similar to that used in regression analysis.[23] Imagine that we were given a number of (*ex post*) observations of the return of the two investments. The points might plot as shown in Figure 8. The scatter of the R_i observations around their mean (which will approximate E_{Ri}) is, of course, evidence of the total risk of the asset—σ_{Ri}. But part of the scatter is due to an underlying relationship with the return on combination g, shown by B_{ig}, the slope of the regression line. The response of R_i to changes in R_g (and variations in R_g itself) account for much of the variation in R_i. It is this component of the asset's total risk which we term the *systematic* risk. The remainder,[24] being uncorrelated

[22] The standard deviation of a combination of g and i will be:

$$\sigma = \sqrt{\alpha^2\sigma_{Ri}^2 + (1-\alpha)^2\sigma_{Rg}^2 + 2r_{ig}\alpha(1-\alpha)\sigma_{Ri}\sigma_{Rg}}$$

At $\alpha = 0$:

$$\frac{d\sigma}{d\alpha} = -\frac{1}{\sigma}\left[\sigma_{Rg}^2 - r_{ig}\sigma_{Ri}\sigma_{Rg}\right]$$

but $\sigma = \sigma_{Rg}$ at $\alpha = 0$. Thus:

$$\frac{d\sigma}{d\alpha} = -\left[\sigma_{Rg} - r_{ig}\sigma_{Ri}\right]$$

The expected return of a combination will be:

$$E = \alpha E_{Ri} + (1-\alpha)E_{Rg}$$

Thus, at all values of α:

$$\frac{dE}{d\alpha} = -\left[E_{Rg} - E_{Ri}\right]$$

and, at $\alpha = 0$:

$$\frac{d\sigma}{dE} = \frac{\sigma_{Rg} - r_{ig}\sigma_{Ri}}{E_{Rg} - E_{Ri}}$$

Let the equation of the capital market line be:

$$\sigma_R = s(E_R - P)$$

where P is the pure interest rate. Since igg' is tangent to the line when $\alpha = 0$, and since (E_{Rg}, σ_{Rg}) lies on the line:

$$\frac{\sigma_{Rg} - r_{ig}\sigma_{Ri}}{E_{Rg} - E_{Ri}} = \frac{\sigma_{Rg}}{E_{Rg} - P}$$

or

$$\frac{r_{ig}\sigma_{Ri}}{\sigma_{Rg}} = -\left[\frac{P}{E_{Rg} - P}\right] + \left[\frac{1}{E_{Rg} - P}\right]E_{Ri}$$

[23] This model has been called the diagonal model since its portfolio analysis solution can be facilitated by re-arranging the data so that the variance-covariance matrix becomes diagonal. The method is described in the author's article, cited earlier.

[24] *Ex post*, the standard error.

FIGURE 9

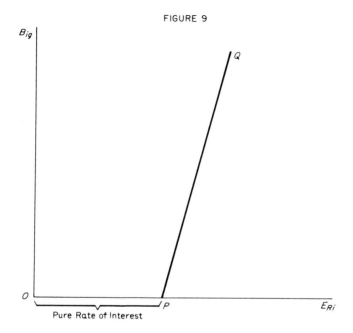

with R_g, is the unsystematic component. This formulation of the relationship between R_i and R_g can be employed *ex ante* as a predictive model. B_{ig} becomes the *predicted* response of R_i to changes in R_g. Then, given σ_{Rg} (the predicted risk of R_g), the systematic portion of the predicted risk of each asset can be determined.

This interpretation allows us to state the relationship derived from the tangency of curves such as *igg'* with the capital market line in the form shown in Figure 9. All assets entering efficient combination *g* must have (predicted) B_{ig} and E_{Ri} values lying on the line PQ.[25] Prices will adjust so that assets which are more responsive to changes in R_g will have higher expected returns than those which are less responsive. This accords with common sense. Obviously the part of an asset's risk which is due to its correlation with the return on a combination cannot be diversified away

[25]
$$r_{ig} = \sqrt{\frac{B_{ig}^2 \sigma_{Rg}^2}{\sigma_{Ri}^2}} = \frac{B_{ig} \sigma_{Rg}}{\sigma_{Ri}}$$

and

$$B_{ig} = \frac{r_{ig} \sigma_{Ri}}{\sigma_{Rg}}$$

The expression on the right is the expression on the left-hand side of the last equation in footnote 22. Thus:

$$B_{ig} = -\left[\frac{P}{E_{Rg} - P}\right] + \left[\frac{1}{E_{Rg} - P}\right] E_{Ri}$$

when the asset is added to the combination. Since B_{ig} indicates the magnitude of this type of risk it should be directly related to expected return.

The relationship illustrated in Figure 9 provides a partial answer to the question posed earlier concerning the relationship between an asset's risk and its expected return. But thus far we have argued only that the relationship holds for the assets which enter some particular efficient combination (g). Had another combination been selected, a different linear relationship would have been derived. Fortunately this limitation is easily overcome. As shown in the footnote,[26] we may arbitrarily select *any* one of the efficient combinations, then measure the predicted responsiveness of *every* asset's rate of return to that of the combination selected; and these coefficients will be related to the expected rates of return of the assets in exactly the manner pictured in Figure 9.

[26] Consider the two assets i and i^*, the former included in efficient combination g and the latter in combination g^*. As shown above:

$$B_{ig} = -\left[\frac{P}{E_{Rg} - P}\right] + \left[\frac{1}{E_{Rg} - P}\right] E_{Ri}$$

and

$$B_{i^*g^*} = -\left[\frac{P}{E_{Rg^*} - P}\right] + \left[\frac{1}{E_{Rg^*} - P}\right] E_{Ri^*}$$

Since R_g and R_{g^*} are perfectly correlated:

$$r_{i^*g^*} = r_{i^*g}$$

Thus

$$\frac{B_{i^*g^*}\sigma_{Rg^*}}{\sigma_{Ri^*}} = \frac{B_{i^*g}\sigma_{Rg}}{\sigma_{Ri^*}}$$

· and

$$B_{i^*g^*} = B_{i^*g}\left[\frac{\sigma_{Rg}}{\sigma_{Rg^*}}\right]$$

Since both g and g^* lie on a line which intercepts the E-axis at P:

$$\frac{\sigma_{Rg}}{\sigma_{Rg^*}} = \frac{E_{Rg} - P}{E_{Rg^*} - P}$$

and

$$B_{i^*g^*} = B_{i^*g}\left[\frac{E_{Rg} - P}{E_{Rg^*} - P}\right]$$

Thus

$$-\left[\frac{P}{E_{Rg^*} - P}\right] + \left[\frac{1}{E_{Rg^*} - P}\right] E_{Ri^*} = B_{i^*g}\left[\frac{E_{Rg} - P}{E_{Rg^*} - P}\right]$$

from which we have the desired relationship between R_{i^*} and g:

$$B_{i^*g} = -\left[\frac{P}{E_{Rg} - P}\right] + \left[\frac{1}{E_{Rg} - P}\right] E_{Ri^*}$$

B_{i^*g} must therefore plot on the same line as does B_{ig}.

The fact that rates of return from all efficient combinations will be perfectly correlated provides the justification for arbitrarily selecting any one of them. Alternatively we may choose instead any variable perfectly correlated with the rate of return of such combinations. The vertical axis in Figure 9 would then indicate alternative levels of a coefficient measuring the sensitivity of the rate of return of a capital asset to changes in the variable chosen.

This possibility suggests both a plausible explanation for the implication that all efficient combinations will be perfectly correlated and a useful interpretation of the relationship between an individual asset's expected return and its risk. Although the theory itself implies only that rates of return from efficient combinations will be perfectly correlated, we might expect that this would be due to their common dependence on the over-all level of economic activity. If so, diversification enables the investor to escape all but the risk resulting from swings in economic activity—this type of risk remains even in efficient combinations. And, since all other types can be avoided by diversification, only the responsiveness of an asset's rate of return to the level of economic activity is relevant in assessing its risk. Prices will adjust until there is a linear relationship between the magnitude of such responsiveness and expected return. Assets which are unaffected by changes in economic activity will return the pure interest rate; those which move with economic activity will promise appropriately higher expected rates of return.

This discussion provides an answer to the second of the two questions posed in this paper. In Part III it was shown that with respect to equilibrium conditions in the capital market as a whole, the theory leads to results consistent with classical doctrine (i.e., the capital market line). We have now shown that with regard to capital assets considered individually, it also yields implications consistent with traditional concepts: it is common practice for investment counselors to accept a lower expected return from defensive securities (those which respond little to changes in the economy) than they require from aggressive securities (which exhibit significant response). As suggested earlier, the familiarity of the implications need not be considered a drawback. The provision of a logical framework for producing some of the major elements of traditional financial theory should be a useful contribution in its own right.

*Eugene F. Fama**

8. Risk, Return and Equilibrium: Some Clarifying Comments

Reprinted from **The Journal of Finance,** Vol. XXIII, No. 1 (March, 1968), pp. 29–40, by permission of the author and the publisher.

Sharpe [12] and Lintner [7] have recently proposed models directed at the following questions: (*a*) What is the appropriate measure of the risk of a capital asset? (*b*) What is the equilibrium relationship between this measure of the asset's risk and its one-period expected return?[1] Lintner contends that the measure of risk derived from his model is different and more general than that proposed by Sharpe. In his reply to Lintner, Sharpe [13] agrees that their results are in some ways conflicting and that Lintner's paper supersedes his.

This paper will show that in fact there is no conflict between the Sharpe-Lintner models. Properly interpreted they lead to the same measure of the risk of an individual asset and to the same relationship between an asset's risk and its one-period expected return. The apparent conflicts discussed by Sharpe and Lintner are caused by Sharpe's concentration on a special stochastic process for describing returns that is not necessarily implied by his asset pricing model. When applied to the more general stochastic processes that Lintner treats, Sharpe's model leads directly to Lintner's conclusions.

I. EQUILIBRIUM IN THE SHARPE MODEL

The Sharpe capital asset pricing model is based on the following assumptions:

(*a*) The market for capital assets is composed of risk averting investors, all of whom are one-period expected-utility-of-terminal-wealth

* Professor of Finance, Graduate School of Business, University of Chicago. In preparing this paper I have benefited from discussions with members of the Workshop in Finance of the Graduate School of Business. The comments of M. Blume, P. Brown, M. Jensen, M. Miller, H. Roberts, R. Roll, M. Scholes and A. Zellner were especially helpful. The research was supported by a grant from the Ford Foundation.

[1] The terms "capital asset" and "one-period return" will be defined below.

maximizers (in the Von Neumann-Morgenstern [16] sense) and find it possible to make optimal portfolio decisions solely on the basis of the means and standard deviations of the probability distributions of terminal wealth associated with the various available portfolios.[2] If the one-period return on an asset or portfolio is defined as the change in wealth during the horizon period divided by the initial wealth invested in the asset or portfolio, then the assumption implies that investors can make optimal portfolio decisions on the basis of means and standard deviations of distributions of one-period portfolio returns.[3]

(b) All investors have the same decision horizon, and over this common horizon period the means and variances of the distributions of one-period returns on assets and portfolios exist.

(c) Capital markets are perfect in the sense that all assets are infinitely divisible, there are no transactions costs or taxes, information is costless and available to everybody, and borrowing and lending rates are equal to each other and the same for all investors.

(d) Expectations and portfolio opportunities are "homogenous" throughout the market. That is, all investors have the same set of portfolio opportunities, and view the expected returns and standard deviations of return[4] provided by the various portfolios in the same way.

Assumption (a) places the analysis within the framework of the Markowitz [10] one-period mean-standard deviation portfolio model. Tobin [15] shows that the mean-standard deviation framework is appropriate either when probability distributions of portfolio returns are normal or Gaussian[5] or when investor utility of return functions are well-approxi-

[2] In the one-period expected utility of terminal wealth model, the objects of choice for the investor are the probability distributions of terminal wealth provided by each asset and portfolio. Each "portfolio" represents a complete investment strategy covering all assets (e.g., bonds, stocks, insurance, real estate, etc.) that could possibly affect the investor's terminal wealth. That is, at the beginning of the horizon period the investor makes a single portfolio decision concerning the allocation of his investable wealth among the available terminal wealth producing assets. All terminal wealth producing assets are called capital assets.

[3] The one-period return defined in this way is just a linear transformation of the units in which terminal wealth is measured; an investor's utility function can be defined in terms of one-period return just as well as in terms of terminal wealth. Note that the one-period return involves no compounding; it is just the ratio of the change in terminal wealth to initial wealth, even though the horizon period may be very long.

Though the remainder of the analysis will be in terms of the one-period return, we should keep in mind that the objects being priced in the market are the probability distributions of terminal wealth associated with each of the available capital assets.

[4] Henceforth the terms "return" and "one-period return" will be used synonomously.

[5] Tobin claims (and properly so) that the mean-standard deviation framework is appropriate whenever distributions of returns on all assets and portfolios are of the same type and can be fully described by two parameters. If the distribution of the return on a portfolio is always of the same type as the distributions of the returns on the individual assets in the portfolio, then that distribution must be a member of the stable (or stable Paretian) class. But the only stable distribution whose variance exists is the normal.

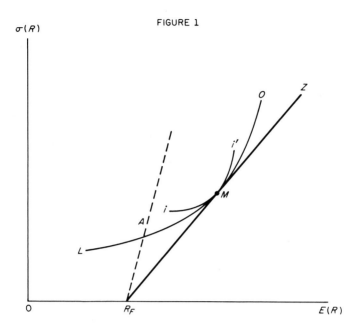

FIGURE 1

mated by quadratics. In either case the optimal portfolio for a risk averter will be a member of the mean-standard deviation efficient set, where an efficient portfolio must satisfy the following criteria: (1) If any other portfolio provides lower standard deviation of one-period return, it must also have lower expected return; and (2) if any other portfolio has greater expected return, it must also have greater standard deviation of return.[6]

Assumptions (b), (c) and (d) of the Sharpe model standardize the picture of the portfolio opportunity set available to each investor. Assumption (b) implies that the portfolio decisions of all investors are made at

[6] The mean-standard deviation model presupposes, of course, the existence of means and variances for all distributions of one-period returns. The work of Mandelbrot [9], Fama [2], and Roll [11] suggests, however, that this assumption may be inappropriate, at least with respect to the standard deviation. Distributions of returns on common stocks and bonds apparently conform better to members of the stable or stable Paretian family for which the variance does not exist than to the normal distribution (the only member of the family for which the variance does exist). This does not mean that mean-standard deviation portfolio models are useless. Fama [3] has shown that insights into the effects of diversification on dispersion of return that are derived from the mean-standard deviation model remain valid when the model is generalized to include the entire stable family. In a later paper [4] it is shown that much of the Sharpe-Lintner mean-standard deviation capital asset pricing model can also be generalized to include the non-normal members of the stable family. Thus it is not inappropriate to reconsider the Sharpe-Lintner models, since resolution of the apparent conflicts between them has implications for the more general model of [4].

the same point in time, and the horizon considered in making these decisions is the same for all. Assumptions (c) and (d) standardize both the set of available portfolios and investors' evaluations of the combinations of expected return and standard deviation provided by each member of the set.[7]

The situation facing each investor can be represented as in Figure 1. The horizontal axis of the figure measures expected return $E(R)$ over the common horizon period, while the vertical axis measures standard deviation of return, $\sigma(R)$. If attention is restricted to portfolios involving only risky assets, Sharpe [12] shows that the set of mean-standard deviation efficient portfolios will fall along a curve convex to the origin, like LMO in Figure 1.[8]

The model assumes, however, that in addition to the opportunities presented by portfolios of risky assets, there is a riskless asset F which will provide the sure return R_F over the common horizon period; it is assumed that the investor can both borrow and lend at the riskless rate R_F. Consider portfolios C involving combinations of the riskless asset F and an arbitrary portfolio A of risky assets. The expected return and standard deviation of return provided by such combinations are

$$E(R_C) = xR_F + (1 - x)E(R_A) \qquad x \leq 1 \tag{1}$$

$$\sigma(R_C) = (1 - x)\sigma(R_A) \tag{2}$$

where x is the proportion of available funds invested in the riskless asset F, so that $(1 - x)$ is invested in A. Applying the chain rule,

$$\frac{d\sigma(R_C)}{dE(R_C)} = \frac{d\sigma(R_C)}{dx} \cdot \frac{dx}{dE(R_C)} = \frac{\sigma(R_A)}{E(R_A) - R_F} \tag{3}$$

This implies that the combinations of expected return and standard devia-

---

[7] Lintner [7, pp. 600–01] considers an extension of the asset pricing model to the case where investors disagree on the expected returns and standard deviations provided by portfolios. The results are essentially the same as those derived under the assumption of "homogenous expectations." Since Lintner's criticism of Sharpe does not depend on this part of his work, our discussion will use the simpler "homogeneous expectations" version of the model. Most of Lintner's discussion is also within this framework, and in all other respects his assumptions are identical to those of Sharpe.

It is important to emphasize that the Sharpe-Lintner asset pricing models, like the Markowitz-Tobin portfolio models, present one-period analyses. For a more complete discussion of the one-period framework see [4].

[8] Strictly speaking this result presupposes that there are at least two portfolios in the efficient set. That is, there is no portfolio which has both higher expected return and lower standard deviation of return than *any* other portfolio. In a market of risk averters with "homogeneous expectations" this is not a strong presumption.

tion provided by portfolios involving F and A must fall along a straight line through R_F and A in Figure 1.

It is now easy to determine the effects of borrowing-lending opportunities on the set of efficient portfolios. In Figure 1 consider the line R_FMZ, touching LMO at M. This line represents the combinations of expected return and standard deviation associated with portfolios where the proportion x $(x \leq 1)$ is invested in the riskless asset F and $1 - x$ in the portfolio of risky assets M. At the point R_F, $x = 1$, while at the point M, $x = 0$. Points below M along R_FMZ correspond to lending portfolios $(x > 0)$, while points above M correspond to borrowing portfolios $(x < 0)$. At given levels of $\sigma(R)$ there are portfolios along R_FMZ which provide higher levels of $E(R)$ than the corresponding portfolios along LMO. Thus (except for M) the portfolios along LMO are dominated by portfolios along R_FMZ, which is now the efficient set.

The conditions necessary for equilibrium in the asset market can now be stated. Since all investors have the same horizon and view their portfolio opportunities in the same way, the Sharpe model implies that everybody faces the same picture of the set of efficient portfolios. If the relevant picture is Figure 1, then all efficient portfolios for all investors will lie along R_FMZ. More risky efficient portfolios involve borrowing $(x < 0)$ and investing all available funds (including borrowings) in the risky combination M. Less risky efficient portfolios involve lending $(x > 0)$ some funds at the rate R_F and investing remaining funds in M. The particular portfolio that an investor chooses will depend on his attitudes toward risk and return, but optimum portfolios for all investors will involve some combination of the riskless asset F and the portfolio of risky assets M.[9] There will be no incentive for anyone to hold risky assets not included in M. If M does not contain all the risky assets in the market, or if it does not contain them in exactly the proportions in which they are outstanding, then there will be some assets that no one will hold. This is inconsistent with equilibrium, since in equilibrium all assets must be held.

Thus, if Figure 1 is to represent equilibrium, M must be the market portfolio; that is, M consists of all risky assets in the market, each weighted by the ratio of its total market value to the total market value of all

---

[9] As noted earlier, Tobin [15] shows that the mean-standard deviation portfolio model is appropriate either when probability distributions of returns on portfolios are normal or when investor utility of return functions are well approximated by quadratics. In either case the indifference curves (i.e., loci of constant expected utility) of a risk averter will be positively sloping and concave to the origin in the $E(R)$, $\sigma(R)$ plane of Figure 1, with expected utility increasing as we move on to indifference curves further to the right in the plane. Since the efficient set of portfolios is linear, equilibrium for the investor (i.e., the point of maximum attainable expected utility) will occur at a point of tangency between an indifference curve and the efficient set or at the point R_F. The degree of the investor's risk aversion will determine whether this will be a point above or below M along R_FMZ in Figure 1.

assets.[10] In addition, the riskless rate R_F must be such that net borrowing in the market is 0; that is, at the rate R_F the total quantity of funds that people want to borrow is equal to the quantity that others want to lend.

As a description of reality, this view of equilibrium has an obvious shortcoming. In particular, all investors hold only combinations of the riskless asset F and M. The market portfolio M is the only efficient portfolio of all risky assets.[11] This result follows from the assumed existence of the opportunity to borrow or lend indefinitely at the riskless rate R_F. Fortunately, in [4] it is shown that the measure of the risk of an individual asset and the equilibrium relationship between risk and expected return derived from the capital asset pricing model will be essentially the same whether or not it is assumed that such riskless borrowing-lending opportunities exist.

----

[10] Figure 1 itself does not tell us that the market portfolio M is the only combination of risky assets with expected return and standard deviation $E(R_M)$ and $\sigma(R_M)$. Suppose there is another portfolio G such that $E(R_G) = E(R_M)$ and $\sigma(R_G) = \sigma(R_M)$. Consider portfolios C where the proportion x $(0 < x < 1)$ is invested in G and $(1 - x)$ in M. Then

$$E(R_C) = xE(R_G) + (1 - x)E(R_M) = E(R_M)$$

$$\sigma(R_C) = [x^2\sigma^2(R_G) + (1 - x)^2\sigma^2(R_M) + 2x(1 - x)\ \text{corr}(R_G, R_M)\sigma(R_G)\sigma(R_M)]^{1/2}$$

It follows that $\sigma(R_C) < \sigma(R_M)$ unless $\text{corr}(R_G, R_M) = 1$, that is, unless the returns on portfolios G and M are perfectly correlated. The condition $\sigma(R_C) < \sigma(R_M)$ is inconsistent with equilibrium, since in equilibrium M must be a member of the efficient set. Thus, if there is a portfolio with the same expected return and standard deviation as the market portfolio M, its returns must be *perfectly* correlated with those of M, an unlikely situation. In any case, such a portfolio would be a perfect substitute for M.

[11] Sharpe [12] himself proposes a slightly different version of equilibrium, one which does not imply that the market portfolio M is the *only* efficient portfolio of risky assets. He argues that in equilibrium an entire segment of the right boundary of the set of feasible risky portfolios may be tangent to a straight line through R_F. He further shows that the returns on all portfolios along such a segment must be perfectly correlated. Since *ex post* returns on portfolios of different risky assets are never perfectly correlated, it is unlikely that investors will expect them to be perfectly correlated *ex ante*, and so multiple tangencies would seem to represent an uninteresting case.

Note, though, that if a segment of the right boundary of the set of feasible risky portfolios is tangent to a line through R_F, to be consistent with equilibrium the market portfolio M must be one of the tangency points along the segment. This is an implication of the fact that when the portfolios of individuals are aggregated, the aggregate is just the market portfolio with zero net borrowing. Thus, it must be possible to obtain the market portfolio by taking weighted combinations of portfolios along the tangency segment.

In sum, given the assumptions of the Sharpe model, equilibrium can be associated (a) with a situation where the market portfolio is the only efficient combination of risky assets or (b) with a situation where there are many efficient combinations of risky assets, one of which is the market portfolio. Fortunately, Sharpe shows that in using the portfolio model to develop the relationship between risk and expected return on individual assets, it does not matter which of these representations of equilibrium is adopted. Because it simplifies the exposition of the model and also seems to be more realistic, we shall concentrate on the case where the market portfolio is the only efficient combination of risky assets. This is also the case dealt with by Lintner [7].

II. THE MEASUREMENT OF RISK AND THE
RELATIONSHIP BETWEEN RISK AND RETURN

We consider now the major problems of the Sharpe capital asset pricing model; that is, (a) determination of a measure of risk consistent with the portfolio and expected utility models, and (b) derivation of the equilibrium relationship between risk and expected return. It is important to note that the development of the Sharpe model to this point is completely consistent with Lintner [7]. In particular, the two models are based on the same set of assumptions, and the resulting views of equilibrium are the same. Thus it seems unlikely that the implications of the two models for the measurement of risk and the relationship between risk and return can be different. In fact it will now be shown that Sharpe's approach leads to exactly the same conclusions as Lintner's. The "conflicts" which they find in their respective results will be shown to arise from the fact that both misinterpret the implications of the Sharpe model.

For any risky asset i there will be a curve, like iMi' in Figure 1, which shows the combinations of $E(R)$ and $\sigma(R)$ that can be attained by forming portfolios of asset i and the market portfolio M. If x is the proportion of available funds invested in asset i, the returns on such portfolios (C) can be expressed as[12]

$$R_C = xR_i + (1 - x)R_M \qquad (x \leq 1) \qquad (4)$$

Now consider portfolios (D) where the proportion x is invested in the riskless asset F and $(1 - x)$ in the market portfolio M. The returns on such portfolios will be given by

$$R_D = xR_F + (1 - x)R_M \qquad (5)$$

As noted earlier, the combinations of expected return and standard deviation of return provided by such portfolios fall along the efficient set line R_FMZ in Figure 1. It is easy to show that the functions underlying iMi' and LMO are both differentiable at the point M. Since R_FMZ is the efficient set, iMi' and LMO must be tangent at M. That is,

$$\frac{d\sigma(R_C)}{dE(R_C)} = \frac{d\sigma(R_D)}{dE(R_D)} \qquad (6)$$

when $x = 0$.

---

[12] When $0 \leq x \leq 1$ portfolios along iMi' between i and M are obtained. At $x = 0$, the market portfolio M is obtained. Since M contains asset i, even when $x = 0$ the portfolio C will contain some of i. When $x < 0$, so that there is a short position in asset i, portfolios along the segment Mi' are obtained.

Though the discussion in the text is phrased in terms of individual assets, the analysis applies directly to the case where i is a portfolio.

The economic interpretation of (6) is familiar. $d\sigma(R_D)/dE(R_D)$ is the marginal rate of exchange of standard deviation for expected return along the efficient set $R_F M Z$. Since all investors have the same view of the efficient set, $d\sigma(R_D)/dE(R_D)$ is in fact the market rate of exchange. On the other hand, $d\sigma(R_C)/dE(R_C)$ is the marginal rate of exchange of standard deviation for expected return in the market portfolio as the proportion of asset i in the market portfolio is changed. In equilibrium excess demand for asset i must be 0. But this will only be the case if when $x = 0$ in (4), the expected return on asset i is such that the marginal rate of exchange $d\sigma(R_C)/dE(R_C)$ is equal to the market rate of exchange $d\sigma(R_D)/dE(R_D)$.

Sharpe's insight was in noting that the equilibrium condition (6) implies both a measure of the risk of asset i and the equilibrium relationship between the risk and the expected return on the asset. Using the chain rule to derive expressions for $d\sigma(R_C)/dE(R_C)$ and $d\sigma(R_D)/dE(R_D)$,[13] and then evaluating these derivatives at $x = 0$, (6) becomes

$$\frac{\text{cov }(R_i, R_M) - \sigma^2(R_M)}{[E(R_i) - E(R_M)]\sigma(R_M)} = \frac{\sigma(R_M)}{E(R_M) - R_F} \tag{7}$$

To get an expression for the expected return on asset i, it suffices to solve (7) for $E(R_i)$, leading to

$$E(R_i) = R_F + \frac{[E(R_M) - R_F]}{\sigma^2(R_M)}\text{ cov }(R_i, R_M) \qquad i = 1, 2, \ldots, N \tag{8}$$

where N is the total number of assets in the market. Alternatively, the "risk premium" in the expected return on asset i is

$$E(R_i) - R_F = \left[\frac{E(R_M) - R_F}{\sigma^2(R_M)}\right]\text{ cov }(R_i, R_M)$$

$$= \lambda \text{ cov }(R_i, R_M) \qquad i = 1, 2, \ldots, N \tag{9}$$

Now (9) applies to each of the N assets in the market, and the value of λ, the ratio of the risk premium in the expected return on the market portfolio to the variance of this return, will be the same for all assets. Thus the differences between the risk premiums on different assets depend entirely on the covariance term in (9). The coefficient λ can be thought of as the market price per unit of risk so that the appropriate measure of the risk of asset i is cov (R_i, R_M). Thus this term certainly

[13] That is,

$$\frac{d\sigma(R_C)}{dE(R_C)} = \frac{d\sigma(R_C)}{dx} \cdot \frac{dx}{dE(R_C)} \quad \text{and} \quad \frac{d\sigma(R_D)}{dE(R_D)} = \frac{d\sigma(R_D)}{dx} \cdot \frac{dx}{dE(R_D)}$$

deserves closer study. In the process we shall find that (9), which is just a rearrangement of the last expression in Sharpe's [12] footnote 22, is exactly Lintner's [7] expression for the risk premium.

Note that by definition R_M, the return on the market portfolio, is just the weighted average of the returns on all the individual assets in the market. That is,

$$R_M = \sum_{j=1}^{N} X_j R_j \qquad (10)$$

where X_j is the proportion of the total market value of all assets that is accounted for by asset j. It follows that

$$\text{cov}(R_i, R_M) = E\{[R_M - E(R_M)][R_i - E(R_i)]\}$$

$$= E\{\sum_{j=1}^{N} X_j[R_j - E(R_j)][R_i - E(R_i)]\}$$

$$= \sum_{j=1}^{N} X_j \text{ cov}(R_j, R_i) \qquad (11)$$

Substituting (11) into (9) yields

$$E(R_i) - R_F = \lambda \sum_{j=1}^{N} X_j \text{ cov}(R_j, R_i) \qquad i = 1, 2, \ldots, N \qquad (12)$$

which is exactly Lintner's [7, p. 596] Equation (11) but derived from Sharpe's model.[14]

Within the context of the Sharpe model (12) is quite reasonable. From (10)

$$\sigma^2(R_M) = \sum_{k=1}^{N} \sum_{j=1}^{N} X_k X_j \text{ cov}(R_j, R_k) = \sum_{k=1}^{N} X_k \sum_{j=1}^{N} X_j \text{ cov}(R_j, R_k) \qquad (13)$$

Now the term for $k = i$ in (13) is just

$$X_i \sum_{j=1}^{N} X_j \text{ cov}(R_j, R_i) = X_i \text{ cov}(R_i, R_M)$$

[14] Lintner [7, 8] makes much of the fact that

$$\text{cov}(R_i, R_M) = \sum_{j \neq i} X_j \text{ cov}(R_j, R_i) + X_i \sigma^2(R_i) \qquad (14)$$

contains a term for the variance of asset i. He stresses the importance of the variance term in empirical studies concerned with measuring the riskiness of an individual asset. Recall, however, that X_i is the total market value of all outstanding units of asset i divided by the total market value of *all* assets. Thus the variance term in (14) is likely to be trivial relative to the weighted sum of covariances—a familiar result in portfolio models.

Thus X_i cov (R_i, R_M) measures the contribution of asset i to the variance of the return on the market portfolio. Since this contribution is proportional to cov (R_i, R_M) and since the market portfolio is the only stochastic component in all efficient portfolios, it is not unreasonable that the risk premium on asset i is proportional to cov (R_i, R_M).

Note that (9) and (12) allow us to rank the risk premiums in the expected returns on different assets, but they provide no information about the magnitudes of the premiums. These depend on the difference $E(R_M) - R_F$, which in turn depends on the attitudes of all the different investors in the market toward risk and return. Without knowing more about attitudes toward risk, all we can say is that $E(R_M) - R_F$ must be such that in equilibrium all risky assets are held and the borrowing-lending market is cleared.

Thus, properly interpreted, the models of Sharpe and Lintner lead to identical conclusions concerning the appropriate measure of the risk of an individual asset and the equilibrium relationship between the risk of the asset and its expected return. What, then, is the source of the "conflict" between the two models which both authors apparently feel exists? Unfortunately Sharpe puts the major results of his paper in his footnote 22 [12, p. 438]; in the text he concentrates on applying these results to the market or "diagonal" model of the behavior of asset returns which he proposed in an earlier paper [14]. But the market model that he uses contains inconsistent constraints which lead to misinterpretation of the capital asset pricing model. Lintner, in his turn, does not appreciate the generality of Sharpe's results, and accepts (and in some ways misinterprets) Sharpe's treatment of the market model.

III. THE RELATIONSHIP BETWEEN RISK AND RETURN IN THE MARKET MODEL

In the "market model" which Sharpe [12, pp. 438–42] uses to illustrate his asset pricing model, it is assumed that there is a linear relationship between the one-period return on an individual asset and the return on the market portfolio M. That is,

$$R_i = \alpha_i + \beta_i R_M + \epsilon_i \qquad i = 1, 2, \ldots, N \qquad (15)$$

where α_i and β_i are parameters specific to asset i. It is further assumed that the random disturbances ϵ_i have the properties,

$$E(\epsilon_i) = 0 \qquad i = 1, 2, \ldots, N \qquad (16a)$$

$$\text{cov}(\epsilon_i, \epsilon_j) = 0 \qquad i, j = 1, 2, \ldots, N \qquad i \neq j \qquad (16b)$$

$$\text{cov}(\epsilon_i, R_M) = 0 \qquad i = 1, 2, \ldots, N \qquad (16c)$$

Thus the assumption is that the only relationships between the returns on individual risky assets arise from the fact that the return on each is related to the return on the market portfolio M via (15).

Applying the market model of (15) and (16) to the equivalent risk premium expressions (9) and (12) will allow us to pinpoint the apparent source of conflict between the results of Sharpe and Lintner. From (15) and (16)

$$\text{cov}\ (R_i,\ R_M) = E\{(\beta_i[R_M - E(R_M)] + \epsilon_i)(R_M - E(R_M))\} \quad (17\text{a})$$

$$= \beta_i \sigma^2(R_M) + \text{cov}\ (\epsilon_i,\ R_M) \quad (17\text{b})$$

$$= \beta_i \sigma^2(R_M) \quad (17\text{c})$$

Substituting (17c) into (9) yields

$$E(R_i) - R_F = \lambda \beta_i \sigma^2(R_M) = [E(R_M) - R_F]\beta_i \quad i = 1, 2, \ldots, N \quad (18)$$

Thus when the stochastic process generating returns is as described by the market model of (15) and (16), the risk premium in the expected return on a given asset is proportional to the slope coefficient β for that asset. The more sensitive the asset is to the return on the market portfolio, the larger its risk premium.

In discussing the implications of his capital asset pricing model Sharpe concentrates on (18). But it is important to remember that the market model assumes a very special stochastic process for asset returns which was not assumed in the derivation of the general expressions (9) and (12) for the risk premium in the capital asset pricing model. The asset pricing model itself, as summarized by expressions (9) and (12), applies to much more general stochastic processes than those assumed in the market model and thus in (18). This point is especially crucial since we shall now see that the market model, as defined by (15) and (16), is inconsistent.

Expression (18) was obtained by applying the market model to (9). Since (12) and (9) are equivalent expressions for the risk premium in the expected return on asset i, it should be possible to apply the market model to (12) and obtain (18):

$$E(R_i) - R_F = \lambda \sum_{j=1}^{N} X_j \, \text{cov}\ (R_j, R_i) \quad (19)$$

$$= \lambda \{\beta_i \sum_{j=1}^{N} X_j \beta_j \sigma^2(R_M) + X_i \sigma^2(\epsilon_i)\} \quad (20)$$

which is exactly Lintner's [7, p. 605] Expression (24). It will presently be shown that the market model implies $\sum X_j \beta_J = 1$. Thus (20) reduces to

$$E(R_i) - R_F = \lambda[\beta_i \sigma^2(R_M) + X_i \sigma^2(\epsilon_i)] \tag{21}$$

or

$$E(R_i) - R_F = [E(R_M) - R_F)]\left[\beta_i + \frac{X_i \sigma^2(\epsilon_i)}{\sigma^2(R_M)}\right] \tag{22}$$

But (22) includes a term involving $\sigma^2(\epsilon_i)$ which does not appear in (18), and this is the major source of controversy between Lintner and Sharpe. In applying the asset pricing model to the market model, Sharpe arrives at (18) while Lintner derives (20) or its equivalent (22). Lintner [7, pp. 607–08] presumes that Sharpe is considering the case where all residual variances [the $\sigma^2(\epsilon_i)$] are 0. But Sharpe clearly did not intend to impose this restriction on his model.[15] In addition, (18) is derived directly from (9), (15), and (16), and there is no presumption in the derivation that the residual variances are 0.

In fact the discrepancy between (18) and (22) arises from an inconsistency in the specification of the market model; neither of these expressions for the risk premium is correct. Note that (10) and (15) together imply

$$R_M = \sum_{j=1}^{N} X_j R_j = \sum_{j=1}^{N} X_j[\alpha_j + \beta_j R_M + \epsilon_j] \tag{23}$$

Thus, since ϵ_i is one of the terms in R_M, (16c) is inconsistent with the remaining assumptions of the market model. Since (16c) is used in deriving both (18) and (22), these are both incorrect expressions for the risk premium in the market model.

Unfortunately, (16c) is not the only inconsistency in the market model of (15), (16) and (23); it is also easy to show that (15), (16b) and (23) cannot hold simultaneously. Recalling that α_j and β_j are constants, (23) implies

$$\sum_{j=1}^{N} X_j \alpha_j = 0 \qquad \sum_{j=1}^{N} X_j \beta_j = 1 \tag{24a}$$

$$\sum_{j=1}^{N} X_j \epsilon_j = 0 \tag{24b}$$

---

[15] Cf., Sharpe [12, pp. 438–39]. "The response of R_i to changes in R_g [our R_M] (and variations in R_g itself) account for much of the variation of R_i. It is this component of the asset's total risk which we term the *systematic* risk. The remainder, being uncorrelated with R_g, is the unsystematic component." Though Sharpe does not explicitly specify the version of the market model he is considering, it seems clear from this quotation and the remainder of his discussion that, for his purposes, (15) and (16) represent the relevant model.

The constraints of (24a) pose no problem; (24b), however, is inconsistent with (16b)—we cannot assume that the disturbances are independent and then constrain their weighted sum to be 0.

One possible specification of the market model which does not lead to the problems discussed above is as follows.

$$R_i = \alpha_i + \beta_i r_M + \epsilon_i \qquad i = 1, 2, \ldots, N \qquad (25a)$$

$$E(\epsilon_i) = 0 \qquad i = 1, 2, \ldots, N \qquad (25b)$$

$$\text{cov}(\epsilon_i, \epsilon_j) = 0 \qquad i, j = 1, 2, \ldots, N \qquad i \neq j \quad (25c)$$

$$\text{cov}(\epsilon_i, r_M) = 0 \qquad i = 1, 2, \ldots, N \qquad (25d)$$

In this model r_M is interpreted as a common underlying market factor which affects the returns on all assets. The relationship between r_M and the return on the market portfolio is then

$$R_M = \sum_{j=1}^{N} X_j R_j = \sum_{j=1}^{N} X_j [\alpha_j + \beta_j r_M + \epsilon_j] \qquad (26)$$

From either (9) or (12) it follows that in this model the risk premium on asset i is

$$E(R_i) - R_F = \lambda \sum_{j=1}^{N} X_j \text{ cov}(R_j, R_i)$$

$$= \lambda \sum_{j=1}^{N} X_j E\{(\beta_j [r_M - E(r_M)] + \epsilon_j)(\beta_i [r_M - E(r_M)] + \epsilon_i)\}$$

$$= \lambda \{\beta_i \sum_{j=1}^{N} X_j \beta_j \sigma^2(r_M) + X_i \sigma^2(\epsilon_i)\} \qquad (27)$$

which is equivalent to Lintner's [7, Equation (23)] expression for the risk premium in this more general version of the market model. But it is again important to note that Lintner's results follow directly from (9) and (12), the *general* expressions for the risk premium developed in Sharpe's model.

Finally, though the issues discussed above are certainly interesting from a theoretical viewpoint, from a practical viewpoint (18), (22) and (27) are nearly equivalent expressions for the risk premium in the market model. The empirical evidence of King [6] and Blume [1] suggests that, on average, $\sigma^2(\epsilon_i)$ and $\sigma^2(R_M)$ in (22) are about equal. Thus the size of the residual term in (22) will be determined primarily by X_i, the proportion of the total value of all assets accounted for by asset i, which will usually be quite small relative to β_i (which is on average 1). The risk premiums given by (18) and (22), then, will be nearly equal.

Next note that it is always possible to scale r_M in (26) so that $\sum X_j \alpha_j = 0$ and $\sum X_j \beta_j = 1$. Then

$$\sigma^2(R_M) = \sigma^2(r_M) + \sum_{j=1}^{N} X_j^2 \sigma^2(\epsilon_j) \tag{28}$$

But again the weighted sum of residual variances will be small relative to $\sigma^2(r_M)$ so that $\sigma^2(R_M) \cong \sigma^2(r_M)$, which implies that the risk premiums given by (22) and (27) are almost equal.

IV. CONCLUSIONS

In sum, then, there are no real conflicts between the capital asset pricing models of Sharpe [12] and Lintner [7, 8]. When they apply their general results to the market model, both make errors which turn out to be unimportant from a practical viewpoint. The important point is that their general models represent equivalent approaches to the problem of capital asset pricing under uncertainty.

REFERENCES

[1] Blume, Marshall E. "The Assessment of Portfolio Performance," unpublished Ph.D. dissertation (Graduate School of Business, U. of Chicago, 1967).

[2] Fama, Eugene F. "The Behavior of Stock-Market Prices," *Journal of Business* (January, 1965), pp. 34–105.

[3] ———. "Portfolio Analysis in a Stable Paretian Market," *Management Science* (January, 1965), pp. 404–19.

[4] ———. "Risk, Return, and Equilibrium in a Stable Paretian Market," unpublished manuscript (October, 1967).

[5] Jensen, Michael. "Risk, the Pricing of Capital Assets, and the Evaluation of Investment Portfolios," unpublished Ph.D. dissertation (Graduate School of Business, U. of Chicago, 1967).

[6] King, Benjamin F. "Market and Industry Factors in Stock Price Behavior," *Journal of Business*, Supplement (January, 1966), pp. 139–90.

[7] Lintner, John. "Security Prices, Risk, and Maximal Gains from Diversification," *Journal of Finance* (December, 1965), pp. 587–615.

[8] ———. "The Valuation of Risk Assets and the Selection of Risky Investments in Stock Portfolios and Capital Budgets," *Review of Economics and Statistics* (February, 1965), pp. 13–37.

[9] Mandelbrot, Benoit. "The Variation of Certain Speculative Prices," *Journal of Business* (October, 1963), pp. 394–419.

[10] Markowitz, Harry. *Portfolio Selection: Efficient Diversification of Investments* (New York, N. Y.: Wiley, 1959).

[11] Roll, Richard. "The Efficient Market Model Applied to U.S. Treasury Bill Rates," unpublished Ph.D. thesis (Graduate School of Business, U. of Chicago, 1968).

[12] Sharpe, William F. "Capital Asset Prices: A Theory of Market Equilibrium under Conditions of Risk," *Journal of Finance* (September, 1964), pp. 425–42.

[13] ——. "Security Prices, Risk, and Maximal Gains from Diversification: Reply," *Journal of Finance* (December, 1966), pp. 743–44.

[14] ——. "A Simplified Model for Portfolio Analysis," *Management Science* (January, 1963), pp. 277–93.

[15] Tobin, James. "Liquidity Preference as Behavior Towards Risk," *Review of Economic Studies* (February, 1958), pp. 65–86.

[16] Von Neumann, John, and Oskar Morgenstern. *Theory of Games and Economic Behavior*, 3d. ed. (Princeton, N. J.: Princeton U. P., 1953).

*Jan Mossin**

9. Security Pricing and Investment Criteria in Competitive Markets

Reprinted from the **American Economic Review,** Vol. LIX, No. 5 (December, 1969), pp. 749–756, by permission of the author and the publisher.

The theory of finance has—or should have—two basic objectives. On the one hand, the theory should be able to explain and interpret phenomena in financial markets. On the other hand, the theory should assist management in making the best decisions with respect to the company's investment and financing decisions by providing useful analytical tools within a realistic theoretical framework.

Everyone would agree that these two aspects of the theory of finance are closely related. The reason is very simple. The most general and universally acceptable formulation of company objectives is maximization of the market value of the company's equity. Through its actions management can *influence* the market value, but is clearly unable to *determine* it completely. The market value is determined by the simultaneous interplay of supply and demand in the capital markets, where other companies also participate as suppliers of securities and where various investors participate in the demand for these securities. No theory of finance can give a satisfactory explanation of security valuation or investment behavior if it fails to take into account the relationships that exist with individual investors' portfolio decisions. This means that all the investment alternatives open to the investor must be taken into account if we want to understand his evaluation of any one of them. Market values are determined by the demand by all investors, and this leads us to establish a theory of general equilibrium in capital markets. For without such a model, management is unable to foresee the effects of alternative investment and financing decisions.

The task of specifying relations constituting such an equilibrium

* Norwegian School of Economics and Business Administration, visiting professor, Graduate School of Business Administration, University of California, Berkeley.

model is not a mean one; so I shall only be able to indicate its structure in broad outline, but I shall also, by means of examples, show how the theory can be utilized to derive meaningful conclusions.

In view of the fundamental theoretical role that the analysis of capital markets should play for the study of the corporate decisions, it is remarkable to what limited extent such an analysis has been brought explicitly into existing financial literature. Even in modern and reputable introductions to the theory of finance, the market plays a highly indirect role. A number of hypotheses are advanced concerning the way in which the market evaluates and reacts (e.g., with respect to discounting for time and uncertainty), but these hypotheses are entirely *ad hoc* and quite arbitrary, since they are not derived from any fundamental assumptions describing market equilibrium.

In the celebrated contribution by Modigliani and Miller [4], the relationship between individual portfolio decisions and market valuation is brought out more clearly, even though no general equilibrium model is explicitly specified. The M-M theory will be discussed in more detail below.

During the past few years there has been a fast-growing interest in models of general equilibrium in markets for uncertain claims, i.e., financial markets. Some of the interest has centered on questions of efficiency (Pareto optimality) of risk allocations under various market arrangements [1]. From the point of view of the theory of finance, however, the main concern is with the description, or characterization, of the equilibrium situation itself (regardless of whether this situation represents an efficient allocation of risk). A pioneering work here is that by William Sharpe [6]. In [5], an attempt was made to sharpen and extend some of his conclusions. The purpose of this paper is to demonstrate, by means of a slightly modified version of this model, some of its implications for the analysis of the firm's optimal investment and financing decisions.

I. A MARKET MODEL

The model we shall consider is very much in the classical tradition. Formally, it is a model of pure exchange, and there are two types of exchange objects: bonds, issued either by firms or by the investors themselves; and company ordinary shares. The analysis takes as given the firms' investment and financing decisions. On the basis of the relationships to be derived between these decisions and market value we can infer the effects of alternative decisions. Thus, the activity carried out by company j is described by a random variable X_j, representing the gross yield of that activity. When the outcome of any such variable becomes known, it is distributed among investors on the basis of the shares and bonds they have acquired through the market exchange. A stylized example may serve to fix ideas.

Each company is a farm which has, at the time of trading, effected its investments (planting of its land) as well as its financing (share sale and borrowing). Thus, the supply of various securities are given data. The trading then determines an allocation of these securities among investors. Crop values are still unknown and represented by random variables X_j. After the harvest is completed, crop values will be used partly for amortizing debt, while the remainder is distributed to shareholders.

The most important assumption we shall make is that the bond market is perfect in the sense that everyone, firms as well as investors, can lend or borrow any amount at a given and certain rate of interest. This is the same as disregarding default risk: all claims will be paid.

With this, the variables entering the model are the following:

For company j:

X_j = gross yield (with $E(X_j) = \mu_j$, $E(X_j - \mu_j)(X_k - \mu_k) = \sigma_{jk}$)
d_j = debt
p_j = market value of shares
$v_j = p_j + d_j$ = market value of company
$R_j = X_j - rd_j$ = return to shares, where r is the certain rate of return on loans[1]

For investor i:

w_i = initial wealth
z_{ij} = fraction owned of company j
$m_i = w_i - \sum_j z_{ij} p_j$ = net bond holdings

$Y_i = rm_i + \sum_j z_{ij} R_j$ = final wealth

The market clearing conditions:

$$\sum_i z_{ij} = 1 \qquad \text{(all } j\text{)} \tag{1}$$

$$\sum_i m_i = \sum_j d_j \tag{2}$$

Apart from the assumption of a perfect bond market, everything written down so far is a definition or accounting identity. Nevertheless, we are

---

[1] That is, we interpret r as one plus the interest rate. This is because, formally, we assume a single period horizon of finite length. This in itself is unimportant, however: the important limitation is that we consider only a single decision—or market—date, rather than a sequence of decision dates. The model and the variables are easily reinterpreted so as to represent an infinite horizon. In that case, r must represent the interest rate (per time unit) itself, while X_j must be taken as an infinite *flow* of yield (or net profit before interest payments), in principle constant through time, but unknown as of the market date.

already in a position to show a very simple result. This is the well-known Proposition I of Modigliani and Miller [4], namely, that total company value is independent of the level of debt. For by substitution of the budget equation and the definition of R_j, we can write final wealth as

$$Y_i = r(w_i - \sum_j z_{ij} p_j) + \sum_j z_{ij}(X_j - rd_j)$$

$$= rw_i + \sum_j z_{ij}(X_j - rv_j) \tag{3}$$

In other words, regardless of the portfolio the investor chooses to buy, the probability distribution for final wealth will be independent of how company values are composed of share values and debt. Then, suppose a change occurred in the d_j's. If $\sum_i z_{ij} = 1$ before the change, i.e., demand for shares equalled the supply of shares, the equality would hold after the change. As a result of this and the fact that $\sum_i w_i = \sum_j v_j$ identically, excess demand for bonds would also remain at zero. In other words, if debt-equity ratios are changed, and company values remain unchanged, all markets will clear; hence the equilibrium values will in fact be independent of debt levels. Given the probability distribution for yields, the amounts of debt will be entirely incidental. This particular formulation is important: if, for some reason, a dependence exists between the funds raised by borrowing and the level of operations carried out by the firm,[2] then a corresponding dependence would be observed between debt level and market value. Yet, as it stands, M-M's Proposition I follows almost as an accounting identity, given of course, the assumption of a perfect loan market. If interest rates differ, either among companies or in relation to private loans, then clearly (3) does not hold.

We have not yet specified investors' demand for shares and bonds. In principle, these are easy to write down. By choosing different sets of values of the z_{ij}, the investor will obtain different probability distributions for final wealth. If he follows certain rules of consistency (the Von Neumann-Morgenstern conditions) in his choice among such probability distributions, then there exists a utility function $U_i(Y_i)$ such that the preferred values of the z_{ij} are those that maximize expected utility, $E[U_i(Y_i)]$. His demand is thus described by the relations

$$\frac{\partial E[U_i(Y_i)]}{\partial z_{ij}} = E[U_i'(Y_i)(X_j - rv_j)]$$

$$= 0 \quad \text{(all } j) \tag{4}$$

[2] As, for example, in Diamond's model [2], to be discussed later.

Formally, the model is now complete. Under normal conditions we may assume that our equations determine the market solution, i.e., the market value of each company and the corresponding equilibrium portfolios.

To see the potentiality of the model for generating meaningful hypotheses, I shall proceed to specify the preference structures of investors by assuming, as an illustration, that these can be represented by quadratic utility functions:[3]

$$U_i(Y_i) = Y_i - c_i Y_i^2$$

This will make it possible to derive an explicit expression for market values, and it is obvious that they will depend only on expected yields and covariances between yields.

II. A MARKET VALUATION FORMULA

The derivation of such a formula is straightforward, although somewhat tedious. By substituting for marginal utility, taking expectations, and rearranging, we shall be able to write the demand relations on the form

$$\sum_k z_{ik}[\sigma_{jk} + (\mu_j - rv_j)(\mu_k - rv_k)] = (\mu_j - rv_j)\left(\frac{1}{2c_i} - rw_i\right) \qquad \text{(all } i, j)$$

which give, for each investor, a system of linear equations with constant coefficients. Taking now the jth equation for each investor and summing (over i), we obtain

$$\sum_k [\sigma_{jk} + (\mu_j - rv_j)(\mu_k - rv_k)] = (\mu_j - rv_j)\left(\sum_i \frac{1}{2c_i} - r\sum_k v_k\right) \qquad (5)$$

On the left-hand side, the z_{ik} have dropped out because of (1). With respect to the right-hand side we have, by summing the budget equations over i:

$$\sum_i w_i = \sum_i m_i + \sum_i \sum_k z_{ik} p_k$$

$$= \sum_k d_k + \sum_k p_k$$

$$= \sum_k v_k$$

[3] I shall refrain from another review of the various shortcomings of, and objections to, quadratic utility functions; any student of the literature on risk taking will be thoroughly familiar (if not fed up) with the topic. The justification here is clearly that of providing a particularly simple and illuminating application of the general theory. It should be added, though, that quadratic utility functions do allow an unconstrained Pareto optimal risk allocation to be achieved by means of markets for bonds and ordinary shares only (see [1]).

The term $r(\mu_j - rv_j) \sum_k v_k$ then drops out on both sides in (5), and we are left with

$$(\mu_j - rv_j) \left(\sum_i \frac{1}{2c_i} - \sum_k \mu_k \right) = \sum_k \sigma_{jk}$$

which, when solved for v_j, gives

$$v_j = \frac{1}{r} \left[\mu_j - \frac{\sum_k \sigma_{jk}}{\sum_i \frac{1}{2c_i} - \sum_k \mu_k} \right] \qquad (6)$$

Here we have a surprisingly simple formula for the company's market value, expressed solely in terms of given market parameters. The interpretation of the formula is also very simple. The second term is, as we shall see, a correction term for risk; so that the market value is computed simply by taking expected yield, allowing a certain deduction for risk, and then discounting the difference at the sure rate of interest.[4] Of course, formulae of this nature have often been suggested in earlier literature, but here we have *derived* the formula from the description of market equilibrium. It is to be emphasized, however, that the formula makes no claim on generality, depending as it does on the particular preference structure we have assumed.

The correction term for risk is seen to consist of two factors. The first one is the magnitude

$$b_j = \sum_k \sigma_{jk}$$

i.e., the sum of the covariances of yield with the yields of all other companies. Thus, in the case of quadratic utilities, this is the relevant risk measure associated with company j's activities. It can be interpreted as the contribution of company j to the market's total variance, since we obviously have

$$\sum_j b_j = \sum_j \sum_k \sigma_{jk} = \mathrm{var} \left(\sum_j X_j \right)$$

It is not very surprising to learn that a company's risk cannot be measured by its own variance (σ_{jj}) alone, but also depends on its correlation with other firms. In traditional approaches to financial analysis, this dependence is often missed, however. Loosely speaking, a rainwear

---

[4] Note that if we consider the model's time span as infinite, with r being the rate of interest (footnote 1), then $1/r$ becomes the appropriate discount factor.

manufacturer is worth relatively more if everybody else produces ice cream and suntan lotion. We even observe that if the yield of a company is sufficiently negatively correlated with other companies' yields, then b_j may well become negative, i.e., its risk premium is negative. Since holdings in such a company strongly reduce the variances of yield on investors' portfolios, demand will be so large as to raise the market value of the company · above its expected present value.

The second factor, which serves as a weighting factor for the company risk factor b_j, is

$$R = \frac{1}{\sum\limits_i \dfrac{1}{2c_i} - \sum\limits_k \mu_k}$$

This factor is seen to be the same for all companies and can be given an interpretation as market risk aversion. I shall skip the details, but it can readily be shown that R is the harmonic mean of investors' expected risk aversion, where by risk aversion we mean the Pratt-Arrow risk aversion measure

$$R_i = - \frac{U_i''}{U_i'}$$

Then

$$R = \frac{1}{\sum\limits_i E\left(\dfrac{1}{R_i}\right)}$$

It is of some interest to observe that the introduction of additional investors, even if each possesses a very small amount of wealth, may influence company values considerably. The explanation of this non-intuitive result is quite simple, however; even though an investor may have an insignificant amount of wealth, he may be able to borrow extensively and in this way affect security demand on roughly the same scale as a wealthy investor.

III. IMPLICATIONS FOR INVESTMENT DECISIONS

We are now in a position to examine some of the implications of our model for the firm's optimal investment policy. It is useful to begin by considering the M-M investment theory, and to do so we must make clear the nature of their risk class assumption, described as follows:

> We shall assume that firms can be divided into "equivalent return" classes such that the return on the shares issued by any firm in any given class is proportional to (and hence perfectly correlated with) the return on the shares issued by any other firm in the same class. This assumption implies that the various shares within the same class differ, at most, by a "scale factor." [4, p. 266]

Even though they use the expression "return on shares", it is clear from the subsequent analysis that the assumption refers to (gross) yield; not necessarily the yield on equity. The assumption therefore, is that firms can be divided into risk classes, such that two firms, j and k, belong to the same class if, and only if,

$$X_j = \alpha X_k$$

According to M-M, this assumption "plays a strategic role on the rest of the analysis". This is because M-M set out to analyze investments undertaken by a firm in a given risk class. Now it is clear that if company j undertakes an investment which changes its yield from X_j to X_j', it will stay within the same risk class only if X_j' and X_j are proportional, i.e., if

$$X_j' = (1 + \lambda) X_j$$

The real meaning of the risk class assumption is therefore that the M-M analysis is restricted to treat investments which change the scale of operations only, or to use modern term, which are such that company yield changes by the same percentage in all "states of the world." The possibility of classifying different companies according to risk seems of less importance.

The theoretical basis for M-M's investment analysis is now that an investment which increases yield by a certain percentage in every state of the world must lead to the same relative increase in the company's market value:

$$v_j' = (1 + \lambda) v_j$$

Looking at the market value Formula (6), we see that this is almost correct, but not entirely. It is easy to see that the new expected yield is

$$\mu_j' = (1 + \lambda) \mu_j$$

and that the same applies to all covariances (and so also to their sum), i.e.,

$$b_j' = (1 + \lambda) b_j$$

If now the risk aversion factor R remained unchanged, we would obviously have $v_j' = (1 + \lambda) v_j$. Yet, R is not entirely unaffected by changes in yields. We see that R depends on expected aggregate yield $\sum_k \mu_k$, and this will necessarily change when the expected yield of any one company

changes. In general, risk aversion will vary with yield, so that strict proportionality will not be observed.[5] What we shall do, however, is to treat
this deviation as a minor and second order effect by assuming that the
number of firms is so large that the change in the risk aversion is negligible. This is essentially the same as assuming that the companies regard
themselves as pricetakers in the security markets.

Under this assumption it is easy to see from the first order conditions
(4) that the proportionality relation holds for arbitrary utility functions:
if a change in one company's yield does not appreciably affect the investor's marginal utility, then Eq. (4) is satisfied only if v_j and X_j are changed
in the same proportion.

If the proportionality relation is accepted, the rest of the analysis
is very simple. To illustrate, we consider an investment priced at I which
will increase yield (and so also market value) by 100λ pct., to be financed
by borrowing. The new level of debt then becomes

$$d_j' = d_j + I$$

and the market value of equity

$$
\begin{aligned}
p_j' &= v_j' - d_j' \\
&= (1 + \lambda)v_j - d_j - I \\
&= p_j + \lambda v_j - I
\end{aligned}
$$

Consequently, the investment will be acceptable only if

$$\lambda v_j \geq I$$

or, equivalently, if

$$\frac{\lambda \mu_j}{I} \geq \frac{\mu_j}{v_j}$$

This is the M-M Proposition III: the criterion for undertaking the investment is that its expected rate of return is at least as high as the current
expected rate of return of the company. As shown by M-M, this rule holds
regardless of the method of financing the investment; borrowing was
meant here as an illustration only.

The M-M analysis is certainly not trivial, but since it can handle
only very special types of investments, its applicability is limited. The
alternative suggested here is to buy increased generality with respect to
the nature of investments at the cost of decreased generality with respect
to the nature of preferences. By means of an explicit market valuation

---

[5] Since quadratic utility functions exhibit increasing risk aversion we have v_j'
somewhat less than $(1 + \lambda)v_j$. Perhaps a more plausible hypothesis is decreasing risk
aversion; in that case the inequality would be reversed.

formula like (6), we are able to analyze investments with completely arbitrary yield characteristics. To see how this is done, consider again loan financing of an investment I, which will generate a yield represented by the random variable Z, which has mean μ_z and covariances σ_{zk} with all other yields (including X_j).[6] With this investment, company yield will be the variate

$$X_j' = X_j + Z$$

and it is easily verified that

$$\mu_j' = \mu_j + \mu_{zj}$$

$$\sigma_{jk}' = \begin{cases} \sigma_{jk} + \sigma_{zk} & \text{for } k \neq j \\ \sigma_{jj} + 2\sigma_{zj} + \sigma_{zz} & \text{for } k = j \end{cases}$$

and consequently

$$b_j' = b_j + b_z$$

where $b_z = \sum_k \sigma_{zk} + \sigma_{zj}$, which is the relevant risk measure for the investment when undertaken by company j. The new market value of the company will be

$$v_j' = v_j + \frac{1}{r}(\mu_z - Rb_z)$$

so that the market value of equity becomes

$$p_j' = p_j + \frac{1}{r}(\mu_z - Rb_z) - I$$

Thus the investment will be undertaken only if

$$\frac{1}{r}(\mu_z - Rb_z) \geq I$$

or, equivalently, if

$$\frac{\mu_z - rI}{b_z} \geq R \tag{7}$$

From currently available data on the firm's activity we can compute the value of R as

$$R = \frac{\mu_j - rv_j}{b_j}$$

---

[6] We have to regard other firms' investments as given independently of the decision of company j. If this assumption is not made, we are conceptually in a very complicated oligopoly situation, but one whose effects on the decisions to be made appear as rather second order.

and assuming, as before, that changes in R are negligible, we can write the investment criterion as

$$\frac{\mu_z - rI}{b_z} \geq \frac{\mu_j - rv_j}{b_j} \tag{8}$$

Again we have, on the right-hand side, objective data on the firm's current activities, its expected yield net of interest costs divided by its current risk factor. On the left-hand side we have corresponding information on the proposed investment, expected net yield divided by its own risk factor. It can easily be shown that this criterion is independent of the method of financing.

A remark on the "social rate of discount" debate

Without going into details, this debate can be summarized as follows. One argument is that individual enterprises are too small to be willing to undertake socially desirable risky investments. The counterargument is that with a market for shares, investors are able to diversify to the extent that the socially optimal risk level is attained. It is seen that the model presented here supports the latter argument. Assume that the investment opportunity Z is technologically independent of the existing firms in the sense that its stochastic properties are the same regardless of which company undertakes it; this means that the left-hand side of inequality (7) will have the same value for all companies. Also, R is the same for all companies, so that the criterion for undertaking the investment is the same for all companies. Even if all existing companies were merged into one, the criterion would not change. Hence, the only barriers to a socially optimal risk level are imperfections in the stock market.

IV. CONCLUSION

I believe that the analysis so far is sufficient to demonstrate both the usefulness and the necessity of tying the theory of market adjustment in with the analysis of firm decision making. The results we have obtained are admittedly specific to the particular preference structure we have assumed, but nevertheless serve to illustrate the structure of the theory. It may also prove possible, by closer analysis of the general model, to develop operational results of the same nature.

Apart from the preference structure, there are two particular directions in which generalization and extension of the theory seem useful and even possible. One is the possibility of removing the assumption of a perfect loan market without default risk. Formally, this requires a substantial increase in the number of markets, since we shall then have to distinguish among as many different types of bonds as there are companies (and possibly even more), each with its particular price. Analytically, such a formulation poses formidable problems. Some work has been done on models incorporating default risk [7]; interestingly, it appears that at least parts of the M-M theory can be rescued also in this case.

A second major task is to make the analysis less partial by extending the model's domain of decision. The theory presented above gives no real explanation of how or why companies have arrived at the yield distribution and the amount of debt they happen to have; rather, we analyze marginal changes in company activity. Clearly, there must be some kind of discretion involved in the relationship between the liability side of the firm's balance sheet and the yield made possible by the corresponding resources on the asset side. One approach to some of the problems involved is represented by the important contribution of Peter Diamond [2]. In Diamond's model there is, in addition to markets for stocks and bonds, a market for a factor of production which firms acquire from the public. Company debt then consists exclusively of claims to compensation for factor input. Company yield becomes a random variable which depends upon the input level:

$$X_j = f_j(d_j, \theta)$$

Here θ is a random variable (the state of nature) representing the stochastic nature of production. A formulation along this line represents a step in the right direction, and it turns out that in such a model the characterization of the firm's optimal investment policy becomes a strangely intricate problem on which future research may hopefully have more to say.

REFERENCES

[1] Borch, K. "General Equilibrium in the Economics of Uncertainty," in K. Borch and J. Mossin, eds., *Risk and Uncertainty* (London, England, 1968).

[2] Diamond, P. A. "The Role of a Stock Market in a General Equilibrium Model with Technological Uncertainty," *American Economic Review*, Vol. 57 (September 1967), pp. 759–76.

[3] Lerner, E. M., and W. T. Carleton. *A Theory of Financial Analysis* (New York 1966).

[4] Modigliani, F., and M. H. Miller. "The Cost of Capital, Corporation Finance, and the Theory of Investment," *American Economic Review*, Vol. 48 (June 1958), pp. 261–97.

[5] Mossin, J. "Equilibrium in a Capital Asset Market," *Econometrica*, Vol. 34 (October 1966), pp. 768–83.

[6] Sharpe, W. F. "Capital Asset Prices: A Theory of Market Equilibrium under Conditions of Risk," *Journal of Finance*, Vol. 19 (September 1964), pp. 425–42.

[7] Stiglitz, J. E. "A Re-Examination of the Modigliani-Miller Theorem," *American Economic Review*, Vol. 59 (December 1969), pp. 784–93.

*Paul A. Samuelson**

10. Lifetime Portfolio Selection by Dynamic Stochastic Programming

Reprinted from **The Review of Economics and Statistics,** Vol. LI, No. 3 (April, 1969), pp. 239–246, by permission of the author and publisher. Copyright 1969 by the President and Fellows of Harvard College.

INTRODUCTION

Most analyses of portfolio selection, whether they are of the Markowitz-Tobin mean-variance or of more general type, maximize over one period.[1] I shall here formulate and solve a many-period generalization, corresponding to lifetime planning of consumption and investment decisions. For simplicity of exposition I shall confine my explicit discussion to special and easy cases that suffice to illustrate the general principles involved.

As an example of topics that can be investigated within the framework of the present model, consider the question of a "businessman risk" kind of investment. In the literature of finance, one often reads; "Security A should be avoided by widows as too risky, but is highly suitable as a businessman's risk." What is involved in this distinction? Many things.

First, the "businessman" is more affluent than the widow; and being further removed from the threat of falling below some subsistence level, he has a high propensity to embrace variance for the sake of better yield.

Second, he can look forward to a high salary in the future; and with so high a present discounted value of wealth, it is only prudent for him

* Professor of Economics, Massachusetts Institute of Technology. Aid from the National Science Foundation is gratefully acknowledged. Robert C. Merton has provided me with much stimulus; and in a companion paper in this issue of the REVIEW he is tackling the much harder problem of optimal control in the presence of continuous-time stochastic variation. I owe thanks also to Stanley Fischer.

[1] See for example Harry Markowitz [5]; James Tobin [14], Paul A. Samuelson [10]; Paul A. Samuelson and Robert C. Merton [13]. See, however, James Tobin [15], for a pioneering treatment of the multi-period portfolio problem; and Jan Mossin [7] which overlaps with the present analysis in showing how to solve the basic dynamic stochastic program recursively by working backward from the end in the Bellman fashion, and which proves the theorem that portfolio proportions will be invariant only if the marginal utility function is iso-elastic.

to put more into common stocks compared to his present tangible wealth, borrowing if necessary for the purpose, or accomplishing the same thing by selecting volatile stocks that widows shun.

Third, being still in the prime of life, the businessman can "recoup" any present losses in the future. The widow or retired man nearing life's end has no such "second or nth chance."

Fourth (and apparently related to the last point), since the businessman will be investing for so many periods, "the law of averages will even out for him," and he can afford to act almost as if he were not subject to diminishing marginal utility.

What are we to make of these arguments? It will be realized that the first could be purely a one-period argument. Arrow, Pratt, and others[2] have shown that any investor who faces a range of wealth in which the elasticity of his marginal utility schedule is great will have high risk tolerance; and most writers seem to believe that the elasticity is at its highest for rich—but not ultrarich!—people. Since the present model has no new insight to offer in connection with statical risk tolerance, I shall ignore the first point here and confine almost all my attention to utility functions with the same relative risk aversion at all levels of wealth. Is it then still true that lifetime considerations justify the concept of a businessman's risk in his prime of life?

Point two above does justify leveraged investment financed by borrowing against future earnings. But it does not really involve any increase in relative risk-taking once we have related what is at risk to the proper larger base. (Admittedly, if market imperfections make loans difficult or costly, recourse to volatile, "leveraged" securities may be a rational procedure.)

The fourth point can easily involve the innumerable fallacies connected with the "law of large numbers." I have commented elsewhere[3] on the mistaken notion that multiplying the same kind of risk leads to cancellation rather than augmentation of risk. I.e., insuring many ships adds to risk (but only as $\sqrt{n}$); hence, only by insuring more ships and by *also* subdividing those risks among more people is risk on each brought down (in ratio $1/\sqrt{n}$).

However, before writing this paper, I had thought that points three and four could be reformulated so as to give a valid demonstration of businessman's risk, my thought being that investing for each period is akin to agreeing to take a $1/n$th interest in insuring n independent ships.

The present lifetime model reveals that investing for many periods does not *itself* introduce extra tolerance for riskiness at early, or any, stages of life.

[2] See K. Arrow [1]; J. Pratt [9]; P. A. Samuelson and R. C. Merton [13].
[3] P. A. Samuelson [11].

BASIC ASSUMPTIONS

The familiar Ramsey model may be used as a point of departure. Let an individual maximize

$$\int_0^T e^{-\rho t} U[C(t)]dt \tag{1}$$

subject to initial wealth W_0 that can always be invested for an exogeneously-given certain rate of yield r; or subject to the constraint

$$C(t) = rW(t) - \dot{W}(t) \tag{2}$$

If there is no bequest at death, terminal wealth is zero.

This leads to the standard calculus-of-variations problem

$$J = \operatorname*{Max}_{\{W(t)\}} \int_0^T e^{-\rho t} U[rW - \dot{W}]dt \tag{3}$$

This can be easily related[4] to a discrete-time formulation

$$\operatorname*{Max} \sum_{t=0}^T (1 + \rho)^{-t} U[C_t] \tag{4}$$

subject to

$$C_t = W_t - \frac{W_{t+1}}{1 + r} \tag{5}$$

or

$$\operatorname*{Max}_{\{W_t\}} \sum_{t=0}^T (1 + \rho)^{-t} U\left[W_t - \frac{W_{t+1}}{1 + r}\right] \tag{6}$$

for prescribed (W_0, W_{T+1}). Differentiating partially with respect to each W_t in turn, we derive recursion conditions for a regular interior maximum

$$\frac{(1 + \rho)}{1 + r} U'\left[W_{t-1} - \frac{W_t}{1 + r}\right] = U'\left[W_t - \frac{W_{t+1}}{1 + r}\right] \tag{7}$$

If U is concave, solving these second-order difference equations with boundary conditions (W_0, W_{T+1}) will suffice to give us an optimal lifetime consumption-investment program.

Since there has thus far been one asset, and that a safe one, the time has come to introduce a stochastically-risky alternative asset and to face up to a portfolio problem. Let us postulate the existence, alongside of the safe asset that makes $1 invested in it at time t return to you at the end

[4] See P. A. Samuelson [12], p. 273 for an exposition of discrete-time analogues to calculus-of-variations models. Note: here I assume that consumption, C_t, takes place at the beginning rather than at the end of the period. This change alters slightly the appearance of the equilibrium conditions, but not their substance.

of the period \$1 $(1 + r)$, a risk asset that makes \$1 invested in, at time t, return to you after one period $\$1Z_t$, where Z_t is a random variable subject to the probability distribution

$$\text{Prob } \{Z_t \leq z\} = P(z) \qquad z \geq 0 \qquad (8)$$

Hence, $Z_{t+1} - 1$ is the percentage "yield" of each outcome. The most general probability distribution is admissible: i.e., a probability density over continuous z's, or finite positive probabilities at discrete values of z. Also I shall usually assume independence between yields at different times so that $P(z_0, z_1, \ldots, z_t, \ldots, z_T) = P(z_t)P(z_1)\ldots P(z_T)$.

For simplicity, the reader might care to deal with the easy case

$$\text{Prob } \{Z = \lambda\} = \tfrac{1}{2}$$
$$= \text{Prob } \{Z = \lambda^{-1}\}, \qquad \lambda > 1 \qquad (9)$$

In order that risk averters with concave utility should not shun this risk asset when maximizing the expected value of their portfolio, λ must be large enough so that the expected value of the risk asset exceeds that of the safe asset, i.e.,

$$\tfrac{1}{2}\lambda + \tfrac{1}{2}\lambda^{-1} > 1 + r$$

or

$$\lambda > 1 + r + \sqrt{2r + r^2}$$

Thus, for $\lambda = 1.4$, the risk asset has a mean yield of 0.057, which is greater than a safe asset's certain yield of $r = .04$.

At each instant of time, what will be the optimal fraction w_t that you should put in the risky asset, with $1 - w_t$ going into the safe asset? Once these optimal portfolio fractions are known, the constraint of (5) must be written

$$C_t = \left[W_t - \frac{W_{t+1}}{[(1 - w_t)(1 + r) + w_t Z_t]} \right] \qquad (10)$$

Now we use (10) instead of (4), and recognizing the stochastic nature of our problem, specify that we maximize the expected value of total utility over time. This gives us the stochastic generalizations of (4) and (5) or (6)

$$\underset{\{C_t, w_t\}}{\text{Max }} E \sum_{t=0}^{T} (1 + \rho)^{-t} U[C_t] \qquad (11)$$

subject to

$$C_t = \left[W_t - \frac{W_{t+1}}{(1 + r)(1 - w_t) + w_t Z_t} \right] \qquad W_0 \text{ given, } W_{T+1} \text{ prescribed}$$

If there is no bequeathing of wealth at death, presumably $W_{T+1} = 0$.

Alternatively, we could replace a prescribed W_{T+1} by a final bequest function added to (11), of the form $B(W_{T+1})$, and with W_{T+1} a free decision variable to be chosen so as to maximize (11) $+ B(W_{T+1})$. For the most part, I shall consider $C_T = W_T$ and $W_{T+1} = 0$.

In (11), E stands for the "expected value of," so that, for example,

$$EZ_t = \int_0^\infty z_t dP(z_t)$$

In our simple case of (9),

$$EZ_t = \tfrac{1}{2}\lambda + \tfrac{1}{2}\lambda^{-1}$$

Equation (11) is our basic stochastic programming problem that needs to be solved simultaneously for optimal saving-consumption and portfolio-selection decisions over time.

Before proceeding to solve this problem, reference may be made to similar problems that seem to have been dealt with explicitly in the economics literature. First, there is the valuable paper by Phelps on the Ramsey problem in which capital's yield is a prescribed random variable. This corresponds, in my notation, to the $\{w_t\}$ strategy being frozen at some fractional level, there being no portfolio selection problem. (My analysis could be amplified to consider Phelps'[5] wage income, and even in the stochastic form that he cites Martin Beckmann as having analyzed.) More recently, Levhari and Srinivasan [4] have also treated the Phelps problem for $T = \infty$ by means of the Bellman functional equations of dynamic programming, and have indicated a proof that concavity of U is sufficient for a maximum. Then, there is Professor Mirrlees' important work on the Ramsey problem with Harrod-neutral technological change as a random variable.[6] Our problems become equivalent if I replace $W_t - W_{t+1}[(1 + r)(1 - w_t) + w_t Z_t]^{-1}$ in (10) by $A_t f(W_t/A_t) - nW_t - (W_{t+1} - W_t)$ let technical change be governed by the probability distribution

$$\text{Prob} \{A_t \leq A_{t-1}Z\} = P(Z)$$

reinterpret my W_t to be Mirrlees' per capita capital, K_t/L_t, where L_t is growing at the natural rate of growth n; and posit that $A_t f(W_t/A_t)$ is a homogeneous first degree, concave, neoclassical production function in terms of capital and efficiency-units of labor.

It should be remarked that I am confirming myself here to regular interior maxima, and not going into the Kuhn-Tucker inequalities that easily handle boundary maxima.

[5] E. S. Phelps [8].

[6] J. A. Mirrlees [6]. I have converted his treatment into a discrete-time version. Robert Merton's companion paper throws light on Mirrlees' Brownian-motion model for A_t.

SOLUTION OF THE PROBLEM

The meaning of our basic problem

$$J_T(W_0) = \underset{\{C_t, w_t\}}{\text{Max}} \; E \sum_{t=0}^{T} (1 + \rho)^{-t} U[C_t] \qquad [11]$$

subject to $C_t = W_t - W_{t+1}[(1 - w_t)(1 + r) + w_t Z_t]^{-1}$ is not easy to grasp. I act now at $t = 0$ to select C_0 and w_0, knowing W_0 but not yet knowing how Z_0 will turn out. I must act now, knowing that one period later, knowledge of Z_0's outcome will be known and that W_1 will then be known. Depending upon knowledge of W_1, a new decision will be made for C_1 and w_1. Now I can only guess what that decision will be.

As so often is the case in dynamic programming, it helps to begin at the end of the planning period. This brings us to the well-known one-period portfolio problem. In our terms, this becomes

$$J_1(W_{T-1}) = \underset{\{C_{T-1}, w_{T-1}\}}{\text{Max}} \; U[C_{T-1}]$$

$$+ E(1 + \rho)^{-1} U[(W_{T-1} - C_{T-1})\{(1 - w_{T-1})(1 + r) + w_{T-1} Z_{T-1}\}^{-1}]$$

$$(12)$$

Here the expected value operator E operates only on the random variable of the next period since current consumption C_{T-1} is known once we have made our decision. Writing the second term as $EF(Z_T)$, this becomes

$$EF(Z_T) = \int_0^\infty F(Z_T) dP(Z_T \mid Z_{T-1}, Z_{T-2}, \ldots, Z_0)$$

$$= \int_0^\infty F(Z_T) dP(Z_T)$$

by our independence postulate.

In the general case, at a later stage of decision making, say $t = T - 1$, knowledge will be available of the outcomes of earlier random variables, $Z_{t-2}, \ldots$; since these might be relevant to the distribution of subsequent random variables, conditional probabilities of the form $P(Z_{T-1} \mid Z_{T-2}, \ldots)$ are thus involved. However, in cases like the present one, where independence of distributions is posited, conditional probabilities can be dispensed with in favor of simple distributions.

Note that in (12) we have substituted for C_T its value as given by the constraint in (10) or (11).

To determine this optimum (C_{T-1}, w_{T-1}), we differentiate with respect to each separately, to get

$$0 = U'[C_{T-1}] - (1 + \rho)^{-1} E U'[C_T]\{(1 - w_{T-1})(1 + r) + w_{T-1} Z_{T-1}\}$$
$$(12')$$

$$0 = E U'[C_T](W_{T-1} - C_{T-1})(Z_{T-1} - 1 - r)$$

$$= \int_0^\infty U'[(W_{T-1} - C_{T-1})\{(1 - w_{T-1})(1 + r) - w_{T-1} Z_{T-1}\}]$$

$$\times (W_{T-1} - C_{T-1})(Z_{T-1} - 1 - r) dP(Z_{T-1}) \quad (12'')$$

Solving these simultaneously, we get our optimal decisions (C^*_{T-1}, w^*_{T-1}) as functions of initial wealth W_{T-1} alone. Note that if somehow C^*_{T-1} were known, $(12'')$ would by itself be the familiar one-period portfolio optimality condition, and could trivially be rewritten to handle any number of alternative assets.

Substituting (C^*_{T-1}, w^*_{T-1}) into the expression to be maximized gives us $J_1(W_{T-1})$ explicitly. From the equations in (12), we can, by standard calculus methods, relate the derivatives of U to those of J, namely, by the envelope relation

$$J_1'(W_{T-1}) = U'[C_{T-1}] \tag{13}$$

Now that we know $J_1[W_{T-1}]$, it is easy to determine optimal behavior one period earlier, namely by

$$J_2(W_{T-2}) = \operatorname*{Max}_{\{C_{T-2}, w_{T-2}\}} U[C_{T-2}]$$

$$+ E(1 + \rho)^{-1} J_1[(W_{T-2} - C_{T-2})\{(1 - w_{T-2})(1 + r) + w_{T-2} Z_{T-2}\}] \quad (14)$$

Differentiating (14) just as we did (11) gives the following equations like those of (12)

$$0 = U'[C_{T-2}] - (1 + \rho)^{-1} E J_1'[W_{T-2}]\{(1 - w_{T-2})(1 + r) + w_{T-2} Z_{T-2}\}$$
$$(15')$$

$$0 = E J_1'[W_{T-1}](W_{T-2} - C_{T-2})(Z_{T-2} - 1 - r)$$

$$= \int_0^\infty J_1'[(W_{T-2} - C_{T-2})\{(1 - w_{T-2})(1 + r)$$

$$+ w_{T-2} Z_{T-2}\}](W_{T-2} - C_{T-2})(Z_{T-2} - 1 - r) dP(Z_{T-2}) \quad (15'')$$

These equations, which could by (13) be related to $U'[C_{T-1}]$, can be solved simultaneously to determine optimal (C^*_{T-2}, w^*_{T-2}) and $J_2(W_{T-2})$.

Continuing recursively in this way for $T - 3$, $T - 4$, ..., 2, 1, 0, we finally have our problem solved. The general recursive optimality equations can be written as

$$0 = U'[C_0] - (1 + \rho)^{-1}EJ'_{T-1}[W_0]\{(1 - w_0)(1 + r) + w_0 Z_0\}$$

$$0 = EJ'_{T-1}[W_1](W_0 - C_0)(Z_0 - 1 - r)$$

$$\cdots\cdots\cdots\cdots\cdots$$

$$0 = U'[C_{T-1}] - (1 + \rho)^{-1}EJ'_{T-t}[W_t]\{(1 - w_{t-1})(1 + r) + w_{t-1}Z_{t-1}\}$$

$$(16')$$

$$0 = EJ'_{T-1}[W_{t-1} - C_{t-1}](Z_{t-1} - 1 - r) \qquad (t = 1, \ldots, T - 1) \qquad (16'')$$

In $(16')$, of course, the proper substitutions must be made and the E operators must be over the proper probability distributions. Solving $(16'')$ at any stage will give the optimal decision rules for consumption-saving and for portfolio selection, in the form

$$C_t^* = f[W_t; Z_{t-1}, \ldots, Z_0]$$

$$= f_{T-t}[W_t] \qquad \text{if the } Z\text{'s are independently distributed}$$

$$w_t^* = g[W_t; Z_{t-1}, \ldots, Z_0]$$

$$= g_{T-t}[W_t] \qquad \text{if the } Z\text{'s are independently distributed.}$$

Our problem is now solved for every case but the important case of infinite-time horizon. For well-behaved cases, one can simply let $T \to \infty$ in the above formulas. Or, as often happens, the infinite case may be the easiest of all to solve, since for it $C_t^* = f(W_t)$, $w_t^* = g(W_t)$, independently of time and both these unknown functions can be deduced as solutions to the following functional equations:

$$0 = U'[f(W)] - (1 + \rho)^{-1} \int_0^\infty J'[(W - f(W))\{(1 + r)$$

$$- g(W)(Z - 1 - r)\}][(1 + r) - g(W)(Z - 1 - r)]dP(Z) \qquad (17')$$

$$0 = \int_0^\infty U'[\{W - f(W)\}\{1 + r - g(W)(Z - 1 - r)\}][Z - 1 - r]$$

$$(17'')$$

Equation $(17')$, by itself with $g(W)$ pretended to be known, would be equivalent to Eq. (13) of Levhari and Srinivasan [4, p. 6]. In deriving (17′) and (17″), I have utilized the envelope relation of my (13), which is equivalent to Levhari and Srinivasan's Eq. (12) [4, p. 5].

BERNOULLI AND ISOELASTIC CASES

To apply our results, let us consider the interesting Bernoulli case where $U = \log C$. This does not have the bounded utility that Arrow [1] and many writers have convinced themselves is desirable for an axiom system. Since I do not believe that Karl Menger paradoxes of the generalized St. Petersburg type hold any terrors for the economist, I have no particular interest in boundedness of utility and consider $\log C$ to be interesting and admissible. For this case, we have, from (12),

$$
\begin{aligned}
J_1(W) &= \operatorname*{Max}_{\{C,w\}} \log C \\
&\quad + E(1 + \rho)^{-1} \log \left[(W - C)\{(1 - w)(1 + r) + wZ\} \right] \\
&= \operatorname*{Max}_{\{C\}} \log C + (1 + \rho)^{-1} \log [W - C] \\
&\quad + \operatorname*{Max}_{\{w\}} \int_0^\infty \log \left[(1 - w)(1 + r) + wZ \right] dP(Z) \quad (18)
\end{aligned}
$$

Hence, Eqs. (12), (16′) and (16″) split into two independent parts and the Ramsey-Phelps saving problem becomes quite independent of the lifetime portfolio selection problem. Now we have

$$
0 = (1/C) - (1 + \rho)^{-1}(W - C)^{-1}
$$

or

$$
C_{T-1} = (1 + \rho)(2 + \rho)^{-1} W_{T-1} \tag{19′}
$$

$$
0 = \int_0^\infty (Z - 1 - r)[(1 - w)(1 + r) + wZ]^{-1} dP(Z)
$$

or

$$
w_{T-1} = w^* \quad \text{independently of } W_{T-1} \tag{19″}
$$

These independence results, of the C_{T-1} and w_{T-1} decisions and of the dependence of w_{T-1} on W_{T-1}, hold for all U functions with isoelastic marginal utility. For example, (16′) and (16″) become decomposable conditions for all

$$
U(C) = 1/\gamma C^\gamma, \quad \gamma < 1 \tag{20}
$$

as well as for $U(C) = \log C$, corresponding by L'Hôpital's rule to $\gamma = 0$.

To see this, write (12) or (18) as

$$J_1(W) = \underset{\{C,w\}}{\text{Max}} \frac{C^\gamma}{\gamma} + (1+\rho)^{-1}\frac{(W-C)^\gamma}{\gamma}$$

$$\times \int_0^\infty [(1-w)(1+r) + wZ]^\gamma dP(Z)$$

$$= \underset{\{C\}}{\text{Max}} \frac{C^\gamma}{\gamma} + (1+\rho)^{-1}\frac{(W-C)^\gamma}{\gamma}$$

$$\times \underset{w}{\text{Max}} \int_0^\infty [(1-w)(1+r) + wZ]^\gamma dp(Z) \quad (21)$$

Hence, (12'') or (15'') or (16'') becomes

$$\int_0^\infty [(1-w)(1+r) + wZ]^{\gamma-1}(Z-r-1)dP(Z) = 0 \quad (22'')$$

which defines optimal w^* and gives

$$\underset{\{w\}}{\text{Max}} \int_0^\infty [(1-w)(1+r) + wZ]^\gamma dP(Z)$$

$$= \int_0^\infty [(1-w^*)(1+r) + w^*Z]^\gamma dP(Z)$$

$$= [1+r^*]^\gamma \quad \text{for short}$$

Here, r^* is the subjective or util-prob mean return of the portfolio, where diminishing marginal utility has been taken into account.[7] To get optimal consumption-saving, differentiate (21) to get the new form of (12'), (15'), or (16')

$$0 = C^{\gamma-1} - (1+\rho)^{-1}(1+r^*)^\gamma(W-C)^{\gamma-1} \quad (22')$$

Solving, we have the consumption decision rule

$$C^*_{T-1} = \frac{a_1}{1+a_1} W_{T-1} \quad (23)$$

where

$$a_1 = [(1+r^*)^\gamma/(1+\rho)]^{1/\gamma-1} \quad (24)$$

Hence, by substitution, we find

$$J_1(W_{T-1}) = b_1 W^\gamma_{T-1}/\gamma \quad (25)$$

[7] See Samuelson and Merton for the util-prob concept [13].

where

$$b_1 = a_1{}^\gamma(1 + a_1)^{-\gamma} + (1 + \rho)^{-1}(1 + r^*)^\gamma(1 + a_1)^{-\gamma} \qquad (26)$$

Thus, $J_1(\cdot)$ is of the same elasticity form as $U(\cdot)$ was. Evaluating indeterminate forms for $\gamma = 0$, we find J_1 to be of log form if U was.

Now, by mathematical induction, it is easy to show that this isoelastic property must also hold for $J_2(W_{T-2})$, $J_3(W_{T-3})$, ..., since, whenever it holds for $J_n(W_{T-n})$ it is deducible that it holds for $J_{n+1}(W_{T-n-1})$. Hence, at every stage, solving the general equations (16′) and (16″), they decompose into two parts in the case of isoelastic utility. Hence,

Theorem. For isoelastic marginal utility functions, $U'(C) = C^{\gamma-1}$, $\gamma < 1$, the optimal portfolio decision is independent of wealth at each stage and independent of all consumption-saving decisions, leading to a constant w^*, the solution to

$$0 = \int_0^\infty [(1 - w)(1 + r) + wZ]^{\gamma-1}(Z - 1 - r)dP(Z)$$

Then optimal consumption decisions at each stage are, for a no-bequest model, of the form

$$C^*{}_{T-i} = c_i W_{T-i}$$

where one can deduce the recursion relations

$$c_1 = \frac{a_1}{1 + w_1}$$

$$a_1 = [(1 + \rho)/(1 + r^*)^\gamma]^{1/1-\gamma}$$

$$(1 + r^*)^\gamma = \int_0^\infty [(1 - w^*)(1 + r) + w^*Z]^\gamma dP(Z)$$

$$c_i = \frac{a_1 c_{i-1}}{1 + a_1 c_{i-1}}$$

$$= \frac{a_1{}^i}{1 + a_1 + a_1{}^2 + \cdots + a_1{}^i} < c_{i-1}$$

$$= \frac{a_1{}^i(a_1 - 1)}{a_1{}^{i+1} - 1} \qquad a_1 \neq 1$$

$$= \frac{1}{1 + i} \qquad a_1 = 1$$

In the limiting case, as $\gamma \to 0$ and we have Bernoulli's logarithmic function, $a_1 = (1 + \rho)$, independent of r^*, and all saving propensities depend on subjective time preference ρ only, being independent of technological investment opportunities (except to the degree that W_t will itself definitely depend on those opportunities).

We can interpret $1 + r^*$ as kind of a "risk-corrected" mean yield; and behavior of a long-lived man depends critically on whether $(1 + r^*)^\gamma \gtrless (1 + \rho)$, corresponding to $a_1 \lessgtr 1$:

(i)   For $(1 + r^*)^\gamma = (1 + \rho)$, one plans always to consume at a uniform rate, dividing current W_{T-i} evenly by remaining life, $1/(1 + i)$. If young enough, one saves on the average; in the familiar "hump saving" fashion, one dissaves later as the end comes sufficiently close into sight.

(ii)   For $(1 + r^*)^\gamma > (1 + \rho)$, $a_1 < 1$, and investment opportunities are, so to speak, so tempting compared to psychological time preference that one consumes nothing at the beginning of a long-long life, i.e., rigorously

$$\operatorname*{Lim}_{i \to \infty} c_i = 0 \qquad a_1 < 1$$

and again hump saving must take place. For $(1 + r^*)^\gamma > (1 + \rho)$, the *perpetual* lifetime problem, with $T = \infty$, is divergent and ill-defined, i.e., $J_i(W) \to \infty$ as $i \to \infty$. For $\gamma \leq 0$ and $\rho > 0$, this case cannot arise.

(iii)   For $(1 + r^*)^\gamma < (1 + \rho)$, $a_1 > 1$, consumption at very early ages drops only to a limiting positive fraction (rather than zero), namely

$$\operatorname*{Lim}_{i \to \infty} c_i = 1 - 1/a_1 < 1, \qquad a_1 > 1$$

Now whether there will be, on the average, initial hump saving depends upon the size of $r^* - c_\infty$, or whether

$$r^* - 1 - \frac{(1 + r^*)^{\gamma/1-\gamma}}{(1 + \rho)^{1/1-\gamma}} > 0$$

This ends the Theorem. Although many of the results depend upon the no-bequest assumption, $W_{T+1} = 0$, as Merton's companion paper shows (p. 247, this *Review*) we can easily generalize to the cases where a bequest function $B_T(W_{T+1})$ is added to $\sum_0^T (1 + \rho)^{-t} U(C_t)$. If B_T is itself of iso-elastic form,

$$B_T \equiv b_T(W_{T+1})^\gamma/\gamma$$

the algebra is little changed. Also, the same comparative statics put forward in Merton's continuous-time case will be applicable here, e.g., the

Bernoulli $\gamma = 0$ case is a watershed between cases where thrift is enhanced by riskiness rather than reduced; etc.

Since proof of the theorem is straightforward, I skip all details except to indicate how the recursion relations for c_i and b_i are derived, namely from the identities

$$b_{i+1}W^\gamma/\gamma = J_{i+1}(W)$$

$$= \underset{c}{\text{Max}} \left\{ C^\gamma/\gamma + b_i(1 + r^*)^\gamma(1 + \rho)^{-1}(W - C)^\gamma/\gamma \right\}$$

$$= \left\{ c^\gamma_{i+1} + b_i(1 + r^*)^\gamma(1 + \rho)^{-1}(1 - c_{i+1})^\gamma \right\} W^\gamma/\gamma$$

and the optimality condition

$$0 = C^{\gamma-1} - b_i(1 + r^*)^\gamma(1 + \rho)^{-1}(W - C)^{\gamma-1}$$

$$= (c_{i+1}W)^{\gamma-1} - b_i(1 + r^*)^\gamma(1 + \rho)^{-1}(1 - c_{i+1})^{\gamma-1}W^{\gamma-1}$$

which defines c_{i+1} in terms of b_i.

What if we relax the assumption of isoelastic marginal utility functions? Then w_{T-j} becomes a function of W_{T-j-1} (and, of course, of r, ρ, and a functional of the probability distribution P). Now the Phelps-Ramsey optimal stochastic saving decisions do interact with the optimal portfolio decisions, and these have to be arrived at by simultaneous solution of the nondecomposable equations (16′) and (16″).

What if we have more than one alternative asset to safe cash? Then merely interpret Z_t as a (column) vector of returns $(Z_t^2, Z_t^3, \ldots)$ on the respective risky assets; also interpret w_t as a (row) vector $(w_t^2, w_t^3, \ldots)$, interpret $P(Z)$ as vector notation for

$$\text{Prob } \{Z_t^2 \leq Z^2, Z_t^3 \leq Z^3, \ldots\} = P(Z^2, Z^3, \ldots) = P(Z)$$

interpret all integrals of the form $\int G(Z)dP(Z)$ as multiple integrals $\int G(Z^2, Z^3, \ldots)dP(Z^2, Z^3, \ldots)$. Then (16″) becomes a vector-set of equations, one for each component of the vector Z_t, and these can be solved simultaneously for the unknown w_t vector.

If there are many consumption items, we can handle the general problem by giving a similar vector interpretation to C_t.

Thus, the most general portfolio lifetime problem is handled by our equations or obvious extensions thereof.

CONCLUSION

We have now come full circle. Our model denies the validity of the concept of businessman's risk; for isoelastic marginal utilities, in your prime of life you have the same relative risk-tolerance as toward the end of life!

The "chance to recoup" and tendency for the law of large numbers to operate in the case of repeated investments is not relevant. (Note: if the elasticity of marginal utility, $-U'(W)/WU''(W)$, rises empirically with wealth, and if the capital market is imperfect as far as lending and borrowing against future earnings is concerned, then it seems to me to be likely that a doctor of age 35–50 might rationally have his highest consumption then, and certainly show greatest risk tolerance then—in other words be open to a "businessman's risk." But not in the frictionless isoelastic model!)

As usual, one expects w^* and risk tolerance to be higher with algebraically large γ. One expects C_t to be higher late in life when r and r^* is high relative to ρ. As in a one-period model, one expects any increase in "riskiness" of Z_t, for the same mean, to decrease w^*. One expects a similar increase in riskiness to lower or raise consumption depending upon whether marginal utility is greater or less than unity in its elasticity.[8]

Our analysis enables us to dispel a fallacy that has been borrowed into portfolio theory from information theory of the Shannon type. Associated with independent discoveries by J. B. Williams [16], John Kelly [2], and H. A. Latané [3] is the notion that if one is investing for many periods, the proper behavior is to maximize the *geometric* mean of return rather than the arithmetic mean. I believe this to be incorrect (except in the Bernoulli logarithmic case where it happens[9] to be correct for reasons quite distinct from the Williams-Kelly-Latané reasoning).

These writers must have in mind reasoning that goes something like the following: If one maximizes for a distant goal, investing and reinvesting (all one's proceeds) many times on the way, then the probability becomes great that with a portfolio that maximizes the geometric mean at each stage you will end up with a larger terminal wealth than with any other decision strategy.

This is indeed a valid consequence of the central limit theorem as applied to the additive logarithms of portfolio outcomes. (For example, maximizing the geometric mean is the same thing as maximizing the arith-

---

[8] See Merton's cited companion paper in this issue, for explicit discussion of the comparative statical shifts of (16)'s C_t^* and w_t^* functions as the parameters ρ, γ, r, r^*, and $P(Z)$ or $P(Z_1, \ldots)$ or $B(W_T)$ functions change. The same results hold in the discrete-and-continuous-time models.

[9] See Latané [3, p. 151] for explicit recognition of this point. I find somewhat mystifying his footnote there which says, "As pointed out to me by Professor L. J. Savage (in correspondence), not only is the maximization of G [the geometric mean] the rule for maximum expected utility in connection with Bernoulli's function but (in so far as certain approximations are permissible) this same rule is approximately valid for all utility functions." (Latané, p. 151, n. 13.) The geometric mean criterion is definitely too conservative to maximize an isoelastic utility function corresponding to positive γ in my Eq. (20), and it is definitely too daring to maximize expected utility when $\gamma < 0$. Professor Savage has informed me recently that his 1969 position differs from the view attributed to him in 1959.

metic mean of the logarithm of outcome at each stage; if at each stage, we get a mean log of $m^{**} > m^*$, then after a large number of stages we will have $m^{**}T \gg m^*T$, and the properly normalized probabilities will cluster around a higher value.)

There is nothing wrong with the logical deduction from premise to theorem. But the implicit premise is faulty to begin with, as I have shown elsewhere in another connection [Samuelson, 10, p. 3]. It is a mistake to think that, just because a w^{**} decision ends up with almost-certain probability to be better than a w^* decision, this implies that w^{**} must yield a better expected value of utility. Our analysis for marginal utility with elasticity differing from that of Bernoulli provides an effective counter example, if indeed a counter example is needed to refute a gratuitous assertion. Moreover, as I showed elsewhere, the ordering principle of selecting between two actions in terms of which has the greater probability of producing a higher result does not even possess the property of being transitive.[10] By that principle, we could have w^{***} better than w^{**}, and w^{**} better than w^*, and also have w^* better than w^{***}.

REFERENCES

[1] Arrow, K. J. "Aspects of the Theory of Risk-Bearing" (Helsinki, Finland: Yrjö Jahnssonin Säätiö, 1965).

[2] Kelly, J. "A New Interpretation of Information Rate," *Bell System Technical Journal* (August, 1956), pp. 917–26.

[3] Latané, H. A. "Criteria for Choice Among Risky Ventures," *Journal of Political Economy* 67 (April, 1959), pp. 144–55.

[4] Levhari, D., and T. N. Srinivasan. "Optimal Savings Under Uncertainty," Institute for Mathematical Studies in the Social Sciences, Technical Report No. 8 (Stanford University, December 1967).

[5] Markowitz, H. *Portfolio Selection: Efficient Diversification of Investment* (New York, N. Y.: Wiley, 1959).

[6] Mirrlees, J. A. "Optimum Accumulation Under Uncertainty," unpublished (December 1965).

[7] Mossin, J. "Optimal Multiperiod Portfolio Policies," *Journal of Business* 41, Vol. 2 (April 1968), pp. 215–29.

[8] Phelps, E. S. "The Accumulation of Risky Capital: A Sequential Utility Analysis," *Econometrica* 30, Vol. 4 (1962), pp. 729–43.

[9] Pratt, J. "Risk Aversion in the Small and in the Large," *Econometrica* 32 (January 1964).

[10] Samuelson, P. A. "General Proof that Diversification Pays," *Journal of Financial and Quantitative Analysis*, Vol. II (March 1967), pp. 1–13.

[10] See Samuelson [11].

[11] ——. "Risk and Uncertainty: A Fallacy of Large Numbers," *Scientia,* 6th Series, 57th year (April–May, 1963).

[12] ——. "A Turnpike Refutation of the Golden Rule in a Welfare Maximizing Many-Year Plan," *Essays on the Theory of Optimal Economic Growth,* Essay XIV, Karl Shell, ed. (Cambridge, Mass.: MIT Press, 1967).

[13] ——, and R. C. Merton. "A Complete Model of Warrant Pricing that Maximizes Utility," *Industrial Management Review* (in press).

[14] Tobin, J. "Liquidity Preference as Behavior Towards Risk," *Review of Economic Studies,* Vol. XXV, 67 (February, 1958), pp. 65–86.

[15] ——. "The Theory of Portfolio Selection," *The Theory of Interest Rates,* F. H. Hahn and F. P. R. Brechling, eds. (London, England: Macmillan, 1965).

[16] Williams, J. B. "Speculation and the Carryover," *Quarterly Journal of Economics* 50 (May 1936), pp. 436–55.

Michael C. Jensen [*]

11. Risk, the Pricing of Capital Assets, and the Evaluation of Investment Portfolios [†]

Reprinted, in abridged form, from **The Journal of Business of the University of Chicago,** Vol. 42, No. 2 (April, 1969), pp. 167–185, 192–202, 241–247, by permission of the author. For Jensen's complete empirical results the reader is referred to the original source.

I. INTRODUCTION

A. Risk and the evaluation of portfolios

The main purpose of this study is the development of a model for evaluating the performance of portfolios of risky assets. In evaluating the performance of portfolios the effects of differential risk must be taken into consideration.[1] If investors are generally averse to risk, they will prefer

[*] Assistant professor, Graduate School of Management, University of Rochester.

[†] The research on this study was supported by fellowship grants from the U.S. Steel Foundation, the American Banking Association and a research grant from the Research Fund in Finance made available by the University of Chicago Graduate School of Business. Extensive computer time at the 7094 Computation Center at the University of Chicago was financed by the Graduate School of Business, and the College of Business of the University of Rochester provided additional time at the 360 Computation Center at the University of Rochester.

I wish to acknowledge a great debt to my dissertation committee; Eugene Fama (chairman), Lawrence Fisher, Merton Miller (who originally suggested this area of research to me), and Harry Roberts, all of whom have given generously of their time and ideas and have continually forced me to rethink and defend my position on numerous issues. I am especially indebted to Professor Fama for his penetrating criticisms of several drafts of this paper. I also wish to thank the members of the Finance Workshop at the University of Chicago for many stimulating and helpful discussions, especially M. Blume, P. Brown, D. Duvel, and M. Scholes. I have also benefited from conversations with M. Geisel, F. Black, and Professors Peter Pashigian, Arnold Zellner, Donald Gordon, and Julian Keilson.

[1] Risk, a critical concept in this paper, will be defined and discussed extensively in Sections II, III, and V.

(*ceteris paribus*) more certain income streams to less certain streams. Under these conditions investors will accept additional risk only if they are compensated for it in the form of higher expected future returns. Thus, in a world dominated by risk-averse investors, a risky portfolio must be expected to yield higher returns than a less risky portfolio, or it would not be held.

The portfolio evaluation model developed below incorporates these risk aspects explicitly by utilizing and extending recent theoretical results by Sharpe [52] and Lintner [37] on the pricing of capital assets under uncertainty. Given these results, a measure of portfolio "performance" (which measures only a manager's ability to forecast security prices) is defined as the difference between the actual returns on a portfolio in any particular holding period and the expected returns on that portfolio conditional on the riskless rate, its level of "systematic risk," and the actual returns on the market portfolio. Criteria for judging a portfolio's performance to be *neutral, superior,* or *inferior* are established.

A measure of a portfolio's "efficiency" is also derived, and the criteria for judging a portfolio to be *efficient, superefficient,* or *inefficient* are defined. It is also shown that it is strictly impossible to define a measure of efficiency solely in terms of *ex post* observable variables. In addition, it is shown that there exists a natural relationship between the measure of portfolio performance and the measure of efficiency.

B. Security price movements, efficient markets, martingales and their implication for security analysis

There has recently been considerable interest in the behavior of security prices in an "efficient market" and more specifically in the martingale hypothesis of price behavior. There seem to be two different forms of the hypothesis which have arisen out of differing definitions of the concept of an "efficient market," definitions which are seldom explicitly enumerated.

One can define a weakly efficient market in the following sense: Consider the arrival in the market of a new piece of information concerning the value of a security. A weakly efficient market is a market in which it may take time to evaluate this information with regard to its implications for the value of the security. Once this evaluation is complete, however, the price of the security immediately adjusts (in an unbiased fashion) to the new value implied by the information. In such a weakly efficient market, the past price series of a security will contain no information not already impounded in the current price. Mandelbrot [39] and Samuelson [47] have rigorously demonstrated that prices in such a market will follow a submartingale—that is, the expected value of all future prices $X(t + \tau)$,

$(\tau = 1, \ldots, \infty)$, as of time t is independent of the *sequence* of past prices $X(t - \tau)$, $(\tau = 1, \ldots, \infty)$, and is equal to:

$$E[X(t + \tau) \mid X(t), X(t - 1), X(t - 2), \ldots] = E[X(t + \tau) \mid X(t)]$$

$$= f(\tau) X(t) \qquad (1.1)$$

where $f(\tau)$ is the "normal" accumulation rate.

Thus, in a market in which security prices behave as a submartingale of the form of Eq. (1.1), forecasting techniques[2] which use only the sequence of past prices to forecast future prices are doomed to failure. The best forecast of future price is merely the present price plus the normal expected return over the period.

The stock market has been subjected to a great deal of empirical investigation aimed at determining whether Eq. (1.1) is an adequate description of the serial behavior of stock prices.[3] The available evidence suggests that it is highly unlikely that an investor or portfolio manager will be able to use the past history of stock prices alone (and hence mechanical trading rules based on these prices[4]) to increase his profits.

However, the conclusion that stock prices follow a submartingale of the form Eq. (1.1) does not imply that an investor cannot increase his profits by improving his ability to predict and evaluate the consequences of *future* events affecting stock prices. Indeed, it has been suggested by Fama [12] that the existence of sophisticated "market participants" who are adept at evaluating current information and predicting future events is one of the reasons why market prices at any point in time represent an unbiased estimate of "true" values and adjust rapidly, and accurately, to new information regarding these values.[5]

This brings us to an alternative definition of an "efficient market," that is, one in which *all* past information available up to time t is impounded in the current price. Within this definition of an efficient market the Mandelbrot-Samuelson proofs imply that the martingale property can be written as

$$E(X(t + \tau) \mid \theta_t) = f(\tau) X(t) \qquad (1.2)$$

where the conditioning variable θ_t now represents all information available at time t.[6] The reader will note that Eq. (1.2) is a much stronger form of the martingale hypothesis than Eq. (1.1), which is conditioned only on the past price series. As such Eq. (1.2) might be labeled the "strong" form of the

---

[2] Charting techniques are one example.
[3] See especially the work by Fama [12] and the works reprinted in Cootner [9].
[4] For an example of the testing of one class of such rules see [12].
[5] For an example of an examination of such adjustment, see Fama *et al.* [19].
[6] See Roll [46] for a discussion of the reasoning which leads to Eq. (1.2).

martingale hypothesis and Eq. (1.1) the "weak" form.[7] Indeed, if security prices follow a martingale of the strong form, no analyst will be able to earn above-average returns by attempting to predict future prices on the basis of *past* information. The only individual able to earn superior returns will be that person who occasionally is the first to acquire a new piece of information not generally available to others in the market. But as Roll [46] argues, in attempting to act immediately on this information, this individual (or group of individuals) will insure that the effects of this new information are quickly impounded in the security's price. Furthermore, if new information of this type arises randomly, no individual will be able to assure himself of systematic receipt of such information. Therefore, while an individual may occasionally realize such windfall returns, he will be unable to earn them systematically through time.

While the weak form of the martingale hypothesis is well substantiated by empirical evidence, the strong form of the hypothesis has not as yet been subjected to extensive empirical tests.[8] The model developed below will allow us to submit the strong form of the hypothesis to such an empirical test—at least to the extent that its implications are manifested in the success or failure of one particular class of extremely well-endowed security analysts.

C. Applications of the model

The portfolio evaluation model developed below will be used to examine the results achieved by the portfolio managers of open-end mutual funds in an attempt to answer the following questions:

1. Do the historical patterns of risk and return observed for our sample of portfolios of risky assets indicate a predominance of risk aversion in the capital markets? If so, do these patterns confirm the implications of the theoretical models of capital asset pricing founded on the assumption of risk aversion?

2. Have open-end mutual funds in general exhibited an ability to select portfolios which earn returns higher than those they may have been expected to earn given their level of risk? Alternatively, have they exhibited an ability to earn returns higher than those which could have been

---

[7] To the best of my knowledge, this terminology is due to Harry Roberts, who used it in an unpublished speech entitled "Clinical vs. Statistical Forecasts of Security Prices," given at the Seminar on the Analysis of Security Prices sponsored by the Center for Research in Security Prices at the University of Chicago, May, 1967.

Subsequent to writing the present paper, an article by Shelton [59] has appeared which contains a very similar statement of the hypotheses.

[8] The only evidence on this question that I am aware of is contained in Fama *et al.* [19], and that evidence suggests that security prices adjust rapidly and in an unbiased fashion to new information.

earned by a naïve selection policy consistent with the theory of capital asset pricing?

The main conclusions will be:

1. The observed historical patterns of systematic risk and return for the mutual funds in the sample are consistent with the joint hypothesis that the capital asset pricing model is valid and that the mutual fund managers on the average are unable to forecast future security prices.

2. If we assume that the capital asset pricing model is valid, then the empirical estimates of fund performance indicate that the fund portfolios were "inferior" after deduction of all management expenses and brokerage commissions generated in trading activity. In addition, when all management expenses and brokerage commissions are added back to the fund returns and the average cash balances of the funds are assumed to earn the riskless rate, the fund portfolios appeared to be just "neutral." Thus, it appears that on the average the resources spent by the funds in attempting to forecast security prices do not yield higher portfolio returns than those which could have been earned by equivalent risk portfolios selected (a) by random selection policies or (b) by combined investments in a "market portfolio" and government bonds.

3. Based on the evidence summarized above, we conclude that as far as these 115 mutual funds are concerned, prices of securities seem to behave according to the "strong" form of the martingale hypothesis. That is, it appears that the current prices of securities completely capture the effects of *all* information available to these 115 mutual funds. Therefore, their attempts to analyze past information more thoroughly have not resulted in increased returns.

Although these results certainly do not imply that the strong form of the martingale hypothesis holds for all investors and for all time, they provide strong evidence in support of that hypothesis. One must realize that these analysts are extremely well endowed.[9] Moreover, they operate in the securities markets every day and have wide-ranging contacts and associations in both the business and the financial communities. Thus, the fact that they are apparently unable to forecast returns accurately enough to recover their research and transactions costs is a striking piece of evidence in favor of the strong form of the martingale hypothesis—at least as far as the extensive subset of information available to these analysts is concerned.

4. The evidence also indicates that, while the portfolios of the funds on the average are "inferior" and "inefficient," this is due mainly to the

---

[9] For example, the total income received by eighty-six investment advisory firms from open-end investment companies amounted to $32.6 million in the fiscal years ending in 1960–61 (cf. Friend *et al.* [26, p. 497]).

generation of too many expenses. Since the evidence indicates that the portfolios on the average are very well diversified, they are "inefficient" mainly because of the generation of too many expenses.

D. An outline of the study

The portfolio evaluation model is developed in Sections II–V. The foundations of the model are discussed in Section II, which proceeds with a brief review of: (1) a theory of rational choice under uncertainty; (2) the normative theory of portfolio selection; and finally (3) a closely associated theoretical model of the pricing of capital assets under uncertainty.

Section III contains a development of the evaluation model under the assumption of homogeneous investor horizon periods. The "market model" and the concept of "systematic risk" are defined, and their application to the evaluation problem is discussed in detail. Finally, measures of portfolio "performance" are derived under alternative assumptions regarding the existence of finite or infinite variances for the distributions of returns.

Section IV contains a discussion of the "horizon problem," a solution to it, and the extension of the evaluation model to a world in which investors have heterogeneous horizon periods.*

Section V contains a discussion of the evaluation criteria, the derivation of a measure of "efficiency," and an examination of the relationship between the concepts of "performance" and "efficiency."

Section VI presents a discussion of (1) the empirical estimates of the concept of "systematic risk" for 115 mutual funds, (2) some empirical tests of the assumptions of the "market model," and (3) an application of the model to the evaluation of these 115 mutual fund portfolios.*

Section VII contains a summary of the theoretical and empirical results and their implications and a brief discussion of some of the main criticisms which will undoubtedly arise regarding the findings. The reader interested mainly in the empirical applications may obtain the general flavor of the model by a close examination of Sections III-A, III-B, and V.

II. THE FOUNDATIONS OF THE MODEL

A. A theory of rational choice under uncertainty

THE EXPECTED UTILITY MAXIM. The problem of choice under uncertainty is characterized by situations in which an individual faces a set of alternative actions, and the outcomes associated with these actions are subject to probability distributions. We shall assume in the development to follow that a rational individual, when faced with a choice under condi-

---

* [Sections IV and VI omitted here.—Ed.]

tions of uncertainty, acts in a manner consistent with the expected utility maxim. That is, he acts as if he (1) attaches numbers (utilities) to each possible outcome and (2) chooses that option (or strategy) with the largest expected value of utility.[10]

THE CONSUMPTION-INVESTMENT PROBLEM. Accepting the expected utility maxim as the objective function, the general problem of the investor in an uncertain world can be stated as the maximization of the expected value of

$$U = U(C_1, C_2, \ldots, C_t, \ldots, C_T, W_T), \tag{2.1}$$

where C_t is the real value of consumption in period t, T is the time of death (which, of course, is a random variable), W_T is the bequest, and U is the utility of the investor's lifetime consumption pattern. The portfolio problem arises within this framework when the investor has assets in one period which he does not wish to consume in that period, but rather desires to carry over into the next period. His portfolio problem at any time t then becomes the selection of a combination of investments which yield him maximum expected utility.

While the consumption-investment problem is most certainly a multi-period problem, the lack of a well-developed multiperiod theory of choice under uncertainty has led most researchers to assume that the portfolio decision can be treated as a *single-period* decision to be made independently of the consumption decision.[11] Necessary and sufficient conditions under which these simplifying assumptions will lead to an optimal solution of the unrestricted multiperiod problem of Eq. (2.1) have been determined only for a very restricted class of utility functions (cf. Hakansson [29] and Mossin [44]. However, Fama [15] has shown under very general conditions that, while the investor must solve a T-period problem like Eq. (2.1) in order to make consumption and investment decisions for period 1, he will behave *as though* he were a single-period expected utility maximizer. That is, the investor will appear to behave *as though* he were maximizing

$$E[U(C_t, W_{t+1})] \tag{2.2}$$

where C_t and W_{t+1} are, respectively, the value of consumption in period t and the terminal value of the portfolio at the end of period t, and his decision variables are C_t and x_i, the fraction of the portfolio invested in

---

[10] An axiomatic derivation of the expected utility maxim is given by Von Neuman and Morgenstern [65] and Markowitz [42]. In chapters x-xiii, Markowitz [42] gives a thorough exposition of the hypothesis and its implications for the portfolio decision in particular.

[11] See, for example, references [7, 13, 14, 22, 36, 37, 40, 42, 43, 51, 52, 61, and 62], all of which (either implicitly or explicitly) are single-period utility of terminal wealth models. That is, they assume the investor's problem can be characterized by the maximization of the expected value of $U(W_{t+1})$, where W_{t+1} is the terminal wealth of the portfolio one period hence.

the ith asset. In addition, if all assets are perfectly liquid[12] and infinitely divisible and there are no taxes,[13] Fama [16] has also demonstrated that, in solving the simultaneous consumption-investment problem of Eq. (2.2), the investor will always choose a portfolio which is efficient in terms of single-period parameters. That is, the investor will always choose a portfolio which is efficient in the sense that for the period under consideration it provides maximum expected return for given level of risk and minimum risk for given level of expected return. This means, of course, that the general conclusions obtained from previous work with single-period utility of terminal wealth models regarding the portfolio decisions of risk-averse investors and the characteristics of general equilibrium remain valid when consumption and investment are jointly considered.

Since a Von Neuman-Morgenstern utility function is unique only up to a positive linear transformation, and since the return on the portfolio is $R_t = \Delta W_t / W_t = (W_{t+1}/W_t) - 1$, we can express the investor's consumption-portfolio problem as

$$\underset{x_i}{\text{Max}}\, E[U(C_t, R_t)] \tag{2.3}$$

and we assume U is monotone increasing and strictly concave in (C_t, R_t). (We state Eq. (2.3) in terms of R because it is more convenient and avoids problems with scale in making comparisons of portfolios later on.)

We have now set the foundation for consideration of the normative mean-variance portfolio models of Markowitz [40, 42] and Tobin [61, 62], which in turn provide much of the motivation for the Sharpe [52] and Lintner [37] models of general equilibrium conditions in the capital asset markets. As we shall see, these results provide the key to the solution of the portfolio evaluation problem.

Thus, let us turn to a brief review of the mean-variance portfolio models. Suffice it to say that all of these models are based on the existence of finite variances for the distributions of security returns. Empirical work by Mandelbrot [38], Fama [12], and Roll [46], however, indicates that the distributions of returns on common stocks and bonds seem to conform to the members of the Stable class of distributions for which the mean

---

[12] An asset is perfectly liquid if (a) at any particular time the buying and selling prices are identical and (b) any quantity can be bought or sold at this price. Thus, transactions costs are assumed to be equal to zero.

[13] In the empirical tests to come later, this may seem to be a significant restriction, for an investor in a high marginal income tax bracket will certainly not be indifferent to the form (capital gains or income dividends) in which he receives his returns. However, in practice this may not be as restrictive an assumption as we might believe. Horowitz [30], examining the properties of a model for ranking mutual funds, finds that the explicit allowance for differential tax rates on income and capital gains results in only minor effects on the relative rankings of ninety-eight funds. In choosing a portfolio for a particular investor, however, these tax considerations must be taken into account.

exists but the variance does not.[14] At this time we merely point out that Fama [13, 16] has demonstrated that with some modifications most of the results obtained for the special case of finite variances also extend to the more general case where the distributions on returns are allowed to be any symmetric member of the class of Stable distributions with finite mean.

We continue the discussion in the mean-variance framework for the moment under the assumption that the probability distributions of all security returns have finite variances. The extension of the mean-variance results to a world characterized by distributions of returns with infinite variances will be considered in Section III-C.

B. The normative theory of portfolio analysis

THE EXPECTED UTILITY MAXIM AND THE DIVERSIFICATION OF IN-VESTMENTS. Markowitz [40, 42] and Tobin [61, 62] have shown that diversification is the logical consequence for risk-averse investors whose objective function[15] can be written as

$$\underset{x_i}{\text{Max }} E[U(R_t)] \qquad (2.4)$$

In particular, the utility maximizing portfolio for any investor will be a mean-variance efficient portfolio in the sense that it offers minimum variance for a given level of expected return and maximum expected return for a given level of variance if (1) the investor's utility function Eq. (2.4) meets the condition that $U' > 0$ and $U'' < 0$, and (2) the distributions of asset and portfolio returns are of the same form[16] and are completely described by two parameters (cf. Tobin [61, 62]). These conditions imply that all asset returns must be normally distributed for mean-variance efficiency to be meaningful.[17] In addition, Fama [16] has demonstrated

---

[14] It may be noted here that the Gaussian or normal distribution is the special case of this class of distributions with characteristic exponent $\alpha = 2$.

[15] By Fama's results [15, 16] we have seen that the conclusions drawn from an investigation of the implications of Eq. (2.4) also hold for the solution to Eq. (2.1). Thus, for simplicity, from this point on we shall ignore the consumption decision, C_t, and couch our discussion in terms of the single-period utility of return function given by Eq. (2.4).

[16] This qualification is extremely important and often overlooked. Samuelson [48] presents a simple example of a two-parameter distribution for which the analysis fails for precisely this reason. It is also interesting to note that the Stable class of distributions (cf. Feller [23, chap. xvii]) are the only distributions which are stable under addition. That is, Stable distributions are the only distributions for which weighted sums of random variables (i.e., a portfolio) will have the same form as the underlying random variables. But this means the only distribution for which the mean-variance version of the Tobin theorem holds is the normal (cf. Fama [16]).

[17] The assumption of quadratic utility functions is often made to guarantee that the utility maximizing portfolio will be mean variance efficient. However, Borch [5] provides an example which illustrates that this line of reasoning must be used very carefully.

FIGURE 1

THE MAXIMIZATION OF INVESTOR UTILITY GIVEN THE
EXISTENCE OF A RISK-FREE ASSET

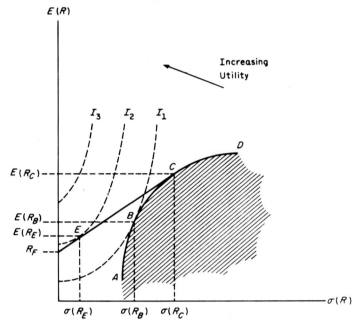

that this theorem can be extended to the general class of symmetric Stable distributions with finite first moment (which, incidentally, seem to describe the empirical distributions of security returns quite well; cf. Fama [12], Mandelbrot [38], and Roll [46]). But we defer discussion of this point to Section III-C.

Figure 1 gives a geometric presentation of the Markowitz mean-variance model. Letting $\sigma(R)$ be the standard deviation of future return, the shaded area in Figure 1 represents all possible combinations of risk and return available from investments in risk-bearing securities. The portfolios lying on the boundary $ABCD$ represent the set of mean standard deviation (or mean variance) efficient portfolios, since they all represent possible investments yielding maximum expected returns for given risk and minimum risk for given expected returns.

As Tobin [61] has shown, the normality of security returns and the existence of risk aversion on the part of the investor are sufficient to yield a family of positively sloping convex indifference curves (represented by I_1, I_2, I_3) in the mean standard deviation plane of Figure 1. The shaded area in Figure 1 represents the opportunity set available to the investor in the absence of a riskless asset, and the boundary of this set $ABCD$

represents the set of efficient portfolios in the Markowitz sense. An investor limited only to investments in *risky assets* who has the particular indifference map shown in Figure 1 will maximize his expected future utility with an investment in portfolio B, yielding $E(R_B)$ and $\sigma(R_B)$ with utility I_1.

IMPLICATIONS OF THE EXISTENCE OF A RISKLESS ASSET. Portfolio B portrayed in Figure 1 represents an optimal solution to the portfolio problem only in the case where investment is restricted to risky assets. Let us now assume the existence of a risk-free asset F, yielding a certain future return R_F as drawn in Figure 1.[18] An investor faced with the possibility of an investment in such a risk-free asset, as well as in a risky asset, can construct a portfolio of the two assets which will allow him to reach any combination of risk and return lying along a straight line connecting the two assets in the mean standard deviation plane (cf. Tobin [61]). Clearly, all portfolios lying below point C along $ABCD$ in Figure 1 are inefficient, since any point on the line R_FC given by

$$E(R) = R_F + \frac{E(R_C) - R_F}{\sigma(R_C)} \cdot \sigma(R) \qquad \sigma(R) < \sigma(R_C) \qquad (2.5)$$

represents a feasible solution. Thus, the investor may distribute his funds between portfolio C and security F such that his combined portfolio, call it E, yields him $E(R_E)$, $\sigma(R_E)$, and maximum utility of $I_2 > I_1$. In addition, if the investor can borrow as well as lend at the riskless rate R_F, the set of feasible portfolios represented by the line R_FC and Eq. (2.5) extends beyond point C.

C. A theory of capital asset prices

Sharpe [52], Lintner [36, 37], and Mossin [43] starting with the normative models of Markowitz and Tobin have developed similar theories of capital market equilibrium under conditions of risk. The following assumptions underlie all three models: (1) all investors have identical horizon periods; (2) all investors may borrow as well as lend funds at the riskless rate of interest; and (3) investors have homogeneous expectations regarding expected future return and standard deviation of return on all assets and all covariances of returns among all assets. Sharpe observed that investors would attempt to purchase *only* those assets in portfolio C and the riskless security F of Figure 1. Thus, we have a situation in which

---

[18] Such an instrument might be cash (yielding no positive monetary return), an insured savings account, or a non-coupon-bearing government bond having a maturity date coincident to the investor's horizon date. In the latter case, of course, the investor can be assured of realizing the yield to maturity with certainty if he holds the bond to maturity. Since we have assumed the investor will not change his portfolio in the interim period, any intermediate fluctuations in price do not present him with risk. We are ignoring the problems associated with changes in the general price level and shall continue to do so in the remainder of the paper.

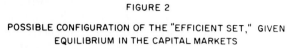

FIGURE 2

POSSIBLE CONFIGURATION OF THE "EFFICIENT SET," GIVEN
EQUILIBRIUM IN THE CAPITAL MARKETS

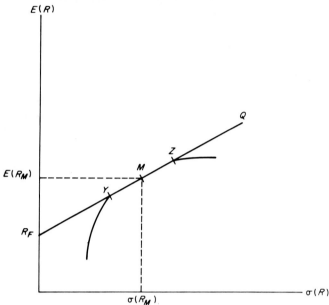

the market for capital assets would be out of equilibrium unless C is the "market portfolio," that is, a portfolio which contains every asset exactly in proportion to that asset's fraction of the total value of all assets. Conceptually, if the market were out of equilibrium the prices of assets in C would be instantaneously bid up and the prices of assets not in C would fall until such time as all assets were held.

In equilibrium, all investors who select *ex ante* efficient portfolios will have mean standard deviation combinations which lie along the line R_FQ in Figure 2, their individual location determined by their degree of risk aversion. Sharpe [52] has asserted that in equilibrium the efficient set may be tangent to R_FQ at multiple points as in Figure 2. However, whether or not this ever occurs,[19] the market portfolio M must always be one of the tangency points (cf. Fama [14] and Fama and Miller [20]).

Most important, however, is the result that in equilibrium the expected return on any *efficient portfolio* ϵ will be linearly related to the ex-

[19] While it is possible for multiple tangency points to exist, it is highly improbable that this would ever occur. The existence of multiple tangency points would require that the returns on one or more individual securities were perfectly correlated with those of the market portfolio M.

pected return on the market portfolio in the following manner:[20]

$$E[R_\epsilon \mid E(R_M), \sigma(R_\epsilon)] = R_F + \frac{E(R_M) - R_F}{\sigma(R_M)} \sigma(R_\epsilon) \qquad (2.6)$$

THE CONCEPT OF SYSTEMATIC RISK. In addition, Sharpe, Lintner, and Mossin have shown that if the capital market is in equilibrium the expected return on any *individual security* (or portfolio) will be a linear function of the covariance of its returns with that of the market portfolio.[21] The function is:

$$E[R_j \mid E(R_M), \mathrm{cov}\ (R_j, R_M)] = R_F + \frac{E(R_M) - R_F}{\sigma^2(R_M)} \mathrm{cov}\ (R_j, R_M) \qquad (2.7)$$

It is important to note that Eq. (2.6) holds *only* for efficient portfolios and Eq. (2.7) holds for any individual security or any portfolio regardless of whether it is efficient. Thus, as long as we are concerned with risk in the context of efficiently diversified portfolios and can assume that the capital markets are in equilibrium, Eq. (2.7) implies that the relevant measure of the riskiness of any security (or portfolio) is the quantity cov (R_j, R_M), and the market price per unit of risk is $[E(R_M) - R_F]/\sigma^2(R_M)$.

We shall see in Section III that this result, Eq. (2.7), will become the foundation of the portfolio evaluation model discussed there. Thus, a detailed discussion of the implications of Eq. (2.7) is given in Section III.

III. THE SINGLE-PERIOD HOMOGENEOUS HORIZON MODEL

The reader will recall that one of the assumptions made in the derivation of the asset pricing model was that all investors are one-period expected utility maximizers having a common horizon date. The assumption of identical investor decision horizons is admittedly unrealistic, but for the moment we proceed with the development of the model within this context. It will be shown in Section IV that the asset pricing model and the portfolio evaluation model based on it can be extended to a world in which investors have horizon periods of different lengths and trading of assets is allowed to take place continuously through time.

A. A standard of comparison

A major problem encountered in developing a portfolio evaluation model is the establishment of a norm or standard for use as a bench mark. The discussion of Section II points to a natural standard—the performance

---

[20] For reasons which will become clear below, we choose to write equations like Eqs. (2.6) and (2.7) recognizing only two of the conditioning variables explicitly on the left-hand side. These variables become crucial to distinctions we wish to maintain below.

[21] We note here that Jack Treynor also had independently arrived at these results at about the same time as Sharpe and Lintner. Unfortunately, his excellent work [64] remains unpublished.

of the market portfolio, M. As long as the market is in equilibrium we know that ex ante this portfolio must be a member of the efficient set. *Ex post*, of course, this portfolio will not dominate all others, since in a stochastic model such as this, realized returns will seldom be equal to expectations.

The market portfolio also offers another interpretation as a standard of comparison, since it represents the results which could have been realized (ignoring transaction costs) by one particular naïve investment strategy, that is, purchasing each security in the market in proportion to its share of the total value of all securities.

Thus, the concept of the market portfolio provides a natural point of comparison. However, as mentioned earlier, we cannot compare returns on portfolios with differing degrees of risk to the same standard; but this problem may be resolved by reference to the asset pricing model discussed in Section II. Recall that the Sharpe-Lintner asset pricing model indicates that the expected return on any asset (or portfolio of assets) is given by Eq. (2.7)

$$E\left[R_j \mid E(R_M), \frac{\text{cov }(R_j, R_M)}{\sigma^2(R_M)}\right] = R_F + [E(R_M) - R_F]\frac{\text{cov }(R_j, R_M)}{\sigma^2(R_M)}$$

Let us define

$$\beta_{1j} = \frac{\text{cov }(R_j, R_M)}{\sigma^2(R_M)} \tag{3.1}$$

so that we now measure the risk of any security[22] j relative to the risk of the market portfolio. (The term β_{1j} will henceforth be referred to as the "systematic" risk of the jth asset or portfolio, and the first subscript, here 1, will be used to distinguish between three alternative interpretations of the coefficient.) Thus, if the asset pricing model is valid and the capital market is in equilibrium, the expected one-period return on any asset (or portfolio of assets) will be a linear function of the quantity β_1 as portrayed in Figure 3. The point M represents the expected return and systematic risk of the market portfolio, and the point R_F represents the return on the risk-free asset. Since we are measuring risk relative to the risk of the market portfolio, it is obvious that the risk of the market portfolio is unity, since

$$\beta_{1M} = \text{cov }(R_M, R_M)/\sigma^2(R_M) = \sigma^2(R_M)/\sigma^2(R_M) = 1$$

Thus, conditional on the expected returns on the market portfolio and the risk-free rate, Eq. (2.7) gives us the relationship between the ex-

---

[22] Henceforth, we shall use the terms "asset" and "security" interchangeably.

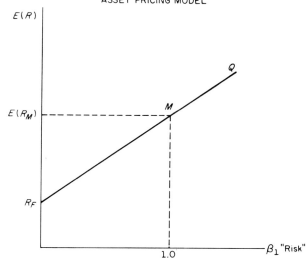

FIGURE 3

THE RELATIONSHIP BETWEEN THE EXPECTED RETURN
ON ANY ASSET (OR COLLECTION OF ASSETS) AND
SYSTEMATIC RISK (β_1) AS IMPLIED BY THE CAPITAL
ASSET PRICING MODEL

pected returns on any asset (or collection of assets) and its level of systematic risk β_{1j}. However, since expectations can be observed only with error, these results will be much more useful if they can be translated into a relationship between *ex post* realizations.[23] We now show how this may be accomplished by utilizing the additional structure imposed on the asset pricing model by the assumptions of what Blume [4] and Fama [14, 16] have called the "market model." In Part B we consider the model under the assumption that the distributions of returns are normal and in Part C under the assumption that the distributions of returns conform to the infinite variance (but finite mean) members of the symmetric Stable family of distributions.

B. Systematic risk in the context of the Gaussian market model

THE MODEL. The market model was originally suggested by Markowitz [42, p. 100] and analyzed in considerable detail by Sharpe [51, 52,

---

[23] For a discussion of the problems and issues which can arise around just this question regarding *ex ante* relationships, see West [66] and Sharpe [58]. While the criticisms raised by West are legitimate, we shall see below that the problems can be completely surmounted in that we can derive explicit relationships between *ex post* variables which still yield testable results. This same issue also arises in the debate contained in [8] and [28].

57], who referred to it as the "diagonal model." Simply stated, the model postulates a linear relationship between the returns on any security and a general "market factor." [24] That is, we express the returns on the jth security as

$$R_j = E(R_j) + b_j\pi + e_j \qquad j = 1, 2 \ldots, N \qquad (3.2)$$

where the "market factor" π is defined such that $E(\pi) = 0$, b_j is a constant, π and e_j are all normally distributed random variables, and N is the total number of securities in the market. The following assumptions are made regarding the disturbance terms e_j:

$$E(e_j) = 0 \qquad j = 1, 2, \ldots, N \qquad (3.3a)$$

$$E(e_j\pi) = 0 \qquad j = 1, 2, \ldots, N \qquad (3.3b)$$

$$E(e_je_i) = \begin{cases} 0 & i \neq j \\ \sigma^2(e_j) & i = j \end{cases} \qquad (3.3c)$$

Now let V_j be the total value of all units of the jth security outstanding. Then

$$x_j = V_j / \sum_{i=1}^{N} V_i$$

is the fraction of the jth security in the market portfolio defined earlier. The returns on the market portfolio R_M are given by

$$R_M = \sum_j x_j R_j = \sum_j x_j E(R_j) + \sum_j x_j b_j \pi + \sum_j x_j e_j. \qquad (3.4)$$

As Blume [4] and Fama [16] have pointed out, the market factor π is unique up to a linear transformation, and thus we can always change the

---

[24] The model described by Eqs. (3.2) and (3.3) is slightly different from the diagonal model originally proposed by Markowitz, analyzed by Sharpe, and empirically tested by Blume [4]. The model is

$$R_j = A_j + B_j I + u_j, \qquad (3.2a)$$

where I is some index of market returns, u_j is a random variable uncorrelated with I, and A_j and B_j are constants. The differences in specification in Eq. (3.2) are necessary in order to avoid the overspecification pointed out by Fama [14] which arises if one chooses to interpret the market index I as an average of security returns or as the returns on the market portfolio M (cf. Lintner [37] and Sharpe [52, 56]). That is, if I is some average of security returns, then the assumption that u_j is uncorrelated with I cannot hold, since I contains u_j.

scale of π such that[25]

$$\sum_j x_j b_j = 1$$

Hence, with no loss of generality, we assume this transformation and reduce Eq. (3.4) to

$$R_M = E(R_M) + \pi + \sum_j x_j e_j \qquad (3.5)$$

Now we saw earlier that the measure of systematic risk is cov (R_j, R_M). By direct substitution from Eqs. (3.2) and (3.5) into the definition of the covariance,

$$\text{cov } (R_j, R_M) = \text{cov } \{[E(R_j) + b_j\pi + e_j],[E(R_M) + \pi + \sum_i x_i e_i]\}$$

$$= b_j\sigma^2(\pi) + x_j\sigma^2(e_j) \qquad j = 1, 2, \ldots, N \qquad (3.6)$$

and

$$\sigma^2(R_M) = \sigma^2(\pi) + \sum_j x_j^2\sigma^2(e_j) \qquad (3.7)$$

Hence, restating the results of the capital asset pricing model given in Eq. (2.7) in terms of the parameters of the market model, we have[26]

$$E[R_j \mid E(R_M), (\cdot)] = R_F + [E(R_M) - R_F]\left[\frac{b_j\sigma^2(\pi) + x_j\sigma^2(e_j)}{\sigma^2(R_M)}\right] \qquad (3.8)$$

where $(\cdot)$ refers to the arguments in brackets on the RHS of Eq. (3.8). Now define

$$\beta_{2j} = \frac{b_j\sigma^2(\pi) + x_j\sigma^2(e_j)}{\sigma^2(R_M)} \qquad (3.9)$$

[25] Reproducing Fama's argument directly, if we have the untransformed market factor π^* and

$$\sum_j x_j b_j^* \neq 1$$

where the b_j^* are defined by $R_j = E(R_j) + b_j^*\pi^* + e_j$, we can create

$$\pi = \pi^* \sum_j x_j b_j^*$$

Now $R_j = E(R_j) + b_j\pi + e_j$, where

$$b_j = b_j^*/\sum_i x_i b_i^*$$

and

$$\sum_j x_j b_j = 1$$

[26] This is essentially the same expression as Lintner [37] arrived at, but as we have seen, and as Fama [14] has already shown, the results of Sharpe originally stated in Eq. (2.7) are in no way inconsistent with Eq. (3.8).

which is the measure of systematic risk in the context of the Gaussian market model. All previous discussion regarding the interpretation of β_{1j} also applies to β_{2j}.

However, Eq. (3.9) can be considerably simplified by noting that we can invoke several approximations and thereby eliminate the strictly unobservable market factor π from the expression. The results of King[27] [34] and Blume[28] [4] imply that the market factor π accounts for approximately 50 percent of the variability of individual security returns.[29] Since $\sigma^2(R_j) = b_j^2\sigma^2(\pi) + \sigma^2(e_j)$, and since the average b_j is equal to unity, the results of King and Blume imply that $\sigma^2(e_j)$ is roughly the same order of magnitude as $\sigma^2(\pi)$.

Let us examine the expression for $\sigma^2(R_M)$ in light of these facts. The last term on the RHS of Eq. (3.7) can be approximately expressed as

$$\sum_j x_j^2\sigma^2(e_j) \cong \frac{N}{N^2}\overline{\sigma^2(e)} = \frac{1}{N}\overline{\sigma^2(e)} \tag{3.10}$$

where $\overline{\sigma^2(e)}$ is the average variance of the disturbance terms. Recall that since x_j is the ratio of the value of the jth security to the total value of all securities, it must on the average be on the order of $1/N$, where N is the total number of distinct securities in the market. Since there are more than 1,000 securities on the New York Stock Exchange alone, x_j will be much smaller than $1/1000$ on the average,[30] and thus Eq. (3.10) will be minute relative to $\sigma^2(\pi)$. Hence,

$$\sigma^2(R_M) \cong \sigma^2(\pi) \tag{3.11}$$

---

[27] King examined sixty-three securities in the period June, 1927, to December, 1960, by methods of factor analysis. He found that the market factor on the average accounts for approximately 50 percent of the variability of the monthly returns on the individual securities, and various industry factors account for another 10 percent. We have ignored these industry factors in constructing the model, since they are relatively unimportant and their inclusion would introduce a great deal of additional complexity.

[28] Blume, using regression analysis, also finds that a market index accounts for an average of 50 percent of the variability of the monthly returns on 251 securities in the period January, 1927, to December, 1960.

[29] There is some indication in Blume's results, however, that this proportion may be declining in recent times.

[30] There are some firms, of course, for which x_j is much larger than $1/1000$. Data obtained from Standard & Poor's indicates that as of December 31, 1964, the four largest firms on the New York Stock Exchange and their percentages of the total values of the Standard & Poor Composite 500 Index were: A.T. & T., 9.1 percent; General Motors, 7.3 percent; I.B.M., 3.7 percent; and DuPont, 2.9 percent. Thus, the largest value that the fraction x_j could take in 1964 was .091, and even this is an overstatement, since the 500 securities were obviously not the total universe—which, of course, includes all other exchanges, unlisted securities, and debt instruments as well.

Substituting for $\sigma^2(\pi)$ in Eq. (3.9), we have

$$\beta_{2j} \cong \frac{b_j\sigma^2(R_M) + x_j\sigma^2(e_j)}{\sigma^2(R_M)}$$

$$= b_j + \frac{x_j\sigma^2(e_j)}{\sigma^2(R_M)} \tag{3.12}$$

For simplicity, let us define

$$z_j = \frac{x_j\sigma^2(e_j)}{\sigma^2(R_M)} \tag{3.13}$$

Substituting for $E(R_j)$ from Eqs. (3.8) and (3.9) into Eq. (3.2), we have

$$R_j = E(R_j) + b_j\pi + e_j$$

$$= R_F(1 - \beta_{2j}) + \beta_{2j}E(R_M) + b_j\pi + e_j \tag{3.14}$$

Adding and subtracting $z_j\pi$ and

$$\beta_{2j} \sum_i x_i e_i$$

on the RHS of Eq. (3.14) gives

$$R_j = R_F(1 - \beta_{2j}) + \beta_{2j}E(R_M) + b_j\pi + z_j\pi$$

$$+ \beta_{2j} \sum_i x_i e_i - z_j\pi - \beta_{2j} \sum_i x_i e_i + e_j \tag{3.15}$$

Noting that $\beta_{2j} \cong b_j + z_j$, using the definition of R_M from Eq. (3.5) and simplifying, we get

$$R_j = R_F(1 - \beta_{2j}) + R_M\beta_{2j} - z_j\pi - \beta_{2j} \sum_i x_i e_i + e_j \tag{3.16}$$

Now we have an *ex post* relationship in which all the important variables are measurable.[31] By assumption Eq. (3.3a), $E(e_j) = 0$. Thus, elim-

---

[31] Note that $z_j\pi$ will be trivially small, since by our previous arguments $\sigma^2(e_j) \cong \sigma^2(\pi) \cong \sigma^2(R_M)$ and x_j is on the average less than 1/1000. Thus,

$$z_j\pi = \frac{x_j\sigma^2(e_j)}{\sigma^2(R_M)}\pi \cong x_j\pi \cong \frac{1}{1000}\pi$$

and is unimportant.
  Note that

$$\beta_{2j} \sum_i x_i e_i$$

will be unimportant also, since by assumption the e_j are independently distributed random variables with $E(e_j) = 0$. We have already seen that the variance of this weighted average (given by Eq. [3.10]) will be minute. But since

$$E\left(\sum_i x_i e_i\right) = \sum_i x_i E(e_i) = 0$$

and its variance is extremely small, it is unlikely that it will be very different from zero at any given time.

inating $z_j\pi$ and $\beta_{2j}\sum_i x_i e_i$ from Eq. (3.16) by the arguments of footnote 31, we see that to a very close approximation the *conditional* expected return on the jth security is given by

$$E(R_j \mid R_M, \beta_{2j}) \cong R_F(1 - \beta_{2j}) + R_M\beta_{2j} \qquad (3.17)$$

Equation (3.17) is an important result. It gives us an expression for the expected return on security j conditional on the *ex post* realization of the return on the market portfolio.[32] Recall that Eq. (2.7), the result of the capital asset pricing model, provides only an expression for the expected return on the jth security conditional on the *ex ante* expectation of the return on the market portfolio. This result (Eq. [3.17]) becomes extremely important in considering the empirical application of the model.[33] We now have shown that we can explicitly use the observed *realization* of the return on the market portfolio without worrying about using it as a proxy for the expected return and without worrying about devising an ad hoc expectations-generating scheme.

THE MEASURE OF PORTFOLIO PERFORMANCE IN THE CONTEXT OF GAUSSIAN DISTRIBUTIONS. Using Eqs. (3.16) and (3.17), we can now define an *ex post* measure of portfolio performance as

$$\delta_{2j} = R_j - E(R_j \mid R_M, \beta_{2j})$$

$$= R_j - [R_F(1 - \beta_{2j}) + R_M\beta_{2j}]$$

$$= z_j\pi - \beta_{2j}\sum_i x_i e_i + e_j \qquad (3.18)$$

But by our previous arguments, the quantity $z_j\pi$ will be minute. In addition, the likelihood of $\beta_{2j}\sum x_i e_i$ ever being much different from zero is extremely small, since its expected value is equal to zero and its variance is close to zero (cf. footnote 31). By these arguments, we may ignore these

---

[32] Of course, as far as the algebraic manipulations are concerned, we do not need the market model to get this result. However, the implications of the results derived in the absence of the market model are not consistent with the observed behavior of the world. That is, consider the formulation in which π always equals zero. The *ex post* returns on the market portfolio would be given by

$$R_M = E(R_M) + \sum_i x_i e_i$$

But in the discussion above, we saw that the last term has expectation equal to zero and an infinitesimal variance. Thus, this formulation implies that the realized returns on the market portfolio would never differ from the expected returns by any amount of consequence—a result clearly contradicted by the behavior of real world prices.

[33] See, for example, the discussions in references [8, 28, 58, and 66] regarding the problems associated with testing models stated in terms of *ex ante* relationships on *ex post* empirical data.

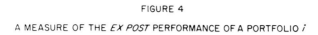

FIGURE 4

A MEASURE OF THE *EX POST* PERFORMANCE OF A PORTFOLIO *i*

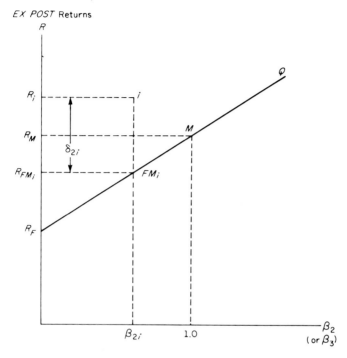

terms in Eq. (3.18), and we have to a close approximation

$$\delta_{2j} \cong e_j \tag{3.19}$$

Figure 4 gives a geometric presentation of these concepts. The point M represents the *realized* returns on the market portfolio, and of course its systematic risk (plotted on the abscissa) is unity.[34] The point R_F represents the returns on the risk-free asset, and the equation of the line $R_F M Q$ is

$$E(R \mid R_M, \beta_2) = R_F + (R_M - R_F)\beta_2 \tag{3.20}$$

Let the point i represent the *ex post* returns R_i on any portfolio i and let β_{2i} be its level of systematic risk. Then the vertical distance between the risk-return combination of any portfolio i and the line $R_F M Q$ in Figure 4 is our measure of the performance of portfolio i.

[34] Note that β_2 merely represents the specific expression for risk in the context of the infinite variance market model and will be defined below.

The measure δ_2 may also be interpreted in the following manner: Let FM_i be a portfolio consisting of a combined investment in the risk-free asset F and the market portfolio M offering the same degree of risk β_{2i} as the portfolio i. Now δ_{2i} may be interpreted as the difference in return realized on the ith portfolio and the return R_{FM_i} which could have been earned on the equivalent risk market portfolio FM_i. If $\delta_{2i} \geq 0$, the portfolio i has yielded the investor a return greater than or equal to the return on a combined investment in M and F with an identical level of systematic risk. It should be noted that since Eq. (3.18) is stated in terms of the *observed* return on the market portfolio, the performance measure δ_{2i} allows for the actual relationship between risk and return which existed during the particular holding period examined.

A discussion of the criteria to be used in judging a portfolio's performance will be postponed until Section V, at which time the entire model will have been developed. Meanwhile, in the next section we shall consider the extension of the model to a world in which the distributions of security returns are non-Gaussian members of the Stable class.

C. Systematic risk and the Stable market model

THE MODEL. As mentioned earlier, there is considerable empirical evidence (Fama [12], Mandelbrot [38], Roll [46]) indicating that distributions of security returns conform to the members of the Stable class of distributions which have finite means but infinite variances. However, Fama [13] has shown that the market model can be used to develop a portfolio model analogous to the mean-variance models of Markowitz, Tobin, and Sharpe in the context of a market in which returns are generated by non-Gaussian finite mean members of the Stable family of distributions. Moreover, Fama [16] has also demonstrated that the Sharpe-Lintner capital asset pricing models can be generalized to a market characterized by returns with infinite variance distributions. The following discussion draws heavily on his extension of the asset pricing model. The reader is referred to Fama [16] for proofs. We begin with a few brief comments on the parameters of Stable distributions.[35]

Stable distributions have four parameters, α, β, δ, and γ. The parameter α is called the characteristic exponent and has range $0 < \alpha \leq 2$. The special case of the Stable distribution with $\alpha = 2$ is the Gaussian or normal distribution and is the only distribution with finite second- and higher-order moments.

The parameter β with range $-1 \leq \beta \leq 1$ determines the skewness of the distribution. When $\beta = 0$ the distribution is symmetric, when $\beta > 0$ the distribution is skewed left, and when $\beta < 0$ the distribution is

[35] For a much more complete description of properties of Stable distributions, see the Appendix in Fama [12] and the references therein.

skewed right. We assume in the following discussion (as does Fama) that we are dealing with symmetric distributions,[36] and therefore $\beta = 0$.

The parameter δ is the location parameter of the distribution, and for distributions with $\beta = 0$ and $1 < \alpha \leq 2$, δ is the expected value or mean. For distributions with $0 < \alpha \leq 1$, the mean does not exist, but for distributions with $\beta = 0$, δ is the median. As Fama [13] has shown, diversification is meaningless in a market characterized by distributions with $\alpha \leq 1$. In addition, Fama [12] and Roll [46] find that estimates of the characteristic exponent α for common stocks and U.S. Treasury bills indicate $\alpha \geq 1$. Thus, we also assume in the following that $1 < \alpha \leq 2$ and therefore $\delta(R) = E(R)$.

The final parameter $\gamma (\gamma > 0)$ defines the scale or dispersion of the Stable distribution. For the Gaussian distribution with $\alpha = 2$, $\gamma = \frac{1}{2}\sigma^2$ where σ^2 is the variance. Unfortunately, as mentioned earlier, when $\alpha < 2$ the variance does not exist and analytical solutions for the exact definition of γ are known only for several special cases; for example, for the Cauchy case $(\alpha = 1)$, γ is exactly equal to the semi-interquartile range.[37] Fama and Roll [21] have demonstrated that for α in the range $1 < \alpha \leq 2$, γ corresponds approximately to the semi-interquartile range raised to the α power.

The Stable market model again consists of Eq. (3.2):

$$R_j = E(R_j) + b_j\pi + e_j \qquad j = 1, 2, \ldots, N \qquad [3.2]$$

with all the variables defined as before. However, in place of Eq. (3.3) it is now assumed that π and e_j $(j = 1, 2, \ldots, N)$ are independently distributed symmetric Stable variables all having the same characteristic exponent α, $(1 < \alpha \leq 2)$. The location parameters of π and e_j are, respectively, $\delta(\pi) = E(\pi) = 0$, $\delta(e_j) = E(e_j) = 0$ $(j = 1, 2, \ldots, N)$, and their dispersion parameters are $\gamma(\pi)$ and $\gamma(e_j)$ $(j = 1, 2, \ldots, N)$. Under these conditions, the location parameter of R_j is $E(R_j)$ and the scale parameter of R_j is given by

$$\gamma(R_j) = \gamma(\pi) \, | \, b_j \, |^\alpha + \gamma(e_j) \qquad (3.21)$$

By the same arguments as in the finite variance case, the return on the market portfolio is given by

$$R_M = E(R_M) + \pi + \sum_j x_j e_j \qquad [3.5]$$

---

[36] The assumption of symmetry seems to be satisfied quite well by the empirical distributions of security returns stated in terms of continuously compounded rates. Furthermore, we shall see in Section IV that the solution to the "horizon" problem implies that all returns must be measured as continuously compounded rates in order for the model to hold. Thus, the assumption of symmetry seems quite appealing.

[37] Defined as half the difference between the .75 and .25 fractiles.

and the scale parameter of the distribution of the returns on the market portfolio is

$$\gamma(R_M) = \gamma(\pi) + \sum_j \gamma(e_j) \mid x_j \mid^\alpha \qquad (3.22)$$

More significantly, Fama has demonstrated (by arguments directly analogous to those of Sharpe and Lintner presented earlier) that, given the assumptions of the Stable market model (and the previously stated assumptions necessary to the Sharpe-Lintner model), the expected return on any security j will be given by

$$E(R_j) = R_F + [E(R_M) - R_F] \left[\frac{\gamma(\pi)b_j + \gamma(e_j) \mid x_j \mid^{\alpha-1}}{\gamma(R_M)} \right] \qquad (3.23)$$

Equation (3.23) is directly comparable to the results given in Eq. (3.8), which were arrived at under the assumption of finite variances. (Note that in the case $\alpha = 2$, Eq. [3.23] reduces directly to Eq. [3.8].)

Now define

$$\beta_{3j} = \frac{\gamma(\pi)b_j + \gamma(e_j) \mid x_j \mid^{\alpha-1}}{\gamma(R_M)} \qquad (3.24)$$

which is the measure of systematic risk in the context of the Stable market model. As before, all previous discussion regarding β_{1j} and β_{2j} also applies to β_{3j}.

Hence, we see that by making use of the characteristics of the market model, the capital asset pricing model can be extended to the case of infinite variance distributions where the concept of a covariance is undefined.

However, as in the finite variance case (and at the expense again of some degree of approximation), the expression for systematic risk Eq. (3.24) can be considerably simplified. As before, the results of King [34] and Blume [4] indicate that on the average the terms $\gamma(\pi)$ and $\gamma(e_j)$ are of about equal size. Likewise as before, the average x_j is on the order of $1/N$, N being very large. Hence, the last term on the RHS of Eq. (3.22) is approximately equal to

$$\sum_j \gamma(e_j) \mid x_j \mid^\alpha \cong \frac{N}{N^\alpha} \overline{\gamma(e)} = \frac{1}{N^{\alpha-1}} \overline{\gamma(e)} \qquad (3.25)$$

where $\overline{\gamma(e)}$ is the average scale parameter of the disturbance terms. But since we have assumed $\alpha > 1$ and since empirical evidence (cf. Fama [12]) indicates $1.6 \leq \alpha < 1.9$, this term will be small relative to $\gamma(\pi)$. Thus,

$$\gamma(R_M) \cong \gamma(\pi) \qquad (3.26)$$

and substituting for $\gamma(\pi)$ in Eq. (3.24), we have

$$\beta_{3j} \cong b_j + \frac{\gamma(e_j) \mid x_j \mid^{\alpha-1}}{\gamma(R_M)} \qquad (3.27)$$

Letting

$$v_j = \frac{\gamma(e_j) \mid x_j \mid^{\alpha-1}}{\gamma(R_M)}$$

we may transform Eq. (3.23) from an *ex ante* relationship into an *ex post* relationship by arguments identical to those for the Gaussian case examined earlier. The result is

$$R_j = R_F(1 - \beta_{3j}) + R_M\beta_{3j} - v_j\pi - \beta_{3j} \sum_i x_i e_i + e_j \qquad (3.28)$$

Similarly, we also define the analogous conditional expected return on the jth security (or portfolio) as

$$E(R_j \mid R_M, \beta_{3j}) = R_F(1 - \beta_{3j}) + R_M\beta_{3j} \qquad (3.29)$$

THE MEASURE OF PORTFOLIO PERFORMANCE IN THE CONTEXT OF NON-GAUSSIAN STABLE DISTRIBUTIONS. The measure of portfolio performance in the context of infinite variance Stable distributions is directly analogous to the finite variation situation and is given by

$$\delta_{3j} = R_j - E(R_j \mid R_M, \beta_{3j})$$
$$= R_j - [R_F(1 - \beta_{3j}) + R_M\beta_{3j}]$$
$$= -v\pi - \beta_{3j} \sum_i x_i e_i + e_j \qquad (3.30)$$

Again, our previous arguments indicate that $v_j\pi$ and $\beta_{3j} \sum_i x_i e_i$ will be extremely small and hence can be ignored, leaving the result

$$\delta_{3j} \cong e_j \qquad (3.31)$$

Since the purpose of all the above has been to arrive at a measure of performance, we shall consider the quantities δ_{2j} and δ_{3j} very closely in determining criteria for judging the performance of a portfolio. Our goal is to arrive at criteria for judging a portfolio's performance to be *superior*, *neutral*, or *inferior*.[38] Given the stochastic nature of the model, it is not surprising that this becomes a probabilistic problem. However, in view of the fact that we are still working within the context of a single-period model, consideration of these questions will be postponed until we have considered the multiperiod model in Section IV.

● ● ●

[38] Formal definitions of these terms will be provided in Section V.

V. THE EVALUATION CRITERIA AND THE CONCEPT
AND MEASUREMENT OF EFFICIENCY*

A. The evaluation criteria

A measure of portfolio performance which provides a measure of a manager's ability to pick "winners" was developed in the preceding sections, culminating in the final form given by Eq. (4.22).* The problem we address at this point is the determination of the criteria by which we judge the performance of any particular portfolio. In Part B of this section we shall derive a measure of a portfolio's "efficiency," and in Part C we shall discuss the relationship between the measures of efficiency and performance. Since all the assumptions made in Section III regarding the disturbance terms e_j also apply to $e_j{}^*$, we are led quite naturally to the following criteria for the evaluation of an estimate (or series of estimates) $\delta_{jt}{}^*$ for a particular portfolio over some time period t.

CRITERION FOR "NEUTRALITY." A portfolio's performance will be defined as neutral if its historical returns are equal to those which the capital asset pricing model implies it should have earned given its level of systematic risk. Formally, this means the results should meet the following conditions:

$$E(\delta_j{}^*) = E(e_j{}^*) = 0 \tag{5.1}$$

$$E(\delta_{j,t}{}^*\delta_{j,t+\tau}{}^*) = E(e_{j,t}{}^*e_{j,t+\tau}{}^*) = 0 \qquad \tau \neq 0 \tag{5.2}$$

That is, we expect the portfolio to experience returns through successive holding periods which will cause it to fluctuate randomly about the market line $R_F M Q$ portrayed in Figure 4.

Thus, a neutral portfolio is one on which the returns are no better or worse than those which could have been earned by a comparable naïve FM portfolio. A neutral portfolio may also be interpreted as one which does no better or worse than that which could have been achieved by a randomly selected portfolio with identical systematic risk.

CRITERION FOR "SUPERIORITY." A superior portfolio will be defined as one which, through successive holding periods, realizes returns such that

$$E(\delta_j{}^*) > 0 \tag{5.3}$$

Thus, a superior portfolio is defined as a portfolio whose returns are consistently greater than those implied by its level of systematic risk. Hence, the returns on such a portfolio would be greater than those which could have been earned by a random selection buy-and-hold policy or by a naïve investment in an FM portfolio having identical systematic risk.

---

* [Section IV, "The Multiperiod Heterogeneous Horizon Problem," has been omitted.—Ed.]

* [Ed.:
$$\begin{aligned} \delta_j{}^* &= R_j{}^* - E(R_j{}^* \mid R_M{}^*, \beta_j) \\ &= R_j{}^* - [R_F{}^*(1 - \beta_j) + R_M{}^*\beta_j] \\ &\cong e_j{}^* \end{aligned} \qquad [4.22]$$
]

Recalling our earlier discussion in Section I regarding the martingale hypothesis, it is clear that Eq. (5.3) also defines the criterion for judging a portfolio manager to be a superior analyst. A portfolio manager who possesses superior economic insight and thus the ability (1) to forecast some of the factors affecting future disturbances $(e_j{}^*)$ for particular securities or (2) to make better than average forecasts of the future realizations on the market factor π, will be able to create a portfolio which consistently dominates the market line $R_F M Q$ of Figure 4. We might mention here that the existence of portfolios satisfying Eq. (5.3) is inconsistent with the strong form of the martingale hypothesis given by Eq. (1.2).

CRITERION FOR "INFERIORITY." We define an inferior portfolio to be one which, through successive holding periods, realizes results such that it is consistently dominated[51] by the market line $R_F M Q$ of Figure 4 and thus has

$$E(\delta_j{}^*) < 0 \qquad (5.4)$$

The martingale property of security price movements implies that the best estimate of future prices (barring superior information) is merely the present price plus a normal expected return. Since any naïve investor or portfolio manager in the market could easily follow this forecasting procedure and expect, on the average, to do as well as the market as a whole, we conclude (if the strong form of the martingale hypothesis is correct) that an inferior portfolio can exist only because the portfolio managers pursue activities which generate expenses. These expenses must be paid out of income, and thus the portfolio returns are reduced.

It should be noted when evaluating mutual funds that there are expenses generated in the provision of services which benefit shareholders (the provision of bookkeeping services is an example), and the value of these benefits to shareholders should be taken into consideration. However, there may be other unnecessary expenses generated which cause the returns to be lower than expected. For example, there may very well be portfolio managers who pursue activities such as attempting to forecast security prices (and trading securities on the basis of these forecasts) while they are unable to increase returns enough to cover their research and commission expenses.

B. The concept and measurement of efficiency

THE CONCEPT OF EFFICIENCY. The reader is cautioned to beware of confusing the above definitions of *performance* with the concept of *efficiency*

---

[51] The exact meaning of "consistently dominated" is left undefined at this point and will be considered below in the context of the empirical results. It will suffice to say at this point that a portfolio can be above or below the efficient boundary either because of random factors or because the portfolio is systematically better or worse than the market portfolio. In addition, if one is examining many portfolios, it is reasonable to expect some of them to be consistently better or worse during the sampling period for purely random reasons. A detailed discussion of this point is contained in Jensen [32].

in the Markowitz-Tobin-Sharpe sense. An efficient portfolio is one which provides maximum expected return for a given level of "risk" and minimum "risk" for a given level of expected return. It is important to note here that "risk" in the definition of efficiency refers to the *total* risk of the portfolio and not just its *systematic* risk (which must always be less than or equal to a portfolio's total risk). Under the assumptions stated in Section II, it was shown that any efficient[52] portfolio ϵ will satisfy

$$E[R_\epsilon \mid E(R_M), \sigma(R_\epsilon)/\sigma(R_M)] = R_F + [E(R_M) - R_F][\sigma(R_\epsilon)/\sigma(R_M)]$$

$$[2.6a]$$

where $\sigma(R_\epsilon)/\sigma(R_M)$ is the total relative risk of the portfolio ϵ. Recall that the results of the capital asset pricing model (given in Eq. [2.7]) merely state the returns which should be expected on any asset given its level of systematic risk. We emphasize that if the capital asset pricing model is valid, Eq. (2.7) applies to *any* asset or portfolio. On the other hand, Eq. (2.6a) will be satisfied only by efficient portfolios as portrayed in Figure 2. The boundary of the opportunity set, the line R_FMQ in Figure 2, is given by Eq. (2.6a). The only portfolios satisfying the requirements for efficiency lie along this line, and (in the absence of superior information about future security returns) all other feasible portfolios lie to the right and below this line.

It should be noted that we are now abandoning the assumption of homogeneous expectations. The reader should now interpret the opportunity set portrayed in Figure 2 as the set which would be determined by knowledge of only the parameters of the market model for each security and the parameters of the distribution on the market factor.[53] Any investor or portfolio manager in possession of information which enables him to (correctly) form expectations on π and e_j which are nonzero will be able to form portfolios which dominate the naïve no-superior-information opportunity set. We shall henceforth use the word *efficient* to refer to this "naïve" concept of efficiency and in particular will *not* use it to refer to the set of "dominant" portfolios which any *individual* investor might observe given any special information he might have regarding the future realizations of the market factor π and the disturbances e_j.

Within this context, then, Eq. (2.6a) gives us the expected returns on any efficient portfolio ϵ conditional on the expected returns on the market portfolio and the total relative risk of the portfolio. (The reader is reminded that it is implicitly assumed in this definition of efficiency that $E[\pi] = 0$ and $E[e_j] = 0$, $[j = 1, 2, \ldots, N]$.)

---

[52] We shall assume throughout the following discussion that security returns are normally distributed. We shall deal with the case of non-Gaussian Stable distributions at the end of Section V.

[53] That is, we assume knowledge of only $E(R_j)$, β_j, $E(e_j) = 0$, $\sigma^2(e_j)$, $E(\pi) = 0$, and $\sigma^2(\pi)$.

Let us now consider the derivation of an expression for the expected return on any *efficient* portfolio ϵ conditional on the *realized* returns on the market portfolio rather than the expected returns. Adding $\beta_\epsilon \pi + e_\epsilon$ to both sides of Eq. (2.6a), we have

$$E[R_\epsilon \mid E(R_M), \sigma(R_\epsilon)/\sigma(R_M)] + \beta_\epsilon \pi + e_\epsilon$$
$$= R_F + [E(R_M) - R_F][\sigma(R_\epsilon)/\sigma(R_M)] + \beta_\epsilon \pi + e_\epsilon \quad (5.5)$$

and since for all *efficient* portfolios

$$E[R_\epsilon \mid E(R_M), \sigma(R_\epsilon)/\sigma(R_M)] = E(R_\epsilon) \quad (5.6)$$

we have, from Eq. (3.2) and the fact that $\beta_\epsilon \cong b_\epsilon$ (by the arguments given in Section III), that to a close approximation

$$E[R_\epsilon \mid E(R_M), \sigma(R_\epsilon)/\sigma(R_M)] + \beta_\epsilon \pi + e_\epsilon \cong R_\epsilon \quad (5.7)$$

Using Eq. (5.7), we can write Eq. (5.5) as

$$R_\epsilon \cong R_F + [E(R_M) - R_F][\sigma(R_\epsilon)/\sigma(R_M)] + \beta_\epsilon \pi + e_\epsilon \quad (5.8)$$

But since, by Eq. (3.5) and the arguments of footnote 31

$$\pi \cong R_M - E(R_M) \quad (5.9)$$

we can substitute into Eq. (5.8) and arrive at

$$R_\epsilon \cong R_F + [E(R_M) - R_F][\sigma(R_\epsilon)/\sigma(R_M)] + [R_M - E(R_M)]\beta_\epsilon + e_\epsilon$$
$$(5.10)$$

Note that

$$\sigma(R_j)/\sigma(R_M) = (1/r_j)\beta_j \qquad r_j \neq 0 \quad (5.11)$$

where r_j is the product-moment correlation coefficient between the returns on the jth portfolio and the returns on the market portfolio.

Using Eq. (5.11), adding and subtracting $\beta_\epsilon R_F$ on the RHS of Eq. (5.10) and rearranging, we have for all efficient portfolios

$$R_\epsilon \cong R_F + (R_M - R_F)\beta_\epsilon + [E(R_M) - R_F]\beta_\epsilon(1/r_\epsilon - 1) + e_\epsilon \qquad r_\epsilon \neq 0$$
$$(5.12)$$

Now, since $E(e_j) = 0$ for all j by Eq. (3.3a), we have $E(e_\epsilon) = 0$ and

$$E[R_\epsilon \mid E(R_M), R_M, \beta_\epsilon, \sigma(R_\epsilon)/\sigma(R_M)] \cong R_F + (R_M - R_F)\beta_\epsilon$$
$$+ [E(R_M) - R_F]\beta_\epsilon(1/r_\epsilon - 1) \qquad r_\epsilon \neq 0 \quad (5.13)$$

Equation (5.13) is an important result. It gives us the expected return on any efficient portfolio ϵ conditional on the realized returns on the market portfolio, its systematic risk, and its total relative risk. But note also that we are left with a term involving $E(R_M)$ which indicates that we cannot define efficiency without taking into account the *ex ante* expected returns on the market portfolio.

In considering this result, note that the first two terms on the RHS of Eq. (5.13) are identical to those in Eq. (3.17) used in the definition of "performance." These two terms tell us what the portfolio should earn given its level of systematic risk. However, if the portfolio is also to be efficient, its returns must be higher by an amount given by

$$[E(R_M) - R_F]\beta_\epsilon(1/r_\epsilon - 1) \qquad r_\epsilon \neq 0 \qquad (5.14)$$

Let us define a perfectly diversified portfolio as one for which the total risk of the portfolio is equal to its systematic risk, and hence one for which $r_j = 1$. Now the quantity

$$\beta_j(1/r_j - 1) = \sigma(R_j)/\sigma(R_M) - \beta_j \qquad (5.15)$$

is just the increment in the portfolio's risk (measured, of course, in a relative sense) which is due to the lack of perfect diversification.

In the absence of transactions costs, a rational manager would never hold an imperfectly diversified portfolio[54] unless he believed he could forecast future security prices to some extent. If he believed he could forecast future prices successfully, it would most certainly be rational to sacrifice some diversification and concentrate some of the portfolio's holdings in those select securities with the highest expected "abnormal" return.[55] But to the extent that the manager accepts additional risk in acting on his forecasts, he must earn higher returns to compensate for it or the portfolio will be inefficient in the sense that a perfectly diversified FM portfolio with the same (higher) level of total risk would earn higher returns. By our previous arguments, $\beta_j[(1/r_j) - 1]$ represents the incremental risk due to the lack of perfect diversification, and the term $[E(R_M) - R_F]$ in Eq. (5.14) is the expected premium per unit of risk. Thus, Eq. (5.14) represents the additional returns which must be earned by an imperfectly diversified portfolio in order for it to be efficient.

Before going on to define an explicit measure of efficiency, let us digress briefly to provide an intuitive interpretation of the foregoing concepts and issues. In considering the definition of a measure of efficiency, one is tempted to simply replace the term $E(R_M)$ in Eq. (2.6a) with R_M and interpret the resulting expression as one defining the expected returns on any efficient portfolio conditional on the realized returns on the market portfolio.[56] That is, it is tempting to simply relabel the vertical axis in Figure 2 as R instead of $E(R)$ and to interpret the line R_FMQ as representing the locus of points about which all efficient portfolios will scatter. It is clear from Eq. (5.12) that the realized returns on all effi-

---

[54] That is, anything other than an FM portfolio defined in Section III.

[55] That is, those for which the manager believes $E(e_j) > 0$ are largest.

[56] Indeed something similar to this is suggested or implied in references [3, 7, 8, 27, 28, 54, 55, 58, and 66].

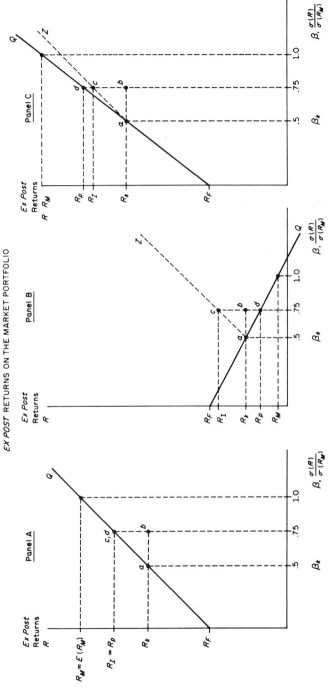

FIGURE 5

THE RELATIONSHIP BETWEEN THE *EX POST* RETURNS EARNED BY A PERFECTLY DIVERSIFIED EFFICIENT PORTFOLIO p, AN IMPERFECTLY DIVERSIFIED EFFICIENT PORTFOLIO I, AND A HYPOTHETICAL PORTFOLIO k, UNDER THREE DIFFERENT ASSUMPTIONS REGARDING THE *EX POST* RETURNS ON THE MARKET PORTFOLIO cient portfolios *will not* scatter about such a simple straight line in the *ex post* return and risk plane, since the *expected* returns on the market portfolio also appear in the equation. To see the issues more clearly, consider the three situations portrayed in panels *A*, *B*, and *C* of Figure 5, in which the *ex post* returns of a hypothetical portfolio *k* are plotted against its systematic risk, β_k, and total relative risk, $\sigma(R_k)/\sigma(R_M)$. The panels differ only in the assumed values of the realized returns on the market portfolio. In panel *A* it is assumed that $R_M = E(R_M)$, in panel *B* it is assumed that $R_M < E(R_M)$, and in panel *C*, that $R_M > E(R_M)$.

Let us now consider our hypothetical portfolio *k* with a level of systematic risk of .5 and managed by an individual who attempts to forecast the future prices of individual securities. In attempting to incorporate his forecasts into the portfolio, the manager is forced to accept additional (and diversifiable) risk in the portfolio. We assume for illustrative purposes that this results in a total relative risk of .75 = $\sigma(R_k)/\sigma(R_M)$. Now Eq. (5.13) (with Eq. [5.15]) indicates that in order for this portfolio to be efficient the manager's forecasting efforts must increase the expected returns on the portfolio by an amount equal to $[E(R_M) - R_F]$ (.25), which is simply the amount of incremental (and diversifiable) risk in the portfolio multiplied by the *ex ante* price per unit of risk.

For illustrative purposes, let us also assume that our hypothetical manager actually cannot forecast any better than a random selection policy, and thus he is reimbursed in the market only for the amount of systematic risk he has taken (in this case, .5). Let us also assume (without loss of generality) that the error terms, *e*, are zero for all portfolios we shall consider in our example.

Now the points labeled *a* in panels *A*, *B*, and *C* denote the *ex post* returns, R_k, and *systematic* risk (.5) of our portfolio under the three different assumptions regarding the value of the realized return on the market portfolio *M*. The points labeled *b* in the figures denote the *ex post* returns and *total relative* risk (.75) of the portfolio *k*. The points labeled *c* in the figures denote the *ex post* returns, R_I, earned by all *imperfectly diversified efficient* portfolios with a total relative risk of .75 and a systematic risk of 0.50. Finally, the points labeled *d* in the figures denote the *ex post* return, R_p, of all *perfectly diversified efficient* portfolios with a total relative (and systematic) risk of 0.75.

In panel *A*, where we have assumed $R_M = E(R_M)$, there is no difficulty at all in interpreting the diagram. All efficient portfolios (whether perfectly diversified or not) will scatter along the line R_FQ when their returns are plotted against their total relative risk. It is clear that our portfolio *k* (which by assumption is inefficient) at point *b* appears to be inefficient, since it is dominated by point *c*, *d*.

However, in panel *B*, where we have assumed $R_m < E(R_m)$, a simple interpretation of the "opportunity set" given by the solid line R_FQ is not valid. That is, all efficient portfolios will not lie along this line; only those portfolios which are perfectly diversified (i.e., for which $\beta_j = \sigma[R_j]/\sigma[R_M]$) will lie along this line. The point b in panel B again denotes the *ex post* returns and total relative risk of our hypothetical portfolio. But, contrary to the situation in panel A, point b appears to dominate point d, which represents the *ex post* return and risk of a perfectly diversified efficient portfolio. This impression is misleading. Point b looks better than point d only because the realized returns on the market portfolio were below the risk-free rate. The realized returns on the manager's imperfectly diversified portfolio were higher than those on the perfectly diversified portfolio p, because $\beta_k = .5$ while $\beta_p = .75$. It is clear that portfolio k cannot be efficient, since it is dominated by a perfectly diversified portfolio with identical returns and total relative risk of 0.5. Therefore, regardless of the realized returns on the market portfolio, if the imperfectly diversified portfolio k is to be efficient, the manager's forecasting ability must be good enough to reimburse the holders of the portfolio for the additional diversifiable risk taken. This increment in return is precisely the quantity given by Eq. (5.14), and the dashed line acZ in panel B denotes the *ex post* returns which must be earned by any imperfectly diversified portfolio with systematic risk equal to .5 in order for it to be efficient. The slope of acZ, of course, is determined by the *ex ante* risk premium per unit of risk. The difference between .75 and .5 is the incremental risk, and the difference between R_I and R_k is the incremental return necessary to compensate for this risk. (The reader will note that the line acZ is just one of an entire family of such lines emanating from every point on the line R_FQ.)

The case in which $R_m > E(R_m)$ is portrayed in panel C. Again, the level of systematic risk and the opportunity set R_FQ determine the *ex post* return R_k on our portfolio, and the *ex ante* risk premium determines the slope of the line acZ. The point c represents the point at which an imperfectly diversified efficient portfolio would lie with returns R_I.

The reader will note that if our hypothetical portfolio with a total relative risk of .75 were perfectly diversified (i.e., $\beta_k = .75$ also), and therefore efficient, it would have earned returns $R_p < R_k$ in the situation portrayed in panel B. Therefore, one might be tempted to conclude that the investor was actually better off with the imperfectly diversified and inefficient portfolio with returns R_p. In a sense this is true, but one must be very careful about giving the manager credit for this situation, which must be due solely to good luck. That is, if he were forecasting R_M to be less than R_F, he would certainly have been far better off to hold only the riskless asset rather than hold an imperfectly diversified portfolio. In addition, as previously mentioned, it is misleading to compare the imperfectly and perfectly diversified portfolios along the return dimension. It is clear that the holder of the imperfectly diversified portfolio k could have earned the same returns R_k with a perfectly diversified portfolio with total relative risk of .5 (rather than .75). Thus, the investor gained nothing from accepting this needlessly higher level of risk.

Moreover, if we consider the point d in panel C, which represents the perfectly diversified efficient portfolio with $\beta_p = \sigma(R_p)/\sigma(R_m) = .75$, it is clear that the returns R_p on such a portfolio are greater than R_k. Hence, in this case, the investor is not better off for having accepted the higher diversifiable risk for which he is not compensated.

In addition, the reader should note that in all three panels, both points c and d represent the locations of *efficient* portfolios with the same degree of total relative risk. Their returns will be coincident *only* when $R_m = E(R_m)$, and the differences are due solely to the random and unpredictable factors determining the returns on the market portfolio. The important point is that both portfolios I and p are *ex ante* efficient by definition; yet they may have vastly different *ex post* returns depending on whether $R_M \gtrless E(R_M)$.

Now we shall consider the definition of a measure of efficiency and the evaluation criteria to be applied to it, and in Part C of this section we shall consider the relationship between the measures of performance and efficiency.

A MEASURE OF EFFICIENCY. Utilizing Eq. (5.13) and taking account of the horizon solution, let us define a measure of efficiency, γ_j^*, as

$$\gamma_j^* = R_j^* - E[R_j^* \mid E(R_M^*), R_M^*, \beta_j, \sigma(R_j^*)/\sigma(R_M^*)]$$

$$= R_j^* - \{R_F + [R_M^* - R_F^*]\beta_j + [E(R_M^*) - R_F^*]\beta_j(1/r_j - 1)\}$$

$$r_j \neq 0 \quad (5.16)$$

where, as before, e_j^* is defined analogously to Eqs. (3.2) and (3.3). We consider now the criteria for judging a portfolio to be "*efficient*," "*inefficient*," or "*superefficient*."

CRITERION FOR "EFFICIENCY." The arguments above imply that an efficient portfolio can be defined as one which through successive holding periods realizes returns such that[57]

$$E(\gamma_j^*) = E(e_j^*) = 0 \quad (5.18)$$

For the moment we shall ignore the problems associated with obtaining empirical estimates of $E(R_M^*)$, which of course are necessary for the estimation of γ^*. We shall consider this point below.

CRITERION FOR "INEFFICIENCY." An inefficient portfolio will be de-

---

[57] Note also that since $\gamma_j^* \cong e^*$ we know also that

$$E(\gamma_{j,t}^* \gamma_{j,t+r}^*) = E(e_{j,t}^* e_{j,t+r}^*) = 0. \quad (5.17)$$

fined as one for which

$$E(\gamma_j^*) < 0 \qquad (5.19)$$

As noted above, it is perfectly possible that a manager is able to forecast security prices to some extent and still manage to create an inefficient portfolio. That is, it is possible that he might not earn returns sufficiently higher than a buy-and-hold policy to adequately compensate the holder of the portfolio for the additional risk taken due to the lack of perfect diversification.

CRITERION FOR "SUPEREFFICIENCY." A portfolio will be defined to be superefficient if

$$E(\gamma_j^*) > 0 \qquad (5.20)$$

One may question the possible existence of a superefficient portfolio, since we usually think of the efficient set of portfolios as dominating the set of feasible portfolios. However, recall that earlier we defined *efficiency* in terms of the opportunity set which would be determined by knowledge of just the parameters of the market model for each security and the parameters of the distribution on the market factor. Hence, it is certainly possible for a manager with superior information or insight to create portfolios which dominate this "naïve" opportunity set.

C. The relationship between the measures of efficiency and performance

THE CASE OF PERFECTLY DIVERSIFIED PORTFOLIOS. The concept of efficiency is extremely important, and it behooves us to investigate its relationship to the measure of portfolio performance, δ^*, suggested above. We have seen that a portfolio may be classified as inferior, neutral, or superior, and its classification depends on the manager's forecasting ability and the amount of expenses generated in the management of the portfolio. If a portfolio is either inferior or neutral, we can make unambiguous inferences regarding its efficiency. From the definition of the measure of performance δ^* given by Eq. (4.22) and the definition of the measure of efficiency γ^* given by Eq. (5.16), we see that

$$\gamma_j = \delta_j^* - [E(R_M^*) - R_F^*]\beta_j(1/r_j - 1) \qquad r_j \neq 0 \qquad (5.21)$$

The second term on the RHS of Eq. (5.21) is just the adjustment for the diversifiable risk in the portfolio and must be taken into account in measuring efficiency. Consider for the moment the case of a perfectly diversified portfolio. Since for such a portfolio $r_j = 1$, we know the last term on the RHS of Eq. (5.21) is zero. Thus, for a perfectly diversified portfolio, $\gamma_j^* = \delta_j^*$, and the measure of performance is also a measure of efficiency.[58]

---

[58] One might wonder at first whether a perfectly diversified portfolio can possibly be inefficient. The answer to such a question is yes, since all a manager of a perfectly diversified portfolio need do to make it inefficient is to generate expenses and therefore lower its returns.

THE CASE OF INFERIOR PORTFOLIOS. If a portfolio is inferior, then it must also be inefficient. That is, if $E(\delta_j^*) < 0$, then $E(\gamma_j^*) < 0$ also. That is, by Eq. (5.21) and the fact that the last term on the RHS of Eq. (5.21) must always be positive,[59] we know that $\gamma_j^* \leq \delta_j^*$ always.

THE CASE OF SUPERIOR PORTFOLIOS. The only case in which some ambiguity exists between the measure of performance, δ^*, and the inference regarding the efficiency of a portfolio is in the case of a superior forecaster with $E(\delta^*) > 0$. We can see from Eq. (5.21) and the definition of efficiency Eq. (5.17) that the superior portfolio will also be an efficient portfolio if

$$E(\delta_j^*) = [E(R_M^*) - R_F^*]\beta_j(1/r_j - 1) \qquad r_j \neq 0 \qquad (5.22)$$

That is, if the positive benefits of the forecaster's ability are just large enough to offset the effects of any imperfect diversification (represented by the difference between r_j and unity), the portfolio will be efficient.

In the situation where

$$E(\delta_j^*) > [E(R_M^*) - R_F^*]\beta_j(1/r_j - 1) \qquad r_j \neq 0 \qquad (5.23)$$

we define the portfolio to be superefficient, since the benefits from the superior forecasting ability are more than enough to offset the effects of the imperfect diversification.

Finally, in the situation where

$$0 < E(\delta_j^*) < [E(R_M^*) - R_F^*]\beta_j(1/r_j - 1) \qquad r_j \neq 0 \qquad (5.24)$$

the portfolio is inefficient, since the benefits from the superior forecasting ability are not large enough to offset the effects of imperfect diversification.

It should be noted that, while a portfolio satisfying Eq. (5.24) is inefficient in and of itself, it most surely is a desirable investment if treated as a single asset in the context of an efficiently diversified portfolio. That is, the investor who realizes that $E(\delta_j^*) > 0$ may combine an investment in that portfolio with investments in other assets and hence create a portfolio which is in a sense superefficient. In effect, as soon as an investor realizes the superiority of a manager's forecasting ability, he may treat that ability as an additional asset in the opportunity set and thereby enable the efficient set (as viewed by himself) to shift upward and to the left.[60]

---

[59] Since, under the assumption of risk aversion, $E(R_M)$ must be greater than R_F or no one would hold risky assets and, as an empirical fact, $\beta_j \geq 0$ and $r_j \geq 0$ always (cf. Blume [4] and Fama et al. [19]).

[60] Of course, there is some question as to why a manager with such superior ability would sell his talents for anything less than their full value. This would imply that none of the benefits would be passed on to the fund investor and raises serious doubts that a superior mutual fund portfolio will ever be found. However, if the superior manager were a risk averter, he might find it advantageous to sell his talents for something less than their full expected value in return for a more stable income flow.

It is also interesting to note that this discussion regarding efficiency implies an economic justification for two very different types of funds: (1) funds which concentrate on maintaining perfectly diversified efficient portfolios and (2) special purpose funds that concentrate on being superior forecasters and perhaps ignore the diversification function entirely. Of course, the investor must realize these differences and treat them accordingly in building his own personal portfolio. The perfectly diversified efficient fund (with the proper risk level) is an appropriate investment for the investor's entire wealth stock. On the other hand, the special purpose fund need not be perfectly diversified (and in general cannot be) and may not be efficient as well, so that while it is a desirable asset to be included in the investor's total portfolio, it is not an appropriate investment for his entire wealth stock. (Of course, there is little if any justification for the existence of special purpose funds in the absence of superior forecasting ability.)

THE CONCEPT OF EFFICIENCY IN THE CONTEXT OF NON-GAUSSIAN STABLE DISTRIBUTIONS. Fama [16] has shown (using arguments analogous to those of Section II) that, in the context of non-Gaussian finite mean symmetric Stable distributions, an efficient portfolio ϵ must satisfy

$$E\left[R_\epsilon^* \mid E(R_M^*), \frac{\gamma^{1/\alpha}(R_\epsilon^*)}{\gamma^{1/\alpha}(R_M^*)}\right] = R_F^* + [E(R_M^*) - R_F^*]\frac{\gamma^{1/\alpha}(R_\epsilon^*)}{\gamma^{1/\alpha}(R_M^*)}$$

$$(5.25)$$

where γ is the dispersion parameter defined in Section III-C. Furthermore, by arguments analogous to those given in Section V-B, we can put Eq. (5.25) in terms of the *ex post* returns R_ϵ^* and R_M^*:

$$R_\epsilon^* = E\left[R_\epsilon^* \mid R_M^*, E(R_M^*), \frac{\gamma^{1/\alpha}(R_\epsilon^*)}{\gamma^{1/\alpha}(R_M^*)}\right] + e_\epsilon^*$$

$$\cong R_F^* + [E(R_M^*) - R_F^*]\frac{\gamma^{1/\alpha}(R_\epsilon^*)}{\gamma^{1/\alpha}(R_M^*)} + [R_M^* - E(R_M^*)]\beta_\epsilon + e_\epsilon^*$$

$$(5.26)$$

Equation (5.26) is analogous to Eq. (5.10), except that all the random variables are Stable variates fulfilling the assumptions stated in Section III-C and $\beta_\epsilon = \beta_{2\epsilon} \cong b_\epsilon$.

Unfortunately, there is no simple relationship between $\gamma^{1/\alpha}(R_\epsilon^*)/\gamma^{1/\alpha}(R_M^*)$ and β_ϵ comparable to Eq. (5.11). The lack of such a relationship prevents further simplification of Eq. (5.26) to a form like that of Eq. (5.13).

From Eqs. (3.21) and (3.26), and the fact that[61] $\beta_j \cong b_j$, we know that

$$\frac{\gamma^{1/\alpha}(R_j{}^*)}{\gamma^{1/\alpha}(R_M{}^*)} \cong \frac{[\gamma(R_M) \mid \beta_j \mid^\alpha + \gamma(e_j)]^{1/\alpha}}{\gamma^{1/\alpha}(R_M)} \tag{5.27}$$

and it is clear that

$$\frac{\gamma^{1/\alpha}(R_j{}^*)}{\gamma^{1/\alpha}(R_M{}^*)} \cong \beta_j \tag{5.28}$$

only when $\gamma(e_j) = 0$. Thus, given Stable distributions, a perfectly diversified portfolio ϵ must have $e_\epsilon{}^* = 0$ always, and this is equivalent to $r_\epsilon = 1$, given Gaussian distributions.

We can also see from Eq. (5.27) that just as in the case of Gaussian distributions, the total relative risk of an imperfectly diversified portfolio will always be greater than its systematic risk.

These arguments imply (1) that δ^*, the measure of performance, is also a measure of efficiency for all perfectly diversified portfolios, (2) that if $E(\delta^*) < 0$, then $E(\gamma^*) < 0$, that is, if the portfolio is inferior it must also be inefficient, and (3) that if the portfolio is imperfectly diversified (i.e., $\gamma^{1/\alpha}(R_j{}^*)/\gamma^{1/\alpha}(R_M{}^*) > \beta_j$), then $E(\delta_j{}^*) > 0$ must hold in order for the portfolio to be efficient.

VII. SUMMARY AND CONCLUSIONS*

A. Summary of the main results

THE THEORETICAL RESULTS. It was shown in Sections II and III that the Sharpe-Lintner theory of capital asset pricing can be used to develop a model for evaluating the performance of portfolios. The model uses the Sharpe-Lintner results to allow explicitly for the effects of differential degrees of "risk" on the returns of portfolios—a problem which prior to this time has never been satisfactorily solved.

The Sharpe-Lintner results (originally derived in the context of a single-period model under the assumption of identical investor horizon periods) were extended to a multiperiod world in Section IV. In this model, investor horizon periods may be of different lengths and trading of assets is allowed to take place continuously.

In addition, the Sharpe-Lintner *ex ante* model was extended to include *ex post* relationships. That is, the resulting model expresses the expected returns on a security (or portfolio) as a function of its level of syste-

---

[61] See pp. 210–11.

* [Section VI, "An Application of the Model to the Evaluation of the Mutual Fund Portfolios," containing the bulk of Jensen's empirical results, has been omitted.– Ed.]

matic risk, the risk-free return, and the *actual realized returns* (instead of the expected future return), on the market portfolio over any holding period.

Given these results, a measure of portfolio performance was defined as the difference between the actual returns on a portfolio in any particular holding period and the expected returns on that portfolio conditional on the riskless rate, its level of systematic risk, and the actual returns on the market portfolio. The criteria for judging portfolio performance to be neutral, superior, or inferior were established in Section V-A.

The concept of efficiency was explicitly defined in Section V-B and a measure of efficiency was derived. It was also shown that it is strictly impossible to define a measure of efficiency solely in terms of *ex post* observable variables. In addition, it was shown that there exists a natural relationship between the measure of portfolio performance and the measure of efficiency.

THE EMPIRICAL RESULTS. The empirical tests presented in Section VI yielded the following results:

1. As implied by the solution to the horizon problem, the estimates of systematic risk seem to be invariant to the length of the interval over which the sample returns are calculated. If this conclusion is valid, the estimates of systematic risk are independent of the investor's horizon period and may be used to evaluate portfolios over a holding period of any length.

2. The measures of systematic risk for the mutual funds seem to be approximately stationary over time, implying that we may use historical data on returns to estimate a portfolio's level of risk.

3. The observed historical patterns of systematic risk and return for the mutual funds in the sample are consistent with the joint hypothesis that the capital asset pricing model is valid and that the mutual fund managers on the average are unable to forecast future security prices.

4. If we assume that the capital asset pricing model is valid, then the empirical estimates of fund performance (summarized in Table 1) indicate that the fund portfolios were "inferior" after deduction of all management expenses and brokerage commissions generated in trading activity. Under these conditions, the average performance measure, $\bar{\delta}^*$, for the 115 funds was -8.9 percent in the period 1955–64. In addition, when all management expenses and brokerage commissions were added back to the fund returns and the average cash balances of the funds were assumed to earn the riskless rate, the fund portfolios appeared to be just neutral. The average δ^* was $+.0009$ in the period 1955–64. Thus, it appears that on the average the resources spent by the funds in attempting to forecast

TABLE 1. SUMMARY OF FUND PERFORMANCE MEASURES (δ^*)
BY TIME PERIOD AND ASSUMPTIONS REGARDING
TREATMENT OF EXPENSES

Definition of Sample and Treatment of Expenses and Transaction Costs	Sample Size	Average δ^*	Funds with Negative δ^*	
			No.	Percent
(1) Total sample—fund returns calculated after subtraction of all expenses; transaction costs ignored............................	115	$-.089$	72	62.5
(2) Fifty-six funds existing over entire 20 years; returns calculated as in (1) above........	56	$-.076$	35	62.5
ten years 1945–54.....................	56	$-.135$	43	76.8
twenty years 1945–64..................	56	$-.196$	39	69.5
(3) Total sample—fund returns calculated after adding back all expenses except interest, taxes, and brokerage commissions; transaction costs on market portfolio ignored....	115	$-.025$	58	50.4
(4) Total sample—fund returns calculated gross of all reported expenses and estimated commission expenses; estimated average cash balances assumed to earn the riskless rate; transaction costs on market portfolio ignored.............................	115	$+.0009$	N.A.[a]	N.A.
(5) Total sample—fund and market portfolio returns calculated as seen by a potential investor; all fund expenses, brokerage commissions, and loading fees subtracted and brokerage commissions of 1 percent on purchase and sales of market portfolio allowed for..........................	115	$-.146$	89	77.4

[a] N.A. = insufficient data available to make calculations.

security prices do not yield higher portfolio returns than those which could have been earned by equivalent risk portfolios selected (a) by random selection policies or (b) by combined investments in the market portfolio and government bonds.

5. Based on the evidence summarized above, we conclude that as far as these 115 mutual funds are concerned, prices of securities seem to behave according to the "strong" form of the martingale hypothesis outlined in the Introduction. That is, it appears that the current prices of securities completely capture the effects of *all* currently available informa-

tion. Therefore, their attempts to analyze past information more thoroughly have not resulted in increased returns.

6. Given the results regarding the average performance measure, we also conclude that on the average the mutual funds provided investors with inefficient portfolios. The explicit estimates of a measure of efficiency yielded an average γ^* of $-.150$ under the assumption $E(R_M{}^*) = R_M{}^*$ for the period 1955–64.

7. The evidence also indicates that, while the portfolios of the funds on the average are inferior and inefficient, this is due mainly to the generation of too many expenses. We know that, since the portfolios on the average are very well-diversified (with an average r_j of .923), they are inefficient mainly because they are inferior, and this apparently is a result of the generation of too many expenses. That is, after adding back all expenses except brokerage commissions and adjusting for the bias involved with the cash balances, the portfolios satisfy the criterion for neutrality with an average δ^* of $+.0009$.

IMPLICATIONS OF THE RESULTS FOR MUTUAL FUND INVESTMENT POLICIES. The results of the analysis imply that in the absence of superior forecasting ability, mutual funds ought to maintain the following policies in order to provide investors with maximum benefits:

1. Minimize management expenses and brokerage commissions. That is, a buy-and-hold policy should be followed as closely as possible.

2. Concentrate on the maintenance of a perfectly diversified portfolio.

In addition to the above implications (which are direct results of the analysis), considerations of the utility model and the manner in which anticipations regarding future risk are formed imply that mutual fund managers should also:

3. Maintain a constant level of systematic risk as closely as possible. A fund which establishes a risk level and attracts investors on this basis should avoid sudden shifts in its risk level, since unexpected changes in its risk are likely to leave its investors with inappropriate portfolios.

B. Some anticipated objections to the results

Realizing that the results of the study are likely to be criticized from many quarters, we shall now try to anticipate some of the objections and criticisms which might be expected.

INSTITUTIONAL FRICTIONS. We would be the first to admit that the empirical results discussed earlier are perfectly consistent with the hypothesis that the security analysts working for mutual funds are indeed able to predict security prices somewhat; but they are prevented from realizing superior returns by institutional frictions or restrictions which prevent them from taking immediate action on their predictions. By institutional frictions we mean, for example, that analysts may not make buy-or-sell decisions themselves but must usually submit their recommendations to an "investment committee" of some sort which reviews the recommendations and makes decisions. If this process sometimes takes as long as a week or two (as has been asserted), and assuming that the analysts on the average can forecast future security prices somewhat, the empirical results imply that whenever deviations of actual price from "true" price exist, they are in general bid away very quickly—so quickly in fact that these relatively minor restrictions on buy-and-sell actions apparently remove all opportunity to earn superior returns. This should be an extremely comforting finding for the naïve investor.

THE EFFECTS OF LARGE SIZE. There are those who claim that the sheer size of most mutual funds is such that their transactions are so large they cannot trade in most securities without significantly affecting their prices (cf. Friend et al. [26, pp. 361 and 387]). That is, it is asserted that in order to significantly affect the returns on a large portfolio, extremely large blocks of securities would have to be turned over in taking full account of the analysts' predictions. It is also asserted that these blocks are so large that they cannot be purchased or sold without "significantly" affecting the price of the security.

While there are no theoretical reasons why the purchase or sale of a "large" block of a particular security will not influence its price, the definition of "large" and the amount of influence on price are essentially empirical questions. Scholes [49] has examined the price effects of sales of large blocks of securities through secondary offerings and the issuance of stock rights. He finds that for 1,207 secondary offerings, the price of the securities fell on the average about 2 percent at the time of the offering. An examination of 669 rights offerings indicates a decline in price of approximately 0.3 percent at the time of offering. Since some of his observations represented sales of up to $185 million worth of securities, his results would certainly seem to indicate that most mutual funds could probably turn their entire portfolios over at a maximum cost of 4 to 5 percent in several weeks.

Thus, if the fund managers have an ability to forecast, but are restricted from taking full advantage of their knowledge by the size of their transactions, then it must be true that it is very rare for the actual price to deviate from the "true" price by more than the transactions costs.

LEGAL RESTRICTIONS. Certain legal restrictions on the holdings of mutual funds may inhibit the full realization of superior forecasting ability if any exists. That is, by law the funds may not hold more than 5 percent of their portfolios in any one security or hold more than 10 percent of the outstanding stock of any company.

THE TIMING OF CASH INFLOWS AND OUTFLOWS. It is also sometimes asserted that the funds do not do as well as might be expected because fund shareholders tend to redeem shares when market prices are low and to purchase shares when market prices are high. This argument is fallacious for two reasons: (1) Because we calculate fund returns on the basis of net asset value per share, and because all redemptions or sales of shares are executed at this net asset value (calculated at least once daily), it is impossible for the cash flows during a period to influence the returns on an outstanding share.[109] (2) Furthermore, the argument is likely to be false since it implies that one could predict the behavior of market prices on the basis of fund redemptions and sales. A vast amount of empirical work has indicated that all other attempts to create models to predict market prices have failed, and there is little reason to believe this case is different.

C. Implications for further research

First and foremost, it is clear that the model tested here ought to be tested further on other managed portfolios, hopefully using monthly or quarterly data—pension funds, bank trusts, and university endowments would seem to be natural candidates. Moreover, the model also should be tested on unmanaged portfolios. That is, since evidence presented here indicates that the capital asset pricing model seems to have empirical as well as theoretical justification, we now need to devote a major effort to testing the capital asset pricing model on data for unmanaged portfolios and for individual securities. Work is now in progress on such a study.

REFERENCES

[1] Aitchison, J., and J. A. C. Brown. *The Log-normal Distribution* (Cambridge, England: Cambridge U. P., 1957).

[2] Arditti, Fred D. "Risk and the Required Return on Equity," *Journal of Finance*, Vol. XXII (March, 1967), pp. 19–36.

[3] Bank Administration Institute (Lorie, J., Cohen, K., Dean, J., Durand, D., Fisher, L., Fama, E., and Shapiro, E.). *Measuring the Investment Performance of Pension Funds* (Park Ridge, Ill.: Bank Administration Institute, 1968).

---

[109] There is one relatively subtle way in which these cash flows might affect the returns on an outstanding share to some small degree. That is, the funds do not explicitly charge the shareholder who redeems shares (or purchases new shares) for the transactions costs involved in investing (or disinvesting) these funds. Hence current shareholders implicitly bear these costs. However, the fund obviously does not execute a transaction for every deposit and withdrawal since these are met out of a cash balance and tend to cancel each other out to a great degree.

[4] Blume, Marshall. "The Assessment of Portfolio Performance" (unpublished Ph.D. dissertation, University of Chicago, 1968).

[5] Borch, Karl. "Indifference Curves and Uncertainty," *Swedish Journal of Economics*, Vol. LXX, No. 1 (March, 1968), pp. 19–24.

[6] Box, G. E. P., and D. R. Cox. "An Analysis of Transformations," *Journal of the Royal Statistical Society*, Series B, Vol. XXVI, No. 2 (1964), pp. 211–43.

[7] Cohen, Kalman J., and Jerry A. Pogue. "An Empirical Evaluation of Alternative Portfolio Selection Models," *Journal of Business*, Vol. XXXX (April 1967), pp. 166–93.

[8] Cohen, Kalman J., and Jerry A. Pogue. "Some Comments Concerning Mutual Fund versus Random Portfolio Performance," *Journal of Business*, Vol. XXXXI (April, 1968), pp. 180–90.

[9] Cootner, Paul H. (ed.). *The Random Character of Stock Market Prices* (Cambridge, Mass.: M.I.T. Press, 1964).

[10] Cramer, Harold. *Mathematical Methods of Statistics* (Princeton, N. J.: Princeton U. P., 1946).

[11] Dietz, Peter. *Pension Funds: Measuring Investment Performance*. (New York, N. Y.: Free Press, 1966).

[12] Fama, Eugene. "The Behavior of Stock-Market Prices," *Journal of Business*, Vol. XXXVII (January, 1965), pp. 34–105.

[13] Fama, Eugene. "Portfolio Analysis in a Stable Paretian Market," *Management Science*, Vol. XI (January, 1965), pp. 404–19.

[14] Fama, Eugene. "Risk, Return, and Equilibrium: Some Clarifying Comments," *Journal of Finance* (March, 1968), pp. 29–40.

[15] Fama, Eugene. "Multi-Period Consumption-Investment Decisions," Report No. 6830 (Chicago, Ill.: University of Chicago, Center for Mathematical Studies in Business and Economics, June, 1968).

[16] Fama, Eugene. "Risk, Return, and Equilibrium," Report No. 6831 (Chicago, Ill.: University of Chicago, Center for Mathematical Studies in Business and Economics, June, 1968).

[17] Fama, Eugene, and Harvey Babiak. "Dividend Policy: An Empirical Analysis," Report No. 6732 (Chicago: University of Chicago, Center for Mathematical Studies in Business and Economics, November, 1967). Forthcoming in the *Journal of the American Statistical Association*.

[18] Fama, Eugene, and Marshall Blume. "Filter Rules and Stock Market Trading," *Journal of Business*, Vol. XXXIX (January, 1966), pp. 226–41.

[19] Fama, Eugene, Lawrence Fisher, Michael C. Jensen, and Richard Roll. "The Adjustment of Stock Prices to New Information," *International Economic Review*, Vol. X (February, 1969), pp. 1–26.

[20] Fama, Eugene, and Merton Miller. "The Theory of Valuation" (unpublished manuscript, University of Chicago, 1967).

[21] Fama, Eugene, and Richard Roll. "Some Properties of Symmetric Stable Distributions," *Journal of the American Statistical Association* (September, 1968), pp. 817–36.

[22] Farrar, Donald E. *The Investment Decision under Uncertainty* (Englewood Cliffs, N. J.: Prentice Hall, Inc., 1962).

[23] Feller, William. *An Introduction to Probability Theory and Its Applications*, Vol. II. (New York, N. Y.: Wiley, 1966).

[24] Friedman, Milton. *A Theory of the Consumption Function* (Princeton, N. J.: Princeton I. P., 1957).

[25] Friedman, Milton, and L. J. Savage. "The Utility Analysis of Choices Involving Risk," *Journal of Political Economy*, Vol. LVI (August, 1948), pp. 279–304.

[26] Friend, Irwin, F. E. Brown, Edward S. Herman, Douglas Vickers. *A Study of Mutual Funds* (Washington, D. C.: U.S. Government Printing Office, 1962).

[27] Friend, Irwin, and Douglas Vickers. "Portfolio Selection and Investment Performance," *Journal of Finance*, Vol. XX (September, 1965), pp. 391–415.

[28] Friend, Irwin, and Douglas Vickers. "Reevaluation of Alternative Portfolio Selection Models," *Journal of Business*, Vol. XXXXI (April, 1968), pp. 174–79.

[29] Hakansson, Nils H. "Optimal Investment and Consumption Strategies for a Class of Utility Functions," Working Paper No. 101 (Los Angeles, Calif.: Western Management Science Institute, 1966).

[30] Horowitz, Ira. "A Model for Mutual Fund Evaluation," *Industrial Management Review*, Vol. VI (Spring, 1965), pp. 81–92.

[31] Horowitz, Ira. "The 'Reward-to-Variability' Ratio and Mutual Fund Performance," *Journal of Business*, Vol. XXXIX (October, 1966), pp. 485–88.

[32] Jensen, Michael C. "The Performance of Mutual Funds in the Period 1945–1964," *Journal of Finance*, Vol. XXIII (May, 1968), pp. 389–416.

[33] Johnston, J. *Econometric Methods* (New York, N. Y.: McGraw-Hill Book Co., 1963).

[34] King, Benjamin F. "Market and Industry Factors in Stock Price Behavior," *Journal of Business*, Vol. XXXIX, Part II (January, 1966), pp. 139–90.

[35] Latané, Henry A. "Portfolio Balance—the Demand for Money, Bonds, and Stocks," *Southern Economic Journal*, Vol. XXIX (October, 1962), pp. 71–76.

[36] Lintner, John. "The Valuation of Risk Assets and the Selection of Risky Investments in Stock Portfolios and Capital Budgets," *Review of Economics and Statistics*, Vol. XLVII (February, 1965), pp. 13–37.

[37] Lintner, John. "Security Prices, Risk, and Maximal Gains from Diversification," *Journal of Finance*, Vol. XX (December, 1965), pp. 587–616.

[38] Mandelbrot, Benoit. "The Variation of Certain Speculative Prices," *Journal of Business*, Vol. XXXVI (October, 1963), pp. 394–419.

[39] Mandelbrot, Benoit. "Forecasts of Future Prices, Unbiased Markets and 'Martingale' Models," *Journal of Business*, Vol. XXXIX, Part 2 (January, 1966), pp. 242–55.

[40] Markowitz, Harry M. "Portfolio Selection," *Journal of Finance*, Vol. VII (March, 1952), pp. 77–91.

[41] Markowitz, Harry M. "The Utility of Wealth," *Journal of Political Economy*, Vol. LX (April, 1952), pp. 151–58.

[42] Markowitz, Harry M. "Cowles Foundation Monograph No. 16," *Portfolio Selection: Efficient Diversification of Investments* (New York, N. Y.: John Wiley & Sons, 1959).

[43] Mossin, Jan. "Equilibrium in a Capital Asset Market," *Econometrica*, XXXIV (October, 1966), pp. 768–83.

[44] Mossin, Jan. "Optimal Multiperiod Portfolio Policies," *Journal of Business*, Vol. XXXXI (April, 1968), pp. 215–29.

[45] Pratt, John W. "Risk Aversion in the Small and in the Large," *Econometrica*, Vol. XXXII (January–April, 1964), pp. 122–36.

[46] Roll, Richard. "The Efficient Market Model Applied to U.S. Treasury Bill Rates" (unpublished Ph.D. dissertation, University of Chicago, 1968).

[47] Samuelson, Paul A. "Proof That Properly Anticipated Prices Fluctuate Randomly," *Industrial Management Review*, Vol. VI (Spring, 1965), pp. 41–49.

[48] Samuelson, Paul A. "General Proof That Diversification Pays," *Journal of Financial and Quantitative Analysis*, Vol. II (March, 1967), pp. 1–13.

[49] Scholes, Myron. "A Test of the Competitive Market Hypothesis: An Examination of the Market for New Issues and Secondary Offerings" (unpublished Ph.D. thesis proposal, University of Chicago, 1967).

[50] Securities and Exchange Commission. *Public Policy Implications of Investment Company Growth* (Washington, D. C.: U.S. Government Printing Office, 1966).

[51] Sharpe, William F. "A Simplified Model for Portfolio Analysis," *Management Science* (January, 1963), pp. 277–93.

[52] Sharpe, William F. "Capital Asset Prices: A Theory of Market Equilibrium under Conditions of Risk," *Journal of Finance*, Vol. XIX (September, 1964), pp. 425–42.

[53] Sharpe, William F. "Reply," *Journal of Finance*, Vol. XX (March, 1965), pp. 94–95.

[54] Sharpe, William F. "Risk Aversion in the Stock Market," *Journal of Finance*, Vol. XX (September, 1965), pp. 416–22.

[55] Sharpe, William F. "Mutual Fund Performance," *Journal of Business*, Vol. XXXIX, Part 2 (January, 1966), pp. 119–38.

[56] Sharpe, William F. "Security Prices, Risk, and Maximal Gains from Diversification: Reply," *Journal of Finance* (December, 1966), pp. 743–44.

[57] Sharpe, William F. "Linear Programming Algorithm for Mutual Fund Portfolio Selection," *Management Science*, Vol. XIII (March, 1967), pp. 499–510.

[58] Sharpe, William F. "Reply," *Journal of Business*, Vol. XLI (April, 1968), pp. 235–36.

[59] Shelton, John P. "The Value Line Contest: A Test of the Predictability of Stock Price Changes," *Journal of Business*, Vol. XL (July, 1967), pp. 251–69.

[60] Standard & Poor's Corporation. *Trade and Securities Statistics: Security Price Index Record* (Orange, Conn.: Standard & Poor's Corporation, 1960).

[61] Tobin, James. "Liquidity Preference as Behavior Towards Risk," *Review of Economic Studies*, Vol. XXV (February, 1958), pp. 65–85.

[62] Tobin, James. "The Theory of Portfolio Selection," in F. H. Hahn and F. P. R. Brechling (eds.), *The Theory of Interest Rates* (New York, N. Y.: St. Martin's Press, 1965).

[63] Treynor, Jack L. "How To Rate Management of Investment Funds," *Harvard Business Review*, Vol. XLIII (January–February, 1965), pp. 63–75.

[64] Treynor, Jack L. "Toward a Theory of Market Value of Risky Assets (unpublished manuscript, undated).

[65] Von Neuman, John, and Oscar Morgenstern. *Theory of Games and Economic Behavior* (Princeton, N. J.: Princeton U. P., 1953).

[66] West, Richard R. "Mutual Fund Performance and the Theory of Capital Asset Pricing: Some Comments," *Journal of Business*, Vol. XLI (April, 1968), pp. 230–34.

[67] Wiesenberger, Arthur. *Investment Companies* (New York, N. Y.: Arthur Wiesenberger & Co., 1955 and 1965).

[68] Wise, John. "Linear Estimators for Linear Regression Systems Having Infinite Variances" (unpublished paper presented at the Berkeley-Stanford Mathematical Economics Seminar, October, 1963).

Jack L. Treynor[*]

12. How to Rate Management of
Investment Funds

Reprinted from **Harvard Business Review,** Vol. 43, No. 1 (January-February, 1965), pp. 63–75, by permission of the author and the publisher.

Investment management has become an important industry in the United States. The responsibilities of investment managers are enormous, and their potential rewards are great. In order to reward management for good performance in this field, however, it is necessary to be able to recognize it. Unfortunately, pension funds, trust funds, and mutual funds all share one serious problem: to the extent that they are heavily invested in common stocks, the return achieved in any one period is subject to wide fluctuations which are beyond the control of investment management. The result has been that, although many believe the quality of investment management is important, no one has devised a satisfactory way to measure its impact on performance.

In this article we shall look at a new way to rate the performance of a fund's investment managers. The comprehensiveness of this rating is a question for the reader to decide for himself, depending on how he thinks about the "quality" of investment management. Most readers are likely to agree, however, that at least one dimension—and a critical one—of the quality of the investment management is analyzed by this new method.

ANALYZING RISK

It is almost ironic that the presence of market risk should pose such a serious problem. The assets controlled by investment managers are remarkably liquid. To a degree almost unmatched in other enterprises, the investment manager is free to act independently of the investment decisions of his predecessors. Furthermore, although there are varying institutional restrictions placed on the investment manager's decisions, by and large he competes directly with other investment managers, buying

[*] Editor, *Financial Analysts Journal.*

and selling securities in the same market. If it were not for the problems created by market risk, therefore, performance comparisons in the investment management industry would be more meaningful than in many other industries.

Actually, of course, there is more than one kind of risk in a diversified fund. There is a risk produced by general market fluctuations—the volatility of the stock market. There is also a risk resulting from fluctuations in the particular securities held by the fund. In any event, here are important practical consequences of either or both of these risks:

1. The effect of management on the rate of return on investments made in any one period is usually swamped by fluctuations in the general market. Depending on whether, during the period in question, the general market is rising or falling, the more volatile funds (stock funds) will look better or worse than the less volatile funds (balanced funds). As the Wharton Report points out, the difficulty is not solved by averaging return over a number of periods.[1] For any sample interval of reasonable length, average return is still dominated by market trends.

2. Measures of average return make no allowance for investors' aversions to risk. The importance of fluctuations in one or a few stocks from the investor's point of view is apparent when one considers that, after all, if this kind of risk were not important, investors would not diversify. It is sometimes argued that because the importance attached to risk varies from investor to investor, no absolute measure of fund performance is possible.

Overcoming difficulties

In order to have any practical value, a measure of management performance in handling a trust fund invested in equities or in handling pension or mutual funds must deal effectively with both problems. It should tend to remain constant so long as management performance is constant—even in the face of severe market fluctuations. Also, it should take into account the aversion of individual shareholders or beneficiaries to investment risk. The method to be described here overcomes both difficulties.

This article has three parts. The first describes a simple graphical method for capturing the essence of what is permanent and distinctive

---

[1] In discussing the cumulative performance of investment funds between January 1, 1953, and September 30, 1958, the report says "...the interpretation of the net result is to be made against the background of the movements in security market prices during this period...general fund performance and comparisons among funds of different types might be quite different in other time periods...," *A Study of Mutual Funds* (Washington, D. C.: Government Printing Office, 1962), p. 308.

about the performance of a fund, including the effects of fund management. The second develops a concept of fund performance which takes investment risk into account. The third develops a measure for rating fund-management performance which can be applied directly, using the graphical technique developed in the first part. For the statistician, an Appendix details certain of the relationships used.

THE CHARACTERISTIC LINE

The first main step to obtaining a satisfactory performance measure is to relate the expected rate of return of a trust, pension, or mutual fund to the rate of return of a suitable market average. The device for accomplishing this is the *characteristic line*. Let us examine its nature and significance.

Application to funds

If the rate of return—taking into account both market appreciation and dividends—is plotted for a fund invested substantially in common stocks, wide swings from period to period are often evident. It is not generally known, however, that most managed funds actually demonstrate a remarkably stable performance pattern over time when viewed in terms of the simple graphical device which I call the characteristic line.

Exhibit 1 summarizes the performance history of four actual managed funds:

● The horizontal and vertical axes in these figures are measured in terms of percent rate of return. (For both individual funds and market averages, rate of return is computed by dividing the sum of dividends, interest, and market appreciation on the funds available at the beginning of the year by the value of the funds available at the beginning of the year. Any increase in asset value during the year due to infusion of new funds is eliminated, as is any reduction due to distributions to beneficiaries or shareholders. Rates of return defined in this way are obviously approximations, because the value of funds available for investment typically fluctuates more or less continuously throughout the year.)

● The horizontal axis measures the corresponding rate of return recorded for a general *market* average (the Dow-Jones Industrial Average); the vertical axis shows the rate of return for the *fund*.

● Each point represents a year in the ten-year interval ending January 1, 1963. The points in orange represent the five years in the latter half of the ten-year interval; the points in black, the years in the former half.

Although the funds exhibited wide swings in rate of return over the ten-year interval, the rate of return in each year fell into a straight-line pattern which remained virtually fixed throughout the ten-year interval. This line—the characteristic line—can be fitted by eye or by statistical methods. The significant thing about it is that it tends to be stationary over time, despite wide fluctuations in short-term rate of return.

EXHIBIT 1
CHARACTERISTIC LINES

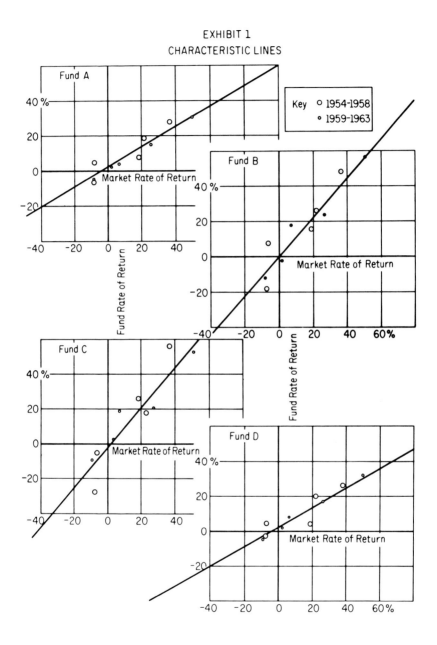

Information revealed

The characteristic line contains information about both expected rate of return and risk. The slope of the line measures volatility. Thus, a steep slope means that the actual rate of return for the fund in question is relatively sensitive to fluctuations in the general stock market; a gentle slope indicates that the fund in question is relatively insensitive to market fluctuations.

The slope angle of the characteristic line obviously provides a more refined measure of a fund's volatility than the usual categories of "balanced fund," "stock fund," or "growth fund." The range of volatilities observed in actual practice is enormous. Among mutual funds, for example, I have found that volatilities range from roughly one-third to about two. A volatility of two means that a 1 percent increase (or decrease) in the rate of return demonstrated by the Dow-Jones Average is accompanied, on the average, by a 2 percent increase (or decrease) in the rate of return demonstrated by the particular fund in question.

For any individual investor who is risk-averse, the observed differences in volatility are surely large enough to be worth measuring. The differences also disclose important contrasts in management policy.

What deviations mean

As users of the characteristic-line method will discover, the plotted points in a typical chart will not all lie on the characteristic line. What this means is that not all of the risk in the fund in question is explained by fluctuations in the general market level.

As pointed out earlier, one can consider that investment risk in a diversified fund is the sum of responses to (1) general market fluctuations and (2) fluctuations peculiar to the particular securities held by the fund. If a fund is properly diversified, the latter risk, which tends to be causally unrelated one security from another, tends to average out. The former risk, being common to all common stocks in greater or lesser degree, does not tend to average out.

If the management of a fund attempts to maintain a constant degree of volatility, then the slope of the characteristic line will tend to measure that volatility. If there are excessive deviations from the characteristic line, we have a strong indication that:

● Either the fund is not efficiently diversified to minimize risk unrelated to the general market (in which case the owner or beneficiary incurs additional risk without any compensating prospects of additional return).

● Or, perhaps inadvertently or perhaps as a matter of deliberate policy, management has altered the volatility of the fund. By increasing fund volatility when it is optimistic and decreasing volatility when it is pessimistic, management can speculate for the fund beneficiaries on fluctuations in the general market.

The appropriateness of such action is an interesting question but outside the scope of this article. It is worth noting, though, that in a sample I have taken of 54 American mutual funds, 4 out of 5 demonstrate fairly clear-cut characteristic-line patterns, with correlation coefficients equal to or exceeding 90 percent.

Possibly this pattern indicates wide agreement that causing fund volatility to vary greatly leaves the individual owner unable to rely on a stable estimate of risk in the portion of his personal portfolio represented by the fund in question. His ability to strike what for him is the optimal overall portfolio balance between expected return and risk is then impaired. But if, in retrospect, fund management has speculated successfully with the volatility of a fund, it is conceivable that beneficiaries may consider the disadvantage more than offset by the improved rate of return.

Suppose the characteristic line itself shifts? This may happen when fund volatility remains constant but fund performance varies widely from year to year. A sweeping change in the personnel constituting fund management, for example, might be accompanied by a sudden shift in fund performance.

Comparing performance

The characteristic line also contains information about management's ability to obtain a consistently higher return than the competition's. If, for example, two trust or mutual funds demonstrate precisely the same volatility, their respective characteristic lines would have the same slope, but one line would be consistently higher than the other (unless they coincide). For instance, suppose a certain fund had exactly the same slope as Fund A in Exhibit 1. If its characteristic line were plotted on the chart, it would run parallel to Fund A's but higher or lower. The fund with the higher line would demonstrate consistently higher performance—in good years and bad.

Although the problem of comparing performances of fund managements is obviously not so simple when the slopes differ, the characteristic line does contain, as we shall see presently, the information necessary to make such comparisons.

Implications for control

The characteristic line has implications for management control, too. No matter how widely the rate of return for a fund may fluctuate, management performance is unchanged so long as the actual rate of return continues to lie on the characteristic line. One can establish control limits on either side of the line; points falling within these limits are assumed to represent a continuation of past management performance, while points falling outside the limits require special scrutiny. Without the characteristic line it is virtually impossible to tell whether the rate of return demonstrated in a given year represents a real change in the quality of fund management. With it, early detection of important changes becomes possible.

In summary, therefore, the graphical method provides a simple test of:

1. The extent to which a fund has adhered, purposely or not, to a single characteristic line.
2. The degree of volatility associated with the fund.
3. The success of fund management in maintaining a high rate of return under a variety of market conditions.

PERFORMANCE MEASURE

We turn now to a second line. This one deals not with an individual fund but with a *portfolio* containing a certain fund. The purpose of the line is to relate the expected return of a portfolio containing the fund to the portfolio owner's risk preferences. This line can be called the *portfolio-possibility* line. We shall see that the slope of this line is a measure of fund performance which transcends differences in investors' attitudes toward risk.

Risk preference

Whether the performance pattern of a given fund rates high or low should depend on whether individual investors choose it in preference to the pattern demonstrated by other funds. During the last few years we have witnessed the rapid development of a theory of rational choice among portfolios.[2] The theory is too complex to be reviewed here in detail, but certain fragments of it provide the basis for a concept of fund-management performance.

It is interesting to note that when one talks about the historical performance pattern of a fund, he is looking at the past; but when he considers the preferences of individual investors and their choices among funds, he is talking about their appraisal of the future. We shall continue to talk about the performance of funds in terms of historical performance patterns, even though actual investor choices among funds are necessarily based on expectations regarding future performance patterns. The implication is that a good historical performance pattern is one which, if continued into the future, would cause investors to prefer it to others.

[2] See, for example, H. M. Markowitz, *Portfolio Selection: Efficient Diversification of Investments* (New York, N.Y.: John Wiley & Sons, 1959); and D. E. Farrar, *The Investment Decision Under Uncertainty* (Englewood Cliffs, N.J.: Prentice-Hall, Inc., 1962).

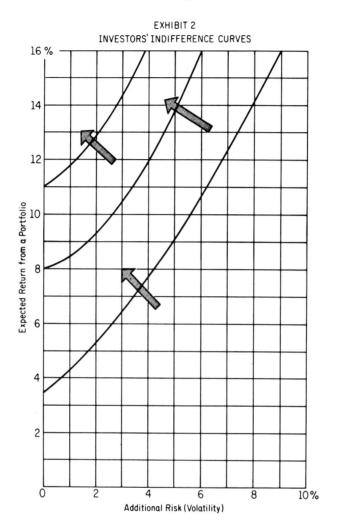

EXHIBIT 2
INVESTORS' INDIFFERENCE CURVES

Economists sometimes study the investor's choice among possible portfolios in terms of a risk-return diagram (like that in Exhibit 2):

● The vertical axis in the exhibit measures the return which the investor would expect to get, on the average, from a given portfolio. The horizontal axis is some appropriate measure of risk.

(As a technical note for those interested in detail, let me add that it is traditional to measure the respective axes in terms of *expected rate of return*, where the rate is a weighted mean of possible future outcomes, and *standard error*, where standard error is a statistical measure of potential variability around the expected performance. Under certain assumptions regarding the nature of investment uncertainty, expected return and standard error completely characterize a given portfolio. These assumptions seem to fit actual stock-market experience fairly well.

When the performance pattern of a mutual fund is clustered closely around the characteristic line, the slope of this line, which is our graphical measure of risk, is statistically an excellent measure of the standard error.)

● The rate of return is for a standard time period—perhaps a month, quarter, or year—per dollar of the individual investor's initial capital.

● The curved lines in the diagram are called indifference curves for the reason that the investor is indifferent to portfolio choices lying on a particular indifference curve; that is, he would just as soon have, say, 5 percent more return at $4\frac{1}{2}$ percent more risk as 8 percent more return at $6\frac{1}{2}$ percent more risk, and so on (see the curve at right of Exhibit 2).[3]

● There is a useful analogy between the investor's relative preference, as shown by indifference curves, and relative heights, as shown by contour lines on a topographical map—that is, lines along which elevation is constant. The arrows in the figure show the direction in which one moves to go from less to more desirable portfolios (or, to complete the topographical analogy, uphill).

Portfolio choices

What kinds of portfolio choices are available to the investor? The assets he can include in his portfolio consist of two fundamentally different kinds:

1. Money-fixed claims, such as checking deposits, savings deposits, government, municipal, and corporate bonds.
2. Equity assets, including equity in personal business and partnerships and corporate common stocks.

The investor who holds money-fixed claims is subject to the risk of changes in both the interest rate and price level. Although both risks are real, in American financial history they have been small compared to the risk entailed in owning equities. The relative insignificance of market risk in money-fixed claims is reflected in the narrow range of net returns available in such claims. We shall simplify slightly and represent all assets of this type by a single point on the vertical axis of the risk-return diagram (point B in Exhibit 3).

If the investor wants to raise the expected rate of return of his overall portfolio above the rate offered by money-fixed claims, he must undertake some equity risk. On the risk-return diagram in Exhibit 3, the investor has available to him the opportunity to invest in shares in a particular balanced or growth fund, Fund A, as well as the opportunity to invest in money-fixed claims, B. If he is free to vary the investment in each outlet more or less continuously, then the locus of portfolio combinations available to him is the straight line—viz., the portfolio-possibility line—joining points A and B. The combination which is best for him will

---

[3] For elegant mathematical proof of the validity of indifference curves, see James Tobin, "Liquidity Preference as Behavior Towards Risk," *Review of Economic Studies* (February, 1958), p. 65; a subsequently written, unpublished manuscript by the author carries the discussion further.

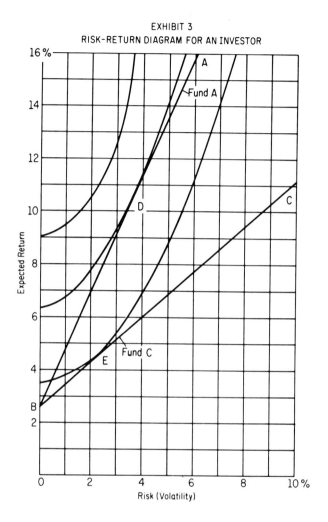

EXHIBIT 3
RISK-RETURN DIAGRAM FOR AN INVESTOR

lie at point D along the line which is farthest "uphill" as indicated by the "contour lines" on his indifference map. The preferred combinations for other investors will differ, depending on the precise shape of their indifference curves.

Now consider a second investment, Fund C (top right of Exhibit 3). The line BC is the locus of possible portfolios made available to our investor by the existence of this investment. As in the case of locus BA, there will, in general, be a single point, E, along BC, which is the farthest "uphill" for the investor.

The significant fact is that, although the location of the points of optimum balance along lines BC and BA will differ from one investor to another, the optimum point D along line BA will always be superior for a given investor to the optimum point E along line BC. For every possible level of risk an investor might choose, the return on a combined portfolio containing Fund A is greater than the return on a portfolio containing Fund C, which provides the same level of risk. This ensures that, whatever the optimum point along line BC may be for a particular investor, the point on BA directly above it (that is, with the same risk) will have a greater expected return. This will be true for every investor who is risk averse, quite independently of the precise shape of his indifference curve.

But if, for every risk-averse investor, line BA is superior to line BC, then, in terms of the portfolio possibilities this line makes available to investors, Fund A is absolutely superior to Fund C. Now it is apparent from Exhibit 3 that lines BA and BC differ only in slope. Line BA, which is superior to line BC, slopes upward more sharply, showing that the rate of gain from shifting the investor's portfolio in the direction of greater risk is greater for Fund A than for Fund C. *The steepness of the portfolio-possibility line associated with a given fund is thus a direct measure of the desirability of the fund to the risk-averse investor.* The force of the preceding argument is not diminished by the fact that many investment funds contain money-fixed claims as well as equities.

Pension and trust funds

All very well for mutual funds, you may say. After all, the investor in mutual funds is free to adjust the fraction of his portfolio invested in each one pretty much as he pleases. But what about cases involving pension funds and trust funds, in which the individual beneficiary has no freedom whatever to alter the fraction of his total assets which are managed by the fund? To answer this question, let us take an illustration:

Suppose a man has a certain fraction of his assets invested in a pension fund. Suppose further that the management performance of the pension fund (measured in terms of the slope of the portfolio-possibility line) ranks just equal to the performance of a certain mutual fund. A certain segment of the portfolio-possibility line for the mutual fund will be unavailable to the investor if part of his funds are irrevocably committed to the pension fund, since he is not free to convert all his assets to money-fixed claims. Within the range of the portfolio-possibility line available to him, however, he can achieve the same portfolio behavior with part of his capital committed to the pension fund as he could achieve if he were free to compose the risky portion of his portfolio entirely from the mutual fund in question. If his attitude toward portfolio risk leads him to choose a portfolio in this range, then he will be indifferent as to a choice of a pension fund or a mutual fund with an equal performance ranking. If, on the other hand, his choice lies outside this range, then the pension fund is less useful to him than a mutual fund with similarly sloped portfolio-possibility line.

Quantitative measure

The performance demonstrated by a fund can be measured by the tangent of the slope angle, symbolized by the figure $\propto$. (For instance, the slope angle for Fund C in Exhibit 3 would be the difference between the slope of line BC and a horizontal line going through B; the slope angle for Fund A, which is larger, is the difference between BA and a horizontal.)

The formula for tangent $\propto$ follows directly from the geometry of Exhibit 3. As detailed in the Appendix, it is:

$$\text{tangent} \propto\ = \frac{\mu - \mu^*}{\sigma}$$

where μ equals the expected fund rate of return at a particular market rate of return, μ^* is measured from a horizontal line through a point that would represent a fund consisting only of fixed-income securities, and σ is the symbol for volatility (which can serve as an approximate measure of investment risk as plotted on the horizontal axis of Exhibit 3).

RATING MANAGEMENT

We are now ready to begin with the practical application of the concepts previously described. We will see how performance ratings can be read directly from the characteristic line.

Relative ranking

In order to plot a fund, and the associated portfolio-possibility line, on a risk-return chart of the type discussed in the last section, one needs both an expected rate of return and an appropriate measure of risk. A measure of risk is provided by the slope of the characteristic line. The characteristic line also enables management to estimate the expected rate of return. In order to obtain a value for the expected rate of return for the fund, however, it is necessary to assume a rate-of-return value for the market. Depending on the choice of market rate of return, expected return for the fund—hence the slope of the opportunity locus—will vary. The effect of changing the assumed market rate is illustrated in Exhibits 4 and 5 as follows:

● Exhibit 4 portrays a sample of characteristic lines for 20 actual managed funds based on rate-of-return data for the years 1953 through 1962. By making specific assumptions about the market rate of return, the characteristic lines for these funds can be transformed into points on the risk-return charts shown in parts a and b of Exhibit 5. (The term "volatility" on the horizontal axes of these charts, as indicated before, refers to the amount of risk in the fund due to fluctuations in the general market.)

EXHIBIT 4
COMPARISON OF 20 MANAGED FUNDS

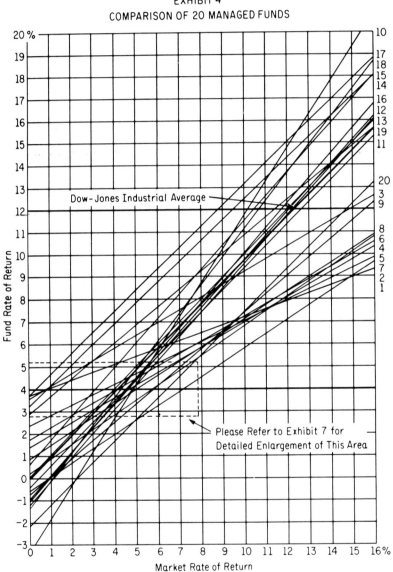

EXHIBIT 5
FUND RANKINGS UNDER DIFFERENT MARKET CONDITIONS

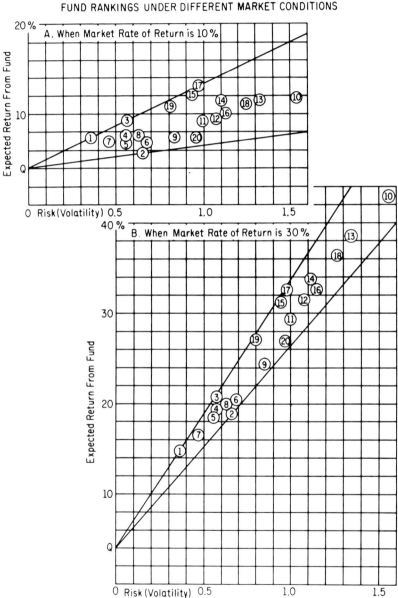

● Part a of Exhibit 5 was plotted by assuming a market return of 10 percent. (The characteristic line for each fund is inspected to determine its pattern of return when the market's return is 10 percent, and this pattern is converted to a point reflecting risk and return.) Given this assumption, the funds in question can easily be ranked visually; by drawing straight lines from point Q to these points, one can obtain the portfolio-possibility lines for the funds in question. The problem is, of course, that the market-return assumption is arbitrary and other returns depend on it.

● Part b results when a market rate of return of 30 percent is assumed instead. Although the risk values for the individual funds are unchanged, the expected rates of return are affected, and a new set of portfolio-possibility lines results.

Inspection shows that the ranking of the funds is unchanged in parts a and b of Exhibit 5. For example, the highest- and lowest-ranking funds in part a are, respectively, the highest- and lowest-ranking funds in part b, despite the fact that the two diagrams are based on widely differing assumptions about the expected rate of return for the general market. This illustrates what is actually a quite general result: although the absolute position of funds on a risk-return chart (and their corresponding portfolio-possibility lines) may vary with the level of market rate of return assumed, *the ranking of funds with respect to each other does not.*

Numerical measure

What is desired, therefore, is a number which will measure the relative ranking of a fund—preferably without being affected by changes in the absolute level of rate of return of the kind illustrated by parts a and b of Exhibit 5. It happens that there is a number which has these properties: it is the level of rate of return for the general market at which the fund in question will produce the same return as that produced by a fund consisting solely of riskless investment. As Exhibit 6 shows, its value can be read directly from the characteristic line.

A horizontal line is drawn so as to intersect the vertical axis at a point representing the rate of return available on money-fixed claims. In Exhibit 6 the horizontal line is drawn at 4 percent. (The choice of rate within the range of $3\frac{1}{2}$ percent to 5 percent is somewhat arbitrary, but not especially critical as regards its effect on performance ratings.) The point at which the horizontal line intersects the characteristic line determines the rating of the fund, which is read off the horizontal axis as a percentage. The lower this percentage, the higher the rating of the pension, trust, or mutual fund. For those interested in a formal proof that the number just defined will have the special properties desired, the Appendix sets forth the steps in the reasoning.

In order to demonstrate the practical significance of the rating technique, let us refer back to Exhibit 4. Each of the performance ratings of the 20 funds whose characteristic lines are shown in this chart could be read directly from the figure if a horizontal line corresponding to the rate

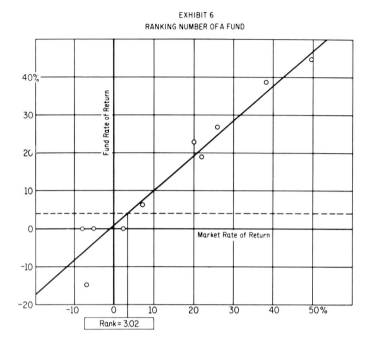

EXHIBIT 6
RANKING NUMBER OF A FUND

of return on a riskless portfolio (here 4 percent) were added. The performance rating for each fund could be determined by the value of market
rate of return at which its characteristic line intersects the horizontal
4 percent line. Now see Exhibit 7. The characteristic lines are the same
as the ones in Exhibit 4, but a 4 percent horizontal has been added, and
the area of intersection with it has been expanded for ease in reading.
Note that the performance ratings for the 20 funds (read off the horizontal axis) range from less than 1 percent to more than 7 percent.

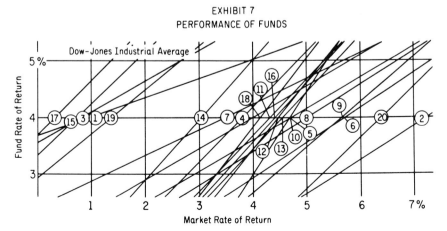

EXHIBIT 7
PERFORMANCE OF FUNDS

Differences important

Is the difference between the best and worst rated fund in Exhibit 7 large enough to be significant to an investor? Let us take an illustration:

Suppose that an investor specifies his portfolio volatility should be equal to one. The amount of "riskless" investment or borrowing which he undertakes will depend on the volatility of the fund. Let us say that Fund XYZ has a volatility of two. Since the desired portfolio volatility is one, then the portfolio must be blended of equal parts (in terms of dollars invested) of the fund and riskless investment. If, for example, the beneficiary's capital is initially worth $10,000, then, since a 1 percent reduction in the market rate of return will be accompanied on the average by a 2 percent reduction in the rate of return on $5,000 invested in the fund, the effective reduction in *portfolio* rate of return is 1 percent since:

$$\frac{.02 \times \$5,000}{\$10,000} = .01.$$

Now assume that the fund in question has a volatility of .75. If the investor's desired portfolio volatility is one, he must invest an amount exceeding his own capital. If his capital is again $10,000, and he borrows $3,333 and invests that sum in Fund XYZ, then a 1 percent reduction in the market rate of return will be accompanied on the average by a .0075 percent reduction in the rate of return on $13,333 invested in the fund. The effective reduction in *portfolio* rate of return is then 1 percent because:

$$\frac{.0075 \times \$13,333}{\$10,000} = .01$$

In both cases the portfolios have a volatility equal to one—the value specified—but the differing fund volatilities necessitate quite different investment strategies.

Is the significance of rating differences for a sample of funds influenced by market conditions? It is to a certain extent. We have already seen that one cannot employ characteristic-line data to obtain an expected rate of return for a fund without first assuming a value for the market rate of return. It is consequently not possible to make categorical statements about the spread in expected portfolio performance between the best and worst managed funds which results when an investor specifies a certain level of portfolio volatility. It is nevertheless possible to get a rough idea of the significance of the spread in performance ratings observed in a sample by making different assumptions about the market. If we take the extreme cases in the sample of 20 funds already described, for instance, we find these differences in investment return:

Expected market rate of return	10 percent	30 percent
Return of highest-ranked fund	13.6 percent	33.4 percent
Return of lowest-ranked fund	6.6 percent	26.6 percent

These figures suggest the following conclusions about differences in ratings:

1. In the range of normal market rate of return, the difference in portfolio rate of return between funds ranked high and low is substantial.
2. The difference seems relatively less important, the higher the performance of the general market is. Hence the consequences of rating differences for portfolio performance will be relatively more significant in a normal market than during the bull market of recent history.

CONCLUSION

In this article we have seen that there is a good way of cutting through the confusion of facts and figures in the marketplace to compare the performance of individual trust, pension, and mutual funds. The new method described is surely not a perfect answer to the needs of fund managers and investment analysts, for it requires the making of certain assumptions about fund performance with which not all men will completely agree (e.g., the desirability of a fund's holding to a consistent investment policy). But the method goes at least part of the way, I believe, to providing answers that have long eluded executives in the investment business.

We have seen that, consistent with any specified level of the market rate of return, there is associated with each fund a range of combinations of expected portfolio return and risk. The slope of the portfolio-possibility line measures the rate at which the individual investor increases the expected rate of return of his portfolio as his burden of portfolio risk increases. A comparison of slopes among funds provides a means of rating funds which transcends variations in individual investors' attitudes toward risk. Although the slopes vary just as the market rate of return varies, it can be proved that the ranking of the funds represented remains unchanged. The relative rankings can be read directly from the characteristic lines of funds to be compared.

Differences in ranking based on the characteristic lines can be quite significant for individual investors, even though they take varying attitudes toward risk. Also, the differences are independent of market fluctuations. Because the ranking measure has these properties, it provides a useful basis for reviewing the performance of fund management.

APPENDIX

Figure A shows the characteristic line for a typical fund. For each possible value of the market rate of return, the characteristic line predicts the corresponding

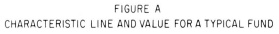

FIGURE A

CHARACTERISTIC LINE AND VALUE FOR A TYPICAL FUND

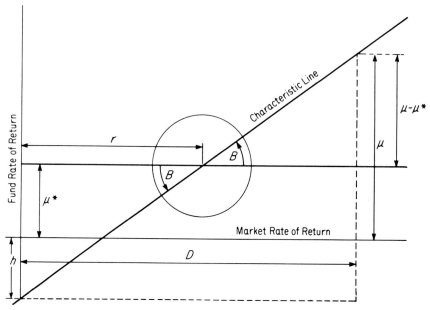

rate of return for the fund pictured. The slope of the characteristic line is measured by tangent B; the vertical intercept is h. For the particular market rate of return D, the expected fund rate of return is μ. A horizontal line drawn a distance μ^* above the horizontal axis depicts the behavior of a fund consisting solely of fixed income securities. The ranking measure r is determined by the intersection of the characteristic line and the horizontal line at height μ^*.

The question is whether the ranking measure r has the properties specified; that is, whether it will

. . . rank funds in the order of their respective values of tangent $\propto$ (the slope of the opportunity locus as discussed earlier in the article);

. . . have the same value for a given fund, independently of fluctuations in the market rate of return.

A moment's reflection shows that no number can have both properties simultaneously unless the general result alluded to in the main text holds true; that is, unless the *relative* ranking of funds—in terms of the slope of the portfolio-possibility line—is unaffected by fluctuations in the general market. Inasmuch as the proof demonstrates that the number in question does indeed have both properties, the general result follows.

From the geometry of the diagram, we have for the volatility:

$$\sigma = \text{tangent } B = \frac{\mu - \mu^*}{D - r}$$

Solving for r, we obtain:

$$r = D - \left(\frac{\mu - \mu^*}{\sigma}\right)$$

The expression in parentheses is the ranking measure discussed in the section on portfolio-possibility lines (see "Performance Measure," p. 240), with the volatility, σ, serving as the approximate measure of investment risk. We conclude that, for any given level of market rate of return D, r is uniquely related to the ranking fraction

$$\frac{\mu - \mu^*}{\sigma}$$ (which equals tangent α).

We note that a relatively large value of r signifies a relatively low level of performance for fund management. A second important property of r is obtained when the following relationship, based on the geometry of the diagram, is substituted in the previous expression for r:

$$\mu = D \text{ tangent } B + h = D\alpha + h$$

Substituting for μ, we find that:

$$r = \frac{\mu^* - h}{\sigma}$$

Now μ^* is the same for all funds and independent of market fluctuations; and h and σ are the intercept and slope, respectively, of the characteristic line. It is clear in this formulation that r is independent of D, the market rate of return. Hence r tends to have the same value independently of fluctuations in the general market.

*Edward F. Renshaw**

13. Portfolio Balance Models in Perspective: Some Generalizations That Can Be Derived from the Two-Asset Case[1]

Reprinted from the **Journal of Financial and Quantitative Analysis,** Vol. II, No. 2 (June, 1967), pp. 123–149, by permission of the author and publisher.

INTRODUCTION

Since the publication of Markowitz's article on "Portfolio Selection,"[2] which was subsequently expanded into a monograph,[3] there has been a great deal of further articulation,[4] a not inconsiderable amount of mathematical programming and sensitivity analysis,[5] the arrival of several

* Professor of Economics and Finance, State University of New York at Albany.

[1] The Author is especially indebted to Keith Smith, who generously incorporated some of the criteria in this paper into the Sharpe program and to Milton Drandell, who was instrumental in securing the correct listing which is necessary to utilize IBM's more general Markowitz program. This integration of diverse contributions to the theory of portfolio selection was a many-year process that has benefited greatly from conversations and comments by John Shelton, Martin Weingartner, Lawrence Fisher, Henry Latané, Norman Johnson, and Alfred Hofflander. Since these gentlemen have not had the opportunity to review this paper, the responsibility for any errors is clearly my own.

[2] *Journal of Finance,* Vol. 8 (March, 1952).

[3] *Portfolio Selection: Cowles Foundation Monograph 16,* (New York, N.Y.: John Wiley & Sons, 1959).

[4] James Tobin, "Liquidity Preference as Behavior Toward Risk," *Review of Economic Studies,* Vol. 25 (February, 1958), p. 73; William J. Baumol, "An Expected Gain–Confidence Limit Criterion for Portfolio Selection," *Management Science,* Vol. 10 (October, 1963), pp. 174–82; William F. Sharpe, "A Simplified Model for Portfolio Analysis," *ibid.,* Vol. 9 (January, 1963), pp. 277–90; John Lintner, "Security Prices, Risk, and Maximal Gains from Diversification," *The Journal of Finance,* Vol. 20 (December, 1965), pp. 587–615.

[5] IBM's three portfolio selection programs are discussed by Milton Drandell in a paper presented at the Institute of Management Sciences/Operations Research Society of America Joint Western Regional Meeting (April, 1965).

competing portfolio balance models,[6] and a near revolution in the theory of money and asset preference.[7] While few formulas for solving a practical problem can claim to have generated as much theoretical fall-out, the new approach to portfolio management apparently has not been very successful at reaching the practitioners for which it was intended.

One of the more important reasons for the lack of application is perhaps the fact that the mathematics are so complicated and/or so abstract as to not be easily understood or responded to in an intelligent way by the persons who are responsible for making the crucial value judgments.

The first part of this paper analyzes various facets of a two-asset case which can easily be expanded into a three-asset model containing two risk assets and one safe asset, such as money or short-term bonds held to maturity. Next, the ways in which a simple index can be constructed to enable the average investor to construct reasonably efficient portfolios of more than two risk assets without resort to an electronic computer are shown.

The second part of this paper considers the question of where on an efficient investment frontier is it rational to be. If wealth maximization is a preferrred criterion, it can be shown that diversification can be justified without resort to the concept of risk aversion on the grounds that it will yield a higher cumulative return if adjustments are made to keep the portfolio in balance.

The Markowitz theory of portfolio selection is essentially a constant ratio plan, if new information does not alter one's estimates of relevant parameters. The concluding section of this paper touches upon the behavioral implications of this theory and points out that simplified models are not necessarily inferior to the original Markowitz model if adjustments are deemed imprudent or so costly as to make a policy of buy and hold the more economical strategy.

A TWO-ASSET PORTFOLIO BALANCE MODEL

The parameters which are required to construct efficient portfolios are: (a) the expected or arithmetic average return for each security, (b) the standard deviation of the individual returns for each security, and (c)

[6] Henry A. Latané, "Investment Criteria—A Three Asset Portfolio Balance Model," *The Review of Economics and Statistics*, Vol. 45 (November, 1963), pp. 427–30; Jack Hirshleifer, "Investment Decision Under Uncertainty: Application of the State Preference Approach," *The Quarterly Journal of Economics*, Vol. 80 (May, 1966), pp. 252–77.

[7] The work of Tobin, Meltzer, Latané, and Chow all appear to have been influenced by the new approach to asset selection. For a more recent summary type article, see Gregory C. Chow, "On the Long-Run and Short-Run Demand for Money," *Journal of Political Economy*, Vol. 74 (April, 1966), pp. 111–29.

the correlation coefficient—the extent to which the returns from different securities either move together or with the market as a whole.

Let A equal the expected return on a portfolio consisting of two assets with expected returns of R_1 and R_2 and standard deviations of s_1 and s_2, respectively. Let p_1 equal the proportion of the portfolio that is invested in the asset with a return of R_1 and let $1 - p_1$ equal the proportion of the portfolio that is invested in the second asset. It has been shown that the expected return on the portfolio as a whole is a weighted sum of the expected returns on the component assets:

$$A = R_1 p_1 + R_2(1 - p_1) = R_2 + (R_1 - R_2)p_1 \qquad (1)$$

Our next requirement is the variance of this weighted sum, S^2. Where C is the correlation coefficient, the variance is equal to:

$$S^2 = p_1^2 s_1^2 + 2p_1(1 - p_1)C s_1 s_2 + (1 - p_1)^2 s_2^2 \qquad (2)$$

The investment frontier

An ordinary investment frontier can now be obtained for any two assets by simply inserting values of p_1 ranging from zero to plus one into Eqs. (1) and (2), solving these equations for A and S, and plotting the resulting values on chart paper. Selected solutions are plotted in Figure 1 for two assets which are assumed to have the same standard deviation equal to .5 (50 percentage points) and expected returns of 1.20 (20 percent) and 1.10 (10 percent). Three different degrees of intercor-

FIGURE 1

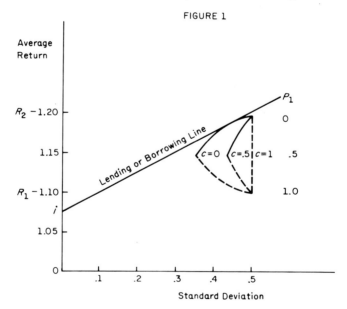

relation are assumed ranging from perfect positive correlation to zero correlation. The dotted portion of each frontier cannot be considered efficient since it is possible to both raise the expected return on the two-asset portfolio and decrease its standard deviation by simply increasing the portion of the portfolio that is invested in the asset with the higher expected return.

When the correlation coefficient is equal to plus one and both assets have the same standard deviation, it is only efficient to invest in the asset with the highest expected return. In this not too unrealistic case which sometimes emerges in connection with mergers, it is theoretically possible to obtain a completely certain return equal to the net difference between R_1 and R_2 by buying the security with the highest expected return R_2 and selling an equal dollar amount of R_1 short, provided the merger is completed on time and according to the original terms. Hedges involving short sales are not a part of ordinary diversification, but should be considered in a context of what I would call sophisticated diversification.

The optimal portfolio

Having utilized Eqs. (1) and (2) to delineate an efficient investment frontier for two risk assets, the next question is where on this frontier is it rational to be? An important step in answering this question was made by Professor Tobin who noted that Eq. (2) will become a simple linear equation if the standard deviation for the second asset is zero.

$$S = s_1 p_1 \tag{3}$$

This means that one can expand a curvilinear investment frontier for two risk assets into a straight line if the two assets are held in fixed proportions and then combined with a much safer third asset such as money, savings deposits or short term bonds held to maturity. The best fixed combination of two risk assets is that point on the investment frontier which is exactly tangent to the highest possible lending or borrowing line, if the risk assets are purchased on margin[8] (see Figure 1). Where i is a lending or borrowing rate and E is an index of efficiency, we can determine this point by maximizing the following expression:

$$E = (A - i)/S \tag{4}$$

---

[8] If margin requirements are restrictive and the investment frontier for risk assets has so little curvature as to be almost parallel to the borrowing line, there may be some advantage in slightly tipping the borrowing line in favor of riskier assets so as to maximize the benefits from limited leverage. This can be accomplished by raising the borrowing rate in the manner of a shadow price to establish a higher point of tangency and then making a judgment as to whether the incremental increase in expected return for the portfolio as a whole is worth the incremental increase in portfolio variance, leverage the same.

If we substitute Eqs. (1) and (2) into Eq. (4) for A and S, differentiate E with respect to p and set the resulting equation equal to zero, we obtain the following quadratic equation:

$$
\begin{aligned}
p_1{}^2[(R_2 - i)(R_1 - R_2)(2Cs_1s_2 - s_1{}^2 - s_2{}^2) + (R_1 - R_2)^2 \\
\times (Cs_1s_2 - s_2{}^2)] + p_1[(R_1 - R_2)s_2{}^2 + (R_2 - i)^2 \\
\times (2Cs_1s_2 - s_1{}^2 - s_2{}^2)] + (R_2 - i)(R_1 - R_2)s_2{}^2 \\
+ (R_2 - i)^2(s_2{}^2 - Cs_1s_2) = 0 \quad (5)
\end{aligned}
$$

While Eq. (5) appears to be complicated, it can easily be solved for the most efficient fixed combination of two risk assets $p_1{}^*$ by using the quadratic formula. When the expected returns on the two risk assets are the same ($R_1 - R_2 = 0$), Eq. (5) simplifies to:

$$
p_1{}^* = \frac{-Cs_1s_2 - s_2{}^2}{s_1{}^2 - 2Cs_1s_2 + s_2{}^2} \quad (6)
$$

Having solved Eqs. (5) or (6) for the optimum fixed combination of risk assets ($p_1{}^*$), one can then substitute this value into Eqs. (1) and (2) and obtain the expected return and standard deviation for the best portfolio of risk assets, i.e., that portfolio of two risk assets which is tangent to the lending or borrowing line. If the expected return on this combination of risk assets is then set equal to R_1 in Eq. (1), if R_2 is set equal to the borrowing or lending rate, and if s_1 in Eq. (3) is set equal to the standard deviation for the two risk assets held in the same fixed proportions, one can convert our two-asset model into a three-asset model and effectively generate all of the points implied by the line of tangency by combining the risk assets with cash or purchasing them on margin.

MODELS CONTAINING MORE THAN TWO RISK ASSETS

Moving from a three-asset model with one safe security to a model containing more than two risk assets has been sufficiently complicated to require an electronic computer to obtain answers which are even approximately correct. There was in the three-asset case, however, the inkling of an index number which can be used to obtain reasonably efficient portfolios of more than two risk assets without resort to mathematical programming.

This can best be appreciated by further analyzing Eq. (6), which has the advantage of being simple enough so that one can easily make sensitivity tests and quickly obtain a feel for optimum proportions when two assets have the same expected return but different correlations and standard deviations.

Let p_1 refer to that security with the highest standard deviation. By substituting a value of zero into Eq. (6) for $p_1{}^*$ we can then derive the conclusion that ordinary diversification will not be justified unless $p_1{}^*$ is positive, which will only be the case if the correlation coefficient is less than the ratio, s_2/s_1.

While this result is strictly true only when both risk assets have the same expected return, we can always use a risk free borrowing or lending rate i to lever the less risky security into what is, in effect, a new asset with the same expected return as a more risky asset. A borrowing or lending line which intersects the most efficient one risk asset can be described by the following equation: $R = i + [(R_2 - i)/s_2]S$. Setting R equal to R_1, solving for S, and substituting this value into the limiting condition $s_2/s_1 > C$ for s_2 yields Eqs. (7) and (8) and allows us to conclude as a more general rule that diversification will not be justified unless $p_1{}^*$ is positive, which will only be the case if

$$\frac{(R_1 - i)s_2}{(R_2 - i)s_1} - C > 0 \tag{7}$$

or

$$\frac{(R_j - i)}{s_j} \cdot \frac{s_0}{(R_0 - i)} - C_j > 0 \tag{8}$$

While Eq. (7) is a limiting condition applicable to a world of two risk assets where it is possible to borrow or lend at a fixed rate of interest, it can also be thought of as an index number which does an extremely good job of delineating those stocks which appear in the Sharpe version of the Markowitz portfolio selection program.

The use of a security index

Let R_0 and s_0 in Eq. (8) be base numbers which are obtained by computing the ratio $(R_j - i)/s_j$ for all risk assets and letting R_0 equal the expected return and s_0 equal the standard deviation for the jth asset with the highest ratio. This is the best risk asset to own if one were given the all-or-none choice of buying only one risk asset on margin or combining it with a risk-free security yielding a safe return i. Let C_j refer to the correlation coefficient between the jth security and a security index describing the average return on all risk assets.

When values for the left-hand side of Eq. (8) were computed for a sample of 150 securities developed by Keith Smith for the years 1953–64[9] and then ranked in order of magnitude, it was discovered that 19 of the

---

[9] Keith Smith, "A Transition Model for Portfolio Revision," *Journal of Finance* (September, 1967, Forthcoming).

TABLE 1. A COMPARISON OF SECURITY PROPORTIONS AND OTHER INFORMATION FOR ASSESSING THE EFFICIENCY OF ALTERNATIVE CRITERIA FOR PORTFOLIO SELECTION

(Average for the Period 1953–64)

Security	Realized Average Return	Standard Deviation	Correlation with		Security Proportions				
			DJIA Index	S&P's Industrials	(I)	(II)	(III)	(IV)	(V)
American Telephone	1.136	.162	.335	.362	.006	.022	.092	.058	.157
Bethlehem Steel	1.196	.362	.808	.863	.024			.014	.021
Chrysler	1.199	.445	.243	.264	.030			.371	.266
Eastman Kodak	1.200	.185	.618	.472		.180	.228		.029
General Electric	1.160	.176	.696	.638	.139	.075	.078	.071	.158
General Foods	1.218	.220	.610	.555	.145	.147	.168	.010	
General Motors	1.219	.280	.899	.940	.175	.050			
Goodyear	1.224	.303	.812	.814	.066	.032	.006	.042	.103
Procter & Gamble	1.206	.235	.480	.515	.181	.088	.120	.053	
Sears Roebuck	1.225	.242	.809	.791		.121	.085	.044	
Standard Oil (NJ)	1.180	.216	.642	.751		.056	.036		.070
Swift	1.116	.193	.410	.262	.199				.141
Texaco	1.228	.198	.774	.856		.229	.161	.323	.033
United Aircraft	1.193	.300	.358	.417			.026	.014	
U.S. Steel	1.200	.402	.878	.895	.036				
Westinghouse Electric	1.111	.248	.357	.228					.023
					(I)	(II)	(III)	(IV)	(V)
Average portfolio return..........					1.220	1.208	1.200	1.207	1.188
Portfolio standard deviation.......					.172	.156	.144	.142	.132
Portfolio efficiency index........					1.045	1.072	1.112	1.175	1.117

TABLE 1 (continued)

Security	Realized Average Return	Standard Deviation	Correlation with		Security Proportions				
			DJIA Index	S&P's Industrials	(VI)	(VII)	(VIII)	(IX)	(X)
American Telephone	1.136	.162	.335	.362	.190	.170	.180	.099	.166
Bethlehem Steel	1.196	.362	.808	.863					
Chrysler	1.199	.445	.243	.264	.029	.079	.129	.067	.058
Eastman Kodak	1.200	.185	.618	.472	.224	.174	.257	.258	.249
General Electric	1.160	.176	.696	.638		.014		.021	
General Foods	1.218	.220	.610	.555					
General Motors	1.219	.280	.899	.940	.146	.142	.193	.105	.152
Goodyear	1.224	.303	.812	.814					
Procter & Gamble	1.206	.235	.480	.515	.131	.155	.029	.040	.077
Sears Roebuck	1.225	.242	.809	.791					
Standard Oil (NJ)	1.180	.216	.642	.751		.024		.061	.015
Swift	1.116	.193	.410	.262		.002			
Texaco	1.228	.198	.774	.856	.219	.134	.212	.260	.224
United Aircraft	1.193	.300	.358	.417	.060	.105		.090	.058
U.S. Steel	1.200	.402	.878	.895					
Westinghouse Electric	1.111	.248	.357	.228					

	(VI)	(VII)	(VIII)	(IX)	(X)
Average portfolio return	1.197	1.193	1.190	1.200	1.198
Portfolio standard deviation	.132	.122	.110	.127	.125
Portfolio efficiency index	1.189	1.259	1.358	1.257	1.265

20 top stocks in this list overlapped the 20 stocks which appeared in the most efficient corner portfolio that was computed by the Sharpe program, assuming a cash return of 1.04, or 4 percent. Subsamples and samples for other periods confirm the power of this statistic to delineate most of those stocks which appear in the most efficient corner portfolio computed by the Sharpe program.

While efforts are still under way to more fully assess the efficiency of various criteria for apportioning an investment budget between risk assets, we can conclude that Eq. (8) and other simple criteria, which are roughly equivalent to this equation, can be used to obtain reasonably efficient portfolios of risk assets. In some instances better portfolios were obtained with simple criteria than with the Sharpe method of approximating the most efficient portfolio.

Various portfolios which were obtained for the Dow-Jones Industrial Average using actual historical returns for the 12-year period from 1953–64 are presented in Table 1 along with the average return, standard deviation, and the correlation between each security and the returns on both the Dow-Jones Industrial Average index and Standard and Poor's industrial index. At the bottom of Table 1 can be found the average return for each portfolio, its standard deviation and an index of portfolio efficiency which was obtained by dividing the true portfolio standard deviation into the average return on risk assets minus a safe return of 4 percent.

The first portfolio was obtained by ranking stocks in the Dow-Jones Industrial Average according to the magnitude of their average return over the 12-year period. The average return for the stock with the eleventh highest return was then subtracted from the average return for each of the ten higher ranking securities. Portfolio proportions were obtained by dividing the sum of the residual returns for the ten highest ranking securities into the individual residuals. This method implies a zero proportion for the marginal security. The eleventh security was arbitrarily considered marginal so as to generate a comparison portfolio with the same number of securities as were obtained using the Sharpe program, Standard and Poor's industrial index and a 4 percent rate of interest.

It can be observed at the bottom of Table 1 that the higher average expected return for this portfolio was more than offset by a relatively higher standard deviation and that its over-all efficiency was less than for any other portfolio.

If C_j in Eq. (8) is set equal to zero for all securities and if the adjustment factor $s_0/(R_0 - i)$ is set equal to one, we are left with an investment criterion $(R_j - i)/s_j$ which has been emphasized by both Lintner and Latané. If the criterion value for the eleventh ranking security is then subtracted from the criterion value for higher ranking securities and if the ten highest ranking securities are apportioned on a residual basis, we obtain the second portfolio (II) in Table 1.

This portfolio is slightly more efficient than the first portfolio, but not as efficient as the other portfolios. It can be made more efficient, however, by dividing $(1 + C_j)$ into each criterion value. See portfolio (III). The criterion $(R_j - i)/s_j(1 + C_j)$ is quite appealing on intuitive grounds. During the period from 1953–64, it produced a portfolio which is almost as efficient as that portfolio generated by the Sharpe program using Standard and Poor's industrial index; see portfolio (V).

While the modified Lintner-Latané criterion does not give as much weight to stocks with low index correlations as the Sharpe program, there are instances in which this property could be a virtue. Correlation coefficients which are obtained from short-run historical data are sometimes subject to the well known phenomenon of regression to higher values. The returns on Standard and Poor's composite stock and high-grade corporate bond indices are a case in point. The correlation between these indices during the 7-year period from 1959–65 was −.59. A person who observed this evidence of negative covariance at the end of 1965 would have been quite disappointed, however, since both markets declined in a rather dramatic fashion. The correlation between these two types of assets over the much longer interval from 1901–65 was .266.

Persons without a good understanding of portfolio theory may find it difficult, moreover, to comprehend why Sears & Roebuck, with an average return almost twice that of Swift and a much better quality image could possibly be omitted from Sharpe's portfolio (V) when Swift is given a rather impressive proportion. The modified Lintner-Latané criterion, which does not give nearly as much weight to low index correlations as the Sharpe program, is easy to apply and will move an unsophisticated investor in the right direction without straining his sense of credulity.

Portfolio (IV) is the same as portfolio (III) except for the fact that the standard deviation for each security was replaced by the difference between the average return for the 12-year period as a whole and the lowest return experienced in any one year. This criterion $(R_j - i)/(R_j - L_j) \times (1 + C_j)$ is even simpler to apply and was also more efficient than the first three portfolios.

Portfolios (III) and (IV) are based on correlations with Standard and Poor's industrial index. Correlation coefficients for the Dow-Jones Industrial Average changed the proportions and overall efficiency of these portfolios very little. The Sharpe program, on the other hand, is quite sensitive to different indices of stock returns. Portfolio (VI) differs from portfolio (V) in that the correlations are based on the Dow-Jones

Industrial Average index rather than the Standard and Poor's index. This substitution caused three stocks to drop out of the Sharpe portfolio and raised the overall efficiency of the portfolio about 6 percent, from 1.117 to 1.189. The most dramatic deletion is Swift, whose correlation coefficient jumped from .262 to .410 with the change in index.

While five of the seven securities in portfolio (VI) also appear in portfolio (I), there is an impressive difference in mix. Stocks with high standard deviations and high index correlations, such as General Motors, Goodyear, U. S. Steel and Bethlehem Steel drop out and are replaced by securities with a lower standard deviation and/or index correlation, such as ATT and United Aircraft. Sears, with a high index correlation, also drops out while Procter and Gamble, with a much lower index correlation, rises in importance.

Portfolio (VII) is composed of the ten stocks which satisfied the condition specified by Eq. (8), using correlation coefficients for the Dow-Jones Industrial Average. Stocks with a positive index value for this equation were simply apportioned on the basis of their relative index values. While three more stocks are included in this portfolio than in the comparable Sharpe portfolio, they are all of marginal importance.

Two other differences should be noted since they seem to be characteristic of other samples. Texaco and Eastman Kodak, which are nominally the most efficient stocks in terms of the criterion $(R_j - i)/s_j$, are given less weight by Eq. (8) than in the Sharpe program, while risky stocks with low index correlations, such as Chrysler and United Aircraft, are given relatively more weight. Whether this difference in properties is a virtue or liability seems to depend, in part, on the security price index that is used to infer the intercorrelations between different securities.

The results for both the Sharpe program and Eq. (8) were improved by shifting from correlations with Standard and Poor's industrial index, which is dominated by the gross market value of motors, steels and other cyclical type stocks, to correlations with the Dow-Jones Industrial Average index which is more nearly neutral with respect to cyclical and more defensive securities, such as Eastman Kodak and General Foods. An index which is dominated by a class of securities that are highly intercorrelated will tend to repel its own securities and may produce a rather inefficient portfolio which is dominated by another class of securities which are not so highly correlated with the first class, but highly correlated with each other.

If this is the case, one ought to be able to improve upon a biased index by constructing a new index which is a weighted average of the first index and the portfolio of securities which it produces. Portfolio (IX) in Table 1 was obtained from the Sharpe program using correlations with an index which is 50 percent dependent on Standard and Poor's industrial index and 50 percent dependent upon the securities in portfolio (V), weighted by their respective proportions. Portfolio (IX) turned out to be quite a bit more efficient than either of the original Sharpe portfolios.[10] Its overall efficiency can be improved a little by carrying the same logic through a second iteration. See portfolio (X), which is 50 percent dependent on the index used to generate portfolio (IX) and 50 percent dependent upon the resulting portfolio.

Neither of these portfolios is as efficient, however, as portfolio (VIII) which was obtained using IBM's original Markowitz program which takes into consideration the entire matrix of intercorrelations between securities. An index based on the six stocks in portfolio (VIII), weighted by their proportional parts, was also inserted into the Sharpe program. It produced a portfolio which was about equal in efficiency to that produced with the Dow-Jones Industrial Average index—portfolio (VI). The rather poor performance of the index constructed from portfolio (VIII) strongly suggests that the index approach to efficient portfolios is inherently inferior to a portfolio based on the true matrix of intercorrelations between securities.[11]

It should be noted, however, that the six stocks which appear in portfolio (VIII) also appear in every other portfolio except the first three. This suggests that one can greatly reduce the effort required to find that portfolio which is close to being the most efficient, by first using the Sharpe program or Eq. (8) to narrow the field of selection before grappling with the more costly and often frustrating problem of providing an entire matrix of intercorrelations for the more general Markowitz program.

WHERE SHOULD AN INVESTOR BE ON THE EFFICIENT FRONTIER?

Given a reasonably efficient portfolio of risk assets which can be expanded into a linear frontier by combining it with a cash return or purchasing the same bundle of risk assets on margin, the next portion of the answer to

[10] This result is especially encouraging considering the lack of success that was experienced by Kalman Cohen and Jerry Pogue in their endeavor to improve upon the single-index model by developing multi-index models. See, "An Empirical Evaluation of Alternative Portfolio Selection Models," *Journal of Business* (Forthcoming).

[11] An arithmetic average, link-relative return index was also inserted into the Sharpe program. It produced a portfolio which was slightly more efficient than that produced by Standard and Poor's index, but not nearly as efficient as portfolio (VI). The main difference was the weight given to United Aircraft: six percent for portfolio (VI), but only 1.7 percent using the arithmetic average, link-relative return index. United Aircraft's index correlation was .358 for the ordinary Dow-Jones index but jumped to .463 for the link-relative return index. The increase in the index correlation coefficient can probably be explained by stock dividends of 50 percent in 1955 and 20 percent in 1957 which, owing to the unique construction of the Dow-Jones Industrial Average, effectively reduced the importance of United Aircraft in the ordinary Dow-Jones Industrial Average index during subsequent years.

this question is provided by Professor Latané, who has argued that while it may be appropriate to use an arithmetic average in averaging returns across securities—since a 50 percent decline in the value of one security can be offset by a 50 percent gain in the value of another security, if the two securities were initially held in equal proportions—it will generally not be appropriate to use an arithmetic average to infer the cumulative gain from holding securities over longer periods of time.

Consider, for example, a nondividend paying collection of growth stocks which have an average price of 100 at the beginning of the first subperiod, a price of 200 at the end of this period, and a price of 100 at the end of the second period. The implied returns for the portfolio as a whole are 2.00 for the first period and .50 for the second period. The arithmetic average return of 1.25 is quite misleading, however, since the ratio of wealth at the end of the second period to wealth at the beginning of the first period is only 1.00. To obtain a true picture of the compound rate of growth over time one should compute a geometric average of the subperiod returns. The geometric return in this instance is $(2 \times .5)^{1/2} = 1.00$, implying no gain in wealth over the two periods as a whole.

While a geometric average can differ substantially from an arithmetic average, the two averages are not unrelated. In the 14th edition of Yule and Kendall,[12] it is noted that the square of the geometric mean G is approximately equal to the square of the arithmetic mean, A, minus the variance of returns around the arithmetic mean S^2.

$$G^2 \simeq A^2 - S^2 \tag{9}$$

Johnson[13] has suggested an alternative approximation:

$$G \simeq A - S^2/2A \tag{10}$$

and Fisher[14] observed that Johnson's formula can be further simplified to:

$$G \simeq A - S^2/2 \tag{11}$$

An important implication to note in connection with these equations is that the cumulative return implied by G in Eqs. (9), (10), and (11) will be greater if the portfolio variance is reduced for any given expected return.

The isolation of portfolios which are efficient in the Markowitz and Tobin sense must, therefore, be considered the first step in the process of finding a composite portfolio which can reasonably be expected to maximize long-run wealth.

---

[12] George U. Yule and Maurice G. Kendall, *Introduction to the Theory of Statistics*, 14th ed. rev. (London, England: Charles Griffin and Co., 1950), p. 150.

[13] Professor of Statistics, University of North Carolina.

[14] Professor of Finance, University of Chicago.

A second implication to note in connection with these equations is that the cumulative return will rise for a time as one moves out along an expanded investment frontier from a safe portfolio with zero standard deviation to more risky portfolios with a higher expected return and a positive standard deviation. The added variance will eventually dominate the linear increase in expected return, however, and cause the geometric return to peak out and decline. Too much financial leverage, in other words, means almost certain bankruptcy, if the game is played for many periods—a point which is clearly recognized by institutional constraints on borrowing.

Fisher's formula for approximating the geometric return is more conservative than Eqs. (9) and (10) and also has the advantage of yielding the simplest equation for apportioning an investment budget between safe and risk assets. If R_2 in Eq. (1) is set equal to a borrowing or lending rate i, and if Eqs. (1) and (3) are then substituted into Eq. (11), we obtain

$$G \simeq i + (R_1 - i)p_1 - s_1^2 p_1^2 / 2 \qquad (12)$$

Taking the derivative of G with respect to p_1, setting that expression equal to zero and solving for that proportion of risk assets p_1' which maximizes G in expression (12) yields the formula[15]

$$p_1' = \frac{(R_1 - i)}{s_1^2} \qquad (13)$$

One point that is worth noting in connection with Eq. (13) is that it does make a difference how one chooses to define the returns from holding different assets. Ordinary percentage returns will lead to something analogous to income maximization in which there is little danger that the investor's principal will ever be in jeopardy. Let R_1 equal 10 percent, i equal 6 percent and s_1 equal 20 percent. If these numbers are substituted into Eq. (13) we obtain a value for p_1' of .01, which tells an income maximizer that he ought not to invest more than one percent of his wealth in risk assets if he wishes to be confident that the income from safe assets will always offset any capital loss on risk assets.[16]

[15] Equation (13) has been derived by Latané in a more indirect manner by assuming a binomial distribution of equally probable good and bad returns and then making certain approximating assumptions which are essentially equivalent to the difference in results which are obtained when Eqs. (1) and (3) are substituted into Eq. (9) rather than Eq. (11). See Henry Latané, "Investment Criteria—A Three Asset Portfolio Balance Model," *The Review of Economics and Statistics*, Vol. 45 (November, 1963), pp. 427–30.

[16] Equation (13) was derived from a formula which is only approximately correct. If i is equal to zero there will obviously be no income to offset capital depreciation. A large i, on the other hand, is likely to produce a portfolio which is overly conservative. The recommended procedure for maximizing income is to define returns as the ratio of expected wealth at the end of the period to wealth at the beginning of the period and then choose the lesser of p_1' or p_1'', where X in Eq. (15) is set equal to one.

If R_1 is redefined to equal 1.10 (expected wealth at the end of the period divided by wealth or principal at the beginning of the period), i is set equal to 1.06, and s_1 is assigned a value of .20, we obtain a strikingly larger value for p_1' equal to 1.0. This result suggests that a wealth maximizer who is not afraid to own assets which will be valued below cost might be justified in putting all his money in risky assets. To further illustrate some of the implications of wealth maximization, let us consider a more complete example.

Suppose that there are two risk assets with returns which are uncorrelated, $C = 0$. Let us further assume that both of these risk assets have the same expected return of 1.10, that both have a standard deviation of .4, and that one can borrow or lend money at a rate of 1.06. The cumulative return which can be estimated from Eq. (11) is only about 2 percent per period if these risk assets are held separately. A higher compound average return of about 6 percent is implied, however, if one computes $p_1' = .5$ from Eq. (6) and then uses Eqs. (1), (2), and (11) to infer the implied geometric average return on a portfolio of two risk assets which is rebalanced at the end of each period (at zero cost) to keep equal amounts of money invested in each security.

A cumulative return of 6 percent on risk assets is not likely to be considered optimal, however, since one can obtain a geometric return of this magnitude by assumption without adjustment costs and without any variation in period-to-period returns by simply lending at 6 percent. To obtain all of the benefits that would seem implicit in wealth maximization, one must consider combinations of loans and risk assets.

The optimum combination for risk assets by themselves was $p_1' = .5$. If this value is substituted into Eq. (2) along with $C = 0$ and $s_1 = s_2 = .4$, we obtain a portfolio variance for risk assets of .08. Setting R_1 in Eq. (13) equal to 1.1, letting i equal 1.06 and s_1^2 equal .08 allows us to conclude that a wealth maximizer ought not to invest more than $p_1' = .5$ of his total portfolio in risk assets. The remaining 50 percent should be lent at 6 percent.

When the new proportions are recycled back into Eqs. (1), (2), and (12) we obtain an overall standard deviation for the three-asset portfolio of .14 and a cumulative return of about 7 percent if adjustments are made at the end of each period to keep the portfolio 50 percent in loans and 25 percent in each of the riskier securities.

Problems in the wealth maximizing model

At least two kinds of criticisms are warranted in connection with wealth maximizing models. All of the formulas which can be derived from Eqs. (9), (10), and (11) are based on approximations which have the unfortunate property of being biased in the direction of going broke if the difference in expected returns on safe and risk assets is large relative to the standard deviation for risk assets. Equation (13) will provide only one standard deviation of protection from going broke, all at once, if the difference in expected returns equals the standard deviation for risk assets—a condition that is not uncharacteristic of the more efficient portfolios in Table 1 during the period from 1953–64.[17]

To avoid the embarrassment of becoming insolvent—which is certainly inconsistent with the philosophy of wealth maximization—or to protect the regular dividend, the investment manager may wish to further adjust the proportion of risk capital so that the probability of a return in any one period below some critical minimum X is less than say one chance in a million. This criterion, which was first proposed in approximately this form by Baumol,[18] will be satisfied if:

$$A - 5S \geq X \qquad (14)$$

When R_2 in Eq. (1) is set equal to i and Eqs. (1) and (3) are substituted into Eq. (14) we can conclude that the highest proportion of risk assets p_1'' which satisfies this inequality is:

$$p_1'' \leq (X - i)/(R_1 - i - 5s_1) \qquad (15)$$

When the minimum acceptable return X in Eq. (15) is set equal to zero, we obtain a Baumol constraint which is approximately equivalent to wealth maximization if the difference in expected returns on risk and safe assets is large relative to the difference in the standard deviation for risk assets. Consider events from 1959–65. The average annual return of Standard and Poor's composite stock index was about 1.115 during this seven-year period and it had a standard deviation of .116. If a person had been able to borrow as much call money as he wished at a cost of 1.05 and had used this information in conjunction with Eq. (13), he might have invested 483 percent of his own wealth in common stock and would

---

[17] While one standard deviation provides almost no protection in a context of repeated investment, investors tend to be protected from mathematical bias of this sort by the existence of margin requirements. A value for X greater than or equal to the maintenance margin should be inserted into Eq. (15) if risk assets are purchased on margin and there is any danger of receiving a margin call.

The purchase of risk assets on margin raises a fairly crucial question as to what is an appropriate investment interval. Professor Shelton has noted, in private conversations, that the expected return tends to increase over the return interval at an exponential rate while the standard deviation may only increase by the square root of the return interval. This means, of course, that the longer the return interval, the higher the proportion of risk assets. When stocks are purchased on margin and subject to call there would appear to exist some danger of being sold out on the basis of a temporary dip in stock prices if the interval of analysis is too long. When risk estimates are obtained from past data one can guard against this unhappy event to some extent by choosing the risk and return interval which encompasses the most severe decline.

[18] William J. Baumol, "An Expected Gain-Confidence Limit Criterion for Portfolio Selection," *Management Science*, Vol. 10 (October, 1963), pp. 174–82.

almost certainly have been sold out during the panics of 1962 or 1966. When the same information is substituted into Eq. (15) with X equal zero, we obtain a more conservative implication that only 204 percent of one's wealth should be invested in common stock. This degree of financial leverage might have been consistent with remaining solvent if our hypothetical investor didn't overdiversify with respect to growth stocks and other speculative issues.

Equation (15) has an added advantage in that the portfolio manager need not assume the degree of risk that would seem implicit in wealth maximization. The investment manager who derived his beliefs about the future from the seven-year period 1959–65 and wished to avoid a one-year loss in the market value of his portfolio greater than 25 percent (an implied $X = .75$) would rationally invest only 58 percent of his portfolio in common stock if he could earn a safe return of 5 percent elsewhere.

While constraints of the Baumol type are quite a bit more flexible than wealth maximizing models and may even provide a superior approximation to the wealth maximizing criterion in some instances, they are not unambiguously better than Eq. (13).

Consider a case where the expected return on risk assets with a standard deviation of .2 is only one-tenth of a percentage point greater than the certain return on insured savings deposits. A wealth maximizer might be tempted to put all his money in risk assets if he simply consults Eq. (15) but will put almost no money in risk assets if he consults Eq. (13). Equation (12) tells us that the true difference in compound average rates of accumulation might be as much as 1.9 percentage points in favor of savings deposits over risk assets in this instance.

The conclusion which should be drawn from this and other numerical examples which have been presented in this essay is that the Latané, Markowitz, and Baumol approaches to portfolio management are not really competing schools of thought but highly complementary approaches to rational decision making. The decision rule which should be followed in a context of repeated selection is to choose the lesser of p_1' or p_1''.

This rule has the virtue of reducing the trade-off between risk and return to a common dimension which is quite familiar and fairly easy to understand. By telescoping risk aversion into a single critical return, many persons who are not adept at translating their attitude toward risk and return into something as abstract as a generalized utility function, will be better able to decide where on an investment frontier it is rational to be.

SOME CONCLUDING REMARKS ON THE COSTS AND RETURNS FROM PORTFOLIO ADJUSTMENT

In this paper we have analyzed various facets of the two-asset case and have shown how a simple index can be constructed to enable the average investor to construct reasonably efficient portfolios without resort to an electronic computer. We have grappled with the question of where on an efficient investment frontier is it rational to be, and also indicated how diversification can be justified on the basis of a higher cumulative return without resort to the concept of risk aversion.

While simplification and integration can be considered a breakthrough that will better enable professors of investments to teach the theory of portfolio selection, it does not answer the more practical question of how one should proceed in estimating relevant parameters. On this score we may be less well prepared to offer useful suggestions than was the case 30 years ago.

In his classic study, Macaulay was greatly intrigued by an index number problem which he chose to call "mathematical drift."[19] Upward drift was particularly evident in an index which measured the changing fortune of an investor who began in any January by investing equal amounts of money in each railroad stock and, in each following January, rearranged his portfolio (without cost of rearrangement) so that once again the market value of his individual holdings would be identical. The value of this index rose from 100 in 1857 to 1150 in 1936 and can be contrasted to ending values of 241 for a Dow-Jones type index and 195 for a price index which was weighted by the total number of shares outstanding.

While upward drift can be caused by random errors and lack of trading, these factors are probably not very important in Macaulay's index of railroad stock prices. A more plausible explanation is that mathematical drift was largely the cumulative gain from following a fairly optimal investment policy in a world where higher risk tended to be offset by either a higher realized return or a smaller covariance. The higher realized return on smaller and presumably riskier railroads is supported by the fact that Macaulay's Dow-Jones type index, which describes the fortune of an investor who held one share of each railroad, outperformed the index which was weighted by the total number of shares outstanding.

In a recent article Fisher has shown that the phenomenon of mathematical drift was not limited to railroad stocks. After applying the link relative arithmetic average index concept to monthly price changes for all stocks listed on the New York Stock Exchange for the period 1926–60, he obtained an implied rate of return of 12.6 percent per annum compared to only 9.0 percent from a policy of mainly buying and holding.[20] While this difference is quite impressive, it should be noted that Fisher's

[19] Frederick R. Macaulay, *The Movements of Interest Rates, Bond Yields and Stock Prices in the United States Since 1856* (New York, N.Y.: National Bureau of Economic Research, 1938), pp. 147–48.

[20] Lawrence Fisher, "Some New Stock-Market Indexes," *Journal of Business*, Vol. 39 (January, 1966), pp. 191–225.

arithmetic link relative price index performed less well than either Standard and Poor's or the Dow-Jones Industrial Average index during the more recent subperiod from 1950 to 1960. Cohen and Fitch have also applied the constant equal ratio concept to annual data for a smaller universe consisting of 337 Compustat securities. The cumulative gain for their index was almost the same as for Standard and Poor's 425 industrials from 1946–62.[21]

The import of the more recent findings may be that we can no longer assume that increased risk will automatically be compensated for in the market place by a higher expected return or a lower covariance. To achieve the gains that would seem implicit in optimum portfolio adjustment, one must grapple with the very difficult task of providing relevant parameter estimates.

That the phenomenon of mathematical drift can still be observed in connection with price-return indices which are based on correct parameter estimates, can easily be shown in connection with portfolio (VIII) in Table 1. One thousand dollars invested in these six stocks at the end of 1952 with reinvestment of dividends and adjustments at the end of each year to maintain the proportions implied by the Markowitz program would have grown to $7,643 by the end of 1964 if taxes and commissions were paid from other sources. To have purchased the same portfolio at the end of 1952 with no adjustment except to reinvest dividends at the end of each year in the security from which they were received would have produced a wealth value of only $6,274. The 21.8 percent difference in cumulative wealth is a return which should be attributed to proper adjustment.

While some, if not all, of this difference could be lost as a result of taxes and extra commissions if dividends and cash accumulations were so small in relation to required adjustments as to necessitate the sale of securities with capital appreciation, it seems likely that part of this difference could be realized by individuals and financial institutions that are either saving or dissaving on balance.

When adjustments are costly there would appear to be an advantage to an index criterion of efficiency, since one obtains an implicit ranking of securities which are not in the optimum portfolio, but might be in an existing portfolio. Partial adjustments involving the sale of some securities can probably be made in a more efficient manner with this additional information.

Large investor liquidity

There is, in addition to taxes and transaction costs, another factor that ought to be considered in connection with adjustments. Real courage

---

[21] Kalman J. Cohen and Bruce P. Fitch, "The Average Investment Performance Index," *Management Science*, Vol. 12 (February, 1966), B, pp. 195–215.

may be required to sell those stocks which have depreciated the least in a bear market and to buy more of those stocks which have declined the most. If uncertainty exists as to the correct parameter estimates, it might not be considered prudent to make the implied adjustments. When no adjustments are made, it is not necessarily the case that the Markowitz program can be expected to yield portfolios which are more efficient than other portfolios.

Under buying and holding with reinvestment of dividends in the same security, the average realized return on portfolio (VIII) in Table 1 declines from 1.19 under proper adjustment to only 1.173 under buy and hold. Its standard deviation increases from .11 to .134. The overall efficiency of this portfolio declines from 1.358 under proper adjustment to .994 with no adjustment. The comparable decline in efficiency for Sharpe's portfolio (VI) was from 1.189 to 1.063. The loss in efficiency under a policy of buy and hold was even more satisfactory for portfolio (IV); its loss was from 1.175 to 1.107.

While a small investor might be able to adjust his portfolio without altering the price of financial assets, this will be less true of large financial institutions and most unrealistic when the theory of portfolio balance is extended to earnings on the book cost of plant and equipment. Our theory says that if assets are purchased with borrowed funds and if there is a bad year, part of the assets should be sold to prepare the investor to withstand the same probability of another bad year.

If all risk takers were highly levered and all tried to sell a portion of their portfolio after a big decline in market values, who would buy and what would be the consequences? In this spectre one can perceive a source of instability in our financial markets, better understand the causal element in inventory recessions, and immediately discern the need for higher order rationality if large corporations and political institutions are to withstand and survive the logic of portfolio adjustment.

If our theory is correct in a normative sense, mutual funds and other financial institutions which are not allowed to buy stock on margin should not allow themselves to become relatively more liquid during bear markets than other times. The behavior of mutual funds during the two most recent panics, however, appears to have been contrary to what one would have predicted on the basis of modern portfolio theory.[22] Herein lies perhaps the greatest opportunity for new knowledge to create a more perfect market.

---

[22] John Slatter, "Mutual Fund Liquidity, the Record Suggests, Often Calls the Turn," *Barron's* (February 6, 1967), p. 5.

Lawrence Fisher[*]

14. Determinants of Risk Premiums on Corporate Bonds[1]

Reprinted from **The Journal of Political Economy**, vol. LXVII, No. 3 (June, 1959), pp. 217–237, by permission of the author and the University of Chicago Press. Copyright, 1959, by the University of Chicago.

I. INTRODUCTION

Economists have long agreed that the rate of interest on a loan depends on the risks the lender incurs. But how lenders estimate these risks has been left largely to conjecture. This paper presents and tests a hypothesis about the determinants of risk premiums on corporate bonds. By risk premium is meant the difference between the market yield on a bond and the corresponding pure rate of interest.

My hypothesis is as follows: (1) The average risk premium on a firm's bonds depends first on the risk that the firm will default on its bonds and second on their marketability. (2) The "risk of default" can be estimated by a function of three variables: the coefficient of variation of the firm's net income over the last nine years (after all charges and taxes), the length of time the firm has been operating without forcing its creditors to take a loss, and the ratio of the market value of the equity in the firm to the par value of the firm's debt. (3) The marketability of a firm's bonds can be estimated by a single variable, the market value of all the publicly traded bonds the firm has outstanding. (4) The logarithm of the average risk premium on a firm's bonds can be estimated by a linear function of the logarithms of the four variables just listed.

[*] Professor of Finance, University of Chicago.

[1] I am greatly indebted to Professor Arnold C. Harberger, who suggested that I undertake this research and guided me throughout the study. Professors Carl Christ and Phillip D. Cagan made valuable comments and criticisms, as did other members of the Research Group in Public Finance of the University of Chicago. An Earhart Foundation Fellowship facilitated the completion of this study.

This paper was read at the September, 1956, meeting of the Econometric Society in Detroit. An abstract was printed in *Econometrica*, Vol. XXV (1957), pp. 366–67.

For convenience, these variables will usually be designated as follows: earnings variability x_1; period of solvency x_2; equity/debt ratio x_3; and bonds outstanding x_4. Risk premium will be called x_0. Capital letters will indicate common logarithms of the variables. Earnings variability and the equity/debt ratio are pure numbers. Risk premium will be expressed in percent per annum, compounded semiannually; bonds outstanding, in millions of dollars; and the period of solvency, in years.[2]

Security analysts generally regard some form of each of these variables to be of value in appraising the "quality" of bonds. But, to the best of my knowledge, this is the first time they have been used together in an attempt to discover how much investors are influenced by various aspects of bond quality.[3]

More precise definitions of the variables will be given later, and the derivation of the hypothesis, alternative hypotheses, and statistical procedures will be explained. But first let us look at some of the main results.

II. THE MAIN RESULTS

The hypothesis was tested by least-squares regressions for cross sections of domestic industrial corporations for five dates: December 31 of the years 1927, 1932, 1937, 1949, and 1953. The cross sections included all firms for which I had meaningful data.[4] The cross sections were for 71 firms in 1927, 45 firms in 1932, 89 firms in 1937, 73 firms in 1949, and 88 firms in 1953.

For each of these cross sections the logarithms of the four variables accounted for approximately three-fourths of the variance in the logarithm of risk premium. Furthermore, I found that the elasticity[5] of risk premium with respect to each of the four variables is relatively stable over time. In view of this stability, it was possible to pool the observed variances and covariances and obtain a single set of "best" estimates of the elasticities. Figure 1 is the scatter of the 366 measured risk premiums against the risk premiums calculated by using this single set of elasticities. The regression equation from which these risk premiums were estimated is

$$X_0 = 0.262X_1 - 0.223X_2 - 0.469X_3 - 0.290X_4 + \text{a constant} \qquad (1)$$

where the constant is equal to 0.966 in 1927; 1.235 in 1932; 0.918 in 1937; 0.847 in 1949; and 0.829 in 1953. This equation accounts for 81 percent of

[2] Some alternative variables will be introduced below. They will be expressed in the following units: equity x_5 and debt x_6—millions of dollars; annual volume of trading x_7—millions of dollars a year; an alternative index of variability of earnings x_8—the reciprocal of years.

[3] The study by Herbert Arkin, discussed in footnote 41, bears a superficial resemblance to this one.

[4] For the sources of data and the criteria used in selecting the firms see Section VI.

[5] Logarithmic regression coefficients are estimates of elasticities.

FIGURE 1

SCATTER OF ACTUAL RISK PREMIUMS AGAINST RISK PREMIUMS
ESTIMATED FROM EQ. 1

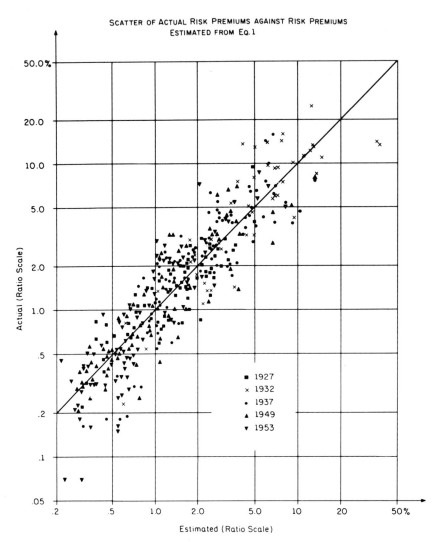

Estimated (Ratio Scale)

the total variance in the logarithm of risk premium. Part of this variance, however, can be accounted for by differences in the mean of X_0 among the cross sections. When that part of the variance is eliminated, Eq. (1) accounts for 74 percent of the remaining or intra-cross-section variance. To make the data strictly comparable among the cross sections, it would have been necessary to make adjustments for such things as changes in tax rates. But, since we do not know whether the determinants of stock prices are stable and since the market value of equity was used in computing one of the variables, these adjustments were not made. Hence there was no reason to expect the constant term of this regression equation to be the same for each date, even if investors' behavior in the bond market was perfectly stable over time.[6]

FIGURE 2

PROPORTION OF INTRA-CROSS-SECTION VARIANCE IN THE
LOGARITHMS OF RISK PREMIUMS ACCOUNTED FOR BY THE
LOGARITHMS OF EARNINGS VARIABILITY, PERIOD OF SOLVENCY,
EQUITY/DEBT RATIO, AND BONDS OUTSTANDING

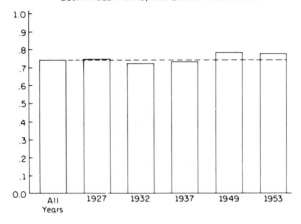

Figure 2 permits us to compare the fraction of the intra-cross-section variance in the logarithm of risk premium X_0 that is accounted for by the pooled-variance regression Eq. (1) with the squares of the multiple correlation coefficients (R^2) obtained by fitting regression equations to each cross section separately.

Figure 3 shows the estimates of elasticities and their standard errors obtained from the pooled-variance regression Eq. (1) and from the regressions for the separate cross sections. The larger bars show the estimated elasticities η. The right ends of the small bars are at points one standard error s greater than the estimated elasticity; the left ends are at $\eta - s$.

---

[6] The regression equation found by keeping the constant term (as well as the elasticities) the same for all cross sections is

$$X_0 = 0.307X_1 - 0.253X_2 - 0.537X_3 - 0.275X_4 + 0.987 \qquad (R^2 = 0.75) \qquad (2)$$

For a complete description of Eq. (2) see Table 1.

TABLE 1. REGRESSION EQUATIONS FOR ESTIMATING LOGARITHM OF AVERAGE RISK PREMIUM ON A FIRM'S BONDS AS A LINEAR FUNCTION OF LOGARITHMS OF EARNINGS VARIABILITY, PERIOD OF SOLVENCY, EQUITY/DEBT RATIO, AND BONDS OUTSTANDING

(Hypothesis that $X_0 = a_0 + a_1X_1 + a_2X_2 + a_3X_3 + a_4X_4$)

Equation	Date	No. of Observations	Degrees of Freedom	R^2	a_0	a_1 (s_1)	a_2 (s_2)	a_3 (s_3)	a_4 (s_4)
1	All	366	357	0.811*	†	+0.262 (.032)	−0.223 (.033)	−0.469 (.029)	−0.290 (.019)
2	All	366	361	.750	0.987	+.307 (.032)	−.253 (.036)	−.537 (.031)	−.275 (.021)
3	1927	71	66	.756	0.874	+.233 (.048)	−.269 (.062)	−.404 (.039)	−.169 (.031)
4	1932	45	40	.726	1.014	+.248 (.128)	−.067 (.114)	−.531 (.092)	−.286 (.071)
5	1937	89	84	.731	0.949	+.286 (.051)	−.254 (.061)	−.491 (.060)	−.271 (.038)
6	1949	73	68	.786	0.711	+.228 (.100)	−.124 (.076)	−.426 (.084)	−.329 (.046)
7	1953	88	83	.773	1.012	+.228 (.091)	−.300 (.089)	−.474 (.085)	−.363 (.043)
A‡	1960	106	101	.803	1.539	+.219 (.048)	−.232 (.060)	−.319 (.044)	−.218 (.035)
B‡	1965	115	110	.747	0.863	+.287 (0.076)	−.321 (0.092)	−.439 (0.053)	−.245 (0.043)

* 0.741 after the effects of differences in a_0 are eliminated.
† 1927: 0.966; 1932: 1.235; 1937: 0.918; 1949: 0.847; 1953: 0.829.
‡ Computed by Luigi Tambini and reported in "Financial Policy and the Corporation Income Tax," p. 221 in A. C. Harberger and M. J. Bailey, eds., The Taxation of Income from Capital (Washington, D.C.: The Brookings Institution, 1969). Used by permission.

The estimates from Eq. (1) may be compared with the estimates from the separate regressions with the aid of the dashed lines. These results

FIGURE 3

ELASTICITIES OF RISK PREMIUM WITH RESPECT TO EARNINGS VARIABILITY,
PERIOD OF SOLVENCY, EQUITY/DEBT RATIO, AND BONDS OUTSTANDING
ESTIMATED FROM CROSS SECTIONS (TOGETHER WITH STANDARD ERRORS
OF ESTIMATE)

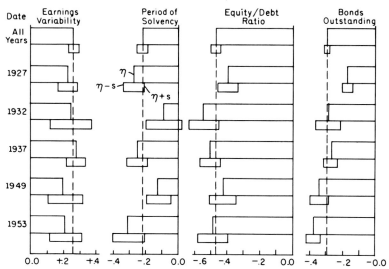

are summarized in Table 1, which shows the elasticities, standard errors of estimate, constant terms, and squares of the coefficients of multiple correlation.

All the coefficients shown in Table 1 have the expected sign.[7] All estimated values of the elasticities are significantly different from zero at the 5 percent level or lower except the estimates for period of solvency x_2 for 1932 and 1949.[8]

III. THEORETICAL FRAMEWORK

The apparent cost of borrowed capital to a firm with publicly traded bonds outstanding is the market rate of return on those bonds (which generally will be the pure rate of interest plus a risk premium) plus the cost of float-

---

[7] See Section IV.

[8] This variable, however, was not measured with any great accuracy (see Section VI). Errors in the measurement of x_2 probably had only a negligible effect on the coefficients of Eq. (1) (see Section VII).

ing the issue.[9] The determinants of the pure rate of interest have long been the subject of extensive study, both theoretical and empirical. Costs of flotation have also been studied.[10] But the matter of what determines risk premiums has been left almost entirely to conjecture.

The basic theory of risk premiums on loans was stated by J. R. McCullough, who wrote:

> There are comparatively few species of security to be obtained in which there is no risk, either as to the repayment of the loans themselves, or the regular payment of the interest. . . . Other things being equal, the rate of interest must of course vary according to the supposed risk incurred by the lender of either not recovering payment at all, or not receiving it at the stipulated term. No person of sound mind would lend on the personal security of an individual of doubtful character and solvency, and on mortgage over a valuable estate, at the same rate of interest. Wherever there is risk, it must be compensated to the lender by a higher premium or interest.[11]
>
> Mercantile bills of unquestionable credit and having two or three months to run, are generally discounted at a lower rate of interest than may be obtained for sums lent upon mortgage, *on account of the facility they afford of repossessing the principal*, and applying it in some more profitable manner.[12]

In other words, the yields on almost all securities include compensation for risk. These risk premiums depend on lenders' estimates of the risk of default and on the ease of turning the securities into cash. Let us consider the risk of default first.

The risk premium on a bond has been defined as the difference between its market yield to maturity and the corresponding pure rate of interest. Market yield is defined as the rate of interest at which the principal and interest payments specified in the bond contract must be discounted if their present value is to equal the current market price of the bond. The corresponding pure rate of interest is defined as the market yield on a riskless bond maturing on the same day as the bond under consideration.

Risk premiums defined in this way must in general be either zero or positive if, other things being equal, bondholders prefer high incomes to low incomes. A bondholder has no expectation of receiving more than the payments called for by his bond and, since corporations have limited

---

[9] This is only the apparent cost because the cost of equity capital probably depends on the firm's capital structure.

[10] For examples see Securities and Exchange Commission, *Costs of Flotation, 1945–1949* (Washington, 1951), and Arthur Stone Dewing, *Financial Policy of Corporations* (5th ed.; New York, 1953), Vol. II, pp. 1131–32.

[11] *The Principles of Political Economy: With a Sketch of the Rise and Progress of the Science* (2d ed.; Edinburgh, London, and Dublin, 1830), pp. 508–9.

[12] *Ibid.*, p. 508 (italics mine).

liability, he may receive less.[13] Hence, regardless of whether he likes or tries to avoid being in situations of uncertain income and wealth, a bondholder will demand a risk premium as compensation for holding any bond that is not certain to be paid.[14]

A lender's estimate of the "risk of default" must depend on his estimates of the probability that a default will occur[15] and of the magnitude of his loss in the event of a default.[16] Let us assume that lenders do not behave capriciously. Then our problem is to find how a rational investor can most readily estimate the probability that a bond will be defaulted. Investors' estimates must be based on information available to them. In general, if a corporation defaults on its bonds, it is because the market value of its assets is less than its liabilities. The value of its assets—that is, the value of its total capital—depends on the earning power of those assets. Hence the "risk of default" is given by the probability that the firm's earnings will not be large enough to meet the payments on its debts.

Recall that risk premium also depends on marketability. The theory of the determinants of risk premiums may then be restated: If investors are rational, the risk premium on any bond will depend on the probability that the issuing firm's earnings will be too small to permit it to pay its debts and on the ease with which the bondholder can turn the bond into cash before it matures.

Let us now turn to the problem of finding ways to measure these variables.

[13] There have been cases in which creditors have received equity interests in firms through reorganizations in bankruptcy, and the firms subsequently made such large profits that the bondholders ultimately received payments larger than those called for by their bonds (but it is doubtful whether, at the time of the reorganizations, the new securities received had a market value as great as the accumulated value of the bonds). But bondholders receive such payments only after expenses of the receivership have been paid and only if the earning power of the firm is underestimated at the time of reorganization. So long as bondholders do not become stockholders, they cannot receive more than the amounts called for by their contracts. (Sinking fund and call provisions in bond indentures complicate this argument slightly, but they limit the bondholders' opportunity for capital gains; hence considering them would probably strengthen these conclusions.) We can conclude that the expectation of a bondholder's receiving more than contractual payments is negligible.

[14] That is, if a bondholder's utility is a function of his income and the first derivative of the function is positive, a dollar a year with certainty must have a greater utility than a dollar a year with probability $p < 1$ plus an amount less than one dollar a year with probability $1 - p$. This proposition is, of course, independent of the sign of the second derivative of the utility function.

[15] More precisely, the probabilities of default at each moment in time.

[16] It can easily be shown that the expected loss in the event of a default is likely to depend on two of the determinants of the probability of default—earnings variability and the equity/debt ratio. My procedure enables one to find an index of the probability of default but not to estimate the probability itself. Hence, to simplify the analysis, the magnitude of loss in the event of a default will not be discussed explicitly. Those who demand rigor may read the phrase "probability of a default" as "expected loss."

IV. AN OPERATIONAL HYPOTHESIS

Risk of default

There are three sorts of variables that it is plausible to use together in estimating risk of default: measures of the variability of the firm's earnings; measures showing how reliable the firm has been in meeting its obligations; and measures depending on the firm's capital structure.

VARIABILITY OF EARNINGS. In 1903, J. Pease Norton suggested the probability that a firm will fail to pay interest on its bonds in any particular year could be found by computing the coefficient of variation of the firm's income in past years, over and above the amount required for fixed charges, and by looking up the probability in a table of the normal distribution.[17] This naïve procedure may be correct for noncumulative income bonds (which are rare), but it is not correct for other types of bonds because corporations often continue to meet fixed charges during periods of losses. Nevertheless, it provides a useful point of departure.

Let us make an assumption which is implicit in Norton's procedure—that a series of observations of a firm's annual net income may be treated as a random sample from a normally distributed population of potential annual net incomes. The coefficient of variation of this series is an estimate of the coefficient of variation of the underlying population.[18] Other things being equal, a firm with a small coefficient of variation of earnings is less likely to default on its bonds than a firm with a large coefficient. Hence the variable suggested by Norton appears to be a promising one, even in analyses of bonds for which his complete procedure is invalid.

In practice, data on the earnings of a firm for its entire history are usually not available. To test the partial hypothesis that investors believe that a bond issued by a firm whose earnings have varied little is a better risk than a bond issued by a firm whose earnings have varied much, one must have comparable earnings data for the two firms. Because my tests covered a large number of firms, it was necessary to place an arbitrary limit on the number of years' earnings used in computing the coefficient of variation. Nine years was the limit selected. During the period considered, nine years was long enough for the earnings of most firms to fluctuate substantially.

In the abstract, one could take as "net earnings" either income after the payment of fixed charges or income after the payment of both charges

---

[17] "The Theory of Loan Credit in Relation to Corporation Economics," *Publications of the American Economic Association*, 3d ser., Vol. V (1904), p. 298. Cf. Irving Fisher, *The Nature of Capital and Income* (New York, 1906), p. 409.

[18] The coefficient of variation is the ratio of the standard deviation of a sample (adjusted for degrees of freedom) to the arithmetic mean of the sample.

and corporation income taxes. If taxes were proportional to income and tax rates did not vary during the nine-year period and if one year's losses could not be deducted from another year's profits in computing taxes, the two methods would give the same computed coefficient of variation. But tax rates do vary from year to year, and there are loss carryback and carryforward provisions in our tax laws; neither measure is ideal. I did not use both measures together because, if I found that risk premium varied with the coefficient of variation in earnings, I wanted to measure the elasticity of risk premium with respect to this measure of the risk of default. And, since the two coefficients of variation were expected to be highly correlated with each other, a precise estimate of either elasticity could not be expected with both variables in the regression.

My choice was made on practical grounds. The appropriate measure of marketability, bonds outstanding, is highly correlated with size of firm. If both coefficients of variation in earnings are equally reliable, the measure that allows the use of the larger range of firms gives the more precise estimate of the elasticity of risk premium with respect to marketability. Issues of *Moody's Manual*, an important secondary source, give data on earnings after taxes for more firms than on earnings before taxes, particularly for very large and for small firms. Therefore, earnings after taxes ("net income") were taken as "earnings" and used in computing x_1, earnings variability.

In many studies it is necessary to adjust data for changes in the general price level. Since bond obligations are in "money" rather than "real" units, no such adjustment was necessary here.

RELIABILITY IN MEETING OBLIGATIONS. The coefficient of variation in earnings computed from a "sample" is only an estimate of the coefficient of variation in the underlying population. This estimate may be either larger or smaller than the actual coefficient. But, other things being equal, the longer a firm has conducted its business without requiring its creditors to take a loss, the less likely it is that its estimated coefficient of variation in earnings is much less than the coefficient in the hypothetical underlying population of annual net incomes. Hence, a measure of the length of time a firm has met all its obligations—the length of time the firm has been solvent—provides a correction for the estimate of risk of default derived from earnings variability. This measure has been designated as x_2. In estimating a firm's period of solvency, I took the length of time since the latest of the following events had occurred: the firm was founded; the firm emerged from bankruptcy; a compromise was made in which creditors settled for less than 100 percent of their claims.

CAPITAL STRUCTURE. Thus far, variations in a firm's earnings have been treated as though they were purely random fluctuations about some mean. Now let us modify this assumption and allow not only for these "random" fluctuations but also for shifts in the underlying mean income (or permanent earning power) of the firm, because we know that industries and firms do rise and fall over the years.

Capital assets have value only because they earn income. If investors believe that the earning power of a particular collection of assets has changed, the market value of those assets will change. When earnings variability is observed, it is impossible to distinguish between "random" fluctuations about the mean and fluctuations due to shifts in the mean itself. It is reasonable to believe that investors attribute variations in earnings to both causes. Earnings variability, then, is no longer a pure measure of random fluctuations. It also gives some information about the likelihood of future shifts in the earning power of the firm—about shifts in the value of the firm's assets. The investor will then be interested in how much the firm's assets can decline in value before they become less than its liabilities and the firm becomes insolvent. A measure of this factor is the ratio of the market value of the firm's equity to the par value of its debts. When this ratio is, say, 19, the firm's assets may fall 95 percent in value before it becomes insolvent. But when the equity/debt ratio is one-fourth, a default can be expected if the assets lose only 20 percent of their value. The equity/debt ratio has been designated as x_3.

Marketability

I have developed the hypothesis that investors believe that the risk that a firm's bonds will be defaulted depends on the firm's earnings variability, its period of solvency, and its equity/debt ratio. Now let us consider the measurement of the other type of risk an investor incurs by holding a corporate bond, the risk associated with the difficulty of turning the bond into cash before it matures.

If securities markets were "perfect" (in the sense that the actions of a single individual could have only an infinitesimal effect on the price of a security), it would not be necessary to take up this topic at all; turning a bond into cash would be no problem. It is true that an investor who disposes of any interest-bearing security before maturity may have to take a loss because of changes in the pure interest rate between the time he buys his bond and the time he sells it. But such losses are allowed for by defining risk premium as the difference between the yield on the bond under consideration and the yield on a bond of the same maturity which is sure to be paid, so that compensation for possible changes in the pure rate of interest is present even in the yields on riskless bonds. Thus marketability can influence the risk premium only if it measures the degree of imperfection—the effect of a single individual's action on price—in the market for a particular security.[19]

How can an investor estimate the degree of imperfection of the market for a particular security? There are several possible ways. Imperfection of the market for bonds can be expected to result in bondholders demanding compensation for risk because it makes the price and yield of a bond at any particular moment uncertain. Ideally, one might measure this uncertainty by finding the "random" fluctuations in the price of a bond over a short period. However, the bond market is often rather inactive.[20] Bond prices are subject both to random fluctuations and to changes caused by changes in the prospects of the firm and in the pure rate of interest. If the period of observation is made so short that the nonrandom changes in bond prices are negligible, it will also be too short to permit much random fluctuation.

The volume of trading and the "spread" between "bid" and "ask" prices are variables sometimes suggested as measures of marketability.[21] The volume of trading can be used only for bonds listed on some securities exchange.[22] In the abstract, "spread" could be applied to both listed and unlisted securities. But published quotations for listed bonds are "inside" (actual) prices, and quotations for over-the-counter securities are generally "outside" (nominal) prices. Hence neither of these measures can be used in this study, which includes both listed and unlisted securities.

The third variable that can be used as a measure of marketability is x_4, the total market value of the publicly traded bonds the firm has outstanding. This variable was used because it is applicable to both listed and over-the-counter securities. One of the reasons for believing that it is a good measure of marketability may be summarized as follows: Other things being equal, the smaller the amount of bonds a firm has outstanding, the less frequently we should expect its bonds to change hands. The less often its bonds change hands, the thinner the market; and the thinner the market, the more uncertain is the market price. Hence, other things being equal, the larger the market value of publicly traded bonds a firm has outstanding, the smaller is the expected risk premium on those bonds.

Thus we have the proposition that risk premium depends on estimated risk of default and on marketability. Risk of default depends on

[19] The holder of a risky bond may demand compensation simply because expectations about his bond may be subject to frequent change. But this type of "risk" is, I believe, merely an aspect of the risk of default itself.

[20] Total sales on the New York Stock Exchange of some of the listed issues included in the cross sections were less than $50,000—50 bonds—a year. An issue may be quoted almost every day but not traded for six months or more.

[21] Cf. Graham and Dodd, *Security Analysis* (3d ed.; New York, 1951), p. 31.

[22] For a comparison of "volume of trading" with "bonds outstanding," the measure of marketability used in this study, see Section VII.

earnings variability x_1; period of solvency x_2; and equity/debt ratio x_3. Marketability depends on bonds outstanding x_4.[23]

Form of the function

My hypothesis may now be stated as

$$x_0 = f(x_1, x_2, x_3, x_4)$$

To test the hypothesis, it was necessary to assume some form of the function.

If the influence of one independent variable on risk premium is independent of the magnitudes of the other independent variables, a linear function may be appropriate. If, however, the influence of one variable depends on the magnitudes of the other variables, then some other form is required.

It would appear that the latter is the case here. Let us again consider the two firms, one with an equity/debt ratio of 19, the other with an equity/debt ratio of one-fourth.[24] The risk of default on bonds of the first firm will probably be very small no matter how unstable its earnings may be; for in order for bondholders to suffer much of a loss if the firm's business should become unprofitable, the resale value of its assets would have to be less than 5 percent of their present value to the business as a

---

[23] This hypothesis might, perhaps, have been derived directly from Alfred Marshall's statements on the considerations involved in determining risk premiums on loans to entepreneurs: "It is then necessary to analyze a little more carefully the extra risks which are introduced into business when much of the capital used in it has been borrowed. Let us suppose that two men are carrying on similar businesses, the one working with his own, the other chiefly with borrowed capital.

"There is one set of risks which is common to both; which may be described as the *trade risks* [A] of the particular business in which they are engaged....But there is another set of risks, the burden of which has to be borne by the man working with borrowed capital, and not by the other; and we may call them *personal risks*. For he who lends capital to be used by another for trade purposes, has to charge a high interest as insurance against the chances of some flaw or deficiency in the borrower's personal character or ability.

"The borrower may be less able than he appears [B], less energetic, or less honest. He has not the same inducements [C], as a man working with his own capital has, to look failure straight in the face, and withdraw from a speculative enterprise as soon as it shows signs of going against him..." [*Principles of Economics* (4th ed.; London, 1898), p. 674; (8th ed.; New York, 1952), pp. 589–90 (italics his)].

My coefficient of variation of earnings can be identified with Marshall's "trade risks" [A] on the ground that the greater is the coefficient of variation, the greater are the trade risks; my period of solvency with Marshall's "the borrower may be less able than he appears" [B] on the ground that the longer a firm has operated successfully, the less likely it is that its success has been due to a run of good luck; and my equity/debt ratio directly with Marshall's "inducements" [C]. Marshall also notes the possible value of marketability (4th ed., p. 673 n.; 8th ed., p. 589 n.) and points out that investors may demand more than actuarial risk premiums (4th ed , p. 196 n.; 8th ed., p. 122 n.).

[24] These numbers are well within the range of the equity/debt ratios of firms included in the cross sections.

going concern. But holders of the bonds of the second firm will be very much interested in how likely it is that the firm will continue to earn enough to meet its obligations; for if its current business should become unprofitable, its assets would probably not be worth enough to pay off the bonds in full. Hence, we should expect the influence of one variable on risk of default to depend on the magnitudes of the other variables. If the risk of default is small, an investor can be quite certain of what the equilibrium price of his bonds is. For when the risk of default is small, estimates of that risk are unlikely to change much over time.[25] Hence if an investor wants to liquidate his holdings, he exposes himself to little uncertainty by borrowing temporarily on the security of his bonds. But when the risk of default is large, his collateral does not enable the bondholder to obtain so large a loan at any given rate of interest. Thus the holder of a risky bond will have more incentive to sell quickly, at less than equilibrium price. Marketability, then, also becomes more important as the other variables indicate more risk of default.

A function which behaves in the manner implied by the preceding paragraph is given in Eq. (8),[25a]

$$x_0 = a_0' x_1{}^{a_1} x_2{}^{a_2} x_3{}^{a_3} x_4{}^{a_4} \tag{8}$$

This form is particularly convenient for multiple regression analysis because the method of least squares may be applied when Eq. (8) is transformed to

$$X_0 = a_0 + a_1 X_1 + a_2 X_2 + a_3 X_3 + a_4 X_4$$

which is the hypothesis described in the introduction.[26]

This hypothesis was tested for cross sections of domestic industrial corporations. The results it gave will be compared with the results given by alternative hypotheses and with the results of some other studies not directly related to this one.

V. SOME ALTERNATIVE MEASURES

The independent variables used in my hypothesis are plausible, but they were selected rather arbitrarily. Some alternatives are also plausible. The use of x_1, the coefficient of variation in earnings for the last nine years, requires the implicit assumption that investors expect the firm's average annual earnings in the future to equal the average for the last nine years. We do not know that this is true. But we do know that the market value of a firm's expected future earnings is given by the market value of the firm's equity and that this market value is highly correlated with expected

---

[25] See any recent *Moody's Manual*, p. v.

[25a] Eqs. (1) to (7) are described in Table 1.

[26] Recall that $X_i = \log_{10} x_i$.

future earnings. Thus an alternative to x_1, earnings variability, for measuring expected variability of earnings is the ratio of the standard deviation in earnings for the last nine years to the market value of the equity in a firm. Let us call this measure x_8.

When the equity/debt ratio is included in the function [Eq. (8)], the measure of marketability x_4 becomes an inefficient measure of the size of a firm, for total debt and bonds outstanding are highly correlated. Is it not possible that investors merely prefer to invest their funds in securities issued by large firms? If the answer to this question is in the affirmative, it would be better to use a more efficient measure of firm size. When the equity/debt ratio is included, such a measure is the market value of the equity in a firm. Let us call this measure x_5.[27]

The results obtained by substituting x_8 for x_1 and x_5 for x_4 will be reported in Section VII.

VI. SUMMARY OF STATISTICAL PROCEDURES

Selection of the cross sections

The hypotheses presented in Sections I and V were tested on cross sections of domestic industrial companies. The tests were restricted to firms domiciled in the United States because a lender to a foreign corporation may incur risks of a kind not present in lending to domestic corporations. Only "industrial" corporations[28] were included because public utilities and transportation companies are subject to forms of regulation which prevent their maximizing profits.[29] In the event of a decline in earnings, the regulatory bodies are presumably required to relax their restrictions enough to allow earnings to return to a "fair" level. Hence there are grounds for believing that, other things being equal, if a public utility and a manufacturing or retailing firm have the same earnings variability, the public utility is less likely to default on its bonds. If this is true, public utilities and industrial firms should not be analyzed in the same cross section.

All domestic industrial corporations were included if meaningful data for testing the hypothesis described in Section I could be obtained for them from the sources consulted. The *Commercial and Financial*

---

[27] Equity is the more efficient measure because, when the equity/debt ratio is held constant, total capital of a firm and equity are perfectly correlated. In this context, total debt is an equally efficient measure of firm size.

[28] For the purposes of this study, industrial firms are defined as firms which would have been included in recent issues of *Moody's Industrial Manual*. This definition includes all types of corporations except public utilities, transportation companies, financial institutions, governments, or corporations not incorporated for profit.

[29] Inclusion of financial institutions would probably require analyzing the structure of their assets.

Chronicle and the *Bank and Quotation Record* were the main sources for security prices; *Moody's Industrial Manual* was the chief source of other data. In general, "meaningful data" were not available for companies with any of the following characteristics:

1. The firm's risk premium could not be estimated if
   (a) Price quotations were not available for at least one bond issue at each significant level of seniority
   (b) The only price quotations available for a class of bonds were for issues quoted at substantially above the call price or for issues whose quotations had obviously been affected by convertibility privileges or by the issue's having been called
   (c) Substantial bond issues were those of subsidiaries or affiliates and the parent firm was not responsible for their debts
   (d) The firm was in or about to go into receivership
   (e) The firm had defaulted or was about to default on at least one of its bond issues
2. Earnings variability could not be estimated if
   (a) Substantially complete and comparable consolidated income statements were not available for either the firm's period of solvency or for nine years
   (b) The firm's period of solvency was less than two years
3. The market value of the firm's equity could not be estimated if quotations were lacking for substantial stock issues

December 31, 1953, was chosen for the initial test because it was the most recent date for which data were available in *Moody's Industrial Manual* when this study was begun (May, 1955). The other dates were chosen in order to get the cross sections spaced over time and from periods of widely differing business and financial conditions.

Measurement of the variables

RISK PREMIUM x_0. I have defined the risk premium on a bond as the difference between its market yield to maturity and the yield on a riskless bond having the same maturity date. When the coupon rate and maturity date of a bond are known, its yield may be found by finding its price and looking up the yield in a book of bond tables. In general, price was found by taking the last sale price on December 31 or the mean of the closing "bid" and "ask" quotations on December 31.[30] In computing yields, this price was adjusted by adding a quarter of a point (for 1927 and 1932) or half a point[31] (for 1937, 1949, and 1953) to allow for a buyer's transactions cost. Thus the yields I computed were estimates of yields facing potential buyers.

Hypothetical pure rates for 1949 and 1953 were obtained from yields

[30] Bond prices are in percent of par value. Stock prices are usually in dollars a share.

[31] For bonds, a point is 1 percent of par value; for stocks, usually one dollar a share.

on fully taxable U. S. treasury bonds. On the earlier dates, interest on government bonds was wholly or partially exempt from income taxes. Hence, yields on governments were not directly comparable with yields on industrials. For 1927, 1932, and 1937, estimates of pure rates were based on "basic yield" series compiled by the National Bureau of Economic Research for the first quarter of the year following.[32]

The average risk premium on a firm's bonds x_0 was taken as a weighted average of the risk premiums on its individual issues.

EARNINGS VARIABILITY x_1. The coefficient of variation in earnings x_1 was generally computed from statements of consolidated net income for nine consecutive years.[33] If a firm engaged in unusual accounting practices—for example, if it had set up surplus reserves out of income or was using last-in-first-out inventory valuation—it was necessary to exclude the firm from the cross section unless its statements could be adjusted.

PERIOD OF SOLVENCY x_2. The methods used to estimate this variable have been described in Section IV. It should be pointed out, however, that for many firms the information in *Moody's* permits only a very rough estimate to be made of x_2, the period of solvency.

EQUITY/DEBT RATIO x_3. In computing the equity/debt ratio, it was first necessary to estimate equity x_5 and debt x_6. Equity was taken as the total market value of all shares of stock (both preferred and common) and all warrants for the purchase of stock outstanding and in the hands of the public. In general, total debt x_6 was taken as total par value outstanding of bonds, notes, debentures, conditional sales contracts, mortgages, and judgments for which the firm was obligor or guarantor. Any current liabilities other than these were not counted because they often vary a great deal during the course of a firm's fiscal year. The equity/debt ratio x_3 was then obtained by dividing x_5 by x_6.

BONDS OUTSTANDING x_4. Bonds outstanding, the market value of publicly traded debt, was found by multiplying the par value of each publicly traded issue included in a firm's total debt by its unadjusted price. I assumed that an issue was publicly traded if I had price quotations for it or if *Moody's* stated that the issue was listed or traded on an organized securities exchange or quoted in some financial center.

---

[32] For a description of these series see David Durand, *Basic Yields on Corporate Bonds, 1900–1942* (Technical Paper No. 3; New York: National Bureau of Economic Research, 1942).

[33] If the firm's period of solvency was less than nine years, years before the beginning of the period of solvency were excluded. Except for 1949, the nine-year period ended approximately on the date for which the cross section was taken. For 1949 the period ended near December 31, 1953. The latter date had been used for the initial cross section; 1949 was used for the first recheck. By using the same period for the computation of x_1 for both cross sections, much labor was saved. The partial regression coefficients of X_1 computed in this manner were identical for both cross sections. In view of this result, it was decided not to make the effort necessary to have the data for 1949 strictly comparable with the data for the other dates.

VOLUME OF TRADING x_7. To find the volume of trading, total sales of each issue on each securities exchange were multiplied by the mean of the high and low sales price of the bond for the year preceding the date of the cross section. The estimates of the volume of trading in each issue for the year were then added to get x_7, the volume of trading in a firm's publicly traded bonds. This variable was computed for firms which had all their bonds outstanding listed or traded on the New York Stock Exchange or the American Stock Exchange, provided that no issue had been offered or retired during the year and there was no issue whose price had obviously been affected by convertibility privileges.

RATIO OF STANDARD DEVIATION IN EARNINGS TO EQUITY x_8. This alternative index of the variability of earnings was computed by dividing the standard deviation of earnings, which had been used in computing x_1, by equity x_5.

Sequence in which the tests were carried out

Before any data were gathered for 1953, I had tentatively concluded that risk premium was a function of earnings variability x_1 and equity/debt ratio x_3. While these data were being collected, it became apparent to me that period of solvency x_2 would probably be an empirically significant variable. The first test of this hypothesis was performed by finding the multiple regression of X_0 on X_1, X_2, X_5, and X_6 for December 31, 1953. All these variables were found to be significant, but it was also found that the simple correlation between X_0 and X_6 was negative and almost as great as the multiple correlation.[34] The necessity for finding a plausible explanation for this phenomenon led to the use of the hypothesis summarized in Section I and developed in Sections III and IV. No further change was made in this hypothesis. When data for the third cross section (1937) were obtained, it was noted that 20 firms had to be excluded only because they had negative values of x_1, and no X_1 could be defined for them. The alternative index of variability of earnings x_8 was thought of as a means of avoiding this restriction on the scope of the hypothesis.

VII. FURTHER RESULTS

The data from the five cross sections are summarized in Table 2. This table and some simple calculations[35] reveal that, although the simple re-

---

[34] For 1953, $r_{06} = -0.76$; $R_{0.1256} = 0.89$. However, r_{06} was unstable. It was not significantly different from zero for 1932.

[35] The simple regression coefficients and simple correlation coefficients may be obtained from Table 2 by applying the formulas

$$b_i = \sigma_{0i}^2/\sigma_i^2$$
$$r_{0i}^2 = b_i\sigma_{0i}^2/\sigma_0^2$$

TABLE 2. MEANS, VARIANCES, AND COVARIANCES OF THE COMMON LOGARITHMS OF THE VARIABLES*

Variable	Date	Mean	Variance or Covariance						
			X_0	X_1	X_2	X_3	X_4	X_5	X_8
X_0	1927	0.1251	0.0740	0.0554	-0.0098	-0.0868	-0.0322	-0.1132	0.1565
	1932	0.6997	.2008	.0871	-.0441	-.1757	-.0976	-.2130	.0853
	1937	0.3385	.1706	.0913	-.0562	-.0936	-.1397	-.2261	....
	1949	0.0261	.1752	.0770	-.0970	-.0861	-.2168	-.2837	....
	1953	-0.0811	.2058	.0907	-.0717	-.0623	-.2405	-.3071	....
	Average	0.1783	.1650	.0808	-.0576	-.0933	-.1533	....	....
	Over-all	0.1783	0.2260	.1176	-.0768	-.1257	-.1684	....	....
X_1	1927	-0.0873	....	.1404	.0141	-.0578	-.0186	-.0739	....
	1932	-0.0134	....	.1238	-.0108	-.1023	-.0044	-.0774	.1426
	1937	0.1650	....	.2430	.0417	-.0289	-.0669	-.0929	.1384
	1949	-0.3240	....	.0882	-.0603	-.0378	-.1010	-.1260	....
	1953	-0.3276	....	.1045	-.0375	-.0250	-.1208	-.1415	....
	Average	-0.1219	....	.1443	-.0095	-.0443	-.0696	....	....
	Over-all	-0.1219	....	0.1843	-.0303	-.0554	-.0855	....	....
X_2	1927	1.3646	....	....	.0759	-.0232	.0118	-.0102	....
	1932	1.3692	....	....	.1163	.0487	.0271	.0642	-.0324
	1937	1.2620	....	....	.1680	.0300	.0389	.0628	.0285
	1949	1.4495	....	....	.1529	.0464	.1349	.1694	....
	1953	1.5717	....	....	.0896	.0116	.0849	.0995	....
	Average	1.4070	....	....	.1219	.0208	.0624	....	....
	Over-all	1.4070	....	....	0.1344	.0257	.0716	....	....

X_3							
1927	0.4688			.2270	−.0735	.1419	
1932	−0.0522			.2628	.0263	.2348	−.1919
1937	0.2942			.1639	−.0101	.1454	−.0594
1949	0.3510			.1011	.0869	.1705	
1953	0.4010			.0896	.0360	.1126	
Average	0.3225			.1567	−.0125		
Over-all	0.3225			0.1799	.0201		
X_4							
1927	1.0117				.3218	.2473	
1932	0.8624				.2819	.2703	−.0287
1937	0.7000				.4217	.3876	−.0594
1949	0.8541				.4249	.4858	
1953	0.9830				.4692	.4967	
Average	0.8792				.3972		
Over-all	0.8792				0.4112		
X_5							
1927	1.5265					.3800	
1932	0.9984					.4418	−.1732
1937	1.1259					.5566	−.1399
1949	1.3035					.6366	
1953	1.5691					0.6360	
X_8							
1932	0.6484						.2274
1937	1.0368						0.1483

* For definitions of variables see text.

gression coefficients all have the signs which would be expected on the basis of the analysis in Section IV, these simple regression coefficients and the coefficients of simple correlation between the logarithm of risk premium, X_0, and the logarithms of the independent variables vary widely between dates.

But, as shown in Section II, both the multiple correlation coefficients and the partial regression coefficients which result from testing the hypothesis stated in the introduction are remarkably stable from cross section to cross section.[36] Thus we have concluded that the partial elasticities of

[36] An approximate test of the significance of the differences of the partial regression coefficients among the cross sections is provided by the following:

Suppose that the estimated partial regression coefficients b_{it} from the separate samples $t = 1 \ldots T$ are all estimates from the same population. Let s_{it} be the standard error of estimate of b_{it} and let

$$b_i{}^* = \frac{\displaystyle\sum_{t=1}^{T} b_{it}/s_{it}{}^2}{\displaystyle\sum_{t=1}^{T} 1/s_{it}{}^2}$$

Then the statistic

$$y = \sum_{t=1}^{T} \frac{(b_{it} - b_i{}^*)^2}{s_{it}{}^2}$$

has approximately the χ^2 distribution with $T - 1$ degrees of freedom. Hence an improbably high value of y is cause for rejecting the hypothesis that the partial regression coefficients are estimates from the same population. (This test was suggested by David L. Wallace.)

When the test was applied to the partial regression coefficients shown in Table 1 for $t = 1927, 1932, 1937, 1949, 1953$, the results in the following table were obtained.

Coefficient (1)	y (2)	Probability of Obtaining as Large a χ^2 (3)	Accept Hypothesis That All Samples Have the Same Coefficient? (4)
a_1	0.72	0.95	Yes
a_2	5.13	.275	Yes
a_3	2.72	.61	Yes
a_4	16.86	0.0022	No

The partial regression coefficient is shown in column 1. The value of y actually obtained is shown in column 2. The probability of obtaining a value of χ^2 as large as that actually found, if the regression coefficients are independent and the differences in a_i among the cross sections are due entirely to random errors of sampling, is shown in column 3. The decision concerning the hypothesis is indicated in column 4.

Although a_4, the coefficient of bonds outstanding, appears to vary significantly, the effects of this variation are small. The root-mean-square standard error of estimate of X_0 from the regressions for the separate cross sections is 0.2076. For the pooled-moments regression Eq. (1) it is only 0.2094—less than 1 percent greater.

risk premium with respect to coefficient of variation in earnings, period of solvency, equity/debt ratio, and market value of publicly traded bonds outstanding are significantly different from zero and are relatively stable over time for domestic industrial corporations.

Comparisons with alternate hypotheses

Equity x_5 was substituted for bonds outstanding x_4 in order to use a better measure of the size of firms in the regression for each of the five cross sections. The resulting coefficient of multiple correlation $R_{0.1235}$ was slightly smaller than $R_{0.1234}$ for all but the 1953 cross section, for which it was slightly larger.[37] The largest difference between corresponding values of a_1 and $b_{01.,235}$ a_2 and $b_{02.135}$, and a_4 and $b_{05.123}$ was 0.035. However, the range of values for $b_{03.125}$ was -0.149 to -0.324, while the range for a_3 was only -0.404 to -0.531. Thus bonds outstanding x_4 appears to be the better variable. It seems to lead to better prediction of risk premiums and, when it is used, the elasticity estimates are more nearly stable. This result was confirmed when it was found that when both variables are used, although the estimates of $b_{03.1245}$, $b_{04.1235}$, and $b_{05.1234}$ are all rather poor because of the multicollinearity among X_3, X_4, and X_5, the minimum ratio of $b_{04.1235}$ to its standard error is 0.86, a value exceeded by the ratio of $b_{05.1234}$ to its standard error in only two of the five cross sections. However, we must distinguish between the two hypotheses chiefly on economic, rather than statistical, grounds. Both risk premium x_0 and bonds outstanding x_4 depend on market price. While the correlation between X_0 and X_4 from this source is undoubtedly very small, the multicollinearity among X_3, X_4, and X_5 is so great that the influence of the autocorrelation on $b_{04.1235}$ may not be negligible. On economic grounds, X_4 is clearly superior to X_5. Large corporations, we find, are able to borrow at lower cost than small corporations, other things being equal. Variable X_4 offers an explanation; X_5 merely repeats the statement.

My tests of the ratio of the standard deviation of earnings to equity x_8 as an alternative to the coefficient of variation of past earnings x_1 are also somewhat inconclusive.[38] For 1932, X_8 appears to be a slightly better variable. For 1937, X_1 appears to be a considerably better variable. Of the two, X_8 has meaning for the larger number of firms; but X_8 is more highly correlated with X_2, X_3, and X_4 than is X_1.[39] It would appear that the

---

[37] The difference between the R's for this sample was the third largest of five.

[38] Compare Eqs. (9) and (10) (Table 3) with Eqs. (4) and (5) (Table 1).

[39] Other things being equal, the standard errors of partial regression coefficients increase as certain elements of the inverse of the variance-covariance matrix of the independent variables increase. These elements depend in part on the collinearities among the independent variables. For 1932 and 1937, five out of six such elements were greater when X_8 was used than the corresponding elements when X_1 was used.

market value of the equity in a firm depends not only on the expectation of the firm's earnings but also on the other factors which determine the risk premiums on the firm's bonds. Since the use of X_1 is based on the arbitrary assumption that investors expect the future average annual earnings of a firm to equal the arithmetic mean of the last nine years' earnings and since neither X_1 nor X_8 is clearly superior to the other, I am sure that an index of expected future earnings can be found that is better than that used in computing either X_1 or X_8. Such a variable could probably best be found in a study of the determinants of market value of equity organized along lines similar to those followed in this study.

The major reason for using X_8, however, was to test the applicability

FIGURE 4

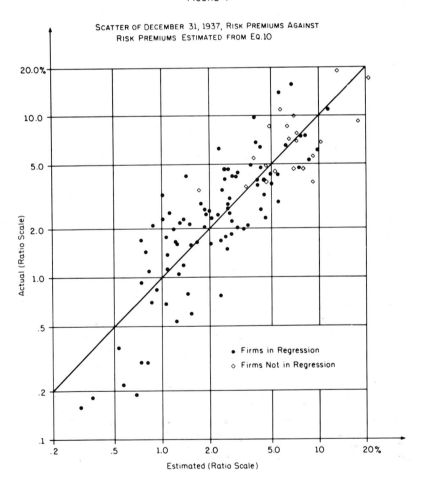

SCATTER OF DECEMBER 31, 1937, RISK PREMIUMS AGAINST
RISK PREMIUMS ESTIMATED FROM EQ.10

• Firms in Regression
◦ Firms Not in Regression

Actual (Ratio Scale)

Estimated (Ratio Scale)

TABLE 3.   REGRESSION EQUATIONS UNDER THE HYPOTHESIS THAT
$$X_0 = d_0 + d_8X_8 + d_2X_2 + d_3X_3 + d_4X_4$$

Equation	Date	No. of Firms	Degrees of Freedom	R^2	d_0	d_8 (s_8)	d_2 (s_2)	d_3 (s_3)	d_4 (s_4)
9...........	1932	45	40	0.738	1.186	+0.295 (.123)	-0.060 (.112)	-0.415 (.117)	-0.272 (.069)
10...........	1937	89	84	0.693	1.304	+.326 (0.080)	-.254 (0.067)	-.423 (0.072)	-.261 (0.042)

of the general hypothesis to firms whose net earnings have been negative. Figure 4 shows the scatter of 1937 risk premiums for the 89 firms included in regression Eq. (10), Table 3, and for 20 firms with negative mean earnings not included in that regression, plotted against values of x_0 estimated from that regression equation. It is obvious from Figure 4 that these 20 risk premiums are predicted with about as much precision as the 89.

Thus it appears that, where applicable, the variables of the main hypothesis, specified in Section I, are superior to the alternative variables suggested in Section V for the purpose of estimating the elasticities of risk premium with respect to factors indicating risks incurred by lenders.

Possible sources of error

When X_0, the logarithm of risk premium, is estimated from Eq. (1), its standard error of estimate is 0.2094, which indicates that approximately two-thirds of the estimates of x_0, risk premium, are between 62 percent and 162 percent of the measured values. Let us consider the possible reasons for the errors in these estimates. If the variables I have used are proper ones and the form of the function I have used is correct, these errors must be due to four causes: errors in the measurement of risk premium; errors in the measurement of the independent variables; omission of relevant variables from the hypothesis; and randomness of bond prices or imperfect adjustment of the market prices of securities to their "equilibrium" values.

ERRORS IN RISK PREMIUMS. Errors in the measurement of risk premium exist for two reasons. There are errors in the yields of bonds, and there are errors in the "pure rate of interest." Errors in the yields of the bonds arose because for many firms I had to rely on the mean of "bid" and "ask" prices. Since these two prices are not the same, one can observe only a range within which the true yield of a bond must lie. Given the "spread" (difference between the bid and ask prices), this uncertainty in the bond yield becomes more serious (since the logarithm of risk premium is used in the regression equations) the nearer the yield is to the pure rate and the shorter the time until the bond matures.

I believe that the errors in X_0, the logarithm of risk premium, introduced by the "random" errors in price are, in general, uniformly distributed over the range of risk premiums. For the spread in price quotations generally narrows as a bond approaches maturity and as its market yield approaches the pure rate. That part of the standard error of estimate of X_0 which is due to the uncertainty of bond prices is perhaps 0.05 (or about 11 percent of the value of x_0). Elimination of random errors of this magnitude would raise the squares of the coefficients of multiple correlation by only about 0.02. Not much of the error in estimating risk premium can be due to this cause.

Errors in the pure rate of interest introduce both random and systematic errors in the values of X_0. Errors in the "pattern" of rates may introduce random errors in X_0. But errors in the general level of the pattern can produce nonlinearities in the function, for an error of given magnitude in the pure rate will cause a larger error in the logarithm of a small risk premium than it will cause in the logarithm of a large risk premium. Overestimating the level of pure interest rates may be the cause of the slight nonlinearities of the scatter in Figure 1 for 1937 and 1953. Since I do not know the errors in the pure rates, I cannot estimate the effects of such errors on the correlation coefficients. It is interesting to note, however, that the multiple correlation coefficients for the dates before World War II are less than the multiple correlation coefficients for the postwar dates. For the former dates basic yield series of the National Bureau of Economic Research were used in estimating pure rates—these series are hypothetical; for the latter dates yields on U. S. government bonds were used—these series were actually observed.

ERRORS IN INDEPENDENT VARIABLES. The errors in the measurement of all independent variables except X_2 are believed to be negligible. Random errors in X_2 resulting in a standard error of estimate of X_2 of 0.0791 (20 percent of the period of solvency x_2) would have a negligible effect on Eq. (1). A standard error of 0.176 (two-thirds of observed values of x_2 between $\frac{2}{3}$ and $\frac{3}{2}$ times the actual values) would have decreased R^2 by about 0.02, a_1 by 0.005, and a_2 by 0.088 and increased a_3 by 0.012 and a_4 by 0.014 (all in absolute magnitude) from their "true" values.[40] I believe that 0.176 is larger than the actual standard error of estimate of X_2. Furthermore, it would appear that the errors in X_2 are negatively correlated with the actual values. Such errors would tend to increase the absolute magnitude of a_2. Hence it appears that the estimates of elasticities in Eq. (1) can be taken at their face value.

OMISSION OF VARIABLES. The problem of the omission of relevant variables is a difficult one. Possible omitted variables are of two kinds: those which would indicate the probability of default and expected loss in the event of a default, and those which take account of the differences in the ways in which interest income and capital gains are taxed.

The latter is a less serious problem. If a bond is brought for par or

---

[40] For a method of finding biases in partial regression coefficients when one independent variable is subject to (known) random error, see Gregory C. Chow, "Demand for Automobiles in the United States" (Doctoral dissertation in the University of Chicago Library), Appendix I.

above, all income from the bond is taxed as ordinary income if the investor holds the bond until maturity. If, however, the investor buys the bond below par, only the interest payments on the bonds are taxed as ordinary income. The difference between the purchase price and the amount for which the bond is redeemed is a capital gain. This difference in tax is difficult to take into account. One would expect the market yield on a bond with a high coupon rate to be higher than the yield on a bond with a low coupon rate because the former is more likely to sell above par if other things are equal. But bonds with the highest coupon rates will tend to be issued by the firms most likely to default. Hence one would expect to find the coupon rate correlated with other independent variables. Another effect also tends to obscure any effect of a high coupon rate. The investor in such a bond will get his income somewhat sooner than the investor in an equivalent bond with a low coupon rate—the high-coupon-rate bond has a shorter "duration." If the term structure of interest rates is higher for long-term securities than for short-term securities, the high-coupon-rate bond will tend to have the lower yield—the tax and duration effects will largely offset each other. Long-term rates were substantially higher than short-term rates for all dates in this study except December 31, 1927.

Other variables that might have been taken into account are various terms contained in the bond indenture. These terms relate to the type of lien the bondholders have; the conditions, if any, under which the firm may issue additional bonds having the same or a higher lien; restrictions on dividends and sale of assets; conditions under which the indenture may be modified; sinking-fund and call provisions; the ratio of current assets to liabilities which the firm must maintain; and possibly other provisions.

One would expect that, if these provisions were included in the regressions, much of their effect on risk premiums would be obscured; for the companies least likely to default usually borrow without incurring many restrictions on their future operations. Even where this is not the case, it is difficult to appraise the effects of many indenture provisions on risk premium. Perhaps an indenture can be modified if holders of two-thirds of the issue consent, or perhaps there is no provision for modification. If the company must extend its bonds to avoid receivership, some bondholders will be better off if the indenture can be modified; others may consider themslves worse off. Hence, it is difficult to say whether a provision permitting modification will tend to raise or lower risk premium. This is an illustration of the difficulties of taking indenture provisions into account. I am not a professional security analyst and was forced to neglect these provisions largely because of my lack of knowledge.[41]

[41] Herbert Arkin, in "A Statistical Analysis of the Internal Factors Affecting the Yields on Domestic Corporate Bonds" [Doctoral dissertation, Columbia University

Relationship between x_4 and x_7

Some attempt was made to compare bonds outstanding x_4 with volume of bonds traded x_7. For each of the prewar cross sections a correlation coefficient of about 0.8 was found between the logarithms of these variables; for the postwar cross sections a correlation coefficient of about 0.7 was found. The annual volume of trading was about 10 percent of bonds outstanding for the prewar years, but only about 1 percent for the postwar years. Furthermore, the data for x_7 appear to be poor. For many issues different publications showed rather different volumes of trading. Moreover, there appears to be no relationship between residual risk premiums estimated from Eq. (1) and residual volume of trading estimated from bonds outstanding. These results, which show lower correlations in years of inactive markets, are consistent with the argument advanced in Section IV for bonds outstanding x_4 as a measure of marketability.

Stability of the level of risk premiums

This study was not designed to measure whether the level of the regression equation is constant between cross sections, since to do so we would have to know whether the determinants of stock prices are stable. Nevertheless, it appears that investors' behavior in the bond market is more stable than one would infer merely from inspecting the spreads between Moody's Aaa and Baa indexes of corporate bond yields. These spreads are shown in Table 4.

The coefficient of variation of the differences between Moody's Baa and Aaa indexes is 0.76. The similar coefficient for the implied indexes is only 0.365. If these spreads are assumed to be normally distributed over time, one must reject the hypothesis that the spreads between Moody's indexes are at least as stable as the spreads between the implied indexes if one uses the 10 percent level of significance, even though each series shown in Table 4 has only four degrees of freedom. The spreads, however, are highly correlated. The coefficient of correlation between the values in columns 4 and 7 of Table 4 is 0.924, which is significantly different from zero at the 2.5 percent level, even though this regression has only three degrees of freedom. However, if the values of x_1 and x_3 were adjusted to

---

(Hewlett, New York, 1940)], attempted to measure the influence on bond yields of factors that are almost all specified by the bond contract. He could account for only 23 percent and 13 percent of the variance in yields of industrials at year-end 1927 and mid-year 1932, respectively. Since Arkin did not take the chief determinants of risk premiums into account (only coupon rate was significant in both of his industrial samples), it is difficult to say what the real importance of indenture provisions is. Arkin's is the only previous study I have found in which multiple regression analysis was used in attempting to discover how market prices of bonds are determined.

TABLE 4. COMPARISON OF MOODY'S DAILY INDEXES OF YIELDS
ON INDUSTRIAL BONDS WITH SIMILAR INDEXES
IMPLIED BY THIS STUDY

Dec. 31 (1)	Moody's Daily Indexes (Percent)			Indexes Implied by This Study (Percent)		
	Aaa (2)	Baa (3)	Difference (4)	High Grade (5)	Medium Grade (6)	Difference (7)
1927.........	4.60*	5.50*	0.90*	4.59	5.71	1.12
1932.........	4.53	7.22	2.69	4.27	6.81	2.54
1937.........	2.95	4.64	1.69	2.60	4.20	1.60
1949.........	2.51	2.87	0.39	2.48	3.68	1.20
1953.........	3.07	3.64	0.57	3.03	4.42	1.39

(SOURCES: Moody's Indexes: *Moody's Investment Survey* and *Moody's Bond Survey*. Implied Indexes: Yields on bonds of firms with risk premiums implied by Equation 1 (1953 constant term) of less than 0.40% for high grade and between 1.00% and 1.50% for medium grade.)

* Read from a graph, not strictly comparable with other dates.

take changes in corporation income tax rates into account, the spread in the implied indexes for 1932 would almost certainly be reduced.

The problem of whether or not the level of risk premiums, given the factors showing risks incurred by investors, is stable over time cannot be answered conclusively on the basis of this study. If the variables I have used should prove to give the most clearly stable level of risk premiums over time, then it is clear that investors' behavior could not be deemed stable over time. For the improvement of the estimates of risk premium which occurs when one goes from Eq. (2), which assumes both a stable level and stable elasticities, to Eq. (1), which does not assume a stable level, is clearly significant.

VIII. CONCLUSION

This study shows that economic and statistical methods are applicable to security analysis. Although by its design it could not show whether investor behavior is rational or even stable, we now know that, at least in the bond market, elasticities are reasonably stable over time.

Robert M. Soldofsky
*Roger L. Miller**

15. Risk-Premium Curves for Different Classes of Long-Term Securities, 1950–1966

Reprinted from **The Journal of Finance,** Vol. XXIV, No. 3 (June, 1969), pp. 429–445, by permission of the authors and the publisher.

An ancient and honorable proposition in economic theory is that a positive relationship exists between risk and return. Irving Fisher wrote, "While the price of the bond will vary inversely with the risk, the rate of interest varies directly with the risk."[1] The existence of risk premiums on securities is a well-known fact which may be documented back to Greek and Roman times.[2] However, very little empirical evidence is available which attempts to ascertain the shape of risk-premium curves by relating the *ex post* yields to some measurement of risk associated with broad classes

* The authors are Professor of Finance, State University of Iowa, and Associate Professor of Finance, California State College at Los Angeles, respectively. The authors wish to acknowledge the support for this project that was provided by the Bureau of Business and Economic Research, College of Business Administration, and the Computer Center of the University of Iowa. Miss Edith Ennis of the Bureau and Mr. Paul Wolfe were especially helpful. We also wish to acknowledge the suggestions of the anonymous Associate Editor of the *Journal of Finance*; his suggestions helped to improve the organization of this article.

[1] Irving Fisher, *The Nature of Capital and Income* (New York, N.Y.: Macmillan, 1906), p. 279. Adam Smith discusses the fluctuations in interest rates and their relationships to profits from the use of productive assets. He took several examples from Roman history. Chapter III, "Of Public Debts," Book V is concerned primarily with the history, interest rates and methods of funding the public debt of England. Adam Smith, *Wealth of Nations*, Modern Library Edition (New York, N.Y.: Random House, 1937), pp. 87–98 and pp. 859–900.

[2] Sidney Homer, *The History of Interest Rates* (New Brunswick, N.J.: Rutgers University, 1963).

of securities from government bonds through the various classes of common stocks.[3]

One of the two major objectives of this paper will be to present risk-premium curves, representing the trade-off between risk and return, for a very wide spectrum of risk classes of securities for the period, 1950–66. Risk-premium curves for various subperiods within this seventeen-year period will also be presented. The risk classes will be limited to long-term securities as described in Section II, but will span the spectrum from government bonds to low-grade common stocks. The risk-premium curves are built upon two-parameter measurements of the performance of the securities included in each risk class. Yield is measured by the geometric mean of the annual rates of return and risk is measured in terms of the standard deviation of these annual rates of return. An analysis of the nature and limitations of the data used and the computational procedures is included in Section II. The two parameter distributions are utilized in Section III and the annual yields are utilized in Section IV.

In Section III our evidence about the shape of risk-premium curves for long-term securities is presented for the entire seventeen-year period and for eight-year and five-year subperiods. This evidence is compared with the normative shape of risk-premium curves as developed by Sharpe.[4] Sharpe also tested his normative theory of the shape of risk-premium curves against evidence based upon mutual fund portfolios. The clear and important difference in Sharpe's empirical results and those present here are discussed.

There is a paucity of theory and evidence about the shape of broad-spectrum risk-premium curves; several reasons for this condition may be suggested. First, the techniques for measuring the yield to maturity on bonds and the expanding arsenal of techniques for measuring the yield on common stock have not been comparable in the sense that neither the information used nor the operations performed were consistent. Any attempts to compare the results of such incongruous methods could only lead to a distorted view of the relative yields and performance of different classes of securities. Second, monetary theory developed in an era in which there was much less information about, and less academic interest in, equity securities than there is today. Some effort, notably that of Gurley and Shaw,[5] has been made to widen the conceptual framework of

---

[3] It should be noted that the concept of risk premium and the approach to its measurement presented in this paper differ from that adopted by some other writers. For example, Lawrence Fisher has defined the risk premium on a bond as the difference between its market yield to maturity and the yield on a riskless bond having the same maturity date. Lawrence Fisher, "Determinants of Risk Premiums on Corporate Bonds," *Journal of Political Economy* (June, 1959), pp. 217–237.

[4] W. F. Sharpe, "Capital Asset Prices: A Theory of Market Equilibrium Under Conditions of Risk," *Journal of Finance* (September, 1964), pp. 425–442.

[5] John G. Gurley and Edward S. Shaw, *Money in a Theory of Finance* (Washington, D.C.: Brookings Institute, 1960).

monetary economics. Third, both the separate traditions of security analysis and monetary theory have been content largely with *ex ante* measures of the yields on securities.

If the explorations and methods presented in this part of the paper are useful, they should give rise to further theoretical and experimental efforts to relate the performance of debt and equity securities within the same framework. The two-parameter distributions should also be useful in furthering the developments of the concept of the cost of money-capital which has made modest progress in the past ten years.

The second major objective of this paper is to present annual profiles of the yields experienced each year from 1950 through 1966 for the spectrum of risk classes studied. These annual profiles will be presented in Section IV. An initial effort will be made to interpret these data as reflections of the recent economic and financial history of the nation. The patterns of yields that emerge will be of considerable interest to many persons concerned with various aspects of economics and finance.

II

In the first part of this section the internal rate of return measurement of the yield on securities will be contrasted with the geometric mean of annual yield measurements. When the latter is used the dispersion of annual yields as measured by the standard deviation may be computed.[6] Next, the *ex post* performance of bonds, preferred stock, and common stock may be measured on exactly the same basis in order to produce results that may be legitimately compared. The meaning of *ex post* yields is contrasted with the meaning of *ex ante* yields.

In the second part of this section, the problems encountered in selecting the securities used and in collecting and processing data are described. The limitations of the data and of our care in preparing the data are discussed. The extent to which these limitations and qualifications affect the results is difficult to judge. Our opinion is that other investigators who replicate our experiments will achieve very similar results.

Method

In order to discuss usefully the extent of the risk premium on long-term securities, a method of measuring that risk premium is essential. The

---

[6] The standard deviation is used in this paper as an appropriate measure of risk rather than the variance or the covariance. For discussions of appropriate measures of risk see the following: John Lintner, "The Valuation of Risk Assets and the Selection of Risky Investments in Stock Portfolios and Capital Budgets," *The Review of Economics and Statistics* (February, 1965), pp. 14 and 23. Harry Markowitz, *Portfolio Selection* (New York: John Wiley and Sons, 1959), pp. 15 and 187.

work of Harry Markowitz has demonstrated the necessity of having a two-parameter distribution in order to attack the problem of efficient investment portfolios.[7] Donald Farrar has summarized the impasse that the certainty-equivalence approach has reached in its attempts to explain diversification as a conscious policy.[8] The analysis of the added rate of return associated with alleged or assumed riskier securities has not progressed, we believe, because of the almost universal use of the internal rate-of-return approach to the measurement of the yield on securities.[9]

The crucial assumption of the internal rate-of-return model—as it is usually used when there is an explicit attempt to measure risk—is that it assumes reinvestment at the average rate of return for the entire period. The implicit behavioral assumption is that funds are reinvested at the single discount rate for the entire period under consideration. This assumption is not warranted because the investor has the option at all times to sell his securities and to reinvest the proceeds in other securities of his choice. If a method were used which provided the actual distribution of rates of return on an annual (or other periodic) basis, the machinery of statistical inference could be utilized to measure the dispersion of annual rates of return. The annual rate of return and the geometric mean of the annual rates of return provide just such a device.[10] The annual rate of return on a security is:

$$k_t = \frac{B_t + (B_t - P_{t-1})}{P_{t-1}} = \frac{B_t + P_t}{P_{t-1}} - 1$$

where k_t = the rate of return in the year t

P_t = price of a unit of the security at the end of the year

P_{t-1} = price of a unit of the security at the beginning or initial point of the year

B_t = is restricted to being the dividend or interest for one year as required by the security being used.

[7] Harry Markowitz, "Portfolio Selection," *Journal of Finance* (March, 1952), pp. 77–91.

[8] Donald E. Farrar, *The Investment Decision Under Uncertainty* (Englewood Cliffs, N.J.: Prentice-Hall, 1962), pp. 11–18.

[9] Two distinct rate-of-return models have been advocated to determine the yield on common stock. For a discussion of these models and their history see James T. Mao, "The Valuation of Growth Stocks: The Investment Opportunities Approach," *Journal of Finance* (March, 1966), pp. 95–102 and Robert M. Soldofsky, "A Note on the History of Bond Tables and Stock Valuation Models," *Journal of Finance* (March, 1966), pp. 103–111.

[10] For a discussion of the superiority of the geometric mean as the better measure of yield as compared with the internal rate of return, see Haim Ben-Shahar and M. Sarnat, "Reinvestment and the Rate of Return on Common Stock," *Journal of Finance* (December, 1966), pp. 737–742.

The average of the annual yields is best expressed as the geometric mean of the annual rates of return which is stated as follows:

$$1 + \bar{k} = \sqrt[n]{\prod_{t=1}^{n} \frac{B_t + P_t}{P_{t-1}}} = \sqrt[n]{\prod_{t=1}^{n} (1 + k_t)}$$

where $\bar{k}$ = geometric mean of the annual rates of return.[11]

One methodological point merits strong emphasis. The yields for all classes of securities calculated for this paper represent their *ex post* yields. In the usual presentation of yields, *ex ante* values are given. For example, if the customarily quoted yield to maturity was 3.1 percent on January 2, 1950, that yield would very likely be shown in an historical series of interest rates as being 3.1 percent. What is done herein is to trace exactly the interest received in 1950, for example, and the change in the market price from January 2, 1950, to January 2, 1951, so that the yield specified for 1950 is the actually experienced or *ex post* yield for that year.

The risk-premium curves developed are historical, and no apology is needed for the importance of historical studies in their own right. The work of many—or, perhaps, most—financial economists, including security analysts, is oriented toward the future. Historical risk-premium curves are likely to be of considerable use to those who probe the future and to those who seek general explanations of economic and financial phenomena.

Data collection

The time period selected, the number of risk classes used, and the number of securities in each class were determined on the basis of a variety of practical considerations. A major consideration was the limited amount of resources available to the investigators. The period of time used obviously had to be at least five to ten years in order to include a wide variety of conditions in the financial markets and in the underlying posture of the economy. Starting with 1950 or 1951—the year of the "Accord" between the Federal Reserve and the Treasury—seemed to be a satisfactory compromise.

Fifteen years was picked as the minimum term to maturity on bonds for two reasons. First, if a longer term had been selected, the number of securities from each risk class would have been drastically reduced. Locating 10 individual securities in each bond risk class and industrial grouping was not possible in some years even with the 15-year minimum period. Second, the remaining 15-year minimum term to maturity was selected

[11] The calculation of the geometric mean is illustrated by Markowitz and the appropriateness of this measure and the related measure of the standard deviations of the logarithms of the relative values is discussed by Robert A. Levy. Harry Markowitz, *Portfolio Selection* (New York: Wiley; 1959), pp. 116–124. Robert A. Levy, "Measurement of Investment Performance," *Journal of Financial and Quantitative Analysis* (March, 1968), p. 44.

in order to minimize any possible influence of the shorter maturities on annual yields; in other words, the objective was to reduce as far as possible the effect of the term structure of interest rates.[12]

Bonds and preferred stock

Fifteen conventionally designated risk classes of long-term securities have been used. One of these classes is government bonds; five classes are corporate bonds;[13] three classes are preferred stocks; and the final 6 classes are common stocks. The selection of each of these classes will be discussed briefly. The reader should be alerted, however, to the fact that a conventionally designated risk class may not fall where it might be expected on a risk-premium continuum.

The yield on the United States government bonds is the average for 3 different long-term bonds only. The differences in the yield among these 3 bonds were sufficiently small to justify the use of this very limited number of issues. The risk classes for corporate bonds designated Aaa, Aa, A, Baa, and Ba by Moody's were used. Data were collected by risk class for industrials, utilities, and railroads. An effort was made in each case to obtain the annual opening and closing prices for each year for 10 individual bonds in each of these 15 subclasses (five risk classes with three categories in each class). In some instances—particularly the industrial Aaa bonds—there were fewer than 10 bonds that met these criteria in individual years. In that event, all of the available securities which did satisfy the criteria were used. In no instance were fewer than 5 bonds used in any one annual industry risk-class set. The use of the same securities each year proved to be impossible because of the term-to-maturity constraint, the continuing appearance of new issues, and the occasional changes in the quality rating of the agency.

No convertible bonds were included in this study. Care was utilized in the final selection of bonds to avoid situations in which the market price reached the ceiling set by the call premium. Using bonds on which this condition appeared in a given year would have distorted the results. Few such cases which had to be eliminated were observed during the period 1950 through 1966 because bond yields were generally rising.

---

[12] See Ramon E. Johnson, "Term Structure of Corporate Bond Yields as a Function of Risk Default," *Journal of Finance, Papers and Proceedings* (May, 1967), pp. 313–345. Johnson shows yields to maturity for five classes of corporate bonds and Durand's basic yields for the period 1920 through 1941. Also see the comments of David Durand on Johnson's paper in the same journal, pp. 348–350. We know of no other systematic published data for the period since World War II for the term structure of yields for various classes of corporate bonds other than basic yield series of Durand which has been kept current for some years by Mr. Atkinson of Scudder, Stevens & Clark. This series appears in the *Statistical Abstract of the United States*.

[13] A history and critique of the commercial agency ratings of corporate bonds is included in Gilbert Harold, *Bond Ratings as an Investment Guide* (New York: Ronald Press, 1938). In Chapter 8, a unique analysis is presented of the relationship between ratings of four different rating agencies, and the risk-class designations.

The preferred stocks were selected on the basis of Standard and Poor's ratings of High Grade, Medium Grade, and Speculative Grade. For each of these risk classes for each year, a minimum of 15 different stocks was used. There were more frequent changes in risk class observed here than was the case for bonds, but no systematic observations were made on this topic. About 60 different preferred stocks were used in preparing the preferred stock yields because of the retirement of some of these stocks during the period being studied, because of the changes in individual ratings, and because of the absence of ratings on some stocks from time to time.

Several possible deficiencies in the procedures and limitations of the bond and preferred stock data should be noted. First, many of the corporate bonds included in this study are traded in what can be considered a "thin" market. Therefore, the annual opening or closing price of an issue may not be representative. When there were no transactions on the opening market day of the year, the opening bid price was used. The hope is that the number of issues used was sufficiently large so that any distortions in prices because of thinness of the market canceled each other. Second, special provisions such as a deferred-call privilege may be worth up to 50 basis points or more when a bond is originally issued but as this provision approaches its terminal date, its value will diminish steadily.[14] Of course, the value of the deferred-call provision will also disappear if market yields do not fall as anticipated.

Third, when more than 10 issues were available for any one industry risk class in one year, more care might have been used to select either the largest issues or the most active issues. Fourth, the quality ratings were based upon agency ratings just prior to the year for which the performance was measured. There could have been changes in the quality of the individual securities during the year for which their performances were measured. This quality change might have been either upward or downward. The general quality of securities is influenced also by changes in the performance of the economy. Fifth, the mean yield-standard deviation measurements of performance were prepared separately for industrial, utility, and transportation company bonds. These three measurements by industry were weighted equally in the data presented in our tables. Other ways of weighting the individual securities could have been used.

COMMON STOCKS. Seventy-five different common stocks divided into six different risk classes were used. The minimum number of stocks in any one class was 10, and the maximum number was 15. In this part of the study the same stocks were used for each year from 1951 through 1966. Almost 300 stocks were initially screened for inclusion when agreement or virtual agreement was found in their 1966 "quality" ratings among the

---

[14] Gordon Pye, "The Value of Call Deferment on a Bond: Some Empirical Results," *Journal of Finance* (December, 1967), p. 632.

three ratings agencies—Standard and Poor, Moody, and Value Line.[15] The ratings for the stocks selected by the initial screening were compared with their ratings by Standard and Poor and Value Line for 1960. When there was an appreciable change in the "quality" of the stock according to these ratings, the stock was eliminated from the sample. The result of these procedures and other problems encountered was to reduce the number of stocks in the universe to 75. Prices were found for the first market day each year for each stock, and cash dividends and stock splits were all carefully accounted for in computing annual rates of return on each stock. The convention of considering the annual dividends as being received at the end of the year rather than quarterly, and reinvested until the end of the year, was used. The impact of this procedure on the rates of return is undoubtedly very small.

III

Table 1 presents the geometric mean μ and standard deviation σ for each of the 15 risk classes of long-term securities for the 17-year period, 1950–66; and for two successive 8-year periods; and for three successive 5-year periods included within the longer 17-year period. Charts 1, 2, and 3 show the least squares linear regression lines for the six sets of data.[16] The purpose of presenting the 17-year period is to examine the relationships between the mean yield on long-term securities and its variability over the longest period of time for which data were prepared. The data for the shorter periods indicate the shift in the position and slope of the risk-premium curves for different unique periods of recent history in the United States.

The results of the linear regression lines fitted to the data are shown in Table 2. The coefficient of determination R^2 for the 17-year period of 0.9099 is much higher than anticipated when these studies were initiated. About 91 percent of the differences in the standard deviation of the mean yields on securities is "explained" by a straight-forward comparison with the mean annual yield on these securities.[17]

---

[15] Richard Stevenson, "The Variability of Common Stock Quality Ratings," *Financial Analysts Journal* (November–December, 1966), pp. 97–101, discusses some of the special problems in matching quality ratings on common stock.

[16] Comparable measurements of performance have also been prepared for all possible time periods included with the 17-year period. For example, data were prepared for the 14 successive, overlapping 4-year time periods included within the 17-year period.

[17] The coefficient of determination of 0.9099 applies to the least squares regression line, $y = a + bx$ where y is the standard deviation and x is the geometric mean of the annual rates of return. When the least squares regression line of the form $y = a + bx + cx^2$ was used, R^2 increased to 0.9258, and the residual variance was lower than for the simpler expression. The residual variances were 0.003911 and 0.0003514 for the first degree and second degree equations, respectively.

TABLE 1.   RISK-PREMIUM CURVES FOR 15 CLASSES OF LONG-TERM SECURITIES, PERIOD 1950 THROUGH 1966

Period	Risk Class	Government Bonds (Long Term) 1	Corporate Bonds*					Preferred Stock†			Common Stock‡ (In order of quality; Class 10 is the highest quality.)					
			Aaa 2	Aa 3	A 4	Baa 5	Ba 6	High 7	Me-dium 8	Specu-lative 9	10	11	12	13	14	15
One 17-Year Period																
1950–1966	μ	.0167	.0131	.0145	.0215	.0130	.0451	.0217	.0455	.0546	.166	.191	.167	.154	.124	.050
	σ	.0512	.0402	.0434	.0421	.0625	.0522	.0583	.0682	.0892	.165	.186	.164	.196	.190	.304
Two 8-Year Subperiods																
1951–1958	μ	.007	.001	.005	.010	—.009	.034	.021	.043	.054	.226	.225	.174	.181	.140	.067
	σ	.046	.039	.044	.042	.071	.056	.054	.075	.108	.151	.197	.161	.205	.198	.313
1959–1966	μ	.030	.025	.023	.030	.032	.048	.026	.042	.052	.110	.159	.165	.127	.109	.034
	σ	.056	.040	.043	.042	.047	.046	.065	.063	.073	.158	.168	.167	.184	.179	.292
Three 5-Year Subperiods																
1952–1956	μ	.009	.006	.007	.018	.023	.044	.023	.048	.057	.203	.237	.158	.179	.138	.068
	σ	.033	.045	.053	.047	.037	.047	.059	.079	.088	.085	.165	.134	.173	.135	.166
1957–1961	μ	.023	.021	.023	.029	.023	.038	.042	.047	.079	.291	.255	.263	.226	.146	—.032
	σ	.080	.035	.038	.036	.038	.057	.044	.055	.106	.158	.194	.178	.230	.273	.424
1962–1966	μ	.031	.023	.021	.024	.021	.050	.018	.046	.035	.032	.109	.098	.059	.092	.087
	σ	.029	.038	.039	.041	.039	.050	.071	.073	.080	.150	.180	.155	.165	.155	.287

* Moody's bond ratings.
† Standard and Poor's preferred stock ratings.
‡ Composite ratings by the investigators based upon Moody's, Standard and Poor's, and Value Line's ratings.

CHART 1

RISK-PREMIUM CURVE,[a] 1950–1966

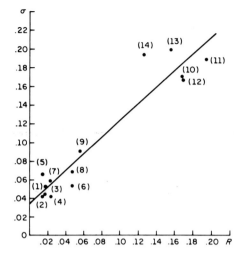

Risk Classes

(1) Government Bonds
(2) Aaa Corporate Bonds
(3) Aa Corporate Bonds
(4) A Corporate Bonds
(5) Baa Corporate Bonds
(6) Ba Corporate Bonds
(7) High Grade Preferred Stock
(8) Medium Grade Preferred Stock
(9) Speculative Grade Preferred Stock
(10) A⁺ Common Stock
(11) A Common Stock
(12) A⁻ Common Stock
(13) B⁺ Common Stock
(14) B Common Stock

[a] Minimum Term to Maturity on Bonds is 15 Years.

Equation for Least Squares Regression Line is
$y = .035 + .8783x$

$R^2 = .90992$
F test: Significant at .01
t test of Variables a and b: Significant at .001
Level with 13 Degrees of Freedom

TABLE 2. LINEAR RISK PREMIUM REGRESSIONS*

$(y = a + bx)$

Length of Period (Years)	Period	σ at 0 Yield a	Coefficient of x (Interest Rate) b	Standard Error a	Standard Error b	R^2 †	F Test
17	1950–1966	.0349	0.878	.00797	.0798	.9099	121.22§
	(t value)	(4.373)‡	(11.01)‡				
8	1951–1958	.0501	0.671	.009862	.08444	.8401	63.05§
	(t value)	(5.080)‡	(7.940)‡				
8	1959–1966	.0201	1.073	.009787	.1135	.8815	89.27§
	(t value)	(2.051)‖	(9.448)‡				
5	1952–1956	.04222	0.512	.009425	.08256	.7623	38.48§
	(t value)	(4.479)‡	(6.203)‡				
5	1957–1961	.04085	0.631	.01958	.1325	.6540	22.69§
	(t value)	(2.087)‖	(4.763)‡				
5	1962–1966	.02136	1.466	.01772	.3177	.6395	21.29§
	(t value)	(1.205)	(4.614)‡				

* Regressions for first 14 risk classes of securities as shown on Table 1.
† 13 degrees of freedom.
‡ Significant at the .001 level.
§ Significant at the .01 level.
‖ Significant at the .1 level.

CHART 2
RISK-PREMIUM CURVES, 1951–1958 and 1959–1966

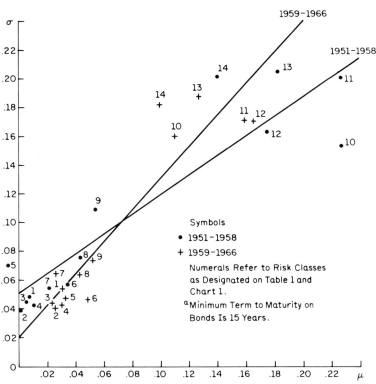

For the period 1950–66, the slope of the regression line is 0.8783, which means that during this period an increase of 1 percentage point in yield was associated with a 0.878 percentage point increase in the standard deviation of the yield around the experienced mean yield. These regression results can now be expressed in terms of a "risk-premium" concept. If risk premium is defined as the additional yield obtained by taking on additional risk (as measured by the experienced standard deviation), these results may be interpreted as follows. During the 1950–66 period, investors obtained an additional 1.148 percent annual yield for each 1 percent increase in standard deviation. Hence, the *less* the slope of the risk-premium curve, the *greater* will be the "risk-premium." Both lower and higher slopes were found in different subperiods.

Before examining the patterns of the risk-premium curves within various subperiods included in this study, mention should be made of the fact that the regression line presented in Chart 1 intercepts the Y axis at a

CHART 3

RISK-PREMIUM CURVES,[a] 1952–1957, 1958–1961, and 1962–1966

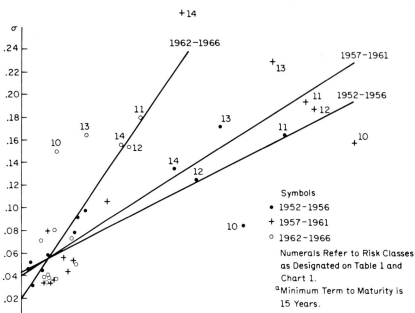

standard deviation of 3.49 percent. This result is interpreted to mean that if a long-term security of a given risk class had experienced a mean yield of zero, the one standard deviation range would be -3.5 percent to $+3.5$ percent.[18]

When attention is focused upon the 8-year and 5-year risk-premium curves, the R^2 is lower as shown in Table 2, but it is still significant at the 0.01 level in terms of an F test.[19] Chart 2 shows the shifts in the two 8-year curves. The slope of the 1951–58 curves is 0.67 and that of the 1959–66 curve is 1.07. Thus, during the period 1951–58 investors obtained an increase of 1.49 percent in yield for each 1 percent increase in standard

[18] Sharpe constructed a similar curve for 34 open-end mutual funds. His data showed that at a positive annual return of 3.8 percent there was zero risk as measured by the standard deviation of the annual returns. William F. Sharpe, "Risk-Aversion In the Stock Market: Some Empirical Evidence," *Journal of Finance*, Vol. XX (September, 1965), pp. 416–422. The differences between the results obtained by Professor Sharpe and the results presented here are discussed below.

[19] An exponential curve was also fitted to the data. Generally the R^2 was lower than it was for the first degree linear regression, but the F test value was still significant at the 0.01 level. The shape of such an exponential curve is consistent with the way in which the efficient frontier of an investment portfolio is usually represented.

TABLE 3.   ANNUAL RATES OF RETURN PLUS UNITY ON LONG-TERM SECURITIES, 1950–1966*

Quality	U.S. Government (Long Term) (1)	Corporate Bonds					Preferred Stock†			Common Stock					
		Aaa (2)	Aa (3)	A (4)	Baa (5)	Ba (6)	High (7)	Me-dium (8)	Specu-lative (9)	I (10)	II (11)	III (12)	IV (13)	V (14)	VI (15)
1950	0.992	1.013	1.024	1.047	1.048	1.109	1.034	1.090	1.083	—	—	—	—	—	—
1951	0.980	0.963	0.967	0.967	0.855	0.997	0.966	0.980	0.996	1.107	1.090	1.110	1.171	1.110	1.223
1952	1.020	1.037	1.046	1.053	1.058	1.081	1.077	1.067	1.061	1.099	1.225	1.064	1.147	0.971	0.973
1953	1.034	1.015	1.004	1.028	1.024	1.031	1.028	1.002	0.982	1.197	1.089	0.969	0.918	1.030	0.881
1954	1.045	1.060	1.075	1.070	0.966	1.095	1.082	1.194	1.215	1.393	1.648	1.405	1.498	1.403	1.378
1955	0.992	0.994	0.994	1.008	1.016	1.058	1.014	1.045	1.090	1.190	1.212	1.181	1.267	1.170	1.148
1956	0.955	0.931	0.925	0.937	0.959	0.962	0.922	0.949	0.957	1.152	1.084	1.216	1.142	1.162	1.024
1957	1.092	1.022	1.016	0.994	0.981	0.955	1.074	0.998	0.927	1.086	0.985	1.014	0.904	0.858	0.619
1958	0.947	0.995	1.022	1.032	1.084	1.109	1.016	1.134	1.250	1.680	1.628	1.540	1.566	1.564	1.539
1959	0.949	0.972	0.963	0.985	1.010	0.993	0.968	0.978	1.023	1.267	1.130	1.356	1.302	1.302	1.147
1960	1.146	1.073	1.081	1.084	1.070	1.073	1.076	1.057	1.082	1.185	1.196	1.069	1.036	0.867	0.677
1961	0.995	1.045	1.037	1.050	1.056	1.073	1.080	1.080	1.139	1.303	1.435	1.421	1.452	1.305	1.112
1962	1.080	1.070	1.073	1.069	1.065	1.081	1.078	1.072	1.073	0.849	0.842	0.876	0.829	0.886	0.801
1963	1.009	1.043	1.031	1.049	1.066	1.095	1.062	1.110	1.055	1.275	1.280	1.188	1.194	1.163	1.286
1964	1.037	1.043	1.045	1.044	1.053	1.079	1.063	1.122	1.133	1.049	1.312	1.245	1.154	1.130	1.190
1965	0.992	0.998	0.999	1.008	1.017	1.043	1.004	1.024	1.029	1.102	1.174	1.258	1.230	1.283	1.510
1966	1.041	0.963	0.959	0.954	0.925	0.958	0.896	0.922	0.898	0.935	1.010	0.980	0.947	0.957	0.819

* Annual rates of return are determined by subtracting unity or 1.000 from the values given. Hence, 1.013 − 1.000 = .013 or 1.3%; 0.963 − 1.00 = −.037 or = −3.7%.

† Standard and Poor's Grades.

deviation. During the more recent period, 1959–66, the relationship was only 0.93 percent additional yield for each additional 1 percent of standard deviation. Consequently, in terms of the definitions and data utilized, the "risk-premium" earned by investors has declined sharply during the period under investigation.

Chart 3 shows the shifts in the three 5-year curves. The equations for these curves are given in Table 2. A point that stands out from the chart is that the position and slope of the risk-premium curves were very similar for the 1952–56 and 1957–61 periods. There were measurable shifts toward lower risk premiums on common stock. For the 1962–66 period there was a very large increase in the variability of the rate of return associated with the average annual rate of return on common stock.

Although data for risk-premium curves for shorter periods were prepared, the authors doubt that much insight would be gained by this presentation. The data in Table 3 present the annual rate of return profiles on the basis of which risk premiums may be built for whatever period the reader wishes.

Risk and the pure rate of interest

Sharpe reached the position that market prices of capital assets should adjust to the point that the relationship between expected risk and expected rate of return of efficient portfolios of assets is linear. He discusses the process which should lead to a linear capital market line under the assumptions that investors are risk-averters, that investors have nearly homogenous expectations about the expected performance of securities, and that investors can borrow and lend at the "pure" rate of interest. Market prices and their rates of return will adjust until portfolios of assets are efficient as Markowitz uses that term. Sharpe shows that for two assets, efficient combinations must lie along a straight line. The same model is shown to apply when more investment opportunities are available.[20]

Sharpe undertook the task of testing his normative model by utilizing *ex post* data for 34 open-end mutual funds for the period 1954–63. His linear regression equation is $E = p + b\sigma$ where E is the expected value of the annual rate of return, p is pure (riskless) interest rate, b is the risk premium, and σ is the standard deviation of the annual rates of return. The values p and b were found to be 3.81 percent and 0.567 percent, respectively; his correlation coefficient was .836 which is significant at the .01 level.

Note, however, that this regression line cuts the expected return axis at 3.81 percent. The interpretation of this intercept must be that at

[20] William F. Sharpe, "Capital Asset Prices: A Theory of Market Equilibrium Under Conditions of Risk," *op. cit.*, pp. 440–442.

zero risk there is a positive interest rate. This result corresponds with his theoretical position that individuals may lend at a pure—and there-fore—riskless rate of interest.

A different position is taken in this paper. Over a period as long as ten years—or shorter periods—the interest rate for government bonds changes, and there will be a mean yield and dispersion of yields for the period. Even the interest rates paid on savings accounts are changed from time to time. If a pure rate of interest existed, the person holding *marketable* securities which yield such a rate would still be exposed to the risk of changes in capital values. In the work being reported here, the yield on long-term government bonds moves through a relatively wide range as measured by the coefficient of variation. Consequently, the implications of the six regression lines presented in this paper, all of which have positive intercepts on the σ axis at zero yields, are viewed as being defensible.

One of the consequences which resulted from Sharpe's use of mutual fund data as a basis for testing his theoretical position is the fact that the lowest yield and standard deviation coordinates included in his sample are 10.0 percent and 9.2 percent, respectively. Therefore an extrapolation of the regression line from the area where the data are located to the x-axis (rate of return) may be questioned.[21]

The very high R^2, $+.9099$, reported here for 14 risk classes of securi-ties for the period 1950–66 is viewed as confirmation of Sharpe's hypothesis that the risk-premium curve would be linear. For the two 8-year periods included in the longer period, the values of R^2 are higher than the $+.836$ reported for mutual funds by Sharpe. Other equations also fitted the evi-dence very well for the μ and σ relationships for the 14 risk classes of long-term securities. Additional explanations of the observed relations may be anticipated. More powerful empirical tests may help in the task of refining and distinguishing between plausible hypotheses for the posi-tion, shape, and movement of risk-premium curves for long-term securities.

The real and financial factors which are present in the economy at every point in time affect the yields in different risk-classes of long-term securities. These effects in terms of annual *ex post* yields for 1951 through 1966 are presented in Table 3.[22] The 8 columns of data in Table 4 represent real and financial factors in the economy each year from 1950 through 1967. Only a few annual yield profiles (AYPs) will be discussed in the attempt to avoid both useless repetition and exposition of the obvious. Some comments will be made about AYPs which approximately repeat

---

[21] Sharpe candidly reported that his correlation coefficient for a quadratic regres-sion equation was slightly higher than it was for his linear regression. He suggested that the result could be due to the presence of inefficient portfolios but that, "...no satis-factory method for testing the validity of this explanation is available." William Sharpe, "Risk Aversion in the Stock Market," *op. cit.*, p. 420.

[22] Charts showing the same data are available from the authors.

TABLE 4. SELECTED REAL AND FINANCIAL FACTORS IN THE UNITED STATES, 1950-68

| Year | Interest Rates | | | DJIA | | GNP | CPI | Unemployment |
	3-Month Treas Bill* (Percent)	10-Year Treas Bonds* (Percent)	Aaa Ind. Bonds* (Percent)	Average†	P/E Ratio (Times)†	(Billions of $)	(1957–59 = 100)	(Percent)
1950	1.06	1.93	2.57	200	8.5	285	83.8	5.3
1951	1.36	2.30	2.66	235	7.7	328	90.5	3.3
1952	1.59	2.57	2.98	269	10.1	346	92.5	3.0
1953	2.04	2.56	3.02	291	11.8	365	93.2	2.9
1954	1.17	2.55	3.06	381	10.3	365	93.6	5.5
1955	1.32	2.56	2.93	404	14.4	398	93.3	4.4
1956	2.40	2.87	3.11	488	13.6	419	94.7	4.1
1957	3.03	3.38	3.77	499	15.0	441	98.0	4.3
1958	2.55	2.98	3.60	454	12.1	447	100.7	6.8
1959	2.63	3.79	4.12	584	20.9	484	101.5	5.5
1960	4.33	4.67	4.61	679	19.8	504	103.1	5.5
1961	2.26	3.74	4.32	616	19.1	520	104.2	6.7
1962	2.70	4.00	4.42	731	22.9	560	105.4	5.5
1963	2.84	3.81	4.21	652	17.9	591	106.7	5.7
1964	3.50	4.13	4.37	763	18.5	632	108.1	5.2
1965	3.83	4.06‡	4.43	874	18.8	684	109.9	4.5
1966	4.60	4.89‡	4.74	969	18.1	743	113.1	3.8
1967	4.76	4.71‡	5.20	786	13.6	785	116.3	3.8
1968	5.10	5.51‡	6.54	905	16.8	807§	118.6	3.5*

* January data
† December 31 of prior year
‡ 3-5 year maturity
§ Fourth quarter, 1967

Periods of Contraction

June 1953–June   1954
Sept. 1957–March 1958
June 1959–March 1960

themselves in response to changes in the economy. The relative movement of corporate and treasury bond yields merits special comment.

Annual yield profiles

The years 1955 through 1958 are convenient to use for this exposition because of the gross differences in the annual yield profiles. The rise in *ex ante* long-term bond yields during 1955 is mirrored in the fall of bond prices. The loss in capital values on bonds that year was generally greater than the interest received; hence, *ex post* yields were negative for governments, Aaa corporates and Aa corporates. The strong upsurge in the economy in 1955 tended to improve the confidence of investors in lower grade bonds and preferred stocks. The prices of these securities were nearly stable and their yields were positive. All classes of common stock yielded about 20 percent. In 1956 interest rates continued to advance strongly and all classes of bonds and preferred stocks showed strong *ex post* negative yields. The first five qualities of common stock (10 through 14) continued to perform exceedingly well but the most speculative class (15) had only a low, positive *ex post* yield.

The impending contraction of the economy, which did not start until the last half of 1957, may have been the cause of the rather poor performance of these very low quality stocks. In 1957 unemployment rose sharply, the GNP rose a mere $6 billion and *ex ante* interest rates fell. These movements are reflected in the high 1957 *ex post* yields in governments. *Ex ante* corporate bond rates dropped less than governments, so their *ex post* yields ranged from slightly positive for Aaa's to negative for Ba's. We suggest that the movements of *ex post* corporate yields reflect both the movement of *ex ante* government yields and the change in degree of confidence in each corporate bond quality class. Lower quality corporates respond as much to the real factors in the economy as to monetary and financial policies. The responses of preferred stocks also reflect quality differences.

The highest quality common stocks gained in 1957 despite the decline in the economy. During the "great bull market" from 1951 through 1962, common stock price-earnings ratios continued to recover from the traumas of the 1930's and World War II and its aftermath. The distinctions between the quality grades of common stock are not as clear-cut as they are between quality grades of bonds. Nevertheless, in 1957 the AYPs for successively poorer common stock classes show the generally expected relationships.

The year 1958 was a year of strong recovery. The increase of 80 basis points in the *ex ante* yield on long-term governments again resulted in capital losses to their owners. The negative yield on long-term governments was 5.3 percent, but the negative yield on Aaa corporates was only 0.5 percent. Other corporate bonds had positive changes in *ex post* yields; lower quality bonds outperformed higher quality bonds. Common stocks all had a banner year as the DJIA increased from 454 to 584; the average yield by class ran from 54 percent to 68 percent.

The annual yield profiles (AYPs) are strikingly different in years of economic expansion as compared with years of contraction. In years of expansion the AYP generally slopes upward from government bonds through common stocks; in years of contraction the AYP generally slopes downward. As expected, volatility of the yields on common stocks is greater than that on bonds.

Cyclical yield patterns: governments versus corporates

Why are *ex post* annual yields experienced on U. S. Treasury Bonds subject to greater variability than the yields on high-quality corporate bonds? As indicated in Table 1, the standard deviation of the annual yields on long-term government bonds during the 17-year period was 5.12 percent, whereas the standard deviations for Aaa, Aa, and A corporate bonds were 4.02 percent, 4.34 percent, and 4.21 percent, respectively.

Treasury securities are generally conceded to be free from any "credit" risk associated with the possibility of default. Thus the only factor which will influence the market price of outstanding, long-term government bonds is the "interest-rate risk" which is reflected in the inverse relationship between the change in market price and the change in *ex ante* yield.

The market prices of corporate bonds, on the other hand, are influenced not only by "interest-rate risk" but also by "credit risk" associated with the quality of the particular issue. Investors' assessments of a corporate bond's quality are likely to vary with the business cycle. During an expansionary phase of the economy there will be a tendency for investors to regard these corporate bonds as improving in quality. This optimistic attitude will tend to exert an upward pressure on the market price which can be associated with the reduced "credit risk" attached to these bonds. This influence can at least partially offset the decline in market price which would result from the rising level of interest rates occurring during the expansionary phase of the cycle. This off-setting feature, which is present in corporate bonds but absent in the case of Treasury securities, tends to add stability to the *ex post* yields experienced on high-grade corporate bonds relative to government bonds. The effects of the two risk components would, of course, be reversed during a period of declining economic activity, but again the net effect would be a more stable pattern of yields for corporate bonds. The relative stability of corporate bond yields may also reflect changes in the attractiveness of other investment opportunities in addition to government securities, such as mortgages.

IV

The major objectives of this article were to present risk-premium curves for long-term securities and to set forth annual yield profiles for the period 1950–66 for a wide spectrum of risk classes of long-term securities. *Ex post* annual yields were defined as the ratio of the sum of the current income (interest or dividends, as appropriate) and the change in the market price of the security to the initial price. This concept of return permits the annual yields of both debt and equity securities to be measured on the same basis and facilitates yield comparisons. The standard deviation of these annual yields for each class of security can then be utilized as a measure of risk associated with these securities.

The 1950–66 risk-premium curve for the 15 risk classes of securities had a coefficient of determination of almost 0.91. The coefficients of determination associated with the shorter subperiods were somewhat lower. The slope and position of the curve shifted among the various subperiods toward lower risk premiums during the more recent periods.

Each of the six risk-premium curves presented in this study exhibited a high standard deviation at zero annual yield for long-term securities. Thus, even Treasury securities are not "riskless" to their owners who might have to sell or evaluate these issues after holding them for one year. The mean yield on long-term government bonds for the period 1950–66 was 1.67 percent and the standard deviation was 5.12 percent.

Annual yield profiles reflecting the *ex post* yields for the fifteen classes of securities exhibit marked cyclical patterns. During periods of economic expansion, the yield on bonds tended to fall below zero as a result of the upward movement in the market rate of interest. Common stock yields, on the other hand, rose sharply during these expansionary periods. When the economy is in a period of contraction, the pattern is reversed. The yields experienced on high-grade corporate bonds did not fluctuate as widely as did the yields on Treasury securities.

The risk-premium curves had a higher coefficient of determination than anticipated but there is a distinct lack of observations near the middle of the curve. Further empirical evidence is needed to attempt to define the exact shape of these risk-premium curves.[23] The development of risk-premium curves relating to earlier historical periods may be useful in augmenting our understanding of the influence of various real and financial factors operating in the economy.

---

[23] Soldofsky completed the preparation of μ-σ measurements of performance for four classes of public utility common stock too late to formally incorporate the results in this article. These results generally fall near the computed regression lines and fill in the upper part of the data gap on the first three charts.

*Lawrence Fisher**
James H. Lorie†

16. Some Studies of Variability of Returns on Investments in Common Stocks[1]

Reprinted, in abridged form, from **The Journal of Business of the University of Chicago,** Vol. 43, No. 2, (April, 1970), pp. 99–111, 114–117, by permission of the authors and the University of Chicago Press. Copyright 1970 by The University of Chicago.

INTRODUCTION

We report here the findings of three studies we have conducted on the variability of returns on investments in common stocks listed on the New York Stock Exchange. One study examines the frequency distributions of returns on individual stocks for 55 specific periods ranging from 1 to 40 years in length during the period 1926–65. A second examines the aggregated distributions of returns from investments in individual common stocks for nonoverlapping periods of equal length from one to twenty years. Aggregating frequency distributions of all such 1-, 5-, 10-, or 20-year periods permits broader generalization about the behavior of the market, since these aggregated distributions are not dominated by the behavior of the market in any single period.

The third study deals with returns from investment in portfolios containing different numbers of common stocks on the New York Stock Exchange. Distributions were found for portfolios of 6 size ranges from 1

* Professor of finance, Graduate School of Business, University of Chicago, and associate director of the Center for Research in Security Prices (sponsored by Merrill Lynch, Pierce, Fenner & Smith, Inc.).

† Professor of business administration, Graduate School of Business, University of Chicago, and director of the Center for Research in Security Prices (sponsored by Merrill Lynch, Pierce, Fenner & Smith, Inc.).

[1] We are indebted to Harry Roberts for aid in understanding Gini's mean difference. Our exposition has benefitted from reactions to presentations at seminars at the University of Chicago and several other universities. Most of the many computer programs required for this study were prepared by Marvin Lipson. Some additional programming was done by Mark Case and Owen M. Hewett.

through 128 and for portfolios containing all such common stocks. The tables dealing with aggregated frequency distributions, paralleling the second study, are of greater general interest, we think, and are discussed in the text. The tables from which they were derived and which deal with specific periods, paralleling the first study, are of less direct interest and are presented in Appendix A.

Before discussing our results, we would like to indicate why we undertook these studies and the ways in which they are related to our earlier studies on average rates of return[2] and on outcomes for random investments.[3]

For several reasons, studies of variability may be interesting. One of the most controversial and important subjects in the field of finance is risk. There is controversy about both methods of estimation and the nature of the relationship between risk and rates of return. The studies reported here do not deal directly with either of those controversial aspects of risk, but they do bear upon the general subject by providing the first comprehensive and well-based estimates of the effect of increasing the size of portfolios on the variability of returns—one of the most widely used estimates of risk. The earlier studies of average rates of return provided bench marks which have been widely used in evaluating the performance of average rates of return from portfolios; the studies reported here can be thought of as providing bench marks for evaluating the effectiveness of diversification in reducing variability of returns.

Another way of looking at the present studies would be to say that the earlier studies on average rates of return indicate only the average experience from investing in common stocks listed on the New York Stock Exchange without any indication of the inherent riskiness. The studies reported here indicate something about riskiness by providing detailed information on frequency distributions of returns.

These studies should prove more useful than the first author's earlier study of outcomes for random investments in common stocks, which also deals with variability of returns, because in these studies we are able to look at the variability of returns on portfolios as well as return on individual stocks. We can now look at portfolios because the current studies hold constant the holding period of the investments whose frequency distributions are reported. Looking at portfolios is obviously desirable, since almost all investors with significant investments hold portfolios of more

[2] Lawrence Fisher and James H. Lorie, "Rates of Return on Investments in Common Stocks," *Journal of Business* 37 (January, 1964), pp. 1–21; Lawrence Fisher and James H. Lorie, "Rates of Return on Investments in Common Stocks: The Year-by-Year Record, 1926–65," *Journal of Business* 41 (July, 1968), pp. 291–316.

[3] Lawrence Fisher, "Outcomes for 'Random' Investments in Common Stocks Listed on the New York Stock Exchange," *Journal of Business* 38 (April, 1965), pp. 149–61.

than one common stock. Moreover, there is much interest in the effect of changing the size of portfolios on variability in return.

The current studies are also superior in that they, unlike the earlier study on outcomes for random investments, take into account the value of investments even after they consist of assets other than the common stock in which the investment was originally made. This change in assets can occur where there are mergers, spin-offs, or delistings.

A section on general methodology follows these introductory remarks. It includes some comments on statistics that we have computed in the course of all three studies. Next are sections on the three studies, and finally appendixes containing the basic data for the last study. The results are presented primarily in tables which, we hope, will provide reference material for specialists in the field. Since we have spent considerable time examining the material in the tables, we will make a few comments. However, most analysis will be left to the reader.

GENERAL METHODS OF ANALYSIS

The distributions which will be described are in all cases the distributions of "wealth ratios." The wealth ratio is the ratio of the value of the investment at the end of the period to the amount invested. Much of the work in this field has been in terms of rates of return, since such rates are necessary in comparing investment results for periods of different lengths. We are free to use wealth ratios because we compare only periods of equal length.

We have used wealth ratios for two reasons. First, introspection and observation have persuaded us that it is extremely difficult to understand the significance of differences among annual rates of return for long periods

TABLE 1. ILLUSTRATION OF RELATIONSHIP
BETWEEN WEALTH RATIOS AND
RATES OF RETURN

Stock	Wealth Ratio After 10 Years	Annual Rate of Return Compounded Annually (Percent)
A	1	0
B	4	14.9
C	7	21.5
Mean	4	12.1

The wealth ratio implied by an investment returning 12.1 percent annually and held for 10 years is 3.14, not 4.0. Thus, using the mean rate of return to deduce the mean wealth ratio would lead to a significant underestimate.

of time. For example, few persons easily see that a difference between 5 percent per annum, compounded annually, and 10 percent per annum over a 40-year period produces wealth ratios which are strikingly different— approximately 7 and 45, respectively. The wealth ratio produced by the 10 percent annual return is 543 percent greater than the ratio produced by the 5 percent return. The corresponding wealth ratios for annual rates of return of 9 percent and 10 percent are 31 and 45, respectively. The wealth ratio for the 10 percent rate of return exceeds that for the 9 percent rate of return by 44 percent.

The second reason for presenting data on wealth ratios rather than on rates of return is that data on rates of return are frequently misinterpreted. The most common mistake is to assume that one can deduce the mean wealth ratio from knowledge of the mean rate of return.[4] Such an attempt leads to an underestimate of the mean wealth ratio if the period in question exceeds the compounding interval, and to an overestimate if the period is less than the compounding interval. This is exemplified in Table 1.

Harry Markowitz[5] uses returns, but they are not necessarily annual rates. They are simply one less than the corresponding wealth ratios, and they are typically expressed as percentages. In Table 1, the Markowitz returns for stocks A, B, and C would be 0, 300 percent, and 600 percent, respectively. We have used wealth ratios rather than Markowitz's returns, since the latter are easily confused with *annual* rates of return.

We recognize, however, that some readers do think about returns from investments as annual rates. In order to facilitate translation from wealth ratios to annual rates of return, we present Table 2, which simply indicates for periods of various lengths the rates of return corresponding to various wealth ratios.

In computing wealth ratios, commissions were charged when investments were originally made and when each dividend was reinvested, but the value of the investment at the end of each period was calculated on the basis of the market price on that date without taking into account any contingent transaction costs or taxes.[6]

---

[4] See, for example, Marc Nerlove, "Factors Affecting Differences among Rates of Return on Investments in Individual Common Stocks," *Review of Economics and Statistics* 50 (August, 1968), pp. 312–31; and Eugene F. Brigham and James L. Pappas, "Rates of Return on Common Stock," *Journal of Business* 42 (July, 1969), pp. 302–20.

[5] Harry Markowitz, *Portfolio Selection: Efficient Diversification of Investments* (New York: John Wiley & Sons, 1959).

[6] The wealth ratios used were, in fact, the wealth ratios used to construct the table of annual rates of return with reinvestment of dividends for the tax-exempt investor in the cash-to-portfolio computations (part a of Table 1 of the Fisher and Lorie 1968 article). For the methods of treating investments in stocks which were merged into or spun off other issues or which were delisted, see the 1968 article, p. 295, and the 1964 article, pp. 15–17.

TABLE 2. WEALTH RATIOS AND CORRESPONDING ANNUAL RATES OF RETURN (COMPOUNDED ANNUALLY) FOR SPECIFIED PERIODS

Holding Period							
5 Years		10 Years		20 Years		39 11/12 Years	
Wealth Ratio	Rate of Return	Wealth Ratio	Rate of Return	Wealth Ratio	Rate of Return	Wealth Ratio	Rate of Return
.01	−60.2	01	−36.9	.01	−20.6	.01	−10.9
.02	−54.3	.02	−32.4	.02	−17.8	.02	−9.3
.03	−50.4	.03	−29.6	.03	−16.1	.05	−7.2
.04	−47.5	.04	−27.5	.05	−13.9	.1	−5.6
.05	−45.1	.05	−25.9	.1	−10.9	.2	−4.0
.07	−41.2	.1	−20.6	.2	−7.7	.3	−3.0
.1	−36.9	.2	−14.9	.3	−5.8	.4	−2.3
.2	−27.5	.3	−11.3	.4	−4.5	.6	−1.3
.3	−21.4	.4	−8.8	.5	−3.4	1.0	0.0
.4	−16.7	.5	−6.7	.7	−1.8	1.5	1.0
.5	−12.9	.6	−5.0	.9	−0.5	2.2	2.0
.6	−9.7	.7	−3.5	1.1	0.5	3.2	3.0
.7	−6.9	.8	−2.2	1.4	1.7	4.6	3.9
.8	−4.4	.9	−1.0	1.8	3.0	6.4	4.8
.9	−2.1	1.1	1.0	2.3	4.3	8.6	5.5
1.0	0.	1.3	2.7	2.8	5.3	12.	6.4
1.1	1.9	1.5	4.1	3.4	6.3	15.	7.0
1.3	5.4	1.8	6.1	4.0	7.2	18.	7.5
1.4	7.0	2.0	7.2	4.7	8.0	22.	8.1
1.6	9.9	2.2	8.2	5.4	8.8	25.	8.4
1.7	11.2	2.4	9.1	5.9	9.3	28.	8.7
1.8	12.5	2.6	10.0	6.4	9.7	31.	9.0
1.9	13.7	2.7	10.4	6.8	10.1	34.	9.2
2.0	14.9	2.8	10.8	7.0	10.2	35.	9.3
2.1	16.0	2.9	11.2	7.1	10.3	36.	9.4
2.2	17.1	3.0	11.6	7.2	10.4	37.	9.5
2.3	18.1	3.1	12.0	7.3	10.5	38.	9.5
2.4	19.1	3.2	12.3	7.4	10.5	39.	9.6
2.5	20.1	3.3	12.7	7.6	10.7	40.	9.7
2.6	21.1	3.4	13.0	7.9	10.9	42.	9.8
2.7	22.0	3.5	13.3	8.3	11.2	44.	9.9
2.8	22.9	3.7	14.0	8.8	11.5	48.	10.2
2.9	23.7	4.0	14.9	9.4	11.9	53.	10.5
3.0	24.6	4.3	15.7	11.	12.7	60.	10.8
3.2	26.2	4.8	17.0	12.	13.2	70.	11.2
3.6	29.2	5.3	18.1	13.	13.7	80.	11.6
4.1	32.6	6.0	19.6	14.	14.1	90.	11.9
4.6	35.7	6.9	21.3	15.	14.5	100.	12.2
5.3	39.6	7.9	23.0	17.	15.2	120.	12.7
6.2	44.0	9.2	24.8	20.	16.2	150.	13.4
7.2	48.4	11.	27.1	22.	16.7	200.	14.2
8.6	53.8	13.	29.2	26.	17.7	250.	14.8
11.	61.5	16.	32.0	30.	18.5	300.	15.4
13.	67.0	19.	34.2	35.	19.5	350.	15.8
16.	74.1	23.	36.8	42.	20.5	400.	16.2
19	80.2	29.	40.0	50.	21.6	500.	16.8
24.	88.8	36.	43.1	60.	22.7	700.	17.8
30.	97.4	46.	46.6	73.	23.9	1,000.	18.9
38.	107.0	58.	50.1	90.	25.2	1,300.	19.7
49.	117.8	75.	54.0	111.	26.6	1,715.	20.5

For each frequency distribution of wealth ratios the following statistics are reported:

1. (a) 5th centile
   (b) 10th centile
   (c) 20th centile
   (d) 30th centile
   (e) 40th centile
   (f) 50th centile (median)
   (g) 60th centile
   (h) 70th centile
   (i) 80th centile
   (j) 90th centile
   (k) 95th centile
2. The maximum
3. The minimum
4. The arithmetic mean
5. Measures of absolute dispersion
   (a) The standard deviation
   (b) The mean deviation
   (c) Gini's mean difference
6. Measures of relative dispersion
   (a) Coefficient of variation
   (b) Relative mean deviation
   (c) Gini's coefficient of concentration
7. Momental skewness
8. Kurtosis

All of the foregoing statistics should be familiar, with the possible exception of Gini's mean difference and Gini's coefficient of concentration. These statistics are discussed, among other places, in Gini's own work[7] and in a text of Kendall and Stuart.[8] Even so, it may be helpful for us to say something here about Gini's statistics.

In principle, to compute Gini's mean difference, one merely finds the absolute value of the difference between the elements of each possible pair of observations and divides by the number of such pairs. For example, consider the following three observations: 2, 4, 7. The following pairs are considered: 2 and 4, 2 and 7, and 4 and 7. The absolute values of the differences between the elements of these pairs are 2, 5, and 3, respectively. Thus Gini's mean difference is 10 divided by 3, or $3\frac{1}{3}$. If there are N observations, the number of possible pairs is equal to $N(N - 1)/2$. When N is very large—as in our third study, for example—the volume of computations necessary for exact calculation is unbearable and estimation must be used.

The relationship between Gini's mean difference and Gini's co-

[7] Corrado Gini, *Memorie di metodologia statistica*, 2d ed. rev. Ernesto Pizzetti and T. Salvemini (Rome: Libreria Eredi Virgilio Veschi, 1955).
[8] Maurice G. Kendall and Alan Stuart, *Advanced Theory of Statistics in Three Volumes*, 2d ed. (New York: Hafner Publishing Co., 1963), Vol. 1.

FIGURE 1

A LORENZ CURVE

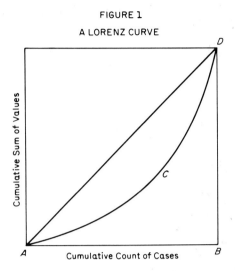

efficient of concentration is nearly analogous to that between the standard
deviation and the coefficient of variation. To compute the coefficient of
variation, one divides the standard deviation by the mean. To compute
Gini's coefficient of concentration, one divides Gini's mean difference by
twice the mean.

The discourteous reader might ask at this point why, instead of
using statistics that are familiar to readers of English, we must refer to
Gini's statistics. In the first place, Gini's mean difference gives us some
information that is interesting in itself. It tells us the expected value of
the difference in returns between two portfolios of any given size, including
portfolios of one stock. In the second place, Gini's coefficient of concentration is useful in summarizing differences in returns to portfolios. The
coefficient was originally developed to summarize differences in wealth or
income and thus applies to our studies of differences among wealth ratios.

Many readers will be familiar with the Lorenz curve as exemplified
in Figure 1. Gini's coefficient of concentration measures the ratio of the
area between the Lorenz curve ACD and the line AD to the total area of
the triangle ABD. When applied to returns on portfolios, the interpretation is straightforward. If portfolios are ranked by the size of returns
from the smallest to the largest, the locus of a Lorenz curve is readily
drawn. The number of portfolios, M, is shown on the horizontal axis; and
the sum of the wealth ratios of these M (smallest) portfolios is shown on
the vertical axis. If all portfolios had equal returns, the Lorenz curve
would be identical with line AD. If all portfolios except one had zero wealth
ratios and that one had a positive wealth ratio, the Lorenz curve would be
virtually identical with curve ABD. In the former case, Gini's coefficient
of concentration would be zero; in the latter case, one.

In the third place, we use Gini's statistics because many of the distributions we report here depart greatly from normality. For such distributions, the standard deviation of even a large sample may not give a very meaningful indication of the dispersion of the population. Gini's mean difference and coefficient of concentration are nonparametric measures and are invulnerable to this consequence of departure from normality. The mean deviation from the mean is also invulnerable to this adverse consequence of departure from normality. Gini's mean difference differs from the mean deviation by giving greater weight to extreme observations, thus taking care of a frequently made criticism of the mean deviation.

We use measures both of absolute and of relative dispersion. The absolute measures are interesting in themselves, but reliance on them exclusively would conceal some relationships which, as we will see, have been remarkably invariant for long periods of time.

THE STUDIES

Study 1: Distributions of wealth ratios for investments in single stocks

The frequency distributions of wealth ratios for investments in single stocks for 55 time periods are summarized in Table 3.[9] Many of their general features should not surprise anyone. In general, the mean wealth ratios shown in column 16 increase with the length of the holding period, although there is substantial overlap. (For example, the greatest mean for a 1-year period is greater than five of the eight means for 5-year periods, and the worst mean for a 5-year period exceeds only four of the 40 1-year means.)

The distributions for longer holding periods tend to have greater dispersion than the distributions for shorter periods, both absolutely and relatively. This tendency may be seen by looking at corresponding entries in columns (17–22) or by comparing ranges defined by columns (6) and (8), (5) and (9), (4) and (10), (3) and (11), (2) and (12), or (13) and (14).

For all periods studied, skewness of the distribution of wealth ratios was positive. This implies, as almost every investor knows, that the probability of deviating from the mean by very large amounts on the high side is greater than the probability of extremely large deviations on the low side. This skewness almost inevitably results from the simple arithmetic fact that it is impossible to lose more than 100 percent of one's investment, assuming that one does not buy on margin, while it is possible to make much more than 100 percent on one's money when one is lucky or wise. For all periods of five years or more, the maximum wealth ratio

---

[9] [Table 3 has been omitted here; the reader is referred to the original source—Ed.]

was at least 4.5 times as large as the mean wealth ratio. In fact, the maximum ratio was more than twice the mean in nine of the forty 1-year periods.

As would be expected with positive skewness, the mean is almost invariably greater than the median. There are a few exceptions for one-year periods when the positive skewness is slight. For almost all 1-year periods and for all periods longer than one year the mean exceeds the median. The longer the period, the greater the difference.

For all periods except 1929, the kurtosis of the frequency distributions is greater than 3.0. That is, a greater proportion of the observations fall near the mean than is true for normal distributions.[10] Nearness to the mean is measured in terms of standard deviations. In these particular distributions, the kurtosis is relatively small when skewness is slight. Thus the "peakedness" is caused largely by the presence of a few very large wealth ratios.

In Table 3, it is interesting to note the lower levels of relative dispersion after 1943. For example, Gini's coefficient of concentration was always at least 0.16 from 1926 through 1943; thereafter, the coefficient was always less than 0.16.

While discussing dispersion, it is interesting to compare the six measures of dispersion: the standard deviation, the mean deviation, the mean difference, the coefficient of variation, the relative mean deviation, and Gini's coefficient of concentration. The important fact is that the standard deviation and measure of relative dispersion derived from it, the coefficient of variation, are more variable from period to period than are the other measures. We believe that the greater instability in the standard deviation and the coefficient of variation lends support to Mandelbrot's hypothesis that the distributions of returns on individual stocks over time have infinite variance.[11]

It is also mildly interesting to note that for our data the relationship between Gini's mean difference and the mean deviation was remarkably stable—always being near the ratio that would be expected if the distributions were normal. For normal distributions, the ratio of Gini's mean difference to the mean deviation is $\sqrt{2}$.[12] Thus, it appears that for the particular distribution we describe here, either measure provides a good estimate of the other. The mean deviation is usually easier to calculate.

[10] As Kaplansky has stated (I. Kaplansky, "A Common Error concerning Kurtosis," *Journal of the American Statistical Association* 40 [June, 1945]: 259), it is a vulgar error blandly or blindly to assume that high kurtosis necessarily implies great concentration around the mean. Since we have examined them in great detail, we know that the common interpretation is correct for these distributions.

[11] Benoit Mandelbrot, "Variation of Certain Speculative Prices," *Journal of Business* 36 (October, 1963), pp. 394–419.

[12] Derived from Kendall and Stuart, pp. 139, 241. For normal distributions the mean deviation is $\sqrt{(2/\pi)}$ (= 0.80) times the standard deviation, and Gini's mean difference is $2/\sqrt{\pi}$ (= 1.13) times the standard deviation. Note also that in Table 3 the standard deviation is usually greater than Gini's mean difference.

Study 2: Distributions of wealth ratios aggregated for nonoverlapping periods

In Table 4 we present data on aggregated frequency distributions of wealth ratios from investments in individual stocks on the New York Stock Exchange. When one considers individual periods separately, as in Table 3, it is hard to make generalizations about the variability of experience in investing in stocks on the New York Stock Exchange because of the substantial changes from period to period.

We cannot, for example, tell the probability of gaining or losing a given amount by selecting a stock at random during a year selected at random. We know only the distribution of experience for the individual periods. To answer a variety of interesting questions (at least for the 40 years 1926–65), we must combine the frequency distributions for each period, giving equal weight to each period's distribution.

Suppose one were interested in knowing the relative frequency with which one would have lost more than 20 percent of his money if he had

TABLE 4. AGGREGATED FREQUENCY DISTRIBUTIONS OF WEALTH RATIOS FROM INVESTMENTS IN INDIVIDUAL STOCKS LISTED ON THE NYSE, 1926–65

	Periods					
Statistic	*Forty* *1-Year*	*Twenty* *1-Year* *(1926–45)*	*Twenty* *1-Year* *(1946–65)*	*Eight* *5-Year*	*Four* *4-Year*	*Two* *2-Year*
5th centile	.466	.356	.663	.201	.130	.052
10th centile	.613	.480	.763	.391	.340	.288
20th centile	.796	.675	.879	.726	.894	1.006
30th centile	.911	.828	.961	.990	1.416	1.871
40th centile	1.003	.958	1.026	1.240	1.833	3.028
50th centile (median)	1.085	1.075	1.091	1.491	2.245	4.222
60th centile	1.173	1.192	1.161	1.762	2.709	5.626
70th centile	1.277	1.326	1.245	2.096	3.282	7.940
80th centile	1.423	1.500	1.359	2.564	4.099	11.194
90th centile	1.675	1.830	1.551	3.581	5.479	17.263
95th centile	1.975	2.230	1.743	4.875	7.451	22.878
Minimum	0.000	0.000	0.000	0.000	0.000	0.000
Maximum	20.841	20.841	5.441	48.855	74.724	110.916
Mean	1.148	1.158	1.138	1.904	2.808	7.064
Standard deviation	.554	.699	.355	2.064	2.892	9.008
Mean deviation	.351	.447	.255	1.145	1.761	5.956
Gini's mean difference	.518	.653	.367	1.640	2.505	8.052
Coefficient of variation	.483	.604	.312	1.084	1.030	1.275
Relative mean deviation	.306	.386	.224	.601	.627	.843
Gini's coefficient of concentration	.226	.282	.161	.431	.446	.570
Skewness	5.339	5.062	1.791	7.197	7.315	3.485
Kurtosis	111.090	86.788	12.734	107.852	144.189	24.393
Number of cases	35,407	14,394	21,013	6,791	3,137	1,363

bought a stock at random and held it for a year during the 40-year period 1926–65. By reference to Table 4, one can see that there was about a 20 percent chance of losing about 20 percent or more of one's money by investing in a stock for one year. Similarly, there was about a 37 percent chance of making 20 percent or more by investing in a stock for one year.

When one turns to the 5-year periods, one can answer the same kinds of questions. For example, one lost about 20 percent or more of his money approximately 23 percent of the time. Conversely, one made at least 20 percent about half of the time. Naturally, the absolute variation in the wealth ratios increases as one moves from a 1-year to a 5-year holding period. Most of the increase is above the mean rather than below, as one would expect during periods when investors in common stocks generally received positive returns. It is important to note, however, that dispersion in the annual rates of return declines as the length of period increases. One can see this by interpreting the data in Table 4 in connection with the conversion table presented earlier (Table 2).

For 10-year periods, one lost 20 percent or more of his money less than 20 percent of the time and made a profit of at least 20 percent about three-quarters of the time (Table 4). It is possible to make other similar observations from Table 4.

Study 3: The effect of increasing the number of stocks in a portfolio on the distribution of returns

SOME PRELIMINARY COMMENTS. Now we shall discuss the most interesting study in this article. The study concerns the wealth ratios resulting from investment in portfolios of specified numbers of stocks, ranging from one through 128 and in all stocks listed on the New York Stock Exchange. The ratios refer to all of the forty 1-year periods, the eight possible nonoverlapping 5-year periods, the four possible 10-year periods, and the two 20-year periods. We also present data for the first 20 years and the last 20 years of the 40-year period so as to permit a comparison of the 20 years ending with the last year of World War II and the first 20 years of the postwar period.

Much of the previous work on the effect of portfolio size on the dispersion of wealth ratios is discussed and summarized in Brealey.[13] Other empirical work has been done by Evans and Archer.[14] This work has generally been concerned only with the effect of diversification on the standard deviation of returns or on the standard deviation of annual rates of return over time. These studies are subject to a serious bias in

[13] Richard A. Brealey, *An Introduction to Risk and Return from Common Stocks* (Cambridge, Mass.: M.I.T. Press, 1969).

[14] John L. Evans and Stephen H. Archer, "Diversification and the Reduction of Dispersion: An Empirical Analysis," *Journal of Finance* 23 (December, 1968): pp. 761–67.

that they are based on investment only in stocks which were listed throughout the period of study. The elimination of stocks which merged into other stocks or were delisted is the source of the bias.

Additional empirical work is not required to find the effect of diversification on the variance or standard deviation of returns when the mean and variance for each period are known. This is true for the following reasons: (1) the variance for any period for portfolios (randomly selected) of more than one stock can be calculated from knowledge of the variance of returns from investment in portfolios of one stock, and (2) the variance for several periods considered together (that is, aggregated) can be calculated from knowledge of the means and variances for the individual periods. The variance among wealth ratios of stocks or portfolios is equal to the sum of their average variances for the periods under consideration and the variance of the means. Diversification by random selection reduces the average variance within each period but does not affect the variance of the means.

If we had been content to rely on the variance and its derivative statistics, we could have avoided much expense in using the computer merely by algebraically calculating the statistics. We incurred the computer expense because the variance and its derivatives have been under suspicion since Mandelbrot's work seven years ago.[15]

Table 5 shows the frequency distribution of returns for portfolios of different sizes.[16] The frequency distributions for portfolios containing one stock were derived from complete enumeration of all possible such portfolios for the nonoverlapping periods selected. These distributions are also shown in Table 4. We also used complete enumeration to find the frequency distributions for portfolios containing two different stocks. We assumed equal initial investment in each stock and also assumed that dividends were reinvested in the stock which paid them.

For portfolios containing 8, 16, 32, and 128 stocks, we used simple random selection of individual stocks without replacement. It is possible, however, that this process produced two or more identical portfolios. We were unable to construct frequency distributions of portfolios of these sizes on the basis of complete enumeration because of the enormous volume of necessary computation. For example, the number of possible portfolios containing eight different stocks that could be selected from a list of 1,000 stocks is more than 24 quintillion.[17] At current costs for computer time, complete enumeration of all such portfolios of eight stocks would have cost approximately $150 trillion. Instead of complete enumeration, we

---

[15] Mandelbrot (n. 11 above).

[16] (Table 5 has been omitted here; the reader is referred to the original source—Ed.)

[17] 2.4115×10^{19}.

TABLE 6. DISPERSION OF RETURNS ON N-STOCK PORTFOLIOS AS
PERCENTAGE OF DISPERSION OF ONE-STOCK PORTFOLIOS
(Based on portfolios of stocks from NYSE for 1926–65 or as specified)

Measure of Relative Dispersion for Holding Period(s)	Number of Stocks in Portfolio						
	1	2	8	16	32	128	All (Market)
Coefficient of Variation							
40 one-year	100	81	64	60	59	57	57
20 one-year (1926–45)	100	81	64	61	59	58	57
20 one-year (1946–65)	100	81	63	59	57	56	55
8 five-year	100	79	58	53	51	49	49
4 ten-year	100	74	46	39	36	33	32
2 twenty-year	100	76	52	47	44	42	41
Relative Mean Deviation							
40 one-year	100	88	75	73	72	71	71
20 one-year (1926–45)	100	89	79	78	77	77	76
20 one-year (1946–65)	100	85	68	65	63	61	61
8 five-year	100	87	72	69	67	65	65
4 ten-year	100	81	56	50	47	45	45
2 twenty-year	100	84	65	63	62	62	62
Gini's Coefficient of Concentration							
40 one-year	100	87	74	71	69	68	68
20 one-year (1926–45)	100	88	76	73	71	70	69
20 one-year (1946–65)	100	84	67	64	62	60	59
8 five-year	100	86	71	68	66	64	62
4 ten-year	100	81	57	50	45	39	34
2 twenty-year	100	84	64	59	55	50	46

used a sample of all possible portfolios. The sample numbers are indicated in the table. The smallest sample size was approximately 32,000 portfolios in a given period.[18] We believe that with random samples of this size there are no significant biases or errors in the portrayals in the frequency distributions for the specified periods.

As indicated earlier, there were two methods of random sampling. The first has already deen described as simple random sampling without replacement. Samples of this type are designated in the table with the letter S. A second method of random sampling was also used, and the results of this method are indicated in the table with the letter R. In the second method, we took steps to insure that the portfolios were well

[18] These sample sizes were selected so as to make the total number of stocks selected approximately the same regardless of the size of the portfolio. The actual numbers (32,768, etc.) are powers of two, which were convenient to use in the computer programming.

TABLE 7.   DISPERSION OF RETURNS ON N-STOCK PORTFOLIOS
AS PERCENTAGE OF DISPERSION OF MARKET PORTFOLIOS
(Based on portfolios of stocks from NYSE for 1926–65 or as specified)

Measure of Relative Dispersion for Holding Period(s)	Number of Stocks in Portfolio						
	1	2	8	16	32	128	All (Market)
Coefficient of Variation							
40 one-year	176	143	112	106	103	101	100
20 one-year (1926–45)	175	142	112	106	103	101	100
20 one-year (1946–65)	180	146	113	107	103	101	100
8 five-year	205	161	118	109	104	101	100
4 ten-year	316	234	145	124	113	103	100
2 twenty-year	243	186	127	114	107	102	100
Relative Mean Deviation							
40 one-year	142	124	107	104	102	101	100
20 one-year (1926–45)	131	117	104	102	101	100	100
20 one-year (1946–65)	165	140	113	107	104	101	100
8 five-year	154	134	111	106	103	100	100
4 ten-year	224	181	126	112	105	100	100
2 twenty-year	161	135	105	101	100	100	100
Gini's Coefficient of Concentration							
40 one-year	148	128	109	105	103	101	100
20 one-year (1926–45)	145	127	110	106	103	101	100
20 one-year (1946–65)	169	141	113	107	104	101	100
8 five-year	161	139	115	109	105	102	100
4 ten-year	291	237	167	146	132	113	100
2 twenty-year	217	183	140	128	120	110	100

diversified by industry. All the common stocks on the New York Stock Exchange were assigned to 34 industry groups.[19] Our method of random selection insured that no more than one stock fell in any single industry group. The greater the number of stocks in an industry, the greater the probability of including that industry in the portfolio. But the greater the number in the industry, the smaller the probability of including any particular stock.

We will not distinguish between these two different random methods of sampling in discussing the results, since the two methods of selecting the sample did not produce significantly different results. Although there was a slight reduction in dispersion within individual periods as a result of the constrained random sampling, this reduction was almost exactly offset by the increased dispersion of the means among periods. Thus, when

[19] See Appendix, Table A1 [omitted here—Ed.].

TABLE 8. PERCENT OF POSSIBLE REDUCTION IN RELATIVE
DISPERSION ACHIEVED THROUGH INCREASING THE
NUMBER OF STOCKS IN THE PORTFOLIO
(Based on portfolios of stocks from NYSE for 1926–65 or as specified)

Measure of Relative Dispersion for Holding Period(s)	Number of Stocks in Portfolio						
	1	2	8	16	32	128	All (Market)
Coefficient of Variation							
40 one-year	0	43	84	92	96	99	100
20 one-year (1926–45)	0	43	84	92	96	99	100
20 one-year (1946–65)	0	43	84	92	96	99	100
8 five-year	0	42	83	91	96	99	100
4 ten-year	0	38	79	89	94	99	100
2 twenty-year	0	40	81	90	95	99	100
Relative Mean Deviation							
40 one-year	0	42	84	91	95	98	100
20 one-year (1926–45)	0	45	87	94	96	99	100
20 one-year (1946–65)	0	39	80	89	94	99	100
8 five-year	0	37	79	89	95	99	100
4 ten-year	0	35	79	90	96	100	100
2 twenty-year	0	43	91	99	100	100	100
Gini's Coefficient of Concentration							
40 one-year	0	41	81	90	94	98	100
20 one-year (1926–45)	0	39	79	87	93	98	100
20 one-year (1946–65)	0	40	81	89	94	98	100
8 five-year	0	36	76	85	91	97	100
4 ten-year	0	28	65	76	84	93	100
2 twenty-year	0	29	66	76	83	92	100

periods were aggregated, the distributions from the two methods of sampling became almost the same.

THE FINDINGS. In considering the findings discussed here, it is important to remember that initial equal investments were made in each stock included in any portfolio and that there was no subsequent reallocation of resources to preserve the equality of investment. This is not an investment strategy we advocate; again, it was chosen to make certain that the distributions were affected only by the number of stocks in the portfolio.

There is only one important generalization about Table 5. It is that portfolios containing eight stocks have frequency distributions strikingly similar to those of portfolios containing larger numbers of stocks—including all listed stocks—except for the tails beyond the fifth and ninetieth centiles. The tails beyond those centiles get progressively shorter as the number of stocks in the portfolio increases. This fact causes the measures of dispersion to get smaller, despite the nearly identical distributions between the fifth and ninetieth centiles.

Tables 6, 7, and 8 summarize the information in Table 5 with respect to the effect on relative dispersion of changing the number of stocks in a portfolio. The tables are easily read. The market as a whole generally had 50–75 percent as much dispersion as did one-stock portfolios, depending on the periods and measure of dispersion (Table 6). Conversely, one-stock portfolios have roughly one and one-third to twice as much dispersion as the market (Table 7). The opportunity to reduce dispersion by increasing the number of stocks in the portfolio is rapidly exhausted (Table 8). Roughly, 40 percent of achievable reduction is obtained by holding 2 stocks; 80 percent, by holding 8 stocks; 90 percent, by holding 16 stocks; 95 percent, by holding 32 stocks; and 99 percent, by holding 128 stocks (Table 8).

APPENDIX A*

Aggregated frequency distributions for portfolios of specified sizes

Table A1 shows the frequency distributions of wealth ratios for portfolios of specified sizes for the fifty-five periods. These distributions were aggregated to produce Tables 4 and 5.

Since the statistics for portfolios having eight or more stocks were based on samples, it is unlikely that the minimum and maximum wealth ratios for any samples were the true minima and maxima. Table A2 shows the true minima and maxima for portfolios of eight or more stocks for each of the fifty-five periods.

* [Appendix A omitted here—Ed.]

*Shannon P. Pratt**

17. Relationship Between Variability of Past Returns and Levels of Future Returns for Common Stocks, 1926–1960

INTRODUCTION

This paper tests the hypothesis that common stocks characterized by relatively high degrees of risk, where risk is measured by instability of historical rate of return, have provided their holders with higher rates of return, on the average and over considerable periods of time, than have common stocks characterized by relatively lower degrees of risk.

A common goal among investors is the optimal balancing of a security portfolio between the desirable characteristic of expected rate of return and the undesirable characteristic of risk. However, a problem which has impeded judgment of what constitutes "optimal" balancing of the portfolio of any given investor has been inadequate empirical knowledge regarding the historical relationship between risk and rate of return in the stock market.

A consensus of written opinion is that investors in general have an aversion to risk; and that investors in general do indeed pay a "premium" to avoid risk, in the sense of accepting lesser average returns in the capital markets on securities characterized by lower degrees of riskiness.

Typical of the statements in the literature on this subject is the following:

> There will ordinarily be a positive market premium on risk. That is, expected risky yields will be higher than sure yields.... That the market does pay positive risk premiums is a statement so refutable that many people (in particular Knight) claim it has in fact been refuted.

* Associate Professor and Director, Investment Analysis Center, Portland State University. The author wishes to express appreciation for assistance in this research and writing from Harry Sauvain, James Lorie, Lawrence Fisher, Benoit Mandelbrot, A. James Heins, William Sharpe, Paul Cootner, and Alexander Robichek. Financial support for the research was provided in part by the Ford Foundation. This essay has not previously been published.

However, I believe that the weight of the evidence indicates that risky media of investment do in fact have higher expected yields than secure media (or, in other words, uncertain expected values are discounted relative to certain values).[1]

Empirical studies have produced substantial evidence to support this position. For example, corporate bonds historically have yielded investors considerably lower returns on the average than the more risky category of securities, common stocks.[2] Similarly, Hickman has shown that more risky bonds have yielded higher returns, on the average, than less risky bonds.[3]

In its 1964 study of research in the capital markets, the Exploratory Committee on Research in the Capital Markets made the following recommendations:

> A reading of Hickman's volumes on the Corporate Bond Research Project leads one to wish that something along similar lines might be done for common stocks. The design of such a study should be broad in scope and cover a considerable time period. . . . It would be extremely useful to examine the *ex post* results of investments in equities of different quality or other characteristics. Yields after losses including capital gains, might be studied as a function of risk.[4]

It is to a portion of that task that this project is directed.

METHOD OF RESEARCH

Data used

The basic data analyzed in this study were developed at the University of Chicago Center for Research in Security Prices. The tape used in the study includes data on every common stock listed on the New York Stock Exchange from 1926 through 1960. The tape gives five pieces of information for each stock as of the close of the last trading day of each month: (1) an identifying number for the particular stock, (2) an industry code number, (3) a month number, (4) an "investment performance relative" (IPR), and (5) a "price relative."[5]

---

[1] Jack Hirshleifer, "Risk, the Discount Rate, and Investment Decisions," *American Economic Review* (May, 1961), p. 117.

[2] See, for example, Lawrence Fisher and James H. Lorie, "Rates of Return on Investments in Common Stocks," *Journal of Business* (January, 1964), pp. 1–21; also Lawrence Fisher, "Outcomes of 'Random' Investments in Common Stocks Listed on the New York Stock Exchange," *Journal of Business* (April, 1965), pp. 149–161.

[3] W. Braddock Hickman, *Corporate Bond Quality and Investor Experience* (Princeton, N.J.: Princeton U.P., 1958).

[4] National Bureau of Economic Research, *Research in the Capital Markets*, published as a supplement to the *Journal of Finance* (May, 1964), p. 15.

[5] For a description of the work of the Center for Research in Security Prices and of the data thus far developed and contemplated for the future, see Fisher and Lorie, *op. cit.* Additional details on the development and content of this tape are given in Fisher, "Outcomes for 'Random' Investments . . .," Appendix, pp. 159–161.

The "investment performance relatives" are the focal point of this study. IPR's represent the price of the stock at the end of the month plus the value of dividends, rights, and other distributions which inure to the stock during the month, divided by the price at the beginning of the month. For example, consider a stock that closed at $50 on January 31, 1950, paid a $1 dividend during February, and closed at $55 on February 28, 1950. The IPR for that stock for February, 1950 would be ($55 + $1)/$50 = $56/$50 = $1.12.

Later reference is made to "quarterly IPR's" and "one-year IPR's." These are derived simply by taking the product of the appropriate number of monthly IPR's. In all cases it is assumed that dividends are reinvested on a monthly basis in the stock of the company making the payment. The IPR minus 1.00 equals the rate of return achieved during the period, on the basis of the price at the beginning of the period.

Risk and return measures

The selection of appropriate measures of risk and rate of return requires consideration. Perhaps the most widely used single statistical measure of risk to date has been the standard deviation of annual rates of return for a security. This measure has been used by Markowitz, Lintner, Sharpe, Baumol, and others.[6] It focuses directly on the variable of ultimate concern to the investor, that is, the rate of return received. This variable reflects a great many underlying influences, such as earnings, dividends, investors' expectations, and psychological and financial market factors.

The present analysis is in full sympathy with the focus on stability of the rate of return to the investor as the relevant variable in an attempt to measure risk. However, if a measure of dispersion around some measure of central tendency is to be meaningful, the dispersion should be measured around that measure of central tendency which is most appropriate to the data. In this study, the average rate of return for a period is derived by finding the geometric mean of the IPR's and subtracting 1.00.

The geometric mean is used to avoid the upward bias which results when the arithmetic mean is employed as a measure of central tendency

---

[6] Harry M. Markowitz, *Portfolio Selection: Efficient Diversification of Investments* (New York, N.Y.: John Wiley & Sons, Inc., 1959); John Lintner, "The Valuation of Risk Assets and the Selection of Risky Investments in Stock Portfolios and Capital Budgets," *Review of Economics and Statistics* (February, 1965), pp. 13–37; William F. Sharpe, "Risk-Aversion in the Stock Market: Some Empirical Evidence," *Journal of Finance* (September, 1965), pp. 416–422; William J. Baumol, "An Expected Gain–Confidence Limit Criterion for Portfolio Selection," *Management Science* (October, 1963), pp. 174–182.

for a compound time series. If we assume reinvestment of all dividends and no withdrawals by the investor, then the arithmetic mean rate of return for an investment over a series of successive time periods is equal to the discounted present value rate of return *only* in the special case where the returns occur at an exactly even rate over the entire series. To the extent that the periodic rate of return fluctuates, the arithmetic mean rate of return will be higher than the discounted present value rate of return. Hence, given the *same* true discounted present value rate of return for several different securities, those with the higher variability of that rate of return among time periods also will have the higher computed arithmetic mean return. Thus, the arithmetic mean is biased upward in the sense that it indicates a rate of return higher than the "discounted present value" rate of return. The magnitude of the bias, which varies with the data selected, may be gauged by a comparison of Tables 3 and 4.

In each of the models used in this study, it is assumed that all dividends are reinvested in the stock of the company which made the payment, and that no withdrawals are made from the investor's portfolio until the entire portfolio is sold at a predetermined date. Under these assumptions, the geometric mean of the IPR's for the series of periods constituting the time the portfolio is held is equal to 1.00 plus the discounted present value rate of return for the time the investment is held. Therefore, the geometric mean of the IPR's, minus 1.00, is the appropriate measure of central tendency to be used to represent the "average" rate of return for the period.

Just as a geometric mean represents a measure of central tendency on a logarithmic scale, the variability of rates of return also should be measured on a logarithmic scale. Specifically, the measure of variability which is of concern is not the absolute amount of deviation from the geometric mean, but is the *ratio* of an observation above the geometric mean to the geometric mean itself, and the *ratio* of the geometric mean itself to an observation below the geometric mean. Measurement of this nature can be achieved very simply by using as the measure of relative stability among the different stocks the standard deviation of the logarithms of the IPR's for the periods of interest, rather than the standard deviations of the absolute rates of return for those periods.

With the foregoing considerations in mind, the objective measure used in the study as a proxy variable for the risk associated with a stock was the *standard deviation of the natural logarithms of the quarterly investment performance relatives* (IPR's) for the stock for a series of quarters immediately preceding the period of time for which the rates of return were compared among the various stocks.

In terms of a formula, the operational measure of the 3-year risk factor may be stated as follows:

$$\sigma_{iq} = \sqrt{\frac{\sum\limits_{q-33,q-30...q-3}^{q} (\ln X_{iq} - \overline{\ln X_{iq}})^2}{n}}$$

where σ_{iq} = "risk factor" for the ith stock measured for the 3-year period ending with the qth quarter;

X_{iq} = IPR for the ith stock for the qth quarter ($\prod\limits_{m-2}^{m} X_{im}$);

X_{im} = IPR for the ith stock for the mth month;

n = number of quarters in observation period over which the "risk factor" was measured.

When the set of experiments was conducted for the second time, computing the risk factor on the basis of five years' (20 quarters') past data, the formula was modified to sum over $q - 57, q - 54, \cdots q$, thus using 60 months instead of 36 months data in determining the risk factor.

The months are numbered 1 through 420, with January, 1926 assigned month number 1 and December, 1960 assigned month number 420. The quarters are numbered 3 through 420, to coincide with the month number of the last month of the quarter. For example, January through March, 1926 is assigned quarter number 3; February through April, 1926 is assigned quarter number 4; and October through December, 1960 is assigned quarter number 420.[7] It should be noted that the quarters thus designated are overlapping rather than discrete.

Time periods studied

The "risk factor" used in this study was computed for each common stock listed on the New York Stock Exchange for each of 372 "base dates," at monthly intervals from January 31, 1929 through December 31, 1959.[8] As of each of the 372 base dates, all the common stocks were divided into five "portfolios" of equal numbers of stocks, the composition of the portfolios determined by the quintile values of the computed risk factor. The five portfolios thus determined for each of the 372 base dates were designated "Grade A," indicating the lowest-risk stocks (those whose past investment performance had been most stable), through "Grade E," the highest-risk stocks (those whose past investment performance had been least stable).

---

[7] As a subscript, q denotes the quarter to which a particular flow variable (such as rate of return) refers, and the end-of-quarter value for a stock variable (such as the risk factor).

[8] An illustration of the computation of the risk factor is shown in Appendix I. The computation shown there is based on quarterly IPR's for the immediately preceding three years.

The returns on each of the five portfolios then were computed for one year forward from each of the 372 base dates. Returns for each portfolio were computed for three years forward from each of 348 base dates (January 31, 1929 through December 31, 1957), for five years forward from 324 base dates (January 31, 1929 through December 31, 1955), and for seven years forward from 300 base dates (January 31, 1929 through December 31, 1953).

FIGURE 1

DIAGRAM OF COMBINATIONS OF OBSERVATION PERIODS AND HOLDING PERIODS USED

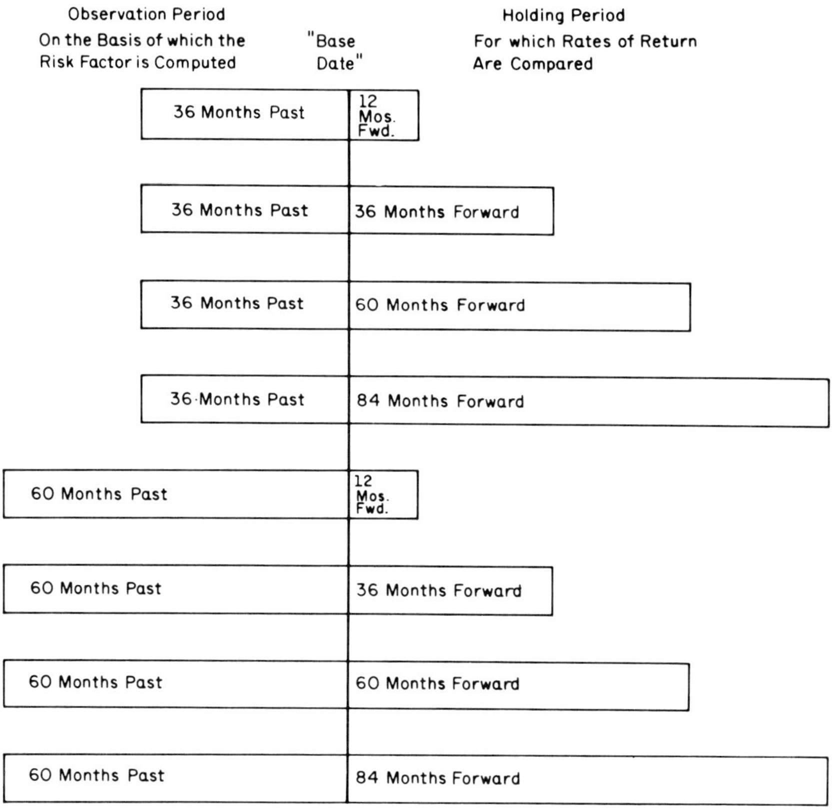

Observation Period On the Basis of which the Risk Factor is Computed	"Base Date"	Holding Period For which Rates of Return Are Compared

A Total of 372 Different "Base Dates" Are Used in the Study.

Figure 1 presents a schematic representation of the combinations of "observation periods" for which the risk factors were measured and "holding periods" for which realized rates of return were measured. An illustration of the computation of the comparative rates of return is shown in Appendix II.

FINDINGS

An overall summary of the relationship that obtained between risk and rate of return for common stocks listed on the New York Stock Exchange from 1929 through 1960 is presented in Tables 1 through 4 and Figures 2 and 3.

The overall arithmetic means of the IPR's for each risk grade for all the holding periods of each of the four durations encompassed in the study are computed by the formula

$$\bar{X} = \frac{\sum \bar{x}_m}{n}$$

where $\bar{x}_m$ = arithmetic mean IPR for the stocks of the particular risk grade for base month m (computed as shown in Appendix II);

n = number of base months included. (For example, base months 37–408, inclusive, would be 372 base months.)

Results of the above are presented in Table 1.

TABLE 1. ARITHMETIC MEAN IPR'S FOR STOCK
PORTFOLIOS OF DIFFERENT RISK GRADES

First Holding Period Beginning January 31, 1929
Last Holding Period Ending December 31, 1960

Risk Grade	Avg. 1-yr. IPR (Base Months 37–408)	Avg. 3-yr. IPR (Base Months 37–384)	Avg. 5-yr. IPR (Base Months 37–360)	Avg. 7-yr. IPR (Base Months 37–336)
A	1.121	1.451	1.847	2.315
B	1.160	1.555	2.085	2.597
C	1.175	1.628	2.215	2.768
D	1.202	1.683	2.305	2.811
E	1.223	1.745	2.321	2.718

First Holding Period Beginning January 31, 1931
Last Holding Period Ending December 31, 1960

Risk Grade	Avg. 1-yr. IPR (Base Months 61–408)	Avg. 3-yr. IPR (Base Months 61–384)	Avg. 5-yr. IPR (Base Months 61–360)	Avg. 7-yr. IPR (Base Months 61–336)
A	1.150	1.531	1.929	2.417
B	1.190	1.638	2.185	2.717
C	1.213	1.703	2.327	2.889
D	1.242	1.775	2.422	2.954
E	1.271	1.834	2.444	2.848

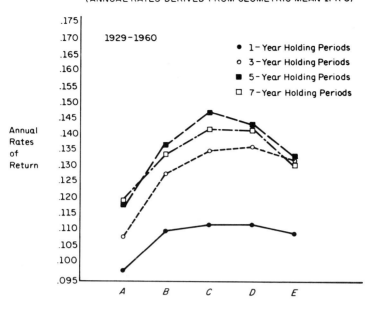

FIGURE 2

AVERAGE ANNUAL RATES OF RETURN FOR STOCK PORTFOLIOS
OF DIFFERENT RISK GRADES
(ANNUAL RATES DERIVED FROM GEOMETRIC MEAN IPR'S)

1929-1960

● 1-Year Holding Periods
○ 3-Year Holding Periods
■ 5-Year Holding Periods
□ 7-Year Holding Periods

Annual
Rates
of
Return

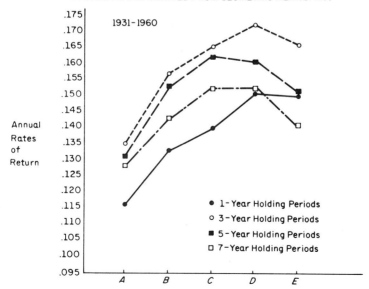

FIGURE 3

AVERAGE ANNUAL RATES OF RETURN FOR STOCK
PORTFOLIOS OF DIFFERENT RISK GRADES
(ANNUAL RATES DERIVED FROM GEOMETRIC MEAN IPR'S)

1931-1960

Annual
Rates
of
Return

● 1-Year Holding Periods
○ 3-Year Holding Periods
■ 5-Year Holding Periods
□ 7-Year Holding Periods

Similarly, geometric means of the IPR's for each risk grade for holding periods of each duration encompassed in the study are computed by the formula

$$\bar{G} = (\prod \bar{x}_m)^{1/n}$$

where $\bar{x}_m$ and n are the same values as those used to compute the arithmetic means.

Results of the above are presented in Table 2.

TABLE 2. GEOMETRIC MEAN IPR'S FOR STOCK PORTFOLIOS OF DIFFERENT RISK GRADES

First Holding Period Beginning January 31, 1929
Last Holding Period Ending December 31, 1960

Risk Grade	$\bar{G}$ of 1-yr. IPR's (Base Months 37–408)	$\bar{G}$ of 3-yr. IPR's (Base Months 37–384)	$\bar{G}$ of 5-yr. IPR's (Base Months 37–360)	$\bar{G}$ of 7-yr. IPR's (Base Months 37–336)
A	1.098	1.35	1.74	2.19
B	1.110	1.43	1.90	2.41
C	1.112	1.46	1.98	2.54
D	1.112	1.47	1.95	2.54
E	1.109	1.45	1.87	2.36

First Holding Period Beginning January 31, 1931
Last Holding Period Ending December 31, 1960

Risk Grade	$\bar{G}$ of 1-yr. IPR's (Base Months 61–408)	$\bar{G}$ of 3-yr. IPR's (Base Months 61–384)	$\bar{G}$ of 5-yr. IPR's (Base Months 61–360)	$\bar{G}$ of 7-yr. IPR's (Base Months 61–336)
A	1.116	1.46	1.85	2.32
B	1.133	1.55	2.04	2.56
C	1.140	1.58	2.12	2.69
D	1.151	1.61	2.11	2.69
E	1.150	1.58	2.02	2.51

Both the arithmetic and geometric means of IPR's for the various risk grades and holding periods then are transformed into equivalent annual rates of return by the formula

$$y = x^{1/n} - 1$$

where y = annual rate of return;

x = the respective figure from Tables 1 or 2;

n = the number of years in the holding period.

These equivalent annual rates of return based on the arithmetic and geometric means of IPR's are presented in Tables 3 and 4, respectively.

Comparison of average investment performance among risk grades

The first of the two sections of Table 1 shows the results based on the 3-year risk factor, starting with base month 37 (January 31, 1929). The second section shows results based on the 3-year risk factor, but excluding base months 37 through 60 and beginning with base month 61 (January 31, 1931).[9]

The averages of the IPR's for the 3-year risk factor are consistently higher for the set of periods beginning with base month 61 than for the set of periods beginning with base month 37. This is because the 2-year span from base months 37 through 60 (January 31, 1929 through January 31, 1931) was a period of large losses in the market as a whole. During that 2-year period, prices of stocks declined nearly 50 percent, as measured by the Dow-Jones Industrial Average.

In spite of the considerable difference in the *level* of the results arising from the difference in starting dates, the *pattern* of the results is exactly the same regardless of which starting date is used. That is, in all cases except the 7-year holding periods, the arithmetic mean of the IPR's for portfolios of stocks of different risk grades over time rises consistently, but at a decelerating rate, as risk grade declines. In the case of the 7-year holding periods, the average IPR's on the Grade E stocks are actually lower than on the Grade C and D stocks.

Table 2 presents the geometric means of the IPR's for each risk grade for all the time periods encompassed in the study. The format of Table 2 is exactly the same as the format of Table 1.

As explained previously, the nature of the geometric mean is such that in all cases the geometric mean of IPR's is lower than the arithmetic mean of the same IPR's. As is the case with the arithmetic mean IPR's, the pattern of the geometric mean of IPR's is almost identical whether the set of observations starts in 1929 or in 1931, and whether the 3-year or the 5-year risk factor is used as the basis of classification.

---

[9] It might also be noted that these rates of return are somewhat higher than the over-all averages shown by Fisher and Lorie, *op. cit.* This is due partly to differences in the respective methods used in arriving at "averages," and partly because their study had many more holding periods ending during the 1930's, with heavy losses depressing their average figures compared to the results shown here.

However, the pattern of the geometric means of IPR's among risk grades differs somewhat from the pattern of arithmetic means of IPR's. As is the case with arithmetic means, the average investment performance of Grade B portfolios consistently outperforms the average investment

TABLE 3. AVERAGE ANNUAL RATES OF RETURN FOR STOCK PORTFOLIOS OF DIFFERENT RISK GRADES
(Annual rates derived from arithmetic mean IPR's)

First Holding Period Beginning January 31, 1929
Last Holding Period Ending December 31, 1960

Risk Grade	1-yr. IPR Basis (Base Months 37–408)	3-yr. IPR Basis (Base Months 37–384)	5-yr. IPR Basis (Base Months 37–360)	7-yr. IPR Basis (Base Months 37–336)
A	.121	.132	.130	.126
B	.160	.159	.159	.146
C	.175	.177	.172	.157
D	.202	.190	.182	.159
E	.223	.203	.183	.153

First Holding Period Beginning January 31, 1931
Last Holding Period Ending December 31, 1960

Risk Grade	1-yr. IPR Basis (Base Months 61–408)	3-yr. IPR Basis (Base Months 61–384)	5-yr. IPR Basis (Base Months 61–360)	7-yr. IPR Basis (Base Months 61–336)
A	.150	.152	.140	.134
B	.190	.179	.169	.154
C	.213	.194	.184	.163
D	.242	.211	.193	.167
E	.271	.224	.196	.161

performance of Grade A portfolios, and the average IPR's on Grade C portfolios is higher in all cases than the average IPR's on Grade B portfolios. However, as measured by the geometric means, the overall average IPR's consistently "top out" at either the C or the D risk grade. In every case, the geometric mean of IPR's over time is lower for Grade E portfolios than for Grade D portfolios; in most cases the geometric mean of IPR's for Grade E portfolios is lower than for Grade C portfolios, and in five instances the geometric mean of IPR's for Grade E portfolios is even lower than for Grade B portfolios.

Tables 3 and 4 simply present the results given in Tables 1 and 2 respectively, transformed into equivalent annual rates of return. (See Appendix II.) When viewed in terms of equivalent annual rates of return, it becomes apparent that using the geometric mean rather than the arithmetic mean as a measure of central tendency has the effect of dampening

TABLE 4. AVERAGE ANNUAL RATES OF RETURN FOR STOCK PORTFOLIOS OF DIFFERENT RISK GRADES
(Annual rates derived from geometric mean IPR's)

First Holding Period Beginning January 31, 1929
Last Holding Period Ending December 31, 1960

Risk Grade	1-yr. IPR Basis (Base Months 37–408)	3-yr. IPR Basis (Base Months 37–384)	5-yr. IPR Basis (Base Months 37–360)	7-yr. IPR Basis (Base Months 37–336)
A	.098	.108	.118	.119
B	.110	.128	.137	.134
C	.112	.135	.147	.142
D	.112	.136	.143	.142
E	.109	.132	.133	.131

First Holding Period Beginning January 31, 1931
Last Holding Period Ending December 31, 1960

Risk Grade	1-yr. IPR Basis (Base Months 61–408)	3-yr. IPR Basis (Base Months 61–384)	5-yr. IPR Basis (Base Months 61–360)	7-yr. IPR Basis (Base Months 61–336)
A	.116	.135	.131	.128
B	.133	.157	.153	.143
C	.140	.165	.162	.152
D	.151	.172	.161	.152
E	.150	.166	.151	.141

the differences between returns for various risk grades more for the shorter holding periods than for the longer holding periods. The results from Table 4 are shown graphically in Figures 2 and 3.

Interpretations of findings

Whether the arithmetic mean or the geometric mean is more representative of an investor's "average" experience depends on whether the investments whose results are being averaged were undertaken concurrently or sequentially. For a group of investments undertaken concurrently, say a portfolio of 10 stocks all purchased on the same date and all sold concurrently on some subsequent date, the arithmetic mean is an appropriate average of the investor's experience with those 10 stocks. But for a series of investments each undertaken with the proceeds of the previous investment, such as a series of 10 stocks or portfolios of stocks purchased in consecutive years with the proceeds of the sale of the stock or portfolio held in the previous year, the geometric mean is the appropriate average of the investor's experience with that sequence of 10 stocks or portfolios of stocks.

Since the holding periods encompassed by this study are partly overlapping and partly sequential, the "average" experience realized by investors as a whole during the entire period of the study was somewhere between the arithmetic and geometric means. Unfortunately, there is no entirely satisfactory method for combining the two.

In any case, the increasing average return from the Grade A stocks down through Grade C stocks is shown consistently in Tables 1 through 4, regardless of what measure of central tendency is employed. Just where, or whether, the return to risk "tops out" depends on the assumptions one makes about investor habits and frequency of portfolio turnover.

The apparent flattening out of the level of returns toward the upper end of the risk scale is one of the most interesting results, since it is inconsistent with the theory that higher average returns should be expected the further out the investor exposes himself on the risk scale. Most of the possible explanations for this result can be subsumed under two general categories: (1) Utility functions of some investors, notably those active in the market at the outer end of the risk scale, may not conform to the so-called "rational" utility function where the utility to the investor of any given level of expected value would decrease with increasing uncertainty; or (2) Some investors may have made erroneous estimates of the expected values and/or degrees of dispersion of future returns.

LIMITATIONS

The general finding of positive incremental returns with increasing risk (up through medium-high-risk stocks) is valid only when applied to large numbers of stocks and adequately long time spans. The study is limited by the fact that no attempt was made to break down the overall time span into two or more shorter periods to attempt to determine whether there was any evidence of change in the general relationship in the later years as compared with the earlier years.

What constitutes an "adequately long time span" depends somewhat on the conditions prevalent in the market during the time span of interest. As long as the market continued in a strong, uninterrupted general upward tre⁻d, the relationship of increasing returns with increasing risk held true quite consistently, regardless of the length of the time span involved. However, negative incremental returns to risk tended to prevail during periods of weak market conditions. Generally speaking, an "adequately long time span" would be one which ended with the general level of the market, as measured by some broad market index, at least as high as at the start of the period. A more conservative statement of what would constitute an "adequately long time span" would be one which ended with a broad market index above the value of the index at the beginning of the period to the extent of the extrapolated difference which would be expected to result from the long-term upward trend of the market index.

The qualification that the relationship is valid only for very large groups of stocks also is important, particularly at the higher risk levels, where the dispersion of results was wide, and extreme outcomes on a small minority of the total number of stocks tended to exert an important effect on the group means. The overall findings are averages based on analysis encompassing nearly 1000 stocks for *each* of more than 2500 combinations of observation and holding periods, during a time span in excess of 30 years.[10] It is quite easy to find examples of, say, 100 stocks, for a single time period, of, say, 10 years, where the risk-return relationship was not consistent with the average results realized by all common stocks listed on the New York Stock Exchange over the entire 30-year-plus span.

SUMMARY AND CONCLUSION

In summary, during the 30 years covered by the study, there was a consistently increasing average rate of return with increasing risk from the lowest-risk stocks up through medium-risk stocks. Regardless of the length of time for which the stocks were held (from 1 to 7 years), and regardless of whether the "average" investment performance was measured by the arithmetic mean of IPR's or by the geometric mean of IPR's, the Grade B portfolios achieved higher average returns than the Grade A portfolios. Similarly, the Grade C portfolios achieved higher average returns than the Grade B portfolios, but not by as wide a margin as the Grade B over the Grade A.

The medium-high-risk stocks (Grade D) also outperformed the medium-risk (Grade C) stocks on the average, although the difference was small. The results for the Grade E vs. the Grade D category were inconclusive, with the Grade E showing slightly higher average returns

---

[10] A total of 1461 different stocks were selected for inclusion in one or more of the 2592 different observation/holding period combinations encompassed by the study.

for the shorter holding periods, and the Grade D showing slightly higher average returns for longer holding periods.

Thus, the results show that, during the historical period covered by this study, the portfolio manager could have increased the expected value of his returns by accepting additional volatility of returns up to some point, perhaps around the eightieth percentile on the variability scale, but that the expected value of his returns would not have been increased by accepting additional risk beyond that point without better than average selection and/or timing expertise.

APPENDIX I

ILLUSTRATIVE COMPUTATION OF RISK FACTOR

Stock #67640 International Packers Ltd.

Quarter Number and Ending Date		Quarterly IPR	$log_e IPR$	Deviation $\mid log_e IPR - (-.009413) \mid$	Deviation Squared
303	3/31/51	1.079766	.076744	.086157	.007423
306	6/30/51	1.003242	.003234	.021647	.000160
309	9/30/51	1.089869	.086058	.095470	.009115
312	12/31/51	1.029747	.029313	.038726	.001500
315	3/31/52	0.810345	− .210295	.200883	.040354
318	6/30/52	0.973231	− .027134	.017721	.000314
321	9/30/52	0.932584	− .069796	.060383	.003646
324	12/31/52	0.993898	− .006121	.003292	.000011
327	3/31/53	1.187500	.171850	.181263	.032856
330	6/30/53	0.918334	− .085194	.075781	.005743
333	9/30/53	0.941176	− .060625	.051212	.002623
336	12/31/53	0.979231	− .020988	.011575	.000134
	Totals*		− .112953		.103878

Mean of logs of IPR's: $-.112953 \div 12 = -.009413$

Mean square deviation (log variance): $.103878 \div 12 = .008656$

Standard Deviation of logs of IPR's (Risk Factor): $(.008656)^{1/2} = .093040$

* Figures shown in columns do not add exactly to totals shown because of rounding.

APPENDIX II

ILLUSTRATIVE COMPUTATION OF RATES OF RETURN FOR
GROUPS OF STOCKS OF DIFFERENT RISK GRADES

Stock	Risk Factor*	1-Year IPR†	3-Year IPR†	5-Year IPR†	7-Year IPR†
67600	.051161	1.464121	1.368867	2.051773	2.552040
67700	.059248	1.485375	1.687547	2.061162	2.322475
		2.949496	3.056454	4.112935	4.874515
No. of stocks per quintile		÷2	÷2	÷2	÷2
Mean IPR for the quintile ($ at end of period for each $1 invested)		1.474748	1.528227	2.056467	2.437257
Take mean IPR to the root of the no. of years.		$\sqrt[1]{1.474748}$ =1.475	$\sqrt[3]{2.528227}$ =1.152	$\sqrt[5]{2.056467}$ =1.155	$\sqrt[7]{2.437257}$ =1.136
Subtract 1		−1.000	−1.000	−1.000	−1.000
Avg. annual compound rate of return for 1st quintile		.475	.152	.155	.136

* Computed as of December 31, 1953, by method shown in Appendix I.

† The 1-year IPR is the product of 12 monthly IPR's for January, 1954, through December, 1954; the 3-year IPR is the product of the 36 monthly IPR's for January, 1954 through December, 1956, etc.

Henry A. Latané
*William E. Young**

18. Test of Portfolio Building Rules

Reprinted from **The Journal of Finance,** Vol. XXIV, No. 4 (September, 1969), pp. 595–612, by permission of the authors and the publisher.

Analyses of *ex post* security price data have in general been concerned with (1) the behavior of stock market prices [2, 5, 9, 12], (2) evaluation of portfolio selection models [1, 8, 10, 11], and (3) security-stock market performance [6, 7]. In this paper *ex post* annual holding period returns (HPRs) are used to test methods for allocating financial resources among portfolio assets (risk free bonds and securities) taking cognizance of the character of security prices, portfolio diversification and portfolio leverage (borrowing or lending). We assume that the objective of portfolio management is to maximize long-run wealth. This is done by maximizing the compound annual average return, that is geometric mean return, on net worth. Hence, we test the effectiveness of various portfolio building rules on the geometric mean return, G, by using past holding period returns to represent probability beliefs of investors faced with building portfolios.

We are using *ex post* distributions of HPR's to test portfolio building rules. This involves two very important assumptions: (1) we assume perfect knowledge as to the statistics of these distributions over time and across securities but no knowledge of the individual HPR's, and (2) we assume that these statistics remain constant over time so that the probability beliefs do not change as actual results become available over time. We are attempting to show the outcome of several portfolio rules given specified statistics for distributions of HPR's. For example, we will use *ex post* data to test the intuitively appealing hypothesis that it would be generally better to reallocate portfolios at the beginning of each investment period rather than to buy and hold, since reallocation would reduce holdings in stocks that had performed well to date (and thus *will* perform relatively poorer over the subsequent periods) and increase holdings that have had

* Professor of Finance and Assistant Professor of Business Administration, respectively, University of North Carolina. Financial support for the paper was provided under a grant from the National Science Foundation.

relatively poor performance (but will wind up with an average perform-ance approximately equal to the other stocks in the portfolio).[1]

No effort is made to determine how investors form probability beliefs about returns on risky ventures; the emphasis of the paper is on the proper financial decisions to be made, given the statistics which summarize such beliefs. It is one of the main functions of security analysis to form opinions as to the expected values, volatility, and reliability of estimates of HPR's in the forthcoming investment period. In short, we are attempting to build portfolios efficiently given such beliefs, and not the equally important but different problem of how to form probability beliefs about the statistics.

TABLE 1. MATRIX OF OVERLAPPING ANNUAL HOLDING PERIOD RETURNS

HPR in 12 Months Beginning with:	Glidden Company	Western Union	Texaco	Market-H_t
Jan., 1953	.8915	1.0930	1.0626	.9517
Feb., 1953	1.0237	1.0956	1.1790	.9950
Mar., 1953	1.0240	1.1264	1.2380	1.0038
$\vdots$				
Nov., 1956	.9564	.9190	1.1978	.8937
Dec., 1956	.9052	.9047	1.2417	.8998
$\vdots$				
Dec., 1959	.8831	.9196	1.0379	.9344
Jan., 1960	.8368	.8084	1.0557	.9456
Statistics:*				
H_i	1.098	1.381	1.227	1.169 $= \bar{H}$
S_i	.2256	.5215	.2020	.2111 $= D$
V_i	.91	2.08	.71	
b_i	.25	.75	1.18	
G_i	1.077	1.297	1.211	1.1508

* H_i, S_i: Mean and standard deviation of HPR for security i
$\quad\quad D$: Standard deviation of the market HPR (.2111 in matrix)
$\quad\quad V_i$: Market elasticity of security i where $H_{it} = H_i + V_i(H_t - \bar{H}) + e$
$\quad SE_i$: Standard error of estimate of the above regression equation. This is the standard deviation of the residual variation which presumably can be greatly reduced by diversification across stocks
$I = 1.05$: the risk free HPR (borrowing or lending rate plus 1)
$\quad\quad G_i$: Geometric mean holding period return for security i
$\quad\quad b_i$: $(H_i - I)/V_iD$—excess yield per unit of nondiversifiable risk (called pure risk yield).

We use hypothetical portfolios composed of bonds (or borrowing on margin) and packages of common stocks. Our basic common stock data are the monthly holding period returns for 224 securities for the period January 1953 through December 1960.[2] From these monthly HPR's we

---

[1] The reallocation portfolio strategy is based on the random character of security prices as pointed out in [3, p. 327] and [19, pp. 10 and 82].

computed a matrix of annual HPR's for each stock for each overlapping 12-month period beginning with the 12 months starting in January 1953 and ending with the 12 months starting in January 1960. The matrix of HPR's is such as that shown in Table 1 for three securities. We denote these returns as H_{it} meaning the annual HPR for security i in the 12 months starting with month t. We use this matrix to determine the statistics in Table 1 such as H_i and S_i, the mean and standard deviation for stock i. The statistics for these annual HPR distributions are more representative of annual returns than if we chose a fixed month, say April, to compute annual returns. Also we have 85 instead of 8 annual observations for each security, and the statistics for each security HPR distribution represent the expected values if we randomly chose a single buy-sell month for each of the eight years to compute the annual return.

The statistics shown in Table 1 were calculated for each of 224 stocks and for the "market" as a whole composed of the average H_{it} of all securities in the sample for each month t. The mean annual HPR for the 1953–60 period is 1.169, the average of the row (or column) averages, and the market standard deviation is .2111. The geometric mean return for the market as a whole is 1.151. This is the compound annual average return which would have been obtained by a hypothetical investor who allocated his portfolio equally among all the stocks at the beginning of each of the constructed 85 annual holding periods.

We use the HPR matrix and statistics to test various portfolio building rules. The test will consist of building hypothetical portfolios using the statistics and then evaluating the results using the HPR's in the matrix. That is, we assume perfect knowledge of the statistics involved in portfolio selection but no knowledge of the occurrence of the individual HPR's. We wish to test the effects of portfolio adjustment policy, amount of diversification, weighting system, selection criterion, and leverage on the geometric mean returns of portfolios for the given matrix of HPR's. In this paper we make no effort to allow for the costs involved in adopting any specified building rule. These costs, such as taxes, transaction costs, and the cost of acquiring and using information, are substantial and will affect both the long-run and short-run performance of the portfolio.

We analyze five general types of questions about building portfolios to maximize the geometric mean return:

1. How often do we readjust the holdings in the portfolio? Do we reallocate the holdings at the end of each year or do we let the holdings stay intact after the portfolio is chosen?

---

[2] The monthly HPR's, $(P_{t+1} + D_t)/P_t$, were taken directly from the January 1926–December 1960 CRSP Price Relative File, University of Chicago.

2. What is the proper number of stocks to include?
3. What is the proper allocation method? Do we put an equal proportion of net worth in each security or do we put smaller amounts in the more risky stocks?
4. On what basis do we select stocks to include in the portfolio? Do unlevered portfolios selected on the basis of the pure risk yields of the individual stocks, for example, perform better than randomly selected portfolios?
5. How do the returns from unlevered portfolios compare with those with optimum borrowing?

It should be emphasized that this is a simulation of portfolio building policy in which actual *ex post* data for 8 years are stretched out to make simulated data for 85 annual holding periods. In effect we ask what are the proper portfolio building rules for maximizing long-run portfolio returns given a specified matrix of HPR's for 224 stocks for 85 holding periods. We do not claim that this matrix will represent future performance over the next 85 years or that it represents performance over any past 85 years. We could have used twelve 224×7 or 8 matrices each representing a 7- or 8-year nonoverlapping period beginning in a different calendar month. Instead we have combined these 12 samples into one. The crucial relationships between the statistics and the individual HPR's in the matrices are not disturbed by this procedure.

I. DISTRIBUTION STATISTICS

The statistics of the HPR distributions are defined in Table 1 and are ranked by size into seven groups in Table 2. We use three of these (H_i, V_i and b_i) as selection criteria in choosing portfolios, and two (S_i and SE_i) are used to allocate net worth among securities in the portfolio. The salient characteristics of the statistics are as follows:

H_i, S_i—The arithmetic mean and standard deviation of the annual holding period returns for security i. The mean as a selection criterion is the expected value of the probability distribution of HPR's for each stock. The standard deviation S_i is the measure of risk for the individual security or a one-stock portfolio.

V_i—Market elasticity of security i where V_i is estimated by regressing the stock HPR's on the market HPR's. V_i measures the variation of H_{it} associated with a unit change in the general market H_t. For example, a stock with $V_i = 2.0$ tends to show a 2 percentage point deviation from its mean for each percentage point change in the market. The regression equation, given at the foot of Table 1, states the market HPR's in deviation form $(H_t - \bar{H})$ and thus shows clearly that the predictive model is based on the security effect H_i and the market effect V_i, with a residual error, SE_i. This is the single index model and assumes that industry effects are zero.

   b_i—pure risk yield as defined in Table 1 which measures the excess yield per unit of nondiversifiable risk. The criterion is based on the assumption of adequate diversification and the single index model. With diversification, the relevant portfolio risk for an individual security is the nondiversifiable risk, which is measured by V_iD where V_i is the market elasticity and D is the standard deviation of the market HPR's (the market HPR's give a 100 percent diversified portfolio composed of all stocks in the market, which is, in our case, 224).[3] The use of the pure risk yield as a selection criterion for building levered portfolios is discussed in [13]. Concepts akin to the pure risk yield are also found in [11, 17, and 18]. The principal hypothesis tested in this paper is that the pure risk yield will prove to be a very valuable ranking criterion when leverage is permitted.

   SE_i—Standard error of estimate of the regression equation in Table 1. This is a measure of the residual variation which presumably can be greatly reduced by diversification across stocks. We test the hypothesis that use

---

[3] The nondiversifiable variance for security i is $R_i^2S_i^2$—the proportion (R_i^2) of variation in H_{it} explained by the market H_t, times the variance S_i^2. The nondiversifiable risk is the square root of $R_i^2S_i^2$ or simply R_iS_i, where R_i is the correlation coefficient. But $R_i = V_i(D/S_i)$ so $R_iS_i = V_iD$. To show that V_iD is on "average" the relevant portfolio risk for the individual security, we can consider the portfolio of n stocks, each with a pure risk of σ_i, which makes up the market index with a standard deviation σ_p. This pure risk by definition represents the variation that is perfectly correlated with the market, so for $n = 2$ with $w_i = 1/n$, the proportion invested in each stock $(\sum w_i = 1)$, the market standard deviation is

$$\sigma_p = (w_1^2\sigma_1^2 + w_2^2\sigma_2^2 + 2w_1w_2R\sigma_1\sigma_2)^{1/2}$$

which reduces to

$$\sigma_p = w_1\sigma_1 + w_2\sigma_2$$

Then in general

$$\sigma_p = \sum_{1}^{n} w_i\sigma_i$$

and with

$$\sigma_i = V_i\sigma_p$$

$$\sigma_p = \sum_{1}^{n} w_i(V_i\sigma_p)$$

$$= \sigma_p(w_i \sum V_i)$$

$$= \sigma_p(1/n \sum V_i) = \sigma_p$$

since the average market elasticity equals 1 or in other words, the market effect of the portfolio of all stocks in the market is 1.

TABLE 2. PORTFOLIO SELECTION AND ALLOCATION CRITERIA: MAXIMUM AND MINIMUM VALUES FOR EACH RANK GROUP AND THE MEAN AND STANDARD ERROR FOR THE 224 STOCKS

		Rank Groups						
Criteria		1	2	3	4	5	6	7
b_i	max	42.899	1.186	.841	.624	.496	.340	.142
	min	1.199	.864	.625	.504	.345	.155	−10.809
V_i	max	4.725	1.556	1.240	1.026	.831	.609	.381
	min	1.558	1.243	1.032	.835	.609	.388	−.038
H_i	max	1.818	1.266	1.204	1.170	1.138	1.109	1.075
	min	1.271	1.204	1.172	1.138	1.111	1.076	.942
S_i	max	1.577	.417	.344	.286	.245	.212	.163
	min	.424	.344	.287	.246	.212	.165	.048
SE_i	max	1.324	.276	.215	.184	.157	.134	.112
	min	.284	.216	.185	.158	.135	.113	.048

	b_i	V_i	H_i	S_i	SE_i
Mean	0.98	1.00	1.169	.3049	.2058
Std. Error	3.77	.63	.115	.1821	.1499

of SE_i in a weighting system to allocate the investment among stocks will improve portfolio returns.

II. METHOD OF ORGANIZING PORTFOLIOS

Securities were selected on the basis of four criteria: random, pure risk yield, market elasticity, and expected value. (See Table 1). In random selection, securities without replacement were ranked in order of selection through use of a random number table. The first security randomly selected was assigned a rank of 1 and the last was assigned a rank of 224. Securities were selected for each of the other three criteria by ranking on the criterion from largest to smallest. For each criterion of selection, non-overlapping portfolios were created for 1, 4, 8, 16, and 32 stocks. For example, when we rank on expected value, the 15th ranking stock would appear in portfolio 15 in the set of one-stock portfolios, in portfolio 4 in the set of 4-stock portfolios, in portfolio 2 in the set of 8-stock portfolios and in portfolio 1 in the sets of 16- and 32-stock portfolios. This gave for each criterion, 224 one-stock portfolios, 56 four-stock portfolios, 28 eight-stock portfolios, 14 sixteen-stock portfolios and 7 thirty-two-stock portfolios. Furthermore the 1-, 4-, 8-, 16-, and 32-stock portfolios are directly comparable since, for example, the first 32-stock portfolio contains the same securities as the first two 16-stock portfolios, the first four 8-stock portfolios, the first eight 4-stock portfolios and the first thirty-two 1-stock portfolios.

This particular method of combining portfolios allows us to measure the effects of diversification and evaluate the selection criterion. Moreover we can do this in summary form by presenting the results for each of 7 groups of ranks on a given criterion where the first group corresponds to the 32 securities with the highest ranks and the seventh group corresponds to the 32 securities with the lowest ranks. Thus to measure the effects of diversification, the performance of the first 32-stock portfolio is comparable to the average of the first two 16-stock portfolios, the average of the first four 8-stock portfolios, etc., since the same 32 stocks make up these portfolios.[4] Also the performance of the ranking criterion is indicated by the performance of the seven groups.

III. PORTFOLIO ADJUSTMENT POLICY

The criterion for evaluating a given portfolio building rule is the net value of the portfolio at the end of the test period and hence the geometric mean return during the test period. If portfolio A produces a net worth of 1.75 per dollar of initial equity at the end of 4 years and hence a geometric mean yield of 15 percent, while portfolio B produces a net worth of 1.57 with a geometric yield of 12 percent, we would say that portfolio A was superior in that test period. For each portfolio without leverage the initial net worth is taken as one and investment in stock i is expressed as a proportion W_i of net worth with $\sum W_i = 1$. The method of computing the geometric mean return on net worth depends on the portfolio adjustment policy. Two policies, reallocation (REA) and buy-and-hold (BH) are evaluated—REA reallocates the intermediate net worth whereas BH considers only the terminal net worth.

Assuming annual compounding, the value of a $1 investment at the end of T years is the product of the HPR's for each of the years and the geometric mean return is the Tth root of this product. That is,

$$G_i{}^T = \prod_{t=1}^{T} H_{it} \tag{1}$$

and

$$G_i = \left(\prod_{t=1}^{T} H_{it}\right)^{1/T} \tag{2}$$

When a buy-and-hold (BH) investment policy is adopted and a proportion, W_i, of the portfolio is put into stock i with $\sum W_i = 1$, the value of

---

[4] Note that by using equal allocation among securities in the portfolio, the arithmetic mean for each group for all portfolio sizes is held constant and is the average of the 32 security means.

that proportion of the portfolio at the end of T years is

$$W_i G_i^T \tag{3}$$

The value of a portfolio of n stocks is the sum of the individual stock holdings, and the BH geometric mean for portfolio k is the Tth root of this value. That is,

$$G_k^T(\text{BH}) = \sum_{i=1}^{n} W_i G_i^T \tag{4}$$

the terminal net worth of a portfolio of n securities held for T years, and

$$G_k(\text{BH}) = (\sum_{i=1}^{n} W_i G_i^T)^{1/T} \tag{5}$$

the buy-and-hold geometric mean.

It is important to note that the BH geometric mean is not the weighted average of the geometric means of the individual stocks as stated in [3, pp. 331–32], except in the case where the geometric means of the individual stock HPR's are *equal*. That is, in general

$$G_k(\text{BH}) \neq \sum_{i=1}^{n} W_i G_i \tag{6}$$

but

$$G_k(\text{BH}) > \sum_{i=1}^{n} W_i G_i \tag{7}$$

The reallocation portfolio policy reallocates the portfolio return, which is the weighted average of the individual stock returns, for each holding period so that the proportion W_i of net worth is allocated to stock i at the beginning of each holding period. This means that for each holding period a portion of those stocks with a HPR larger than the portfolio return are sold and reinvested in the stocks with a HPR smaller than the portfolio return. That is, with equal allocation among n stocks ($w_i = 1/n$), an equal proportion of the portfolio return is reinvested in each stock. The value of portfolio k with reallocation at the end of T periods is the product of the portfolio HPR's, and the compound annual average return $G_k(\text{REA})$ is the Tth root of this value. That is,

$$H_{kt} = \sum_{i=1}^{n} W_i H_{it} \tag{8}$$

the portfolio HPR for $t = 1, 2, \ldots T$

$$G_k{}^T(\text{REA}) = \prod_{t=1}^{T} H_{kt} \qquad (9)$$

the terminal value of the portfolio with reallocation, and

$$G_k(\text{REA}) = (\prod_{t=1}^{T} H_{kt})^{1/T} \qquad (10)$$

the reallocation geometric mean.

The two adjustment policies are illustrated in Table 3 where results from investing equal amounts in each of 3 stocks (hence $W_i = .333$) at the beginning of the period and holding to the end (buy-and-hold policy) is contrasted to the results of the REA adjustment policy where funds

TABLE 3. GEOMETRIC MEANS FOR BUY-AND-HOLD (BH) AND REALLOCATE (REA) PORTFOLIO ADJUSTMENT BASED ON TWO ILLUSTRATIVE MATRICES OF HPR'S

Stock i	HPR's for Year				G^4 *	G_i	w_i	BH Value $w_i G_i{}^4$
	1	2	3	4				
			Matrix A					
A	1.01	1.25	1.49	.69	1.2980	1.0674	.333	.432
B	1.50	1.00	1.00	1.20	1.8000	1.1583	.333	.600
C	.70	.90	1.80	.90	1.0206	1.0050	.333	.340
Average	1.07	1.05	1.43	.93	1.494 = REA Value			1.372

$G(\text{BH}) = (1.372)^{1/4} = 1.0823$
$G(\text{REA}) = (1.494)^{1/4} = 1.1056$

			Matrix B					
D	1.01	1.25	1.49	.69	1.2980	1.0674	.333	.432
E	1.50	1.30	1.30	1.20	3.0420	1.3207	.333	1.014
F	.70	.60	1.50	.90	.5670	.8678	.333	.189
Average	1.07	1.05	1.43	.93	1.494 = REA Value			1.635

$G(\text{BH}) = (1.635)^{1/4} = 1.1308$
$G(\text{REA}) = (1.494)^{1/4} = 1.1056$

* G^4: Product of HPR's or average HPR's for four years.

are reallocated at the beginning of each year. In Table 3, Matrix A, the buy-and-hold value of an initial \$1 investment in stock A is the product of the 4 holding-period returns from stock A ($= 1.298$) and the value of 1 dollar in the 3 stocks on a buy-and-hold basis is 1.372. In similar fashion, if the portfolio is reallocated at the beginning of each year, the average return is earned in each year and the value of the portfolio is the product of the four average returns, which is 1.494. In this case the reallocation policy produced the greater return.

In general, the reallocation and buy-and-hold adjustment policies are an evaluation of the tradeoff between (1) the beneficial effects of *diversification of the portfolio across time*, given by reallocation, and (2) the effects of the *divergence of two or more series with different geometric means* (growth rates), given by buy-and-hold.[5] The performance of the two policies is a function of

(a)   the difference among the geometric means of the security HPR's across time (average growth rate of HPR's or trends in prices),

(b)   the number of holding periods (i.e., the number of periods of compounding the geometric means),

(c)   the covariance among the security HPR's, and

(d)   the portfolio size.

The effects of pronounced differences among geometric means (and hence price trends) is shown in Table 3, Matrix B where stock E is a strong growth stock and stock F is losing growth. Here the BH policy is superior because it leads to greater and greater concentration of the portfolio investment in stock E as its price increases; and, if these "trends" continued with an infinite number of holding periods, the asymptotic terminal net worth of the BH portfolio would be the compounded geometric mean return for stock E.

On the other hand, if the random element is the predominant factor in security prices relative to the growth rates and the HPR's are randomly high and low, the reallocation policy, which redistributes the intermediate net worth for each holding period and maintains a constant proportion invested in each security, is superior. This is shown in Table 3, Matrix A, where the reallocation policy produced the larger geometric mean return, even though the geometric means are considerably different (1.005 to 1.158).

The results for the two adjustment policies using our matrix of 85 overlapping holding periods for 224 stocks is shown in Table 4, Parts I and II. For the four selection criteria, we present the geometric mean for each of the seven 32-stock portfolios and also an enumeration (in II) of the number of individual portfolios for each portfolio size for which the BH return was greater than the REA return. It is clear from the 32-stock portfolio results that the performance of the two policies depend on the selection criterion and rank group. With random and V_i selection, diverse

---

[5] Perhaps a better statement is that reallocation maintains a diversified portfolio over time by preventing the investment from becoming concentrated in a few securities.

TABLE 4. ANALYSIS OF REALLOCATE (REA) AND BUY-AND-HOLD (BH) PORTFOLIOS FOR FOUR SELECTION CRITERIA WITH EQUAL ALLOCATION

I. 32-Stock Portfolio—Geometric Means:

Selection Criteria	Rank Groups						
	1	*2*	*3*	*4*	*5*	*6*	*7*
Random							
REA	1.115	1.192	1.166	1.143	1.154	1.157	1.123
BH	1.115	1.256	1.153	1.146	1.145	1.163	1.131
b_i							
REA	1.241	1.208	1.210	1.162	1.126	1.086	1.004
BH	1.284	1.201	1.200	1.137	1.106	1.069	.987
V_i							
REA	1.185	1.154	1.133	1.131	1.137	1.155	1.118
BH	1.202	1.152	1.139	1.143	1.140	1.229	1.115
H_i							
REA	1.326	1.210	1.169	1.139	1.112	1.082	1.007
BH	1.319	1.191	1.155	1.125	1.096	1.066	.998

II. Number of Individual Portfolios with BH Return Greater Than REA:

Portfolio Size	Number of Portfolios	Random	b_i	V_i	H_i
4	56	24	6	23	0
8	28	9	4	16	0
16	14	6	2	7	0
32	7	4	1	5	0
Total	105	43	13	51	0

price trends often are dominant so that 9 out of 14 comparisons favor the BH adjustment policy and only 4 out of 14 favor reallocation and there is one tie. The diversity of price trends is reduced by the selection process when the remaining selection criteria are used. Hence we would look for reduced performance by BH portfolios. This proves to be the case. The BH portfolios were better in only 1 out of 14 instances.

The results for all portfolio comparisons are shown in Table 4, Part II. In all there were a total of 105 paired comparisons possible for each selection criterion. Where diversity of price trends was reduced by the selection criterion (that is, where H_i and b_i are used as a ranking device), there were only 13 out of a total of 210 paired comparisons (105 for each criterion) in which the buy-and-hold portfolios surpassed the reallocated portfolios. On the other hand, where selection was random or on the basis of market elasticity, the buy-and-hold portfolios were superior in 94 out of the 210 paired comparisons.

These latter results strongly contradict the results for John Evans in [3]. Evans built a very large number of randomly selected portfolios to compare the BH and the REA adjustment policies and found the REA significantly better. However, he used the average of the geometric mean returns from the stocks in his portfolios to get his buy-and-hold geometric mean return and we previously have shown that this estimate is biased downward. We believe that a recalculation of his data to eliminate this systematic error would show results similar to ours.

The remainder of our analysis is framed in terms of the reallocation adjustment process. We conceive of portfolio management as involving repeated choices with cumulative effects. However, this does not mean that strict readjustment to the ideal balance is essential at all times. The average gain from annual reallocation as compared with buy-and-hold is only around 1 percentage point even in those selection processes which reduce price divergence. Long-run return is significantly affected by the reallocation process but is not highly sensitive to that process.

IV. DIVERSIFICATION

The number of different stocks to be included in a portfolio depends on a number of factors such as record keeping, information getting and cost of buying and selling a large number of small holdings if the portfolio is widely diversified. The number of stocks to be included also depends on factors intrinsic to diversification in itself. It is these factors, especially the variance and the covariance, of the holding period returns from the individual stocks, with which we are concerned. Consider a cluster of 9 stocks with approximately equal standard deviations and expected returns. If an equal amount is invested in each stock and the HPR's are not correlated, the standard deviation of the package would be only $1/\sqrt{9} = \frac{1}{3}$ of that for the individual stocks and, in fact, the standard deviation could be made as small as desired if only enough stocks are included in the portfolio. On the other hand, if the HPR's are perfectly correlated there would be no reduction in standard deviation when the portfolio size is increased. The standard deviation of the package of stocks depends on the inter-correlations among the HPR's from the stocks.

We have data on the average standard deviations for portfolios of various sizes in our sample which we can use to breakdown the variation between diversifiable and nondiversifiable variation.[6] This is done by use of the equation

$$S_n = NS + DS(1/\sqrt{n}) \tag{11}$$

---

[6] The separation of risk is well stated in [10, p. 94]. "In portfolio management the standard deviation of the probability distribution of portfolio returns often can be reduced, without lowering the mathematical expectation of the distribution, by proper diversification among the underlying securities. When returns from a group of stocks fluctuate together, however, it is impossible to eliminate all risks. This dissertation attempts to deal with risks which cannot be eliminated by diversification—that is, it deals with choices among whole portfolios." See also [4, 14].

TABLE 5. ACTUAL AND ESTIMATED STANDARD DEVIATIONS OF PORTFOLIOS OF VARIOUS SIZES

n	$1/\sqrt{n}$	$DS(1/\sqrt{n})$	S^*	Actual	Error S-Actual
1	1.0	.1025	.3006	.3049	− .0043
4	.5	.0513	.2494	.2435	+ .0059
8	.3535	.0362	.2343	.2292	+ .0051
16	.2500	.2056	.2237	.2223	+ .0014
32	.1768	.0181	.2162	.2181	− .0019
224	.0668	.0068	.2049	.2111	− .0062

* Estimated Standard Deviation using Eq. (11)

$$S_n = NS + DS(1/\sqrt{n})$$

$$= .1981 + .1025(1/\sqrt{n})$$

where S_n is the average standard deviation for a portfolio of size n, NS is the nondiversifiable part and DS is the diversifiable part which is assumed to vary (be reduced) by the square root of the number of stocks in the portfolio. The results are shown in Table 5. In our sample with equal amounts in each stock, it is possible to eliminate only one-third of the average security variation by diversification and the amount varies inversely with the square root of the number of stocks in the portfolio.

In [4], Evans and Archer also use the format of Eq. (11) but use $1/n$ rather than $1/\sqrt{n}$ as the explanatory variable. The results from using

TABLE 6. REGRESSION OF AVERAGE PORTFOLIO STANDARD DEVIATION (S) VS PORTFOLIO SIZE TO ESTIMATE NONDIVERSIFIABLE (NS) AND DIVERSIFIABLE (DS) RISK: $S_x = NS + DS(X)$

X	Data*	NS	DS	R^2
$1/n$	1	0.1190	0.0865	.9854
	2	.2160	.0904	.9901
	3A	.2380	2.0313	.9540
	3B	.2242	.0919	.9995
$1/\sqrt{n}$	1	0.1044	0.0859	.9590
	2	.1981	.1025	.9794
	3A	.0073	2.2333	.9993
	3B	.2147	.0971	.9657

* 1—Evans-Archer [4, Appendix 1]. $n = 1, 2, \ldots, 40$ and 470. Standard deviation of "market" (470 stock portfolio) $= .1161$.

2—Data in Table 5. $n = 1, 4, 8, 16, 32$ and 224. Standard deviation of 224 stock portfolio $= .2111$.

3—Markowitz [14, p. 112]. Portfolio A: Stocks with independent returns and equal variances of 5. Portfolio B: Stocks with correlation of returns of 0.5 and equal variances of 0.1. $n = 1, 10, 25, 50, 100, 250, 500$ and 1000.

these two variables with Evans-Archer [4] and our data and Markowitz simulation data [14, p. 112] are shown in Table 6. The $1/n$ estimation gives a higher R^2 with three out of four of the sets of data but both give good results except with data set 3 where the nondiversifiable risk is incorrectly determined by $1/n$. In any event, it is clear that the portfolio standard deviation can be reduced by diversification but that the incremental reduction in the standard deviation drops off fast as the number of stocks increases.

The effects of diversification can also be measured by the geometric mean for different portfolio sizes as is shown in Table 7 for the seven rank

TABLE 7. AVERAGE GEOMETRIC MEAN RETURNS FOR PORTFOLIOS OF 1, 4, 8, 16 AND 32 STOCKS FOR THE SEVEN RANK GROUPS BASED ON EXPECTED VALUE, H_i, SELECTION AND FOR THE FOUR STOCK SELECTION CRITERIA*

	Portfolio Size				
H_i Group	1	4	8	16	32
1	1.271	1.309	1.319	1.325	1.326
2	1.188	1.205	1.208	1.209	1.210
3	1.154	1.166	1.168	1.168	1.169
4	1.123	1.136	1.138	1.139	1.139
5	1.094	1.108	1.110	1.111	1.112
6	1.061	1.076	1.079	1.082	1.082
7	.989	1.003	1.005	1.006	1.007
Mean:					
H_i	1.126	1.143	1.147	1.149	1.149
Random	1.126	1.143	1.147	1.149	1.150
b_i	1.126	1.142	1.145	1.147	1.148
V_i	1.126	1.140	1.143	1.144	1.145

* The geometric mean of the 224-stock portfolio is 1.151

groups for the expected value criterion and the means for each criteria. In these portfolios the expected portfolio return is held constant and thus the geometric mean increases as the standard deviation is reduced by diversification.[7] This effect is apparent in the numerical example $3 \times 3 > 2 \times 4 > 1 \times 5$ in which the expected value (arithmetic mean) of the two numbers is constant and the variance increases as the product of the numbers decreases.

The average results for all selection criteria (see Table 7) for each portfolio size are as follows:

[7] Geometric mean approximations based on the arithmetic mean (H) and standard deviation (S) are discussed by Renshaw [15, p. 139]. The approximation, $G^2 \simeq H^2 - S^2$, is derived in [19, p. 230], and several geometric mean approximations including skewness and kurtosis are derived and evaluated in [20].

PORTFOLIO SIZE

	1	4	8	16	32	224
H	1.169	1.169	1.169	1.169	1.169	1.169
S	.3049	.2450	.2303	.2231	.2190	.2111
G	1.126	1.142	1.145	1.147	1.148	1.151

This shows that 1.126 is the expected geometric return if we randomly selected a one-stock portfolio, and 1.151 is the geometric mean of a 100 percent diversified portfolio of 224 stocks. This represents a gain of 2.5 percentage points due to diversification. Similarly, if we randomly selected a 4-stock portfolio, the expected geometric mean return is 1.143, an increase of 1.7 percentage points. This 1.7 percentage points is more than two-thirds of the potential gain from 100 percentage diversification. Eighty-four percent of the potential gain is reached with an 8-stock portfolio and 96 percent with a 16-stock portfolio. It is important to note that the percentage of the possible gain from diversification accomplished by 4-, 8-, 16- and 32-stock portfolios remains remarkably consistent over selection criterion and rank group. This indicates strongly that 85–95 percent of the possible gains through diversification can be achieved with 8- to 16-stock portfolios. The dispersion of geometric mean returns about the average also follows the same general pattern as the gain in return from diversification. For the one-stock portfolios, the range is .840, which is the difference between the largest (1.715) and the smallest (.875) geometric mean return for individual securities in our sample. For the randomly selected 4-, 8-, and 16-stock portfolios the reduction of range is 62 percent, 75 percent, and 86 percent of the range for the one-stock portfolios. The range of returns by rank group for selection criteria other than random is affected by the criterion used and, of course, is one of the measures of the effectiveness of the selection criterion.

V. PORTFOLIO ALLOCATION

We next discuss the allocation of net worth among the securities in the portfolio. Three sets of weights are used. The first is equal allocation for each stock so that $W_i = 1/n$ where $n = 4$, 8, 16 and 32 and W_i is the proportion put in stock i. The second is an allocation among securities such that the portfolio variance is minimized. Here we use

$$W_i = (1/S_i)/\sum(1/S_i)$$

where S_i is the standard deviation of stock i HPR's. For example, with a two-stock portfolio with $S_1 = .10$ and $S_2 = .20$, $W_1 = \frac{2}{3}$ and $W_2 = \frac{1}{3}$. The third method attempts to minimize the residual variation. Here

$$W_i = (1/SE_i)/\sum(1/SE_i)$$

TABLE 8. REALLOCATE GEOMETRIC MEANS OF 4- AND
32-STOCK PORTFOLIOS FOR THREE METHODS OF
ALLOCATION (WEIGHTS) AND FOUR SELECTION CRITERIA

Rank Group	4-Stock Portfolios*			32-Stock Portfolios		
	Equal	Min S_i	Min SE_i	Equal	Min S_i	Min SE_i
Random:						
1	1.111	1.111	1.107	1.115	1.116	1.112
Mean	1.143	1.134	1.134	1.150	1.137	1.136
b_i:						
1	1.234	1.201	1.204	1.241	1.199	1.202
Mean	1.142	1.131	1.133	1.148	1.133	1.136
V_i:						
1	1.172	1.160	1.153	1.185	1.168	1.157
Mean	1.140	1.134	1.131	1.145	1.137	1.133
H_i:						
1	1.309	1.323	1.320	1.326	1.311	1.301
Mean	1.143	1.150	1.148	1.149	1.152	1.148

* Average geometric mean for eight portfolios.

where SE_i is the standard error of estimate for security i HPR's regressed on the market index. (See Table 2 for the range of values of S_i and SE_i).

Note that the second and third methods of allocation change the expected value of the portfolio return as well as the variance. Thus the portfolios are comparable only within a given portfolio size. Although the geometric means for each rank group were computed for the 4-, 8-, 16- and 32-stock portfolios, only the 4- and 32-stock results for the top rank group and the mean are presented in Table 8. For each rank group the 4-stock results are averages of eight portfolios and the mean is an average of the fifty-six 4-stock portfolios. The 32-stock portfolio results are the geometric means of the seven individual portfolios.

With the exception of portfolios selected on the expected value criterion, the method of equal allocation gives the best results on average for the 4- and 32-stock portfolios as shown by the results for each of the selection criteria. This means that minimizing the portfolio variance and residual variation also led to a disproportionate reduction in the portfolio mean return. The two methods of minimizing variation gave about the same results. This was to be expected as the standard deviation and standard error of estimate proved to be highly correlated ($r > .95$). The reduction in variance through the use of $MinS_i$ and $MinSE_i$ lead to higher long-run returns for all of the portfolios selected on the basis of expected value; but, with this exception, the method of equal allocation proved superior. For this reason we use equal allocation among selected stocks in portfolio building.

VI. PORTFOLIO SELECTION AND LEVERAGE

The performance of the four selection criteria with unlevered portfolios is shown in Table 9 which is based on the same data as that used in Table 7. In Table 9 we show the mean return from randomly selected portfolios of each size—with size measured by number of stocks in the portfolio rather than total net worth invested. We also show returns from the first rank group for each selection criterion. Table 9 shows unlevered portfolios made from the top-ranked 32 stocks from our sample of 224 all consistently outperform random selection even though the gain from ranking on market elasticity is relatively small. Gains from ranking on pure risk yield average out to around 9 percentage points while ranking on expected returns leads to increased returns of upwards of 15 percentage points. Perfect information as to H_i would have been of much more value in building unlevered

TABLE 9.   AVERAGE GEOMETRIC MEAN RETURNS ON TOP RANK GROUP PORTFOLIOS OF 1, 4, 8, 16 & 32 STOCKS FOR FOUR SELECTION CRITERIA

	Portfolio Size				
Selection Criterion:	*One Stock*	*4*	*8*	*16*	*32*
Random*	1.126	1.143	1.147	1.149	1.150
Market Elasticity	1.138	1.172	1.178	1.182	1.185
Pure Risk Yield	1.217	1.234	1.238	1.240	1.241
Expected Value	1.271	1.309	1.319	1.325	1.326

* Mean of all portfolios.

portfolios than perfect information as to market elasticity or as to pure risk yields.

VII. LEVERAGE

Initially we hypothesized that the pure risk yield would be a valuable ranking criterion. But this assumes that we can invest some ratio q to original net worth in risk assets by borrowing $(q - 1)$ or lending $(1 - q)$ of net worth at a riskless HPR, which we assume to be 1.05. Thus we must consider leverage in order to evaluate the selection criteria.

This study deals only with optimum leverage $q*$ or the amount of investment with borrowing or lending that maximizes the geometric mean return on net worth. The computation of the geometric mean with leverage is as follows: Let R_t be the return on the package of stocks making up the portfolio for period t and assume that the portfolio owner can borrow or lend freely at 5 percent. Then when the portfolio consists of bonds and stocks, the portfolio return in period t is

$$R_t(q) = qR_t + (1 - q)1.05 \tag{12}$$

and when the portfolio is levered by borrowing to buy stock, the return in period t is

$$R_t(q) = qR_t - (q - 1)1.05 \tag{13}$$

The two equations of course are exactly equivalent. The geometric mean

TABLE 10. REALLOCATE GEOMETRIC MEAN RETURNS OF 1-, 4-, AND 32-STOCK PORTFOLIOS USING OPTIMUM LEVERAGE AND EQUAL ALLOCATION FOR FOUR SELECTION CRITERIA

Selection Criteria	Rank Group							
	1	2	3	4	5	6	7	Mean
Random:								
1stk	1.178	1.461	1.280	1.357	1.203	1.341	1.258	1.297
4stk	1.201	1.751	1.476	1.247	1.259	1.340	1.179	1.350
32stk	1.163	1.637	1.336	1.240	1.264	1.295	1.191	1.304
Market Elasticity:								
1stk	1.340	1.178	1.177	1.232	1.242	1.594	1.313	1.297
4stk	1.245	1.205	1.179	1.232	1.361	1.661	1.524	1.345
32stk	1.213	1.200	1.177	1.195	1.295	2.028	1.735	1.406
Expected Return:								
1stk	1.829	1.350	1.344	1.267	1.152	1.083	1.052	1.297
4stk	1.906	1.530	1.351	1.264	1.148	1.102	1.051	1.336
32stk	2.569	1.584	1.388	1.272	1.160	1.090	1.050	1.445
Pure Risk Yield:								
1stk	2.005	1.368	1.305	1.163	1.111	1.075	1.051	1.297
4stk	4.057	1.685	1.432	1.225	1.145	1.104	1.051	1.671
32stk	7.803	1.996	1.530	1.271	1.152	1.150	1.050	2.279

return with reallocation for a levered portfolio is the geometric mean of the $R_t(q)$. Optimum leverage or optimum bond-holding q^* within an increment of .05 was determined by iterating values of q and comparing the resulting geometric means for each of the 1-, 4-, 8-, 16- and 32-stock portfolios. For the multiple stock portfolios the three methods of allocation among stocks were also evaluated, but even with leverage, there was very little advantage to minimizing the standard deviation or the residual variation.

The portfolio results, G^*—average geometric means for 1- and 4-stock portfolios and geometric means for 32-stock portfolios—are given in Table 10 for optimum leverage using equal allocation. These results show the impressive returns which would have been possible by setting up portfolios with optimum leverage during the time period under consideration. It must be emphasized that the amount of borrowing involved in these portfolios is unrealistically high even though it could have been undertaken without ruin in this period. The results confirm the hypothesis that pure risk yield is a superior criterion to use with optimum leverage. This criterion was not as good as the expected return criterion with unlevered portfolios but is far superior when optimum leverage is available. In passing it is interesting to note that when portfolios are ranked on market elasticity, the riskiest portfolios do best when unlevered (from Table 9) and the least risky do best when levered (Table 10).

VIII. CONCLUSION

Results of the tests of the effects on portfolio geometric mean returns of various portfolio management policies are summarized in Table 11 which shows the average geometric mean returns on various portfolios. It leads to the following conclusions:

1. Diversification pays, as is shown by the superiority of portfolio 2 over 1, 5 over 4, and 8 over 7 over 6. This advantage of diversification results entirely from the reduction of variance and hence increases in the geometric mean return. It is not necessary to appeal to risk aversion on the part of investors to justify diversification.

TABLE 11. AVERAGE GEOMETRIC MEAN RETURNS ON VARIOUS EQUALLY ALLOCATED PORTFOLIOS

	Portfolio Leverage	Portfolio Description			Average Geometric Mean Return
		Selection Criterion	Number of Stocks	Group	
1	Unlevered	Random	1	All	1.126
2	Unlevered	Random	16	All	1.149
3	Unlevered	Expected Value	16	Top	1.325
4	Optimum	Random	1	All	1.297
5	Optimum	Random	4	All	1.350
6	Optimum	Pure Risk Yield	1	Top	2.005
7	Optimum	Pure Risk Yield	4	Top	4.057
8	Optimum	Pure Risk Yield	32	Top	7.803

2. Expected value of HPR is a good criterion for ranking stocks for inclusion in unlevered portfolios. The actual value of the criterion, however, depends on the ability of the investor to predict average returns from individual stocks.

3. Optimum leverage leads to major gains. The proper use of debt can increase returns greatly. The gain from optimum leverage with random selection is just as great as the gain from selection on the basis of expected returns. This is shown by comparing portfolios 4 and 5 with 3.

4. Ranking on pure risk yield when combined with optimum leverage leads to extremely favorable portfolio performance.

REFERENCES

[1] Cohen, K. J., and J. A. Pogue. "An Empirical Evaluation of Alternative Portfolio-Selection Models," *The Journal of Business*, Vol. XXXIX (January, 1966), pp. 166–93.

[2] Cootner, P. H. (ed.). *The Random Character of Stock Market Prices* (Cambridge, Mass.: M.I.T. Press, 1964).

[3] Evans, J. L. "The Random Walk Hypothesis, Portfolio Analysis and the Buy-and-Hold Criterion," *Journal of Financial and Quantitative Analysis*, Vol. III (September, 1968), pp. 327–42.

[4] ——, and S. H. Archer. "Diversification and the Reduction of Dispersion: An Empirical Analysis," *Journal of Finance*, Vol. XXIII (December, 1968), pp. 761–67.

[5] Fama, E. "The Behavior of Stock-Market Prices," *The Journal of Business*, Vol. XXXVIII (January, 1965), pp. 34–105.

[6] Fisher, L. "Outcomes for 'Random' Investments in Common Stocks Listed on the New York Stock Exchange," *The Journal of Business*, Vol. XXXVIII (September, 1965), pp. 148–61.

[7] ——, and J. H. Lorie. "Rates of Return on Investments in Common Stocks," *The Journal of Business*, Vol. XXXVII (January, 1964), pp. 1–21.

[8] Friend, I., and D. Vickers. "Portfolio Selection and Investment Performance," *The Journal of Finance*, Vol. XX (September, 1965), pp. 391–415.

[9] King, B. F. "Market and Industry Factors in Stock Price Behavior," *The Journal of Business*, Vol. XXXIX (January, 1966), pp. 139–90.

[10] Latané, H. A. "Rational Decision Making in Portfolio Management," Ph.D. Thesis, University of North Carolina, 1957, Chapel Hill, North Carolina.

[11] ——. "The Rationality Model in Decision Making" in H. J. Leavitt (ed.), *The Social Science of Organizations* (Englewood Cliffs, N. J.: Prentice-Hall, 1963).

[12] Latané, H. A., and D. L. Tuttle. "An Analysis of Common Stock Price Ratios," *The Southern Economic Journal*, Vol. XXXIII (January, 1967), pp. 343–54.

[13] ——. "Criteria for Portfolio Building," *The Journal of Finance*, Vol. XXII (September, 1967), pp. 359–72.

[14] Markowitz, H. *Portfolio Selection: Efficient Diversification of Investments* (New York, N. Y.: John Wiley and Sons, 1959).

[15] Renshaw, E. F. "Portfolio Balance Models in Perspective: Some Generalizations That Can Be Derived from the Two-Asset Case," *Journal of Financial and Quantitative Analysis*, Vol. II (June, 1967), pp. 123–49.

[16] Sharpe, W. F. "A Simplified Model for Portfolio Analysis," *Management Science*, Vol. IX (January, 1963), pp. 277–93.

[17] ——. "Capital Asset Prices: A Theory of Market Equilibrium Under Conditions of Risk," *Journal of Finance*, Vol. XIX (September, 1964), pp. 425–42.

[18] Tobin, J. "Liquidity Preference as Behavior Towards Risk," *Review of Economic Studies*, Vol. XXV (February, 1958), pp. 65–86.

[19] Young, W. E. "Common Stock *Ex Post* Holding Period Returns and Portfolio Selection," Ph.D. Thesis, University of North Carolina, 1968, Chapel Hill, N. C.

[20] ——, and R. H. Trent. "Geometric Mean Approximations of Individual Security and Portfolio Performance," *Journal of Financial and Quantitative Analysis*, Vol. IV (June, 1969).

part Two

INVESTMENT ANALYSIS

*Nicholas Molodovsky**

19. The Many Aspects of Yields

Reprinted, in abridged form, from the **Financial Analysts Journal,**
Vol. 18, No. 2 (March-April, 1962), pp. 49–62, 77–86, by permission
of the author and the publisher.

For some time now, stock yields have been declining while bond
yields were rising. They have been moving so long in such appallingly
"wrong" directions that they finally landed where finance is not often
featured—on *Life Magazine*'s editorial page. On January 12, 1962, *Life*'s
second editorial was captioned "Odd Views in Wall Street."

"The greatest bull market in history," wrote *Life*, "roaring on almost
without interruption, started in 1949 and has turned many of the one
time 'basic principles' of investment topsy-turvy. It used to be assumed,
for example, that whenever the yields of common stocks fell below those
of preferred stocks or bonds, the disparity would have to be corrected by
(1) a drop in stock prices to bring their yields up, or (2) a big enough
rise in earnings to do the same thing.

"Instead, look what has happened: the pre-tax yield on common
stocks by 1958 dropped below the average yield on corporate bonds. By
1959—incredibly enough—it even dropped below the yield on *tax-exempt*
bonds. Good tax-exempt bonds today yield about $3\frac{1}{2}$ percent compared
with a pre-tax yield of 2.75 percent for typical industrial stocks."

Life's preoccupation was shared not only by many investors but by
their advisors as well. On December 26, 1961, only two days before this
writer addressed the American Statistical Association on the same subject, Dr. Jules I. Bogen, a famed New York University economist and
former editor-in-chief of the *Journal of Commerce*, discussed this topic in
his weekly column on the front page of that *Journal*, stating that "the
widening of the differential between stock and bond yields during 1961
presents a major issue to every class of investors."

Some financial analysts called this differential "the reverse yield

* Deceased. Formerly editor of the *Financial Analysts Journal* and vice-president
of White, Weld & Co., Inc.

gap" and saw in it a financial revolution brought about by many complex causes. Others, on the contrary, made no attempt to explain the unexplainable. They showed readiness to accept it as a manifestation of providence in the financial universe.

I. STOCK PRICES AND DIVIDENDS

The curtain of the drama rises on the inception of the stock market's postwar advance. While the rise of stock prices was progressing, with cyclical interruptions, from its 1949 low to its present exalted heights, stock yields were noticeably shrinking.

Dividends were increasing too; but not at the same rate as the prices of common stocks. The fastest postwar advance in annual dividend payments took place between 1945 and 1950. Then their engine stalled for several years. When it got going again, it did so at a much reduced speed and with occasional sputtering and sighing, contrasting sadly with the joyful flight of the prices of stocks.

Stock yields are a ratio of dividends to prices. When dividends—standing in the numerator—increase at a stingy rate, while the price denominator is quite generously enlarged, the ratio falls. People looking at yield charts in the fall of 1959 could not help but observe—and probably not without a spine-tingling sensation—that stock yields had dropped below those of 30 years ago. The figure on the chart for 1959 is 2.92 percent. The 1929 yield was 3.1 percent. And 1929 is a date inscribed in flaming figures in the memories of all market students. A foreboding of disaster was apparently being written by history's hand on the walls of security marts as once before on the wall of Nebuchadnezzar's palace. Yet the real lesson proved to be rather that analogy and analysis are not necessarily identical twins.

The center section of Figure 1 shows stock and bond yields since 1871. Even the best among equities carry a larger degree of investment risk than certificates of indebtedness, especially when the latter are bonds of the highest grade. It is a logical thought that in order to compensate the investor for accepting the greater risk of holding common stocks, he should enjoy a richer return from his investment. During most of the years plotted on Figure 1, the ratio of stock yields to bond yields was appropriately high—the return on equities being larger and, at times, twice or three times as large as the return on high-grade corporate bonds.

But in more recent years, an irreverent note began creeping into this eminently proper picture. By 1955, the ratio of the two yields dropped below the level it had formed at the tops of the two preceding bull markets—those of 1946 and 1937—and yet no reversal of stock prices took place. A

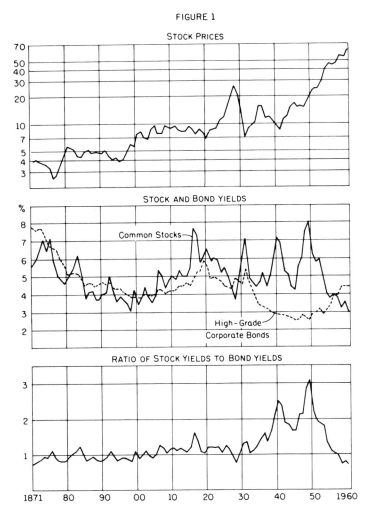

FIGURE 1

STOCK PRICES

STOCK AND BOND YIELDS

Common Stocks

High-Grade
Corporate Bonds

RATIO OF STOCK YIELDS TO BOND YIELDS

few years later, the ratio was already below the point marking the ill-fated peak of 1929. Yet still no disaster followed. As it happened—and this was downright embarrassing—a bull market was born in October, 1960, when the ratio of stock yields to bond yields was close to the lowest point it had registered since the beginning of this century.

How can we account for all these strange happenings?

As we look at Figure 1, several observations come to mind. (The indexes used are described in the Appendix.) The wide gulf which developed since the middle of the 1930's, completely separating, for a period of 20 years, stock and bond yields, stands out as a unique occurrence strangely isolated from the entire previous historical experience. This is illustrated by both the spread between stock yields and bond yields, and by the curve of their ratio.

Yet the ratio's tallest peak did not constitute a point of no return. Within five years it came back to a level more in line with its customary historical range. Reflecting this decline of the ratio of stock and bond yields, their own gap began to narrow until the two lines crossed a few years ago, forming a reverse gap.

Even before this recrossing of stock yields and bond yields took place (and while the two curves, coming from opposite directions, were gradually approaching each other), there came a rising tide of outpourings of dire forecasts. Some so-called "Services" were particularly persistent in promenading before their readers signboards strapped to their statistical shoulders announcing the imminence of doomsday.

To certify that this presentation is not facetious, a few quotations may be in order. They come from nationally known publications.[1]

It was towards the end of 1952 that declining stock yields began to impress investors. Our first quotation is dated January 5, 1953:

> When optimism is full to overflowing, the signs of it that are easiest to read are in stock yields. . . . To date, stock yields have fallen considerably. They are still above the lowest yields in 1929 and in 1937, which preceded serious bear markets, and on the surface it could, accordingly, be argued that today's stock yield level has entered the shadows of suspicion . . . but it is not highly suspect.

Many investment counselors sensed real danger when, after the middle of 1954, the two blades of the scissors of stock and bond yields started coming closer together. A quotation dated July 12, 1954, uses the following dramatic terms:

> Warning—A Dangerous Stock Market. . . . We believe the stock market is in serious jeopardy. . . . If the stock yields after income tax are compared to the yields from highest grade tax-exempt bonds, the stock market position becomes alarming. . . .

And five months later, the same service wrote:

> We find a rising differential between stock yields and bond yields which suggests that relative to bond yields stock yields are already in the zone of danger, as historically determined. . . . A drop in prices of the magnitude of 150 points on the D. J. Index of Stock Averages is within the realm of probability.

While the order of magnitude of the anticipated price change was not far out of line, the change itself was in the opposite direction. Some

[1] Names are withheld. Margins of error in stock market judgments are notoriously high. The author's aim in using quotations is to illustrate; not to undermine prestige.

16 months later, the Dow-Jones Industrial Average was floating approximately 140 points higher. And despite two cyclical declines which later did take place, we stood at the 1961 year-end at a level which, in terms of Dow-Jones Industrials, was almost twice as high as at the end of 1954.

In the summer of 1958, bond yields were about to rise above those of stocks for the first time since 1929. When this event took place, an advisory service suggested to its subscribers:

> The Investor in today's market has been here before—at the stock market peaks of 1929, 1937, 1946 and 1957. . . . The current yield on stocks is only in the order of 3.7%. High grade corporate bonds on average yield 3.8%. . . . The times when stock yields fell to the level of bond yields in the past . . . were times of important top formations in the stock market. . . . The rational adjustment for the investor would be to hold some portion of his investment capital in cash or government bonds.

II. SOME OBSERVATIONS

We stand now three and a half years away from this last advice. Another cyclical decline has come and gone. A new period of cyclical expansion is under way and a new bull market started in October, 1960. Yet Figure 1 reveals that only once before did annual averages of stock yields register a point as low as in 1959. This was in 1899. The historical sequence that followed was not one of calamity and collapse, but rather of brilliant structural change and growth, of unprecedented technological progress and economic prosperity. During this period, stock prices, as well as the yields on stocks and bonds, all advanced.

In the light of the long historical perspective offered by Figure 1, what other additional observations may be noted?

The ratio of stock and bond yields pictured on the bottom panel shows that until the beginning of this century, stock yields remained often below the yields on bonds. This is also quite visible on the center section of Figure 1, which traces the changes in the stock and bond yields themselves. Yet the curve of the latter could almost serve as a trend line—or at least as a guideline for the wider fluctuations of stock yields. There is visible also an inverse relation between the peaks and troughs of stock prices and stock yields. But it was irregular and had no specific numerical characteristics.

The powerful bull market which began just before the turn of the century witnessed, at its inception, the lowest stock yields in recorded statistical annals. And the 1919–21 bear market which was much more severe than it looks in retrospect on Figure 1—severe enough to enable the Du Ponts to acquire General Motors from a ruined Durant—was underway when stock yields were high. We may also stress once more that stock yields were often below the yields of bonds. Investors were apparently sufficiently smart to realize the constructive implications for equity values of growing corporate earnings and this, surprisingly enough, without the benefit of ever having read Edgar Lawrence Smith's *Common Stocks as Long Term Investments* or, still more frustratingly, this author's articles on this subject in the *Financial Analysts Journal*.

III. THE GREAT DISRUPTION OF YIELDS

It is probably fair to say that for the first 60 years of the period covered by Figure 1, stock yields and bond yields showed a propensity of traveling in the same direction. What brought about their separation in the 1930's?

Since 1932 the yields of high-grade bonds were rolling down the slope like an avalanche. In two years they dropped 100 basis points. And, by 1946, they came down all the way from about 5.3 percent to 2.6 percent, losing more than half of the return they were bringing to investors.

This rapid descent of bond yields was caused by the depression. And subsequently, the yields were pinned down by a structural change in money and credit policies. Bond yields became managed, while stock yields remained free.

Yields on highest-grade corporate bonds remained below the 3 percent line for many years—as long as interest rates remained artificially "pegged." And the gap between them and current returns on stocks was widened to almost fantastic proportions between 1946 and 1949 by a decline of stock prices, which was not caused by cyclical forces.

From 1942 to 1946, the cash income of many individuals and corporations exceeded their expenditures because of lack of goods to buy. This left balances which have been used in many instances to purchase stocks, driving them upwards and pushing yields down. But following the cessation of hostilities, conversion to peacetime production created an enormous need for capital goods. Corporations began selling stocks just at a time when the return of consumer goods to the free markets was transforming many individuals also into sellers of stocks.

This selling turned into quite a scenic waterfall when numerous other investors began getting rid of their equities in the expectation of a postwar depression which did not materialize. It was a costly error of judgment. But its psychology was deeply rooted and took years to dispel. In the meantime, these concerted actions sent stock prices down and their yields reached unprecedented heights by the end of the decade of the 1940's.

By 1949, the deep undervaluation of stocks in the face of sharply rising earnings and dividends, and the enforcement of a cheap money policy, were a combination of factors quite adequate in themselves to originate a great bull market. This potential thrust was boosted by events which were to gain a cumulative and lasting effect on the demand-supply relations of common stocks.

Bond yields came back to life when a free money market was re-established in 1951. And the rapid decline in the ratio of stock yields beginning with the early 1950's, which is depicted on Figure 1, coincided with changes instituted in the investment laws of the key state of New York. The law authorized life insurance companies and savings banks to invest in equities. This change came about when the impact of pension fund buying also began to make itself felt in the demand for common stocks. During the early phase of their existence, pension funds had to take care not only of their current investment needs, but also of their accumulated pension liabilities for employees' past services. The great flowering of investment companies, and the birth of monthly investment plans shifted more investment demand towards equities and away from bonds and mortgages where it would have gone under the more tradi-tional auspices of savings institutions where much of this money would otherwise have been lodged.

Finally, the numbers of private stockholders and the means at their command also grew. All these developments swelled the demand for stocks which were already being driven upwards by the momentum of the bull market and their undervaluation. Yet no corresponding increase in their supply took place. Capital gains taxes, a more favorable tax treatment of bond issues, and depreciation policies limited the offers of stocks to the anxiously bidding buyers.

Perhaps equally important as the shift in the demand and supply equation was a change in the very philosophy of stock investment through the return and renewed lease on life of the growth stock idea. This idea was widely accepted in the late 1920's, but its popularity had been under-mined by the depression. As already mentioned, investors may have been consciously or instinctively applying this philosophy in practice long be-fore it was used by financial writers. So far, however, private individuals were its principal adherents. Yet, this philosophy is infinitely more suited to the policies of immortal institutions. Any initial small stock yield, with dividends growing even at a slow rate, is bound to exceed, at some point, the rate of return from fixed income securities.

IV. EARNINGS YIELDS

The yields we have been dealing with so far represented all actual pay-ments of money. But there exists one so-called "yield" which is not a payment at all. It lies in hiding, so to speak, between stock prices and yields. From this secreted position it wields considerable power by its

FIGURE 2

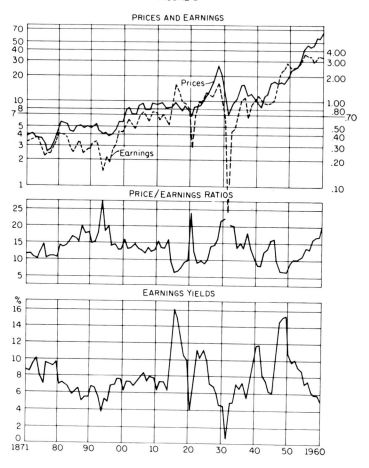

bearing on the complex problem of cost of equity capital. We refer to "earnings yield." We cannot pretend to treat it rightly in a few lines, but we hope someday to be able to give it the undivided attention of a king-sized report. In the meantime, earnings yields may be found graphically depicted in the last panel of Figure 2.

Developed by the Federal Power Commission, the cost of capital theory of the rate of return resulted in the famous 1952 decisions in the Northern Natural Gas and Colorado Interstate cases. Originally, the cost of money was measured by the interest and dividends that investors were willing to accept as a return on their capital. But dividends can be reduced or omitted. This is not the case of the earnings yields.

However, whether a single earnings/price ratio is used, or many of them are averaged covering a period of years, such ratios can have a meaning only under conditions of earnings stability. Both for theoretical and practical considerations discussed by us so often on the pages of the *Financial Analysts Journal*, in connection with price/earnings ratios, their reciprocals, i.e., earnings yields, have also to be transcribed, after taking into account projected rates of earnings growth, into present value terms.

V. THOSE DYNAMIC EARNINGS

Of the three principal stock market factors—prices, earnings, and dividends—without much doubt earnings are the most dynamic. Compared to them, stock prices are relatively stable, while dividends are still more tame. The differences in the amplitudes of the relative movements of earnings and dividends are brought out in the top sections of Figures 2

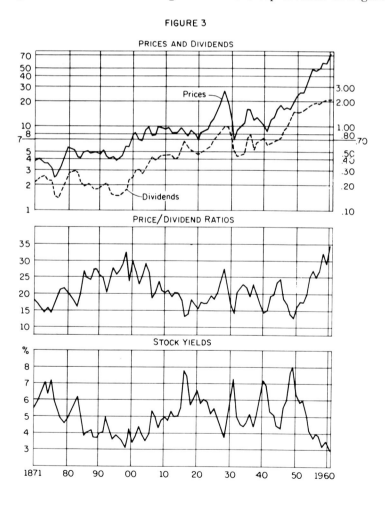

FIGURE 3

and 3. When discussing Figure 1 we noted that stock prices and stock yields frequently move in opposite directions. Their divergence was more pronounced than that of stock prices and dividends. In other words, changes in stock prices tended to dominate—and often to account for—the changes in stock yields.

In the case of Figure 2, it is the factor of earnings which dominates the picture. The inverse relation of earnings and price/earnings ratios (as illustrated by the top and center panels of Figure 2) is practically perfect. It demonstrates why price-to-earnings ratios are meaningless when used as capitalizers of current earnings. They cannot serve in the double capacity of quotients and multipliers without merely reproducing the price curve and adding nothing to the information it provides.

The interwoven curves of earnings and dividends at the top of Figure 2 help also to understand why current earnings cannot serve as a capitalization base. To reach this "finding" we do not have to dive into great depths of theoretical analysis. So often we hear—especially more recently—that stock prices are too high simply because they have been rising while earnings were falling off. Yet where should we cast the anchor of comparison? Why not begin with 1932? And if this destroys the presentation of their arguments, let's grant to the proponents of this demonstration a generous 10 years' grace. Let them begin with 1942 and use that year as the point of departure of their reasoning.

We do not deny that average stock prices are now above average investment values. But the analysis should offer richer substance.

In point of fact, no correlation exists between the *amplitudes* of fluctuations of stock prices and current earnings. Nor could the latter be used as standards of value. Only when earnings are stretched out into significant trends can they become usefully measurable and lead to appraisals of investment values.

VI. BACK TO THE WORKBENCH

Investors have a wide range of yields from which to choose when making commitments these days. . . . The spread between bond yields and stock yields is unusually wide. . . . As time goes on, people who are partly or wholly dependent on their savings for living expenses are more and more pressed for income. . . . A man who has saved $100,000 finds it hard to be satisfied with a return of $2,000 or $2,500 a year, and is tempted to transfer an increasing part of his funds into equities. He could secure $6,500 now by making the transfer complete.

We trust he did! The above quotation is taken from an investment review dated December, 1949. At that time, the DJIA was around 200. His capital would have more than tripled and he would have enjoyed a vastly increased income from his investments.

But now he stands at the other end of the rainbow. And while he cannot hope to ride back to its crest again and triple his capital once more by reverting to bonds, he considers the switch for the sake of preserving his funds. He could considerably enlarge the income from his investments and even make it at least partially tax-exempt. He hesitates, having heard a lot about inflation and even some rumblings of the weakening position of the dollar in foreign trade. From experience, he knows that money does not buy as much as it used to. He has some other dollar assets: insurance, some savings in the bank and social security income when he is ready to retire.

Mulling the situation over, he recalls that the decision of switching back into bonds had been pressed upon him by well-meaning advisers for well over five years. They were so wrong! But, in the meantime, the income spread between the returns from stocks and bonds has become wide enough to make the temptation to benefit from it an almost irresistible force.

Yet business is good and seems to be improving. The government will apparently continue to spend more and more. Stocks should benefit from all this. Their latest weakness scared him somewhat. He sold a few stocks at the worst possible time, using the proceeds to buy some short-term bills. He is glad that he did not sell more, now that stocks seem to be again on the up-and-up. He knows nothing about the economics of stock and bond yields and cares even less. But his instinctive shrewdness makes him feel that pretty soon he might resolve all these doubts and indecisions by rolling his money into two bundles of about equal size—half stocks and half bonds.

We envy the simplicity of his common sense decision and shall not trouble his peace of mind by sending him a reprint of this paper. But we shall drag out our blueprints and, before making any decision, shall pour over them and suffer through every nook and cranny of their design for financial living.

VII. BOND YIELDS

Yields of high-grade bonds measure long-term interest. The latter is an economic factor of the highest order.

As long as the soundness of the money of payment is not in doubt, values of all fixed income producing assets vary inversely with changes of the rate of interest. The higher the prevailing rate of interest, the smaller the multiplier applicable to a given return for estimating the amount of capital necessary to produce it. When interest rates rise, a relatively smaller capital produces the same income as before the rise. Rising interest rates tend to lower values, and declining interest rates to lift them.

Changes in interest rates are determined by the intensity of demand by borrowers and the supply of funds available for lending. The most frequent changes in the demand and supply equation of money occur in response to cyclical fluctuations in business and to policy action of monetary authorities. But as may be observed from the center section of Figure 1, there are discernible also longer trends of rising and declining interest rates corresponding to longer periods of economic contractions or expansions.

Cyclically, interest rates are affected by the profitability of industry. When their profits are mounting, business enterprises seek additional capital, and their cumulative demand pushes interest rates up.

Since higher interest rates, through their inverse relation to income producing assets, tend to cause stock prices to decline, rising earnings—by stimulating interest rates—have in the later stages of cyclical expansions conflicting effects on stock prices. Their direct effect is to push prices up. Indirectly, by lifting interest rates, rising earnings have a dampening effect on stock prices in the final phase of a cyclical expansion.

At first, the tendency toward declining stock prices brought about by the rise in interest rates is more than offset by the continued growth of earnings. In other words, the rise in interest rates then acts merely as a brake on the further rise of stock prices; it is not yet able to reverse their upward trend. But interest rates react upon the economic environment in which they were born. The interest rate is a derivative factor only as far as the profits of yesterday are concerned; it is itself a determinant of the profits of tomorrow. Higher interest rates ultimately bring lower earnings.

In sum: the conflicting influences of earnings and interest rates on the trends of stock prices are rooted in earnings. The growing profitability of industry—a phase of the rising tide of the cycle—becomes reflected in higher equity prices. But through a slow and subtle process it contains within itself its own countermeasure—its stimulating effect on the interest rate. Many other economic factors also carry within themselves opposing forces of propulsion and regression, revealing the fundamental balance of economic life. They themselves reverse the very trends they originate. The fact that fundamentally the rise in interest rates is due to higher earnings suggests that between them there may exist a characteristic lead and lag in cyclical timing.

Interest rates also reveal, as already mentioned, more lasting trends than fluctuations caused by business cycles. Figure 1 shows the final years of the expansion that followed the Civil War. But in 1873 a financial panic ushered in a period of depression. It lasted through 1877, which saw a strong recovery in earnings, stock prices, and dividends. Dividends are traced in the top diagram of Figure 3.

However, as may be seen on these charts, the 1880's and 1890's were again a poor period for business. Accordingly, the demand for loans dried up and interest rates continued to decline through the turn of the century. The center section of Figure 1 shows the downward trend of bond yields during these years.

This trend was reversed early in the twentieth century when mass production methods carried industrial activity to new heights. Peacetime expansion was succeeded by wartime inflation. Bond yields were carried by the resulting demand for loans and rise of interest rates to a level which, so far, has remained unequaled.

The changes in bond yield trends that occurred in the 1920's were caused once more by shifts in the demand for and supply of loanable funds. The redemption of the public debt and the boom during the last few years of this period were primarily responsible for them.

Finally, the sharp decline of bond yields and/or interest rates from 1933–46, and their steep subsequent recovery, were brought about by the great depression with subsequent war finance "pegging" and postwar expansion and inflation.

During the "pegging" period, open market purchases of government bonds by Federal Reserve authorities resulted, of course, in a monetization of the public debt on a large scale. But in March, 1951, the Federal Reserve "unpegged" bond prices after reaching an agreement with the U. S. Treasury. As bond yields moved upward, institutions (banks in particular) were no longer able to sell their long-term government bonds at all times with complete impunity. When banks repurchased them during recessions of 1953–54 or 1957–58, they had to face losses in selling them during subsequent recoveries to meet the demands for loans by their business clients.

On Figure 1, bond yields are plotted as annual averages. They gloss over fluctuations occurring within the same calendar year. Yet even on that smoothed out chart we can observe that during the 1953–54 recession, for instance, the decline in yields was quite marked and that their rise was exceptionally rapid during the subsequent bull market which ended in the summer of 1957. An increase of some 50 percent occurred during this period in the long-term rate. This meant quite a fall in bond prices.

A new element was injected during the postwar period into the bond yield structure and added to its complexity. The monetary authorities were entrusted with the mission of helping to iron out business cycles. Rates of interest are among the chief levers they use to achieve credit ease or stringency.

Extraneous forces may also make sudden inroads into the bond market. Figure 1 shows that bond yields declined between 1957 and 1958 as a result of the recession. They recovered briskly when business improved and the demand for capital returned. On June 15, 1958, the U. S. Treasury made a new bond offering. Promptly, its price fell six points. For three months, yield changes in long-term government bonds were sharper than price changes of common stocks which were at the time rising quite vigorously. This was an aftermath of a sudden emergence of widespread gambling in thinly margined holdings of government securities. Heavy losses were suffered by countless small and ignorant speculators trying to make a killing in what they knew to be the safest of all investments. But they failed to realize that highly leveraged positions are quite impartially loaded with magnified potentials of profit and loss.

Substantial investors are now more conscious of the serious risks involved in possible interest rate changes. In the past they were more inclined to disregard them, concentrating their attention, when they were studying corporate securities, on the financial strength of the issuer, as well as the grade and the maturity of the bond. A wide gap between bond and stock yields certainly is tempting. But conditions accounting for its existence prevent a hasty conclusion that a massive switch from stocks into bonds should be made in a hurry.

At the time of this writing, i.e., at the beginning of February, 1962, there is as usual no unanimity of thought among the experts as to the outlook for long-term interest rates during the remainder of this year. The balance of opinion seems to lean to the belief that the prospective flow of new institutional long-term investment funds will be sufficient to prevent severe pressures on the long-term capital markets. However, some pressure is expected in the short-term sector, which should cause a moderate increase in long-term rates as well. Yet they are expected to rise less than in previous periods of cyclical expansion in business. This opinion is predicated on various underlying assumptions which may—or may not—materialize. And it also postulates that while the balance of payments could continue to deteriorate, a dollar crisis will be avoided.

VIII. STOCK YIELDS

"History amply demonstrates the great importance of yield trends to the long-term course of stock prices." This sentence concludes two scholarly studies published some years ago, in two of its weekly reviews, by one of the most respected investment services. In developing their train of thought, the authors of these studies remarked:

> The matter of the major trend of yields is highly important to the stock price level. The market valuation of a dollar of dividends tends broadly to fluctuate with the trend of financial sentiment or the degree

of investment confidence. When financial sentiment declines and investment confidence ebbs, the market's valuation of dividends tends also to decline and yields widen; conversely, when confidence strengthens, the market tends to set a higher value on a dollar of dividends and yields narrow.

This trend of yields can, too, be more potent in its market effect than the trend of dividends as was the case in recent years, when dividend rates were rather steadily advancing, but price/dividend ratios declined more than enough to offset the effects of rising dividends. The result was declining market prices.

The summary heading the study in the first of these two issues concluded by a recommendation stating that

> ... the prospect of further declines in average yields over a period is a long range factor supporting to the average level of stock prices. There is no occasion for disturbing selected shares bought for long range purposes. Buying with new funds should be confined to individually attractive situations.

It is not important that, in point of fact, soon after this opinion was rendered, stock yields did decline to a somewhat lower level from which, however, they proceeded to double before a new decline of stock yields set in. We all know that investment forecasts are often more fragile than the most precious of china. Nor are we at odds with the opinion that investment confidence is an important contributor to the formation of stock prices. We are also willing to grant that a market valuation of a dollar of dividends illustrated by the center panel of Figure 3—or by its reciprocal panel of stock yields—does sometimes reflect financial sentiment. Yet it impresses us as a curiously backhanded way of analyzing and projecting trends of stock prices by accepting them as the result of changes in stock yields. Stock prices and dividends are the primary economic factors whose movements are determined by the long-term trends of the economy, as well as by its cyclical fluctuations. Stock yields are effects of the different combinations into which these primary factors can enter. And depending on the nature of such combinations, identical levels of stock yields can have at various times different economic meaning.

IX. THE DEVIL'S DOZEN

The complexity of stock yields may be illustrated by the fact that its changes, i.e., changes in the dividend/price ratio, are subject to 13 possible different combinations of directions in which dividends and prices may be moving.

Stock yields can decline under five different sets of conditions governing the ratios of dividends to prices:

1. When both dividends and prices are declining, but dividends are declining relatively more
2. When dividends are declining and prices move sideways
3. When dividends are declining, but prices are rising
4. When dividends remain unchanged, but prices are rising
5. When both dividends and prices are rising, but prices are rising relatively more

Of course, stock yields can *rise* under five different sets of conditions also. These will be symmetrically inverse to the above. A little probing will reveal the three possible combinations under which no change would take place in the direction of the ratio.

Variations in the economic significance of different combinations producing an identical result in stock yield changes can be manifold, to say the least.

X. SOME NOTES ON FIGURE 3

We should bear in mind that this chart's center and lower panels are reciprocals. If we use P as the symbol of stock prices and D to represent dividends, the algebraic transcription of the two ratios traced on the panels in question could be respectively written as P/D and D/P. The inverse relation of the two panels is also quite visible graphically despite the difference in the statistical nature and proportions of their scales.

The curve of price/dividend ratios P/D was not included on Figure 1. We have inserted it in Figure 3 because some investors like to think of stock levels in terms of multiples of dividends. Stocks are more richly priced when one has to pay for them, on the average, $30 for each $1 of dividends, than when their dividends can be purchased at a $20 rate.

Let us focus our attention on the movements of the top and bottom curves of Figure 3: those of stock prices and stock yields. Or, if we like, we can make the same comparison on Figure 1 where these two curves stand nearer to each other.

One of the aspects of the interrelations of stock prices and stock yields is their tendency to move in opposite directions. The amplitudes of these divergent movements vary; but the opposite movements recur.

We may note that most of the time dividends move in the same direction as stock prices. The divergencies of stock prices and stock yields must be therefore accounted for by the wider amplitude of price movements.

However, during periods when prices are relatively stable, dividends may become the more dynamic element, taking over the leadership of stock yield trends. The earliest of such cases shown on Figure 3 covered the years from 1884 to 1899 during which stock yields were dominated by dividends. And this happened again in the few years immediately preceding the outbreak of World War I in Europe, and also when the stock market refused to capitalize the rise of wartime dividends, causing a sudden upward thrust of stock yields.

XI. UNRELATED SERIES

The review of the main trends of stock and bond yields over a 90-year period points up the differences in their economic natures and in the mechanisms of their directional changes. It is probably safer to use them as separate economic guides than try to draw conclusions from their confrontation. And, needless to say, stock yields must be each time carefully disentangled and read in the light of the meaning of the action of their underlying factors.

Another reason for caution was pointed out in a recent letter by Jules I. Bogen, Professor of Finance of New York University:

> Qualitative questions raised by a comparison of bond and stock yields in the nineteenth century are frightening. In an era when substantially all earnings were paid out as dividends, dividend yields meant something quite different from what they do when only half of earnings are paid out on the average, and that after a very large depreciation allowance and heavy research outlays. There is no practical way to allow for such qualitative factors in yield indices, but they are vital to an interpretation of yield comparisons going back so many years.

In addition to these various pragmatic considerations, there also exist strong theoretical reasons throwing considerable doubt on the validity of using stock yields and their ratios to the yields on bonds as indicators of impending trend changes in stock prices.

To quote from Macaulay, "It is highly undesirable to call the function a 'yield' and thus, by the use of terms, insidiously to suggest that it is of the same nature as the ('hypothetical') yield of a bond."[2] He is referring to stock yields. Bond yields are based on an assumption of payments. The assumption may or may not materialize. However, it introduces the element of time *which enters into a mathematical relationship with all the other factors that are part of the concept.*

[2] Frederick R. Macaulay, *Some Theoretical Problems Suggested by the Movements of Interest Rates, Bond Yields, and Stock Prices in the United States since 1856* (New York, N.Y.: National Bureau of Economic Research, 1938), p. 133.

We can scarcely hope to reach reliable conclusions concerning the state and outlook of the stock market by drawing them from comparison of factors whose very natures are different.

XII. STOCK YIELDS AND STOCK VALUES

Do so-called stock yields, i.e., current returns from common stocks, have then any meaning at all? They do.

They are a basic point of departure for measuring the total return from dividends. Such an overall effective yield—including not only the current return but future payments as well—could be legitimately compared with bond yields because it also introduces the factor of time which is an essential ingredient of all investment concepts. This is the road towards appraising investment values.

During the five years elapsed between 1897, when Charles H. Dow devised the Dow-Jones Industrial and Rail Averages, and his death in 1902, Dow often referred in his editorials in the *Wall Street Journal*, of which he was a founder, to stock values. Regardless of temporary fluctuations in stock prices, he felt that values were the determining factor in the long run. He believed that values were measurable by the return to the investor.

The idea was sound. But as in the case of many another pioneer, Dow's tools were primitive. The number of stocks in the original averages was small. And only five years elapsed between the time he constructed them and the time he died. All his observations were made on a narrow base and over a short period. If he had lived longer he might have come to realize that values cannot be meaningful if they take in the present only; they should discount the future as well.

On the basis of such observations as he had been able to accumulate, Dow thought that when a stock sells at a price which returns only about $3\frac{1}{2}$ percent on the investment, it is "obviously" dear, unless there existed some special reason for supporting so high a price.

Present-day Dow theorists continue to be faithful to the founder's concept of value. On December 19, 1960, a well-known follower of *the Theory* related that after studying the action of the DJIA from 1920 onwards, he found that the average yield on the D.J. Industrials was subject to wide swings coinciding with the major bull and bear markets. According to him, investors tended to distribute stocks when the average yield on the D.J. Industrials receded to the $3\frac{1}{2}$ percent area and tended to accumulate them when the average yield on the D.J. Industrials rose above the 6 percent level.

The practical usefulness of such observations is quite limited. The date on which these remarks were published in a financial periodical happened to stand in the midst of the earliest swirling weeks of a powerful bull market that was just under way. Yet the center panel of Figure 1, which is traced in terms of D.J. Industrials, shows that, under Dow's measures of value, stocks were a sale rather than a purchase. The same diagram reveals that stocks were not good values even at the bottom of the preceding bear market.

The Cowles Commission, which had the time and the organization needed for a much more thorough job, published indexes of not just a few selected equities, but of all stocks covering a very extended period—from 1871 to 1938. And it did the additional work of computing stock yields not only on an actual annual average basis, but also as monthly indexes of yield expectations. It drew the following conclusions from its observations of the movements of stock yields:

> An examination of the All Stock monthly index for yield expectations shows that four times in the last 68 years the expected yield has dropped below 3 percent. These were in February-March-April, 1899, April, 1901, August-September, 1929, and July, 1933. Each of these four periods was a favorable one for the sale of stocks, since in each case lower prices developed in the next year. There have also been three cases where yield expectations rose above 8 percent. These occurred in October, 1873, October-November-December, 1917, and April-May-June 1932. In each of these three instances stock prices averaged higher in the subsequent 12 months. It would thus appear that, when average yields are below 3 percent, stocks are priced too high, and when average yields are above 8 percent, stock prices are too low.[3]

In the course of the very long period covered by the Cowles Commission study, the upper and lower limits were exceeded only a few times. Twenty-eight years elapsed between the second and third recurrence of the lower limit; and 44 and 15 years separated the second from the first, and the third from the second occurrence of the upper. Furthermore, and paradoxically, yields were low also in periods when they could not possibly be regarded as warning signals. In some part of every year between 1932 and 1940 industrial stock yields were lower than at the bull market's turning point of 1937.

These examples show how unreliable such comparisons are. The basic idea behind them—the search for investment values—is sound. But an adequate technique is lacking. Perhaps the weakest point in trying to use current yields for appraising stock values is the fact that they depend so much on the action of stock prices themselves whose validity they set out to measure.

[3] Alfred Cowles 3d and Associates, *Common-Stock Indexes* (Principia Press, 1939), pp. 46–47.

XIII. STOCK MARKET ANALYSIS

A growing number of financial analysts are developing new techniques for the valuation of common stocks. We have also made some contributions to this area of the science and art of investment on the pages of the *Financial Analysts Journal*. John G. McLean, a Vice President of Continental Oil, and a former member of the Faculty of the Harvard Business School, in *"How to Evaluate New Capital Investments"* (*Harvard Business Review*, November-December, 1958) uses as the article's motto the good counsel, "Don't count your cash before it is discounted!" We also use the principle of present worth adapted to stock valuation needs. We use stock yields only as the point of departure for finding a universal discount rate capable of placing all stocks on a comparable basis. We must be able to determine an overall "effective yield" before we can make a significant appraisal of a stock's investment value. The essential factor of time must be recognized in the appraisal of common stocks.

In the years following 1949, the stock price curve of Figure 3 shows three barely perceptible indentations in the steep slope of its climb. When we lived through them, our senses responded to them more sharply than is now done by our chart. But feelings aside, the 1953 cyclical contraction took place when the market *prices* of most stocks were still very much lower than their investment *values*. This was no longer quite as much the case in 1957. And when the current cyclical rise of stock prices began in October, 1960, the DJIA had barely shifted from its previous high of an *overpriced* position to the neutral gear of *fair value*.

Exactly a year ago, in the March-April, 1961, issue of the *Financial Analysts Journal*, we published an appraisal for 1961 of the *investment values* of DJIA and each of its 30 component stocks. Many among them were clearly *overpriced*. Yet it was equally clear that the cyclical upswing was in its early stages. Economic indicators were only beginning to form their troughs. It seemed difficult to discourage investors from participating in a powerful bull market despite the flagrant *overpricing* of many stocks. The best advice we could give them was to keep closer to earth by increasing the proportion of holdings of realistically *priced* stocks.

As we are penciling these lines, it is of interest to observe that while DJIA, despite its January, 1962, decline, stands quite a bit higher than a year ago, many among those of its stocks which we then found to be overpriced are now selling considerably below their last year's level.

And yet, our valuation appraisals were done without much refinement—on a mass production basis and mostly for purposes of illustration. Earnings growth rates were projected in each case for the same period: 10 years. And at exactly that point a uniform "ignorance rate" of $2\frac{1}{2}$ percent was invariably spliced to the earnings trend line of each stock in complete disregard of whether it was Alcoa, American Tobacco, Procter & Gamble, or U. S. Steel. It is clear that the nature of the industry to which a given company belongs—as well as that corporation's particular characteristics—should in reality determine both the length of the period for which earnings are projected into the future and also the delicate process of the "splicing" with an overall historical rate. Depending on each individual case, such a transition may well take the form of mathematical curves with very different gradations of diminishing rates of growth.

Nevertheless, last year's rough appraisals taught a valuable lesson. They showed that much of what happened in the stock market since then may be described as a struggle between the impulse of cyclical momentum and the investment value of each particular stock.

The picture which this analysis discloses is different from the concept that all stocks are uniformly subject to overriding cyclical tides. To be sure, few will remain immune to the rises and falls of cyclical expansions and contractions. But the magnitudes of their responses will differ and some will show contracyclical trends.

If this analysis is substantially correct, it could conceivably place investment policy decisions into a different perspective. The traditional shifts between stocks and bonds would lose much of their previous compulsion. Only in the presence of overpowering actuarial reasons would a major withdrawal from equities seem justified. For the majority of institutional and private investors a greater flexibility inside their common stock portfolios would probably offer a sounder road to investment success. And in the presence of sufficient indications of impending cyclical reversals they could temporarily use the shelter of instruments equivalent to cash.

We would stand on firmer ground in confronting bond yields with the *prices* of common stocks rather than with their current returns. If we invert bond yields and plot them, as bond prices, together with prices of common stocks, we shall be looking at two related and significant cyclical series. And we can further refine our observations by constructing various indexes of bond and stock prices and price and volume ratios based on their relative investment grades and other special characteristics.

APPENDIX

We do not always realize how fortunate we are in having at our disposal well-constructed indexes covering extended periods. When Frederick Macaulay was writing, not so long ago, the book referred to in this article, it took him five years to complete it. He had not only to solve arduous theoretical problems, but also to construct his own indexes going back to 1856. More than 350 pages of his volume consist of appendixes and tables computed by him to do the job. And when, a year later, the Cowles Commission published its Common-Stock Indexes, only 10 percent of the monograph was devoted to discussion, while many hundreds of remaining pages consisted of the figures of the new indexes themselves. As stated in its preface, some idea of the magnitude of the project may be indicated by the fact that over 1,500,000 work sheet entries were made, requiring 25,000 computer hours. In the process of doing this job, the Cowles Commission used portions of Macaulay's and Standard Statistics indexes and prepared the ground for having its own work eventually incorporated into the new Standard & Poor's "500" series.

All the data on all the charts in the article itself and this Appendix are annual averages or their ratios.

No choice existed for stock indexes. Two series only explore the past sufficiently: the Cowles Commission and Standard & Poor's "500." They take us back to 1871.

Stock yields used from 1926 to date are those of the Standard & Poor's "500" indexes. But as "500" dividends are not available prior to 1926, Cowles Commission figures were used for the earlier years.

Several indexes could be used for tracing the curves of high-grade bond yields. Our problem here is not due to lack of data but to what the French call an embarrassment of riches.

Difficulties of Selecting Bond Yield Indexes

For the most recent period, a suitable yield index of bonds of the highest grade is the Standard & Poor's index for U.S. Government long-term taxable bonds. It begins in 1942. There exist no yield indexes of long-term taxable government bonds prior to that date.

Both Moody's Investors Service and Standard & Poor's Corporation have indexes of high-grade corporate bonds. Moody's highest bond grade rating is designated by the letters *Aaa*. Standard & Poor's also uses a Triple A designation for highest grade bonds, but writes it with three capital letters: *AAA*. Prior to November, 1960, Standard & Poor's used, for the identical bonds, the symbol A1+. But in the interest of standardizing symbols throughout the industry, Standard & Poor's adopted all-letter symbols at the above-mentioned date. This change was made possible by its acquisition of the Fitch publications, including the use of the Fitch rating symbols which graded bonds in all-letter symbols.

When they are plotted on the same chart, the differences between the yields on Moody's and Standard & Poor's Triple A bond are almost imperceptible. Both are indexes of corporate bonds of the highest grade. To use a phrase from Macaulay's book, "bonds of the highest grade are bonds than which there are none better." Both indexes qualify under this definition as far as corporate bonds are concerned. The difference between them is not in quality but in the periods for which they were computed. Moody's index goes back to 1919, while the Standard index extends to 1900.

Macaulay's own yield indexes of bonds of the highest grade go back all the way to 1856. They consist of railroad bonds only—for obvious historical reasons. But Macaulay constructed two series of yields of high-grade railroad bonds: the unadjusted and the adjusted series.

Figure A traces all these bond yield indexes since 1871. As noted, Macaulay's bond indexes probe a much earlier past as well, but no stock yield indexes exist prior to 1871. On the other hand, Macaulay's book was published in 1938, and his indexes do not extend beyond 1936. Since Moody's and Standard & Poor's Triple A indexes are practically identical, Figure A uses the Standard index because it applies to a longer period.

FIGURE A

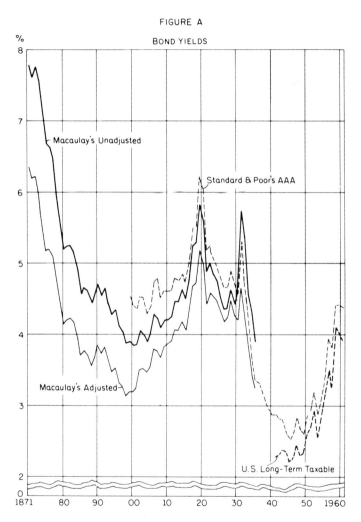

We are facing a double problem: (1) which of the two Macaulay indexes should we use? (2) Which of the latter day indexes should be spliced to the selected Macaulay index?

In thinking about the choice of the most appropriate index, we are not indulging in irrelevant technicalities. Figure B brings out that depending on the bond yield index selected, its comparison with stock yields produces a very different historical lesson.

In all three panels of Figure B, identical stock yield curves are used. They are based on Standard "500" and Cowles Commission data.

FIGURE B

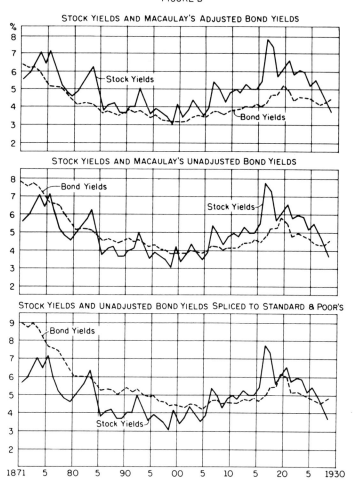

The top panel of Figure B compares stock yields with Macaulay's adjusted index, while the middle panel uses his unadjusted bond yields. In the lowest section, stock yields are confronted with Standard & Poor's Triple A yield index spliced, in 1900, to Macaulay's unadjusted yields. A splicing to the adjusted index would have produced similar results, the difference being absorbed by the splicing factor.

The three panels of Figure B tell completely different stories about the relative historical action of stock and bond yields. And yet it was on the presumed knowledge of past yield interrelations that so much of recent advice was based. If investors should take into account historical yield relations, policy decisions must be quite different depending on which of the three panels we select.

Construction of Macaulay's Indexes

In confronting stock yields and bond yields, investors and financial writers compare the returns from equities with long-term interest rates. Unless they are studying some special aspect of investments, the bond yield indexes they use are those of the highest grade long-term corporate bonds.

Since their return to economic freedom in 1951, the yields of long-term taxable government bonds are, for this country, the truest measure of long-term interest rates. This was not the case for the period covered by Macaulay's work, extending from 1856 to 1936. As pointed out by Macaulay, the yields of U.S. Government bonds were seriously affected by their circulation privileges. Bank notes could be issued against them. Their yields were consequently lower than if they had been valued for interest payments alone. Even after the formation of the Federal Reserve system, they continued to carry special banking privileges.

During the long period of Macaulay's study, bonds matured and disappeared, and had even to be discarded years before maturity to preserve the long-term nature of the index. Substitutions were made annually. This created the problem of what Macaulay describes as the "economic drift." The index of yields of bonds of the highest grade contained secular and cyclical changes in the grades of the bonds and alterations in the values of underlying properties, liens, and financial strengths of the issuing corporations.

Macaulay's unadjusted index was directly computed from average monthly yields of specific individual long-term railroad bonds. Each of these bonds is named and its monthly yield is shown. For 1871—the first year of our period—he used 21 separate bond issues. For 1935—the last full year appearing in his book—he used 28 issues.

As to his adjusted index, we shall let him speak for himself.

> The index number that we calculated from the sigma equations to present a picture of the course of the yields of railroad bonds of the highest possible grade, a grade often slightly higher than that of any actual bond, was constructed by assuming a yield of 4.50 percent in January 1925 and working backward to January 1857 and forward to January 1936. The lowest yield of any bond we used in January 1925 was 4.50 percent. However, this is quite accidental. Throughout the entire period from January 1857 to January 1936, the sigma index, though it is more often lower than it is higher, tends to run fairly close to the yields of the lowest yield bonds. But it has no rigid relation to any individual yield. It weaves in and out among the lowest yields only because, in its character as an index from which "drift" was presumed to be eliminated, it was designed to do so....
>
> A study of the corporations themselves gives us considerable reason to believe that the very best railroad bonds in the early period were inferior to the best bonds in the later period. But, from the yields of the best bonds in the early period, or even from the yields of all the bonds in all the periods, it is difficult if not impossible to calculate plausibly what would have been, in the early period, the yield of a railroad bond of apparently as high grade as the very best railroad bonds in the latter period (pp. 117–121).

Conclusion

We believe that the choice from among the various indexes shown on Figure A should be determined by the nature of the proposed study.

To students of interest rates in this country, we would suggest the use of Macaulay's adjusted index continued, after 1942, by Standard & Poor's index of U.S. Government taxable long-term bond yields. The few missing years from 1937 through 1941 could be easily bridged by using, for splicing, the differentials between the two suggested selections and Standard & Poor's yield index of *AAA* corporate bonds.

For a study like ours, which compares the yields from stock and bonds, Macaulay's unadjusted index, spliced at some suitable point to the Standard & Poor's Triple A index, appears a logical solution. We spliced the two indexes by connecting their respective points for the years 1928 and 1929.

Macaulay himself points out that

> All existing index numbers of the prices of common stocks contain "economic drift." This is not merely almost inevitable but also desirable and necessary *if the indexes are to present faithful pictures of what actually occurs.* [Emphasis ours.] Economic drift is the essential characteristic of the movements of common stock prices. Those prices are the prices of radically junior securities and economic drift is the very badge of their "juniority." To eliminate it from an index, if that were feasible, would be nothing short of emasculating the index (p. 148).

It seems to us that by using Macaulay's unadjusted index in conjunction with a stock index that is unadjusted *per se* and *ex officio* we make a comparison presenting a more *faithful picture of what actually occurred.* On the other hand, Macaulay's adjusted index comes probably closer to economic truth in showing the movements of long-term interest rates.

In practice, this counsel, which we not only offer, but also follow, has not been generally applied. Numerous students of economic history have used Macaulay's indexes. But we have the distinct impression that they rarely give careful attention to the selection of the index which is better suited to the nature of their problem and is least likely to distort the results. Some authoritative investment services have used Macaulay's adjusted bond yield index in conjunction with Cowles Commission indexes of common stock prices and dividends. In so doing they are apt to "discover" an "economic law" that stock yields cannot decline below bond yields without calamitous declines of stock prices.

*Burton G. Malkiel**

20. Expectations, Bond Prices, and the Term Structure of Interest Rates[1]

Reprinted by permission of the author and publisher from the **Quarterly Journal of Economics,** Vol. LXXVI (May, 1962), pp. 197–218 (Cambridge, Mass.: Harvard University Press; copyright 1962, by the President and Fellows of Harvard College).

I. INTRODUCTION

The relation of short-term to long-term yields has often intrigued both economic theorists and investment analysts. This relationship, usually referred to as the *structure* of interest rates, has been characterized by significantly divergent patterns. Despite the considerable attention devoted to the question, rate-structure theory remains in an uncomfortable state of confusion. In addition, an unfortunate lacuna still exists between the writings of economic theorists and the practices of bond traders and institutional investors. This study examines briefly the principle hypotheses which have been offered to explain the relationship of short to long rates. Then, a new theoretical apparatus is offered which, it is hoped, will at once provide a useful framework for amending and reconciling our current body of theory and also bring into closer conformity the beliefs of academic economists and of those close to the debt market.

Traditional doctrine has typically formulated and analyzed the rate-structure problem in terms of a combination of "spot" and "forward" trading.[2] The rate of interest for a two-year loan is conceived as being compounded out of the "spot" rate for loans of one year and the "forward" rate of interest for one-year loans to be executed at the beginning of the second year. Writing the two-year rate (the "long" rate) as R_2, the current one-year ("short") rate as r_1, and the forward one-year "short" rate as

---

* Professor of Economics, Princeton University.

[1] I am greatly indebted to Professors W. J. Baumol and R. E. Quandt, who have offered several useful suggestions and criticisms. The helpful comments of Professors L. V. Chandler and F. Machlup are also gratefully acknowledged.

[2] E.g., J. R. Hicks, *Value and Capital*, 2d ed. (New York, N Y.: Oxford U.P., 1946), pp. 144–45.

r_2, we have $(1 + R_2)^2 = (1 + r_1)(1 + r_2)$. Thus, the system of rates for various maturities can be reduced to the short rate combined with a series of relevant forward short rates.[3] It is then possible to account for different rate structures. If future short-term rates are expected to fall, then the long-term average of those rates must necessarily be below the current short rate. Similarly, long rates will exceed the current short rate if future short rates are expected to rise. Perhaps the most articulate spokesman for this doctrine, F. A. Lutz, abstracting from costs of investment and institutional rigidities, is able to explain any pattern of rates in this manner.[4]

The short-rate expectational theory has been beleaguered by critics. Building on the Keynesian theory of "normal backwardation" in the futures market, Hicks offered one of the earliest qualifications. Hicks argued that even if short rates are expected to remain unchanged, the forward short rate can normally be expected to exceed the current short rate by a risk premium which must be offered the holder of a bond to compensate him for assuming the risks of price fluctuations.[5] Thus, the "normal relationship" is for long rates (which are averages of forward short rates) to exceed short rates. Only if the short rate is considered abnormally high could long rates be below short rates.[6] Other critics have confuted the Lutz theory's basic behavioral postulate, i.e., that investors do in fact decide whether to invest in bonds or bills on the basis of their expectations of future short rates. Investors faced with the choice now of buying either a five-or a ten-year government bond are simply not capable of accurately predicting bill rates from 1967–72. More important, it is doubtful whether any bond investors believe they are capable of doing so. The *reductio ad absurdum* of the argument has been offered in a well-known quip by Mrs. Robinson: If the investor happens to buy consols then he must think he knows exactly what the rates of interest will be every day from today until Kingdom Come.[7]

Recently, the Lutz theory has come under increasingly severe attack. Rather than offering suggestions as modifications, the newer critics have attacked the basic foundations of the theory.[8] J. M. Culbertson lays stress

---

[3] Hicks assumes that all funds are retained in the investment until maturity.

[4] Friedrich A. Lutz, "The Structure of Interest Rates," *Quarterly Journal of Economics*, Vol. LV (November, 1940), pp. 36–63.

[5] Cf. J. M. Keynes, *A Treatise on Money*, Vol. II (New York, N.Y.: Harcourt, Brace, 1930), pp. 142–44. Hicks, *op. cit.*, pp. 138–39, 144–47.

[6] Hicks, *op. cit.*, p. 147.

[7] Joan Robinson, "The Rate of Interest," *Econometrica*, Vol. 19 (April, 1951), p. 102 n.

[8] A notable exception is J. W. Conard's *Introduction to the Theory of Interest* (Berkeley, Calif.: U. of California P., 1959), Part Three. Conard makes a valiant attempt to incorporate many of the modifications and criticisms using the Lutz analysis as the cornerstone of an overall theory of the term structure.

on the institutional impediments to perfect mobility and to changes in the maturity structure of the supply of debt instruments as determinants.[9] But Culbertson's assault is not merely confined to the simplifying assumptions of the Lutz hypothesis; it is directed at the whole structure of the theory. Culbertson finds the expectational explanation theoretically unsatisfactory and doubts that expectations are a major determinant of the term structure of rates. Moreover, Luckett has argued forcefully that once Lutz leaves the world of perfect certainty, awkward logical difficulties arise which are sufficient to throw the entire internal consistency of the theory into question.[10] As a result, a very appealing theory has been thrown under considerable suspicion.

This paper takes the position that the basic expectational approach of the Lutz theory is both correct and of substantial importance in understanding the actual behavior of market interest rates of securities with different terms to maturity. Nevertheless, we assert that the yield-maturity relationship is more clearly perceived when *explicit* recognition is given to bond prices. We propose to examine rigorously the nexus between market interest rates and bond prices. Then the Lutz theory will be recast in terms consistent with the practices of bond investors and traders. Expectations will be introduced through explicit expected price changes rather than expected future short rates. Finally, we shall examine the implications of relaxing some of the assumptions inherent in the analytical model and of introducing expectations into the supply as well as the demand side of the market.

II. THE MATHEMATICS OF BOND PRICES

Economists have typically formulated theories of the structure of interest rates in terms of bond yields to the exclusion of bond prices. Keynes probably came closest to an explicit realization of the effect of price risks as a major determinant in the desire for liquidity and, therefore, of interest rates.[11] Even Keynes, however, did not adequately call attention to the precise relationship between changes in bond yields and bond prices. Keynes argued that with a long-term rate of interest of 4 percent, if it were feared that the rate would rise faster than 0.16 percent, per annum, then cash would be preferred to bonds. He reasoned that the fall in bond prices associated with the rise in the interest rate would more than offset the coupon interest received.[12] But if the issue in question were a ten-year

[9] J. M. Culbertson, "The Term Structure of Interest Rates," *Quarterly Journal of Economics*, Vol. LXXI (November, 1957), pp. 485–517.

[10] Dudley G. Luckett, "Professor Lutz and the Structure of Interest Rates," *Quarterly Journal of Economics*, Vol. LXXIII (February, 1959), pp. 139–40.

[11] J. M. Keynes, *The General Theory of Employment, Interest and Money* (New York, N.Y.: Harcourt, Brace, 1935), Ch. 15.

[12] *Ibid.*, p. 202.

(4 percent coupon) bond, it would take a 0.50 percent rise in yields to satisfy his argument. For a five-year bond, rates would have to rise by more than 0.91 percent to wipe out an amount of capital equivalent to the interest received. Keynes was not careful to point out that his analysis is approximately correct only in the case of a perpetual bond. I feel the implication of yield changes on bond prices has usually received inadequate or imprecise attention in the literature. Bonds are traded in terms of price, not yield. They are bought and sold by speculators, long-term investors, and financial institutions who are vitally concerned with price movements. We hope to show that a rigorous examination of the nexus between bond yields and market prices can be enormously helpful in understanding the actual fluctuations of yields in the bond markets.[13]

The market value of a bond is determined by four factors: (1) the face value of the bond, i.e., the principal amount to be paid at maturity which we denote by F; (2) the coupon or interest paid periodically to the bondholder, denoted by C; (3) the effective interest rate per period i, which is referred to as the net return per period or, where we assume annual compounding, the annual yield to maturity; and (4) N, the number of years to maturity. The market price P is simply the sum of the present values of all the coupons to be received as interest and the principal amount to be paid at maturity:

$$P = \frac{C}{(1+i)} + \frac{C}{(1+i)^2} + \cdots + \frac{C}{(1+i)^N} + \frac{F}{(1+i)^N} \tag{1}$$

Summing the geometric progression and simplifying, we obtain

$$P = \frac{C}{i}\left[1 - \frac{1}{(1+i)^N}\right] + \frac{F}{(1+i)^N} \tag{2}$$

As N goes to infinity the expression approaches the limit C/i. Thus, for a perpetual bond paying $1.00 per annum, the market value becomes simply the reciprocal of the market rate of interest.

It will be useful to review certain well-known preliminary relationships. Rewriting Eq. (2) above as

$$P = \frac{C}{i} + \frac{F - C/i}{(1+i)^N} \tag{3}$$

---

[13] The need for a study of the term structure of interest rates to go behind the yields themselves and consider bond prices has been suggested, but not explored, by David Durand. Cf. David Durand, "Basic Yields of Corporate Bonds, 1900–1942" (Technical Paper 3; New York, N.Y.: National Bureau of Economic Research, 1942), p. 19.

and defining the nominal or stated rate of yield i_0 as

$$i_0 \equiv \frac{C}{F} \tag{4}$$

we can observe that when the market yield to maturity i is equal to the nominal yield then

$$\frac{C}{i} = F \quad \text{and} \quad P = F \tag{4a}$$

The bond sells at par. When $i > i_0$, then

$$\frac{C}{i} < F \quad \text{and} \quad P < F \tag{4b}$$

The bond sells at a discount. When $i < i_0$, then

$$\frac{C}{i} > F \quad \text{and} \quad P > F \tag{4c}$$

The bond sells at a premium.

We may now proceed to examine the relationship between yield changes and bond price movements.

Theorem 1: Bond prices move inversely to bond yields.

Proof: Differentiating Eq. (1) with respect to i we obtain

$$\frac{\partial P}{\partial i} = -\frac{C}{(1+i)^2} - \frac{2C}{(1+i)^3} - \cdots - \frac{NC}{(1+i)^{N+1}} - \frac{NF}{(1+i)^{N+1}} < 0 \tag{5}$$

Theorem 2: For a given change in yield from the nominal yield, changes in bond prices are greater, the longer is the term to maturity.

Proof: We wish to evaluate $\dfrac{\partial[P(i) - P(i_0)]}{\partial N}$. But $\dfrac{\partial P(i_0)}{\partial N} = 0$ since for $i = i_0$, $P = F$, a constant, by Eq. (4a). Therefore, it is sufficient to evaluate the sign of $\partial P(i)/\partial N$. Rewriting Eq. (2) we have

$$P = \frac{C}{i} - (1+i)^{-N}\left[\frac{C}{i} - F\right]$$

Differentiating with respect to N we obtain

$$\frac{\partial P}{\partial N} = \left[\frac{C}{i} - F\right][1+i]^{-N}[\ln(1+i)] \tag{6}$$

When $i < i_0$, the bond sells at a premium,

$$\left[\frac{C}{i} - F\right] > 0 \tag{6a}$$

from Eq. (4c) and therefore $\partial P/\partial N > 0$. Therefore, if the market yield is below the nominal yield i_0, the price of the bond (P) will be higher the longer the time to maturity. When $i > i_0$, the bond sells at a discount,

$$\left[\frac{C}{i} - F\right] < 0 \tag{6b}$$

from Eq. (4b) and therefore $\partial P/\partial N < 0$. Thus if the market yield is above the nominal yield, the price of the bond (P) will be lower as the length of time to maturity increases. Since the absolute and percentage change in bond prices is measured by the difference between the derived P and F ($F = 100$) we find that bond-price movements are amplified as time to maturity is increased.

Theorem 3: The percentage price changes described in Theorem 2 increase at a diminishing rate as N increases.

Proof: Differentiating Eq. (6) with respect to N we obtain

$$\frac{\partial^2 P}{\partial N^2} = -\left[\frac{C}{i} - F\right]\left[\ln (1 + i)\right]^2\left[(1 + i)^{-N}\right] \tag{7}$$

Repeating the same argument as above we have for i below the nominal rate i_0, $\partial^2 P/\partial N^2 < 0$. The percentage price rise from par increases with N but at a diminishing rate. Similarly, for i above i_0, $\partial^2 P/\partial N^2 > 0$. The percentage price decline from par increases with N at a diminishing rate.

Theorem 4: Price movements resulting from equal absolute (or, what is the same, from equal proportionate) increases and decreases in yield are asymmetric; i.e., a decrease in yields raises bond prices more than the same increase in yields lowers prices.

Proof: We will show that in order to prove asymmetry it is sufficient to show that $\partial^2 P/\partial i^2 > 0$. Differentiating Eq. (5) with respect to i we have

$$\frac{\partial^2 P}{\partial i^2} = \frac{2C}{(1 + i)^3} + \frac{2 \cdot 3C}{(1 + i)^4} + \cdots + \frac{N(N + 1)C}{(1 + i)^{N+2}} + \frac{N(N + 1)F}{(1 + i)^{N+2}} > 0 \tag{8}$$

Thus the slope of the function $P = f(i)$ becomes less negative as i increases. Consequently, for any i', the average slope of the function over the range between i' and $(i' - \Delta i)$ is steeper than over the range between i' and $(i' + \Delta i)$. Therefore, a (say 10 percent) increase in yield will result in a smaller absolute and percentage price decline than a 10 percent decrease in yield will raise bond prices.

Theorem 5: The higher is the coupon carried by the bond, the smaller will be the percentage price fluctuation for a given change in yield except for one-year securities and consols.

Proof: We wish to prove $\dfrac{\partial[(\partial P/\partial i)\cdot(i/P)]}{\partial C} > 0$, for all finite $N \geq 2$.

Differentiating Eq. (2) with respect to i we obtain:

$$\frac{\partial P}{\partial i} = \frac{-C(1+i)^{N+1} + C(1+i+Ni) - FNi^2}{i^2(1+i)^{N+1}}$$

Multiplying through by i/P (where we use Eq. 2 for P) and simplifying we obtain:

$$\frac{\partial P}{\partial i}\cdot\frac{i}{P} = \frac{-C(1+i)^{N+1} + C(1+i+Ni) - FNi^2}{C(1+i)^{N+1} - C(1+i) + Fi(1+i)} \tag{9}$$

Let us write $\Delta(N) = (1+i)[C(1+i)^N - C + Fi]^2$ so that

$$\frac{Fi}{(1+i)[C(1+i)^N - C + Fi]^2} = \frac{Fi}{\Delta(N)} > 0 \tag{10}$$

for all finite N. Differentiating Eq. (9) with respect to C we obtain:

$$\frac{\partial[(\partial P/\partial i)\cdot(i/P)]}{\partial C} = \frac{Fi}{\Delta(N)}[1 + i + (1+i)^N(Ni - 1 - i)] \tag{11}$$

When $N = 1$, Eq. (11) $= 0$. Equation (11) is positive for all finite $N \geq 2$ as will now be shown by induction. Write

$$\emptyset(N) = 1 + i + (1+i)^N(Ni - 1 - i)$$

First note that for $N = 2$, $\emptyset(N) = (i^2 + i^3) > 0$ for all $i > 0$. We now prove that $\emptyset(N)$ is an increasing function of N so that since $\emptyset(N) > 0$ for $N = 2$, $\emptyset(N) > 0$ for $N > 2$.

$$\emptyset(N + 1) = 1 + i + (1+i)^N(1+i)(Ni - 1)$$

that is,

$$\emptyset(N + 1) = \emptyset(N) + Ni^2(1+i)^N$$

therefore

$$\emptyset(N + 1) > \emptyset(N) \quad \text{for all} \quad N > 0, \quad i > 0$$

Thus we conclude

$$\emptyset(N) > 0 \tag{12}$$

for all finite $N \geq 2$. Hence, since Eq. (11) can be written $[Fi/\Delta(N)]\cdot\emptyset(N)$, we conclude by Eqs. (10) and (12) that

$$\frac{\partial[(\partial P/\partial i)\cdot(i/P)]}{\partial C} > 0 \qquad \text{Q.E.D.}$$

But note that when $N \to \infty$, $Fi/\Delta(N) \to 0$ and Eq. (11) $\to 0$.

Table 1 summarizes several of the relationships described by the theorems. The greater absolute and diminishing marginal volatility of long-term bond prices is patently revealed.

A two-year bond is shown to rise or fall about twice as far from par as a one-year bond. Similarly, a four-year bond fluctuates almost twice as much as a two-year security. A 64-year bond will not, however, fluctuate in price significantly more than a 32-year bond, particularly for an increase in yield. Thus, the implications for an investor of extending the maturity of his bond portfolio can be quite different depending on the maturity sector of the curve to which it is applicable.[14] Furthermore, an asymmetry of price movements on either side of the axis from par is revealed. There is a natural cushion which exists simply in the mathematics of bond prices which limits a long-term bond's price decline as yields rise.[15]

An examination of these relationships alone brings us immediately to an important conclusion. Empirical investigations of the shape of the yield curve[16] show that the curve invariably flattens out as term to maturity is extended. We have shown that the price risks inherent in holding long-term bonds over a wide range of maturities are roughly similar. Therefore, it is not surprising that these bonds, which are mathematically almost equivalent securities in terms of potential price fluctuations, will sell in the market at roughly similar yields. Conversely, in the short and inter-

---

[14] Frederick R. Macaulay has argued that years to maturity is a very inadequate measure of the true length of a loan. It tells only the date of the final payment and nothing about the size and frequency of all intermediate payments. In the case of a very long-term bond, the importance of the maturity date may be so small as to be negligible. Macaulay uses the term "duration" to describe the true length of the bond. The duration of any loan is simply the weighted average of the maturities of the individual loans that correspond to each future payment. The present values of the individual payments are used as weights. As bonds lengthen in time to maturity, true length or duration increases at a decreasing rate. A 25-year bond is surprisingly little different from a 50-year bond, but a 6-year bond is approximately twice as long as a 3-year issue. This is consistent with and helps explain the actual price relationships described by our theorems. Cf. Frederick R. Macaulay, *Some Theoretical Problems Suggested by the Movements of Interest Rates, Bond Yields and Stock Prices in the United States Since 1856*. (New York: National Bureau of Economic Research, 1938), pp. 44–53.

[15] Another important factor is the tax implication of bond discounts. The effective after-tax yield to maturity is much larger for a discount bond selling at a given yield to maturity than for a bond selling at par with the same pre-tax yield. In the case of the discount bond, part of the yield to maturity is taxed at preferential capital-gains rates. In addition, the remoteness of possible call features lends added attraction to deep-discount bonds.

[16] A graphic device used for examining the relationship between the yield and term to maturity of comparable debt securities.

TABLE 1. SELECTED PRICE DATA FOR A BOND WITH NOMINAL YIELD (i_0) 3 PERCENT*

Years to Maturity (N)	Price (P) to Yield 4 Percent (i) to Maturity	Loss Incurred if Market Yields Rise from i_0 to 4 Percent (Percent)	Marginal Loss Incurred by Extending Maturity One Additional Year (Percent)	Price (P) to Yield 2 Percent (i) to Maturity	Gain Realized if Market Yields Fall from i_0 to 2 Percent (Percent)	Marginal Gain Realized by Extending Maturity One Additional Year (Percent)
1	99.029	.971	.971	100.985	.985	.985
2	98.096	1.904	.933	101.951	1.951	.966
4	96.337	3.663	.862	103.826	3.826	.928
8	93.211	6.789	.736	107.359	7.359	.857
16	88.266	11.734	.536	113.635	13.635	.731
32	82.039	17.961	.285	123.551	23.551	.531
64	76.982	23.018	.080	136.009	36.009	.281
Consol	75.000	25.000	.000	150.000	50.000	.000

* All examples assume semiannual compounding.

mediate areas of the yield curve, the extension of maturity even for a few years implies considerably different price risks and opportunities for capital gains. Thus it is reasonable to expect that these areas of the yield curve are the ones which will exhibit the more dramatic responses to changes in expectations.[17] We shall show this result specifically in our analytical models which follow.

III. EXPECTATIONS AND THE TERM STRUCTURE OF RATES

We now approach the very difficult area of expectations. Fortunately, our *modus operandi* enables us to move gingerly at first. We shall begin by introducing the theoretical construct "the expected normal range of interest rates." This range will be defined in terms of the level rather than the structure of rates. Our problem is one of finding some correspondence between our *ex ante* theoretical construct and the observable *ex post* empirical data at our disposal, i.e., the historical level of rates.[18] As a first approximation, the aggregate of individuals comprising the "market" will be assumed to believe that the historical range of interest rates will prevail in the future. We shall assume, in the examples which follow, that the expected normal range for government bonds is roughly between 2 percent and 5 percent.

First, let us suppose that interest rates for securities of all maturities are fixed at $4\frac{1}{2}$ percent by an arbitrary decree of a *deus ex machina*. For simplicity, we shall consider that all bonds carry coupons of $4\frac{1}{2}$ percent and, therefore, the prices of all securities are fixed at par. Now, in stages, we shall examine the effects of removing completely all controls from the market. In the first stage, we shall assume the "market" has formed no expectation as to whether bond prices will rise or fall. However, in consonance with our construct of the normal range, investors are well aware of the fact that this level of rates leaves less to be feared than hoped. The worst situation that could confront an investor is for him to suffer a rise in interest rates to 5 percent. On the other hand, rates could fall to 2 percent and still lie within the normal range. Historical interest rate movements would suggest, however, that such a drastic drop in the level of rates has been associated with secular rather than cyclical movements. Thus, investors could not reasonably anticipate that the lower end of the normal range would be realized within, say, one year. Under these circumstances we might believe that a plausible one-year normal range might be

[17] It is interesting to compare the above explanation with that offered by Lutz. To form a "shoulder," short rates would have to be expected to change in the near future and then reach a certain level where they would stay constant.

[18] Our method here follows that used by Milton Friedman, in *A Theory of the Consumption Function* (Princeton, N.J.: Princeton U.P., 1957), Ch. III.

between 5 percent and $3\frac{1}{2}$ percent. Any precise figures are really irrelevant. We simply wish to explore the effects of a subjective expectation of a normal range on the structure of rates. The critical assumption is that the investor has more to gain than to fear. Therefore, whatever the expected normal fluctuations for the coming year may be, our assumption demands that the "market" believe that these will be contained in a range where the lower limit is further from $4\frac{1}{2}$ percent than the upper limit. Again we must remind our reader, however, that investors have collectively made no judgment as to the likelihood of interest rates in general moving up or down.

Columns 2 through 5 of Table 2 summarize the resulting price action of bonds of varying maturities if yields should move to the extremities of the one-year normal range in one year.[19] Thus, investors collectively are faced with the matrix consisting of the array of percentage gains and losses (negative gains) contained in columns 3 and 5, which we can call states of nature A and B. We next assume, as a first approximation, that utility is linear in gains. Furthermore, we postulate that investors' preferences can be represented by a von Neumann-Morgenstern utility index. We may now choose that particular relationship where the utility numbers are made equal to the gains.[20] There are at least two grounds upon which one could quarrel with this assumption. In the first place, it is doubtful that utility is linear in money. Second, and in addition to the diminishing utility of money payoffs, it is well known that losses are especially unpleasant. Thus on both counts losses will be more negatively preferred than equivalent gains are desirable, particularly for institutional investing officers. We shall examine later the implications of relaxing this assumption of linearity but, as an initial approximation, we feel justified in considering that the unadjusted gains and losses make up the game matrix facing our collective investor.

We may now proceed to consider this situation as a classical example of a game against nature. The investor must choose among several acts (i.e., the array of maturities available to him) where the desirability of each act depends on the state of nature which will prevail. We have postulated that the decision-maker believes that one state of nature (i.e., either A or B) will exist, but he does not know the relative probabilities of each. The standard literature on decision theory suggests a group of criteria to

[19] Note that we have substituted a one-year outlook for the long-run horizon implied by the Lutz theory. Expectations, to the extent that they are made concerning the likelihood of interest rate changes, are often very vague beyond the near future. Moreover, the one-year horizon is consistent with the practices of institutional bond investors.

[20] Cf. John von Neumann and Oskar Morgenstern, *Theory of Games and Economic Behavior*, 3d ed. (Princeton, N.J.: Princeton U.P., 1953), pp. 15–31. The index chosen has minus 100 as its zero point. Minus 100 is the worst possible outcome. The investor cannot lose more than his investment. No such limitation exists for his gains.

TABLE 2.   ASSUMED 4½ PERCENT BONDS

N	Market Price of Bond if Interest Rates Rise to 5 Percent in One Year*	Resulting Price Appreciation (Percent)	Market Price of Bond if Interest Rates Fall to 3½ Percent in One Year	Resulting Price Appreciation (Percent)	Mathematical Expectation of Gain (p: A, B) p = .50	Market Prices Equalizing Mathematical Expectation of Gain (Col. 6) among Maturities	Derived Structure of Rates from Col. 7	Derived Structure of Rates (p: A, B) p = .25
1	2	3	4	5	6	7	8	9
		A		B				
1	100.†	—	100.†	—	—	100.00	4.50	4.50
1½	99.76	−.24	100.49	+.49	+.13	100.13	4.41	4.29
2	99.52	−.48	100.97	+.97	+.25	100.25	4.37	4.18
5	98.21	−1.79	103.70	+3.70	+.96	100.96	4.28	3.98
10	96.41	−3.59	107.66	+7.66	+2.04	102.04	4.25	3.91
20	93.91	−6.09	113.79	+13.79	+3.85	103.85	4.21	3.86
50	90.89	−9.11	123.35	+23.35	+7.12	107.12	4.16	3.82
Consol	90.00	−10.00	128.66	+28.66	+9.33	109.33	4.12	3.78

* I.e., Price in one year to yield 5 percent from "present plus one year" to maturity.
† In one year a one-year security matures at par.

deal with these types of problems.[21] The theoretical justification for using any one of these is shaky. We shall select the Laplace principle of insufficient reason to solve the game matrix.[22] This criterion asserts that since the decision-maker is ignorant of the probabilities of the different possible states of nature, he should treat them all as equally likely. He will then assign to each act A_i its expected utility index

$$\frac{U_{i1} + \cdots + U_{in}}{n}$$

and choose that act with the largest index. In our case, which has only two states of nature, this is equivalent to attaching a probability of .50 to each state.

Unfortunately, from an empirical point of view, this principle is confronted with serious difficulties. There is really an infinite number of states of nature which could be regarded as "equally likely." For example, yields might remain unchanged, rise 0.5 percent, fall 0.5 percent, etc. Why should the extremes of our one-year normal range be singled out as the natural parametrization of the states for which this criterion is appropriate? Our answer is simply that for our purposes it makes no difference which states of nature we select so long as they conform to our critical assumption which demands that for states to be equally likely they must leave the investor more to hope than fear. By selecting the extremes of the possible range of price movements we achieve the same results as would be obtained by using the uniform distribution over the entire range. The narrower is the expected range of fluctuations, the smaller will be the derived yield differentials. But the differences in results will be only differences in degree. If, however, investors believe that there will be no range of fluctuation during the coming year then the derived yield curve would be horizontal, which is precisely what we would expect.

We may now proceed quickly to some results. Column 6 of Table 2 presents the mathematical expectation of gain for each maturity. Longer-term securities are clearly more desirable to our collective investor than

[21] Cf. John W. Milnor, "Games Against Nature," Thrall, Coombs and Davis, *Decision Processes* (New York, N.Y.: John Wiley and Sons, 1957), pp. 49–60; or R. Duncan Luce and Howard Raiffa, *Games and Decisions* (New York, N.Y.: John Wiley and Sons, 1957), pp. 275–326.

[22] The Hurwicz solution which utilizes a subjective "optimism-pessimism index" is inconsistent with our assumption that our representative investor has made no judgment as to the likelihood of interest rates moving up or down. Applying the Wald "maximin" criterion is tantamount to saying that normal backwardation will always force the investors to buy the shortest security available if there exists any possibility of loss. Similarly, the Savage "minimax regret" criterion would lead investors to confine their purchases toward the long end of the yield curve. These latter two criteria may be rejected on empirical grounds as not being in accord with the normal behavior of bond investors.

short-term issues.[23] Hence the bond market will not remain at the equilibrium which was formerly imposed upon it by decree. Assuming that the prices of long-term securities are bid up to remove the differences in opportunities for gain among maturities, the prices listed in Column 7 will be realized in the market.[24] At these prices, the derived yields to maturity listed in Column 8 will represent the new equilibrium term structure of rates.[25] There will be no net tendency to shift from one maturity to another from a partial equilibrium-comparative statics point of view.[26] We have, therefore, explained a descending term structure of interest rates when the level of rates is near the upper limit of its normal range. Expectations have been introduced only to the extent of assuming that the normal range of the past will also continue into the future. Our major tool has been an analysis of the mathematics of bond prices. We find that an analysis of potential market-price changes can provide important insights into the behavior of yields of securities with different terms to maturity.

Having started with almost complete uncertainty as the foundation of our analytical model, it is now incumbent on us to introduce expectations in a less passive manner. We suggest that if interest rates appear to be high relative to the normal range, investors may also attach a higher subjective probability to that state of nature in which interest rates fall. This transforms our game matrix from a game against nature into the domain of decision-making under risk. We can now associate with state of nature A, the probability p, and with state B, the probability $(1 - p)$. The new utility index becomes $U_{iA}(p) + U_{iB}(1 - p)$ and again the decision-maker will choose that act having the maximum utility index. If we assume that the "market" attaches a probability of .75 to the state of nature in which rates fall, Column 9 presents the new derived yield-

---

[23] One additional element serving to dampen potential price fluctuations of short-term securities should be noted. The passage of time changes the maturity of the security and thus diminishes the issue's characteristic price fluctuations. The passage of one year cuts the potential volatility of a two-year bond approximately in half.

[24] There are, of course, several ways in which the market could equalize the mathematical expectation of gain among maturities. We shall return to this point.

[25] We should actually equalize the (discounted) value of the expected price appreciation (depreciation) and the coupons to be received during the holding period, all as a percentage of the purchase price paid for the bond. In our examples we have eliminated the entire mathematical expectation of gain (loss) but the value of the two coupons as a percentage of the market price of the securities will not be equalized. Our approximation was used to permit simplicity of computation. The differences in the derived yield are generally in the order of magnitude of .01 percent and therefore have no effect on our results.

[26] We must assume, however, that investors' expectations as to what constitutes the normal one-year range are tied to the level of the one-year short rate and are, therefore, unchanged. Otherwise, the structure of rates derived after the process of adjustment is likely to set up changed expectations concerning the one-year normal range and further adjustments would be required. This restriction is not, in general, necessary, as we shall later show.

maturity curve. We notice that the expectations introduced have made the curve more sharply descending then before. Nevertheless, the new curve shows the same tendency to level out as term to maturity is extended.

Table 3 describes a similar case starting from an initial fixed interest rate level of $2\frac{1}{2}$ percent for all maturities. All bonds are assumed to bear a $2\frac{1}{2}$ percent coupon. Analogously to our first example, the one-year normal range is postulated to be between 2 percent and $3\frac{1}{2}$ percent. In this case, investors have more to fear than hope. The result (Column 8) is an ascending structure of rates which becomes flat for long-term maturities. One curious result should be noted. We find that our theoretical apparatus indicates that a consol should yield less than a 50-year dated issue despite the fact that the general shape of the yield curve is ascending. This is not a peculiarity of the particular numerical example chosen. The same result will be obtained for any p, $.01 \leq p \leq 1$, i.e., except where there is essentially no prospect for gain. This "anomaly" results solely from the mathematics of bond prices.[27] Furthermore, our finding is consistent with the empirical evidence. British consols have typically sold to yield less than long-term dated issues irrespective of the general shape of the yield curve.[28] It is one of the strengths of our theory that it is consistent with some of the more bizarre relationships of the yield curve.

Let us now push our expectational analysis one step further. Empirical evidence discloses that short-term interest rates have exhibited a greater volatility than long-term rates. Indeed, our theoretical apparatus indicates that this must occur because investor expectations will cause an ascending curve to be formed when interest rates are low relative to the historical range and a descending curve when rates are relatively high. Therefore, we are neither begging the question nor guilty of circular reasoning if we include in our expectations the belief that long-term interest rates will fluctuate less than do short rates. Thus, instead of assuming that 2 percent will be the lower limit to which all interest rates can fall, we could hypothesize that short rates would fall .75 percent to 1.75 percent but long rates would decline only .25 percent to 2.25 percent. Similarly, for the upper limit we shall allow short rates to rise to 4 percent while long rates rise to 3.50 percent. Intermediate rates would be scaled accordingly between the two limits. All other assumptions remain identical with those in our pre-

---

[27] This relationship can be explained with the aid of Theorem 4: Note that the asymmetry of bond price movements provides a natural cushion limiting a consol's potential price decline whereas no such restraint exists to dampen the consol's possible price appreciation (cf. Columns 3 and 5 for a 50-year and perpetual bond). Thus, even though the mathematical expectation of loss (Column 6) is greatest for a perpetual bond, it is not so great as Theorem 2 would require to equalize the derived yields of Column 8 (cf. Columns 4 and 7 for a 50-year and perpetual bond).

[28] We do not suggest that this can be entirely explained by the mathematics of differential potential price actions. Undoubtedly another powerful determinant is the greater protection from call offered by the deeper discount.

TABLE 3. ASSUMED 2½ PERCENT COUPON BONDS

N	Market Price of Bond if Interest Rates Fall to 2 Percent in One Year	Resulting Price Appreciation (Percent)	Market Price of Bond if Interest Rates Rise to 3½ Percent in One Year	Resulting Price Appreciation (Percent)	Mathematical Expectation of Gain $(p: A, B)$ $p = .25$	Market Prices Which Equalize Mathematical Expectation of Gain (Col. 6) among Maturities	Derived Structure of Rates from Col. 7	Derived Structure with Expectation of Greater Fluctuations in Short Rates
1	2	3	4	5	6	7	8	9
		A		B				
1	100.00	—	100.00	—	—	100.00	2.50	2.50
1½	100.25	+.25	99.51	−.49	−.31	99.69	2.71	2.76
2	100.49	+.49	99.03	−.97	−.61	99.39	2.81	2.87
5	101.91	+1.91	96.30	−3.70	−2.30	97.70	3.00	3.09
10	104.10	+4.10	92.34	−7.66	−4.72	95.28	3.05	3.15
20	107.87	+7.87	86.21	−13.79	−8.38	91.62	3.06	3.15
50	115.57	+15.57	76.65	−23.35	−13.62	86.38	3.03	3.12
Consol	125.00	+25.00	71.40	−28.60	−15.20	84.80	2.95	3.07

vious illustrations. We find in Column 9, Table 3, that an ascending yield curve is again formed, but in this case it traces a more sharply upward course than in our previous example. This is an important qualification to the expectational theory. To the extent that institutional rigidities lead to relatively greater volatility in short rates, it is not true that the activities of arbitrageurs will necessarily work in the direction of smoothing these additional yield fluctuations. It is far more likely that the market will recognize these tendencies and that these expectations will tend to be self-fulfilling.[29]

IV. ALTERING SOME OF THE ASSUMPTIONS

Let us now examine the effects of altering certain of the explicit and implicit assumptions contained in our analysis. We have alluded to some of these in passing. First, let us assume that the investors' utility functions weigh losses more heavily than equivalent gains. This will have the effect of making the slope of ascending yield curves steeper and the slope of the descending curves flatter. The basic shapes of the curves in our examples will, in general, not be changed even by making fairly substantial adjustments in the game matrix.[30] This does suggest, however, that it is somewhat more difficult for descending curves to be formed and may be offered as a partial explanation for the somewhat greater number of ascending curves which are found in the historical data. Thus we find that the Keynes-Hicks analysis easily can be incorporated into our theoretical apparatus. We suggest, however, that the hypothesis of a "normal relationship" can be supported neither by our analytical model nor by the empirical evidence.

Next, we might relax the assumption of the invariance of the normal range. Is it not plausible that investors' expectations will be influenced to a greater degree by the more immediate past? Thus, when interest rates have been low for a considerable period of time, investors will come to reduce their idea of a normal range. The effect of this suggestion is to make it possible for expectations to form a descending curve at a lower level of interest rates (when rates in the immediate past have been par-

[29] Of course, we have implicitly assumed in our analytical model that sufficient flexibility exists in the maturity needs of different investors to make arbitrage possible. We do not disagree that institutional impediments to perfect mobility do exist to a sufficient degree that any expectational theory must be modified. Nevertheless, the considerable amount of interchangeability between the maturity sectors which exists on both the demand and supply sides of the debt market can be easily underestimated. Even if the maturity needs of many classes of financial institutions are rigid, maturity indifference on the part of a small number of investors and issuers may be sufficient to prevent serious market segmentation, and independence in the behavior of different segments of the yield curve.

[30] For example, if in the game matrix presented in Table 2 we double the negative utility values of all losses, we still obtain a descending yield curve which falls from 4.50 percent to 4.31 percent (for $p = .50$).

ticularly low) than would be possible had proximate rates been at a higher level. Thus, for example, the yield curve on governments in late 1957 descended gently at a level of interest rates of about 3.90 percent. Yet, during the early summers of 1960–61 when the level of rates was again at 3.90 percent, the curve was either relatively flat or rising. One difference was that investors in 1960–61 had become accustomed to a significantly higher level of interest rates and, therefore, their expectations as to what would constitute a normal range of rates were considerably changed from those extant in 1957.[31]

In our examples we have employed only two illustrative values of p, .50 and .75. If investors attach a probability greater than .75 to the possibility that bond prices will rise (fall), a more sharply descending (ascending) curve will result. And if coupons on existing maturities are not all identical, we can expect differing price reactions, all of which will obey Theorem 5. These price reactions will then alter the yield-maturity pattern, for bonds will now be more or less attractive to the investor depending upon their coupons. This is one reason for the many kinks which exist in the yield curve for government securities.[32] Only a model cast in terms of price changes can deal effectively with this type of adjustment. The introduction of considerations such as call features and the special tax advantages of discount bonds strengthens our analytical findings. When interest rates fall to low levels, many long-term bonds rise in price to where they sell at premiums over their call prices. This diminishes their attractiveness and tends to raise the yields of these long-term securities. Alternatively, high interest rates and accompanying low bond prices free the bondholder from call risks and deep bond discounts lend added attraction because of their higher effective after-tax yields.

[31] Expectational theories have often been criticized on the basis of an empirical analysis of holding-period yields. We have derived hypothetical rate structures assuming that investors will act in such a way that the mathematical expectations of gain or loss are equalized among maturities.

But even if an expectational analysis constructed in this manner could provide a complete explanation of the actual rate structure in the market, empirical investigations would not, in general, show that holding-period yields are identical for securities of different terms to maturity. Only in the unusual event that yields move exactly to the limits set by the mathematical expectation of our collective investor will holding-period yields be equalized. Since the mathematical expectation is compounded out of several variables, including individual attitudes toward risk aversion, past interest rates, expected future rates, etc., a resulting equality of holding-period yields should hardly be expected.

[32] The reader is cautioned to consider that even for governments, the most similar group of securities, there is a myriad of special features inherent in individual issues which may also alter their yield relationship, e.g., optional maturities on many issues differentiate them in the minds of the buyers. Other securities may be "put" to the Treasury at the option of the holder. Some issues are partially tax exempt. Most, when owned by a decedent and part of his estate, are redeemable at par for payments of federal estate taxes irrespective of the current market price. Finally, prices of maturing issues are often influenced by possible exchange privileges at call or maturity.

Finally, let us consider alternative methods of equalizing the mathematical expectation of gain among securities of various maturities. In our examples, we equalized opportunities for gain by eliminating them, i.e., we allowed all bond prices to rise or fall so that the entire expectation of differential gain was removed. It is interesting to examine what would happen if investors sold shorts and bought longs when prices were expected to rise. In this case short-term bond prices would fall and long-term prices would rise less than in our examples. The resulting level of rates would be higher than in our example solution. Furthermore, it can be shown that the yield curve would become steeper because even small price declines in the short-term area would have a greater effect in raising short yields than the smaller increases in price in the long-term area would tend to raise long yields.[33]

We have no quarrel with the position taken by Culbertson and others that changes in the maturity structure of the supply of debt instruments are important determinants of the rate structure. One should not expect that arbitrage would neutralize their effect.[34] It is useful, however, to look behind these changes, to examine the possible role which expectations may play in causing those disturbances which are claimed to impede expectations on the demand side from determining the shape of the yield curve. An analysis of the introduction of expectations to the supply side of the market is completely analogous to our previous argument. If issuers of securities believe that interest rates are relatively high compared with their expectations of what constitutes a normal range, they will tend, to whatever extent possible, to issue short-term securities rather than longer bonds. Conversely, if rates appear attractive, issuers will take advantage of the opportunity and issue long-term securities. The motivation of issuers cannot be cast in terms of price risks but must rather be explained by considering the desire to minimize long-run financing costs. Most Secretaries of the Treasury have placed the objective of minimizing the cost of debt service among the primary goals of prudent debt management. Similarly, corporate treasurers are keenly aware of the cost of debt capital and

---

[33] When we allow alternative methods of equalizing mathematical expectations of gains and losses we need no longer assume that the one-year normal range is tied to the level of the one-year short rate (cf. footnote 26). If investors are allowed to arbitrage by selling shorts and buying longs when yields were expected to fall, then the level of rates (assuming it is a function of both long and short rates) may not be changed after the adjustment. Short rates will be higher but long rates will be lower so that the one-year normal range may remain unchanged and therefore no further adjustment is required. If we assume that the level of rates (and, therefore, the one-year range) does change, we cannot a priori tell whether it will be higher or lower and, consequently, it is impossible to make any definite statement about the secondary adjustments in the term structure which will occur.

[34] As we have mentioned, impediments to perfect arbitrage do exist. Moreover, the actual or potential increase in supply itself changes the expected normal range for any maturity area.

attempt to time their trips to the long-term capital market to avoid, insofar as possible, periods of high interest rates.[35]

I believe a careful examination of the empirical evidence would indicate that long-term borrowing and refunding are, to an important extent, postponable, thus allowing expectations to exert considerable influence. There is a tendency for a high level of interest rates to have a self-regulating influence on the supply of new long-term issues. During periods of relatively high long-term interest rates the Treasury has seldom floated long bonds despite its desire to lengthen the maturity of the debt.[36] "Poor" market conditions have also tended to remove many corporations from the capital markets. They may postpone coming to the market and may meet their immediate needs by drawing down their liquid assets or by short-term borrowings from commercial banks and other lenders. Similarly, state and local governments often have found it difficult to enter the long-term market during periods of stress, whereas they have responded to reduced levels of long-term rates by accelerating the financing of construction programs. Thus the introduction of expectations on the supply side of the market has the effect of dampening the fluctuations in long-term rates while causing additional pressures in the short-term sector as both the Treasury and corporations finance their needs with bills and certificates, on the one hand, and bank loans on the other.

The pressures on the bond market from both the demand and supply side are reinforcing in their effect. When interest rates are believed to be high in relation to historical precedent, investors will prefer to buy long-term bonds while issuers will prefer to sell short-term securities. Conversely, low interest rates will encourage investors to buy shorts and issuers to sell longs. We have opened, with care, the Pandora box of expectations and the direction, if not the magnitude, of their effect is unambiguous. Perhaps we may be charged with the Hicksian accusation that this leaves the rate of interest uncomfortably hanging by its own bootstraps.[37] We can only answer, with Mrs. Robinson, that the price today of any long-lived object with negligible carrying costs must be strongly influenced by expectations about what its price will be in the future.[38] If the rate of interest hangs by its own bootstraps, so does the price of a Miró painting.

---

[35] Curiously, the desire to minimize interest costs may not be their most important motivation. There is also a definite stigma attached to the financial reputation of corporations which have included in their capitalizations securities which bear such high interest coupons that they are considered "undignified."

[36] During 1959 and early 1960, the Treasury was prevented from issuing securities with a maturity longer than five years because of the $4\frac{1}{4}$ percent interest ceiling on these issues.

[37] Hicks, *op. cit.*, p. 164.

[38] Joan Robinson, *op. cit.*, p. 103.

V. CONCLUDING REMARKS

It will now be useful to summarize our findings and underline the advantages of the model which has been presented. First, we have shown that an explicit examination of theoretical bond price movements takes us a good part of the way toward understanding the observable structure of market interest rates. The inevitable tendency of the yield curve to flatten out as term to maturity is extended was explained and later demonstrated. Next we derived from our model an ascending and descending yield curve with behavioral assumptions far less demanding than in the Lutz theory. In fact, expectations were introduced only to the extent that future interest-rate fluctuations were anticipated to be contained within the range which has existed in the past. At a level of interest rates close to the upper end of the historical range we could explain a descending yield curve even where investors have formed no expectations as to the probable direction of interest-rate changes. When later we introduced stronger elements of foresight, our model had the advantage of being in closer conformity with the practices of bond investors who had always considered the Lutz theory chimerical. Furthermore, the Keynes-Hicks modifications were easily assimilated into the analytical framework. Finally, our model could be modified to take account of differences in yield which result from coupon differences, call features, tax advantages of discount bonds and institutional rigidities as they might apply to a particular maturity area. Thus, at least we have clothed the traditional expectational theory with new raiments which fit more closely the investing practices of bond investors and make the theory both simpler in its assumptions, and more tractable to modification. Hopefully, we have also gained added insights into the behavior of yields of securities with different terms to maturity.

*Lawrence Fisher**
James H. Lorie†

21. Rates of Return on Investments in Common Stocks[1]

Reprinted, in abridged form, from **The Journal of Business of the University of Chicago,** Vol. XXXVII, No. 1 (January, 1964), pp. 1–9, by permission of the authors and the University of Chicago Press. Copyright, 1964, by the University of Chicago.

This article presents data on rates of return on investments in common stocks. It answers the question of how much gain or loss an individual investor might have realized if he had bought all New York Stock Exchange common stocks—at five different dates and held them for varying lengths of time during the 35 years from 1926–60, a total of 22 time periods. This work is the first to emerge from the Center for Research in Security Prices (sponsored by Merrill Lynch, Pierce, Fenner & Smith Inc.). For that reason we shall describe the facilities and plans of the Center before presenting the results and methods of its first research.

I. THE CENTER FOR RESEARCH IN SECURITY PRICES

Purpose

The sole purpose of the Center for Research in Security Prices is to conduct research and to disseminate the results throughout the academic and financial communities. This is what Merrill Lynch, Pierce, Fenner & Smith Inc. had in mind when they provided the funds to establish the

* Professor of Finance and Associate Director of the Center for Research in Security Prices, Graduate School of Business, University of Chicago.

† Professor of Business Administration and Director of the Center for Research in Security Prices, Graduate School of Business, University of Chicago.

[1] Funds to support the work reported in this article came primarily from Merrill Lynch, Pierce, Fenner & Smith Inc. Support also came from the Graduate School of Business through funds granted by the Ford Foundation. In addition, the work was supported by the National Science Foundation through their grant to the Computation Center of the University of Chicago. We also would like to acknowledge the invaluable help of Frederick J. Meier and Milton Davis in the collection of data and the direct assistance of at least 19 computer programmers, most notably that of Sergius Kunitzky, Ann Walinski Loidl, Daniel I. Rosenfels, Lee H. Hook, and Haym L. Rabinovitz.

Center, and this is what the Graduate School of Business had in mind when it sought support.

Despite the enormous quantities of available data on security prices and related things, the amount of scientific research based on these data is inadequate for many purposes. As a result, a number of controversies and unresolved issues about security prices have continued. For example, there is controversy about whether successive changes in the prices of common stocks are statistically independent or are serially correlated. If the former is true, technical analysis such as that based on the Dow Theory is not likely to be helpful; if the latter is true, regularities in the patterns of change can be detected by appropriate analysis.

Another controversy revolves about the question of what effect, if any, dividends exert on stock prices. Some feel that only earnings matter and that payout ratios are therefore of no consequence. Others feel that the declaration of a dollar dividend affects the price of a stock differently from a dollar of earnings retained. This matter is of great consequence to American corporations, but the issue remains unresolved.

Another difficult problem is the subject of stock market averages. Averages are a lot like the weather in that everyone talks about them—usually with dissatisfaction—but no one does anything. It is time that a serious effort be made to devise averages which do more than report descriptively the movement of some stock prices.

Many people would like to have more detailed and refined information regarding the relationship of movements in stock prices to changes of other sorts in the economy. More work needs to be done on the relationships between earnings and prices and on the relevance of balance sheet data in understanding and predicting the financial fate of corporations.

The Center for Research in Security Prices will work on all of the problems mentioned above and many others. It is intended to be a permanent institution which will work as rapidly as financial resources and the imagination and abilities of research workers will permit. The facilities of the Center will be available not only to the faculty and graduate students of the University of Chicago but also to persons at other educational institutions and in the financial community who have serious problems for which the Center's facilities can be helpful. The Center's facilities will be described below.

Facilities

In March, 1960, Merrill Lynch, Pierce, Fenner & Smith Inc., made an initial grant of $50,000 to the University of Chicago to establish the Center for Research in Security Prices. The initial funds and additional resources equivalent to more than $150,000 have been used to establish a "laboratory" consisting of a very large volume of data on security prices and related things appropriately arranged and stored on computer tape. These data together with appropriate computer programs, make possible a large variety and number of analyses of security prices, of their determinants, and of their relationships to other things in the economy.

SECURITY PRICES. Monthly closing prices of all common stocks on the New York Stock Exchange from January, 1926, through December, 1960, have been placed on tape. Their accuracy has been appraised in several ways, and, after three years of checking and rechecking, it is estimated that the incidence of error is extremely low and that remaining errors do not bias the results.

Further, there are on tape—though at present in less useful form— daily high, low, and closing prices of all common stocks on the New York Stock Exchange from July 1, 1960, to the present. This information is being kept up to date, but has not yet been integrated with the file on monthly prices; and its accuracy has not been tested adequately.

CAPITAL CHANGES. In order for the information on security prices to be useful for refined analyses, it is essential that information be recorded on all types of capital changes. This has been done. Such changes include, for example, cash dividends, stock dividends, stock splits, rights, exchange of shares, etc. One way to summarize the data that have been placed on tape is to say that almost all pertinent information in the Commerce Clearing House series, *Capital Changes Reporter*, has been coded, checked for possible error, and placed on tape. The accuracy of these data has been exhaustively checked.

An additional comment is warranted on the treatment of cash dividends. Where available, four dates are recorded for each dividend: (1) the date of declaration, (2) the ex-dividend date, (3) the date of record, and (4) the date of payment. Further, the tax status for each dividend is recorded; there are seven different tax categories.

OTHER DATA. A wide variety of national economic statistics has been coded and is ready to go on tape. These data cover such things as commodity prices, interest rates, industrial production, and national income.

For each period for which there is a security price, data on trading volume have also been recorded.

Data on earnings have been placed on IBM cards and ultimately will be transferred to tape. This information is in the form reported by the company and requires extensive adjustment before its use for refined analysis will be worthwhile.

Plans for the future

It is planned to keep the basic file of information up to date and to include new data of various kinds, depending on the projects that the

Center undertakes. Undoubtedly there will be experimentation with balance sheet data, and certainly an effort will be made to include data on securities other than common stocks listed on the New York Stock Exchange. Priority will be given to research of general interest, but other projects will also be undertaken.

II. RATES OF RETURN ON INVESTMENTS IN COMMON STOCKS

It is surprising to realize that there have been no measurements of the rates of return on investments in common stocks that could be considered accurate and definitive. There have been many efforts, but each has been deficient in at least one crucial respect. Some have lacked comprehensiveness, having dealt only with a selection of individual securities such as those in one of the popular stock market averages. This study embraces all common stocks listed on the New York Stock Exchange during the time periods covered—some 1700 of them. Again, earlier studies have dealt only with one or two brief time periods in contrast to the 22 time periods within a 35-year span covered here. Finally, all other studies have been deficient because they have ignored taxes and transaction costs. In this study actual New York Stock Exchange round-lot commission rates, as they existed on all purchase, sale, and re-investment dates, have been included in the calculations; and all federal taxes, as they applied to income from dividends or capital gains at specific times in selected tax brackets, have been taken into consideration. As can be seen from Tables 1 and 2, taxes and commissions can have large effects on rates of return. This study has shortcomings, but we believe that they are less pronounced than those of previous work.

Rates of return with reinvestment of dividends

Table 1 shows the results of investing an equal sum of money in each company having one or more issues of common stock listed on the New York Stock Exchange at the beginning of each period *and* of reinvesting dividends as received throughout the periods in the stock of the company making the payment. The results referred to thus include dividends and capital appreciation. Stocks listed at the beginning of any time period receive equal weight. A stock listed after the beginning and before the end of a particular time period is included whenever holders of other stocks receive its shares and also to whatever extent funds for reinvestment become available through the delisting of stocks that still possess value. To be more specific, when a stock is delisted, it is sold over the

TABLE 1. RATES OF RETURN ON INVESTMENT IN COMMON
STOCKS LISTED ON THE NEW YORK STOCK EXCHANGE
WITH REINVESTMENT OF DIVIDENDS*
(Percent per annum compounded annually)

	Income Class					
	Tax Exempt		$10,000 in 1960		$50,000 in 1960	
Period	Cash-to-Portfolio†	Cash-to-Cash‡	Cash-to-Portfolio	Cash-to-Cash	Cash-to-Portfolio	Cash-to-Cash
1/26–12/60	8.8	8.7	8.2	7.9	7.2	6.6
1/26–9/29	20.3	20.2	20.3	20.2	20.3	19.4
1/26–6/32	−17.2	−17.3	−17.2	−17.3	−17.1	−13.8
1/26–12/40	1.9	1.9	1.9	1.9	1.8	2.0
1/26–12/50	6.5	6.5	6.0	5.9	5.3	4.9
9/29–6/32	−48.8	−49.1	−48.8	−49.1	−48.7	−40.9
9/29–12/40	−3.1	−3.2	−3.1	−3.0	−3.2	−2.4
9/29–12/50	4.8	4.8	4.3	4.1	3.5	3.2
9/29–12/60	7.6	7.6	7.0	6.7	5.9	5.3
6/32–12/40	20.9	20.8	20.9	20.4	20.4	19.2
6/32–12/50	18.5	18.4	17.7	17.3	16.4	15.4
6/32–12/60	17.3	17.3	16.5	16.1	14.9	14.1
12/50–12/52	12.4	11.9	11.0	10.0	8.9	7.1
12/50–12/54	17.9	17.6	16.5	15.3	14.3	11.6
12/50–12/56	17.0	16.8	15.8	14.8	13.7	11.4
12/50–12/58	16.5	16.4	15.4	14.6	13.4	11.4
12/50–12/60	14.9	14.7	13.9	13.1	12.0	10.3
12/55–12/56	6.5	5.4	5.8	4.6	4.1	2.9
12/55–12/57	−3.7	−4.2	−4.4	−4.0	−6.0	−4.2
12/55–12/58	13.0	12.6	12.2	11.1	10.5	8.2
12/55–12/59	14.0	13.7	13.2	12.1	11.6	9.2
12/55–12/60	11.2	11.0	10.5	9.6	8.9	7.2

* Revised Table A1 reprinted with permission of the University of Chicago Press
from *The Journal of Business of the University of Chicago*, Vol. 41, No. 3 (July, 1968),
p. 314. Copyright 1968 by the University of Chicago.

† "Cash-to-Portfolio" means the net rate of return which would have been realized
after paying commissions and taxes (if any) on each transaction but continuing to hold
the portfolio at the end of each period.

‡ "Cash-to-Cash" means the net return which would have been realized after
paying commissions and taxes (if any) on each transaction including the sale of the
portfolio at the end of each period.

TABLE 2. RATES OF RETURN ON INVESTMENT IN COMMON
STOCKS LISTED ON THE NEW YORK STOCK EXCHANGE
WITHOUT REINVESTMENT OF DIVIDENDS*
(Percent per annum compounded annually)

| | Income Class | | | | | |
| | Tax Exempt | | $10,000 in 1960 | | $50,000 in 1960 | |
Period	Cash-to-Portfolio†	Cash-to-Cash‡	Cash-to-Portfolio	Cash-to-Cash	Cash-to-Portfolio	Cash-to-Cash
1/26–12/60	6.8	6.8	6.6	6.6	6.1	5.7
1/26–9/29	19.9	19.8	19.9	19.8	19.8	18.9
1/26–6/32	−13.8	−13.9	−13.8	−13.9	−13.8	−11.2
1/26–12/40	1.5	1.4	1.5	1.5	1.4	1.6
1/26–12/50	5.1	5.0	4.8	4.7	4.5	4.2
9/29–6/32	−48.7	−49.0	−48.7	−49.0	−48.5	−40.7
9/29–12/40	−4.9	−5.0	−4.9	−4.7	−4.8	−3.8
9/29–12/50	2.4	2.3	2.1	2.0	1.9	1.7
9/29–12/60	4.9	4.9	4.7	4.5	4.3	3.8
6/32–12/40	24.0	23.9	24.0	23.6	23.4	22.0
6/32–12/50	21.1	21.1	20.5	20.2	19.0	18.1
6/32–12/60	20.2	20.2	19.4	19.2	17.5	17.0
12/50–12/52	12.5	12.0	11.1	10.1	9.0	7.1
12/50–12/54	17.3	17.1	16.1	14.9	14.1	11.4
12/50–12/56	16.6	16.5	15.5	14.6	13.6	11.3
12/50–12/58	16.2	16.1	15.2	14.4	13.3	11.3
12/50–12/60	15.0	14.9	13.9	13.2	12.1	10.4
12/55–12/56	6.6	5.5	5.8	4.7	4.1	2.9
12/55–12/57	−3.3	−3.8	−4.1	−3.7	−5.8	−4.1
12/55–12/58	12.6	12.2	11.9	10.8	10.3	8.1
12/55–12/59	13.7	13.4	13.0	11.9	11.4	9.1
12/55–12/60	11.1	10.9	10.4	9.6	8.9	7.2

* Revised Table A2 reprinted with permission of the University of Chicago Press from *The Journal of Business of the University of Chicago*, Vol. 41, No. 3 (July, 1968), p. 315. Copyright 1968 by the University of Chicago.

† "Cash-to-Portfolio" means the net rate of return which would have been realized after paying commissions and taxes (if any) on each transaction but continuing to hold the portfolio at the end of each period.

‡ "Cash-to-Cash" means the net return which would have been realized after paying commissions and taxes (if any) on each transaction including the sale of the portfolio at the end of each period.

counter and the proceeds are spread evenly over all stocks listed on that date.

It should be emphasized that Table 1 represents the rates of re-turn—or rates of capital appreciation—that result from the adoption of only one of a large number of possible investment policies. An illustrative alternative would be the allocation of investment funds in proportion to the value of shares outstanding.

Except for the large amount of double-counting involved, this latter policy, in contrast to the one underlying Tables 1 and 2, would indicate the rates of return available to all the investors considered together.[2] That is, new investors as a group might be able to allocate funds among securi-ties in proportion to the value of shares outstanding but could not invest equal amounts in each security without changing many prices by a sub-stantial amount.

The decision to invest equal amounts in each company with common stock listed on the Exchange was based on the desire to calculate rates of return that would on the average be available to the individual investor who selected stocks at random with equal probabilities of selection—that is, exercised no judgment. A policy of allocating funds in proportion to shares outstanding or according to any other criterion implies less neu-trality of judgment in making investments.[3]

Since dividends constitute income, the results of reinvesting divi-dends would obviously vary with the individual investor's tax bracket. For the purposes of this study, three brackets were chosen, although any other set of tax rates could easily be substituted for those used.

The first category, "Tax Exempt," shows the rate of return that might have been realized by a tax exempt institution.

Results in the $10,000 income class were computed in the following manner:

1.   The marginal income tax rate as of 1960 was figured for a married man with standard deductions and an adjusted gross income of $10,000.

---

[2] By "double-counting" we mean the ownership by one company of stock in another listed company. For example, Du Pont owns large amounts of stock in General Motors. Allocation of investment funds in proportion to the value of Du Pont and General Motors stock outstanding involves counting some of the General Motors shares twice.

[3] We made an estimate of the rates of return available from investing in proportion to the value of shares outstanding by using the Standard and Poor's Index of Common Stocks on the New York Stock Exchange—an index weighted according to the value of shares outstanding—and the Standard and Poor's dividend series. For three of the five starting dates covered in Table 1, the Standard and Poor's rate of return was generally higher; for two of the starting dates, the yield was lower. No systematic differences were detectable, and on the average the yields based on the two different investment policies were similar.

2. For each previous year, a tax rate was determined for a man who held the same relative position in the pattern of income distribution existing in those years as the man with $10,000 income in 1960.
3. The appropriate tax rate for such a married man was then applied in all preceding years.

A precisely analogous procedure was used in computing results in the third category, the $50,000 income class.[4]

For each period in each income class, two rates of return are shown. The first, "Cash-to-Portfolio," shows the after-tax rate of interest, compounded annually, which an individual would have had to get on a sum equal to the gross purchase price of the portfolio at the beginning of a period in order to equal the value of the portfolio at the end of the period. The second figure, "Cash-to-Cash," indicates the rate of interest, compounded annually, that would be required on the value of the initial portfolio in order to equal the value of the sum at the terminal date after selling the portfolio and paying the commissions and the capital gains tax applicable.

These rates of return speak for themselves and require little comment. The periods were chosen for obvious reasons. The period from 1926 to 1960 is a long span with booms and depressions—prime examples of each!—and war and peace. The periods beginning in September, 1929, were included to indicate the experience of those who invested at the height of the stock market boom of the 1920's. The periods beginning in June, 1932, were included to show the results of investing at the nadir of this country's worst depression. The numerous brief, recent periods were included to bring details of postwar experience into sharp focus.

Aside from most periods ending in 1932 or 1940, the rates of return are surprisingly high. For half the 22 periods, the rates are above 10 percent per annum compounded annually; and for two-thirds of the periods, the rates exceed 6 percent.

Rates of return without reinvestment of dividends

Table 2 presents the rates of return on common stocks listed on the New York Stock Exchange with no reinvestment of dividends, that is, under the assumption that dividends are spent for consumer goods and services at the time they are received. The method of calculation is analogous to that used to compute the yield-to-maturity of a bond. The cost

[4] For example, men with incomes of $10,000 or $50,000 in 1960 would have had incomes of $1780 or $8950, respectively, in 1933. The ranges of marginal tax rates were from 0 to 25 percent for dividends for the $10,000 man and from 0 to 62 percent for the $50,000 man. The capital gains tax rates ranged from 0 to 13 percent for the $10,000 man and from 5 to 42 percent for the $50,000 man.

TABLE 3. RATES OF CHANGE IN VALUE OF INVESTMENT IN
COMMON STOCKS LISTED ON THE NEW YORK STOCK
EXCHANGE, IGNORING DIVIDENDS*
(Percent per annum compounded annually)

| | *Income Class* | | | | | |
| | *Tax Exempt* | | *$10,000 in 1960* | | *$50,000 in 1960* | |
Period	*Cash-to-Portfolio†*	*Cash-to-Cash‡*	*Cash-to-Portfolio*	*Cash-to-Cash*	*Cash-to-Portfolio*	*Cash-to-Cash*
1/26–12/60	3.9	3.9	3.9	3.6	4.0	3.3
1/26–9/29	16.1	16.0	16.1	16.0	16.1	15.2
1/26–6/32	−21.0	−21.1	−21.0	−21.1	−20.9	−17.6
1/26–12/40	−2.7	−2.8	−2.7	−2.7	−2.6	−2.3
1/26–12/50	1.5	1.5	1.5	1.3	1.7	1.3
9/29–6/32	−51.7	−52.0	−51.7	−52.0	−51.5	−43.5
9/29–12/40	−7.8	−7.9	−7.8	−7.5	−7.4	−6.3
9/29–12/50	−0.4	−0.4	−0.3	−0.4	0.0	−0.2
9/29–12/60	2.5	2.5	2.6	2.3	2.8	2.2
6/32–12/40	16.8	16.6	16.8	16.2	16.7	15.1
6/32–12/50	13.1	13.0	13.1	12.5	13.0	11.7
6/32–12/60	12.0	12.0	12.0	11.5	11.9	10.9
12/50–12/52	6.0	5.5	6.0	4.9	6.0	4.1
12/50–12/54	11.5	11.2	11.5	10.2	11.4	8.7
12/50–12/56	11.0	10.8	11.0	10.0	10.9	8.6
12/50–12/58	10.9	10.7	10.9	10.0	10.8	8.7
12/50–12/60	9.7	9.6	9.7	8.9	9.7	7.8
12/55–12/56	2.0	0.9	1.9	0.8	1.9	0.7
12/55–12/57	−8.0	−8.6	−8.1	−7.7	−8.1	−6.3
12/55–12/58	8.2	7.9	8.2	7.1	8.2	6.0
12/55–12/59	9.5	9.2	9.5	8.4	9.5	7.1
12/55–12/60	7.0	6.7	6.9	6.1	6.9	5.2

* Revised Table A3 reprinted with permission of the University of Chicago Press from *The Journal of Business of the University of Chicago*, Vol. 41, No. 3 (July, 1968), p. 316. Copyright 1968 by the University of Chicago.

† "Cash-to-Portfolio" means the net rate of change which would have been experienced after paying commissions and taxes (if any) on each transaction but continuing to hold the portfolio at the end of each period.

‡ "Cash-to-Cash" means the net change which would have been experienced after paying commissions and taxes (if any) on each transaction including the sale of the portfolio at the end of each period.

of the stock at the beginning of a time period is analogous to the purchase price of the bond; dividends are analogous to interest payments; and the value of the stock at the end of the period is analogous to the sum received by the holder of a bond when it matures. The rate of return is the rate of discounting which makes the stream of after-tax cash flows have a present value of zero.

At first, one might expect the rates in Table 2 to be significantly lower than in Table 1, whereas in fact the rates are quite similar for most of the periods. This similarity merely reflects the fact that the rate of appreciation in the prices of stocks after the receipt of dividends was on the average about the same as the rate of appreciation before the receipt of dividends. When the latter rate was higher, the rates in Table 2 are lower than those in Table 1 and vice versa. The individual who reinvests his dividends is obviously wealthier at an ending date than is the individual who spends them. On the average he also has a great deal more invested in his portfolio. Thus, some rates in Table 1 are higher than the corresponding rates in Table 2; some are lower; and several are the same.

Table 3 shows rate of capital appreciation or gain, ignoring dividends.

Comparison with other investment media

Comparable data for other investment media are not available, but there is some information on realized rates of return on a *before-tax* basis. The most nearly complete data are for savings in commercial banks, mutual savings banks, and savings and loan associations. Savings in these institutions never earned as much as 6 percent per annum for any of the 22 time periods listed in Table 1, and for most of the period 1926–60 earned less than 4 percent.[5]

Data on mortgage loans made by commercial banks and life insurance companies on nonfarm homes are available for 1920–47 and for some subperiods.[6] When all types of mortgages are considered together,

---

[5] Based on (1927–60) figures of U.S. Savings and Loan League *Fact Book*, 1955 and 1962 editions, whose sources are as follows: (1) (savings and loan associations) data of members of Federal Home Loan Bank System, (2) (mutual savings banks) National Association of Mutual Savings Banks, (3) (commercial banks) data of Board of Governors of the Federal Reserve System and Federal Deposit Insurance Corporation. The yields for these years were computed by dividing the total cash and credited dividends or interest by the average of deposits at the beginning and end of each year.
1926 figures: (savings and loan associations) R. W. Goldsmith, *A Study of Saving in the United States* (Princeton, N.J.: Princeton U.P., 1955), Vol. I, p. 447; and (savings and commercial banks) J. V. Lintner, *Mutual Savings Banks in the Savings and Mortgage Markets* (Boston, Mass.: Division of Research, Graduate School of Business Administration, Harvard University, 1948), p. 477.
[6] J. E. Morton, *Urban Mortgage Lending: Comparative Markets and Experience* (Princeton, N.J.: Princeton U.P., 1956), p. 114.

realized yields never exceeded 6 percent, never fell below 4 percent, and averaged about 5 percent.

Realized yields on municipal and U.S. government bonds, as indicated by Standard and Poor indexes, ranged from −7.0 to +7.8 percent and averaged less than 4 percent during the 22 time periods listed in Table 2.

Average realized yields on large issues of corporate bonds are available for 1900–58.[7] These yields ranged from −6 percent to just over 15 percent during periods from 1920–43. The very high yields were achieved during the recovery from the depression of 1929–32 when prices of industrial bonds, in particular, advanced sharply in price. During most periods, yields varied between 5 and 8 percent and in recent periods have been lower.

The fact that many persons choose investments with a substantially lower average rate of return than that available on common stocks suggests the essentially conservative nature of those investors and the extent of their concern about the risk of loss inherent in common stocks. And yet their experience with mortgage foreclosures during the 1930's and the substantial rate of default on bonds during the same period shows that even such "conservative" investments carry considerable risks.

The Center for Research in Security Prices is currently at work on another study that will focus more sharply on this question of risk in common stock ownership. While the present study is concerned with rates of return on common stocks for various periods, the above-mentioned study will seek to answer the questions of how often and how much the investor might have gained or lost on every stock listed on the New York Stock Exchange from 1926 to 1960.

III. CONCLUSIONS

During the entire 35-year period, 1926–60, the rates of return, compounded annually, on common stocks listed on the New York Stock Exchange, with

[7] W. B. Hickman, *Statistical Measures of Corporate Bond Financing Since 1900* (Princeton, N.J.: Princeton U.P., 1960), pp. 291, 298–301. Hickman's sample included all straight corporate bond issues of $5 million or more.

See also David Durand, "A Quarterly Series of Corporate Basic Yields, 1952–57, and Some Attendant Reservations," *Journal of Finance*, Vol. XIII, No. 3 (September, 1958).

Basic yields, together with some discussion of the basic-yield concept, appeared in David Durand, *Basic Yields of Corporate Bonds, 1900–1942* (Technical Paper No. 3; New York, N.Y.: National Bureau of Economic Research, 1942). The series was later brought up to date, with additional discussion, in David Durand and Willis J. Winn, *Basic Yields of Bonds, 1926–1947: Their Measurement and Pattern* (Technical Paper No. 6; New York, N.Y.: National Bureau of Economic Research, 1947). Later basic-yield figures have appeared in the *Economic Almanac* and the *Statistical Abstract of the United States*.

reinvestment of dividends, were 9.0 percent for tax exempt institutions; 8.2 percent for persons in the $10,000 income class; and 6.8 percent for persons in the $50,000 income class. These rates are substantially higher than for alternative investment media for which data are available. It is probably worth noting here that a dollar earning 9.0 percent per annum, compounded annually, would be worth over $20 in 35 years.

The rates for the postwar periods are substantially higher than for the periods prior to the war except during the period of recovery after 1932. It will perhaps be surprising to many that the rates have consistently been so high. For the postwar period (1950–60), as a whole, rates have exceeded 10 percent for all tax brackets considered, even after payment of capital gains taxes, and this has been true for most subperiods as well.

Rates of return without reinvestment of dividends varied from period to period above and below rates with reinvestments, but on the whole the rates were similar. This merely reflects the fact that, on the average, rates of appreciation in the prices of stocks after the receipt of dividends were similar to rates before the receipt of dividends.

Lawrence Fisher[*]

22. An Algorithm for Finding Exact Rates of Return

Reprinted from **The Journal of Business of the University of Chicago,** Vol. XXXIX, No. 1, Part II (January, 1966), pp. 111–118, by permission of the author and the University of Chicago Press. Copyright 1966 by the University of Chicago.

I. INTRODUCTION

Computation of the realized rate of return on an investment has been a problem for the financial community for a very long time. Calculations required to solve such problems are frequently thought to be difficult and are certainly tedious. In the past, two ways have been developed to reduce the tedium. Tables showing present values of lump sums and of income streams arising from annuities and bonds have been produced. With the tables available, one can often cast one's problem in a form where the tables are useful. The other method of circumventing the problem has been through the use of formulas that provide approximate answers in the hope that they are "good enough."

Now there is another way to avoid the tedium. High-speed computers are available and are used by many financial institutions for their routine bookkeeping operations. Proper use of computers is far more economical than use of the old techniques.

This paper presents an algorithm for solving what is, perhaps, the most complex of all common compound-interest problems: the determination of a realized rate of return on an investment portfolio where funds have been added to and withdrawn from the portfolio after the initial investment. Because it is a rather general algorithm, it can also be applied to problems that are less complex, such as finding the promised yield of a bond.

[*] Professor of Finance, Graduate School of Business, University of Chicago, and Associate Director, Center for Research in Security Prices. The basic algorithm described here was developed in consultation with the Trust Department of the First National Bank of Chicago.

Except for some special cases, problems where an effective compound rate of interest must be found cannot be solved directly. Instead, what must be performed in solving them is the selection of a trial discount rate and determination of the error in net present value that would result from using this trial rate. This process is repeated until an acceptable solution has been found. A good algorithm for the computation of rates of return is simply an efficient way of selecting successive trial values of the discount rate and discovering when the acceptable solution has been found. For the particular problem at hand, the algorithm must have an additional feature. In some cases no discount rate—or more than one discount rate[1]— exists. It is then impossible to state *the* discount rate. Hence a good algorithm must also show that no solution is feasible.

The specific problem for which this algorithm was developed is that of finding the realized rate of return since its beginning on the portfolio of a pension fund. The pattern of receipts and disbursements of typical pension funds is one that makes obtaining an exact answer completely infeasible with old techniques. Indeed, with such techniques obtaining an even approximate answer is costly.[2]

The rate of return realized by the portfolio of a pension fund is that discount rate which reduces the net present value of the following income stream to zero: "positive" elements of the income stream are the contributions to the fund; "negative" elements are payments to beneficiaries of the fund. For some computational purposes, the market value of the portfolio as of the date to which it is decided to find the rate of return is also a negative element. Contributions are generally made in very unequal installments and at unequal time intervals. Withdrawals for the payment of pensions are generally made in increasing amounts each month as the fund and the beneficiaries get older. However, lump-sum withdrawals are also likely to take place when employees leave the company if the employees have made contributions to the fund or if they have vested rights.

The algorithm presented here is simple enough so that it can be represented by an almost trivial program on nearly every digital computer extant. It is, nevertheless, so efficient that on some computers the machine time used in finding the rate of return on virtually any income stream for which a rate of return exists costs less than one cent.

In Section II the usual formula for finding the rate of return for an income stream is stated. It is then restated in the context of continuous

---

[1] For an example see James H. Lorie and Leonard J. Savage, "Three Problems in Rationing Capital," *Journal of Business*, Vol. XXVIII (October, 1955), pp. 236–38.

[2] E.g., the management of a large corporation computes the rate of return realized on its pension fund's portfolio since inception at the end of each month. It takes approximately a half-hour each month to make the computation. To compute the realized rate of return for the pension fund to the end of each month during a 10-year period by hand methods would thus require several hundred dollars' worth of the managers' time.

compounding of interest. Another concept required by the algorithm is then introduced. This concept is that of *duration* as defined by Frederick R. Macaulay.[3] It, too, is put into the context of continuous compounding of interest. Section III presents the algorithm itself, which is a simple Newtonian approximation. Section IV provides a brief discussion of some other applications of the algorithm. An illustrative FORTRAN II program is presented in the Appendix.

II. A STATEMENT OF THE EQUATION TO BE SOLVED

The formula for finding the realized rate of return of a pension fund since its inception may be stated as follows:

$$P_j(1 + r)^{T-t_1} + P_2(1 + r)^{T-t_2} + \cdots + P_n(1 + r)^{T-t_n} = V_T$$

or

$$\sum_{j=1}^{n} P_j(1 + r)^{T-t_j} = V_T \tag{1}$$

where P_j = the amount of the jth payment into the fund (P_j is positive if it represents a net contribution and negative if it represents a withdrawal);

t_j = the date of the jth payment;

r = the rate of return, compounding annually;

V = the assets of the fund (at market), and

T = the date to which rate of return is to be found.

This formula is inconvenient if $(T - t_j)$ is a fraction of a year because in such a case $(1 + r)^{T-t_j}$ must be found by (a) finding the logarithm of $1 + r$, (b) multiplying it by $(T - t_j)$, and (c) finding the antilogarithm of $(T - t_j) \log (1 + r)$. Since several (say K) values of r must be used before the correct one is found, K logarithms and Kn antilogarithms must be found.

If we express Eq. (1) in terms of continuous compounding, it becomes

$$\sum_{j=1}^{n} P_j e^{i(T-t_j)} = V_T \tag{2}$$

where i = the rate of return compounding continuously and e = the base of natural logarithms (2.7182818285...). Once i has been found, we can find r by means of the relationship

$$r = e^i - 1 \tag{3}$$

[3] *Some Theoretical Problems Suggested by the Movements of Interest Rates, Bond Yields and Stock Prices in the United States since 1856* (New York, N.Y.: National Bureau of Economic Research, 1938), Chap. ii, esp. pp. 44–53.

Whenever we use natural logarithms, finding the antilogarithm of x is the operation of finding e^x.

By using Eqs. (2) and (3) instead of Eq. (1) to find the discount rate, the computation of logarithms is completely eliminated at a cost of finding only a single additional antilogarithm. Thus we can eliminate the coding, testing, use, and storage required for one computer routine.

In short, instead of trying successive values of r and having to find the logarithm of $1 + r$ each time, by using continuous compounding we simply try successive values of i, which is the logarithm of $1 + r$.

Duration, as defined by Macaulay,[4] is the average time to maturity of an investment, where the number of years *to* the receipt of each rent (other than a current one) is given a weight proportional to the present value of that rent. Using the notation of Eqs. (1), (2), and (3) at time T, we find

$$D = \frac{\sum_{j=1}^{n} (t_j - T)P_j(1 + r)^{T-t_j}}{\sum_j P_j(1 + r)^{T-t_j}}, \tag{4}$$

$$D = \frac{-\sum_j (T - t_j)P_j e^{i(T-t_j)}}{\sum_j P_j e^{i(T-t_j)}} \tag{5}$$

or

$$D = \frac{-\sum(T - t_j)P_j(1 + r)^{T-t_j}}{V_T}$$

$$= \frac{-\sum(T - t_j)P_j e^{i(T-t_j)}}{V_T} \tag{6}$$

where D = duration.

The concept of duration provides a convenient way of describing securities that may have the same promised yield but different forms of contract. Macaulay uses it, for example, to point out why, when interest rates change, the change in the price of a bond with one year to maturity will be quite different from the change in price of a 10-year bond, and the price change in the 10-year bond will also differ appreciably from the change of a 40-year bond; but 40-year and 100-year bonds will move almost exactly together.

Duration combined with continuous compounding is also useful in

[4] *Ibid.*, p. 44.

another way. Suppose one wonders what will happen to the value of a bond if its yield rises by, say, ten basis points. It can be shown that

$$\frac{dV}{V} = -D\,di \tag{7}$$

or

$$\frac{\Delta V}{V} \approx -D\,\Delta i \tag{8}$$

where Δx means "the change in x." It should be noted that Eq. (7) is simpler than the corresponding equation using annual compounding, viz.,

$$\frac{dV}{V} = -D\,\frac{dr}{1 + r} \tag{9}$$

Macaulay shows that a 6 percent bond, selling at par, and having 15 years to maturity has a duration of approximately 10 years.[5] Thus if its yield should rise to 6.10 percent, its price would fall to about 99.

In the specific problem we are concerned with here, payments have been made into the fund in the past—in our computations we are not dealing with rents to be received in the future. Thus, at time T, duration is always a negative number.

III. THE ALGORITHM

Let i_k = the kth approximation of i^*, the true rate of return. Then

$$V_k = \sum_j P_j e^{i_k(T-t_j)} \tag{10}$$

and

$$D_k = \frac{-\sum(T - t_j)P_j e^{i_k(T-t_j)}}{\sum P_j e^{i_k(T-t_j)}} \tag{11}$$

or

$$D_k = \frac{-\sum(T - t_j)P_j e^{i_k(T-t_j)}}{V_k} \tag{12}$$

In finding the rate of return i^* by successive approximation, the problem is to eventually choose a value of i_k such that $V_k \approx V_T$.

[5] *Ibid.*, p. 51.

Until the proper value of i_k is found, V_k will be either too large or too small.

Define

$$E_k = V_T - V_k \tag{13}$$

Then applying equation (8), we want to choose Δi so that $\Delta V = E_k$. Thus

$$\frac{E_k}{V_k} \approx -D_k \Delta i_k \tag{14}$$

or

$$\Delta i_k = \frac{-E_k}{V_k D_k} \tag{15}$$

And

$$i_{k+1} = i_k + \frac{V_T - V_k}{V_k \{ [\sum (T - t_j) P_j e^{i_k(T-t_j)}]/V_k \}} \tag{16}$$

that is,

$$i_{k+1} = i_k + \frac{V_T - \sum P_j e^{i_k(T-t_j)}}{\sum (T - t_j) P_j e^{i_k(T-t_j)}} \tag{17}$$

Equation (17) is a computational algorithm for finding i^* (the value of i for which $V_k \approx V_T$). The method of computation is as follows:

1. Start with any value of i, e.g., let $i_1 = 0.00$ if this is the first time computations are being done since the computer was started, or let $i_1 = i^*$ for the previous case.
2. Apply equation (17), and keep applying equation (17) until the difference between i_{k+1} and i_k is smaller than some acceptable degree of error. On most computers it is probably feasible to carry the computation to the point where $|i_{k+1} - i_k| < 0.00009005$, or even further. However, requiring that $|i_{k+1} - i_k|$ be <0.00005 will give an answer that is virtually always correct to the nearest basis point.

Let us illustrate the use of this algorithm by taking two trivial examples, which do not require its use.[6]

EXAMPLE 1: 292 days ago, $100.00 was received and later invested. The current value of the assets of the fund is $108.00. Two hundred ninety-two days are 0.8000 years. Let $i_1 = 0.0000$.

---

[6] The numbers presented are rounded from those of the calculations used in constructing these examples.

Then

$$i_2 = 0.0000 + \frac{108.000 - 100.000}{80.000} = 0.1000$$

$$i_3 = 0.1000 + \frac{108.000 - 108.329}{86.66} = 0.0962$$

$$i_4 = 0.0962 + \frac{108.000 - 108.000}{86.400} = 0.0962$$

$$i^* = 0.0962$$

$$r^* = e^{0.0962} - 1.0 = 10.10 \text{ percent}$$

$$\left\{ \begin{array}{l} Check: \quad \log_e (1.08) = 0.07696 \\[1em] \qquad\quad \dfrac{0.07696}{0.8} = 0.09620 = i^* \end{array} \right\}$$

EXAMPLE 2: Two years ago $2.00 was received and invested; one year ago, $1.00 was withdrawn; the value of the fund today is $1.32.

$$i_1 = 0.0000$$

$$i_2 = 0.0000 + \frac{1.3200 - (2.0000 - 1.0000)}{4.0000 - 1.0000} = 0.1067$$

$$i_3 = 0.1067 + \frac{1.3200 - (2.4756 - 1.1126)}{4.9511 - 1.1126} = 0.0955$$

$$i_4 = 0.0955 + \frac{1.3200 - (2.4207 - 1.1002)}{4.8414 - 1.1002} = 0.0953$$

$$i_5 = 0.0953 + \frac{1.3200 - (2.4200 - 1.1000)}{4.8399 - 1.1000} = 0.0953$$

$$i^* = 0.0953$$

$$r^* = 0.1000 = 10.00 \text{ percent}$$

$$\left\{ \begin{array}{l} Check: \\[1em] \quad 2(1 + r)^2 - (1 + r) - 1.32 = 0 \\[1em] \quad 1 + r = \dfrac{1 \pm \sqrt{1 + 10.56}}{4} = 1.10 \\[1em] \qquad r^* = 10.00 \text{ percent} \end{array} \right\}$$

In Example 2 note that the algorithm can also be used in the form

$$r_{k+1} = r_k + \frac{V_T - \sum P_j(1 + r_k)^{T-t_j}}{\sum(T - t_j)P_j(1 + r_k)^{T-t_j}} \tag{18}$$

Thus

$$r_1 = 0.0000$$

$$r_2 = 0.0000 + \frac{1.3200 - (2.0000 - 1.0000)}{4.0000 - 1.0000} = 0.1067$$

$$r_3 = 0.1067 + \frac{1.3200 - (2.4494 - 1.1067)}{4.8987 - 1.1067} = 0.1007$$

$$r_4 = 0.1007 + \frac{1.3200 - (2.4230 - 1.1007)}{4.8459 - 1.1007} = 0.1001$$

$$r_5 = 0.1001 + \frac{1.3200 - (2.4203 - 1.1001)}{4.8407 - 1.1001} = 0.1000$$

$$r_6 = 0.1000 + \frac{1.3200 - (2.4200 - 1.1000)}{4.8401 - 1.1000} = 0.1000$$

$$r^* = 0.1000$$

Equation (18) converges more slowly than Eq. (17) because the factor $(1 + r_k)$ is missing from the numerator of the fractional part. If the factor were present, each form of the algorithm would converge at about the same rate.

In the actual application of the algorithm, V_T can be treated in the same manner as any other element of the income stream. When this is done, Eq. (17) becomes

$$i_{k+1} = i_k - \frac{\sum P_j e^{i_k(T-t_j)}}{\sum(T - t_j)P_j e^{i_k(T-t_j)}} \tag{19}$$

In Eqs. (17) and (19), time is given its origin as of the date at which the market value of the portfolio is known. But the origin of time can also be taken as some other date. Define τ as the arbitrary origin of time. The algorithm then becomes

$$i_{k+1} = i_k - \frac{\sum P_j e^{i_k(\tau-t_j)}}{\sum(\tau - t_j)P_j e^{i_k(\tau-t_j)}} \tag{20}$$

For finding the rate of return since inception on the portfolio of a pension fund, the algorithm will usually converge more rapidly if τ is set equal to $T - 1$.

If, in Example 2, Eq. (20) is used instead of Eq. (17) and τ is set equal to $T - 1$, we will find that

$$i_1 = 0.0000$$

$$i_2 = 0.0000 - \frac{2.0000 - 1.0000 - 1.3200}{2.0000 + 1.3200} = 0.0964$$

$$i_3 = 0.0964 - \frac{2.2024 - 1.0000 - 1.1987}{2.2024 + 1.1987} = 0.0953$$

$$i_4 = 0.0953 - \frac{2.2000 - 1.0000 - 1.2000}{2.2000 + 1.2000} = 0.0953$$

$$i^* = 0.0953$$

Thus, the number of iterations is cut substantially. However, when $\tau \neq T$, there is a danger that the denominator will be zero. If it should become zero, it is necessary to choose another arbitrary value for τ.

IV. SOME OTHER APPLICATIONS

In addition to computing the realized rate of return on an investment portfolio, the algorithm can be used to find the discount rate for any other "cash flow" where the flows are made up of discrete elements. For example, it may be used to find the promised yield on a bond.[7] It can also be used for finding the realized rate of return on a portfolio between any two dates for which the value of the portfolio is known. Thus, availability of the algorithm makes it convenient to find rates of return for short periods (still taking exact account of contributions to and withdrawals from a fund) and find the kinds of measures of performance used by William F. Sharpe[8] but at more frequent intervals. These measures may include an average annual rate of return (computed by finding the arithmetic mean of rates compounded continuously) stated at any desired frequency of compounding.

[7] For most bonds, however, a modified form of the algorithm would be far more efficient because it could make use of the standard formula for the present value of an annuity.

[8] "Mutual Fund Performance," *Journal of Business*, Vol. XXXIX, No. 1, Part II (Supplement, January, 1966).

APPENDIX

An illustrative computer program using the algorithm

The illustrative computer program shown here uses the algorithm as given in Eq. (17). It has been tested on the IBM 7094. It assumes that input is in the form of images of punched cards on magnetic tape. There is to be a group of cards for each case for which the rate of return is to be computed. The first card of each group contains T, V_T, n, and an identification of the case. It is followed by n cards each containing a value of t_j and P_j. The format for T and t is $mm/dd/yy$, where mm is month, dd is day of month, and yy is the last two digits of the year. (Other symbols are as defined in the text.) The program finds i and r for each case.

The main program is coded in FORTRAN II. In addition to standard library subroutines for input and output, it uses the library function "EXP" for finding e^x and the FAP-coded subroutine "TIME" for converting T and each t into floating-point numbers.

It should be emphasized that this program is for illustrative purposes only. It should not be used for actual computations for several reasons:

1. Equation (17), which is less efficient than Eq. (20), is used.
2. The format in which results are presented is inconvenient for everyone but the programmer.
3. Most importantly, the illustrative program makes no attempt to check dates for validity nor does it provide any assistance in determining why no rate of return has been found when Eq. (17) fails to converge within 100 trials.

Figure A is a listing of the main program. Figure B is a listing of subroutine "TIME." Figure C is a listing of data cards for three examples. Figure D is the output produced with these data.

FIGURE A

```
SAMPLE APPLICATION OF RATE OF RETURN ALGORITHM (EQ.17)

      DIMENSION T DIFR(999), P(999), CASE(9)
      LIMIT = 100
   10 READ INPUT TAPE 5, 20, MONTH, DAY, YEAR, V, N, CASE
   20 FORMAT (I2, 2(1XF2.0), F11.2, I3, 9A6)
      BIGT = TIME(MONTH, DAY, YEAR)
      DO 30 J = 1, N
      READ INPUT TAPE 5, 20, MONTH, DAY, YEAR, P(J)
   30 T DIFR(J)=BIG T - TIME(MONTH, DAY, YEAR)
      SMALL I = 0.
      DO 200 K = 1, LIMIT
      SUM VAL = V
      DENOM   = 0.
      DO 100 J = 1, N
      PRSNTV = P(J) * EXPF(SMALL I * T DIFR(J))
      SUM VAL = SUM VAL - PRSNTV
  100 DENOM = DENOM + TDIFR(J)*PRSNTV
      DELTA I = SUM VAL/DENOM
      SMALL I = SMALL I + DELTA I
      IF(ABSF(DELTA I) - 0.00005) 300, 300, 200
  200 CONTINUE
      WRITE OUTPUT TAPE 6, 210, CASE
      GO TO 10
  210 FORMAT (17H FAILURE ON CASE 9A6)
  300 R = EXPF(SMALL I) - 1.0
      WRITE OUTPUT TAPE 6,320, SMALL I, R, CASE
      GO TO 10
  320 FORMAT (1H  2F8.5, 9A6//)
      END(1,0,0,0,0,0,1,0,0,1,0,0,0,0,0)
```

FIGURE B

FUNCTION TO MAKE MONTH-DAY-YEAR INTO DATE

```
                      00000              ENTRY   TIME
00000   0500 60 4 00003    TIME  CLA•    3,4           CHECK FOR LEAP YEAR--PICK UP YEAR
00001  -0300 00 0 00051          UFA     =15588        UNNORMALIZE IT
00002   0560 00 0 00045          LDQ     =0            CLEAR MQ
00003   0765 00 0 00002          LRS     2             'DIVIDE' BY 4
00004   0131 00 0 00000          XCA                   PLACE REMAINDER IN AC
00005  -0100 00 0 00007          TNZ     •+2           TRANSFER IF COMMON YEAR
00006  -0625 00 0 00044          STL     FLAG          LEAP YEAR SET FLAG
00007   0500 60 4 00001          CLA•    1,4           PICK UP MONTH
00010   0634 01 1 00026          SXA     SAVE1,1       SAVE XR1
00011  -0734 00 1 00000          PDX     ,1            MONTH TO XR1
00012   0500 00 1 00044          CLA     TABLE,1       CLEAR, ADD DAYS IN PREVIOUS MONTHS OF YEAR
00013   0300 60 4 00002          FAD•    2,4           ADD DAYS
00014  -0520 00 0 00044          NZT     FLAG          LEAP YEAR
00015   0020 00 0 00023          TRA     COMYR           NO. COMMON YEAR
00016  -3 00002 1 00020          TXL     •+2,1,2       JANUARY OR FEBRUARY
00017   0300 00 0 00046          FAD     =1.             NO. ADD A DAY
00020   0600 00 0 00044          STZ     FLAG          CLEAR FLAG
00021   0241 00 0 00050          FDP     =366.         FIND FRACTIONAL PART OF YEAR
00022   0020 00 0 00024          TRA     BACK
00023   0241 00 0 00047    COMYR FDP     =365.         FIND FRACTIONAL PART OF YEAR
00024   0131 00 0 00000    BACK  XCA
00025   0300 60 4 00003          FAD•    3,4           ADD YEAR
00026   0774 00 1 00000    SAVE1 AXT     ••,1          RESTORE XR1
00027   0020 00 4 00004          TRA     4,4           RETURN
00030  +211516000000             DEC     334.,304.,273.,243.,212.,181.,151.,120.,90.,59.,31.,0
00031  +211460000000
00032  +211421000000
00033  +210746000000
00034  +210650000000
00035  +210552000000
00036  +210456000000
00037  +207740000000
00040  +207550000000
00041  +206730000000
00042  +205760000000
00043  +000000000000
00044                      TABLE BSS     0
00044   0 00000 0 00000    FLAG  PZE
                                 END
```

```
   LITERALS
00045   000000000000
00046   201400000000
00047   211555000000
00050   211556000000
00051   233000000000
```

FIGURE C

SAMPLE INPUT DATA

```
10/31/65      108.00   1 EXAMPLE 1
 1/12/65      100.00
12/31/65      132.00   2 EXAMPLE 2
12/31/64     -100.00
12/31/63      200.00
 1/ 1/66     1000.00  11 EXAMPLE 3--A 4 PER CENT BOND AT PAR
 1/ 1/66      -20.00
 7/ 1/61      -20.00
 1/ 1/62      -20.00
 7/ 1/62      -20.00
 1/ 1/63      -20.00
 7/ 1/63      -20.00
 1/ 1/64      -20.00
 7/ 1/64      -20.00
 1/ 1/65      -20.00
 7/ 1/65      -20.00
 1/ 1/61     1000.00
```

FIGURE D

SAMPLE RESULTS

0.09620 0.10098 EXAMPLE 1

0.09531 0.10000 EXAMPLE 2

0.03961 0.04040 EXAMPLE 3--A 4 PER CENT BOND AT PAR

*Seymour Kaplan**

23. Computer Algorithms for Finding Exact Rates of Return

Reprinted from **The Journal of Business of the University of Chicago,** Vol. 40, No. 4 (October, 1967), pp. 389–392, by permission of the author and the University of Chicago Press. Copyright 1967 by the University of Chicago.

I. INTRODUCTION

In a recent paper in this *Journal*,[1] Lawrence Fisher has proposed an algorithm for finding exact rates of return on investments. The aims of the present paper are (1) to demonstrate that the proposed procedure need not converge to the actual rate of return in many realistic investment situations having a unique rate of return, and (2) to suggest an improved algorithm which will converge to the exact rate of return in the vast majority of investment situations where a unique rate of return exists.

The relationship employed by Fisher to obtain the rate of return is

$$i_{k+1} = i_k + \frac{V_T - \sum_{j=1}^{n} P_j e^{i_k(T-t_j)}}{\sum_{j=1}^{n} (T - t_j) P_j e^{i_k(T-t_j)}} \tag{1}$$

where (using Fisher's definitions),

P_j = the amount of the jth payment into the fund (P_j is positive if it represents a net contribution and negative if it represents a withdrawal),

t_j = the date of the jth payment,

i = the rate of return, compounding annually,

V = the assets of the fund (at market), and

T = the date to which rate of return is to be found.

* Associate professor, Department of Industrial Engineering and Operations Research, New York University.

[1] "An Algorithm for Finding Exact Rates of Return," *Journal of Business*, Vol. XXXIX, No. 1, Part II (January, 1966).

Fisher states that one can arbitrarily select an acceptable degree of error (call it α) and carry the computations to the point where the error is less than α. That is, if $i_{k+1} - i_k$ is defined as the error, one can carry the computations to the point where

$$| \, i_{k+1} - i_k \, | < \alpha$$

The value of the exact rate of return r at such a point is found from the relationship

$$r = e^{i_k} - 1$$

Fisher suggests a value of 0.00005 for α, and implies that the non-convergence of any problem after a large number of trials means that no rate of return exists. We shall see that nonconvergence can take place after 100 or more trials for many reasons in situations where a unique value for the rate of return does exist.

II. DISCUSSION

Let $f(i_k)$ represent the net value of the fund at time T if all contributions and withdrawals are compounded at the continuous rate i_k, and if V_T is considered to be withdrawn at T. This net value is just

$$f(i_k) = -\Big[V_T - \sum_{j=1}^{n} P_j e^{i_k(T-t_j)}\Big] \tag{2}$$

The first derivative of $f(i_k)$, $f'(i_k)$, is given by

$$f'(i_k) = + \sum_{j=1}^{n} (T - t_j) P_j e^{i_k(T-t_j)} \tag{3}$$

Thus, Fisher's algorithm can be written

$$i_{k+1} = i_k - \frac{f(i_k)}{f'(i_k)} \tag{4}$$

In most cases, such as in the examples presented by Fisher, the function $f(i_k)$ appears as shown in Figure 1. That is, $f(i_k)$ is positive monotone increasing and has a nondecreasing first derivative $[f'(i_k) > 0, f''(i_k) < 0]$, for values of $i_k \geq 0$. Thus, the algorithm correctly indicates the direction of change of i_k in order to arrive at the true rate of return and will always guarantee convergence. If $f(i_k) < 0$, i_{k+1} will be greater than i_k by use of the algorithm, whereas if $f(i_k) > 0$, i_{k+1} must be made smaller than i_k if the algorithm is employed.

The trouble with the algorithm lies in the fact that for many realistic investment situations, $f(i_k)$ may not be monotone increasing but may have a minimum point in the region $i_k \geq 0$ as shown in Figure 2. In such

FIGURE 1

MINIMUM OF $f(i_k)$ TO THE RIGHT OF THE ORIGIN

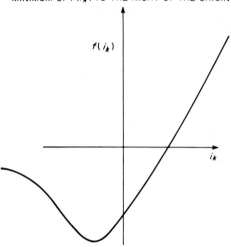

cases, consider what would happen, using the algorithm, if we started at a point such as $i_k = 0$. At this point, $f'(i_k)$ would be <0 and so would $f(i_k)$. Thus, the indicated direction of change would be to *decrease* i_k, which of course would lead us in a direction away from the true rate of return at i^*. To illustrate the above, consider the following example: 2 years ago,

FIGURE 2

MINIMUM OF $f(i_k)$ TO THE RIGHT OF THE ORIGIN

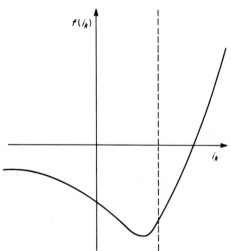

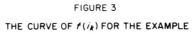

FIGURE 3

THE CURVE OF $f(i_k)$ FOR THE EXAMPLE

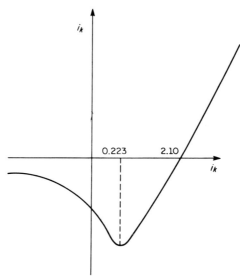

$1.00 was received and invested; 1 year ago, $2.50 was withdrawn; the value of the fund today is $2.00. Find the rate of return for this fund.

Simple algebra will show that the rate of return for the above investment has a unique positive value of approximately 210 percent (i^* approximately 1.13). The function $f(i_k)$ (plotted in Figure 3) has a unique minimum point at $i_k = 0.223$. It has a negative slope for $i_k < 0.223$ and a positive slope for $i_k > 0.223$. The use of the algorithm starting at $i_1 = 0.0000$ leads to:

$$i_2 = 0.0000 + \frac{2.0000 - (1.0000 - 2.5000)}{2.0000 - 2.50000}$$

$$= 0.0000 + \frac{3.50000}{-0.50000}$$

$$= -7.0000$$

The continued use of the algorithm would reverse the direction of change when $f(i_k)$ became positive, and the solution would eventually diverge. The reason for the divergence is that at $i_2 = -7.0000$, $f'(i_k)$ is very small and negative, and $i_3 = i_2 + f(i_2)/f'(i_2)$ has a large positive value of approximately $0.8e^7$. The next iterations will give $i_{k+1} \sim i_k + \frac{1}{2}$, and hence the solution will fail to converge.

There are various modifications of Fisher's algorithm which will guarantee that the proper direction of change takes place. For example, one can, at each stage of the iteration, examine the function $f'(i_k)$ for sign. If $f'(i_k)$ is positive, the algorithm can be used as given. If $f'(i_k)$ is negative, the algorithm can be written as

$$i_{k+1} = i_k + \frac{f(i_k)}{f'(i_k)} \tag{5}$$

The possibility also exists that $f'(i_k)$ may be exactly zero or near zero at some point i_k. In such cases, the jump from i_k to i_{k+1} may be of an unreasonably large magnitude. It is suggested that when this happens i_k be advanced by some small arbitrary increment. That is, if the absolute value of $f'(i_k)$ is less than some arbitrarily preassigned number, advance i_k by some arbitrary amount and continue the modified algorithm.

In the above description, we have assumed that there exists a unique positive value for the internal rate of return. Thus, the possibility of a nonunique positive rate (as in Figure 4, for example) has not been considered.

FIGURE 4

NONUNIQUE VALUE OF RATE OF RETURN

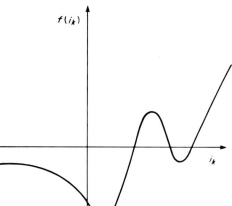

Of course one must know a priori that there is a unique positive value for the internal rate of return. There is nothing in Fisher's paper to indicate how this might be done. One recommended procedure that can easily be programed for a digital computer and has been suggested by this author involves the use of Sturm's Theorem.[2]

Let us now return to the given example and recalculate, using the modified algorithm discussed above. Let us also arbitrarily decide that, if at any stage $f'(i_k)$ is less than 0.1 in absolute value, we shall increment i_k by 0.03. The first iteration, of course, gives $i_2 = +7.0000$. (Because $f'[0]$ was negative, we have chosen to increase i_k. Also, $f'[0]$ was greater than 0.1 in absolute value.) At this new value of i_k, we have

$$f'(7) = \sum (T - t_j) P_j e^{7(T-t_j)}$$

$$= (2)(1)e^{14} - (1)(2)e^7$$

$$= 2(1,202,604) - 2(1096.6)$$

$$= 2,403,014.8$$

Thus, $f'(7)$ is positive and greater than 0.1 in absolute value. The next steps in the iteration are:

$$i_3 = 7.0000 + \frac{2.00 - (1.000e^{14} - 2.5e^7)}{2,403,014.8}$$

$$= 7.0000 - \frac{1,199,860.5}{2,403,014.8}$$

$$= 7.0000 - 0.4993 = 6.5007$$

$$i_4 = 6.0019, \text{ etc.}$$

In the above example, the solution converges quite slowly. About sixteen iterations are needed before the solution will converge to the correct value of $i_k = 1.13 (r = 2.10)$. Undoubtedly, more efficient programing routines can be developed. One possible approach, in the presence of a unique minimum point to the right of the origin, is to translate the origin forward to a point somewhat to the right of the minimum (*broken line* in Fig. 2) and then proceed using Fisher's method. It is not difficult to see that the solution will always converge in such a case. However, considerable computing time may be required to determine the position of the minimum and how far to the right of it one has to go to find an acceptable

---

[2] "A Note on a Method for Precisely Determining the Uniqueness or Non-Uniqueness of the Internal Rate of Return for a Proposed Investment," *Journal of Industrial Engineering* (January–February, 1965).

starting point. The suggested procedure of this paper is probably one of the simplest ways in which Fisher's method can be easily modified.[3]

III. SUMMARY

There are still certain types of unusual mathematical difficulties which might still arise with the use of the modified algorithm, but for the over-whelming majority of realistic investment situations, it should prove quite adequate and be a practical tool of great value. In addition to the reasons for usefulness given by Fisher, sensitivity analyses of various types could be carried out efficiently. For example, the algorithm would serve as a device for quickly determining the changes to be expected in rates of re-turn for anticipated capital investments when some of the variables con-cerning these investments (such as the annual cash flows) varied over different sets of values.

---

[3] It should be pointed out that the suggested procedure can also lead to difficulties in situations where the rate of return is unique but where there is more than one local maximum or minimum. However, such shapes for $f(i_k)$ will occur relatively rarely in practice. Cases with a single minimum point, such as in the example given, will occur much more frequently.

part Three

THE INVESTMENT ENVIRONMENT

*Daniel S. Ahearn**

24. Investment Management and Economic Research

Reprinted from the **Financial Analysts Journal,** Vol. 20, No. 1 (January-February, 1964), pp. 15–20, by permission of the author and the publisher.

It is hard to think of a business which can offer the economist more scope to use his skills or greater opportunity to participate in key decisions than investment management. This is in sharp contrast to the situation in most businesses—steel, chemicals, autos, department stores—where production, distribution, and selling are the heart of the operation, and the economic function sits off on the sidelines.

Why should economic analysis be more important in the business of investment management? Simply because the investment decision is almost always in large part an economic decision: the purchase or sale of future economic performance. The stream of potential income which the investor buys or sells will fluctuate, grow, or decline depending on how the economic environment affects it. Moreover, the capitalized value of this potential income—the price of the investment—will also be influenced by economic developments.

To be most fruitful, the economist should be involved at every stage of the investment operation. Investment policy is naturally heavily influenced by his description and analysis of the economic and political environment in which investment decisions are made. The investment program—that is, which industries and which companies should be bought or sold—is importantly affected by the economist's evaluation of changing trends in the economy and their impact on specific industries and companies. Finally, the economist's thinking can be a valuable aid to the security analyst who often has a natural bias toward a narrow focus on an individual company and who needs in any case an economic framework for the estimation of individual company earnings. It goes without saying, of course, that the economist gains as much as he gives in the common effort with other members of the investment management team. The goal,

* Wellington Management Company.

in every stage of the investment management process, is to produce a better result than the market technician, security analyst, or economist could have achieved on his own.

I. INVESTMENT MANAGEMENT VERSUS SECURITY ANALYSIS

It is important to remember that investment management is more than good security analysis. Stocks cannot be considered in isolation, and constructing an investment portfolio involves a great deal more than just collecting a long list of good stocks and bonds. What is required is the *selection* of a balanced portfolio which meets the investor's objectives and also provides adequate protection and opportunities with respect to a wide range of risks and other contingencies.

This task has become more difficult in recent years. Paradoxically, the investment universe has become larger and smaller at the same time. On the one hand, investment opportunities are available all over the world, and they range from the certainty of a small return on 90-day Treasury bills to the uncertain but possibly spectacular gain to be derived from the common stock of a new company with a revolutionary but untried idea. But, on the other hand, international and inter-industry competition have sharpened to the point where virtually no investment can be considered in isolation; a steel plant in Belgium is in some markets a next door neighbor of a Pittsburgh producer.

To be successful in this vast, complex, and interdependent investment environment, the investment manager needs perspective. The economist, trained to see the economy as a whole, ought to be able to supply the broad view, including analysis of the implications of political as well as economic events.

How valuable is perspective? Compare the likely experience of two investors considering investment in steel stocks a few years back. The investor whose perspective led him to avoid the steel industry as a whole because it seemed to be in for difficult times has had a far better investment experience over the past few years than even the most acute security analyst who picked the top-performing steel company. Note also the recent return of the railroads to investment favor. The catalyst here has not been the income statements or balance sheets of individual railroads but rather the shifts in the industry's climate of government regulation, taxation, labor relations, and technology—that is, in the political economics of the industry.

The ability to supply perspective depends, of course, on keeping in close touch with current economic and political developments. Economic research may be divided into roughly three areas, though there is naturally cross-fertilization at all times: analysis of business, the money market, and international developments, with a strong awareness of political influences in all three areas. Each of these will be taken up in order and then specific investment applications will be discussed.

II. BUSINESS ANALYSIS AND FORECASTING

Business activity is not the only thing that affects security markets, as witness the decline in stock prices in 1962, a year of rising business. But a considered view of the business outlook is essential in investment management. It sets out the investment planning environment. It is helpful in interpreting current developments, in deciding whether, say, a tire price increase is likely to stick. It provides a consistent framework and guide for the earnings estimates of security analysts. It avoids the situation in which the auto analyst estimates auto earnings on the basis of a 7 million car year, while the steel analyst is figuring steel output and earnings on the basis of a 5 million car year.

The business forecast is developed and presented in the usual GNP model framework. But in arriving at this global judgment, an investment economist enjoys some special advantages. He has the benefit of continuing reports from security analysts on current and future company and industry developments, including capital spending plans. In addition, Wellington Management takes advance notice of changes in corporate profit margins and the profit outlook, both sensitive indicators of change in business activity and capital spending, from Wellington's sample of 110 major companies which are surveyed periodically to check on the earnings outlook for each major industry and industrial sector. The special attention paid to corporate profits reflects their vital role in the American economy. Profits provide both incentive and financing for capital investment and business expansion. Moreover, to a major common stock investor, profits are even more directly important, since they are probably the single most important determinant of stock prices.

The investment manager has a special need to discern coming changes in business and profits long before they are generally visible, because the stock market is extremely sensitive to changes in these key areas. To do a good job he has to be ahead of the stock market; in other words, he has to be able to lead what itself is regarded as a leading indicator. Hence, the stress on shifts in profits estimates.

To get a still longer lead on profit trends and capital spending plans, it would seem more useful to place greater weight on the behavior of prices than seems currently fashionable. Published price indices, of course, have well-known deficiencies, so it has proved useful to make systematic independent surveys of price changes as they occur, using our own contacts in the industries as well as the published announcements which appear in the general and trade press. Price changes have much more powerful impacts on profit margins and net income than is generally realized. Take a company which has net income equal to 15 percent of sales. A 5 percent price increase which leaves sales unchanged can improve its profit margin by no less than 27 percent and raise net income by 33 percent. The possible impact on profits and capital investment plans is obviously powerful.

Most business analysts in recent years have focused on identifying cyclical turning points. Longer-term appraisals of the business outlook have been out of favor ever since the "Soaring Sixties" got off on the wrong foot. Nevertheless, longer-term business forecasting still is important, particularly for long-term investors. It is highly useful to make 3- to 5-year appraisals of the business and profit outlook. Cyclical fluctuations, after all, have been relatively mild. The bigger problem has been a rate of industrial growth which has been too slow to absorb all the new entrants to the labor force or to provide the profit incentives needed to stimulate more capital investment and faster growth.

Taking this longer look ahead, a major question for both investors and the economy as a whole is whether corporate profits are in process of rising off the flat plateau they have been on since 1955. This is something the economist is more likely to be aware of than the security analyst who concentrates on the individual company. The question deserves real study. A sustained uplift in the profitability of American business would change the entire investment climate and obviously would be of crucial significance to the decisions of the investment manager. It could justify more fully invested positions in common stocks, on the average, than had been appropriate in the past few years of flat earnings and slackened economic growth. Our own tentative conclusion is that a substantial improvement in business profitability is taking place.

What about common stock selection? Economic analysis can also contribute importantly here by stressing differential industry profit trends and pointing out interrelationships between political developments, business activity, the money market, and international affairs. In the political area, for example, a tax cut which lowers corporate taxes and quickens economic growth has bullish implications for stocks and, because of the federal budget deficit involved, bearish implications for bonds. The overall strength of the economy, particularly the anticipated behavior of capital spending, has obvious implications for a choice between aggressive and defensive stocks. A monetary policy which stresses higher short-term rates and relative stability in long-term rates has implications worth noting for the profit margins of financial institutions which live on the spread between the rates they pay and the rates they earn. A continuing deficit in the U. S. balance of payments could have favorable implications for companies which would benefit if export incentives were used to correct the problem. It might have unfavorable implications for overseas transport industries if any curbs were imposed on American tourist travel.

III. MONEY MARKET ANALYSIS

The second major area of economic research is the money market. This has had special importance for institutional investors. Many millions of dollars of their portfolios are in bonds or other fixed income securities. Moreover, unlike many fixed income investors, Wellington, for instance, does not buy bonds steadily regardless of yield; instead a real effort is made to concentrate buying when interest rates are high. This, of course, makes accurate interest rate forecasts essential.

Forecasting interest rates has never been easy but it used to be simpler than it is today. Until about three years ago, interest rates rose whenever business activity rose; when business activity declined, so did interest rates. This was a natural result of the fact that prosperity brought bigger credit demands from both businessmen and consumers at the same time that the Federal Reserve, fearful of inflation, was tightening money. In recessions, all these influences went into reverse and interest rates dropped sharply. Moreover, under these circumstances, bond yields and prices swung widely so the investor had easily visible landmarks by which he could steer a course. In 1959, for example, the rise in yields of high-quality corporate bonds to beyond 5 percent, the highest level in over 30 years, provided a clear buy signal.

Recently, bond investing has been more difficult. Wide price and yield swings have just about vanished. Since the middle of 1960, yield fluctuations in long-term U. S. Government bonds rarely have exceeded $\frac{1}{8}$ percent; in the 1950's $\frac{1}{2}$ percent and 1 percent swings were common. Price swings have been dampened correspondingly; the Treasury $3\frac{1}{2}$s of 1990, which rose 7 points in 1958 and dropped 23 points in 1959, have held within a 7 point range since mid-1960. Moreover, as Sidney Homer, partner of Salomon Bros. & Hutzler and a well-known authority on the money market, has pointed out, bond market movements are no longer closely correlated with business activity; in fact, bond yields today are appreciably below their levels in December, 1961, even though industrial production has risen 10 percent since then.

Clearly, things have changed. Understanding why they have changed is essential for successful bond investing. One reason yields have not risen more is that corporate cash flow has been rising far faster than needs for cash to finance plant and equipment investment or business inventories. Plant and equipment investment in 1962 barely exceeded the 1957 peak of $37 billion, but cash flow was $12 billion larger than in 1957. Another reason is the record flow of personal savings into major savings institutions, not to mention the amortization payments on $263 billion of mortgage debt which reinforce the funds seeking investment. Meanwhile, with persistently high unemployment levels and substantial unused plant capacity making inflation less of a danger, the Federal Reserve monetary managers have been keeping credit more easily available than was the case in past periods of business expansion.

One might conclude that bond yields should have fallen dramatically under these circumstances, but here a new element entered. The emergence of a serious balance-of-payments problem for the United States led both the Treasury and the Federal Reserve to exert substantial efforts to raise and maintain short-term interest rates at levels attractive enough to keep foreign funds invested here. These short-term rates have, in effect, been a floor for long-term rates.

This new environment, in which no single element has been dominant, calls for an eclectic approach to money market analysis. Developments in the U. S. balance of payments, increasing or decreasing pressure for higher interest rates to keep foreign funds invested here, can provide valuable clues to the next direction in Federal Reserve and Treasury policy. Less obviously, financial and economic developments abroad are also important since they determine the foreign interest rates with which U. S. rates must compete. The demand for and supply of long-term funds is important, but here one needs to recognize the dynamic elements involved as well as take account of the fact that commercial banks and individuals in recent years have not been reluctant residual suppliers of funds to the long-term markets but instead aggressive seekers of fixed income. Also, it is vital to pay close attention to the flow of private placements. This is difficult to keep track of, but it is a crucial index to overall money flows. In the first half of 1963, for example, privately placed issues ran $1.2 billion or 60 percent above 1962, even though the volume of publicly offered corporate bonds was slightly below 1962. The attitudes and objectives of the Federal Reserve authorities are, of course, vital subjects for continuing study; they are crucial determinants of the balance of the supply and demand for funds.

Investment managers should set up their own monthly surveys of savings and time deposit flow to get early warning of shifts in trend of this key variable. They should also closely watch bank portfolio attitudes; the banks link the long-term markets with the deposits newly created by Federal Reserve policy, and time deposits in recent years have been of central significance in the long-term markets. Less formally, investment managers can keep in touch with the attitudes of major institutional investors, specifically including their preferences between stocks and bonds, and their maturity preferences in fixed income securities.

To sum up, what is required is a careful study of the attitudes of the Treasury, the Federal Reserve, and private investors against the background of a sources and uses of funds analysis continually rechecked in the light of current developments.

IV. INTERNATIONAL DEVELOPMENTS

Investors today are much more aware of international financial developments as a result of the publicity given to the U. S. balance-of-payments problem. But most of the attention paid to the problem has focused on the more dramatic elements. For example, a number of financial observers and journalists have jumped to the conclusion that a devaluation of the dollar and an increase in the price of gold is imminent. Clearly, if this took place, it would have massive significance in the investment world. It deserves the most careful analysis before it is either accepted or rejected. If the past is any guide, those who act without careful analysis will have reason to regret their decision, as will be shown shortly. But first some less dramatic but more immediate implications for investors need to be noted.

For one thing, the balance-of-payments problem has already affected American investors by leading the Federal Reserve to raise interest rates and also, though few outside government would credit it, by leading to a slowing down of federal government spending. The impact on bond prices and on the prices of defense industry stocks has been appreciable. In July the President proposed an interest equalization tax on American purchases of foreign stocks and bonds. No one knows what further actions may be taken, but a prudent investment manager must consider all the possibilities: tax incentives to benefit U. S. exporters, curbs on American tourist travel, restraints on U. S. direct investment overseas. All of these would have measurable impact on security values.

But the significance of foreign developments for the U. S. investor goes much further. This is obvious once it is realized that many U. S. companies have very sizable operations abroad, accounting for 20 percent to 50 percent of sales and earnings. In 1962, devaluations in Brazil, Canada, and Argentina wiped out the better part of a year's earnings growth for some American companies. Less striking, but not less important, are the impacts of foreign government policies, labor problems, taxation, and monetary developments on the earning power of American subsidiaries abroad.

Even for companies without foreign subsidiaries, foreign developments can be crucial. Consider, for example, the increasing importance of foreign competition in our own market. When business is bad abroad, the pressure to export here grows. An investor considering the impact of foreign competition needs to pay special attention to the forthcoming general tariff negotiations. Few American industries will fail to be affected.

Having given a general outline of investment-oriented economic research and analysis, a few specific examples of its relevance to investment problems and practice will be taken up.

V. GOLD STOCKS AND THE PRICE OF GOLD

Possible devaluation of the dollar and increase in the price of gold has been a recurrent theme in some quarters since 1949. Investors have been advised to buy gold or gold stocks in order to profit from devaluation even though the case for devaluation has not been convincing up to the present day. That devaluation would not help the U. S. balance of payments if other countries followed suit, as was and still is likely, has been shrugged off. The argument has been that devaluation is needed to increase international liquidity. What is often overlooked is that the foreign currency reserves which today make up five-sixths of world liquidity are about half gold and half dollars. A devaluation of the dollar would raise the value of gold reserves, but it would simultaneously penalize central bankers who had trusted the dollar. If this were to reduce future willingness to hold dollars, as would seem likely, world liquidity might not increase as much as some proponents of devaluation anticipate. A sober assessment of the prospects for devaluation also must consider the political impact in a world which has made a stable dollar the keystone of its financial structure and a symbol of U. S. political and military leadership.

Responsible economic opinion in the past 15 years has argued repeatedly that dollar devaluation was neither necessary nor likely. What has been the experience of those who ignored this counsel and invested in gold?

Let us first take the central banker who distrusted the dollar and who, therefore, has concentrated his country's currency reserves in gold since 1949. He may have gained peace of mind. But it is certain that he gave up interest earnings, for gold is a nonearning asset. Currency reserves invested in U. S. Treasury bills would by now have appreciated 38 percent more than reserves placed in gold. Such is the power of accumulating interest, even at 2 percent and 3 percent interest rates. This 38 percent appreciation, it may be noted, now constitutes a sizable devaluation reserve.

What about the individual or institutional investor who invested in gold mining stocks back in 1949? (In the following evaluation of their experience, dividend income is not considered, since it is believed that most gold stock purchases are motivated by desire for capital appreciation.) The investor could have bought Homestake Mining, a major domestic gold producer, as low as \$35 and as high as \$50 in 1949. Had he bought at \$50, he would have a loss of \$3 a share, certainly not a happy outcome after 15 years' holding. But suppose he bought at the low price, \$35. He would now have a profit of \$12 or 34 percent. This looks good. But is it? An appreciation of 34 percent over a 15-year period is only 2 percent a year compounded. Moreover, the purchase of the gold mining stock meant that alternative investment choices were rejected. Standard & Poor's 500 stock average, for example, is now more than five times its 1949 low and four and one-half times its high. This is what the investor missed by choosing this gold stock in 1949. A decision not to invest is often as important as a decision to invest.

VI. COMMON STOCK SELECTION

Economic analysis can help to focus attention on industries likely to fare best or worst under existing and prospective economic conditions. This helps the security analysts to concentrate their attention where it is likely to be most rewarding. The chances of catching a big fish, investment-wise, are better if you cast your line where the big fish swim. Of course, big fish and good investment opportunities sometimes are found in surprisingly unpromising areas so the security analyst must be alert for such targets of opportunity as well. But by and large a good working assumption is that profitable and growing companies are most likely to be found in expanding sectors of the economy.

Individual companies may not be able to escape their industries, even when they recognize adverse future trends, though some make the attempt via diversification. The investment manager, however, has no excuse for not avoiding sectors of the economy or industries which are on the verge of a declining phase. This is the way to protect profits. Conversely, there are few things more profitable than early recognition of a turn for the better in a depressed industry; the investor gets the compound benefit of rising earnings and an increase in the multiple at which these earnings are valued. In short, early recognition of a shift in the major trend of an industry, for better or for worse, can be extremely profitable and economic research can be extremely helpful in this task.

Back in 1959, Edmund A. Mennis, of Wellington Management Company, made a basic economic study of the steel industry. At the time, steel stocks could hardly have been more highly regarded. Their prices were at all-time peak levels and there was even talk of the steels as growth stocks, reflecting a spreading belief that steel industry earnings and dividends would continue to push upward and would be much less cyclical than in the past. Taking a minority view, Dr. Mennis' study, published under the title "A Reappraisal of the Steel Industry" in the August, 1959,

Analysts Journal, expressed skepticism that steel stocks could do as well in the future as in the past. It noted a number of adverse considerations dictating a more cautious investment attitude: the failure of steel demand to expand, the threat of foreign competition, possible government intervention, and probable inability to continue to raise prices to offset cost increases. It is hard to find a better illustration of the dollars and cents value of good economic analysis. Standard and Poor's steel stock index made an all-time high of 100 in September, 1959, and has since been as low as 45.

VII. BOND INVESTMENT TIMING

Two recent specific examples may illustrate the value of careful money market analysis. The author will be forgiven for drawing his examples from the investment experience with which he is most familiar.

Back in late 1961, it will be recalled, most economists and money market observers were forecasting higher interest rates into 1962, mostly because business activity was rising, yields had already increased appreciably from the 1961 recession low, and a tightening in Federal Reserve policy was expected. This was the first business recovery after the 1959 money squeeze and some prople were anticipating a repetition of that experience. But there were a number of reasons to doubt this standard forecast. The failure of the Federal Reserve to cut back banks' free reserves as industrial production rose suggested a new and easier approach to credit policy. The autumn rise in business loan demands on the banking system had been less than seasonal. The high level of the stock market had made a number of institutions inclined to channel money away from stocks and into fixed income securities. Conversations with investment bankers and major institutional investors suggested that huge amounts of cash had been accumulated to take advantage of better long-term yields when they appeared. When the Federal Reserve raised the rate that banks could pay on time and savings deposits to 4 percent, and major banks quickly adopted higher rates, there was an additional source of demand for long-term fixed income obligations as the banks tried to earn enough to cover the higher deposit rates.

In this environment, it seemed apparent that bond yields would not go much higher and could go lower once the market recognized that its yield expectations were unrealistic. Accordingly, the Wellington Fund bought $104 million long-term bonds, with most yielding $4\frac{1}{2}$ percent to 5 percent, from December, 1961, through May, 1962, a period when many other investors were still waiting for 1959 to happen all over again. Later in 1962 and early 1963, U. S. corporations subsequently sold bonds to yield as little as 4.19 percent and the bonds Wellington had acquired all rose to premiums.

In the autumn of 1962 a reappraisal of the outlook indicated that the decline in yields had about run its course. Analysis suggested that improvement in the balance of payments in the first half of the year, which was encouraging to the bond market, had been temporary and was being followed by a serious deterioration. This seemed to spell bad news psychologically for the bond market and also threatened an increase in the Federal Reserve discount rate which at that time had been unchanged for $2\frac{1}{2}$ years. Prospects for lower interest rates abroad, which some hoped would avoid necessity for higher rates here, did not seem promising in view of emerging inflation in Europe. Bank portfolio extension, which had been sizable in 1962 under necessity to get high yields to cover higher savings deposit rates, seemed unlikely to be as much of a support to the bond market in 1963. Moreover, a substantial Federal budget deficit was in the offing, with or without a tax cut. Wellington's business forecast looked for rising business rather than a recession in 1963, and this suggestion of better credit demands seemed to be reinforced by a rising volume of private placement activity.

Putting all of this together with an optimistic attitude toward stocks, Wellington decided to retrace its steps and shorten its bond portfolio a little. The new issue corporate market is now down about 4 points since the January peak. It seems clear that economic analysis was the important factor in building the conviction that it was desirable to sell bonds.

VIII. STOCK—BOND SHIFTS

Flexible balanced investing, shifting buying power to bonds only when their yields seem high and to stocks only when they appear attractively priced, brings the best results.

An illustration of this approach is provided by the cyclical shifts in 1961–62. In May, 1961, economic analysis suggested that both the business recovery and corporate profits would be less dynamic than generally expected. When this economic outlook was combined with the high level of the stock market, Wellington Management Company recommended that the fund ought to trim its stock position back by reducing or eliminating holdings for which one could not make a strong case. The sales proceeds were put first in short-term U. S. Treasury obligations and then, as higher long-term interest rates came along, into bonds.

Later in the year, as noted earlier, a reappraisal of business and money market analysis suggested an opposite move, from bonds back into stocks. Accordingly, the round-trip was completed by reducing the fund's fixed income securities and by moving the money into stocks which were now available at favorable prices. This, too, proved beneficial since stock prices subsequently rose and bond prices declined.

IX. CONCLUSION

The examples chosen in this review have, obviously, been favorable illustrations of how sound economic analysis can play a valuable role in investment management. The economist's role has been highlighted for emphasis. It goes without saying that many other people—security analysts and market technicians—are essential in arriving at profitable investment decisions. Moreover, it must be frankly acknowledged that the right decisions are neither easy nor unanimous. But economic research can help to keep mistakes to a minimum and assure a good professional batting average, one that is better than the average investor could achieve for himself.

The task of applying economic research in the investment management field is clearly both challenging and rewarding. But it must be stressed that an attitude of responsibility is essential for the economist working in the investment management field. His findings may be quickly reflected in investment decisions involving millions or tens of millions of dollars. They cannot be arrived at casually. The economist in investment management is not in a position to say: "I think automobile sales next year will be about 7 million, but I wouldn't want to bet on it." The investment management business does bet on it, so judgments have to be carefully considered. Yet they have to be timely, too. The gains from awaiting more complete data must be weighed against the possible loss of an investment opportunity if decision is delayed too long.

Thus, the economist's job in investment management is not easy and it certainly is no ivory tower. But it is almost impossible to match for variety, breadth of activities, the sense of having made a real contribution, and, last but not least, the challenge of having one's judgments subject to the test of the market place.

*Arthur F. Burns**

25. Progress Towards Economic Stability[1]

Reprinted from **The American Economic Review**, Vol. L, No. 1 (March, 1960), pp. 1–19, by permission of the author and the publisher.

The American people have of late been more conscious of the business cycle, more sensitive to every wrinkle of economic curves, more alert to the possible need for contracyclical action on the part of government, than ever before in our history. Minor changes of employment or of productivity or of the price level, which in an earlier generation would have gone unnoticed, are nowadays followed closely by laymen as well as experts. This sensitivity to the phenomena of recession and inflation is a symptom of an increased public awareness of both the need for and the attainability of economic progress. It is precisely because so much of current industrial and governmental practice can be better in the future that our meetings this year are focused on the broad problem of improving the performance of the American economy. However, as we go about the task of appraisal and criticism, it will be well to discipline our impatience for reform. In the measure that we avoid exaggerating our nation's failures or understating its successes, we shall make it easier for ourselves as well as for economists in other countries to see current needs and developments in a just perspective.

It is a fact of the highest importance, I think, that although our economy continues to be swayed by the business cycle, its impact on the lives and fortunes of individuals has been substantially reduced in our generation. More than 25 years have elapsed since we last experienced a financial panic or a deep depression of production and employment. Over

* Presently, Chairman of the Board of Governors of the Federal Reserve System. Formerly, Professor of Economics, Columbia University.

[1] Presidential address delivered at the Seventy-second Annual Meeting of the American Economic Association, Washington, D.C., December 28, 1959. The author is indebted to his colleagues—M. Abramovitz, S. Fabricant, M. Friedman, Jane Kennedy, L. Wolman, and especially G. H. Moore—for counsel and criticism in the preparation of this paper.

20 years have elapsed since we last had a severe business recession. Between the end of the second world war and the present, we have experienced 4 recessions, but each was a relatively mild setback. Since 1937 we have had 5 recessions, the longest of which lasted only 13 months. There is no parallel for such a sequence of mild—or such a sequence of brief—contractions, at least during the past hundred years in our own country.

Nor is this all. The character of the business cycle itself appears to have changed, apart from the intensity of its overall movement. We usually think of the business cycle as a sustained advance of production, employment, incomes, consumption, and prices, followed by a sustained contraction, which in time gives way to a renewed advance of aggregate activity beyond the highest levels previously reached. We realize that changes in the price level occasionally outrun changes in production, that employment is apt to fluctuate less than production, and that consumption will fluctuate still less; but we nevertheless think of their movements as being roughly parallel. This concept of the business cycle has always been something of a simplification. For example, during the early decades of the nineteenth century, when agriculture dominated our national economy, occasional declines in the physical volume of production, whether large or small, had little effect on the number of jobs and sometimes had slight influence even on the flow of money incomes. As agriculture diminished in importance, the nation's production, employment, personal income, consumption, and price level fell more closely into step with one another and thus justified our thinking of them as moving in a rough parallelism. In recent years, however, and especially since the second world war, the relations among these movements have become much looser.

The structure of an economy inevitably leaves its stamp on the character of its fluctuations. In our generation the structure of the American economy has changed profoundly, partly as a result of deliberate economic policies, partly as a result of unplanned developments. In considering problems of the future, we can proceed more surely by recognizing the changes in economic organization which already appear to have done much to blunt the impact of business cycles.

I

In the early decades of the nineteenth century the typical American worker operated his own farm or found scope for his energy on the family farm. Governmental activities were very limited. What there was of industry and commerce was largely conducted through small firms run by capitalist-employers. Corporations were rare and virtually confined to banking and transportation. As the population grew and capital became more abundant, individual enterprise expanded vigorously but corporate enterprise expanded still more. An increasing part of the nation's business therefore came under the rule of corporations. By 1929, the output of corporate businesses was already almost twice as large as the output of individual proprietorships and partnerships. The gap has widened appreciably since then. Corporate profits have therefore tended to increase faster than the incomes earned by proprietors, who still remain very numerous in farming, retail trade, and the professions. Fifty years ago the total income of proprietors was perhaps two and a half times as large as the combined sum of corporate profits and the compensation of corporate officers. By 1957 this corporate aggregate exceeded by a fourth the income of all proprietors and by two-thirds the income of proprietors outside of farming.

The great growth of corporations in recent decades has occurred preponderantly in industries where the firm must operate on a large scale to be efficient and therefore must assemble capital from many sources. But a corporation whose stock is held publicly and widely has a life of its own, apart from that of its owners, and will rarely distribute profits at the same rate as they are being earned. While profits normally respond quickly and sharply to a change in sales and production, the behavior of dividends is tempered by business judgment. In practice, dividends tend to move sluggishly and over a much narrower range than profits. Corporations have therefore come to function increasingly as a buffer between the fluctuations of production and the flow of income to individuals. In earlier times the lag of dividends was largely a result of the time-consuming character of corporate procedures. More recently, the advantages of a stable dividend—especially its bearing on a firm's financial reputation—have gained increasing recognition from business managers. Meanwhile, modern trends of taxation have stimulated corporations to rely more heavily on retained profits and less on new stock issues for their equity funds, and this development in turn has facilitated the pursuit of stable dividend policies. Thus the evolution of corporate practice, as well as the growth of corporate enterprise itself, has served to reduce the influence of a cyclical decline of production and profits on the flow of income to individuals.

The expansion and the means of financing of governmental enterprise, especially since the 1930's, have had a similar effect. The increasing complexity of modern life, a larger concept of the proper function of government, and the mounting requirements of national defense have resulted in sharp increases of governmental spending. Fifty years ago the combined expenditure of federal, state, and local governments was about 7 percent of the dollar volume of the nation's total output. Governmental expenditures rose to 10 percent of total output in 1929 and to 26 percent in 1957. This huge expansion of governmental enterprise naturally led to increases in tax rates and to an energetic search for new sources of revenue. In time, taxes came to be imposed on estates, gifts, employment, sales, and—most important of all—on the incomes of both corporations and individuals. Fifty years ago customs duties still yielded about half of the total revenue of the federal government, and none of our governmental units as yet collected any tax on incomes. Twenty years later, personal and corporate income taxes were already the mainstay of federal finance. Subsequently, the activities of the federal government increased much faster than local activities and taxes followed suit. By 1957 the income tax accounted for nearly 70 percent of federal revenue, 8 percent of state and local revenue, and a little over half of the combined revenue of our various governmental units.

This dominance of the income tax in current governmental finance, together with the recent shift of tax collection toward a pay-as-you-go basis, has measurably enlarged the government's participation in the shifting fortunes of the private economy. During the nineteenth century, taxes were not only a much smaller factor in the economy, but such short-run elasticity as there was in tax revenues derived almost entirely from customs duties. Hence, when production fell off and private incomes diminished, the accompanying change in governmental revenues was usually small. In recent years, however, governmental revenues have become very sensitive to fluctuations of business conditions. When corporate profits decline by, say, a billion dollars, the federal government will collect under existing law about a half billion less from corporations. When individual incomes decline by a billion, the federal government may be expected to collect about $150 million less from individuals. State income taxes accentuate these effects. In short, when a recession occurs, our current tax system requires the government to reduce rather promptly and substantially the amount of money that it withdraws from the private economy for its own use. The result is that the income from production which corporations and individuals have at their disposal declines much less than does the national income.

Moreover, the operations of government are now so organized that the flow of personal income from production is bolstered during a recession by increased payments of unemployment insurance benefits. Unemployment insurance was established on a national basis in 1935, and the protection of workers against the hazards of unemployment has increased since then. Not all employees are as yet covered by unemployment insurance and the benefits, besides, are often inadequate to provide for essentials. Nevertheless, there has been a gradual improvement in the ability of families to get along decently even when the main breadwinner is temporarily unemployed. At present, over 80 percent of those who work for a wage or salary are covered by unemployment insurance, in contrast to 70 percent in 1940. The period over which benefits can be paid to an unemployed worker has become longer and the typical weekly benefit has risen in greater proportion than the cost of living. Furthermore, arrangements have recently been concluded in several major industries whereby benefits to the unemployed are supplemented from private sources.

Other parts of the vast system of social security that we have devised since the 1930's have also served to support the flow of personal income at times when business activity is declining. Payments made to retired workers kept increasing during each recession of the postwar period. The reason is partly that workers handicapped by old age or physical disability experience greater difficulty at such times in keeping their jobs or finding new ones and therefore apply for pensions in somewhat larger numbers. Another factor has been the intermittent liberalization of statutory benefits. But the most important reason for the steady increase of old-age pensions is the maturing of the social security system. In 1940, only 7 percent of people of age 65 and over were eligible for benefits from the old-age insurance trust fund, in contrast to 23 percent in 1948 and 69 percent in 1958. The trend of other public pension programs and the various public assistance programs has also been upward. Between 1929 and 1957 the social security and related benefits paid out by our various governmental units rose from 1 percent of total personal income to 6 percent. In 1933, with the economy at a catastrophically low level, these benefit payments were merely $548 million larger than in 1929. On the other hand, in 1958—when business activity was only slightly depressed— they were $4.4 billion above the level of 1957. Even these figures understate the difference between current conditions and those of a quarter century ago, for they leave out of account the private pensions which are beginning to supplement public pensions on a significant scale.

As a result of these several major developments in our national life, the movement of aggregate personal income is no longer closely linked to the movement of aggregate production. During the postwar period we have had several brief but sizable setbacks in production. For example, in the course of the recession of 1957–58, the physical output of factories and mines fell 14 percent, the physical output of commodities and services in the aggregate fell 5.4 percent, and the dollar volume of total output fell 4.3 percent. In earlier times personal incomes would have responded decisively to such a decline in production. This time the government absorbed a substantial part of the drop in the dollar volume of production by putting up with a sharp decline of its revenues despite the need to raise expenditures. Corporations absorbed another part of the decline by maintaining dividends while their undistributed profits slumped. In the end, the aggregate of personal incomes, after taxes, declined less than 1 percent and the decline was over before the recession ended.

Although the details have varied from one case to the next, a marked divergence between the movements of personal income and production has occurred in each of the postwar recessions. Indeed, during 1953–54 the total income at the disposal of individuals defied the recession by continuing to increase. This unique achievement was due to the tax reduction that became effective soon after the onset of recession as well as to the structural changes that have reduced the dependence of personal income on the short-run movements of production.

II

When we turn from personal income to employment, we find that the imprint of the business cycle is still strong. During each recession since 1948, unemployment reached a level which, while decidedly low in comparison with the experience of the thirties, was sufficient to cause serious concern. But although the fluctuations of employment have continued to synchronize closely with the movements of production, the relation between the two has been changing in ways which favor greater stability of employment in the future.

As the industrialization of our economy proceeded during the nineteenth century, an increasing part of the population became exposed to the hazards of the business cycle. Manufacturing, mining, construction, freight transportation—these are the strategic industries of a developing economy and they are also the industries in which both production and jobs have been notoriously unstable. Shortly after the Civil War, the employees attached to this cyclical group of industries already constituted 23 percent of the labor force. Employees of industries that have remained relatively free from cyclical unemployment—that is, agriculture, merchandising, public utilities, financial enterprises, the personal service trades, and the government—accounted for another 32 percent. The self-employed in farming, business, and the professions, whose jobs are especially steady, made up the rest or 45 percent of the work force. This was the situation in 1869. Fifty years later, the proportion of workers engaged in farming, whether as operators or hired hands, had shrunk drastically, and this shrinkage was offset only in part by the relative gain of other stable sources of employment. Consequently, the proportion of employees in the cyclical industries kept rising, decade after decade, and reached 36 percent in 1919.

Clearly, the broad effect of economic evolution until about 1920 was to increase the concentration of jobs in the cyclically volatile industries, and this was a major force tending to intensify declines of employment during business contractions. Since then, the continued progress of technology, the very factor which originally was mainly responsible for the concentration in the cyclical industries, has served to arrest this tendency. The upward trend of production in manufacturing and the other highly cyclical industries has remained rapid in recent decades. However, advances of technology have come so swiftly in these industries as well as in agriculture that an increasing part of the nation's labor could turn to the multitude of tasks in which the effectiveness of human effort improves only slowly, where it improves at all. Thus the employees of "service" industries constituted 24 percent of the labor force in 1919, but as much as 44 percent in 1957. The proportion of self-employed workers in business and the professions, which was 9.4 percent in the earlier year, became 10.6 percent in the later year. True, these gains in types of employment that are relatively stable during business cycles were largely canceled by the countervailing trend in agriculture. Nevertheless, the proportion of employees attached to the cyclically volatile industries has not risen since 1919. Or to express this entire development in another way, the proportion of workers having rather steady jobs, either because they work for themselves or because they are employed in industries that are relatively free from the influence of business cycles, kept declining from the beginning of our industrial revolution until about 1920, and since then has moved slightly but irregularly upward.

Thus, the changing structure of industry, which previously had exercised a powerful destabilizing influence on employment and output, particularly the former, has ceased to do so. The new stabilizing tendency is as yet weak, but it is being gradually reinforced by the spread of "white-collar" occupations throughout the range of industry. For many years now, the proportion of people who work as managers, engineers, scientists, draftsmen, accountants, clerks, secretaries, salesmen, or in kindred occupations has been increasing. The white-collar group, which constituted only 28 percent of the labor force outside of agriculture in 1900, rose to 38 percent in 1940 and to 44 percent in 1957. Workers of this category are commonly said to hold a "position" rather than a "job" and to be paid a "salary" rather than a "wage." Hence, they are often sheltered by a professional code which frowns upon frequent firing and hiring. Moreover, much of this type of employment is by its nature of an overhead character and therefore less responsive to the business cycle than are the jobs of machine operators, craftsmen, assembly-line workers, truck drivers, laborers, and others in the "blue-collar" category. For example, during the recession of 1957–58, the number of "production workers" employed in manufacturing, who approximate the blue-collar group, declined 12 percent, while the employment of "nonproduction workers," who approximate the white-collar group, declined only 3 percent. This sort of difference has been characteristic of recessions generally, not only the most recent episode, and on a smaller scale it has also been characteristic of industry generally, not only of manufacturing.

It appears, therefore, that changes in the occupational structure of the labor force, if not also in the industrial structure, have been tending of late to loosen the links which, over a considerable part of our economic history, tied the short-run movement of total employment rather firmly to the cyclical movement of total production, and especially to the cyclical movement of its most unstable parts—that is, the activities of manufacturing, mining, construction, and freight transportation. This stabilizing tendency promises well for the future, although up to the present it has not left a mark on records of aggregate employment that is comparable with the imprint that the stabilizing influences we discussed previously have left on personal income. In the postwar period, as over a longer past, the number of men and women at work, and even more the aggregate of hours worked by them, has continued to move in fairly close sympathy with the fluctuations of production.

We can no longer justifiably suppose, however, when employment falls 2 million during a recession, as it did between July, 1957, and July, 1958, that the number of people who receive an income has declined by any such figure. In fact, the number of workers drawing unemployment insurance under the several regular plans rose about 1.3 million during these twelve months, while the number of retired workers on public pensions rose another million. Hence, it may be conservatively estimated that the number of income recipients increased over 300 thousand despite the recession. In the other postwar recessions our experience was fairly similar. In other words, as a result of some of the structural changes on which I dwelt earlier, the size of the income-receiving population has grown steadily and escaped cyclical fluctuations entirely.[2]

III

Turning next to consumer spending, we must try once again to see recent developments in historical perspective. The fact that stands out is that the impact of business cycles on consumption has recently diminished, while the effects of consumption on the business cycle have become more decisive.

In the classical business cycle, as we came to know it in this country, once business investment began declining appreciably, a reduction of con-

[2] This upward trend would appear steeper than I have suggested if recipients of property income and of public assistance were included in the count. In the present context, however, it has seemed best to restrict the income-receiving population to the working class, or more precisely, to members of the labor force or those recently in the labor force who receive an income as a matter of right and on some regular basis.

sumer spending soon followed. Sometimes the expansion of investment culminated because the firms of one or more key industries, finding that their markets were growing less rapidly than had been anticipated, made an effort to bring their productive capacity or inventories into better adjustment with sales. Sometimes the expansion culminated because the belief grew that construction and financing costs had been pushed to unduly high levels by the advance of prosperity. Sometimes it culminated for all these or still other reasons. But whatever the cause or causes of the decline in investment, it made its influence felt over an increasing area of the economy. For a while consumer spending was maintained at a peak level or even kept rising. But since businessmen were now buying on a smaller scale from one another, more and more workers lost their jobs or their overtime pay, financial embarrassments and business failures became more frequent, and uncertainty about the business outlook spread to parts of the economy in which sales and profits were still flourishing. If some consumers reacted to these developments by curtailing their spending in the interest of caution, others did so as a matter of necessity. Before long, these curtailments proved sufficient to bring on some decline in the aggregate spending of consumers. The impulses for reducing business investments therefore quickened and the entire round of events was repeated, with both investment and consumption declining in a cumulative process.

As the contraction continued, it tried men's patience, yet in time worked its own cure. Driven by hard necessity, business firms moved with energy to reduce costs and increase efficiency. Consumers whose incomes were declining often saved less or dissaved in order not to disrupt their customary living standards. Hence, even if sales and prices were still falling, profit margins improved here and there. In the meantime, bank credit became more readily available, costs of building and terms of borrowing became more favorable, the bond market revived, business failures diminished, and the investment plans of innovators and others began expanding again. When recovery finally came, it was likely to be led by a reduced rate of disinvestment in inventories or by a new rush to make investments in fixed capital. At this stage of the business cycle, consumer spending was at its very lowest level, if not still declining.

Many of these features of earlier business cycles have carried over to the present. However, the behavior of consumers in the postwar recessions has departed from the traditional pattern in two respects. In the first place, consumers maintained their spending at a high level even after business activity had been declining for some months, so that the tendency of recessions to cumulate was severely checked. During the recession of 1945 consumer spending actually kept increasing. In each of the later recessions it fell somewhat; but the decline at no time exceeded 1 percent and lasted only a quarter or two. In the second place, instead of lagging at the recovery stage of the business cycle, as it had in earlier times, consumer spending turned upward before production or employment resumed its expansion. This shift in cyclical behavior appears clearly in department store sales, which have been recorded on a substantially uniform basis for several decades and are widely accepted as a tolerably good indicator of consumer spending. In the recoveries of 1921, 1924, 1927, and 1938, these sales lagged by intervals ranging from two to four months. In 1933 their upturn came at the same time as in production and employment. It thus appears that, during the 1920's and 1930's, consumer spending in no instance led the economy out of a slump. In the postwar period, on the other hand, department store sales have led successive recoveries by intervals stretching from two to five months. Of course, department store sales cover only a small fraction of consumer expenditure, and correction for price changes would alter their historical record somewhat. But the main features of the cyclical behavior of dollar sales by department stores are broadly confirmed by other evidence on consumer spending, which is extensive for recent years. We may therefore conclude with considerable assurance that consumer spending has played a more dynamic role in recent times. Not only have consumers managed their spending during recessions so that the cumulative process of deflation has been curbed, but consumer spending has emerged as one of the active factors in arresting recession and hastening recovery.

This new role of the consumer in the business cycle reflects some of the developments of the postwar period that we considered earlier, particularly the greatly enhanced stability in the flow of personal income, the steady expansion in the number of income recipients, and the relative increase in the number of steady jobs. It reflects also the improvements of financial organization and other structural changes which have strengthened the confidence of people, whether acting as consumers or investors, in their own and the nation's economic future. Whatever may have been true of the past, it can no longer be held that consumers are passive creatures who lack the power or the habit of initiating changes in economic activities. There is no harm in thinking of consumer spending as being largely "determined" by past and current incomes, provided we also recognize that the level of current incomes is itself shaped to a significant degree by the willingness of people to work hard to earn what they need to live as they feel they should. The evidence of rising expectations and increased initiative on the part of consumers is all around us. It appears directly in the rapidly rising proportion of women in the labor force, in the sizable and increasing proportion of men who hold down more than one job, in the slackening of the long-term decline of the average work week in manufacturing despite the increased power of trade unions, as well as indirectly in the improvement of living standards and the great upsurge of population. Indeed, the expansive forces on the side of consumption have been so powerful that we must not be misled by the cyclical responses of consumer spending, small though they were, to which I referred earlier. There are no continuous records of inventories in the hands of consumers; but if such statistics were available, we would almost certainly find that consumption proper, in contrast to consumer spending, did not decline at all during any of the postwar recessions.

In view of these developments in the realm of the consumer, it is evident that the force of any cyclical decline of production has in recent years been reduced or broken as its influence spread through the economy. Production has remained unstable, but the structure of our economy has changed in ways which have limited the effects of recessions on the lives of individuals—on the numbers who receive an income, the aggregate of personal incomes, consumer spending, actual consumption, and to some degree even the numbers employed. It is, therefore, hardly an exaggeration to assert that a good part of the personal security which in an earlier age derived from living on farms and in closely knit family units, after having been disrupted by the onrush of industrialization and urbanization, has of late been restored through the new institutions that have developed in both the private and public branches of our economy.

IV

In concentrating, as I have thus far, on the changes of economic organization which have lately served to reduce the impact of business cycles on the lives of individuals, I have provisionally taken the cyclical movement of production for granted. Of course, if the fluctuations of production had been larger, the impact on people would have been greater. On the other hand, the stabilized tendency of personal income and consumption has itself been a major reason why recent recessions of production have been brief and of only moderate intensity. Many other factors have contributed to this development. Among them are the deliberate efforts made in our generation to control the business cycle, of which I have as yet said little.

In earlier generations there was a tendency for the focus of business thinking to shift from the pursuit of profits to the maintenance of financial solvency whenever confidence in the continuance of prosperity began to wane. At such times experienced businessmen were prone to reason that it would shortly become more difficult to collect from their customers or to raise funds by borrowing, while they in turn were being pressed by their creditors. Under the circumstances it seemed only prudent to conserve cash on hand, if not also to reduce inventories or accounts receivable. Such efforts by some led to similar efforts by others, in a widening circle. As pressure on commodity markets, security markets, and on the banking system mounted, the decline of business activity was speeded and the readjustment of interest rates, particularly on the longer maturities, was delayed. More often than not the scramble for liquidity ran its course without reaching crisis proportions. Sometimes, however, as in 1873, 1893, and 1907, events took a sinister turn. Financial pressures then became so acute that doubts arose about the ability of banks to meet their outstanding obligations and, as people rushed to convert their deposits into currency, even the soundest banks were forced to restrict the outflow of cash. With the nation's system for making monetary payments disrupted, panic ruled for a time over the economy and production inevitably slumped badly.

It was this dramatic phase of the business cycle that first attracted wide notice and stimulated students of public affairs to seek ways and means of improving our financial organization. The Federal Reserve Act, which became law under the shadow of the crisis of 1907, required the pooling of bank reserves and established facilities for temporary borrowing by banks. The hope that this financial reform would ease the transition from the expanding to the contracting phase of business cycles has been amply justified by experience. But the Federal Reserve System could not prevent the cumulation of financial trouble during business expansions. Nor could it prevent runs on banks or massive bank failures, as the Great Depression demonstrated. The need to overhaul and strengthen the financial system became increasingly clear during the 'thirties and led to numerous reforms, among them the insurance of mortgages, the creation of a secondary market for mortgages, the insurance of savings and loan accounts, and—most important of all—the insurance of bank deposits. These financial reforms have served powerfully to limit the propagation of fear, which in the past had been a major factor in intensifying slumps of production.

But more basic than the financial innovations or any other specific measures of policy has been the change in economic and political attitudes which took root during the thirties. The economic theory that depressions promote industrial efficiency and economic progress lost adherents as evidence accumulated of the wreckage caused by unemployment and business failures. The political belief that it was best to leave business storms to blow themselves out lost its grip on men's minds as the depression stretched out. In increasing numbers citizens in all walks of life came around to the view that mass unemployment was intolerable under modern conditions and that the federal government has a continuing responsibility to foster competitive enterprise, to prevent or moderate general economic declines, and to promote a high and rising level of employment and production. This new philosophy of intervention was articulated by the

Congress in the Employment Act of 1946, which solemnly expressed what had by then become a national consensus.

In recent times, therefore, the business cycle has no longer run a free course and this fact has figured prominently in the plans of businessmen as well as consumers. During the 1930's, when the objectives of social reform and economic recovery were sometimes badly confused, many investors suspected that contracyclical policies would result in narrowing the scope of private enterprise and reducing the profitability of investment. These fears diminished after the war as the government showed more understanding of the need to foster a mood of confidence so that enterprise, innovation, and investment may flourish. In investing circles, as elsewhere, the general expectation of the postwar period has been that the government would move with some vigor to check any recession that developed, that its actions would by and large contribute to this objective, and that they would do so in a manner that is broadly consistent with our national traditions. This expectation gradually became stronger and it has played a significant role in extending the horizons of business thinking about the markets and opportunities of the future. The upsurge of population, the eagerness of consumers to live better, the resurgence of Western Europe, the revolutionary discoveries of science, and the steady flow of new products, new materials, and new processes have added impetus to the willingness of investors to expend huge sums of capital on research and on the improvement and expansion of industrial plant and equipment. Some of these influences have also been effective in augmenting public investment. The fundamental trend of investment has continued to move cyclically; but it is now a smaller fraction of total national output and it has displayed a capacity to rebound energetically from the setbacks that come during recessions.

The specific measures adopted by the government in dealing with the recessions of the postwar period have varied from one case to the next. In all of them, monetary, fiscal, and housekeeping policies played some part, with agricultural price-support programs assuming special prominence in one recession, tax reductions in another, and increases of public expenditure in still another. Taking a long view, the most nearly consistent part of contracyclical policy has been in the monetary sphere. Since the early 1920's, when the Federal Reserve authorities first learned how to influence credit conditions through open-market operations, long-term interest rates have tended to move down as soon as the cyclical peak of economic activity was reached, in contrast to the long lags that were characteristic of earlier times. Since 1948 the decline of long-term interest rates in the early stages of a recession has also become more rapid. This change in the cyclical behavior of capital markets reflects the increased vigor and effectiveness of recent monetary policies. Inasmuch as optimism, as a rule, is still widespread during the initial stages of an economic decline, a substantial easing of credit, provided it comes early enough, can appreciably hasten economic recovery. This influence is exerted only in part through lower interest rates. Of greater consequence is the fact that credit becomes more readily available, that the money supply is increased or kept from falling, that the liquidity of financial assets is improved, and that financial markets are generally stimulated. The effects of easier credit are apt to be felt most promptly by smaller businesses and the home-building industry, but they tend to work their way through the entire economy. There can be little doubt that the rather prompt easing of credit conditions, which occurred during recent setbacks of production, was of some significance in keeping their duration so short.

Business firms have also been paying closer attention to the business cycle, and not a few of them have even tried to do something about it. These efforts have been expressed in a variety of ways—through the adoption of long-range capital budgets, closer control of inventories, and more energetic selling or some relaxation of credit standards in times of recession. I do not know enough to assess either the extent or the success of some of these business policies. Surely, business investment in fixed capital has remained a highly volatile activity—a fact that is sometimes overlooked by concentrating attention on years instead of months and on actual expenditures instead of new commitments. There is, however, strong evidence that the businessmen of our generation manage inventories better than did their predecessors. The inventory/sales ratio of manufacturing firms has lately averaged about a fourth less than during the 1920's, despite the increased importance of the durable goods sector where inventories are especially heavy. The trend of the inventory/sales ratio has also moved down substantially in the case of distributive firms. This success in economizing on inventories has tended to reduce the fluctuations of inventory investment relative to the scale of business operations, and this in turn has helped to moderate the cyclical swings in production. Not only that, but it appears that the cyclical downturns of both inventories and inventory investment have tended to come at an earlier stage of the business cycle in the postwar period than they did previously, so that any imbalance between inventories and sales could be corrected sooner. Since consumer outlays—and often also other expenditures—were well maintained during the recent recessions of production, the rising phase of inventory disinvestment ceased rather early and this naturally favored a fairly prompt recovery of production.

Thus, numerous changes in the structure of our economy have combined to stimulate overall expansion during the postwar period and to keep within moderate limits the cyclical declines that occurred in production. Indeed, there are cogent grounds for believing that these declines were even more moderate than our familiar statistical records suggest. The line of division between production for sale and production for direct use does not stand still in a dynamic economy. In the early decades of the industrial revolution an increasing part of our production was, in effect, transferred from the home to the shop and factory. This trend has continued in the preparation of foods, but in other activities it appears on balance to have been reversed. The great expansion of home ownership, the invention of all sorts of mechanical contrivances for the home, longer vacations, the general eagerness for improvement, if not also the income tax, have stimulated many people to do more and more things for themselves. Consumers have become equipped to an increasing degree with the capital goods they need for transportation, for the refrigeration of food, for the laundering of clothes, as well as for entertainment and instruction. They have also been doing, on an increasing scale, much of the carpentry, painting, plumbing, and landscaping around their homes. Such activities of production are less subject to the business cycle than the commercial activities which enter statistical reports. Yet these domestic activities have undoubtedly been expanding rapidly, and perhaps expanding even more during the declining than during the rising phase of the business cycle. Hence, it is entirely probable that the cyclical swings of production have of late been smaller, while the average rate of growth of production has been higher, than is commonly supposed.

V

It is in the nature of an economic vocabulary to change slowly, when it changes at all. We keep speaking of the price system, the business cycle, capitalism, socialism, communism, and sometimes we even refer to the "inherent instability" of capitalism or of communism; but the reality that these terms and phrases are intended to denote or sum up does not remain fixed. I have tried to show how a conjuncture of structural changes in our economy has served to modify the business cycle of our times. Some of these changes were planned while others were unplanned. Some resulted from efforts to control the business cycle while others originated in policies aimed at different ends. Some arose from private and others from public activities. Some are of very recent origin and others of long standing. The net result has been that the intensity of cyclical swings of production has become smaller. The links that previously tied together the cyclical movements of production, employment, personal income, and consumption have become looser. And, as everyone knows, the once familiar parallelism of the short-term movements in the physical volume of total production, on the one hand, and the average level of wholesale or consumer prices, on the other, has become somewhat elusive.

To be sure, special factors of an episodic character played their part in recent business cycles, as they always have. For example, a pent-up demand for civilian goods was highly significant in checking the recession of 1945. The tax reduction legislated in April, 1948, helped to moderate the recession which began towards the end of that year. The tax cuts announced soon after business activity began receding in 1953 merely required executive acquiescence in legislation that had been passed before any recession was in sight. Again, the sputniks spurred the government's response to the recession of 1957–58. Special circumstances such as these undoubtedly weakened the forces of economic contraction at certain times; but they also strengthened them at other times. In particular, governmental purchases from private firms have not infrequently been an unsettling influence rather than a stabilizing force. We need only recall the drop of federal expenditure on commodities and services from an annual rate of $91 billion in the early months of 1945 to $16 billion two years later, or the fall from $59 billion to $44 billion soon after the Korean hostilities came to a close. The ability of our economy to adjust to such major disturbances without experiencing a severe or protracted slump testifies not only to our good luck; it testifies also to the stabilizing power of the structural changes that I have emphasized.

It seems reasonable to expect that the structural changes in our economy, which have recently served to moderate and humanize the business cycle, will continue to do so. The growth of corporations is not likely to be checked, nor is the tendency to pay fairly stable dividends likely to be modified. The scale of governmental activities will remain very extensive, and so it would be even if the communist threat to our national security were somehow banished. Our methods of taxation might change materially, but the income tax will remain a major source of governmental revenue. Governmental expenditures might fluctuate sharply, but they are not likely to decline during a recession merely because governmental revenues are then declining. The social security system is more likely to grow than to remain stationary or contract. Private pension arrangements will multiply and so also may private supplements to unemployment insurance. Our population will continue to grow. The restlessness and eagerness of consumers to live better is likely to remain a dynamic force. Research and development activities will continue to enlarge opportunities for investment. Governmental efforts to promote a high and expanding level of economic activity are not likely to weaken. Private businesses will continue to seek ways to economize on inventories and otherwise minimize the risk of cyclical fluctuations in their operations. Employment in agriculture is already so low that its further decline can no longer offset future gains of the service industries on the scale experienced in the past. The spread of white-collar occupations throughout the range of industry will continue and may even accelerate. For all these reasons, the business cycle is unlikely to be as disturbing or troublesome to our children as it once was to us or our fathers.

This is surely a reasonable expectation as we look to the future. Yet, it is well to remember that projections of human experience remain descriptions of a limited past no matter how alluringly they are expressed in language of the future. A lesson of history, which keeps resounding through the ages, is that the most reasonable of expectations sometimes lead nations astray. If my analysis is sound, it supports the judgment that the recessions or depressions of the futre are likely to be appreciably milder on the average than they were before the 1940's. It supports no more than this. In view of the inherent variability of business cycles and our still somewhat haphazard ways of dealing with them, there can be no assurance that episodic factors will not make a future recession both longer and deeper than any we experienced in the postwar period.

Nor can there by any assurance that the conjuncture of structural changes on which I have dwelt will not be succeeded by another which will prove less favorable to economic stability. For example, although the stabilizing influence of the rising trend of white-collar employment in manufacturing has been more than sufficient to offset the cyclically intensifying influence of a greater concentration of employment in the durable goods sector, the balance of forces might be tipped the other way in the future. This could happen all the more readily if, as white-collar work continues to grow, the need to cut costs during a recession should make this type of employment less stable than it has been. Again, our exports in recent decades have tended to intensify the business cycle somewhat, and this factor may become of larger significance. Also, it still remains to be seen whether the rising trend of prices—to say nothing of the rapidly growing consumer and mortgage debt—may not serve to complicate future recessions.

A generation ago many economists, having become persuaded that our economy had reached maturity, spoke grimly of a future of secular stagnation. Parts of their analysis were faulty and their predictions have proved wrong; yet their warning helped to mobilize thought and energy to avert the danger of chronic unemployment. Of late, many economists have been speaking just as persuasively, though not always as grimly, of a future of secular inflation. The warning is timely. During the postwar recessions the average level of prices in wholesale and consumer markets has declined little or not at all. The advances in prices that cus-tomarily occur during periods of business expansion have therefore be-come cumulative. It is true that in the last few years the federal govern-ment has made some progress in dealing with inflation. Nevertheless, wages and prices rose appreciably even during the recent recession, the general public has been speculating on a larger scale in common stocks, long-term interest rates have risen very sharply since mid-1958, and the yield on stocks relative to bonds has become abnormally low. All these appear to be symptoms of a continuation of inflationary expectations or pressures.

Such developments have often led to economic trouble. They could do so again even if our balance of payments on international account re-mained favorable. That, however, has not been the case for some time. The "dollar shortage" which influenced much of our economic thinking and practice during the past generation seems to have ended. The econ-omies of many areas of the Free World, especially of Western Europe and Japan, have lately been rebuilt and their competitive power has been restored. This re-establishment of competitive and monetary links be-tween our country and others may cause us some inconvenience, but it is basically a promising development for the future. It should stimulate our economic growth as well as contribute to the economic progress and political stability of other nations of the Free World. Our financial policies, however, will gradually need to be adjusted to the changed international environment. Although our gold stocks are still abundant and the dollar is still the strongest currency in the world, we can no longer conduct our economic affairs without being mindful of gold, or of the short-term balances that foreign governments and citizens have accumulated here, or of the levels of labor costs, interest rates, and prices in our country relative to those in other nations. Unless the deficit in our balance of payments is soon brought under better control, our nation's ability to pursue contracyclical policies during a business recession may be seriously hampered.

We are living in extraordinarily creative but also deeply troubled times. One of the triumphs of this generation is the progress that our nation has made in reducing economic instability. In the years ahead, no matter what we do as a people, our economy will continue to undergo changes, many of which were neither planned nor anticipated. However, the course of events, both domestic and international, will also depend—and to a large degree—on our resourcefulness and courage in deliberately modifying the structure of our economy so as to strengthen the forces of growth and yet restrain instability.

Great opportunities as well as difficult problems face our nation.

Monopoly power, which is still being freely exercised despite all the exhortation of recent years, can be curbed by moving toward price and wage controls or, as many economists still hope, by regenerating competition. Higher protective tariffs, import quotas, and "Buy American" schemes can be embraced or, as many economists hope, avoided. A tax structure that inhibits private investment and directs people's energy into activities that contribute little to the nation's economic strength can be retained or reformed. Costly farm surpluses can be further encouraged by government or discontinued. The problems posed by the slums and the inefficient transportation of many of our cities can be neglected or attacked with some zeal. The inadequacy of our unemployment insurance system can be ignored until the next recession or corrected while there is opportunity for a judicious overhauling. In general, our governmental authorities can deal with recessions by trusting to improvisations of public spending, which often will not become effective until economic recovery is already under way, or by providing in advance of any recession for fairly prompt and automatic adjustment of income tax rates to a temporarily lower level of economic activity. The coordination of governmental policies, which may make the difference between success and failure in promoting our national objectives, can be left largely to accidents of personal force and ingenuity or it can be made systematic through an economic policy board under the chairmanship of the President. These and other choices will have to be made by the people of the United States; and economists—far more than any other group—will in the end help to make them.

*Theodore A. Andersen**

26. Trends in Profit Sensitivity

Reprinted from **The Journal of Finance,** Vol. XVIII, No. 4 (December, 1963), pp. 637–646, by permission of the author and the publisher.

Various journals of economics and business in recent years have contained numerous articles which have discussed the effect of changing profit margins on economic growth rates, inflation, and wage rates.[1] Also, the decline in profit margins and the contributing factors have been discussed.[2] There is, however, another important characteristic of profits which has developed since World War II and which has received very little attention. This is their increasing sensitivity to business recessions.[3]

* Associate Professor of Business Economics, University of California, Los Angeles.

[1] N. Kaldor, "Economic Growth and the Problem of Inflation," *Economica* (August, 1959), pp. 212–26, and (November, 1959), pp. 287–98. Mr. Kaldor discusses the dependence of profit margins on the growth rate of the economy. P. W. S. Andrews and Elizabeth Brunner, "Business Profits and the Quiet Life," *Journal of Industrial Economics* (November, 1962), pp. 72–78. Their article emphasizes the importance of the individual firm's strenuous efforts to maximize profits. Richard G. Lipsey and M. D. Stener, "The Relation between Profits and Wage Rates," *Economica* (May, 1961), pp. 132–55. The authors contend that the rate of increase in wage rates is more sensitive to unemployment than profit rates in the postwar period in the United Kingdom. Rattan J. Bhatia, "Profits and the Rate of Change in Money Earnings in the U.S., 1953–59," *Economica* (August, 1962), pp. 255–62. Mr. Bhatia argues that both the level of profits and the rate of change in profits influence strongly changes in the U.S. money earnings. He sees one of two implications in his findings. One is the so-called cost inflation which has been of the profit-push rather than the wage-push variety. The other is that the entire postwar period has been characterized by demand-pull inflation which first increases prices and profits and then wages.

[2] Sidney Cottle and Tate Whitman, "Twenty Years of Corporate Earnings," *Harvard Business Review* (May–June, 1958), pp. 100–114. The authors note that while 1955 was in general a much more prosperous year than 1935, in most industries profit margins were lower. J. Roger Morrison and Richard F. Neuschel, "The Second Squeeze on Profits," *Harvard Business Review* (July–August, 1962), pp. 49–66. The authors note that the business recession in 1960–61 was mild, but profits declined more sharply than in previous recessions. They cite evidence and arguments which indicate that increasing severity of competition rather than a wage-price squeeze was the major cause of the recent declines in profit margins.

[3] Charles L. Schultze, *Recent Inflation in the United States,* Joint Economic Committee, Congress of the United States (September, 1959), pp. 78–96. The author provides empirical evidence of the substantial rise in overhead costs for manufacturing industries between 1947 and 1957. From this it can be inferred that profits would become more sensitive to decreases in sales.

The purpose of this article is to evaluate the postwar trend in this characteristic of profits. Part I analyzes the changing sensitivity of total corporate profits and also compares the stability of profits in the manufacturing industries with those in the nonmanufacturing industries. In addition to presenting the empirical evidence, an attempt is made in Part II to evaluate the underlying causes of the trends that are shown. The changing patterns of business policies and costs, as well as the shifts in profit margins, are analyzed to determine their effect on profit sensitivity. Part III discusses the implications of these trends from the standpoint of such business policies as pricing, expansion of productive capacity, and marketing.

I. TRENDS IN PROFIT SENSITIVITY

Table 1 shows the trend in profit sensitivity during the four postwar recessions. The periods of decline were selected to show the peak level of

TABLE 1.   MEASURES OF PROFIT SENSITIVITY DURING FOUR POSTWAR RECESSIONS

Period of Decline	Percent Change in GNP	Percent Change in Corporate Profits	Profit Sensitivity Ratio*
4Q48–4Q49	−4.3	−15.4	3.6
2Q53–2Q54	−2.8	−18.8	6.7
3Q57–1Q58	−3.8	−27.3	7.2
2Q60–1Q61	−0.8	−14.2	17.8

* Percent decline in profits divided by percent decline in GNP. For example, 15.4 ÷ 4.3 = 3.6, the profit sensitivity ratio for the 1948–49 recession.
NOTE: (1) All data are on a seasonally adjusted basis. SOURCE: calculated from data on GNP and profits published by the U.S. Department of Commerce, *National Income* (1951), pp. 205, 207; *Business Statistics* (1955), pp. 2, 3; (1959), pp. 1, 2; *Economic Report of the President* (January, 1963), pp. 171, 246. (2) During the 1953–54 recession, the Korean War tax on excess corporate profits was eliminated, while in the other recessions there were no changes in tax rates. Thus, to put all recessions on a comparable basis, it has been necessary to examine the profit data on a pretax basis. With the exception of the 1953–54 recession, the trends in profit sensitivity on an after-tax basis show the same pattern as on a pretax basis.

GNP before the recession got under way and the lowest peak reached during the recession. In the first postwar recession, for example, GNP was $267.0 billion in the fourth quarter of 1948, and it declined in each succeeding quarter until it reached $255.5 billion in the fourth quarter of 1949.[4] This represented a 4.3 percent decline.

[4] *National Income*, 1951, U.S. Department of Commerce, p. 207.

TABLE 2.   TRENDS IN PROFIT SENSITIVITY OF MANUFACTURING AND NONMANUFACTURING INDUSTRIES

	Profit Sensitivity Ratio	
Period of Decline	Manufacturing	Nonmanufacturing
4Q48–4Q49	5.6	.56
2Q53–2Q54	7.8	5.1
3Q57–1Q58	8.9	4.2
2Q60–1Q61	24.0	11.25

SOURCE: Federal Trade Commission-Securities Exchange Commission, *Quarterly Financial Report for Manufacturing Corporations* (fourth quarter, 1949), p. 5; (second quarter, 1954), p. 3; (first quarter, 1958), p. 30; for the 1960–61 recession, the U.S. Department of Commerce's figures on manufacturing profits were used rather than FTC-SEC, because the former's were on a seasonally adjusted basis. For the 1957–58 and prior recessions, only FTC-SEC data on manufacturing profits were available on a quarterly basis. These were seasonally adjusted by the author.

The striking feature of this table is the strong, steady increase in the profit sensitivity ratio. Before attempting to explain the causal factors underlying this trend, it should be noted that for manufacturing industries the level of sensitivity ratios is different from that of nonmanufacturing industries, although the trend for the two groups is the same. This can be seen in Table 2 and Chart 1, which were prepared on the same basis as Table 1.

The sensitivity in profits shown in Tables 1 and 2 reflects the well-known fact that costs usually drop less than sales during recessions. Be-

CHART 1

TRENDS IN PROFIT SENSITIVITY RATIOS

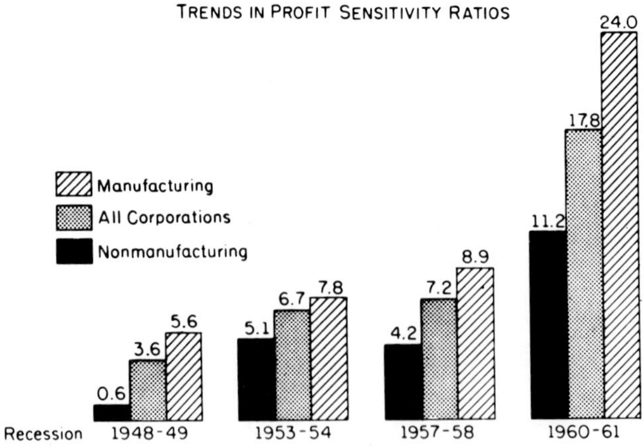

NOTE: Sensitivity ratios show ratio of percent decline in profits to percent decline in GNP from business cycle peak to bottom.
SOURCE: Tables 1 and 2.

cause of the data available on sales, profit margins, and aggregate profits, it is possible to construct a reasonably accurate model of the proportionate decline in costs that occurred in each of the postwar recessions. For example, if the business statistics show that (a) sales in a given recession drop by 4 percent and aggregate profits by 20 percent, and (b) that profits are 10 percent of sales just prior to the downturn, then it can be deduced that costs decline by 2.2 percent. This is illustrated in Table 3.

TABLE 3. THEORETICAL MODEL SHOWING THE EFFECT ON COSTS OF A 4 PERCENT DECLINE IN SALES*

	Period I	*Period II*	*Percent Change*
Given			
Sales	100	96	−4
Profits, before taxes	10	8	−20
Computed (sales less profits)			
Costs	90	88	−2.2

* Assumptions: In Period I, sales = 100, profits are 10 percent of sales and decline by 20 percent from Period I to Period II.

The results of applying this method to the business statistics available on the four postwar recessions are shown in Table 4.

The computed 0.5 percent rise in total corporate costs during the 1960–61 recession is substantiated by the fact that the total wage and

TABLE 4. ESTIMATED CHANGES IN COSTS DURING THE POSTWAR RECESSIONS

Period of Decline	*Percent Change in:*		
	Sales	*Costs*	*Profits*
4Q48–4Q49	−4.3	−2.8	−15.4
2Q53–2Q54	−2.8	−0.8	−18.8
3Q57–1Q58	−3.8	−1.2	−27.3
2Q60–1Q61	−0.8	+0.5	−14.2

Note: Allowance has been made for the fact that the ratio of profits to sales at the beginning of each recession became progressively lower after the 1948–49 slump.

salary payments fell by only $1.5 billion in this period, while depreciation expense and business contributions to U. S. social security systems (because of an increase in tax rates) rose by $1.7 billion. Other business expenses which increased include aggregate bond interest expense and property taxes.

It may be generalized that in view of the low ratio of profits to sales—usually under 5 percent after taxes, even during periods of relatively low unemployment—a small drop in sales not accompanied by a proportionate drop in costs can easily produce a percentage drop in profits that is many times greater than the percentage drop in sales. Table 3 showed that the combination of a 4 percent drop in sales and a 2 percent drop in aggregate costs produced a 20 percent drop in profits. This is about what happened in the 1948–49 recession.

II. FACTORS REDUCING COST FLEXIBILITY

The statistics on profit sensitivity indicate that business operating costs are becoming less and less susceptible to reduction during periods of sales decline.[5] There appear to be two major reasons for this trend. First, many firms are accelerating their expenditures on product development, and these costs tend to keep rising even during periods of economic recession. In 1958, for example, expenditures for research and development (R&D) were up about $1 billion or 10 percent from 1957, while between 1948 and

TABLE 5. AGGREGATE INDUSTRIAL RESEARCH AND
DEVELOPMENT EXPENDITURES BY DECADES, 1940–70

Period	Amount (Billions)
1941–50	$ 13
1951–60	60
1961–70	172

SOURCES: *Statistical Abstract of the United States, 1954,* p. 514; National Science Foundation, "Review of Data on R&D" (September, 1961), pp. 1–3; 1941–42 and 1961–70 estimates are by the author.

1949 these expenditures remained stable. Then, too, in the 1957–58 recession, employment of engineers, scientists, and technical workers increased from 6.6 million in October, 1957, to 7.2 million in October, 1958. Again, in the 1960–61 recession, industrial R&D expenditures continued to rise and were about $1 billion higher in 1961 than in 1960.

Because R&D costs have been growing larger relative to total costs, they obviously are becoming an even more important deterrent to cost reduction. Table 5 and Chart 2 show the trends in these expenditures.

Product development, of course, involves costs other than just research. The building and testing of prototype products, tooling up to produce the new or changed product, retraining of workers, and customer education and sales promotion are extra costs which often follow industrial R&D expenditures. This complex of expenditures may well continue to expand during recessions to help contribute over the long

[5] Schultze, *op. cit.,* pp. 78–84.

run to a strong competitive position for the firm. With consumer discretionary income both very large and expanding rapidly, with the consumer stock of durable goods at a record high level, and with technology accelerating, it seems likely that the emphasis on product development will continue to increase. This means that this upward pressure on business costs may serve over time to reduce cost flexibility continuously.

The second major factor working against major cost reductions during sales declines is the trend toward greater mechanization of production and increased efforts to plan and control business operations. For either the highly mechanized or automated business operation, costs cannot be cut as rapidly when output slumps as they could have been had that operation been handled largely or entirely by direct labor. Depreciation, obsolescence, and costs of capital have been rising as a per-

CHART 2

TRENDS IN INDUSTRIAL R&D EXPENDITURES, 1940-70
(Billions of Dollars)

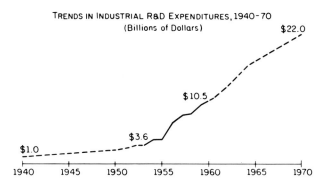

SOURCE: *Statistical Abstract of the United States, 1954*, p. 514;
National Science Foundation, "Reviews of Data on R&D" (September,
1961), pp. 1-3; 1941-42 and 1961-70 estimates are by the author.

centage of total costs, and these types of costs, of course, do not lend themselves to reduction during periods of production decline as well as do factory direct labor costs. Between 1948 and 1958, for example, the ratio of depreciable assets to annual sales rose from 28 to 33 percent. Thus the continuous substitution of capital for production labor means decreasing downward flexibility in total costs.

In the categories of employment which have been rising, such as industrial and systems engineers, research, accounting, finance, training, market planning, and sales promotion, little opportunity is found for reductions in employment during recessions. Thus, with the trend toward fewer workers engaged in the types of activities where employee cuts can be made during production slumps, it is becoming increasingly difficult to reduce costs when sales decline. These shifts in the way employees

TABLE 6. EFFECT OF RISING PRODUCT DEVELOPMENT AND DEPRECIATION COSTS ON PROFIT SENSITIVITY FOR A GIVEN COMPANY

	Assumption of Proportion of Sales Represented by Product Development Plus Depreciation Expenses			
	Period I: 10 Percent		Period II: 20 Percent	
	Business-Cycle Peak	Business-Cycle Bottom	Business-Cycle Peak	Business-Cycle Bottom
Sales	100	95	100	95
Development and depreciation costs	10	10.5 (up 5%)	20	21.0 (up 5%)
Variable costs	80	76.0 (down 5%)	70	66.5 (down 5%)
Total costs	90	86.5	90	87.5
Profits	10	8.5 (−15%)	10	7.5 (−25%)

are used make for higher productivity and more rapid product change, but they also make for less downward flexibility in costs.

Profit sensitivity has increased faster for manufacturing than for nonmanufacturing firms because both research and depreciation expenses are much larger percentages of total sales for the former group than for the latter. Table 6 shows that if for a given company in Period I its product development plus depreciation costs equaled 10 percent of sales and are rising, a 5 percent sales decline would produce a relatively small drop in profits of 15 percent. If, however, by Period II these costs equaled 20 percent of sales and are rising, then a 5 percent drop in sales would be accompanied by a 25 percent drop in profits. Manufacturing firms in general have experienced an upward trend in these costs from 10 percent of sales toward 20 percent over the past 15 years, and these costs have tended to rise even during recessions.

TABLE 7. EFFECT OF PROFIT SQUEEZE ON PROFIT SENSITIVITY

	Assuming 3 Percent Sales Decline and a 13 Percent Profit Margin*		Assuming 3 Percent Sales Decline and a 9 Percent Profit Margin*	
	Period I	Period II	Period I	Period II
Sales	100	97	100	97
Costs	88	88	91	91
Profits	12	9 (−25.0%)	9	6 (−33.3%)

* The ratio of profits to GNP was 12 percent as of 4Q48, the beginning of the first postwar recession. It was 9 percent as of 2Q60, the beginning of the fourth postwar recession.

Table 7 shows that profit sensitivity is in part a function of the size of profit margins. Thus a 3 percent decline in sales from Period I to II accompanied by no change in costs produces (a) a 25 percent drop in profits if the profit-to-sales ratio is 12 percent and (b) a 33.3 percent drop in profits if the profit-to-sales ratio is 9 percent. With the higher profit margin, the profit sensitivity ratio proved to be 8.3 and with the lower profit margin, 11.1. It is believed, however, that the decline in profit margins over the postwar period was less of a contributing factor to the increase in profit sensitivity than the relatively rapid increase in the various types of overhead costs. The profit sensitivity ratios increased about fivefold over the postwar period, whereas the decline in profit margins as shown in Table 7 tended to increase the sensitivity ratio by less than 30 percent.

III. BUSINESS POLICY IMPLICATIONS OF RISING PROFIT SENSITIVITY

The trend toward rising fixed costs might well encourage the individual business firm to become more aggressive during or in anticipation of sales slumps in attempting to maintain its unit sales in the following ways: (1) Cut prices where competition is unlikely to retaliate. (2) Cut prices if demand is quite elastic. (3) Where improvements in the product or services or both can be made in a comparatively short period of time, initiate such improvements. (4) Broaden the distribution of company products into new domestic and foreign markets. (5) Budget more for sales promotion.

Also, with rising fixed costs, manufacturing firms need to become more careful in expanding their productive capacity. The automated firm,

TABLE 8

(In Period II prices are 2 percent higher than in Period I, unit sales are off 3 percent, and revenue is down 1.06 percent*)

	Fixed Costs Are 40 Percent of Total Costs		Fixed Costs Are 80 Percent of Total Costs	
	Period I	Period II	Period I	Period II
Fixed costs	4,000	4,000	8,000	8,000
Variable costs	6,000	5,820 (−3%)	2,000	1,940 (−3%)
Total costs	10,000	9,820 (−1.8%)	10,000	9,940 (−0.6%)

* Assumes unit volume of 1,000 and price of $11 in Period I. Thus, total revenue in each model drops from $11,000 to $10,883, a decline of 1.06 percent, or $117. Total costs declined by $180 when fixed costs were 40 percent of total costs. When fixed costs were 80 percent of total costs, however, the decline in total costs was only $60, or less than the decline in revenue.

for example, often cannot cut its costs as much when sales slump as it could if there were greater reliance on direct labor. Of course, the savings produced by automation when the utilization rate is high may more than offset the cost disadvantage incurred during periods of low production.

The growing inability to cut costs as much as previously during sales slumps may also have the effect of discouraging price increases. To illustrate this point, two models have been constructed (see Table 8) which show the effect on profits of raising prices when costs are relatively (*a*) flexible and (*b*) inflexible.

When fixed costs were only 40 percent of total costs, the 3 percent decline in output was accompanied by a 1.8 percent decline in costs. When fixed costs were 80 percent, the drop in total costs was only 0.6 percent. In general, the higher the percentage of fixed costs the less the decline in total costs when a given cut in output occurs. Since the price increases tend to exert downward pressure on unit sales, it is more and more likely that the loss of revenue which could occur if prices were raised would be greater than the decline in costs that would occur.

The assumptions used in Table 8, of course, are not always consistent with what happens in the economy. For example, rising prices and rising sales may occur simultaneously, particularly when national income is rising. For an individual firm, however, in competition with firms in its own industry and those in other industries (which produce substitute goods), an increase in price may well tend to reduce its sales volume from the level which might have been secured had prices not been raised.

In past economic recessions, a large segment of the business community has opposed federal tax reduction because it would cause the government to experience, at least in the short run, a larger budgetary deficit. Now, with fixed costs rising as a percentage of total costs, the majority of business management will be under increasing financial pressure during economic slumps to support the aggressive use of federal fiscal policies to counteract the slump. It cannot, of course, be predicted with much certainty how the businessman's attitude in the future will change toward federal fiscal policy as a countercyclical force. It seems likely, though, that the growing loss of cost flexibility will increase the amount of business support for stronger federal action to counter business downturns.

With the trend toward greater profit sensitivity, it may well be that many firms will want to depend more heavily on equity financing in the future. When costs were more flexible, debt capital could be used with less risk; but with decreasing flexibility, debt financing is becoming riskier. Creditors may also become increasingly concerned about profit instability and insist that borrowers rely more heavily on equity capital in the future.

IV. SUMMARY

There appear to be strong and persistent reasons for rising profit sensitivity, particularly in the manufacturing industries. Product development appears to be an increasingly important part of total costs and so do mechanization and automation. Expenditures for planning and control also appear to be rising as a percentage of total costs and are relatively inflexible in the short run.

Business firms can therefore be expected to undertake progressively greater efforts to stabilize revenue, but the acceleration of technological advance is doing much to unstabilize sales for a given firm. Products have a shorter and shorter life span. This probably can explain in large part the trend toward product diversification and corporate mergers. It may also lead to more conservative financing in the future and greater business support for vigorous use of the federal government's power to moderate business cycles.

Francis A. Mlynarczyk, Jr.[*]

27. An Empirical Study of Accounting Methods and Stock Prices

Reprinted from **Empirical Research in Accounting: Selected Studies, 1969** (Supplement to Volume 7 of **Journal of Accounting Research**), pp. 63–81, by permission of the publisher. Copyright, Institute of Professional Accounting, 1970.

This study constitutes an attempt to determine from empirical data the effects of one set of specific alternative accounting methods on security prices by means of multivariate statistical techniques. After a brief introduction dealing with the accounting process and resource allocation, literature relevant to the study is discussed. The setting of the study is then presented, followed by the conceptual framework, the research design, the results, and the conclusions drawn.

INTRODUCTION—NATURE OF ACCOUNTING AND THE ACCOUNTING PROCESS

It has been stated that accounting deals with the measurement and communication of economic information.[1] The measurement process generally takes place when an accountant expresses his judgment about the nature of an economic event in the form of a decision to make (or not to make) an entry into the accounting records. The communication process generally takes place when the information contained in the accounting system is summarized and classified into the forms of income statements, balance sheets, and other supplementary statements, along with additional verbal notes. The statements prepared might be intended solely for internal use (i.e., for management purposes), or for external use (i.e., for financial reporting purposes), or for both purposes.

The financial statements prepared for publication must be developed according to "generally accepted accounting principles," and usually must

[*] Research Officer, First National City Bank, New York, and Adjunct Assistant Professor, New York University. The bulk of the work performed for this study was done at Purdue University.
[1] See Bevis [3, p. 27].

be audited by an independent member of the public accounting profession. That is, an independent member of the public accounting profession is called upon to express his judgment concerning whether or not the judgment of the accountant who prepared the statements was a "fair" or "reasonable" estimate of the "true" nature of the underlying economic facts. If in the opinion of the independent public accountant, after an adequate examination of the accounting system and transactions, the statements in question conform with generally accepted accounting principles, a "clean opinion" will be attached to the statements. If the statements do not appear to conform, the independent accountant will qualify or disclaim their fairness, as the circumstances require.

INVESTORS AS USERS OF PUBLISHED FINANCIAL STATEMENTS

Among the users of published financial statements are investors who must base decisions to supply or not to supply capital to a great extent upon information contained in published accounting statements. Presumably, identical economic events, *ceteris paribus*, should give rise to identical behavior on the part of a given investor. However, because two or more differing generally accepted accounting principles (e.g., specific identification, FIFO, LIFO, and average cost for inventory accounting) may be used to report identical economic events (e.g., the physical flow of a given quantity of goods out of an enterprise resulting from sales), the important question arises: Do investors recognize the underlying economic event for what it is and base their decisions upon it, or do they base their decisions upon the reported information per se? If investors grounded their portfolio decisions on the reported information on its face, then reporting variations for a class of economic events that play a material role in the determination of income for a firm could cause a misallocation of resources, even though enough information might be conveyed to allow adjustments to be made for purposes of comparison with other firms. Of course, if reporting variations prevail and enough information to allow adjustments for comparison purposes to be made is *not* provided, then misallocation of resources is a highly probable result.

It might be argued that accounting fulfills satisfactorily its intended purposes, namely, the measurement and communication of economic data, even if generally accepted accounting principles do allow different accounting methods for reporting purposes to be used to describe the same economic event, if enough information is provided to allow for adjustments to be made for purposes of comparison. On the other hand, it can be argued that investors should not be expected to be expert in accounting, and, consequently, only if identical economic events give rise to identical decisions is accounting fulfilling its purpose satisfactorily. The argument is that the accounting process should not affect resource allocation. Only economic "facts" should affect resource allocation.

The latter position takes a broader view of the role of the accounting process. It maintains that to provide information that can be adjusted for comparative purposes is not enough, if the adjustment is not made.[2] It maintains that investors should not be persuaded to supply a greater amount of capital, or a given amount on more favorable terms, simply because of the accounting methods used, if the underlying economic facts are the same. It maintains that investors have enough problems of their own, such as developing operational theories of rational investment policy, and that the task of becoming expert accountants should not be thrust upon them. This is the position taken in this study.

An important question, then, is: Does accounting *method* influence investor behavior? Many opinions have been ventured that imply that the wide latitude of choice of accounting methods within generally accepted accounting principles has indeed had an impact on investor behavior. The following are some examples from *Forbes* [30, p. 28, et seq.] of the kinds of opinions held by various influentials in the investment management environment:

> ... the annual net earnings figure tends to have a magical significance not only for the ordinary investor but for security analysts and even for acquisition-minded managements.
> ... single, conveniently packaged net earnings figure has always seemed to fill the bill perfectly. ... On their reliability, billions of investment dollars are wagered.
> Professional investors, the men who manage large portfolios of stocks, regard published earnings with the utmost skepticism.

and from *Barron's* [32, pp. 29–30]

> ... no one on Wall Street is making much of an allowance for the way earnings are reported. This is surprising since the market is now supposedly dominated by professionals.
> We've always had differing methods of reporting earnings, but in the past the professionals have made allowances for them.

Statements such as the above suggest that some question exists as to whether investors act upon the facts behind the figures or merely upon the figures. Accounting research in this area appears to be potentially fruitful to shed light on the effects of the accounting process on resource allocation.

---

[2] By a "very large" proportion of investors. How large is "very large," of course, is an open question.

RELEVANT LITERATURE

In the area of alternative accounting methods and decisions, the research to date has fallen into four broad categories: empirical study, experimental study, simulation study, and theoretical exposition. The studies in the area of specific alternative accounting methods and security prices are few in number, and have been primarily experimental or empirical.

Empirical studies

Only three empirical studies of specific alternative accounting methods and security prices have been published. These are the two studies of O'Donnell [24], [25] (depreciation/tax accounting) and the work of Summers [28] (tax accounting). Empirical study of the *type* of published accounting data (e.g., annual reports, quarterly reports) used by investors has been done by Benston [2]. Empirical study of the correlation of common stock values and various financial accounting variables (e.g., reported earnings, funds flows) has been performed by Staubus [27].

The work of O'Donnell [24] is the earliest empirical study to be found on specific alternative accounting methods and security prices. In his first study, O'Donnell [24, p. 135] attempted to examine two questions:

(a) Under what circumstances does the market regard specific accounting changes as producing "real" or "fictitious" profits?

(b) How long does it take the market to correctly evaluate such changes?

The specific accounting method he chose to study was the depreciation and related tax accounting methods used for financial reporting purposes by electric utility companies. All electric utility companies during the period of the study used straight-line depreciation (or methods producing substantially similar effects on reported profits) for financial reporting purposes. For federal income tax purposes many companies, though not all, used an accelerated method of depreciation for new plant and equipment allowed under the Revenue Act of 1954. Of the companies that did use an accelerated method, (1) some flowed-through the resulting reduction of income tax payments to the income statement for financial reporting purposes; (2) the others normalized the tax payment reduction by charging (debiting) a taxes expense account by an amount based upon the profit before taxes figure on the financial reporting income statement, with corresponding credits to a taxes payable account, and, usually, a deferred tax liability account.[3]

---

[3] See Appendix A for an example of the two methods of reporting.

O'Donnell's test consisted of examining trends in the price-earnings ratios of a sample of 37 electric utility operating and holding companies for the period 1949 through 1961. Since the change in the tax laws relating to admissible depreciation charges took place in 1954, the period chosen for his study allowed comparison before and after the change. O'Donnell's 37-company sample was broken down into three subsamples, consisting of 12 companies that did not switch to an accelerated method of depreciation for tax purposes during the period, and 25 that did. Of the latter, 18 of those normalized the tax reduction benefits, and the remaining 7 flowed-through the benefits.

O'Donnell's comparisons of the mean yearly price-earnings ratios and the trends of means over time led him to conclude that investors appeared to view flow-through earnings as overstatements of profits.

There is strong evidence that the univariate analysis used by O'Donnell was inadequate to test his hypothesis. He did not take into account arguments supporting the contention that a structural change in market demand for electric utility common stocks occurred during the last half of the 1950's (see, for example, Graham, Dodd, and Cottle [16, p. 299]). The nature of the change in demand was such that investors appeared willing to pay a premium for a company whose earnings per share were expected to grow relatively faster than those of other companies.

Empirical support for the arguments can be found (see, for example, Brigham [5, p. 30], and Miller and Modigliani [22, pp. 385–86]). Consequently, O'Donnell's results cannot be regarded as definitive until a more soundly grounded methodology has been used to test his hypothesis. A sounder methodology would include explicit treatment of earnings-per-share growth.

O'Donnell's second study [25] suggested no new methodology for dealing with the accounting method/securities prices problem. The results of that study were consistent with those of his first. The new results presented dealt with the fact that fixed-charge coverage ratios of flow-through companies generally were lower than, and had declined relative to, those of both normalizing and not-using companies over the period 1961–1966.

The work of Summers [28] constituted an attempt to determine the effects on investors of "accounting efficiency." Using the domestic airline industry as a source of data, he examined the effects of investment credit accounting, interperiod tax allocation, and the use of funds-flow statements on investors. On the basis of his univariate tests, he found no statistically significant impact of any of the accounting treatments, implying that investors were indifferent to any of the accounting treatments. These results conflict with O'Donnell's [24 and 25].

The study by Benston [2] did not deal with the effects of specific alternative accounting methods on stock prices but with the kinds of published information used by investors. He concluded that the effects of published accounting data on stock prices were not very great.

The study by Staubus [27] dealt with measuring the association between several financial accounting variables and common stock values. He concluded that income before depreciation was more useful to investors than income after depreciation.

The study by Livingstone [19] revealed that a "learning set" was formed by regulatory bodies in adapting to new accounting methods. Regulatory bodies have shown a pronounced tendency to require flow-through treatment of taxes for electric utilities under Sec. 167 of the Revenue Act of 1954. He attempted [19, chs. 7 and 8] to demonstrate mathematically that flow-through tax accounting is the normatively correct accounting alternative in the case of electric utilities. He pointed out that since regulatory bodies began to require over time flow-through tax accounting in rate decisions, the normatively preferred alternative, they exhibited a "learning set." One is tempted to conclude, however, that the learning set formed was for choosing an accounting method that resulted in immediately lower consumer power bills, rather than for the normatively preferred alternative.

Experimental studies

Several experimental studies of the effects of alternative accounting methods on decisions have been performed. The most noteworthy of these were published by Jensen [18], Bruns [10], and Dyckman [12], [13], [14]. Of these, the study by Jensen [18] dealt with security price valuation, and one study by Dyckman [14] dealt with the valuation of a hypothetical firm.

The study by Jensen [18] was an attempt to examine the effects of alternative depreciation and inventory accounting methods on investor decision making by means of an experimental field study. Jensen analyzed data derived from questionnaires sent to professional security analysts. The most important weakness in his study is the fact that he tested analysts' opinions, as opposed to actual investors' decisions.[4] Jensen con-

---

[4] Other criticism centers about some of the details of his methodology. For example, one of the questions he asked in the questionnaire, upon the analysis of which he partially based his conclusions, contained a potentially serious source of experimental error (see [18, p. 229, Question A]). The analyst was asked to recommend for a hypothetical client the allocation of a sum of money *between* the common stocks of two hypothetical companies. Because the question requested an allocation between two securities, the feelings of the analysts about diversification should have been taken into consideration.

cluded that the accounting variations did affect the opinions of the analysts, primarily through their impact on earnings-per-share figures.

The study by Bruns [10] dealt primarily with inventory valuation methods and their effects on management decisions. He used a sample of 52 businessmen and 56 students with some business training, for a set of sequential decisions. His analysis indicated he had to reject hypotheses that pricing, advertising, and production decisions were affected by method of inventory valuation.

Dyckman's first study [12] dealt with LIFO vs. FIFO cost flow assumptions and valuations of hypothetical firms. When given two sets of financial statements, identical except for inventory methods and scaling for size, Dyckman reported that a large proportion of the participants were influenced by the accounting variations. These results conflict with those of Bruns [10].

Dyckman's second study [13], a continuation of the first, produced some conflicting results with the first. Using a three-firm oligopolistic market structure, he had participants make pricing and marketing decisions. His results indicated that the participants did not make significantly different decisions.

Dyckman's third study [14] indicated that the participants of his experiment were influenced by inventory accounting variations. These results are in accord with the results of his first study, but in conflict with those of the second.

Simulation studies

Two simulation studies of note have been published that bear upon the decision problem. The one by Bonini [4] dealt with the simulation of a firm using various decision rules, derived from an analysis of the literature, to test the effects of changes in certain variables on various management decisions. He used a deterministic simulation methodology, and analyzed the results with an analysis of variance for a factorial design. He found LIFO a generally superior inventory cost-flow method, under varied conditions, in inducing a higher average-level of profit.

The study by Brigham [7] was a deterministic simulation of the effects of alternative depreciation and tax accounting methods on utility rates and earnings. He concluded that utility company reported profits under flow-through or normalization tax accounting were generally comparable without adjustment [7, pp. 6–7].

Theoretical exposition

The most noteworthy theoretical exposition in the area of accounting alternatives and (management) decisions has been written by Ijiri,

Jaedicke, and Knight [17]. The paper builds a framework for viewing accounting in the decision making process. The paper points out that a decision maker's adjustment to a change in accounting method will depend upon (1) whether the decision maker receives feedback that the accounting method has changed, and if so (2) whether the decision maker suffers from "functional fixation." "Functional fixation" is a term to describe the situation in which a "... person attaches a meaning to a title or object ... and is unable to see alternative meanings or uses" [17, p. 194]. While the paper focuses upon management decisions, the applicability to investor decisions is obvious.

DISCUSSION OF STUDY

Since there are many alternative accounting methods, to determine whether a specific method influences the valuation of security prices the field of possibilities should be narrowed down. As many variables as possible that are likely to have major impact upon the valuation of security prices, other than the accounting variables, should be either held constant or suitably adjusted for. Also, the larger the sizes of the samples used, the more reliable the statistical results are likely to become. In an initial study the number of accounting variables under examination should be kept as small as possible.

In line with the foregoing, this study will focus upon alternative accounting methods for federal income taxes in the electric utility industry to determine if the principal methods influenced the common stock prices of electric utility companies during the period 1957–1961. The electric utility industry was chosen for the following reasons: (1) it is about as uniform in its basic operations, economics, and technology as can be found; (2) it is comprised of a large number of large companies (more than 100); (3) the long-term capital structures of the companies are similarly divided between long-term debt and stockholders' equity (typically about 50 percent each, with common stock equity ranging from one-half of the stockholders' equity to all the stockholders' equity); (4) for an extended period of time it had only one set of accounting alternatives with major impact on the financial reporting process (i.e., from 1954–1962 the accounting for federal income taxes resulting from Section 167 of the Revenue Act of 1954); (5) it is a mature industry whose common stocks tend to sell on a capitalized (earnings, and/or dividends, for example) basis rather than on a liquidation basis. (This assumption is implicit in O'Donnell's studies [24 and 25] and most other studies dealing with the valuation of earnings.)

The central problem to be examined in this study is the determination of an answer to the question:

> Did investors distinguish between deferred tax accounting (normalizing) and flow-through tax accounting in valuing the earnings of companies in the electric utility industry in the period 1957–1961?

The negative answer to this question is hereafter referred to as the principal hypothesis. This is essentially the problem examined by O'Donnell [24], whose conclusions, rationale, and methodology were discussed above. The time period chosen allows a suitable number of companies using each of the accounting methods to be included in the analysis, and allows a comparison of results with those of O'Donnell [24].

CONCEPTUAL FRAMEWORK

This section discusses the assumptions underlying the stock-price valuation model used in the research design, and the role of accounting information in the valuation process.

Under conditions of certainty, stock price valuation theory suggests that rational investors would discount the future dividends and the final-sale proceeds of a security to a present value figure. The literature along this line begins with Williams [31] and can be traced through Durand [11] and Miller and Modigliani [21], with the latter two articles touching upon the well-known "growth stock paradox." Since this study deals with a real world problem, the discussion of certainty will not be carried further.

. Under conditions of risk the problem becomes more difficult. Conceptually, a rational investor should choose a portfolio of securities such that the expected return and the expected variability of the return are consistent with his risk-return utility function. Operationally, problems such as (1) obtaining accurate forecasts, (2) conceptualizing and measuring risk-return preference, and (3) developing efficient computational procedures to evaluate the information, muddy the water quickly. Literature dealing with some of these problems can be traced from Markowitz [20] through Sharpe [26] and Wallingford [29], among others.

In this study it is assumed that (1) investors estimate expected future returns and variability of those returns and choose securities consistent with their risk-return preference functions; (2) the prime vehicles used by investors to value securities are current reported accounting earnings and expected growth of those earnings; (3) risk considerations are handled by investors by examination of size and capital structure of the various corporations under study, as well as by examination of the inherent business risks facing the corporations considered.

The principal hypothesis to be tested in this study is linked with assumption (2) of the conceptual framework, and its test will serve to test that assumption.

RESEARCH DESIGN

To determine from empirical data whether or not the principal hypothesis can be rejected, the following model is used for each of the years, 1957–1961.

$$P_{it} = b_{0t}E_{it}{}^{b_{1t}}G_{it}{}^{b_{2t}}R_{it}{}^{b_{3t}}C_{it}{}^{b_{4t}} \exp\ (b_{5t}M_{it} + b_{6t}A_{it})e_{it}{}^{*} \qquad (1)$$

where P_{it} = price of the ith company's stock at time t;

E_{it} = latest 12-month reported accounting earnings available at the time of estimation t;

G_{it} = an index for the expected future earnings growth of earnings per share of the ith company at time t (see discussion below about surrogates used for this variable);

R_{it} = latest reported annual revenues for the ith company at time t;

C_{it} = proportion of common equity in long-term capital structure of the ith company at time t;

M_{it} = market where the shares of the ith company are traded at time t (dummy variable with 1 = NYSE, 0 = other);

A_{it} = accounting method of ith company at time t (dummy variable with 1 = normalization, 0 = flow-through tax accounting);

$e_{it}{}^{*}$ = error term.

That the model (1) is inherently linear is readily seen. The model to be estimated is, then,

$$\ln P_{it} = \ln b_{0t} + b_{1t} \ln E_{it} + b_{2t} \ln G_{it} + b_{3t} \ln R_{it}$$
$$+ b_{4t} \ln C_{it} + b_{5t}M_{it} + b_{6t}A_{it} + e_{it} \quad (2)$$

where $e_{it} = \ln e_{it}{}^{*}$. The model will be estimated cross-sectionally once for each of the years 1957–1961 by using data available as of the third week in January in the succeeding year. Thus, the data collection points include dates of January 1958 through January 1962.

The test of the principal hypothesis consists of an examination of the statistical significance of the estimated coefficient b_{6t}. If b_{6t} is statistically different from zero at a high level of probability, then the price of the stock of a company that used deferred tax accounting was valued systematically differently from the stock of a company that used flow-through tax accounting.

A discussion of the model and the individual variables is in order at this time. A multiplicative model is entertained because aspects of certainty theory suggest $P = pE[f(G)]$ where P is price per share, p payout ratio, E current earnings per share, and G future growth rate (see Miller and Modigliani [21], Durand [11], or Mlynarczyk [23, pp. 140–45]). The revenue term R_{it} and the capital structure term C_{it} are treated multiplicatively for ease of estimation and since they should be of minor influence on price once E_{it} and G_{it} are taken into consideration. The market-where-traded term and the accounting method term are treated in the manner shown since the use of 0, 1 dummy variables allows the interpretation of $\exp(b_{5t}) - 1$ or $\exp(b_{6t}) - 1$ as the percent premium (or discount) of the shares of companies more marketable and/or using normalization tax accounting, respectively.

The G_{it} term[5] is the most difficult to handle operationally. All other variables are empirically observable; since G_{it} is not, some estimate of it must be surrogated. Several techniques were tried: (1) perfect knowledge of the future by the market for some long period (five years) was assumed and an average of future growth in earnings per share was calculated; (2) past information was used to predict future growth in earnings per share by regressing future earnings growth on past earnings growth in combination with other variables; and (3) a simple past five-year average growth rate in earnings per share was used. (All three surrogate variables were tried, and each had similar effects on the estimated equation in terms of reducing the error sum-of-squares, and in terms of impact on b_{6t}. The results below include method (3) treatment of expected future earnings growth rate.)

The R_{it} term is used as a measure of size of the companies. The C_{it} term is computed by dividing common equity by total long-term capital, and serves as a measure of leverage. These two terms are included to account for business and financial risk. The M_{it} variable is included to account for marketability risk.

THE RESULTS

The regression results appear in Table 1. The b_{6t} coefficient is statistically significant at the .05 level or higher for the years 1961, 1960, and 1959. The sign of the coefficient is positive, indicating that in each of those years the normalizing companies systematically enjoyed a premium in price over the flow-through companies of about 10 percent, 9 percent, and 7 percent, in 1959, 1960, and 1961, respectively, as indicated in Table 3.

---

[5] The variable $G_{it} = 1 + [E_i(t-1) - E_i(t-5)]/[E_i(t-5)]$, which under the conditions of the study can never be zero or negative.

TABLE 1. REGRESSION RESULTS AND SAMPLE BREAKDOWN

Estimated equation: $\ln P = \ln b_0 + b_1 \ln E + b_2 \ln G + b_3 \ln R + b_4 \ln C + b_5 M + b_6 A$

Year	$\ln b_0$	b_1	b_2	b_3	b_4	b_5	b_6	R	s.e.e.
1962	2.021	.774	.717	.044	− .254	.055	.068*	.920	.136
(s.e.)		(.044)	(.095)	(.016)	(.127)	(.087)	(.033)		
1961	1.956	.734	.519	.051	− .186	.021	.090*	.897	.152
(s.e.)		(.051)	(.093)	(.018)	(.127)	(.040)	(.037)		
1960	1.673	.841	.505	.046	− .304	.028	.097*	.929	.135
(s.e.)		(.044)	(.087)	(.017)	(.112)	(.037)	(.035)		
1959	2.229	.847	.398	.039	− .021	.042	.028	.934	.126
(s.e.)		(.045)	(.076)	(.015)	(.083)	(.033)	(.033)		
1958	1.983	.893	.281	.044	.031	.030	.017	.952	.115
(s.e.)		(.037)	(.077)	(.013)	(.078)	(.029)	(.035)		

Sample Breakdown of Companies

	1962	1961	1960	1959	1958
Normalizing	66	67	67	72	80
Flow-through	29	28	27	22	14
Total	95	95	94	94	94

* Significant .05 level or higher.

These results are consistent with those reported by O'Donnell [24]. These results indicate that the principal hypothesis must be rejected for 1959, 1960, and 1961.

Examination of the regression residuals plotted (1) against the independent variables did not reveal any undesirable correlations, and (2) against the predicted value of the dependent variable did not reveal heteroscedasticity. In order to interpret the regression results as interpreted above, the accounting method variable should be uncorrelated with the other independent variables. Table 2 indicates that the simple correlation coefficients between the accounting method variable and the other independent variables in each of the years studied are all small and/or spurious. An additional test performed (but not reported here) involved computing a discriminant function in each year to classify the companies

TABLE 2. SIMPLE CORRELATION COEFFICIENTS BETWEEN ACCOUNTING METHOD AND OTHER INDEPENDENT VARIABLES

Variable/Year	Accounting method				
	1962	*1961*	*1960*	*1959*	*1958*
E	− .003	.079	.179	.059	− .024
G	.047	.030	− .074	.005	.055
R	− .224	− .158	− .086	− .120	− .113
C	.312	.292	.252	.165	− .078
M	− .142	− .026	.009	.078	.028

by accounting method, using the five other independent variables as discriminatory variables. A statistically significant discriminant function could not be formed for any of the five years studied.

Finally, a histogram of the regression residuals in each year appeared to be approximately normally distributed, with about 4 to 8 percent of the residuals falling beyond the range of $\pm 2X$ (standard error of the estimate (s.e.e.)).

With the rejection of the principal hypothesis for three of the years, the important question arises: Were the shares of the normalizing companies valued higher by the "appropriate amount"? The affirmative answer to the question is referred to hereafter as the secondary hypothesis.

TABLE 3. MEASURED (b_{6t}) NORMALIZING PREMIUMS

1961	$\exp (b_6) - 1 = .0704 \doteq 7.04$ percent
1960	$\exp (b_6) - 1 = .0940 \doteq 9.40$
1959	$\exp (b_6) - 1 = .1017 \doteq 10.17$

To test the secondary hypothesis a random sample of size seven of normalizing companies was selected, and the deferred tax expense relating to Section 167 of the Revenue Act of 1954 charged as a percentage of reported income was computed for 1959, 1960, and 1961. This percentage, as indicated in Appendix B, is equal to the theoretical normalizing premium, i.e., the appropriate amount mentioned above. A confidence interval about the theoretical mean-normalizing premium was constructed for each of the three years 1959, 1960, and 1961. The random sample data and confidence interval constructions appear in Table 4. The measured normal-

TABLE 4.   95 PERCENT CONFIDENCE INTERVALS FOR
THEORETICAL MEAN PREMIUMS

Deferred tax expense charged as a percentage of reported income (Random sample)

Company	1961	1960	1959
Boston Edison	13.27 percent	12.66 percent	12.71 percent
Central Illinois Public Service	11.35	9.47	8.41
Commonwealth Edison	16.79	16.97	17.56
Florida Power Corporation	13.64	12.38	13.05
Gulf States Utilities	15.97	14.68	11.65
Idaho Power	13.20	13.67	10.29
Public Service Co. Indiana	8.22	14.17	10.85
Theoretical Premium ($\bar{x}_M$)	13.20 percent	13.42 percent	12.07 percent
Standard Deviation (s)	2.84	2.31	2.88
Standard Error of Mean ($s_{\bar{x}_M}$)	1.072	.872	1.088

95 Percent Confidence Interval Construction for Theoretical Premium True Mean M

1961	10.57 percent $\leq M \leq$ 15.83 percent
1960	11.28 $\leq M \leq$ 15.56
1959	9.29 $\leq M \leq$ 14.75

izing premiums, indicated in Table 3, fall within the 95 percent confidence intervals for the 1959 study only. For 1960 and 1961 the measured premiums fall below the lower limit of the theoretical premium confidence interval. Thus, the secondary hypothesis must be rejected for 1960 and 1961, but cannot be rejected for 1959.

SUMMARY AND CONCLUSIONS

The regression results indicated that the principal hypothesis had to be rejected for 1959, 1960, and 1961, but could not be rejected for 1957 and 1958. The principal hypothesis stated that investors did not distinguish between the alternative accounting methods examined in valuing the earnings of electric utility companies in the period 1957–61.

The secondary hypothesis stated that, given the principal hypothesis was rejected, investors distinguished between the earnings by the "appropriate amount." The appropriate amount was determined for the three years of rejection of the principal hypothesis, and was compared with the regression results relating to the test of the principal hypothesis. The secondary hypothesis had to be rejected for 1959, but could not be rejected for 1960 and 1961.

During 1959, 1960, and 1961, then, it appeared that the shares of normalizing companies were valued systematically higher than those of flow-through companies by about 10 percent, 9 percent, and 7 percent, respectively. Had virtually all investors distinguished between the alternative accounting methods, the valuation premiums would have been about 12 percent, 13 percent, and 13 percent for 1959, 1960, and 1961, respectively.

On the basis of these results, it can be tentatively said that during the 1959–61 period some investors did take into consideration the alternative tax accounting methods available to companies in this industry in formulating their portfolio decisions. It appeared that a large proportion of investors first became concerned with the alternative accounting methods during 1959, since for that year the two hypotheses had to be rejected. After 1959 a large proportion of investors remained concerned, although the size of the proportion dwindled somewhat.

The inability to reject the principal hypothesis in the two earliest years of the study could perhaps be attributed to a learning factor on the part of investors. Examination of annual reports of flow-through and normalizing companies during the entire period did not reveal any salient changes in the communication process. Perhaps in the three later years studied some investors began to look upon the additional tax charges made by normalizing companies as more or less permanent deferrals, and consequently viewed the normalizing reported earnings as being understated by the amount of the deferred tax expense charges.

The conclusion can be drawn that federal income tax accounting procedures for financial reporting purposes in the electric utility industry during 1959–61 did convey information that investors were able to use in formulating portfolio decisions. This conclusion has implications for the accounting process: it appears that if alternative accounting measures having major impact on reported profits are few in number (in this case, one), and if the alternatives are communicated in the reporting process, investors are able to adjust for the measuring variations.

In this admittedly special case, it appears that the accounting process did fulfill its intended purpose, namely, the measurement and communication of economic information in a way useful to decision makers.

The results above differ from those of Jensen [18] and Dyckman [12] and [14]. Jensen [18] indicated that the security analysts participating in his study either did not perceive the accounting variations there, or, if they did, they suffered from "functional fixation" with respect to reported earnings per share. In that study, however, there were two types of transactions subject to accounting variations, viz., inventory and depreciation transactions. The study here focused on one depreciation-related variation, it being unnecessary to consider inventory variations since electricity cannot be stored in economically useful quantities. The study here indicated that a large proportion of investors could adjust, although they appeared to question whether they should adjust as the period studied wore on. The adjustments required in Jensen's [18] study were more difficult to perform than those in the present study and could perhaps explain the different results.

The results of Dyckman [12] and [14] indicated his subjects did not adjust for the accounting variations affecting reported profits. Again, the calculations necessary for proper adjustment were more complicated than those required in the present study.

The results of the present study indicated that the conclusions of O'Donnell [24] were justified, although they could not be justified by the research methodology he employed.

Another result of the present study, interesting, but not relevant to any hypothesis here, was that the shares of electric utility companies traded on the New York Stock Exchange enjoyed a systematic premium over those traded elsewhere of about 4 percent over the period studied. An interesting exercise would be to examine the benefits of a systematically higher stock price, *ceteris paribus*, versus the annual costs of having the stock listed on the NYSE. An intuitive feeling suggests that the benefits would far outweigh the costs, indicating that electric utilities should be encouraged to have their shares listed as soon as they can meet the listing requirements of size, profitability, and ownership distribution.

Finally, it appears that multivariate statistical techniques can be effectively utilized to test hypotheses about the effects of accounting variations on security prices. This subject is extremely important in an economy in which profit is a key determinant in the resource allocation process.

APPENDIX A

Numerical Example of Deferred vs. Flow-through Tax Accounting

Utility A charges straight-line depreciation for financial reporting purposes, but uses an accelerated method for federal income tax purposes. The difference in depreciation charges is assumed to be $1,000,000. Assuming a 50 percent tax rate, and that all other items on the two income statements are the same, the following financial reporting tax accounting methods are possible [see *Accounting*

Research Bulletin No. 44 (Revised)]:

Utility A

Financial Reporting Statement   Tax Return

	Financial Reporting Statement	Tax Return
Revenues	$20,000,000	$20,000,000
Expenses	8,000,000	8,000,000
	$12,000,000	$12,000,000
Depreciation	2,000,000	3,000,000
Profit before taxes	$10,000,000	$ 9,000,000
Taxes	?	4,500,000
Profit after taxes	?	(Irrelevant)

Method 1: Flow-through

Let taxes for financial reporting purposes be the actual legal tax liability, i.e., $4,500,000.

Accounting entry:

Taxes	4,500,000	
Taxes Payable		4,500,000

Result: Reported profits are $5,500,000.

Method 2: Normalize

Let taxes for financial reporting purposes be 50 percent $\times$ $10,000,000. (Tax rate times profit before taxes on the financial reporting statement), i.e., $5,000,000.

Accounting entry:

Taxes	5,000,000	
Taxes payable		4,500,000
Deferred tax liability		500,000

Result: Reported profits are $5,000,000.

APPENDIX B

Determination of "Appropriate Amount" of Normalizing Company Earnings Valuation Premium

Let P_n, E_n and P_f, E_f be the price and reported earnings of a normalizing and flow-through company, respectively. For $P_n = P_f$ the valuation differential for a normalizing company is k in $P_n/E_n = kP_f/E_f$. Then the relation between reported earnings is $k = E_f/E_n$. Since $E_{fi} = E_{ni} + T_{di}$ for company i to adjust from normalizing to flow-through earnings, where T_{di} is the amount of deferred tax expense charged relating to Section 167 of the Revenue Act of 1954, $E_{fi}/E_{ni} = 1 + T_{di}/E_{ni} = k_i$.

A random sample of size seven was selected from the available normalizing companies for 1959, 1960, and 1961, and $x_m = T_d/E_d$ was computed in Table 4. The statistic x_m is called the valuation premium for normalizing companies' earnings. Since $\bar{k} = 1 + \bar{x}_m$, working with $\bar{x}_m$ is equivalent to working with $\bar{k}$.

A 95 percent confidence interval can be constructed about M, where $M = E(\bar{x}_m)$, by use of the relation

$$\bar{x}_M - 2.447 \, s_{\bar{x}_M} \leq M \leq \bar{x}_M + 2.447 \, s_{\bar{x}_M}$$

where the 2.447 $= t_{(.025, \, 6)}$.

APPENDIX C

Sample Companies

Allegheny Power System
American Electric Power
Arizona Public Service
Atlantic City Electric
Black Hill Power and Light
Boston Edison
California Electric Power
Carolina Power and Light
Central Hudson Gas and Electric
Central Illinois Electric and Gas
Central Illinois Lighting
Central Illinois Public Service
Central Louisiana Electric
Central Maine Power
Central and Southwest
Central Vermont Public Service
Cincinnati Gas and Electric
Citizens Utilities
Cleveland Electric Illuminating
Columbus and Southern Ohio Edison
Commonwealth Edison
Community Public Service
Connecticut Light and Power
Consolidated Edison
Consumers Power
Delaware Power and Light
Detroit Edison
Duke Power
Duquesne Light
Eastern Utilities Association
El Paso Electric
Empire District Electric
Florida Power Corporation
Florida Power and Light
General Public Utilities
Gulf States Utilities
Hartford Electric
Idaho Power
Illinois Power
Indianapolis Power and Light
Iowa Electric Light and Power
Iowa Power and Light
Iowa Public Service
Iowa Southern Utilities
Kansas City Power and Light
Kansas Power and Light
Kentucky Utilities
Lake Superior District Power

Long Island Lighting
Madison Gas and Electric
Maine Public Service
Middle South Utilities
Montana Power
New England Electric
New England Gas and Electric
New York State Electric and Gas
Niagara Mohawk Power
Northern Indiana Public Service
Northwestern Public Service
Ohio Edison
Oklahoma Gas and Electric
Orange and Rockland Utilities
Pacific Gas and Electric
Pacific Power and Light
Pennsylvania Power and Light
Philadelphia Electric
Portland General Electric
Potomac Electric Power
Public Service of Colorado
Public Service Electric and Gas
Public Service of Indiana
Public Service of New Hampshire
Public Service of New Mexico
Puget Sound Power and Light
Rochester Gas and Electric
St. Joseph Light and Power
Sierra Pacific Power
Southern California Edison
South Carolina Electric and Gas
Southern Company
Southern Indiana Gas and Electric
Tampa Electric
Toledo Edison
Tuscon Gas Electric Light and Power
Union Electric
United Illuminating
Upper Peninsula Power
Virginia Electric Power
Washington Water Power
West Penn Power
Western Light and Telephone
Western Massachusetts Companies
Wisconsin Electric Power
Wisconsin Power and Light
Wisconsin Public Service

REFERENCES

[1] American Institute of Certified Public Accountants. *Accounting Research and Terminology Bulletins.* Final ed. (New York, N. Y.: AICPA, 1961).

[2] Benston, George J. "Published Corporate Accounting Data and Stock Prices," *Empirical Research in Accounting: Selected Studies, 1967,* Supplement to Vol. 5, *Journal of Accounting Research.*

[3] Bevis, Herman W. "The Accounting Function in Economic Progress," *Journal of Accountancy* (August, 1958).

[4] Bonini, Charles P. *Simulation of Information and Decision Systems in the Firm* (Englewood Cliffs, N. J.: Prentice-Hall, Inc., 1963).

[5] Brigham, Eugene F. "Cost of Equity Capital to Electric Utilities," *Public Utilities Fortnightly* (September 24, 1964).

[6] ——. "Public Utility Depreciation Practices and Policies," *National Tax Journal* (June, 1966).

[7] ——. "Depreciation and Reported Profits: The Effects of Alternative Accounting Policies on Utility Rates and on Utility and Nonutility Companies' Reported Profits." University of California, Los Angeles, 1966 (mimeographed).

[8] ——. "The Effects of Alternative Tax Depreciation Policies on Public Utilities Rate Structures," *National Tax Journal* (June, 1967).

[9] ——. "The Effects of Alternative Depreciation Policies on Reported Profit," *The Accounting Review* (January, 1968).

[10] Bruns, W. J., Jr. "Inventory Valuation and Management Decisions," *The Accounting Review* (April, 1965).

[11] Durand, D. "Growth Stocks and the Petersburg Paradox," *Journal of Finance,* (September, 1957).

[12] Dyckman, T. R. "On the Investment Decision," *The Accounting Review* (April, 1964).

[13] ——. "The Effects of Alternative Accounting Techniques on Certain Management Decisions," *Journal of Accounting Research* (Spring, 1964).

[14] ——. "On the Effects of Earnings-Trend, Size and Inventory Valuation Procedures in Evaluating a Business Firm," in *Research in Accounting Measurement,* Jaedicke, Ijiri, and Nielsen (eds.), American Accounting Association (1966).

[15] Eiteman, David K. "Interdependence of Utility Rate-Base Type, Permitted Rate of Return and Utility Earnings," *The Journal of Finance* (March, 1962).

[16] Graham, E., D. Dodd, and S. Cottle, with the collaboration of C. Tatham. *Security Analysis,* 4th ed. (New York, N. Y.: McGraw-Hill Book Company, 1962).

[17] Ijiri, Y., R. Jaedicke, and K. Knight. "The Effects of Accounting Alternatives on Management Decisions," in *Research in Accounting Measurement, op. cit.*

[18] Jensen, R. E. "An Experimental Design for Study of Effects of Accounting Variations in Decision Making," *Journal of Accounting Research* (Autumn, 1966).

[19] Livingstone, J. L. "The Effects of Alternative Accounting Methods on Regulatory Rate of Return Decisions in the Electric Utility Industry," unpublished Ph.D. dissertation, Stanford University, December, 1965.

[20] Markowitz, H. "Portfolio Selection," *The Journal of Finance* (March, 1952).

[21] Miller, M., and F. Modigliani. "Dividend Policy, Growth, and the Valuation of Shares," *Journal of Business* (October, 1961).

[22] ———. "Some Estimates of the Cost of Capital to the Electric Utility Industry, 1954–57," *The American Economic Review* (June, 1966).

[23] Mlynarczyk, F. A. "A Study of the Effects of Alternative Accounting Methods on Common Stock Prices," unpublished Ph.D. dissertation, Purdue University, 1969.

[24] O'Donnell, J. L. "Relationships Between Reported Earnings and Stock Prices in the Electric Utility Industry," *The Accounting Review* (January, 1965).

[25] ———. "Further Observation on Reported Earnings and Stock Prices," *The Accounting Review* (July, 1968).

[26] Sharpe, W. F. "A Simplified Model for Portfolio Selection," *Management Science* (January, 1963).

[27] Staubus, George J. "The Association of Financial Accounting Variables with Common Stock Values," *The Accounting Review* (January, 1965).

[28] Summers, Edward L. "Observation of Effects of Using Alternative Reporting Practices," *The Accounting Review* (April, 1968).

[29] Wallingford, B. A. "A Survey and Comparison of Portfolio Selection Models," *Journal of Financial and Quantitative Analysis* (June, 1967).

[30] "What *Are* Earnings? The Growing Credibility Gap," *Forbes* (May 15, 1967).

[31] Williams, J. B. *The Theory of Investment Value* (Cambridge, Mass.: Harvard U. P., 1938).

[32] Wilson, Bob. "Two-Thirds' Exposure," *Barron's* (May 6, 1968).

part Four

EQUITY VALUATION

*Robert M. Soldofsky**

28. Growth Yields

Reprinted from the **Financial Analysts Journal,** Vol. 17, No. 5
(September–October, 1961), pp. 43–47, by permission of the author
and the publisher.

What are the dividend yield and price/earnings ratio on a (very high
rate of) growth stock that is selling for $600 per share, paying $4.00 per
year in dividends, and earning $10 per year? What are the dividend yield
and price/earnings ratio on a (medium rate of) growth stock that is selling
for $100 per share, paying $2.00 per year in dividends and earning $5.00
per year? What are the dividend yield and price/earnings ratio on a public
utility share that is selling for $100, paying $4.00 per year in dividends,
and earning $7.00 per year? The dividend yields and price/earnings ratios
on these three hypothetical shares are as follows:

	Dividend Yield	Price/Earnings Ratio	Earnings Yield*
Rapid growth stock.............	0.67%	60 times	1.7%
Medium growth stock..........	2.00	20 times	5.0
Public utility.................	4.00	14.3 times	7.0

* The earnings yield and price/earnings ratio are reciprocals.

Which of these shares is the best buy? Is a high grade bond yielding
4.50 percent (on a yield to maturity basis) a better buy? Of course, the
answer depends in part on the degree of certainty with which the buyer
(or owner) holds his projection for the company, for the industry of which
the company is a part, and for the entire national economy. Each financial
analyst may have some rule of thumb for comparing the types of situations
illustrated. Even if the dividends and earnings projections were certain,
how could the dividend yields be compared directly with one another and
with the yield on bonds? Clearly, the three dividend yields specified are
not stated on a strictly comparable basis. In fact, analysts' rules of thumb
are developed largely because the yields are not strictly comparable.

* Professor of Finance, State University of Iowa.

Is there a method by which yields can be specified on a precisely comparable basis? Yes! Yields can be calculated by discounting the expected *rising* dividend streams and relating the sum of the discounted values to the market prices of common stock; this yield may then be called the growth yield. For example, according to Table 2, if a share of common stock is now paying a $1 dividend per year, and the dividend is expected to increase at the rate of 4 percent per year for 20 years, the growth yield will be 3 percent when the market price is $62.41. The current yield on the market price is 1.6 percent; alternatively, to obtain 3 percent on a current yield basis the market price would have to be $33.33.

Some analysts may point out that even if growth yields can be constructed, they would still be of limited usefulness because a major motivation in the purchase of growth stocks is the hope of obtaining capital gains. Although the problem of calculating growth yields including capital gains will not be discussed, the procedure is only slightly more time consuming and very little more complicated than that of determining the dividend growth yield itself.

In the balance of this article the meaning of growth yield will be described more fully, and the major limitations of the "current" dividend yield and payout systems of evaluating alternative stocks with rising dividends will be reviewed. The limitations of the growth yield concept itself will be admitted, and illustrations of growth yield tables will be given. The growth yield concept will be used to restate the spread between bond yields and stock yields.

The usual dividend yield on common stocks is called here the "current" dividend yield because it is in some ways comparable to the "current" yield on bonds. The current yield is defined as the current dividend divided by the market price or $D \div MP = DY$. What does this equation imply?

It implies that a dividend of some amount, say $1 per year, divided by the market price is the correct dividend rate under the conditions implicit in the formula. The formula is virtually always taken to imply that the present value of a series of *equal payments* extended *indefinitely* into the future and discounted at a *uniform rate* will be identical with the amount determined by the formula. In other words, a dividend of $1 per year discounted at some rate is equal to the market price. If the rate is 5 percent, the market price is $20, or $1 over .05 = $20. Five percent is the true yield or rate of interest. But, again note the precisely specified conditions: (1) the dividends continue indefinitely into the future; and (2) the amount of dividends per period remains unchanged.

In the case of the vast majority of well-known stocks, it is true that dividends are expected to continue into the future without any forseeable limit, but it is not true that the dividend payment is expected to remain

TABLE 1. DETERMINATION OF A GROWTH YIELD

Year	Projected Dividends Per Year	Present Worth Factors at 9 Percent	Present Worth of Dividends for Each Year
1.....................	$1.00	.9174	$ .9174
2.....................	1.04	.8417	.8745
3.....................	1.08	.7722	.8340
4.....................	1.12	.7084	.7934
5.....................	1.17	.6499	.7604
6.....................	1.22	.5963	.7275
7.....................	1.27	.5470	.6947
8.....................	1.32	.5019	.6625
9.....................	1.37	.4604	.6307
10....................	1.42	.4224	.5998
11....................	1.48	.3875	.5735
12....................	1.54	.3555	.5475
13....................	1.60	.3262	.5219
14....................	1.67	.2992	.4997
15....................	1.73	.2745	.4749
Beyond 15 years........	1.73	3.0504*	5.2772*
Total estimated value of stock			$15.3905

* The sum of the present worth factors at 9 percent for a perpetual income earning asset approaches $11.111,111. This is the same factor used in capitalizing income at 9 percent ($1 ÷ .09 = X or Income ÷ Rate = Principal.) The sum of the present worth factors for 15 years at 9 percent is $8.060688. The difference between $11.111,111 and $8.060688 or $3.050423 is the value of the present worth factors from the fifteenth year on. Assuming the income remains $1.73 per share, the present value of the income stream beyond the fifteenth year is $1.73 × $3.050423.

unchanged. Investors expect dividends to rise more or less regularly for some period of time and such expectations are very likely to be fulfilled. In the case of such common stocks, then, the current dividend yield, which implies a constant amount of dividends continuing indefinitely into the future, does not state the yield on a basis that conforms with expectations.

What is needed is a growth yield, a yield which equates the expected rising stream of dividends with the market price. Once the problem is stated in this way two new bits of information are needed, namely, the rate of growth of dividends and the period that the growth is most likely to continue. The analyst must now specify these two variables on the basis of available information and his projection of future dividends.

Assume that a well-known common stock is selling for $15.50 per share and paying $1 per year in dividends; furthermore, it is expected that the dividends will rise at the rate of 4 percent for 15 years and will stabilize thereafter. Under these conditions as shown in Table 1 the true rate of return is virtually 9 percent, not 6.3 percent as determined by dividing $1 by $15.50. The growth yield is that rate of interest (discount) which equates the rising stream of dividends with the market price of the stock. Earnings growth yield may be computed by the same method and stated in terms of its reciprocal, the price/earnings ratio.

The growth yield of 9 percent illustrated in Table 1 is a true compound rate of interest that is developed on the basis of the same fundamental concept as the yield to maturity on a bond; this concept is *present value* as the term is used in the mathematics of finance. With the aid of growth yield tables the hypothetical rapid growth stock, the medium growth stock, and the utility stock may be precisely compared with one another in terms of dividend yields if the analyst specifies growth rates and growth periods. The growth yields may be strictly compared with the yield to maturity on a bond because both rates are computed on the basis of the same concept.

Pay-off periods are sometimes recommended as a basis for discriminating between growth stocks. When this technique is used the analyst is required to specify the rate of growth of dividends for the securities under consideration. The rising stream of annual dividends is totaled and the number of years required until this rising accumulation of dividends is equal to the purchase price is noted. The number of years to pay-off is compared for various stocks and the one with the shortest pay-off period is the "best buy," other things being equal.

The major problem here is that the pay-off period is not a rate of return concept. Dividend yields cannot be specified and compared directly with one another or with bond yields. For the same general reasons that the discounted cash-flows method is strongly recommended for corporate managers in evaluating alternative investment opportunities rather than the more widely used pay-off criteria, the growth yield concept is greatly superior to the pay-off criteria in evaluating alternative purchases (or holdings) of securities. The growth yield and discounted cash-flows concepts are both present value methods that result in true rates of interest or discount. The pay-off period measures only the *amount* of cash flow. It may be useful in discriminating between alternatives when the future is extremely uncertain; when availability of cash is a paramount concern; or when alternatives are otherwise acceptable on rate of return criteria.

One method of computing the growth yield has been illustrated, and reasons for superiority of the growth yield as compared with the current dividend yield and the pay-off period have been reviewed. Growth yield tables will now be illustrated and the limitations of the growth yield technique will be discussed. Finally, the growth yield concept will be used to restate the spread between bond and stock yields.

Table 2 is abstracted from growth yield tables. Only a limited number of items are reported, but these may be sufficient to indicate some of the uses of such tables. In Table 2, the rate of growth of dividends is specified for a selected set of numbers and the effects of different growth

TABLE 2. GROWTH YIELDS ON COMMON
STOCK—SELECTED VALUES*

Growth Yield	3 Percent	4 Percent	5 Percent	6 Percent	7 Percent	8 Percent
Growth Period (Years)	Rate of Growth 3 Percent					
0†	$ 33.33	$ 25.00	$20.00	$16.67	$14.25	$12.50
5	38.23	28.65	22.71	18.97	16.25	14.20
10	43.21	32.17	25.31	21.00	17.84	15.56
15	48.19	35.51	27.65	22.77	19.20	16.61
20	53.17	38.68	29.79	24.29	20.38	17.45
25	58.14	41.71	31.70	25.62	21.30	18.12
35	68.08	47.35	35.00	27.73	22.69	19.04
50	82.94	54.85	38.29	29.92	23.98	19.82
	Rate of Growth 4 Percent					
5	$ 40.04	$ 29.99	$23.75	$19.83	$16.96	$14.81
10	47.12	34.99	27.44	22.71	19.30	16.74
15	54.59	39.98	30.97	25.35	21.34	18.33
20	62.41	44.98	34.30	27.75	23.09	19.64
25	70.61	49.97	37.47	29.92	24.61	20.73
35	88.23	59.96	43.31	33.66	27.08	22.38
50	117.99	74.93	50.86	38.03	29.63	23.93
	Rate of Growth 5 Percent					
5	$ 41.88	$ 31.33	$24.81	$20.69	$17.69	$15.45
10	51.39	38.05	29.75	24.57	20.83	18.02
15	61.83	45.04	34.68	28.26	23.68	20.24
20	73.35	52.40	39.60	31.78	26.26	22.18
25	86.01	60.10	44.49	35.14	28.60	23.85
35	115.26	76.67	54.16	41.34	32.67	26.57
50	171.01	104.67	68.26	49.44	36.99	29.43

* The values in the growth tables are prepared by a formula and computational routine different from the very time consuming procedure illustrated in Table 1. Even with "short cut" methods the computations are surprisingly time consuming. All values are based upon a $1 dividend paid in the first year.

The growth values are selected and reproduced from Robert M. Soldofsky and James T. Murphy, *Growth Yields on Common Stock: Theory and Tables* (Iowa City, Iowa: Bureau of Business and Economic Research, State University of Iowa). The "Mathematical Appendix" to this monograph states the exact method of computation.

† The growth period of 0 years gives the same result as the traditional current dividend yield computation. This same line and same set of values could be repeated for the 4 percent and 5 percent growth tables.

periods and discount rates are noted. All figures in these tables are based upon a $1 dividend paid in the first year so adjustments may easily be made in terms of any actual payment.

If the market price of a share is $20 and the dividend is $1, and not expected to rise, the yield is 5 percent. If dividends are expected to rise on the average at 4 percent per year for the next five years and remain constant thereafter at the level of $1.17 per share (which will be reached at the end of that period), and if the stock were purchased at $23.75, the growth yield would be 5 percent.

If the rate of growth is again taken as 4 percent, the growth period extended to 10 years, and if the market price is $27.44, the growth yield would still be 5 percent. In other words, $7.44 ($27.44 − $20.00) more could be paid for a stock whose dividends were expected to rise at the rate of 4 percent per year for 10 years than indicated on a current yield basis and the yield would still be a true 5 percent return. The relationships between the growth period, dividend growth rate, and market prices that will yield a given rate of return, may be observed in any column in Table 2.

Given the rate of growth and the period of growth, it is instructive to observe the market prices for a series of growth yields. For example, if the rate of growth of dividends of 4 percent is selected again and the growth horizon is held constant at 20 years, the following figures may be read out of growth tables:

Market Price	Growth Yield
$96.29*	2 percent
76.23*	$2\frac{1}{2}$
62.41*	3
52.44*	$3\frac{1}{2}$
44.98	4
34.30	5
27.75	6
23.09	7
19.64	8
17.01	9
14.95	10

* These prices are based on a 200-year dividend stream.
The rest of the prices are based on 100-year dividend streams.

The materials in growth tables may be arranged so that the effect of different rates of growth may be observed. Thus, assume that the growth horizon and the growth yield are fixed and observe how the market price will vary with changes in the rate of growth of dividends. A few figures drawn from growth tables arranged to highlight the effect of different rates of growth are given in Table 3. Given the growth period, successive increases of 1 percent in the dividend growth rate have successively larger impacts on the amount that will result in a given growth yield. The longer the growth period, the greater also is the effect of a given increase in the rate of dividend growth.

Growth yields may also be of interest in evaluating the spectacular

TABLE 3.   PRICES WHICH GIVE CONSTANT GROWTH YIELDS*

(Assuming 10- and 20-year growth periods)

Rate of Dividend Growth	10-Year Growth Period Growth Yield		20-Year Growth Period Growth Yield	
	4 Percent	*5 Percent*	*4 Percent*	*5 Percent*
0 percent	$25.00	$20.00	$25.00	$20.00
2	29.59	23.33	33.55	25.93
3	32.17	25.31	38.68	29.79
4	34.99	27.44	44.98	34.30
5	38.05	29.75	52.40	39.60
6	41.35	32.25	61.15	45.82
7	44.94	34.95	71.14	53.12
8	48.83	37.89	83.57	61.67

* All values in the table are based upon a $1.00 dividend paid in the first year. Also see notes to Table 2.

prices of individual stocks. For example, say a certain stock is selling for $143 and paid a $1 dividend last year; its dividends are expected to grow at the rate of 5 percent per year. The current yield is 0.70 percent. If the dividends are expected to rise steadily at a rate close to 5 percent per year for 75 years, the growth yield would be 4 percent!

The growth yield concept has many limitations; one is that no adjustment has been made for the price appreciation of shares. It was suggested at the outset that such computations can be made with a little more work on the analyst's part. Many individuals may point out that projections of dividends are required for the growth yield method and none are required by the current yield method. After a little reflection, however, it should be clear that in buying a stock or any other investment, a projection of the future income is essential. The current dividend yield and the price/earnings ratio imply that present dividends and earnings will continue indefinitely into the future. Another serious criticism of the growth yield technique is that it requires the analyst to specify the rate of growth and the period of growth.

No one has knowledge of this sort and the nature of things is such that no one can have certain knowledge of the future. This criticism may be turned about and the objector may ask whether a projection of the present per share dividend or a rising dividend per share for some period of time will more nearly represent the picture of his anticipations. The answer will probably be the latter, the rising dividend payment. The analyst's problem is to specify the future dividend pattern as best he can on the basis of his knowledge of the past and his skill at economic and political analysis. For most well-known stocks of large established companies an analyst is very likely to have more confidence in his projection of a specific rising dividend stream than a constant dividend stream.

The confidence that the analyst has in his projection will depend upon the particular company and industry with which he is concerned. The approximate rates of growth of dividends of the stocks included in the Dow-Jones series for three periods of time have been as follows:

	1929–1959	1939–1959	1947–1959
30 industrials..................	1.62%	6.25%	7.0%
15 public utilities..............	...	7.2*	4.7
20 rails......................	0.52	8.6	7.2

* Since 1945, the earliest date for which information is available.

Admittedly, the growth of dividends of some companies and industries has been more erratic than others. Another problem in using growth rates based upon the past is the fact that accounting techniques used in preparing net income have not been consistent. New policies adopted for accounting for inventory and depreciation are the two best known and probably most important illustrations of changing accounting practices that have affected reported net income. Most large manufacturing companies, including those now in Dow-Jones lists, have been adopting the Last-In, First-Out basis of accounting for inventory since this method was authorized for tax purposes in 1939. Several companies among the Dow-Jones Industrials adopted LIFO in the 1950's. The 1954 Internal Revenue Code authorized the sum-of-years' digits and declining balance methods for large corporations. Both of the techniques mentioned generally have the effect of reducing reported net income as compared with the method that had previously been used.

In the growth tables the projected dividends have been discounted at one uniform rate. This practice is consistent with the construction of bond tables and the interpretation of the current yield formula as the latter has been widely used. An analyst may consider that his dividend projection is a probability distribution of possible results and make no further adjustments. Other analysts may use the growth yield as a first step and handicap their results for the degree of confidence they have in their projects. Professor Clendenin has also constructed brief growth yield tables, but he has discounted different parts of the projected dividend stream at different rates. Professor Clendenin uses three different discount rates, and dividends more distant in time are discounted at arbitrarily selected higher discount rates.[1]

[1] John C. Clendenin, *Theory and Technique of Growth Stock Valuation* (Los Angeles, Calif.: Bureau of Business and Economic Research, UCLA, 1957). See also Clendenin, "Dividend Growth as Determinant of Common Stock Values," *Trusts and Estates Magazine* (February, 1957), and Clendenin and Maurice Van Cleave, "Growth and Common Stock Values," *Journal of Finance*, Vol. IX, No. 4 (December, 1954), pp. 365–376.

One minor problem is the matter of interpolation. In the completed tables that have been copyrighted by this author, the market values are a maximum of about $5 apart at the 20-year growth horizon. Even though interpolations between successive prices in the tables should be made along the curve rather than along a straight line, any very small errors in growth yields that are the result of straight line interpolation between successive figures in the growth tables can be disregarded given the nature of the projections of the dividend stream. Very minor computational errors arising from straight line interpolation will not influence the decisions made with the aid of the growth yield tables.

The analyst may believe that for some growth companies a higher rate of growth will prevail during the more immediate years than for more distant years. Growth yields for such cases are worthwhile, but they are too complex to warrant the preparation of tables by any hand tabulating technique. A computer program has been developed for obtaining growth yields in these more complex cases.

The spread between the current dividend yield on Dow-Jones Industrials and Barron's highest-grade bonds is one measure of the "highness" or reasonableness of prices on the stock market. Since the great breakthrough of September, 1958, the bond yield has been above the current dividend yield on the Dow-Jones Industrials. At times the spread has been as much as 1.6 percent in favor of bonds. Why buy or hold common stocks under these circumstances? Each individual can give an array of answers, but generally they believe that their return from shares will be sufficiently higher than the bond yield to compensate them for the added risks of owning shares. Because of the way the spread is computed this higher dividend rate is not reflected in the spread.

The true dividend yield on the Dow-Jones Industrials is understated because no consideration is given to the probable future growth of these dividends. If it is assumed, for example, that the dividends on the Dow-Jones Industrials will rise on the average at 6.25 percent per year for the next 15 years, the growth yield will be approximately 6.4 percent when the DJIA is at 600.

If the growth period is taken to be 25 years, the growth yield will be about 7 percent with the DJIA at 630. If dividends grow at 6.25 percent for the 15 years and at 3 percent for the following 10 years the growth rate will again be approximately 7 percent when the DJIA is at 608. On the basis of the application of the growth yield concept it is clear that the spread between the yield on Barron's high grade bonds and the Dow-Jones Industrials is at least 2.00 percentage points in favor of the Industrials.

Institutional investors such as mutual funds, pension fund trustees, and insurance companies, are especially interested in the long-term yield they can expect from securities. The "current" dividend yield (the current dividend divided by the market price) does not give much of a clue as to what dividend yield may be expected over a period of 10, 20, 30 or more years when dividends are expected to rise in the future. Pension costs from the employer's point of view are related to the long-run dividend yield, that is the growth yield. The appraisal of variable annuities as compared with the traditional fixed dollar annuities depends in large part upon the differences between yields on fixed income securities and the growth yield on common stocks.

Incidentally, the rate of return on the variable annuity, CREF (College Retirement Equities Fund), from the time it began operations, in July, 1952, through December, 1960, is 14 percent. Administrators of university endowment funds are extremely interested in the long-run yield on common stocks in making investment decisions. Each investor is likely to have one or more investment objectives for which the use of growth yields will be exceedingly helpful.

Growth yields are relatively simple to use. They should be of considerable interest in appraising individual stocks as well as the general level of stocks.

Editor's Note:

Growth yield tables have been published by the author for two growth rates and two corresponding growth periods, such as a 12 percent dividend growth rate for 5 years, a 6 percent dividend growth rate for the next 10 years, and level or constant dividends thereafter. Special tables also have been published to facilitate the computation of an overall yield on common stock, which includes both the growing dividend stream and capital gains. The "two-step" tables, the tables to facilitate the computation of the "overall" yield, and the method for making this computation are in Robert M. Soldofsky and James T. Murphy, *Growth Yields on Common Stock: Theory and Tables* (Iowa City, Iowa: Bureau of Business and Economic Research, State University of Iowa, 1964). Three-step tables have also been prepared and duplicated, but are not included in the above monograph.

In addition to these and the Clendenin tables (cited *supra*, footnote 1), "Comprehensive Stock Value Tables" have been compiled and published by George E. Bates in the *Harvard Business Review*, Vol. 40, No. 1 (January-February, 1962), pp. 53–67. These are versatile tables but require the user to make a number of simple calculations. A mathematical appendix is included.

Tables which consider a period of constant growth, a transitional period which the rate of growth declines to zero, and zero growth indefinitely thereafter, are included in "Common Stock Valuation," by Nicholas Molodovsky, Catherine May, and Sherman Chottiner, *Financial Analyst Journal*, Vol. 21, No. 2 (March-April, 1965), pp. 104–123.

Charles C. Holt[*]

29. The Influence of Growth Duration on Share Prices[†]

Reprinted from **The Journal of Finance,** Vol. XVII, No. 3 (September, 1962), pp. 465–475, by permission of the publisher.

I. INTRODUCTION

The spectacular investment performance of "growth stocks" in recent years has focused attention on the problem of evaluating the securities of fast-growing companies. Unfortunately, methods for placing valuations on such securities are not yet adequately developed, and investors make their buy-and-sell decisions as best they can.

That a company's high rate of "growth" may come to an end is an important, but little-emphasized, investment consideration in the evaluation of growth stocks. To call attention to this point, we present in this paper an exploratory analysis of the relationship between price/earnings ratio, rate of growth, and the duration of growth. In omitting risk from the present analysis, we are explicitly neglecting the fact that investments in growth stocks are often riskier than in nongrowth stocks. Consistent with this, the capitalization rates for both kinds of securities are assumed to be the same, and hence any differences in their price/earnings ratios are attributable to differences in their growth of earnings.

The obvious investment success of growth stocks has led investors to seek out these securities for purchase, with the result that their prices have been driven up so that growth stocks now generally carry high price/earnings ratios. But just how high it is wise for investors to drive price/earnings ratios is not clear. If a growth stock is evaluated by discounting future growing dividends back to the present, the paradoxical result is obtained that an infinite price/earnings ratio is justified for a stock whose dividends per share are expected to grow at a (percent per annum) rate that is higher than the discount rate. This clearly untenable result

---

[*] Professor of Economics, University of Wisconsin.
[†] Conversations with M. H. Miller and F. Modigliani supplied much of the stimulation for writing this paper.

comes from the implicit assumption of an *indefinite* continuation of exponential growth and may be avoided by limiting the assumed growth period.[1] Another method[2] has received considerable attention in investors' literature and seems to have had considerable influence. The growth in earnings per share of a company is extrapolated, say five years into the future, at the growth rate indicated from the recent past. The current price of the stock is divided by this forecast of earnings five years hence, to obtain a price/earnings ratio. In this way, more normal, i.e., lower price/earnings ratios are obtained for growth stocks and some useful indication is given on whether the existing price of the security is justified or not. However, this method is rather crude in ignoring any dividends that might be received during the five-year period or growth that might occur after this arbitrarily selected period.[3]

II. DURATION OF GROWTH

If investments in the common stocks of growth companies were expected to continue growing indefinitely at a constant exponential rate, then the investor's problem would be largely one of selecting the companies with the highest forecasted growth rates.[4] But before anyone chose to follow such an investment policy, he would be well advised to question seriously the assumption of indefinitely continued growth. Studies of the past growth in the applications of inventions and in the sales of companies and industries show growth curves in which very high rates of growth are achieved initially, but ultimately the growth rates tend to slow down or stop as maturity is reached. This logistic type of growth curve is rather complicated, and the forecasting of its leveling-off is quite difficult from

[1] O. K. Burrell, "A Mathematical Approach to Growth Stock Valuation," *Financial Analysts Journal*, Vol. XVI (May–June, 1960), pp. 69–76; John C. Clendenin and Maurice Van Cleave, "Growth and Common Stock Values," *Journal of Finance*, Vol. IX (1954), pp. 365–76.

[2] Julian G. Buckley, "A Method of Evaluating Growth Stocks," *Financial Analysts Journal*, Vol. XVI (March–April, 1960), pp. 19–21.

[3] The more subtle point that the dividend returns from a growth stock are farther in the future than those from nongrowth stocks and hence that forecasts of the dividends are riskier has not been adequately treated as yet, nor will it be considered here. See David Durand, "Growth Stocks and the Petersburg Paradox," *Journal of Finance*, Vol. XII (September, 1957), pp. 348–63; and Henry Allen Latané, "Individual Risk Preference in Portfolio Selection," *Journal of Finance*, Vol. XV (March, 1960), pp. 45–52.

[4] For a more refined analysis of growth see M. H. Miller and F. Modigliani, "Dividend Policy, Growth, and the Valuation of Shares," *Journal of Business*, Vol. XXXIV (October, 1961), p. 22. Growth in earnings of itself does not necessarily justify a high price/earnings ratio, if dividends are correspondingly low—i.e., the growth requires some form of expanding opportunities for profit. The present paper will not analyze the source of "growth" but only the problem of determining its value.

both the statistical and the forecasting points of view. Although we shall not attempt this degree of refinement, it does seem desirable to assume that the growth opportunities of a "growth" company are likely at some point in time to slow down to the rate that is normally achieved by companies generally. Presumably, this more modest growth rate can be maintained indefinitely. As the period of high growth passes, the price/earnings ratio of a company will drop back to the normal level characteristic of "nongrowth stocks." This perhaps distant, but almost inevitable, decline in price/earnings ratio constitutes one of the important risks of investing in a growth stock, especially since the termination of rapid growth is so difficult to forecast.

To simplify matters, we shall make the assumption that the growth in earnings per share (adjusted for stock dividends and splits) of a company will continue at a high constant exponential rate until some point in time when the rate drops abruptly to the average rate for nongrowth companies. Under this assumption, the *duration of growth* for a company becomes a simple concept, i.e., the time duration of the high growth rate. Clearly, companies with long durations of growth should be valued more highly than those with short durations of growth, other things being equal. Also companies with high growth rates of earnings should be valued higher than companies with low growth rates, other things being equal.

Both the duration and the rate of growth need to be taken into account in valuing a growth stock. One way to do this is to consider the following question. How long, at a minimum, will the present high rate of earnings growth of a company have to continue in order to attain the same level of earnings that can be achieved by an alternative investment in nongrowth stocks of comparable risk? Assume that beyond this time the high growth rate drops to the normal rate, the low dividend payout rises, and the high price/earnings ratio falls, so that the two investments become virtually equivalent. In saying this, we have, of course, roughed over the uncertainty problem by assuming comparable risk for both investments. This time is the *minimum* required growth duration for the growth stock to justify its high price/earnings ratio. Of course, in both cases we need to take into account the dividend yields.

If we can formulate an analysis for determining the duration of growth estimate that is implicit in the market price of a growth stock, this may be useful to investors in making judgments as to whether the high price/earnings ratio of the growth stock is justified or not. We can obtain the market's estimate of duration of growth as follows: If we let $E'(t)$ be the earnings per share (adjusted for stock splits and stock dividends) of a common stock in the year t (measured from the present, when $t = 0$) and let ΔE be the percent per annum growth rate of earnings per share, then an estimate of future earnings per share as long as this growth rate continues is given by the following expression:

$$E'(t) = E'(0)(1 + \Delta E)^t \tag{1}$$

It is convenient for analysis to assume the reinvestment of dividend income to obtain additional "growth" so that it can be combined simply with the above expression.[5] This is done by pretending that the dividends are used to buy more (perhaps fractional) shares of the same stock. This assumption is purely for analytical purposes, to put all securities on a common "no dividend payment" basis.

Thus if D is the constant percent per annum dividend yield (i.e., ratio of dividends to market price), the number of shares $N(t)$ at the end of year t is

$$N(t) = (1 + D)^t \tag{2}$$

assuming that one share was bought originally when $t = 0$. The total earnings $E(t)$ at the end of year t on the original and purchased shares combined are

$$E(t) = E'(t)N(t) = E'(0)[(1 + \Delta E)(1 + D)]^t \tag{3}$$

Since D and ΔE are "small" and for the one original share $E'(0) = E(0)$, we obtain

$$E(t) \approx E(0)(1 + \Delta E + D)^t \tag{4}$$

This growth measurement of investment return is equally applicable to growth and nongrowth stocks. We apply it to both and introduce the subscript g to indicate a growth stock and the subscript a to indicate an alternative nongrowth stock of comparable risk.

After the *duration of growth*, which we designate as τ, we have assumed that the growth stock has the *same* general characteristics as the nongrowth stock. Hence in the year τ their market values will be in direct proportion to their earnings of that year.[6] Since uncertainty has been left out of our analysis and since no dividends are withdrawn, we would expect that the market would tend to value the shares of the two stocks for current purchase in direct proportion to their value in year τ and hence in direct proportion to the forecasted earnings in the year τ. If this proportionality condition were not satisfied, investors would tend to buy the relatively underpriced stock, in order to be in a better position in the year τ, thereby driving up the low price. Thus the market will tend to

---

[5] There is little meaningful distinction between dividend income and capital gains aside from factors that we are not considering now, namely, risk, taxes, brokerage commissions for odd-lot transactions, and administrative convenience.

[6] $E(t)$ is given by substituting τ for t in expression (4).

satisfy this relation between the current share prices of the growth and the nongrowth stocks, $P_g(0)$ and $P_a(0)$, respectively:

$$\frac{P_g(0)}{P_a(0)} \approx \frac{E_g(0)(1 + \Delta E_g + D_g)^\tau}{E_a(0)(1 + \Delta E_a + D_a)^\tau} \tag{5}$$

or, equivalently,

$$\left(\frac{P_g(0)/E_g(0)}{P_a(0)/E_a(0)}\right) \approx \left(\frac{1 + \Delta E_g + D_g}{1 + \Delta E_a + D_a}\right)^\tau \tag{6}$$

Here we see that the ratio between the price/earnings ratios of the two stocks is equal to the ratio of their composite growth rates raised to the τth power. The compounded growth offsets the high price/earnings ratio of the growth stock.

We may solve for τ by taking logarithms. For simplicity, we have dropped the time parentheses indicating current prices and earnings but without changing the meaning:

$$\ln\left(\frac{P_g/E_g}{P_a/E_a}\right) \approx \tau \ln\left(\frac{1 + \Delta E_g + D_g}{1 + \Delta E_a + D_a}\right) \tag{7}$$

Since this equation is linear in the logarithms, we may graph it on semilog paper to obtain the simple relation shown in Figure 1. Fortunately, the log scales on the graph avoid any necessity of dealing with logarithms. The intersection of a horizontal line representing the relative price/earnings ratio with a sloping line representing the relative growth rate determines a point. Dropping vertically, we can read the market estimate of growth duration τ. In this way, by plotting the point of intersection, we can obtain τ for a security. An example will clarify the results of the analysis. Suppose that the current price/earnings ratio for a growth stock is 45 and for a nongrowth stock of comparable risk is 15. Then the relative price/earnings ratio is $(P_g/E_g) \div (P_a/E_a) = 45/15 = 3$, as shown by the heavy horizontal line on Figure 1. Suppose, further, that the growth in earnings per share of the growth stock is expected to continue at the rate of 30 percent per year but the dividend yield is only 1 percent per year. The nongrowth stock, on the other hand, is expected to have only a 5 percent growth in earnings but has a 5 percent dividend yield. Thus the relative growth rate is $(1 + \Delta E_g + D_g) \div (1 + \Delta E_a + D_a) = (1 + 0.30 + 0.01) \div (1 + 0.05 + 0.05) = 1.31/1.10 = 1.2$, as shown by the heavy sloping line through the origin of Figure 1. The intersection of these two lines determines a point labeled A. Dropping vertically, we can read from the horizontal scale that the market estimate of duration of growth is evidently six years. That is to say, the market is valuing the growth stock *as if* its

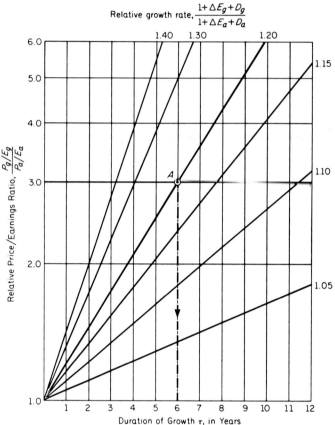

FIGURE 1

GROWTH VERSUS NONGROWTH COMPANIES

Relative growth rate, $\dfrac{1+\Delta E_g+D_g}{1+\Delta E_a+D_a}$

present high rate of growth would continue for six years and then decline sharply to the normal level. The graph has made it easy to find that $\tau = 6$. This value, of course, satisfies Eq. (6) for this example:

$$\frac{45}{15} \approx \left(\frac{1 + 0.30 + 0.01}{1 + 0.05 + 0.05}\right)^6$$

Another way to interpret the six-year growth duration is in terms of total growth potential. A 30 percent growth rate is, say, 25 percent above the normal growth rate, taking the nongrowth stock as the standard. If this rate continues for six years, we would have a total growth potential of $(1.25)^6 = 3.82$ or 382 percent. This amounts to forecasting that the ratio of earnings per share of the growth stock to the nongrowth stock will ultimately improve by almost a factor of four.

III. AN ILLUSTRATION USING MARKET DATA

The use of this analysis may be illustrated by selecting the Dow-Jones index as a representative alternative nongrowth investment, and selecting the following growth common stocks: Ampex, International Business Machines, Litton, Polaroid, and Texas Instruments. The dividend yields and price/earnings ratios for May, 1960, were used.

For the Dow-Jones index, the price/earnings ratio P_a/E_a was 18, D_a was 3 percent per year, and ΔE_a was 5 percent per year. These forecasts were extrapolations of the previous five years' history. We have obtained ΔE_g for each of the growth companies by plotting on semilog paper the earnings per share, adjusted for stock splits and stock dividends, for 1956 through 1959 and estimating the slope.

Before plotting points for each growth company, Figure 1 was modified by changing its scales to incorporate the Dow-Jones index as the

FIGURE 2

GROWTH COMPANIES VERSUS DOW-JONES INVESTMENT (AS OF MAY, 1960)

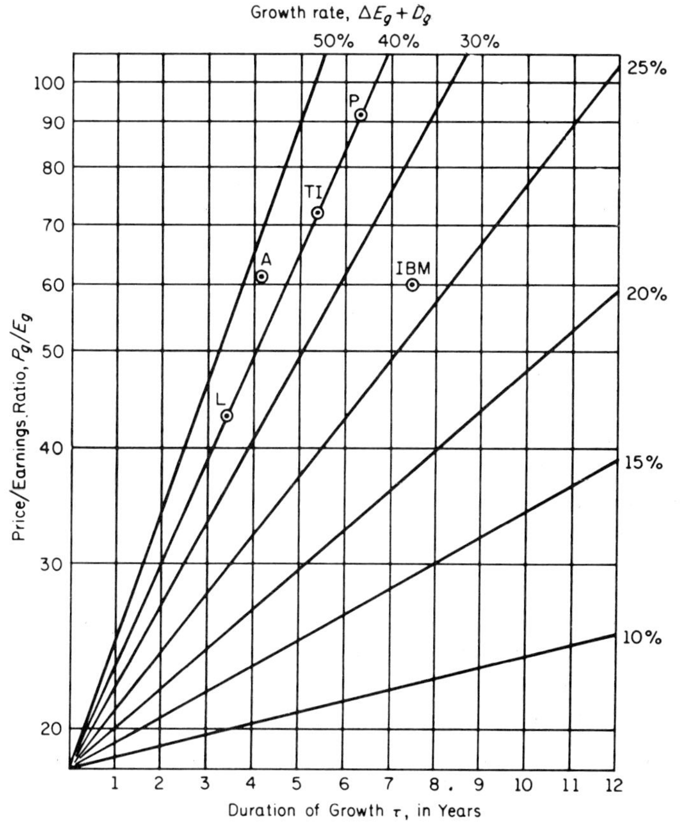

TABLE 1

Company	Market Estimate of Duration of Growth (Years)	Adjusted for Taxes (Years)
Ampex......................................	4.1	4.2
International Business Machines................	7.5	7.5
Litton..	3.4	3.4
Polaroid......................................	6.3	6.8
Texas Instruments............................	5.3	5.7

standard nongrowth alternative[7] (see Figure 2). Plotting these data on Figure 2 indicates the growth duration periods shown in the second column of Table 1. In interpreting these results, one is tempted, at first blush, to say that Litton is the better buy because it will justify its high price/earnings ratio relative to a Dow-Jones investment in a shorter period of time than the other companies. However, valid conclusions require a comparison for each company between the market estimate of duration of growth and the investor's own estimate. The investor can compare his judgments with those of the market and act accordingly where he feels the market is in error. Clearly, if growth duration actually proves to be longer than the market's estimate, the stock will have proved to be a bargain purchase. A stock with growth duration shorter than the market estimate will prove to have been a poor investment. As always, the investor must bet that his forecast is better than that of the market. If he can forecast growth durations successfully, growth stocks may offer important investment opportunities.

This analysis may be used in another way. An estimate of the growth duration for a company may be made by the investor and the corresponding line drawn vertically on Figure 1 or Figure 2 until it intersects the sloping growth-rate line. By moving left horizontally from the point of intersection, the investor may read the price/earnings ratio that would be warranted by this duration of growth. This could be compared with the price/earnings ratio existing in the market and purchase-sell decisions made accordingly.

IV. ADJUSTMENT FOR TAXES

An extension of the analysis might well take into account the fact that long-term capital gains are taxed at an advantageously low rate, so that income through price appreciation is more desirable than dividend income. An exact adjustment for taxes would greatly complicate the analysis, but,

---

[7] The growth-rate scale on Figure 2 plus 1 equals the relative growth-rate scale of Figure 1 multiplied by $(1 + 0.05 + 0.03)$.

by ignoring the fact that capital gains taxes are postponable, we may make an approximate adjustment. By making the simplifying assumption that capital gains are taxed in the year in which they occur, we can modify Formula (7) to reflect growth after taxes.

The growth from dividend reinvestment is reduced by taxes to $(1 - K_D)D$, where K_D is the marginal tax rate applicable to dividend income. Similarly, the growth of earnings is reduced to $(1 - K_C)\Delta E$, where K_C is the marginal tax rate applicable to capital gains income. A person whose marginal income tax rate was 30 percent would be taxed at half that rate on capital gains, i.e., $K_D = 0.3$ and $K_C = 0.15$. The maximum K_C is, of course, 0.25.

Recalling that the price/earnings ratio of the growth stock falls as the termination of the high growth rate approaches, we need to recognize that all the gain in earnings is not reflected in gain in market price of the shares. Since we have applied the capital gains tax to the full earnings appreciation, we need to make an offsetting adjustment by applying the capital gains tax to the decline in price/earnings ratio. If we rewrite the left parentheses of Formula (7),

$$\frac{P_g/E_g}{P_a/E_a} \approx \frac{P_a/E_a + (P_g/E_g - P_a/E_a)}{P_a/E_a} \tag{8}$$

we can interpret the right parentheses in Formula (8) as the capital "loss" component for the growth stock as the result of the reduction in price/earnings ratio to that of the nongrowth stock. We apply the capital gains tax to this "loss" adjustment by multiplying the "loss" term by $(1 - K_C)$:

$$\frac{P_a/E_a + (P_g/E_g - P_a/E_a)(1 - K_C)}{P_a/E_a} \approx 1 + \left(\frac{P_g/E_g}{P_a/E_a} - 1\right)(1 - K_C) \tag{9}$$

Incorporating the above adjustments in Formula (7), we obtain

$$\ln\left[1 + \left(\frac{P_g/E_g}{P_a/E_a} - 1\right)(1 - K_C)\right]$$

$$\approx \tau \ln\left[\frac{1 + (1 - K_C)\Delta E_g + (1 - K_D)D_g}{1 + (1 - K_C)\Delta E_a + (1 - K_D)D_a}\right] \tag{10}$$

The inclusion of the tax adjustment does not complicate the graphs, but it does complicate somewhat the computation step before entering the graphs. The effect of the adjustment will be to reflect the preference of the high-income person for companies that do not pay out their growth in the form of dividends. Applying this adjustment to the companies that we have already considered and assuming an investor whose tax rates are $K_D = 0.5$ and $K_C = 0.25$, we obtain the overtake periods shown in the third column of Table 1. In this case, the overtake periods were not greatly affected by the adjustment for taxes.

V. CONCLUSION

Four limitations of this analysis need to be noted. First—and most important—the uncertainty of forecasting earnings in the distant future is a much more important consideration for growth stocks than for nongrowth stocks. Hence, ignoring the risk inherent in probabilistic forecast errors is an important omission which will tend to make growth stocks appear more attractive than they really are. Second, the analysis rests on forecasts of constant earnings-per-share growth rates and constant dividend-per-share yields. Such forecasts on a per share basis need to be made critically because past data may reflect purely financial transactions, such as increasing leverage, etc., which may reflect increasing risk rather than growth. Third, the relative tax advantage of capital gains income, which is the principal return from growth stocks, is somewhat understated by neglecting the deferred collection of the capital gains tax, so that growth stocks appear less attractive than they really are—especially for high-income investors. Fourth, we hardly expect the growth of earnings to terminate sharply but, rather, would expect the growth rate to decline gradually as the special advantages enjoyed by the growth company are whittled away by increasing competition, expiration of patents, appearance of substitute products, etc. Thus the high growth rate would tend to last longer than the above analysis would indicate, but the rate of growth would be reduced.

The need for a really adequate theory of investment under certainty is emphasized by the gross approximations that were used in this exploratory analysis. Granting these limitations, the analysis does offer a systematic framework for evaluating growth stocks that includes many of the relevant variables with a minimum of complexity and computation. Hopefully, the analysis is simple enough—even using the adjustment for taxes—to be useful to investors.[8]

[8] An independent, but equivalent, analysis by Robert Ferguson has recently yielded a nomograph which reduces the computations to a simple mechanical procedure ["A Nomograph for Valuing Growth Stocks," *Financial Analysts Journal*, Vol. XVII (May–June, 1961), pp. 29–34]. Unfortunately, the underlying assumptions of his analysis are not fully explicit.

*David Durand**

30. Growth Stocks and the Petersburg Paradox[1]

Reprinted from **The Journal of Finance,** Vol. XII, No. 3 (September, 1957), pp. 348–363, by permission of the publisher.

At a time like the present, when investors are avidly seeking opportunities for appreciation, it is appropriate to consider the difficulties of appraising growth stocks. There is little doubt that when other things are equal the forward-looking investor will prefer stocks with growth potential to those without. But other things rarely are equal—particularly in a sophisticated market that is extremely sensitive to growth. When the growth potential of a stock becomes widely recognized, its price is expected to react favorably and to advance far ahead of stocks lacking growth appeal, so that its price/earnings ratio and dividend yield fall out of line according to conventional standards. Then the choice between growth and lack of growth is no longer obvious, and the astute investor must ask whether the market price correctly discounts the growth potential. Is it possible that the market may, at times, pay too much for growth?

Most problems encountered in appraising growth stocks seem to fall into two categories. First there are the practical difficulties of forecasting sales, earnings, and dividends. Then come the theoretical difficulties of reducing these forecasts to present values. For a long time it seems to have been assumed, altogether too casually, that the present value of a forecasted dividend stream could be represented simply as the sum of all expected future payments discounted at a uniform rate. Doubts, however,

* Professor of Industrial Management, Massachusetts Institute of Technology.

[1] Financial assistance was received from a grant by the Sloan Research Fund of the School of Industrial Management at Massachusetts Institute of Technology. Intellectual assistance, in the form of ideas, helpful suggestions, and critical comment was received from William Beranek, Joseph N. Froomkin, Myron J. Gordon, J. Arthur Greenwood, Avram Kisselgoff, Paul A. Samuelson, Eli Shapiro, Volkert S. Whitbeck, and from various persons interviewed by the author while touring Wall Street as a guest of the Joint Committee on Education representing the American Securities Business. All this assistance is gratefully acknowledged, but the author must assume full responsibility, since some of the views expressed here are controversial.

are beginning to manifest themselves. As early as 1938, J. B. Williams suggested nonuniform discount rates, varying from payment to payment.[2] More recently, Clendenin and Van Cleave have shown that discounting forecasted dividends at a uniform rate in perpetuity may lead to absurdities or paradoxes, since implied present values of infinity sometimes result. "We have not yet seen any growth stocks marketed at the price of infinity dollars per share," they remark, "but we shall hereafter be watching. Of course, many investors are skeptical and would probably wish to discount the very large and remote dividends in this perpetually growing series at a high discount rate, thus reducing our computed value per share to a figure somewhat below the intriguing value of infinity."[3] Clendenin and Van Cleave might have made a good point even better had they noticed a remarkable analogy between the appraisal of growth stocks and the famous Petersburg Paradox, which commanded the attention of most of the important writers on probability during the eighteenth and nineteenth centuries.

I. THE PETERSBURG PARADOX

In 1738 Daniel Bernoulli presented before the Imperial Academy of Sciences in Petersburg a classic paper on probability, in which he discussed the following problem, attributed to his cousin Nicholas: "Peter tosses a coin and continues to do so until it should land 'heads' when it comes to the ground. He agrees to give Paul one ducat if he gets 'heads' on the very first throw, two ducats if he gets it on the second, four if on the third, eight if on the fourth, and so on, so that with each additional throw the number of ducats he must pay is doubled. Suppose we seek to determine the value of Paul's expectation."[4]

One may easily obtain a solution according to the principles of mathematical expectation by noting the sequence of payments and probabilities in Table 1: Paul's expectation is the sum of the products of probability by payment or

$$\tfrac{1}{2} + \tfrac{2}{4} + \tfrac{4}{8} + \tfrac{8}{16} + \tfrac{16}{32} + \cdots$$

If the players agree to terminate the game after n tosses, whether a head shows or not, the series will contain n terms and its sum will be $n/2$; but

[2] John B. Williams, *The Theory of Investment Value* (Cambridge, Mass.: Harvard U.P., 1938), pp. 50–60.

[3] John C. Clendenin and Maurice Van Cleave, "Growth and Common Stock Values," *Journal of Finance*, Vol. IX (1954), pp. 365–76. Quotation appears on p. 369.

[4] Daniel Bernoulli, "Exposition of a New Theory on the Measurement of Risk," *Econometrica*, Vol. XXII (1954), pp. 23–36, which is a translation by Dr. Louis Sommer of Bernoulli's paper "Specimen Theoriae Novae de Mensura Sortis," *Commentarii Academiae Scientiarum Imperialis Petropolitanae*, Vol. V (1738), pp. 175–92.

TABLE 1

Sequence of Tosses	Probability	Payment
H...	1/2	1
TH..	1/4	2
TTH...	1/8	4
TTTH..	1/16	8
TTTTH...	1/32	16

if they agree to continue without fail until a head shows, as the rules of the game stipulate, then n is infinite and the sum $n/2$ is infinite as well. Thus the principles of mathematical expectation imply that Paul should pay an infinite price to enter this game, but this is a conclusion that virtually no one will accept. A variety of explanations have been given to show that the value of the game to Paul is, in fact, only a finite amount—usually a small finite amount; and all of these explanations are relevant to growth stock appraisal. But before considering them, we shall do well to examine an important modification of the original Petersburg problem.

One modification, which is obvious enough, consists in stipulating some figure other than $\frac{1}{2}$, say $1/(1 + i)$, for the probability of tossing a tail and some figure other than 2, say $1 + g$, for the rate of growth; but this has no particular interest for security appraisal. A more extensive modification, which is of interest, provides for a series of increasing payments, instead of a single lump sum. In effect, Peter agrees to pay D ducats if the first toss is a tail, $D(1 + g)$ if the second is a tail, $D(1 + g)^2$ if the third is a tail, $D(1 + g)^3$ if the fourth is a tail, and so on until a head shows—at which point the game ceases. Then, if the probability of a tail is $1/(1 + i)$, the mathematical expectation is (see Appendix)

$$\frac{D}{1 + i} + \frac{D(1 + g)}{(1 + i)^2} + \frac{D(1 + g)^2}{(1 + i)^3} + \cdots \tag{1}$$

This series is arithmetically equivalent to a discounted series of dividend payments, starting at D ducats, growing at a constant rate g, and discounted at rate i.[5] The summation of the series is a simple exercise in

---

[5] Possibly the objection may be raised that Series (1) is conceptually quite different from a discounted series of dividends on the grounds that the discount rate ordinarily represents the price paid for waiting in addition to the price paid for assuming risk. To meet this objection, it suffices to discount the dividend series twice, first, by an amount just sufficient to cover the price of waiting, and second, by the amount required to cover the risk of dividend termination when Peter finally tosses a head. Then, the growth rate g in Series (1) would represent the real growth rate less an adjustment for waiting, and i would represent only the risk of termination.

actuarial mathematics. The sum of the first n terms is[6]

$$D\frac{1 - (1 + g)^n/(1 + i)^n}{i - g} \tag{2}$$

provided i is different from g; and the sum of an infinite or very large number of terms approaches the very simply formulated quantity

$$\frac{D}{i - g} \tag{3}$$

provided that i exceeds g. If, however, $g \geq i$, the sum of an infinite number of terms would again be infinite—as in the original Petersburg problem—and a reasonable Paul might again object to paying the price.

The applicability of Formulas (2) and (3) to growth stock appraisal is not new. In 1938, for example, J. B. Williams[7] derived (3), or its equivalent, in order to appraise the retained portion of common stock earnings. He made the derivation, using quite different notation, on essentially the following assumptions: first, that in any year j, earnings per share E_j bear a constant ratio r to book value B_j; second, that dividends D_j bear a constant ratio p to E_j. Then,

$$B_{j+1} = B_j + E_j(1 - p) = B_j[1 + r(1 - p)]$$

Hence, book value, dividends, and earnings are all growing at the same constant rate $g = r(1 - p)$ and Formula (3) can be rewritten

$$\frac{D_1}{i - g} = \frac{E_1 p}{i - g} = \frac{B_1 p r}{i - g} \tag{3a}$$

Williams realized, of course, that these formulas are valid only when i exceeds g, and he mentioned certain other limitations that are best discussed with some of the proposed solutions for the Petersburg Paradox.

II. ATTEMPTS TO RESOLVE THE PETERSBURG PARADOX[8]

The many attempts to resolve the paradox, summarized very briefly below, fall mostly into two broad groups: those denying the basic assump-

[6] See, for example, Ralph Todhunter, *The Institute of Actuaries' Text-Book on Compound Interest and Annuities-Certain*, 4th ed., revised by R. C. Simmonds and T. P. Thompson (Cambridge, England: U.P., 1937), pp. 48–49.

[7] *Op. cit.*, pp. 87–89, 128–135.

[8] For a general history of the paradox, see Isaac Todhunter, *A History of the Mathematical Theory of Probability from the Time of Pascal to that of Laplace* (reprint, New York, N.Y.: G. E. Stechert & Co., 1931), pp. 134, 220–22, 259–62, 275, 280, 286–89, 332, 345, 393, 470. For a briefer treatment, see John Maynard Keynes, *A Treatise on Probability* (London, England: Macmillan and Co., 1921), pp. 316 ff.

tions of the game as unrealistic, and those arguing from additional assumptions that the value of the game to Paul is less than its mathematical expectation.

The basic assumptions of the game are open to all sorts of objections from the practically minded. How, in real life, can the game continue indefinitely? For example, Peter and Paul are mortal; so, after a misspent youth, a dissipated middle age, and a dissolute dotage, one of them will die, and the game will cease—heads or no heads. Or again, Peter's solvency is open to question, for the stakes advance at an alarming rate. With an initial payment of one dollar, Peter's liability after only 35 tails exceeds the gold reserve in Fort Knox, and after only three more, it exceeds the volume of bank deposits in the United States and approximately equals the national debt. With this progression, the sky is, quite literally, the limit. Even if Peter and Paul agree to cease after 100 tosses, the stakes, though finite, stagger the imagination.

Despite these serious practical objections, a number of writers chose to accept the assumption of an indefinitely prolonged game at face value, and to direct their attention toward ascertaining the value of such a game to Paul. First among these was the Swiss mathematician Gabriel Cramer, who early in the eighteenth century proposed two arbitrary devices for resolving the Petersburg Paradox by assuming that the utility of money is less than proportional to the amount held.[9] First, if the utility of money is proportional to the amount up to $2^{24} = 166,777,216$ ducats and constant for amounts exceeding 2^{24}, so that the utility of the payments ceases to increase after the 24th toss, Paul's so-called moral expectation is about 13 ducats. Second, if the utility of money is assumed equal to the square root of the amount held, Paul's moral expectation is only about 2.9 ducats. Cramer believed that 2.9 was a more reasonable entrance fee than 13.

A little later and apparently independently, Daniel Bernoulli devised a solution only slightly different from Cramer's. Assuming that the marginal utility of money is inversely proportional to the amount held, he derived a formula that evaluates Paul's expectation in terms of his resources at the beginning of the game. From this formula, which does not lend itself to lightning computation, Bernoulli estimated roughly that the expectation is worth about 3 ducats to Paul when his resources are 10 ducats, about 4 ducats when his resources are 100, and about 6 when his resources are 1000.[10] At this rate, Paul must have infinite resources before he can value his expectation at infinity; but then, even his infinite valuation will constitute only an infinitesimally small fraction of his resources.

An interesting variant of Bernoulli's approach was proposed about

[9] Cf. Bernoulli, *op. cit.*, pp. 33 ff.
[10] *Ibid.*, pp. 32 ff.

a century later by W. A. Whitworth[11]—at least some of us would consider it a variant, though its author considered it an entirely different argument. Whitworth was, in fact, seeking a solution to the Petersburg Problem that would be free of arbitrary assumptions concerning the utility of money; and he derived a solution by considering the risk of gamblers' ruin, which is always present when players have limited resources. Thus, for example, if A with one dollar matches pennies indefinitely against B with $10, it is virtually certain that one of them will eventually be cleaned out; furthermore, A has 10 chances out of 11 of being the victim. Accordingly, a prudent A might demand some concession in the odds as the price of playing against B. But how much concession? Whitworth attacked this and other problems by assuming a prudent gambler will risk a constant proportion of his resources, rather than a constant amount, on each venture; and he devised a system for evaluating ventures that entail risk of ruin. Applied to the Petersburg Game, this system indicates that Paul's entrance fee should depend upon his resources. Thus Whitworth's solution is reminiscent of Bernoulli's—particularly when one realizes that Whitworth's basic assumption implies an equivalence between a dime bet for A with $1 and a dollar bet for B with $10. Bernoulli, of course, would have argued that the utility of a dime to A was equal to the utility of a dollar to B. Finally, the notion of a prudent gambler seeking to avoid ruin has strong utilitarian undertones, for it implies that the marginal utility of money is high when resources are running out.

But Whitworth's approach—regardless of its utilitarian subtleties—is interesting because it emphasizes the need for diversification. The evaluation of a hazardous venture—be it dice game, business promotion, or risky security—depends not only on the inherent odds, but also on the proportion of the risk-taker's resources that must be committed. And just as the prudent gambler may demand odds stacked in his favor as the price for betting more than an infinitesimal proportion of his resources, so may the prudent portfolio manager demand a greater than normal rate of return (after allowing for the inherent probability of default) as the price of investing more than an infinitesimal proportion of his assets in a risky issue.[12]

Although the preceding historical account of the Petersburg Paradox has been of the sketchiest, it should serve to illustrate an important point. The various proposed solutions, of which there are many, all involve

---

[11] W. A. Whitworth, *Choice and Chance*, 4th ed., enlarged (Cambridge, England: Deighton, Bell & Co., 1886), Ch. 9.

[12] Section 87 of the New York Insurance Law states: "Except as more specifically provided in this chapter, no domestic insurer shall have more than ten percent of its total admitted assets invested in, or loaned upon, the securities of any one institution;..." Section 81, subsection 13, places additional restrictions on common stock investment.

changing the problem in one way or another. Thus some proposals evaluate the cash value of a finite game, even when the problem specifies an infinite game; others evaluate the utility receipts, instead of the cash receipts, of an infinite game; and still others foresake evaluation for gamesmanship and consider what Paul as a prudent man should pay to enter. But although none of these proposals satisfy the theoretical requirements of the problem, they all help to explain why a real live Paul might be loath to pay highly for his infinite mathematical expectation. As Keynes aptly summed it up, "We are unwilling to be Paul, partly because we do not believe Peter will pay us if we have good fortune in the tossing, partly because we do not know what we should do with so much money ... if we won it, partly because we do not believe we should ever win it, and partly because we do not think it would be a rational act to risk an infinite sum or even a very large sum for an infinitely larger one, whose attainment is infinitely unlikely."[13]

III. IMPLICATIONS OF PETERSBURG SOLUTIONS FOR GROWTH-STOCK APPRAISAL

If instead of tossing coins, Peter organizes a corporation in a growth industry and offers Paul stock, the latter might be deterred from paying the full discounted value by any of the considerations that would deter him from paying the full mathematical expectation to enter the Petersburg game. And again, these considerations fall into two categories: first, those denying the basic assumptions concerning the rate of indefinitely prolonged growth; and, second, those arguing that the value of the stock to Paul is less than its theoretical discounted value.

Underlying J. B. Williams' derivation of Formula (3) is the assumption that Peter, Inc., will pay dividends at an increasing rate g for the rest of time. Underlying the derivation in the Appendix is a slightly different assumption: namely, that Peter will pay steadily increasing dividends until the game terminates with the toss of a head, and that the probability of a head will remain forever constant at $i/(1 + i)$. Under neither assumption is there any provision for the rate of growth ever to cease or even decline. But astronomers now predict the end of the world within a finite number of years—somewhere in the order of 10 billion—and realistic security analysts may question Peter, Inc.'s ability to maintain a steadily increasing dividend rate for anywhere near that long. Williams, in fact, regarded indefinitely increasing dividends as strictly hypothetical, and he worked up formulas for evaluating growth stocks on the assumption that dividends will follow a growth curve (called a logistic by Williams) that increases exponentially for a time and then levels off to an asymptote.[14]

[13] Keynes, *op. cit.*, p. 318.
[14] Williams, *op. cit.*, pp. 89–94.

This device guarantees that the present value of any dividend stream will be finite, no matter how high the current, and temporary, rate of growth. Clendenin and Van Cleave, though not insisting on a definite ceiling, argued that continued rapid growth is possible only under long-run price inflation.

The assumption of indefinitely increasing dividends is most obviously objectionable when the growth rate equals or exceeds the discount rate ($g \geq i$) and the growth Series (1) sums to infinity; then Formula (3) does not even apply. If Peter, Inc., is to pay a dividend that increases at a constant rate $g \geq i$ per year, it is absolutely necessary, though not sufficient, that he earn a rate on capital, $r = E/B$, that is greater than the rate of discount—more exactly, $r \geq i/(1 - p)$. But this situation poses an anomaly, at least for the equilibrium theorist, who argues that the marginal rate of return on capital must equal the rate of interest in the long run. How, then, can Peter, Inc., continually pour increasing quantities of capital into his business and continue to earn on these accretions a rate higher than the standard rate of discount? This argument points toward the conclusion that growth stocks characterize business situations in which limited, meaning finite though not necessarily small, amounts of capital can be invested at rates higher than the equilibrium rate. If this is so, then the primary problem of the growth-stock appraiser is to estimate how long the departure from equilibrium will continue, perhaps by some device like William's growth curve.

If, for the sake of argument, Paul wishes to assume that dividend growth will continue indefinitely at a constant rate, he can still find reasons for evaluating Peter's stock at somewhat less than its theoretical value just as he found reasons for evaluating his chances in the Petersburg Game at less than the mathematical expectation. The decreasing-marginal-utility approach of Cramer and Bernoulli implies that the present utility value of a growing dividend stream is less than the discounted monetary value, because the monetary value of the large dividends expected in the remote future must be substantially scaled down in making a utility appraisal. Or again, Whitworth's diversification approach implies that a prudent Paul with finite resources can invest only a fraction of his portfolio in Peter's stock; otherwise he risks ruinous loss. And either argument is sufficient to deter Paul from offering an infinite price, unless, of course, his resources should be infinite.

IV. THE PROBLEM OF REMOTE DIVIDENDS

There is, moreover, another important limitation on Paul's evaluation of a growth stock that has not arisen in the discussion of the Petersburg Paradox, namely, the remoteness of the large dividend payments. Conventional theory argues that a dividend n years hence is adequately evaluated by the discount factor $1/(1+i)^n$, but this is open to question when n is very large. The question is, of course, academic for ordinary instruments like long-term bonds or preferred stock, since discounted coupons or preferred dividends many years hence are negligible when discounted in the conventional manner. Thus, for example, if \$5.00 a year in perpetuity is worth exactly \$100.00 (assuming 5 percent compounded annually), then \$99.24 is attributable to the first 100 payments. But for a stock growing according to Series (1) and with $g \geq i$, the discounted value of remote dividends, say 10,000 years hence, is anything but negligible; in fact, it may be astronomic. But how should Paul evaluate such remote growth dividends?

If Paul is a real live person without heirs or other incentives for founding an estate, his problem is fairly clearcut. Dividends payable beyond his reasonable life span are useless to him as income, although claims on them may be convertible into useful income through the medium of the market place. At retirement, for example, he might easily be able to increase his income for the remainder of his life by selling long-term securities and buying an annuity. If, however, Paul has heirs, he may look forward several generations and place a very real value on dividends that will be payable to his grandchildren and great-grandchildren. But even here his investment horizon may be limited by the uncertainty of planning for offspring not yet born.

If Paul is a life insurance company, he has a special interest in evaluating remote dividends; for the shades of obligations currently contracted may extend far into the future as the following fanciful though not impossible sketch will indicate. In 1956 John Doe, aged 21, buys for his own benefit a whole life policy containing the customary guaranty of a rate of interest if the insured elects to settle the proceeds in instalments. In 2025, aged 90, John Doe decides to settle this policy on his newborn great-grandson Baby Doe and directs the insurance company to accumulate the proceeds at the guaranteed rate of interest until Baby Doe shall reach the age of 21 and thereupon pay them out to him as a life income, according to the table of guaranteed rates in the policy. Encouraged by his monthly checks, Baby Doe now lives to the ripe old age of 105, so that only in 2130 does the insurance company finally succeed in discharging its obligation of 1956, based on the then current forecasts of long-term interest rates.

Even though the case of John Doe may be a bit out of the ordinary, it illustrates forcefully why life insurance companies must concern themselves with dividend income up to perhaps 200 years hence and how a future decline in the earning rate on assets may threaten the solvency of an insurance fund. Although the purchase of long-term bonds is an obvious form of protection against falling interest rates, it is not entirely effective when the liabilities extend too far into the future. To illustrate the difficulty of long-term protection, it will be convenient at this point to introduce a concept called "duration" by Macaulay,[15] which may apply to an individual security, a portfolio of securities, or even to a block of liabilities. Duration, incidentally, must not be confused with a related concept known as "equated time."

The duration of an individual security or a portfolio is the arithmetic mean of the several coupon or maturity dates, each date weighted by the present value at the valuation rate of interest of the expected income on that date. The duration of an E bond or noninterest-bearing note is simply the term to maturity; and the duration of a portfolio consisting, for example, of two $100 E bonds due two years hence and a $500 E bond due five years hence would be

$$\left[\frac{2 \times 200}{(1.03)^2} + \frac{5 \times 500}{(1.03)^5}\right] \div \left[\frac{200}{(1.03)^2} + \frac{500}{(1.03)^5}\right]$$

if evaluated at 3 percent compounded annually. The duration of an interest-bearing bond is less than the term to maturity, because the long term of the principal payment at maturity must be averaged against the shorter terms of the various coupons. Macaulay's formula for the duration of interest-paying bonds is somewhat complex; but for perpetuities, such as Canadian Pacific debenture 4's, it simplifies to $(1 + i)/i$.[16] At $i = .03$, the duration of a perpetuity is therefore about 34 years.

In seeking suitable methods for matching the assets of a fund to its liabilities so as to minimize risk of loss from fluctuations in the interest rate, British actuaries have shown that the possible loss is very small when both present value and duration of the assets equal present value and duration of the liabilities; and, indeed, they have given examples where the "loss" is a small gain for fluctuations either up or down.[17] But although the

---

[15] F. R. Macaulay, *Some Theoretical Problems Suggested by the Movement of Interest Rates, Bond Yields and Stock Prices in the United States since 1856* (New York, N.Y.: National Bureau of Economic Research, 1938), pp. 44–51.

[16] Macaulay, *ibid.*, pp. 49–50. In Macaulay's formula for perpetuities (p. 50) let $R = 1 + i$.

[17] See, for example, J. B. H. Pegler, "The Actuarial Principles of Investment," *Journal of the Institute of Actuaries* (England), Vol. 74 (1948), pp. 179–211; F. M. Redington, "Review of the Principles of Life-Office Valuations," *ibid.*, Vol. 78 (1952), pp. 286–340; G. V. Bayley and W. Perks, "A Consistent System of Investment and Bonus Distribution for a Life Office," *ibid.*, Vol. 79 (1953), pp. 14–73; A. T. Haynes and R. J. Kirton, "The Financial Structure of a Life Office," *Transactions of the Faculty of Actuaries* (Scotland), Vol. 21 (1953), pp. 141–218; D. J. Robertson and I. L. B. Sturrock, "Active Investment Policy Related to the Holding of Matched Assets," *ibid.*, Vol. 22 (1954), pp. 36–96. Also see Paul A. Samuelson, "The Effect of Interest Rate Increases on the Banking System," *American Economic Review*, Vol. XXXV (1945), pp. 16–27, especially p. 19.

Interest of the British in this subject, which seems to be greater than that of the Americans, may be due in part to their relative freedom from liability for policy loans. Although the British companies are prepared to make such loans, they are not forced to do so.

portfolio manager can ordinarily achieve satisfactory matching by merely selecting long- and short-term bonds in such proportions that their average duration equals that of the liabilities, he runs into difficulty when the duration of the liabilities is exceptionally long. Thus, for example, the duration of the liability of a pension fund with many young workers and only a few pensioners can easily exceed 40 years: and this is too long to be matched by a portfolio consisting wholly of perpetuities, whose duration at current interest rates is only about 30 years. In such a difficulty, however, growth stocks offer a possible solution; for when dividends are growing according to Series (1), the duration is longer than a perpetuity. In fact, if we define

$$1 + b = \frac{1 + i}{1 + g}$$

then $(1 + b)b$ is the duration of the series.[18] Thus growth stocks provide a possible means of increasing the average duration of a portfolio when the composition of the liabilities requires this. W. Perks has, in fact, hinted as much.[19]

There is, in fact, no theoretical limit to the duration of a stock with dividends growing as in Series (1). When $g = .05$ and $i = .06$, say, the duration is approximately 100 years; and as the difference between g and i decreases, durations of 1,000 years, 10,000 years, or even 1 million years might result. Moreover, when $g \geq i$, $b \leq 0$ and formula $(1 + b)/b$ is no longer valid; then the duration is infinite as well as the present value. But although securities with a duration of 100 years might be useful to British life companies for increasing average duration of pension fund assets, or for providing protection against contingencies illustrated by the case of John Doe above, securities with much greater duration would begin to lose appeal. The essential characteristic of a very long duration is that the security holder or his legatees must expect to wait a long time before the security begins to pay a substantial return; and with those hypothetical securities having infinite duration, the legatees must literally expect to wait forever. Even the most forward looking of investors, who are probably those who leave bequests to such institutions as universities and religious organizations, cannot afford to look that far into the future; for, to paraphrase Keynes, it would not be a rational act to risk an infinite sum or even a very large sum for an infinitely larger one, whose attainment is infinitely remote. In effect, the very remote dividends in Series (1) cannot be worth their actuarially discounted value when g is large; whether they are worth it when g is small is probably academic, for then the discounted value will be negligible.

---

[18] This can be proved by using Macaulay's method of finding the duration of a perpetuity and making the substitution $b = i$.

[19] See his remarks following the paper by Redington, *op. cit.*, p. 327.

To allow for various uncertainties in evaluating dividends in the very remote future, Clendenin and Van Cleave made a significant suggestion, namely, to increase the discount rate applicable to the more remote dividends. The difficulty, of course, is to find some reasonable, objective basis for setting up an appropriate schedule of rates. To illustrate their suggestion, Clendenin and Van Cleave worked out valuations for hypothetical securities by discounting the first 20 years of dividends at 4 percent, the second 20 at 6 percent, the third 20 at 8 percent, and considering all subsequent dividends as worthless. But although such a schedule, totally disregarding all dividends after 60 years, might appeal to a man aged 40 without heirs, it would not appeal to insurance companies and pension managers, who have to look forward 150 to 200 years; and it would certainly not appeal to the loyal alumnus, who wishes to leave a bequest to alma mater. But the essential point is that by setting up a schedule of discount rates that increase fast enough to render very remote dividends negligible, one can assure himself that the present value of any increasing stream of dividends will be finite. And although many investors would object to neglecting dividends after 60 years, few would object to neglecting them after 600.

V. SUMMARY AND IMPLICATIONS FOR SECURITY APPRAISAL IN GENERAL

There are, to sum up, a number of potent reasons any one of which suffices to dissuade Paul from paying an infinite price for a growth stock under even the most favorable circumstances, namely when $g \geq i$ and the sum of Series (1) is infinite. Moreover, these reasons do not lose all their force when $g < i$ and the sum of Series (1) is finite. In appraising any growing stream of dividends, Paul might wish to make provision for eventual decline and perhaps cessation of the growth rate, as suggested by J. B. Williams; he might adjust large dividends to allow for the decreasing marginal utility of money, somewhat in the manner of Cramer and Bernoulli; or again he might apply Whitworth's reasoning and scale down his valuation to a sum he can afford to risk, given his resources; or finally he might, following Clendenin and Van Cleave, apply a very high discount rate to remote dividends that have no significance to him. And he might, of course, apply a combination of such approaches.

But, oddly enough, the very fact that Paul has so many good reasons for scaling down the sum of Series (1) when g is high, and so many ways to accomplish this end, leaves him with no clear basis for arriving at any precise valuation. Thus, the possible adjustments for the decreasing marginal utility of money are many and varied. Cramer's two proposals yielded very different solutions for the Petersburg Problem and would yield very different appraisals if applied to rapidly growing growth stocks; and Daniel

Bernoulli's proposal would yield yet another result. Or again, there are many ways by which Paul can allow for an eventual decline in the current rate of growth, all of which entail major forecasting problems. Williams' formula, for example, which is stated here in the form[20]

$$V = D \left[\frac{(1 + g)^n - (1 + i)^n}{(g - i)(1 + i)^n} + \frac{(2g + i + 2gi)(1 + g)^n}{i(g + i + gi)(1 + i)^n} \right]$$

after the substitution $D = \Pi_0(1 + g)$ and some rearrangement, rests on the somewhat restrictive assumption that dividends grow annually at a constant rate g for n years and then taper off exponentially to a level equal to exactly twice the dividend in the nth year. Even when the assumptions are acceptable in principle, practical application of the formula may require more accurate information on g, i, and n than one could possibly expect to obtain. This is particularly true when n is large and g is only slightly larger than i; then $g - i$ in the denominator of the first fraction is small and tremendously sensitive to errors in either g or i. Nor is this difficulty peculiar to Williams' formula. Table 2, abridged from Clendenin and Van Cleave,[21] gives the present value of 60 dividend payments dis-

TABLE 2

Growth Period	Rate of Growth	
	5 Percent	4 Percent
0..	$18.93	$18.93
10...	$28\frac{1}{4}$	26
20...	37	$32\frac{1}{4}$
30...	$45\frac{1}{4}$	$37\frac{1}{2}$
40...	$52\frac{1}{4}$	$41\frac{1}{2}$
50...	$57\frac{3}{4}$	$44\frac{1}{4}$
60...	60	$45\frac{1}{2}$

counted at 5 percent. It is assumed that the initial dividend rate of $1.00 grows at either 4 percent or 5 percent for a period of years and then remains constant for the remainder of the 60-year period, after which dividends either cease or are considered worthless. This table again illustrates the difficulty of making appraisals without an accurate forecast of the growth rate and the length of the growth period.

More conventional securities such as bonds and preferred stocks, though much less troublesome than growth stocks, still present some of the same difficulties of evaluation, and a single example should make this clear. In evaluating bonds—even bonds of supposedly uniform quality—

[20] Williams, *op. cit.*, formula (27a), p. 94.
[21] *Op. cit.*, Table 4, p. 371.

one must make some adjustment for term to maturity. Ordinarily one does this by summing a discounted series of coupons and principal

$$\frac{C}{1 + i_n} + \frac{C}{(1 + i_n)^2} + \cdots + \frac{C}{(1 + i_n)^n} + \frac{P}{(1 + i_n)^n}$$

in which the uniform discount factor depends on the number of years to maturity. Alternatively, however, one could follow the suggestion of Clendenin and Van Cleave, which would entail summing the series

$$\frac{C}{1 + i_1} + \frac{C}{(1 + i_2)^2} + \frac{C}{(1 + i_3)^3} + \cdots + \frac{C}{(1 + i_n)^n} + \frac{P}{(1 + i_n)^n}$$

in which each discount factor i_1, i_2, etc. depends on the date of the coupon or principal payment discounted. But whether one prefers the conventional method or the alternative, the issue is clear: one cannot apply a standard discount factor i uniformly to all bonds; some adjustment for the length, or duration, of the payment stream is essential.

The moral of all this is that conventional discount formulas do not provide completely reliable evaluations. Presumably they provide very satisfactory approximations for high-grade, short-term bonds and notes. But as quality deteriorates or duration lengthens, the approximations become rougher and rougher. With growth stocks, the uncritical use of conventional discount formulas is particularly likely to be hazardous; for, as we have seen, growth stocks represent the ultimate in investments of long duration. Likewise, they seem to represent the ultimate in difficulty of evaluation. The very fact that the Petersburg Problem has not yielded a unique and generally acceptable solution to more than 200 years of attack by some of the world's great intellects suggests, indeed, that the growth-stock problem offers no great hope of a satisfactory solution.

APPENDIX

Proof of formula (1) for Paul's expectation in the modified Petersburg Game

The table below lists a few possible outcomes, with associated probabilities, for the modified Petersburg Game, in which Peter pays Paul a series of dividends according to the number of tails that occur before a head finally shows. There is, of course, an infinite number of such possible outcomes, because every finite sequence

Sequence of Tosses	Probability	Dividend	Total Pay (Cumulated Dividends)
H....................	$i/(1 + i)$	0	0
TH...................	$i/(1 + i)^2$	D	D
TTH..................	$i/(1 + i)^3$	$D(1 + g)$	$D + D(1 + g)$
TTTH................	$i/(1 + i)^4$	$D(1 + g)^2$	$D + D(1 + g) + D(1 + g)^2$

of tails, no matter how long, has a finite, though possibly very small, probability of occurring. It is assumed, moreover, that throughout even the longest sequence, the probability of a tail remains constant at $1/(1 + i)$, leaving $i/(1 + i)$ as the probability of a head.

Paul's mathematical expectation is obtained by summing the products of probability in the second column by payout in the fourth. Thus, the sequence TTH, for example, has probability $i/(1 + i)^3$ and results in the payout of two dividends, D and $D(1 + g)$. The product appears in the table below along with similar products for the sequences H, TH, and TTTH.

Sequence	Product
H............................	0
TH...........................	$Di/(1 + i)^2$
TTH..........................	$[D + D(1 + g)]i/(1 + i)^3$
TTTH.........................	$[D + D(1 + g) + D(1 + g)^2]i/(1 + i)^4$

To sum these products, it is convenient to break them up and to rearrange the parts in powers of $1 + g$. Thus, for example, all elements containing $(1 + g)^2$ form an infinite series

$$\frac{Di(1 + g)^2}{(1 + i)^4}\left[1 + \frac{1}{1 + i} + \frac{1}{(1 + i)^2} + \cdots\right]$$

where the factor in the bracket is a well-known actuarial form having the sum to infinity $(1 + i)/i$. Thus, the sum of all elements in $(1 + g)^2$ is $D(1 + g)^2/(1 + i)^3$, which is one of the terms in Series (1). The other terms are obtained in an analogous manner.

*James E. Walter**

31. Dividend Policy: Its Influence on the Value of the Enterprise

Reprinted from **The Journal of Finance,** Vol. XVIII, No. 2 (May, 1963), pp. 280–291, by permission of the author and the publisher.

The question before the house is whether dividends are in some sense of the word weighted differently from retained earnings at the margin in the minds of marginal investors. As evidenced by the current literature on the subject, the answer is by no means self-evident.

Although the problem that confronts us can be approached in a variety of ways, our preference is to commence with net cash flows from operations and to consider the effect of additions to, and subtractions from, these flows upon stock values.[1] Not only does this starting point by-pass certain measurement problems, but it also directs attention to the relevant variables in a manner that other approaches may not.

Net cash flows from operations are available for (1) the payment of interest and principal on debt or the equivalent and (2) capital expenditures and dividend payments. Operating cash flows can, of course, be supplemented in any period by debt or equity financing. Debt financing creates obligations to pay out cash in future periods and thereby reduces cash flows available for capital expenditures and dividends in those periods. Equity financing, in turn, diminishes the pro rata share of total cash flows available for dividends and reinvestment.

The stockholder shares in the operating cash flows of each period to the degree that cash dividends are declared and paid and in future cash flows insofar as they are reflected in the market price of the stock.[2] In like

---

[*] Professor of Finance, University of Pennsylvania.

[1] As a point of departure, *net cash flows from operations* lie somewhere between (1) net cash flow and (2) net operating income. See, for example, Bodenhorn [1]. (Bracketed numbers refer to readings listed at the end of this article.) For an illustrative breakdown and an explanation of the manner in which net operating cash flows are derived from balance sheets and income statements, refer to Ch. 11 of Walter [12].

[2] It almost goes without saying that an existing shareholder periodically compares the objective market price with his subjective version of anticipated dividend streams and terminal prices to determine whether to hold or liquidate. In this respect, his behavior resembles that of a prospective buyer.

fashion, the purchaser of a share of stock acquires (1) a finite stream of anticipated cash dividends and (2) an anticipated market price at the end of his holding period. The market price of the stock at any time can be said to be determined by the expectations of marginal investors (as these anticipations pertain to the dividend stream and to the terminal market price) and by their system of weighting the possible outcomes per period and through time.

To focus directly upon the potential influence of variations in dividend policy in this scheme of things, it is useful, first, to draw an analogy to the stream-splitting approach to the cost of capital. Consideration is then afforded (1) the conditions under which adjustments in dividend payout exert no effect upon stock price and (2) the consequences of modifying these conditions to take account of the economic power of large corporations and other aspects of observed behavior. The final item treated in this article is that of statistical testing.

The assumptions that prevail throughout the analysis are commonplace. One is that the satisfaction which investors derive from owning stock is wholly (or almost wholly) monetary in character. A second is that investors do the best that they can; they operate, however, in a competitive capital market and are unable to stack the results.

Corporate management—we may add—is also keenly aware of the potential impact of its actions upon stock price (if only because of stock options). Management may nonetheless be confronted with such *mixed* motivations as self-preservation and avoidance of antitrust action. The consequence is that maximization of stock price need not be the sole objective.[3]

So far as uncertainty is concerned, it is supposed that—unless otherwise stated—people think whatever they think about the future. Whether this assumption is appropriate remains to be seen.

No attempt is made in this treatment of dividend policy to run the gamut from perfect foresight to generalized uncertainty. Papers by Miller and Modigliani [10] and Lintner [7]—among others—have already proceeded along these lines. Rather, the intention is to show where dividends fit into the underlying analytical scheme, to spotlight certain assumptions that underlie recent statements pertaining to the neutrality of dividend policy, and to propose extensions in the theory designed to recognize deficiencies in the perfectly competitive model.

I. ANALOGY TO COST OF CAPITAL

Before the thrust shifted to dividends, the basic issue in the cost of capital discussion was one of dividing the stream of operating cash flows (or some

---

[3] For justification, we have only to refer to the statistics on concentration of economic power.

reconcilable variant thereof) between debt and equity in such a manner as to maximize the market value of the enterprise. Modigliani and Miller [8], it may be remembered, dramaticized the stream-splitting aspect by drawing an analogy to the price effect of separating the whole milk into cream and skim milk. Their contention that, even in the face of institutional limitations, the farmer cannot gain by splitting the milk stream was subsequently subjected to empirical testing by Durand [3] and shown to be invalid.

When dividends enter the picture, the issue becomes one of dividing the stream of operating cash flows among debt, dividends, and reinvestment in such a way as to achieve the same result. The principal difference in the character of the analysis is that it may no longer be feasible to assume that the size and shape of the stream of operating cash flows is independent of the manner in which it is subdivided.[4]

Much the same as contractual interest payments and other financial outlays, the continuation of cash dividends at their prevailing (or regular) rate can be—and commonly is—assigned a priority by management.[5] In such instances, the burden of oscillations in operating cash flows is placed upon lower-priority outlays, namely, capital and related expenditures, unless management is both willing and able to compensate by adjusting the level of external financing.[6] Even if management is willing to seek funds outside the firm, moreover, the uncertainties inherent in the terms under which external financing can be obtained in the future reduce the likelihood of such action in the event of operating cash deficiencies in any period. The upshot is that current cash dividends may well be capitalized somewhat differently from anticipated future cash flows (net of current dividends, to avoid double-counting).

It may be observed that the relative instability of expenditures designed to augment future cash flows shows up even in the aggregate. The change from year to year for new plant and equipment averaged 19 percent for all manufacturing corporations in the postwar period (to 1961), as compared with 9 percent for cash dividends. The maximum declines from one year to the next were 40 percent for new plant and equipment and but 2 percent for dividends.

---

[4] Although the milk-separating analogy implies that the dimensions of the stream are unaffected by its division between debt and equity, even this need not be a fundamental difference in character. As evidenced by Donaldson [2], decisions by management to borrow or not to borrow sometimes affect growth, that is, the level of future cash flows.

[5] Cf., for example, Lintner [6], in which observed corporate behavior involves gradual adjustments of dividends to earnings and "greater reluctance to reduce than to raise dividends...."

[6] The term "capital and related expenditures" refers to all outlays that affect operating cash flows over several periods. Either by reason of previous commitments or because of their importance to the continued operation of the business, certain elements of these expenditures may have priorities that equal or exceed those connected with the payment of cash dividends.

Again, as in the case of debt versus equity, investor reactions to dividend policy changes can nullify in whole or in part their price effect. Whenever the stockholder is dissatisfied with the dividend payout, the balance between present and future income can be redressed by buying or selling shares of stock and perhaps by other means as well (for instance, by "lending" or "borrowing" on the same *risk* terms that cash dividends are paid). If dividends are deemed insufficient, the desired proportion of current income can be obtained by periodically selling part of the shares owned. If current income is too high, cash dividends can be used to acquire additional shares of stock.

The one thing that shareholders cannot do through their purchase and sale transactions is to negate the consequences of investment decisions by management. If—as may well be the case—investment decisions tend to be linked with dividend policy, their neglect in the analysis of dividend effect seems inappropriate.

II. CONDITIONS FOR NO DIVIDEND EFFECT

The conditions under which changes in dividend payout have minimal influence upon stock values can now be stated. For the most part, they follow from the logics of stream-splitting.

1. *Condition No. 1: The level of future cash flows from operations (that is, the growth rate) is independent of the dividend-payout policy.*—In essence, this condition implies that the impact of a change in dividend payout upon operating cash flows will be *exactly* offset (or negated) by a corresponding and opposite change in supplemental (or external) financing.

For those who believe that the cost of capital is unaffected by the capital structure, either debt or equity financing is a legitimate means of neutralizing dividend policy changes. For those who believe otherwise, an increase in dividends can be offset only by the sale of equity shares. In the latter instance, then, the capital structure must also be taken as independent of the dividend-payout policy.

If attention is confined to offsetting transactions in equity shares for the sake of simplicity and generality, the following result obtains: An increase in dividend payout will leave operating cash flows unchanged in the aggregate, but the share of future cash flows accruing to existing stockholders will decline, since additional stock has to be sold to finance the planned capital outlays. The existing shareholder can, of course, reconstitute his former pro rata position by purchasing shares in the market with his incremental dividends.

Implicit in these remarks is the presumption that the market completely capitalizes anticipated growth in operating cash flows. New shares are thus acquired at a price that returns new investors *only* the going market rate for the relevant class of risks. The present value of extraordinary returns from investment by the corporation goes to existing stockholders (or whoever was around at the time when the prospect of these returns was first recognized by the market), rather than to new shareholders.

To the degree that the anticipated level of operating cash flows, that is, the growth rate, is connected with the dividend payout for one reason or another, the market value of the firm may be conditioned by variations in dividend payout. The policy changes must, of course, be unexpected, and their price effect hinges at least partly upon the relation between the *internal* and *market* rates of return. If the former exceeds the latter, the present value of a dollar employed by the firm (other things being equal) will be greater than a dollar of dividends distributed and invested elsewhere. This issue was considered in my 1956 paper [11].

Condition No. 1 can readily be extended to take account of tax differentials. The amended version is that operating cash flows *net* of taxes paid thereon by shareholders are unaffected by the dividend payout. As things stand, this criterion simply does not hold; neither—it might be added—does the corresponding condition hold in the case of debt versus equity.[7]

2. *Condition No. 2: The weights employed are independent of the dividend-payout policy.*—In other words, the discount factors or weights, that is, the ratios of indifference values between one period and the next, are invariant with respect to changes in dividend payout.

Gordon [4] argues that the weights employed must also be constant between periods and that such is unlikely to be the case under uncertainty. That is to say, looking forward from period zero, the ratios of the indifference values between periods 0 and 1, 1 and 2, and so on have to be all the same.

In order to evaluate this possible addition to Condition No. 2, it is pertinent to recall Condition No. 1. If the level of total operating cash flows is unaffected by the policy revision, a change in current cash dividends will alter the stockholder's stake in future cash flows. The gain or loss in current dividends will just equal the gain or loss in the present value of future cash flows (or dividends, if you wish), provided that the system of weights remains unchanged. Gordon's point is thus unacceptable because the firm has to go into the market for funds to replace those paid out in dividends and, in so doing, has to pay the market rate.

Returning to the question of the independence of the weights used from the dividend-payout policy, a change in dividend payout undoubtedly disturbs the investors in that stock to some extent unless the modification

---

[7] The price effect of tax differentials may well be less than might be supposed. For example, the marginal tax rates implied in a comparison of recent yields on tax-exempts of high quality with those on U.S. government securities are on the order of 15–25 percent.

was anticipated previously. Insofar as costs of one kind or another, indivisibilities, and other factors prevent the shareholders thus activated from completely reconstituting their *old* position and thereby give rise to a new and different equilibrium point, the weights employed will adjust in some measure. The role played by friction in the system is, however, well known, and there is little need to dwell upon this aspect.

More significant, perhaps, is the fact that the substitution of future cash flows for present dividends superimposes an element of market risk upon the basic uncertainty of the operating cash-flow stream. As contrasted with cash dividends in which the stockholder receives a dollar for each dollar declared, there is no telling what price the shareholder will realize in the market at any given time for his stake in future cash flows.

It is, of course, true that the corporation would confront the same market risk if it—rather than the shareholder—were forced to enter the capital market. It is also true that realized prices may average out over a period of time. The fact remains that the firm may well be better able to adjust for—as well as to assume—this class of risk.

Whether further conditions ought to be introduced is a moot point. A recent article by John Lintner [7], for example, concludes that "generalized uncertainty" is itself sufficient to insure that shareholders "will *not* be indifferent to whether cash dividends are increased (or reduced) by substituting new equity issues for retained earnings to finance given capital budgets."

As a generalization, this conclusion is suspect, for it appears to be inconsistent with a logical extension of Lintner's earlier analysis under idealized uncertainty. It is difficult to see why two or two million investors cannot be indifferent at a given price for a variety of reasons. If so, generalized uncertainty can—but perhaps need not—produce the same *surface* result as idealized uncertainty.[8]

In any event, Condition No. 2 is sufficiently broad to embrace the foregoing aspect of the uncertainty issue. To the degree that Lintner's proposition is valid, generalized uncertainty produces an effect that resembles that associated with the presence of costs and frictions in the system.

III. IMPERFECT COMPETITION, REGULATED ENTERPRISE AND NONECONOMIC CONSIDERATIONS

That the conditions for no dividend effect fail to hold in certain important respects has already been established here and elsewhere. At this stage, there is little point in discussing further the consequences of differences in tax treatment, new-issue and other costs associated with external financ-

---

[8] To add to the confusion, moreover, see n. 35 in Lintner [7].

ing, and uncertainty itself (although the *on balance* effect will be considered toward the end of the paper). It is nonetheless relevant—in view of their neglect in the literature—to extend the examination of dividend effects beyond the oft-used competitive model that presupposes rational behavior in the traditional economic sense and to consider the influence of such things as management leeway, economic slack, and intramarginal pricing policies. The following remarks represent a preliminary effort in this direction.

In the bulk of corporations with which it is possible to deal statistically, management has considerable leeway in decision making. Their histories of earnings and dividends—not to mention their economic power— are such that their survival in the foreseeable future seemingly does not hinge upon single modes of behavior. The presence of generalized uncertainty implies, moreover, that there is often no best *visible* course of action.

The frequently observed association between dividend-payout policy, capital structure, and rate of growth is a useful case in point; the survival of the corporation ordinarily does not depend, in the short run at least, upon any specific rate of growth. The prime considerations affecting growth, apart from profit opportunities, are (1) the willingness of corporations to go into the public market place for additional funds and (2) their attitude toward dividends (including their willingness to return unneeded funds to the investors).

For firms that are reluctant to get involved in external financing (and there appear to be many), then, the burden of expansion rests upon residual internal sources, that is, operating cash flows *less* cash dividends and debt servicing *net* of additions to debt. Decisions to increase or decrease dividends thus condition the value of the enterprise as long as the returns on new investments differ from the market rate.

The sword cuts both ways. Wherever the available investment opportunities are unable to earn their keep, the specter of liquidating dividends or repurchase of shares or debt retirement arises. If there is no debt outstanding and if the repurchase of shares is not contemplated, the burden of liquidation falls upon dividend payout.

The fact that many of the corporations that normally constitute the statistical samples used in testing dividend hypotheses are characterized by negatively sloping demand curves is also worth noting. Suppose, for instance, that such firms do not charge what the traffic will bear in the sense of equating discounted marginal revenues with discounted marginal costs. Instead, let us assume that they employ some sort of a full-cost pricing policy.

Insofar as these companies assign priorities to the payment of dividends and regard them as a cost (that is, as an obligation of the firm that should be met if possible), the dividend-payout policy will affect stock prices. Decisions to alter the dividend payout under the full-costing approach will, sooner or later, be reflected in product prices (although the impact may be barely visible to the naked eye). If the new prices more nearly approach optimum prices from a profit-maximization standpoint, the effect is to increase stock values. If the reverse obtains, values diminish.

The foregoing consideration may be especially significant in the case of regulated companies whose prices are set by edict rather than by competitive forces. The dividends that regulatory bodies explicitly or implicitly permit to be incorporated in the elements that determine product or service prices will be reflected in stock values.

Closely connected with, but extending beyond, the matter of product or service pricing is the question of operating slack. Our experience has been that most profitable firms are able in some measure to curtail their nonoperating and operating outlays without interfering with future cash flows. To the extent that a change in dividend-payout policy conditions the amount of slack in the system, the value of the firm is modified by such changes.

The impact of a revision in dividend policy need not show up immediately; it may await a softness in operating cash flows. As mentioned previously, Lintner [6] and others cite evidence that some fraction of cash dividends is commonly placed well up on the priority scale. The upshot is that managements' reactions to unanticipated reductions in operating cash flows may lead not only to the adjustment of lower-priority outlays but also to the elimination of slack from the system before dividend-payout policies (once established) are altered.

In summary, it is not our purpose to overemphasize the importance of the foregoing extension of the competitive model. The point is simply that hypothesis building in this area has barely begun to scratch the surface. With this in mind, let us turn to the important matter of statistical testing.

IV. STATISTICAL TESTING

The woods are currently replete with statistical analyses designed to demonstrate the significance (or nonsignificance) of the diverse factors that may influence stock prices. While it is not our aim to add further to the mounting pile, it is meaningful to mention certain problems of a statistical nature, referred to in the recent literature, that have a bearing on the testing of most hypotheses and, in particular, on the testing of an imperfectly competitive model. Specifically, the comments that follow focus upon the notion of a random variable and collinearity.

In their 1958 article, Modigliani and Miller [8] alluded to the peril of relying upon "a single year's profits as a measure of expected profits." Later [9], they argued—as have others—that investors may accept current dividends as an indirect measure of profit expectations.

The difficulties inherent in the use of a random variable to reveal expectations are well known. The realized value of a random variable in any period is ordinarily but one of several values that might have obtained; it may bear little relation—in any visible sense of the word—to the underlying expectation. With this in mind, recent studies have tended to employ averages of one kind or another for the earnings variable. Kolin [5], using an exponential weighting system, has found earnings thus measured to be superior to current dividends in explaining the relative valuation of stocks.

Notwithstanding the fact that current dividends test out more significantly than current earnings, it is important to remember that they, too, are random variables. There is on the surface (apart from their relative stability) little more to recommend current dividends as a measure of expected dividends than there is to presuppose that current earnings adequately reflect anticipated earnings.

Looking to Lintner's earlier work [6], in which dividends were said to adjust gradually to a target payout ratio, an interesting and relevant reversal of the information-content proposition comes to mind. It is entirely possible (as well as quite reasonable) for some weighted average of earnings to be a good surrogate for dividend expectations. In other words, the improved results obtained by Kolin [5] may well be entirely consistent with the *dividend* hypothesis.

In a subsequent piece [10], Miller and Modigliani remarked upon the omission of relevant variables. Pointing a critical finger at certain studies (one of mine and two of Durand were cited!), they stipulated that "no general prediction is made (or can be made) by the theory [i.e., theirs] about what will happen to the dividend coefficient if the crucial growth term is omitted."[9] Except by oblique footnote reference to Gordon's work, however, they neglected to add that specification of the dividend coefficient may be difficult even if a growth term is included.

The issue in question is *collinearity*. In his analysis of a linear function that includes both dividends and earnings, Gordon [4] pointed to the instability present in the coefficients whenever a strong correlation existed between two explanatory variables. His finding was: "They [i.e., the coefficients] vary over a very wide range and they cannot be used to make reliable estimates on the variation in share price with each variable." Kolin [5], in turn, referred to the danger of a "severe loss of accuracy due to near singularity of the correlation matrix of independent

[9] Actually, my study should not be castigated on this score, for it incorporated variables that measure both growth and internal rate of return.

variables that would occur if the two highly collinear variables were present in the same regression." His concern was with the stochastic properties that might be introduced by computer programs that treat "all digits of the words that are input to the inversion program as error free digits."

It follows that the correlation between dividend payout and growth (that is, the level of future cash flows), which seems likely to exist in many instances, contributes to the difficulty of interpreting results obtained from regression analyses. At the extreme, as Miller and Modigliani [10] affirmed, there may be "no way to distinguish between the effects of dividend policy and investment policy."

Other pitfalls to statistical testing readily come to mind. Perhaps the most significant (in the context of this paper) is the character of the sample used in relation to the hypothesis being tested. More specifically, it seems incongruous to utilize samples drawn from the universe of either regulated monopolies or very large corporations to test competitive behavior.

V. CONCLUSIONS

The implication of the foregoing treatment is that the choice of dividend policies almost always affects the value of the enterprise. The general conditions for neutrality are simply not satisfied in the world as we know it. The dimensions of the cash-flow stream (both before and after account is taken of taxes imposed on recipients of dividends and capital gains) are conditioned by dividend-payout policy; efforts by investors to negate the effects of policy changes are frequently of limited avail; and so on.

In the real world (again, as we know it), it is insufficient to contemplate the effects of dividends under perfectly (or even purely) competitive circumstances. The fact that a great many firms exercise some control over their own destinies deserves to be recognized. Once the possibility of imperfections is admitted, the potential association between dividends and the level of future cash flows, among other things, becomes clear.

Standard objections to dividend neutrality, that is, differences in tax treatment and costs of external financing, ordinarily favor the retention of earnings. Interdependence between dividend-payout policy and capital outlays, on the other hand, can work either way; it all depends on the profitability of the enterprise.

Statistical analyses designed to support the "pure earnings" hypothesis—or any other hypothesis, for that matter—remain ambiguous. For one thing, uncertainties exist as to precisely what is being measured. For another, the closer the linkage between dividend policy and dimensions of the total stream, the less meaningful are the coefficients attached to each independent variable.

Be that as it may, we are not opposed to statistical analyses. What we do say, however, is that judgment must ultimately rest on the power of the theory generated.

REFERENCES

[1] Bodenhorn, D. "On the Problem of Capital Budgeting," *Journal of Finance*, Vol. XIV (December, 1959), pp. 473–92.

[2] Donaldson, G. *Corporate Debt Capacity* (Boston, Mass.: Harvard Business School, 1961).

[3] Durand, D. "The Cost of Capital in an Imperfect Market: A Reply to Modigliani and Miller," *American Economic Review*, Vol. XLIX (June, 1959).

[4] Gordon, M. *The Investment, Financing and Valuation of the Corporation* (Homewood, Ill.: R. D. Irwin, 1962).

[5] Kolin, M. "The Relative Price of Corporate Equity with Particular Reference to Investor Valuation of Retained Earnings and Dividends." Unpublished manuscript.

[6] Lintner, J. "Distribution of Incomes of Corporations among Dividends, Retained Earnings and Taxes," *American Economic Review*, Vol. XLVI (May, 1956), pp. 97–113.

[7] ———. "Dividends, Earnings, Leverage, Stock Prices and the Supply of Capital to Corporations," *Review of Economics and Statistics*, Vol. XLIV (August, 1962), pp. 243–70.

[8] Modigliani, F., and M. Miller. "The Cost of Capital, Corporation Finance and the Theory of Investment," *American Economic Review*, Vol. XLVIII (June, 1958), pp. 261–97.

[9] ———. "The Cost of Capital, Corporation Finance and the Theory of Investment: Reply," *ibid.*, Vol. XLIV (September, 1959), pp. 655–69.

[10] ———. "Dividend Policy, Growth and the Valuation of Shares," *Journal of Business*, Vol. XXXIV (October, 1961), pp. 411–33.

[11] Walter, J. "Dividend Policies and Common Stock Prices," *Journal of Finance*, Vol. XI (March, 1956), pp. 29–41.

[12] ———. *The Investment Process* (Boston, Mass.: Harvard Business School, 1962), Ch. xi.

Volkert S. Whitbeck[*]
Manown Kisor, Jr.[†]

32. A New Tool in Investment Decision Making

Reprinted from the **Financial Analysts Journal**, Vol. 19, No. 3
(May-June, 1963), pp. 55–62, by permission of the authors and the
publisher.

What makes stock prices? Why should the common shares of International Business Machines sell at more than 35 multiples while those of General Motors are priced at less than 18 times earnings?

If we look at Chart 1, which depicts the historical earnings records of both, we shall find two clues to the reasons why.

Let us note first that IBM's rate of growth in net income per share, as indicated by the slope of its historical earnings path, has been considerably more rapid than that of GM. We note also that IBM's growth has been more stable, in the sense that the deviations from its trend in earnings have been much less marked than those of GM.

This double fact that IBM's growth has been both more rapid and more stable than GM's progress is readily apparent from informal, visual inspection. We may wish, however, to have more formal, statistical expressions of the past growth and stability of the two companies. Measures of this sort are easily constructed by the method of "least-squares" regression. Without attempting to conduct a course in statistics, we may describe this procedure as a method by which the trend line of "best-fit" is drawn through the historical earnings path. More specifically, the trend line is constructed so that the sums of the *squares* of the deviations of the actual earnings from the trend line are a *minimum*—hence the term "least-squares."

Actually, if we were to take a rubber band and stretch it across the plotted data for each stock on Chart 1, trying to get the trend line of best visual "fit," we probably would locate lines approximating the "least-squares" trends. Any two of us, however, would find slightly different

[*] The Bank of New York.
[†] Paine, Webber, Jackson & Curtis.

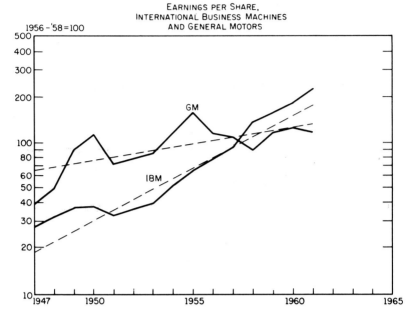

lines, while the "least-squares" procedure yields one and only one path through the data. Using the logarithmic value of the actual earnings per share, as we did for the historical earnings chart, we are able to express the trend line in terms of a constant percentage rate of growth, a rate of growth which is a true "annual average" in that it does not depend directly on the selection of any two particular terminal years.

The trend lines on the historical earnings chart for IBM and GM were constructed in just such a fashion, the trend line for IBM showing an annual average rate of growth of 16.1 percent while that of GM indicates an average rate of only 5.3 percent per annum over the 15-year period.

The same least-squares procedure we attempted to describe above also provides us with a measure of the stability of the historical earnings record. Called the *standard deviation*, this measure reports the range about the trend line within which the actual earnings tended to fluctuate during the historical period. In order to provide ourselves with a measure which permits direct comparison of the stability records of different companies, we may express the standard deviation in terms of a percentage fluctuation from the trend line.

In general, this percentage figure denotes the range, on either side of the trend line, within which, in two years out of three, actual earnings were reported. In other words, if the standard deviation over the historical period were 15.0 percent, we might expect to find that two out of three years' actual earnings fell within 15.0 percent on either side of the trend line. Another way of expressing this relation is to say that the "chances" are two out of three that actual earnings in any given year were within 15.0 percent of the trend-line value of earnings for that year.

The lower the standard deviation in percentage terms, then, the more stable the historical record. For IBM over our 15-year period, the standard deviation of earnings about trend was 22.1 percent; for less stable GM, 29.9 percent.

It was suggested earlier that we would find, in the historical record, two clues to the reasons why IBM currently commands a price/earnings multiple more than twice that of GM. We have seen that IBM's expansion has been more stable, as well as more rapid, than GM's growth in earnings per share, and this combination of historical occurrence might itself be utilized in an attempt to explain the more generous current pricing of IBM.

The real rationale for the price differential is, however, more subtle. IBM commands a higher price/earnings (P/E) ratio not because of its past performance, but, rather, because the market, on balance, expects more *in the future* from IBM than it does from GM. As investors, we buy common stocks not simply for their records prior to our purchase, but, more fundamentally, for what we anticipate from them after our commitment.

The historical record is relevant only to the extent that past performance can provide an insight into prospective growth. To the extent that we can form an expectation (whether based on the relative growth and stability of earnings exhibited by the two companies over the past 15 years or on some other, supplemental information) that IBM will continue to outgrow GM, we are justified in paying more for a share of IBM, in terms of price/earnings multiples, than for one of GM.

The question becomes: "How much more?" This is what the valuation study attempts to answer.

I. THE VALUATION STUDY

Assuming that we are in agreement in our anticipations of the future relative earnings progress of IBM and GM—that IBM's per-share earnings growth will be both more rapid and more stable than GM's—we should be willing to pay more, in terms of price/earnings multiples, for a share of IBM than for one of GM. The critical question of "How much more?" is the one to which we now direct ourselves.

In attempting to provide an answer to this vital query, we must introduce several special concepts, the most fundamental of which is that

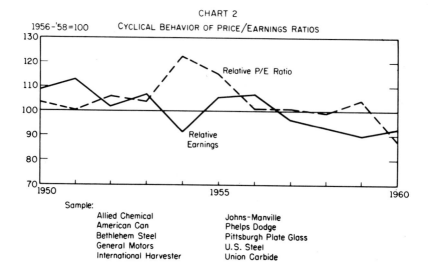

CHART 2

1956-'58=100   CYCLICAL BEHAVIOR OF PRICE/EARNINGS RATIOS

Relative P/E Ratio

Relative Earnings

Sample:

Allied Chemical	Johns-Manville
American Can	Phelps Dodge
Bethlehem Steel	Pittsburgh Plate Glass
General Motors	U.S. Steel
International Harvester	Union Carbide

of "normalized" earnings. Most of us are well aware of the fact that, over the course of a cycle in general business, the price multiples attached to the earnings of many firms tend to behave in a contracyclical fashion, falling as earnings rise and rising as earnings fall. Chart 2 provides an illustration of this phenomenon.

Constructed by plotting the ratio of the sample's mean earnings and earnings multiples to those of Standard and Poor's Industrials, the chart abstracts from trends in the general market, portraying the movement of the variables *relative* to their counterparts in the market as a whole. The tendency of price/earnings ratios to move contracyclically with earnings is readily apparent, especially in the earlier years.

Revelation of this aspect of the market for shares carries with it an important implication for our analysis. The fact that earnings multiples tend to fall as earnings rise and rise as earnings fall suggests that the market possesses an awareness of the inherent periodicity in the earnings of many companies.

To be emphasized is the point that the market differentiates between the absolute cyclicality of corporate earnings as a whole and the *relative* cyclicality of the net income of individual firms. This is demonstrated in the chart, which portrays the path of the sample's earnings and price/earnings ratios relative to those of the market as a whole. And if the market recognizes the relative cyclicality of earnings of different companies, it follows that the market also has some concept of earnings normality for each firm. Reasoning from the fact that the market does not apply a constant multiplier to cyclically varying earnings, we infer that investors on balance conceive of some mid-cyclical or average level of earnings for each company.

This notion of normalized or mid-cyclical earnings is not as nebulous as it may seem at first. For purposes of our analysis, we may conceive of the normalized earnings of a given firm as that level of net income which would prevail currently if the economy as a whole were experiencing mid-cyclical business conditions. In terms of widely-used, general measures, we might denote the current mid-cyclical or "normal" level of the economy by a Gross National Product of $550 billion and an F.R.B. Index of Industrial Production of 117. The normalized earnings of a given company, then, would be those which would result from these general economic conditions if the company itself were experiencing "normal" operations; that is, operations not affected by such nonrecurring items as strikes, natural disasters, and the like.

Since another part of this discussion is devoted entirely to the estimation of normalized earnings (and other variables which we will find fundamental to our analysis), let us, for now, simply assume that we have predetermined IBM's current normalized earning power at $10.50 per share and GM's at $3.30 per share. We will assume also that we have projected growth in earning power from these levels at 17.0 percent per annum for IBM and 3.0 percent for GM.

The very fact that we expect IBM to grow more rapidly than GM might engender a willingness on our part to pay a higher P/E ratio for the shares of the former. Ignoring for the moment additional aspects of valuation—important considerations such as the prospective standard deviation of earnings discussed earlier—let us attempt to quantify this P/E ratio differential. Chart 3 contains the key to our analysis. This "scatter diagram" demonstrates the relationship between the earnings multiple and the projected rate of growth, and is constructed as follows:

> Utilizing prices for all issues in the sample as of the close of business on a given date, in this case June 8, 1962, we determine the "normalized P/E ratio" for each stock by dividing price by current normalized earnings. This normalized earnings multiple is then plotted against the projected rate of growth in earnings per share; e.g. 15.4 vs. 3.0 for GM and 35.3 vs. 17.0 for IBM.

With the entire 135 stocks in the sample so plotted, we have a visual record of the relation prevailing in the market, on June 8, between price/earnings ratios and prospective rates of growth. This visual record is readily translated into formal statistical terms by means of the least-squares procedure discussed earlier. The dashed line on the chart was computed in just such a fashion.

In the terminology of simple high school algebra, the relevant char-

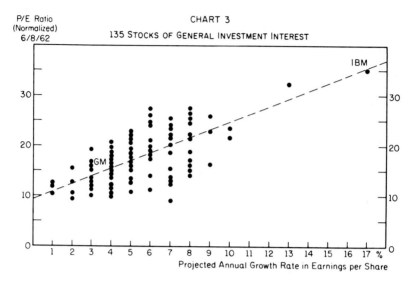

P/E Ratio
(Normalized)
6/8/62

CHART 3

135 STOCKS OF GENERAL INVESTMENT INTEREST

Projected Annual Growth Rate in Earnings per Share

acteristics of this line of average relationship are a slope of approximately 1.5, and a Y-intercept of 9.3, as indicated by the point where the line crosses the P/E ratio axis. Translated into terms more germane to the analysis of common stock values, a Y-intercept of 9.3 tells us that, on June 8, 1962, the market relationship was such that a stock with a zero rate of growth in earnings per share commanded, on the average, a price of slightly more than 9 times earnings.

A slope of 1.5 denoted that, on our pricing date, each percentage point of positive growth added 1.5 P/E ratios to the 9.3 base multiple. In the case of GM, for example, our projected rate of growth of 3.0 percent indicated that we add 1.5 $\times$ 3.0, or 4.5, to the base multiple of 9.3, giving us a "theoretical" multiple for GM of 13.8 times earnings. For IBM, our growth projection of 17.0 percent combined with the base multiple to yield a theoretical P/E ratio of 9.3 plus 1.5 $\times$ 17.0, or 34.8 times earnings.

How much more should we pay for IBM than for GM? Valuing stocks solely on the basis of our expectations of their future growth, the market, on June 8, told us that IBM should sell at 34.8 times earnings and GM, at 13.8 times earnings. The differential, with the issues valued on the basis of growth alone, was, then, 21.0 multiples.

Obviously, prospective growth rates are not the only constituent in common stock valuation. We have already mentioned that the relative stability of growth is a significant factor, and it goes without saying that consideration of dividend payout is of fundamental importance in determining common stock values. Before we introduce these factors into our analysis, however, let us retrace our steps and emphasize the high points of our progress thus far.

Having assumed IBM's current level of normal earning power to be $10.50 and GM's to be $3.30 per share, we agreed that, if IBM were to grow at 17.0 percent per annum from this level while GM grew at only 3.0 percent, we would be willing to pay more, in terms of price/earnings ratios, for a share of IBM than for one of GM.

The vital question of "How much more?" was the one to which we directed ourselves. To answer it, we addressed *the market as a whole*, as represented by a sample of 135 stocks of general investment interest. In order to determine how much we should pay for IBM and GM, we sought the relationship between price/earnings ratios and growth rates in the general market. Through the method of least-squares, we found the *average* price-earnings ratio attached to each level of projected growth. For IBM's 17.0 percent rate of growth, this market-average or theoretical multiple was 34.8; for GM's 3.0 percent rate of growth, 13.8 times earnings. The market, in other words, told us, through our simple regression analysis, that, if both issues were selling at their June 8 theoretical price/earnings ratios, we would be justified in paying, on the basis of prospective growth alone, 21.0 multiples more for IBM than for GM.

What, now, about the other factors in common stock valuation? Earlier, we discussed in detail the concept of the standard deviation of earnings about trend, agreeing that, in general, a relatively low anticipated standard deviation was a desirable investment characteristic. In our discussion of the cyclical behavior of price/earnings ratios, we emphasized the tendency of multiples to rise as earnings fall, and fall as earnings rise. Important to note now is that fact that, although price/earnings ratios tend to move contracyclically with earnings, in general their progress is not in direct proportion to the movement of earnings.

Multiples rise as earnings fall, but not as rapidly. The prices of stocks with high standard deviations of earnings do fall relative to the market as a whole as their earnings decline. And, conversely, as earnings of these issues increase again, their prices rise relative to the general market. On the other hand, stocks with more stable earnings, those with low standard deviations, tend to fluctuate in price less widely than the market as a whole. For investors desiring price stability, then, a relatively low prospective standard deviation of earnings becomes a distinctly desirable investment characteristic.

For these investors, an anticipated standard deviation of zero—in other words, an absolutely straight earnings path—would be an optimum trait, and anything less than this optimum would be a detractor from investment value. And if it is this category of investor which dominates the market as a whole, we would expect that, of two stocks with identical growth prospects, the one with the lower anticipated standard deviation would command the higher price/earnings ratio.

Having concluded that high prospective rates of growth and low expected standard deviations of earnings per share are, in general, characteristics which enhance investment value, let us turn now to the consideration of a third factor in common stock valuation, *dividend payout*.

To the extent that investors as a whole consider current dividends a desirable investment characteristic, we would expect high dividend payout ratios to contribute positively to the prices of common stocks. That is to say, if we had two issues identical with respect to anticipated growth and stability, we might expect to find the one with the greater prospective payout selling at a higher P/E ratio than the one with the smaller dividend/earnings ratio.

On the other hand, if investors on balance did *not* desire current income, the opposite relation could be anticipated. In this case, of our two otherwise identical stocks, the one with the *lower* payout policy would command the higher price/earnings ratio. The effect on price of the dividend-payout ratio is, then, determined by the balance of market sentiment.

A study 'in combination'

We have examined individually the three principal constituents of common stock valuation—growth, stability, and payout of earnings. Our task now is to consider them in combination, to analyze their joint effect on common stock prices. To do so, we must expand the concepts introduced in our discussion of growth alone. There, we saw the nature of a two-dimensional scatter diagram and the use of a simple least-squares analysis.

The problem there was to determine the statistical relation between two variables—the normalized price/earnings ratio and the expected rate of growth in earnings per share. Here, we must examine the multiple relationship among four variables—the normalized price/earnings ratio, the projected growth rate, and anticipated standard deviation, and the prospective ratio of dividends to earnings. The tool we can utilize is directly akin to the two-dimensional least-squares analysis employed before. In the terminology of statistics, our tool before was "simple regression"; now it will be *"multiple* regression," a least-squares analysis in four dimensions.

The simple regression of earnings multiples and growth rates gave us the average price/earnings ratio prevailing in the market for each rate of growth. The multiple regression analysis to which we now turn will give us the average price/earnings ratio for each *combination* of prospective growth, stability, and payout of earnings.

Utilizing the same sample of 135 stocks of general investment interest, all priced as of June 8's closing, as before, and applying our multiple regression procedure, we are able to express the then prevailing market relationships in terms of a simple equation:

Theoretical P/E ratio $= 8.2 + 1.5$ (growth rate) $+ 6.7$ (payout)

$$- 0.2 \text{ (standard deviation)}$$

Remembering that this equation describes the relationships existing in the market as of a given date, let us analyze its composition in some detail, utilizing our old friends for examples.

The first component of the equation, the constant term, gives us our base multiple. It is to this base multiple that we add to (or subtract from) the effects of the valuation factors—the prospective growth, stability, and payout of earnings. The second component of the equation describes the contribution made by each percent of projected growth. The effect of dividend payout is denoted by the third segment of the equation.

As we can see from the positive sign attached to the factor by which we multiply the prospective payout ratio, the market on June 8 considered current dividends a desirable investment characteristic. The equation's fourth segment describes the effect on valuation of the anticipated stability of earnings. Anything less than perfect stability, as denoted by a zero standard deviation, is a detractor from investment value.

Utilizing our 17.0 percent projected growth rate for IBM, and assuming that its dividend payout will be .25 and its standard deviation, 5.0 percent, we compute the company's theoretical price/earnings ratio as follows:

Theoretical P/E ratio $= 8.2 + 1.5(17.0) + 6.7(.25) - 0.2(5.0)$

$$= 8.2 + 25.5 + 1.7 - 1.0$$

$$= 34.4$$

For GM, given a growth rate of 3.0 percent, a prospective payout of .75, and an expected standard deviation of 20.0 percent, we have:

Theoretical P/E ratio $= 8.2 + 1.5(3.0) + 6.7(.75) - 0.2(20.0)$

$$= 8.2 + 4.5 + 5.0 - 4.0$$

$$= 13.7$$

With these two theoretical price/earnings ratios so computed, we are in a position now to introduce the vital concept of the *price ratio*— the ratio of market price to theoretical price. On June 8, IBM was selling at 371, 35.3 times normalized earnings of $10.50 per share. Priced at 15.4

times normalized earnings, GM was selling at 51 on that date. Dividing market price by theoretical price (market P/E ratio by theoretical P/E ratio) for each stock, we arrive at a price ratio of 1.02 for IBM and one of 1.13 for GM. On June 8, then, IBM's market price was almost identical with its theoretical price, while GM, on the other hand, was being marketed at a level 13.0 percent above its theoretical price.

In order to evaluate the above information, we must remind ourselves of the exact nature of the theoretical price/earnings ratio—it is that earnings multiple prevailing in the market, at a given moment of time, for a particular combination of prospective growth, stability, and payout of earnings per share. Remembering this, we shall say, for purposes of our analysis, that a stock is "undervalued" if it is selling for less than its theoretical P/E ratio and "overvalued" if it is priced in excess of its theoretical P/E ratio.

The shares of IBM, by this definition, were but 2.0 percent overvalued on June 8, while those of GM were overvalued by 13.0 percent, given our expectations of their prospective growth, stability, and payout. (To the extent that another investor's expectations for IBM were less favorable, and/or those for GM more favorable, he might reach an altered, even opposite, conclusion with regard to the proper pricing of the two issues—even if he were to utilize the same valuation procedure.)

On the face of our projections and analytical concepts, it would appear that, on June 8, IBM was more attractively priced than GM and that a commitment in the former would prove more successful than one in the latter. This, indeed, is the conclusion which we wish to manifest. We would draw it, however, not simply from the primarily theoretical analysis which we have undertaken so far, but from real-world results, results which are discussed here later in detail.

The point to make here concerns one more piece of pure theory—the keystone on which the entirety of our analysis rests.

Our efforts have been directed toward measuring the relative valuation of common stocks on a particular pricing date. We have answered the question "What makes stock prices?" from the standpoint of the market at a given moment in time, while the "market" itself is a succession of such moments. Because we have determined our theoretical price/earnings ratios on the basis of a single, static moment, we should expect these average relationships to change from day to day.

Underlying the average earnings multiple for each combination of prospective growth, stability, and payout is the aggregate of investor "feelings," concepts, beliefs, and we know that these forces are themselves transitory in nature. The fact remains, however, that changes in market psychology come, by and large, in a slow and orderly fashion, and it is the premise which underlies our principal hypothesis:

> Given the theoretical or normal price of any stock, we assume that the market price of the stock will seek this level faster than the theoretical price itself will change—this is the key to our analysis.

II. PRICE PERFORMANCE: PAST AND PROSPECTIVE

During the year which followed the pricing date of the original valuation study, September 23, 1960, we accumulated a wealth of data concerning the price movements of common stocks. The purpose of this part of our treatise is to examine that data and to consider future performance in the perspective of past results. In doing so, we will be dealing with what is formally termed *statistical* or *empirical* probability.

The nature of the forces inherent in stock price movements is such that we cannot calculate exactly the *mathematical probability* that a given stock will or will not increase in price. But if we cannot reduce our projections to pure mathematical form, we *can* base them upon knowledge of what has occurred on similar occasions in the past. By examining our data on past price movements, and by making the quite reasonable assumption that analogous movements will occur in the future, we are able to offer quantified projections of future performance.

Let us begin our discussion by considering the 12-month performance of the valuation study in the aggregate. In doing so, we will be examining the validity of our hypothesis that, given the theoretical or normal price for any given stock, the market price of the stock will seek its normal level more rapidly than the theoretical price itself will change.

The criterion of success we choose is quite simple. We say that the valuation study is successful whenever the group of stocks labeled "undervalued" in relation to the general market outperforms Standard and Poor's 500-Stock Index, at the same time that the "500" outperforms those issues denoted "overvalued" in relation to the market as a whole.

In the discussion which follows, we will be examining the performance of the valuation study groups over the three months following each of four pricing dates. The "undervalued" group consists of those stocks with price ratios—ratios of market price to theoretical price—of less than .85, while the "overvalued" group contains issues with price ratios of 1.15 or greater.

As can be seen in Table 1, our criterion of success was met in all four valuation studies. In each of the 3-month periods following the pricing dates, the undervalued group had a mean price performance superior to that of Standard and Poor's "500," and the "500," in turn, consistently outperformed those stocks labeled overvalued in relation to the market as a whole.

TABLE 1. VALUATION STUDY PERFORMANCE

	Undervalued Group		S & P's 500		Overvalued Group	
	3 Months' Change	Cumulative Change	3 Months' Change	Cumulative Change	3 Months' Change	Cumulative Change
9/23/60 Study..........	+11.9% (1.050)	+11.9% (1.050)	+6.6%	+6.6%	+5.7% (.992)	+5.7% (.992)
12/23/60 Study........	+16.8 (1.040)	+30.7 (1.092)	+12.3	+19.7	+8.3 (.964)	+14.5 (.956)
3/24/61 Study.........	+3.0 (1.020)	+34.6 (1.113)	+1.0	+20.9	−1.4 (.976)	+12.9 (.933)
6/23/61 Study.........	+3.2 (1.008)	+38.9 (1.122)	+2.4	+23.8	+2.1 (.997)	+15.3 (.931)

Note: Figures in parentheses represent performance of group relative to that of Standard and Poor's "500." E.g., for the 3/24/61 Study:

(a) Undervalued Group $\frac{1.03}{1.01} = 1.020$

(b) Overvalued Group $\frac{98.6}{1.01} = .976$

If we examine the relative-to-market action of the undervalued group, we note that the average percentage difference in 3-months performance was approximately 3.0 percent. Noting this fact from the past, we might be led directly to conclude that if Standard and Poor's "500" were to appreciate 10 percent over a 3-month period in the future, we could expect that the mean percentage price increase of the stocks in the undervalued group would be $1.03 \times 1.10 - 1.00$ or 13.3 percent.

How right would be in voicing this expectation? Isn't it possible that the seeming success of the valuation study in the past was due simply to the working of chance? Let us consider this possibility. We know that, for any given study, the price performance of the three groups could be ordered by chance in six different ways, so that the probability of success as defined is $\frac{1}{6}$. One of the rules of probability theory tells us that the probability of four consecutive chance successes, if the probability of one success is $\frac{1}{6}$, is given by $\frac{1}{6} \times \frac{1}{6} \times \frac{1}{6} \times \frac{1}{6}$ or $1/1296$.

The odds, then, are more than 1,000 to 1 against the random occurrence of four consecutive performance orderings of the sort experienced by the valuation study during the year after its inception. The performance of the valuation study was far too consistent to be attributable to the workings of chance. One must conclude, therefore, that this performance flowed directly from the study itself, that it was the logical concomitant of a tool which is both relevant and reliable, and that the relative-to-market appreciation of the undervalued group will continue to approximate 3.0 percent per quarter or 12.5 percent per annum.

III. ROLE OF THE FINANCIAL ANALYST

Throughout our discussion of the theoretical aspects of common stock valuation, we simply assumed that the various factors influencing share prices all were predetermined. The time has come now to part the veil of pure theory and examine the practical aspects of projecting future growth, stability, and payout of earnings. The task of projection falls to the financial analyst, for it is he who is best prepared to assay the future prospects of individual firms.

His task, however, is not an easy one, for it involves a unique combination of analytic talent, sustained effort, and, in some cases, intellectual wizardry. The starting point for his analysis is a graphic record of whatever historical information he considers relevant, a record similar to our Chart 1. In addition to portraying the past path of earnings per share, the "growth chart," as it is commonly called, contains the complementing record of per-share sales or revenues. Placing current results in a longer-term perspective, the chart permits easy examination of several fundamental relationships:

1. The current progress of earnings may be placed in the light of the long-term trend. Between 1958 and 1960, for example, GM's earnings expanded more rapidly than those of IBM. A quick glance at the chart, however, would dispel any notion that this relative progress would be likely to prevail in the future. IBM's 2-year movement was from a level above the 15-year trend; GM's expansion sprang from a cyclical low.

2. Casual comparison of the growth charts of several firms will reveal the relative stability of earnings over the longer-term. As we noted earlier, the fact that IBM's earnings progress has been more stable than GM's is readily apparent from the record portrayed in Chart 1.

3. With the path of sales per share to complement the earnings record, inspection will manifest trends in profit margins, as well as the relative stability of sales or revenue. An earnings line of greater slope than the path of sales would, of course, indicate rising margins; the opposite, declining margins. We must emphasize that a rising trend in profit margins seldom can be projected indefinitely into the future, and this lack of projectability is especially operative where the company's margins exceed those typical of the industry. With regard to the relative stability of sales per share, we may point out that a sales record substantially more stable than that of earnings would emphasize a high cyclicality of profit margins and engender detailed investigation of "leverage" relationships.

Other factors forming a basis for projection of future growth and stability may be revealed by inspection of growth charts, but these are the most important. They must, however, be subjected to further analysis. Merely extending a stable trend from the past is not enough. The historical paths of sales and earnings per share provide a starting point for the projection of growth—but only a starting point. If our projections are to be tenable, our analysis must be more thorough. One prerequisite of projection is an examination of the physical side of growth. We must have an awareness of potential product demand, and this awareness must encompass physical amounts as well as dollar volume. We need, in other words, an estimate of the prospective growth in product units, be they widgets, data processors, or tons of cold-rolled steel.

A second prerequisite of projection concerns the *financial* aspects of growth. One of the paramount problems facing the analyst concerned with the projection of per-share earnings is the question of the firm's ability to finance future growth. If our growth projections are to be realistic, they must be consistent with the present and potential capital structures of the firm. In other words, they must be consistent with the company's capital budgeting policy, as revealed in its financial structure and payout practice.

The projected rate of growth in per share earnings which enters our valuation study is that rate which is expected to prevail over a future of at least five years' duration. It is also that rate which could be considered "normal" for the 5-year period, in that it abstracts from cyclical elements indigenous to the firm itself or the economy as a whole.

If, for example, we had estimated the current normal or mid-cyclical earning power of a given firm at $2.00 per share, as contrasted with actual earnings of $2.50 per share, and if we projected its earnings five years into the future at a mid-cyclical level of $3.00 per share, the firm's normalized rate of growth would be in the order of 8.5 percent per annum, even though its actual rate of growth (from the current level of $2.50 per share to the $3.00 anticipated five years hence) would be less than 4.0 percent per year. Our choice of the first concept for our measure of "growth" is based, obviously, on one of the arguments presented previously, that investors on balance make allowance for cyclical phenomena.

The standard deviation

Our direct allowance for cyclical phenomena rests, of course, with the inclusion of the standard deviation as an independent valuation factor. Since we discussed this concept of earnings stability in considerable detail earlier, we need comment now only on the general procedure for its estimation. Because this variable is of a formal statistical nature, the analyst is given the computed measure for the historical period.

It then becomes his task to review the measure as calculated and to determine whether revision is required. Because the standard deviation used in the valuation study is the percentage range about trend within which earnings are *expected* to fluctuate over the next five years, the analyst is responsible for examining the factors influencing past stability to determine if they may be anticipated to prevail in the future. Maturity of growth in product demand, alteration in capital structure, and changes in proportion of revenues derived from leasing are the sort of modifications of past relationships which would engender a revision in the calculated standard deviation.

The third principal factor of valuation, the anticipated payout of earnings, is, perhaps, the factor most readily projected. The procedure generally followed is to divide the sum of the past 10 years' dividends by the sum of earnings over the same period. This measure of average or normal payout may then be compared with payout ratios in the individual years to determine if a trend is in evidence. Final adoption of a measure for valuation work requires examination of the consistency of anticipated payout with projected growth.

Having taken a brief look at the means of projecting valuation variables, let us stress again the vital role played by the analyst. It is his projections which enter the valuation procedure outlined here previously. No matter how correct in concept our method may be, the ultimate success of the valuation study rests with the analyst. Our procedure is to examine the market at a given moment in time and to determine the average price/earnings ratio for each combination of projected growth, stability, and payout of earnings.

Given this theoretical earnings multiple for each stock, we then compare it with the actual price/earnings ratio in order to measure the share's relative valuation. The ratio of market price to theoretical price, the *price ratio*, becomes the final product of our analysis. It is this variable upon which we base our projections of price performance. The past success of these price projections has been discussed. Suffice it to say here that this success has been both impressive and persistent. It has demonstrated that combination of valuation procedure and security analysis has provided a highly efficient tool for comparing the relative attractiveness of investment alternatives. This combination is inseparable, however. Regardless of the efficiency of the valuation element, the results of our studies—both past and prospective—are dependent on the accuracy of the inputs. If our staff of analysts were systematically to misconceive growth, stability, and income prospects, the outcome, of course, would be negative. The results of the past studies demonstrate that the *combination* of analysis and valuation has proved itself successful. And as individual analysts become even more adept in applying our valuation approach and at anticipating the prospective paths of earnings and dividends, the results of future studies should be even more rewarding.

Michael Keenan*

33. Models of Equity Valuation: The Great SERM Bubble

Reprinted from **The Journal of Finance,** Vol. XXV, No. 2 (May, 1970), pp. 243–273, by permission of the author and the publisher.

I. INTRODUCTION

1.1 The subject

There was a foolish hen that sat brooding upon a nest of snake eggs. A swallow, that observed it, went and told her the danger of it. Little do you think, says she, what you are at this instant doing, and that you are just now hatching your own destruction; for this good office will be your ruin.

MORAL: 'Tis the hard fortune of many a good natured man to breed up a bird to peck out his own eyes, despite all cautions to the contrary.[1]

It is the thesis of this paper that economic scientists doing empirical research on models of equity valuation have focused on a methodology that has brought this field to a state of crisis. In the past two decades there has been an explosive increase in research on share price models. Over one hundred doctoral dissertations have now been written in this area and probably an even greater number of master's theses. Researchers at dozens of academic institutions and a comparable number of private organizations have spent thousands of man-hours and millions of dollars in trying to find the determinants of equity value.[2]

What are the benefits of such a large expenditure of time and money? In terms of research findings, there seem to have been some advances in the theoretical structure of the models. But in terms of empirical results we know only this:

---

* Assistant Professor of Finance, Graduate School of Business Administration, New York University. Helpful comments on this paper were made by my colleagues Edwin Elton and Martin Gruber. Additional insights came from discussions on methodology with doctoral students in our advanced topics course and with some of our working masters students who are a part of this first computer generation of security analysts.

[1] The fable "A Hen and a Swallow" from *Fables of Aesop* according to Sir Roger L'Estrange [43], p. 80.

[2] Documentation for statements in this section can be found in Keenan [39], pp. 4–10. Parts of Sections 2, 3, and the appendix are also excerpted from the author's thesis [39] under Professor Kalmon J. Cohen at Carnegie Mellon University.

For empirically tested models of equity valuation extant results suggest that, in general, the greater majority of the estimated parameters for the variables of these models are neither statistically significant nor stable. About all one can conclude from existing evidence is that there is usually (for screened samples) a positive relationship of unspecified magnitude between equity share prices and dividends, earnings, and growth rates. The performance of other variables, especially risk-type variables (as measured by firm financial data), is poor as parameter signs are often indeterminant and magnitudes highly unstable.

These results on parameter estimates seem rather meager in view of the vast resources expended and in view of the fact that the indicated results are apparent to almost any amateur looking at the equity markets.

1.2 Structure of the paper

The remainder of this paper will develop the theme that routinized methodology—the availability of historical financial data, computers, and standardized regression procedures—has led to a significant distortion of the expectations propositions that are a part of the theory of financial instruments paradigm. We begin in Section 2 with a retrospective look at highlights in equity model development; Section 3 examines the question of parameter stability of existing empirical estimates. Section 4 discusses technique as a limiting force in this research area and Section 5 looks at prospective directions that might be taken once we are free of current methodological restrictions. We conclude in Section 6 with a note on the relevance of this discussion to the general question of methodology in the field of finance.

II. RETROSPECTIVE HIGHLIGHTS

In this section we take a retrospective look at selected highlights of work in the past two decades in the area of equity valuation. Our theme is a simple one. It is that the work that has evolved is mostly based on one paradigm and one test methodology. The paradigm suggests that security prices can be functionally related to expectations about firm financial variables. The test methodology suggests that these expectations are closely related to real financial variables and that the functional relationship can be specified in terms of relatively simple, constant parameter, equations.

2.1 The early models

2.1.1 There have probably been attempts to find explanatory predictors for equity share prices so long as equity securities have existed. Present day equities evolved from the financial instruments created in the Middle Ages to finance exploration and trade. The lack of knowledge and of even an implicit model to relate security value to underlying real values led to some spectacular excesses in market pricing in former times. The bubble created by public and private speculation in the shares of the Mississippi Company in the early part of the Eighteenth Century is but one of a series of instances where share prices took on disingenuous values relative to real underlying worth.[3] Gradually, however, a set of customary procedures evolved for professional evaluation of equity shares.

Formal attempts to develop models of equity valuation closely parallel the development of analytic economics. Such models seem to have evolved as applications of interest rate theory and relate to similar attempts to develop models for interest bearing instruments. Actually, there are few academic articles before 1945 in the area of equity valuation models.[4] Probably the three most often noted works are papers by Macaulay [48], Tinbergen [68], and Williams [74].

2.1.2   The paper by Tinbergen is one of the early attempts to develop an econometric model of share price formation. He begins with a discussion of what he calls the simple static law: "share prices vary proportionally with dividends and, inversely, proportionally with the rate of interest, for which the long term rate may be taken."[5] As Tinbergen suggests, this is a reasonable hypothesis only if (a) the market consists of investors and not speculators and (b) the dividend is expected to be constant through time. Since these conditions are seldom fulfilled the simple static law is elaborated into a "generalized static law." In this case expected dividends may differ from current constant dividends so price may vary less than proportionally with dividend changes. Finally, to adjust in a simple way for speculative mood the assumption is made that the attractiveness of a share will be greater, the greater has been the rise in prices some time before. Tinbergen's dynamic theory of share price formation can thus be summarized as[6]

$$P = f(X_1, X_2, X_3) \tag{1}$$

where X_1 = long-term interest rates;
  X_2 = dividend yields on nominal capital;
  X_3 = rate of change in share price (P).

The model was tested in a simple linear form on time series indexed data for different countries as a part of Tinbergen's larger study of business cycles. By today's standards the model is clearly deficient in the

---

[3] For a fascinating discussion of this and other financial madnesses see Mackay [49], pp. 1–45.

[4] I am distinguishing here between articles on equity valuation appearing in the academic professional journals and the more implicit models appearing in the various publications from Wall Street. The latter source, while it may be just as relevant, is generally not indexed, not accessible, and not decipherable because it is mixed in with literally tons of superfluous materials that are churned out by Wall Street institutions.

[5] See Tinbergen [68], p. 153.

[6] *Ibid.*, p. 154.

statistical procedures employed; but judged in its historical perspective—
or even by today's standards in terms of the insight of the theory formulation—the study remains an important contribution to the received
literature on theory and research methodology in the area of equity valuation.

2.2 The Durand model

2.2.1   Durand undertook his study of bank stock prices in 1952 as
part of the National Bureau of Economic Research's financial research
program.[7] The purpose of the study was to measure the relative importance
of some basic variables that might affect the market price of bank stocks.
Durand was concerned that some stocks were selling for less than book
value, for he believed that in the long run the ability of a bank to raise
capital through a stock flotation depends on whether or not a stock is
selling for more than its book value. While a bank could certainly sell
stock even if present book value were greater than present market price,
it appeared at the time of the study that such equity financing could
only be done at rather prohibitive costs.

2.2.2   The question that concerned Durand was, "Given a ratio of
market price (P) to book net worth (nw), what level of the bank's rate of
return (net income divided by book net worth or ni/nw) would be necessary to maintain a (P/nw) ratio of at least 100 percent?"[8] At least one
additional factor was thought to influence this relationship, and that was
the dividend payout rate dv/ni (all figures are per share data). An increase in this rate, ceteris paribus, was assumed to decrease the rate of
return necessary to maintain (P/nw) at a given level. The basic relationship can be written as[9]

$$P/nw = a \cdot (ni/nw)^e \cdot (dv/nw)^f \tag{2}$$

Durand decided to test Eq. (2) in a slightly different form. The actual
test equation is indicated by Eq. (4).

$$P = a \cdot (ni/nw)^e \cdot (dv/ni)^f \cdot (nw)$$
$$= a \cdot (ni)^{e-f} \cdot (dv)^f \cdot (nw)^{1-e} \tag{3}$$

$$P = a \cdot (ni)^b \cdot (dv)^c \cdot (nw)^d \tag{4}$$

Since the coefficients of (nw) are now unconstrained, one test of the reasonableness of Eq. (2) is to see whether or not the parameter sum ($b + c + d$)
is approximately equal to one.

Durand examined several other variables to see whether additional
factors besides the (dv/ni) ratio should be incorporated into the basic

[7] See Durand [23] and [24].
[8] See Durand [23], pp. 2–5.
[9] Ibid., pp. 30, 52–59.

model. These factors included: (a) total equity capital, as a measure of bank size, (b) ratio of assets to capital, (c) ratio of risk assets to capital, (d) ratio of current dividend rate to average past dividend rate, (e) average annual rate of increase in earnings as measured by the slope coefficient of the regression of earnings on time for each bank, and (f) the stability of earnings as measured by the standard deviation of earnings about the trend line in (e). None of these variables performed well enough to warrant being added to the basic regression.

2.2.3 A sample set of six groups of banks and the 8-year period 1946–53 (making 48 basic samples) was used to derive estimates for Eq. (4). The groups were geographic clusters. The parameter estimates were quite variable from group to group and from year to year. Durand documented this variability by performing a series of covariance analysis tests on the data. He concluded that the samples could not be regarded as coming from the same underlying population either on a cross-section (pooling of groups) or time-series (pooling of years) basis.[10] Nor could additional variables be found that would reduce these sample heterogeneities.

Thus the parameter estimates for this model turned out to be almost completely sample sensitive. While it is possible to make generalizations about parameter signs and very crude orders of magnitude, it is not possible to generalize about quantitative magnitudes. In this work Dr. Durand explicitly sounded a warning on the theoretical and statistical problems that would arise for those pursuing this type of research strategy in the area of equity valuation. That most researchers who followed him chose to ignore his findings is but one of the many directional misfortunes that plague the history of science.

2.3 Cost of capital models

2.3.1 Instead of working directly on an equity valuation model some researchers have preferred to work on solving the relative valuation problem. In such work the theory and testing relate cost of equity capital or stockholder required rate of return to variables that attempt to specify risk-return expectations in terms of operational measures. The obvious gain of such a structure is the relativistic nature of most of the variables. But there are also problems in that statistical estimating procedures are often more complicated in cost of capital formulations and, until recently, the model forms tended to be even more *ad hoc* than the models for explicit price expectations.[11]

---

[10] See Durand [24], pp. 34–37.

[11] In recent years there has been an explicit attempt to relate the structural form of cost of capital models to basic portfolio and utility theory frameworks. Even in this work however the relation between model constructs and firm financial variables is quite tenuous. See for example Arditti [4], Sharpe [65].

2.3.2 The most famous cost of capital model is undoubtedly the Modigliani-Miller model.[12] Professors Modigliani and Miller did not set out explicitly to develop an explanatory model of equity valuation. Nevertheless, Proposition II in their set of conjectures is a partial model relating cost of equity capital (k) to firm risk class (ρ), corporate income tax rate (t), and market value debt-equity ratio (B/S).[13]

$$k = f(\rho, t, B/S) \tag{5}$$

This proposition has been tested by different researchers in variations of the form:[14]

$$NI^*/S = a + b \cdot (B/S) \tag{6}$$

$$NI^* = \text{some measure of expected earnings}$$

It should be noted that since this is a partial model, the researchers were not so much interested in parameter magnitudes as in the sign of the (b) parameter. But the specification is so incomplete it turned out to be virtually impossible to detect even the sign of that parameter without model elaboration.[15]

In 1966 Professors Modigliani and Miller presented their own elaboration of their original model.[16] In this version there is a shift of focus to (1) the development of explicit firm valuation (V) theory—and hence shareholder value (S) models, and (2) the development of more sophisticated statistical testing procedures. A two-stage least squares regression procedure is used to develop a model incorporating the following variables[17]

$$V = f(t, D, NI^*, A, g, \rho) \tag{7}$$

$$NI^* = h(t, D, A, g, PR, DV) \tag{8}$$

where t = income tax rate;
D = utility debt;
NI^* = expected net income;
A = total assets;
g = asset growth rate;
PR = preferred stock;
DV = expected dividend measure;
ρ = risk class index.

[12] See Modigliani and Miller [53], [54], [55], [56] for the primary discussion of their theory.
[13] See Modigliani and Miller [55], p. 439.
[14] For some of the variations empirically tested see Modigliani and Miller [53], pp. 281–287, Weston [71], and Barges [5].
[15] For a test of the original version see Keenan [39], pp. 126–135. Model elaborations can be found in Beranek [11], Wippern [75], White [73], and in the references cited in footnotes 14, 19, and 20.
[16] See Modigliani and Miller [56], pp. 333–352.
[17] *Ibid.*, pp. 353–364.

There is an important shift in the type of output demanded from the new research. For the discussion deals not only with parameter signs but also with parameter magnitudes. But the parameters are not stable.[18] Indeed, there is ample evidence to suggest that despite substantial model elaborations we still cannot even answer qualitatively the question of whether or not there are nontax advantages of leverage for the modern corporation.[19]

2.3.3   Other researchers have tried to formulate cost of capital models in terms of a more elaborate risk space.[20] Risk is viewed as a multidimensional concept that cannot be reduced to a one or two dimensional index. But there is little agreement about what the relevant protocol experiences are and even some doubt about the appropriate constructs necessary to structure the global concept of risk.[21] The result from a methodological viewpoint has been an almost completely *ad hoc* procedure in the specification of risk measures and the way such measures are incorporated into the model structure.

Typical of such approaches is the model formulated by Benishay in 1961. The model attempts to examine empirically the determinants of the differences in rates of return on corporate equities. The rate of return is hypothesized to be a function of seven variables: (1) the trend in earnings, (2) the trend in the market price of the common stock, (3) the payout ratio, (4) a stability of income index, (5) a stability of equity value measure, (6) firm size as measured by the market value of the equity, (7) the debt-equity ratio.[22] The statistical results are not sharp enough to determine most parameter signs, let alone orders of magnitude. The strongest result, the significance of firm size, is almost certainly due to parameter bias introduced by the structure of the estimating equation.

2.4 The Gordon model

2.4.1   Perhaps the most elaborate attempt to find explanatory variables to describe the equity valuation process is the model proposed

[18] The need to deal with parameter magnitudes has really existed since the Modigliani and Miller tax correction note [55], but the problem did not become an empirical issue until the Wippern [75] and 1966 Modigliani and Miller article [56].

[19] See comments by Crockett and Friend [22], Gordon [31], Robichek, McDonald, and Higgins [62], Archer and Faerber [3], Sarma and Rao [64]. One of the unfortunate aspects of this indetermination has been the conflicting testimony presented to regulatory agencies about appropriate debt strategy for regulated utilities.

[20] See Arditti [4], Benishay [8], Gonedes [30], and Caltagirone [17] for different measure spaces of risk.

[21] Most theoretical constructions that have empirical counterparts continue to relate risk to second (or higher) moments of return probability distributions. As Markowitz himself suggested, however, there are alternatives (such as the semi-variance) that may be better measures of risk. More recently the question as to whether some of the distributions of certain variables in valuation theory even have finite variances has been raised. For a discussion of these issues see Markowitz [51], Fama [27], Samuelson [63].

[22] See Benishay [8], pp. 81–86.

by Myron Gordon [32]. The model is constructed by extending earlier certainty-perpetuity models on which Gordon had worked. Unlike some of the cost of capital models, this is a model which is explicitly designed to answer the question as to what variables might explain the value of common stock equities.

There are six variables that are suggested as possible contributants to an equity valuation process: (1) the dividends of the firm, (2) the expected growth rate in dividends, (3) a measure of earnings instability, (4) a measure of the firm's leverage, (5) an index of operating asset liquidity, and (6) a measure of firm size. In the empirical specification of this model the six variables are postulated to have a simple multiplicative relation to the dependent variable price.[23]

2.4.2   From a methodological viewpoint Gordon's monograph may be the penultimate in single equation least squares models of equity valuation. Indeed, there has been subsequent work directed at simplifying and weeding out some of the overly complex indexes of this model.[24] Basically Gordon followed a linear procedure in developing this model. A simplified model framework was used to specify an initial relationship between price and the variable under consideration. Then, after the variable had been logically defined under a restrictive set of *ceteris paribus* conditions, an empirical specification of the variable was appended to the overall model and ignored while the next variable type was considered. Thus, while Gordon's analysis attempted to specify a consistent underlying theoretical framework his methodological procedures and simplifications led him to almost the same end result as those studies where variables are added on the basis of introspective considerations. The index variables are not really independent, of course, so parameter estimates may be biased.

Despite these limitations, the Gordon model is an important work for two reasons. First, using standard statistical criteria applied by others to their own work, this model (or variations of it) performs about as well as any other model reported in the literature—at least for those models that rely on firm financial variables as the basic explanatory agents. Thus it is a useful benchmark to measure future progress against.[25] Second, the Gordon methodology contains a very important innovation. His dividend variable depended not only on the firm's actual dividend payments but

---

[23] For an exact definition of each variable type see Gordon [32] or the appendix to this paper.

[24] See for example Peterson [60], Gruber [34], and Gordon himself in Brigham and Gordon [14].

[25] Unlike other potential benchmarks in equity valuation models the Gordon model can be replicated without too much difficulty. Many of the models in this area of research contain a "my-own" variable. My-own variables are measures that can only be calculated at great cost or are nonexistent for many firms. Hence these models are never replicated and, for better or worse, pass from the literature.

also on the level of those payments[26]:

> When income falls sharply or the firm feels a strong temporary need for
> cash, the dividend may be cut sharply as a temporary expedient. To
> deal with these situations 2 percent of the book value per share was used
> whenever the dividend was below this figure.

This implies, of course, that dividend expectations may sometimes be
best approximated by ignoring actual dividends (or nondividends). Limited
testing suggests that this is not an insignificant alteration in the Gordon
model.[27] Performance is substantially improved by including this dual
evaluation functional variable specification.

2.5 Synthetic models

In recent years increasing attention has been focused on the partial
nature of most valuation models. The result has been a number of attempts to reconcile existing models and to synthesize from these partial
theories a more general theory of equity valuation. The basic paradigm
and research methodology have not shifted however. The new models
still relate value to a complex set of expectations about firm financial
variables, and still specify equilibrium-stable parameter-testable hypotheses
which are evaluated using standard regression procedures.

2.5.1   The clearest example of this synthesis is the work of Eugene
Lerner and Willard Carleton.[28] Briefly, Lerner and Carleton argue that as
is true of all economic markets the equilibrium price of equity capital depends on demand and supply considerations—in this case related to expectations about future firm flows. Share price is said to be jointly determined by capital budgeting (investment opportunities), dividend, and
capital structure decisions. To analyze each of these decisions in terms
of a partial theory is to impose restrictions, usually arbitrary and sometimes misleading, on the other decision variables.

Lerner and Carleton develop a two-equation system, a stock valuation equation (P) and an investment opportunities model (LC). The
basic model takes the form[29]:

$$P = f(b_I, r_I, A, i^*, T, L/E, \sigma) \tag{9}$$

$$LC = h(b_C, r_C, T, L/E, \sigma) \tag{10}$$

where the independent variables are either investor (I) or corporate (C)

---

[26] See Gordon [32], p. 157.

[27] A substitution of book value figures for only one or two firms sometimes changed
parameter estimates significantly. This, of course, reflects the increasing nonlinearity of
log dividends below $1.00 per share.

[28] See Lerner and Carleton [44], [45], and [46].

[29] See Lerner and Carleton [44], pp. 695–697 and Lerner and Carleton [45],
pp. 191–196.

expectations about firm retention rate (b), rate of return (r), asset level (A), risk-free, nongrowth interest rate (i^*), income tax rate (T), debt-equity ratio (L/E), and risk class measure (σ). The equilibrium conditions $(b_I = b_C, r_I = r_C)$, implying consistent expectations, are imposed to generate model solutions.[30] The scope and complexity of the Lerner-Carleton theory would seem to be an order of magnitude greater than any single equation valuation model. Indeed, so extensive are the parameters that are implicitly or explicitly subsumed by this theory, it has barely been tested.[31] It may be that this theory has outrun the available "technology" and that it cannot be adequately tested by existing regression methodology. If that is so the theory is an important contribution not only because of its increased generality, but also because it provides a justifiable basis for reconsideration of existing test methodology.

2.5.2   There have been other attempts to integrate and elaborate existing theory in the area of equity valuation. We briefly note the work by Weston and Brigham, Sloane and Reisman on model reconciliation[32]; the attempt by Myers to formulate valuation risk dimensions in terms of a time-state preference model[33]; the allusions by Weingartner and Jaaskelainen as to how valuation might be incorporated into mathematical programming planning models of the firm.[34] Deriving sharp testable implications from such general models is not an easy task so it may be some time before we know whether such frameworks solve (except in an idealized normative sense) any of the problems inherent in more restrictive models.

III. PARAMETER STABILITY

The essence of scientific methodology is the development of testable hypotheses that can relate real world phenomena to idealized structures. In this section we begin by summarizing evaluative criteria ordinarily used to validate hypotheses in the area of equity valuation. We then apply these criteria to tests of models by Benishay, Gordon, and others. The evidence suggests that existing models do not meet the specified evaluative criteria. Hence the use of such models in explaining observable phenomena remains limited.

[30] Part of the power of the Lerner-Carleton theory is that it explicitly incorporates the possibility of differing expectations on the part of managers and investors. Even if the notion of equilibrium is dropped, the theory remains viable if one specifies some sort of linkage relating (b_I, r_I) to (b_C, r_C).

[31] Some idea of the number of dimensions that have been parameterized in this theory can be gleaned from Lerner and Carleton [45], *passim*, or from a working paper by Simkowitz [66]. See also the note by Boseworth, Kuhlman, and Spurdle [12].

[32] See Weston and Brigham [72], and Sloane and Reisman [67].

[33] See Myers [59].

[34] The inferences can be found in Weingartner [70] and Jaaskelainan [37]. But note that these are normative models, not scientific hypotheses.

3.1 Evaluative criteria

What sort of criteria must a "good" model of equity valuation satisfy? As to the theory we can only speak generally in terms of certain precepts that have evolved in most scientific disciplines. The model should be internally consistent.[35] The theory that displays a certain aesthetic simplicity and yet has constructs that can be extended to a more global theory is to be preferred.[36] The form of the model should have some meaning or justification.[37]

As to the statistical criteria there are at least three objectives that might be specified for good models (within the framework of current test methodology):

1. Estimated parameters should be significant. This can be interpreted two ways. First, at the grossest level, parameter signs should be consistent. Second, variable-parameter contributions should not be trivial explanative agents.[38]

2. The estimated parameters should exhibit reasonable stability in different cross-section samples unless there are obvious market imperfections or anomalies that have not been incorporated into the model.

3. The parameters should exhibit reasonable stability over time. If the parameters are not stable it should at least be possible to infer some of the events causing the parameter changes.[39]

The statistical problems associated with the testing of equity valuation models are not inherently different from the statistical complications that arise in testing most economic models. The problem is somewhat more acute in equity valuation models however, for the parameter results must be sharper to have a useful theory. Whereas in the tests of many economic hypotheses it is sufficient to know the parameter signs, in equity valuation models it is necessary to know magnitudes if the results are to be useful to investors or firms for decision purposes.

Estimated parameters may be biased or subject to undue variation

---

[35] This is apparently not as easy as one might suppose for equity valuation models. The constructs (as well as their empirical specifications) of "earnings" and "risk" are particularly susceptible to shifts in meaning.

[36] It is difficult to specify this intuitive criterion concretely, but it has long been a standard for most scientific theories. See for example the discussion on this subject by Koestler [40] and Margenau [50].

[37] Almost always the form specified for valuation models is linear or log-linear. This is a reflection of the technology available as a tool in this area, a subject we consider in Section 4.

[38] This relates to the difficulty in imposing closure on microeconomic systems. Some interesting comments on the problem are made by Emile Grunberg [35].

[39] For a study that does infer some of the factors causing temporal shifts in parameters of the Gordon model see Gruber [34].

because of a variety of well known statistical problems: (*a*) measurement errors in the variables, (*b*) autocorrelation in the disturbance terms, (*c*) multicollinearity among explanatory variables, (*d*) omitted variables, (*e*) least-squares weighting biases, and (*f*) mis-specification of the model form.[40] These are problems that can generally be corrected by additional sampling of the population of interest or by slight modifications of the existing model or test procedures. What cannot be corrected are parameter variations due to sampling from a universe that does not constitute a uniform parent population or due to fundamentally mis-specifying the theoretical constructs.

3.2 Tests of three models

3.2.1   If parameters are to be quantitatively meaningful they must not be completely sample sensitive. Drawings of firms from an *a priori* specified population should give parameter estimates that fall within a probabilistically acceptable range of the population parameters. In order to replicate tests of several models of equity valuation we selected a number of firms for some standard sample sets. Four sample groups of firms were selected and data were gathered to provide tests for each of the four years 1956–59. Thus there were 16 samples available for each of the models tested.[41]

The firms selected are not random samples of companies with publicly traded stock but are major corporations listed on the tapes of the Standard and Poor Corporation's Compustat Service. All firms for which there were missing data for the years 1951–59 were excluded and almost all the firms selected had positive earnings and dividends for the period under consideration. Three of the samples can be loosely characterized as industry type samples while the fourth sample is a cross-section of large firms. The samples include: (1) a food-related industry sample of 55 firms (Group I), (2) a group of 62 firms from machinery-related industries (Group II), (3) a chemical process-related sample of 50 firms (Group III), (4) a sample of 55 of the largest firms from about 50 different industries (Group IV). The years 1956–59 are a period containing a significant stock market and business cycle.[42]

None of the samples are in any sense perfect "pure industry" samples

[40] Standard discussions of the problems can be found in Johnston [38]; see also the comments by Friend and Puckett [29].

[41] Lists of the firms selected for each sample are available upon request. The design of the sample set matrix as well as other aspects of the test methodology owes much to the book by Edwin Kuh [42].

[42] Groups I and II are almost the same as Myron Gordon's samples. The samples are not completely independent since some of the firms in Groups I–III are in Group IV. It is not obvious that initial classification by industry is really desirable. The "industry" necessary to get a sample of 50 or more industrial firms is not usually an industry anyway.

or "homogeneous risk class" samples. This should not be so important in the Benishay or Gordon models where risk measures are already an explicit part of the model structure but it could be a problem in the capital gains model. In any event it simply will not do to say *a posteriori* that the parameter estimates are not satisfactory because the sample was not homogeneous in an important omitted variable. If the concept "risk class" is to be meaningful some *a priori* screening procedure must be specified.[43]

3.2.2 Results of test replications of three of many models examined are reported in the Appendix of this paper. The three models are formulations by Benishay, Gordon, and an adaptation of the Tinbergen model. The basic structures of these models were described in Section 2, and the exact specifications tested are reported in the first part of the Appendix. In general the results conform closely to the results originally reported by the authors.

Most of the parameters in the Benishay model are not significant. The most often significant parameters are the coefficient associated with the size measure (significant in 11 of 16 tests) and the coefficient associated with the debt-equity measure (significant in 8 of 16 cases). But the magnitude and significance of these two parameters may be due more to statistical bias than to a true functional relation, for the denominator of the dependent variable and the numerator of the size variable are the same measure (aggregate market equity value, which is presumably not free of measurement error).

In the Gordon replications most of the parameters are significantly different from zero for the majority of the 16 regressions. We could not quite get significance in the earnings instability index or the operating asset liquidity index; both of these were also variables that gave Gordon trouble. Given the relative parameter significance what about the stability of the parameter estimates? Can it be assumed that the samples are drawn from one underlying population? In the case of the Gordon formulation we should expect homogeneity across cross-section samples (Groups I–IV for each year) since risk measures are explicitly part of this model. It is less likely there will be intertemporal stability (years 1956–59 pooled for each group); for even though the variables are all smoothed, market level fluctuations have not been removed from the data. A series of covariance tests was performed to evaluate parameter stability. These tests essentially compare the residuals from the sample regressions assumed to come from the same population with the residuals from a pooled regression

---

[43] In this respect the Gonedes paper [30] and other work on applying factor analytic techniques to possible risk measures is certainly preferable to unmeasured *ad hoc* assertions about what firms constitute a risk class. To the extent the risk measures can be reduced to one or a few indexes, they can be incorporated directly into the valuation equation.

made up of all the sample data under consideration.[44] The results of these covariance tests indicate that assumptions about the equivalence of population parameters must be rejected whether one considers possible pooling cross-sectionally or inter-temporally. That is, the magnitudes of the parameters are sample unique and should not be averaged, pooled, or otherwise grouped with other sample results to derive inferences from a nonexistent underlying universe.[45]

The third set of parameters examined relate to a modified form of the Tinbergen model. Price is assumed to be a function of expected dividends—measured as the greater of actual reported dividends or 40 cents per share, and capital gains—measured as the greater of an exponentially smoothed function of past gains or $2.00 per share.[46] This simple investor expectations model does not, of course, postulate relative valuation in terms of firm financial variables but instead formulates a model in terms of variables directly observed by investors in the market. As the Appendix results indicate, all parameters are highly significant.[47] The variability across groups or over time is still too great however for the estimates to be accepted as coming from the same underlying population. Several attempts to incorporate into this model market rate fluctuations and Lintner-Sharpe risk indexes to reduce parameter variability failed.

3.3 Other test considerations

3.3.1 The results reported above seem to be typical of what one finds in empirical studies of equity valuation models. There are a group of variables which, for the restricted sample sets used by most researchers, usually have significant parameters. Such variables include earnings, dividends, retained earnings, growth measures, lagged prices, capital gains, size measures. For these measures smoothing the historical series used will often improve significance. There is another group of variables where parameter significance or sign is often indeterminant. Such variables include most risk measures derived from standard firm financial statistics. Whether the parameters are significant or not there seems to be almost

---

[44] For a discussion of the test procedures see Kuh [42], Johnston [38], or the original article by Chow [19].

[45] This makes it virtually impossible to make quantitative inferences or test sharp hypotheses since we have only broad "ranges" in which the true parameter for a firm (sample) may lie. There are also problems (see Section 3.3) in assuming standard Normal regression theory is applicable to equity valuation models.

[46] The 40 cents and $2.00 figures are arbitrary, but not completely so. They are a consensus of minimum expectations of a small group of investors on a hypothetical $40.00 stock. Variations of this model keep appearing in related forms. See for example the discussion by Bushow and Clower [16] or Douglas [85].

[47] There are reasons for believing these parameters may be biased (but note that these are cross-section and not time-series regressions). The intercept term is constrained to be zero, and sometimes in each sample the variables took on their minimum values, so the relative magnitude of the bias is not obvious.

no equity valuation model that is not wholly sample sensitive.[48] Thus it is not possible to make quantitative generalizations about parameter values. We must be satisfied with crude benchmark intervals that ordinarily turn out to be useless for the refined hypotheses we wish to test or inferences we wish to make.

Actually, the results may be even worse than they appear, for an examination of the regression residuals of several equity valuation models suggests that they violate every assumption of standard Normal regression theory.[49] This is partially a reflection of the fact that we have not been able to find variables to measure all "firm" effects, but it could also be indicative of the fact that the basic generating functions in financial markets have complex moments.[50] It would also appear that the same problems are being encountered in other countries with different institutional arrangements and different disclosure rules. Fisher [28] for example reports results of tests on samples of British steel stocks that are consistent with the results reported above for tests using American data.

3.3.2   We cannot of course replicate tests of every model.[51] First of all it is infinitely easier to generate new model variations than it is to test them. We suspect that in this past decade most model "innovations" have been new measure specifications (test variables) for a hypothetical construct of the theory (for example "financial risk"). There have been fewer innovations in the theoretical structure itself (such as the Lerner-Carleton focus on the simultaneity of certain decisions or the Lintner-Sharpe risk index for individual securities). It is very easy to generate new measure variables. Thus every researcher can have his own measure of say financial risk. And when that measure does not work (as it probably will not) he or the next researcher can specify a new measure. And so it proceeds, with little questioning of whether the theoretical construct itself may be unsound. In this frenetic search for the "golden measure" we might at least hope for a list of wrong measures, but alas this has not been the case.

[48] We are tempted to say no reported equity valuation model that has been tested except that Bruce Fitch (University of California, Berkeley) in some unreported work and Richard Bower [13] have achieved some success in stabilizing parameters by incorporating an index of firm residuals from previous years' regressions as a variable in this year's regression. It is an intriguing feedback mechanism and although it emasculates the statistical properties of the regression analysis, may be worth exploring.

[49] The sampling variances could not be considered constant; there seem to be too many residuals greater than four standard deviations from the mean; there are strong firm effects and moderately strong industry effects. A working paper on this subject, "The Misbehavior of Regression Residuals for Some Models of Equity Valuation," is in preparation.

[50] See for example Fama [27] for a discussion of the generating functions associated with stock price changes.

[51] It is not clear that replication is even necessary. In some cases the parameter variations reported by the original researchers are so great there is little likelihood they would pass Chow-type stability tests. See for example the results reported by Benishay [8] or Friend and Puckett [29].

The second problem in replicating tests as we indicated earlier is the specification of a "my-own" variable. If a researcher claims success for a model because it contains a measure variable that can only be calculated at very great cost or for relatively few firms we must play a waiting game. Eventually the model will be validated by new data, by other more testable implications of the model framework, or it will be forgotten. Such models can seldom be explicitly rejected. It may be that by playing the "add a variable, drop a variable, add a variable again" game too much the researcher has created an *ad hoc* set of relations that has little or no theoretical basis.[52] We have little appetite for replicating models that are in search of a theory.

IV. TECHNIQUE AS A LIMITING FORCE

Technique is sometimes a limiting force in science. The absence of technique with its associated instruments and data structures delimits the progress that can be made in a field. Thus the air pump and pneumatic chemistry were prerequisites to the analysis of air, the cathode tube a prerequisite of the discovery of X-rays, refined X-ray pictures necessary for the discovery of DNA structure.[53] In economics, data manipulation techniques such as the structuring of modern financial statements, regression procedures and linear programming formulations preceded significant rapid expansions in the level of economic analysis.[54] Just as the absence of technique can limit progress, technique too firmly entrenched can become a limiting force. For example the power of Newtonian mechanics probably delayed the development of relativistic physics; the success of phlogiston theory made it extremely difficult to even conceive the questions necessary to develop the oxygen theory of combustion. In economics various methodological schools continue to vie for dominance as "the correct approach" to the study of economic problems.[55]

As we have already suggested, the rapid expansion of man-hours spent on the development of equity valuation models has been made possible by technique that includes the availability of computer facilities, financial data banks, and standard regression theory as a statistical analysis

[52] An old football cry at some Institutes of Technology: "Add a variable, drop a variable, add a variable again; add a variable, drop a variable, that's the way to win." It wasn't a formula for winning many football games and it's not likely to win many research awards.

[53] See Kuhn [76], pp. 52–76 and the autobiographical report on the discovery of DNA structure by Watson [69].

[54] For an interesting description of the development of published financial statements in America see Hawkins [36].

[55] Indeed in the short history of economics there have been so many schools (historical, institutional, mathematical, econometric, fiscal, monetary, etc.) some would characterize the field as having only recently emerged from prescience.

vehicle. In the remainder of this section we discuss some of the problems associated with such technique and indicate several anomalies that have not been adequately resolved within the present methodological framework.

4.1 Information structure biases

The structure of financial statements plays a critical role in modern stock valuation models, for it is mostly from balance sheet and income statements that expectational measures are derived. But the items in these statements are only representations of the underlying stocks and flows (protocol activity) that are the source of real value. There is no income in the natural world, no current assets, no depreciation, no net worth. These are measures created to summarize certain types of information about real corporate goods and processes. To the extent that our accounting measure variables misrepresent the real activity or give us only a dimensionally incomplete view of the process we are likely to bias model structures that incorporate such measures.

The balance sheet for example is a fundamentally misleading document. It purports to be a static picture of corporate value just as a movie still is a static glimpse of some ongoing activity. For a large corporation, however, the probability that a balance sheet actually summarizes a state through which the firm actually passed is very small. Nor for large firms are individual items on the balance sheet likely to be an accurate measure of actual or historical values.

The situation may be even more serious for current income statements. As the complexity of firms and the rigidity-flexibility of accounting rules have increased, it has become increasingly difficult to relate income statement flows to actual firm activity.[56] Income taxes paid, economic depreciation taken, actual research and development done, actual sales, nonoperating revenues and expenses, subsidiary activity—in all these areas and more the measures reported are often gross distortions of the real activity. Different accounting procedures by firms in the same industry, by holding companies as compared to simply structured corporations, by regulated companies as compared to nonregulated firms, by companies in different industries makes it dangerous to relate a uniquely defined theoretical construct (say revenues or profits) to its apparent protocol measure (accounting revenues or profits).

There are also problems in that balance sheets and income statements are incomplete and inconsistent over time. The information on quarterly

---

[56] The phrase rigidity-flexibility is a contradiction but some of my colleagues feel that this may portray the current situation. As the Accounting Board substitutes an increasing list of specific rules and guidelines for "professional standards of conservatism, consistency, materiality, and stewardship" some would argue it becomes easier to violate the rules.

statements does not match in detail or accuracy the information provided in annual reports. It is often impossible to make comparative analyses between statements for the current period and statements for previous periods.[57] The detail in published reports does not necessarily conform to the detail of reports filed with the Securities and Exchange Commission.

The question of what data may actually be used by investors is one we consider in the next section. Here it is sufficient to note that even within the existing structural framework there are variations in measures reported. For example per share net income may be reported one way in a company's annual report, another way in the news media, a third way to the SEC, a fourth way to regulatory or tax agencies, a fifth way by the investment advisory or financial data services.[58] Existing techniques and assumptions associated with models of equity valuation do not generally allow for the consideration of such variations.

Suppose there were other information structures available; would that lead to different variables in the valuation model structure? We can conceive of entirely different schemes where "boogles, bits, and nits" would replace our current measures of revenues, costs, and profits. Even given the existing basic accounting framework there are many ways the data might be assembled to make clearer underlying real activity. It is possible that detailed sources and uses of funds statements, value added statements, capital expenditure statements, revenue product-matrix statements, standard budget and budget variance statements would lead to better surrogate indexes than current balance sheet and income statements.[59]

4.2 Test procedure biases

The proliferation of empirical research on equity valuation models has been made possible by a standardized methodology or technique.[60] We have already indicated that the technique includes Normal regression theory as a test procedure and in Section 3.3 we indicated some doubt about whether the economic phenomena under consideration met the prerequisite population assumptions of standard regression theory. In

---

[57] The published comparative figures for last year are of course often very different from the figures actually available to investors last year.

[58] Now some companies are reporting several net income per share figures in their annual reports, but the same statement of differing figures could be made for other items in the financial statements.

[59] There is also interesting work in progress that attempts to aggregate economic bits of information into entirely different types of planning and analysis documents. See for example Ijiri [77] and Theil [78].

[60] The research community is greatly indebted to the Standard Statistics Division of Standard and Poor Corporation for making their Compustat tapes available on reasonable terms. These computer tapes have been an essential tool in this area of research.

this section we consider two additional biases that have developed from an over-concentration on simple regression methodology.

The first bias relates to what will happen to outriders or anomalies in a regression model. In regression estimation the objective is usually to minimize a set of squared residuals, so any observation vector in a sample of size (N) that has a large residual will have a more than proportionate effect in determining the estimated regression plane. A large residual is usually associated with anomalies in the observation vector, so such observations tend to be excluded from the sample set. In some cases the exclusions are deliberate. Researchers have in various cases excluded as observations (a) firms with a series of negative earnings, (b) firms with no dividend payments, (c) firms with negative growth rates, (d) firms with extreme capital structures, or (e) other individual firms where one or more variables in the observation vector appear anomalous. Sometimes the same sort of exclusion is implicitly achieved. For example, those researchers using the Compustat tape and demanding a history of 20 years will get a population of large firms generally not having characteristics (a)–(d). As we suggest in Section 4.3, such exclusions tend to lead to serious misconceptions about both the generality and validity of current models.

The second bias relates to the type of parameters being estimated.[61] The functional specification of most equity valuation models has been in terms of relatively simple linear or multiplicative (log-linear) formulations. This means that the parameters are usually constants throughout the range of the observation vectors. Whether this is a reasonable assumption for market cross-sections is an open question. There is increasing evidence however that such constant parameter formulations are not accurate representations of the way individuals assess equity value. Individuals seem to formulate value by looking at variables in a sequential manner, by dividing each variable up into fairly simple network alternatives (such as high, low, average), and then by comparing the end results to already established benchmarks.[62]

Consider the following hypothetical possibility: net income (NI) is regarded as an important variable and its level enters into valuation as $(a \cdot NI)$ if $(NI \geq X)$. If $(NI < X)$ however the individual looks to other variables for valuation and the partial contribution of income is given a value $(b \cdot NI)$. Such discontinuous or highly nonlinear or inter-related weighting schemes (suppose the earnings parameter (a) above depends on the level of dividends) cannot easily be approximated or tested by the simple regression procedures heretofore used. Regression "packages" tend to

---

[61] The fact that parameters are even being estimated within the system is of course one type of methodological constraint.

[62] For a codification of the analytic procedures employed by one investor see Clarkson [20]; a related discussion can be found in Ahlers [1].

prejudice the case in favor of constant parameter estimates both because of the simplicity of linear forms and because of the small populations available for sampling.[63]

4.3 Excluded anomalies

So far we have suggested that functional specifications and test methodology associated with existing theories of equity valuation lead to unstable parameters such that we cannot sharply specify parameter levels or in some cases even parameter signs. In this section we pose several valuation problems. These problems have one thing in common. They are all situations that tend to be excluded from consideration in existing theories of equity valuation; they must be excluded from empirical tests of such theories whenever the measure variables are standard firm financial variables.

The problems include:

1. The valuation of companies with no financial history. This is a problem investment bankers and the investing public face for many new issues. Yet such issues are priced.
2. The valuation of companies with several quarters of losses, or companies with negative growth rates, or bankrupt companies. Such companies are almost always excluded from empirical tests even though they may give us the clearest evidence as to how expectations are actually formed.[64]
3. The valuation of holding companies, either of the operating conglomerate form or the closed-end mutual fund type. What is the financial structure or relevant flows of a conglomerate with legally separate and publicly valued subsidiaries? What factors determine the discount (premium) on different types of closed-end funds?
4. The valuation of stocks with different shareholder compositions. Sometimes securities with very thin markets or with ownership concentrated with some group or individual are excluded from test samples. Current models of equity valuation do not consider shareholder composition a first order determinant of value, but there is suggestive evidence that it is a measurable factor.[65]
5. The valuation of companies who make per share net income a function of share price. Current models of equity valuation

---

[63] There are probably fewer than 2000 firms with data sufficient for existing models, and any one researcher is probably drawing from a smaller universe because of imposed constraints.

[64] Firms do have value before, during, and after bankruptcy; see Altman [2].

[65] See for example Elton and Gruber [25] on the impact of personal taxes on share price changes.

generally assume that net income (or dividends) is an independently determined variable influencing share price. There are indications, however, that some firms sometimes "program" earnings (or dividends) to reach targets they think appropriate for the current level of their stock prices. With recent accounting changes it is literally true that reported per share net income (exclusive of transactions in other company securities) in some cases is a function of market price.

6. The valuation of stocks in multinational markets. There are several questions here. Are current models satisfactory for valuing domestically traded shares of foreign corporations? Are current models satisfactory for valuing foreign traded shares of foreign corporations? Even when standard balance sheet and income statement information is available (say for the class of Canadian mining stocks selling for less than $5.00 per share), it is clear that existing models (or more exactly the model test methodologies) will fail under certain institutional settings.

There are undoubtedly other types of firms that are also ignored or excluded from current models of equity valuation but this list is sufficiently long to make the point. These anomalies exist not because they could not be incorporated into the existing theory of equity valuation (they can), but because they cannot be incorporated into existing test methodology for the theory without radically altering test procedures.

By binding ourselves to a methodology that requires standard balance sheet and income statement information as inputs, and the estimation of constant parameters through standard Normal regression techniques as the validation procedure, we mostly exclude from consideration those very elements that would truly validate equity theory and contribute to its elaboration. The pattern of exclusion in the problem firms above is obvious, and so is the solution. In the following section we turn to the consideration of prospects for shifting existing methodology in the study of equity valuation models.

V. PROSPECTIVE DIRECTIONS

5.1 The dynamic expectations paradigm

5.1.1   The classic paradigm for a theory of financial instruments valuation suggests that security value is a function of investor expectations about the underlying real or financial flows and stocks associated with a particular instrument. In a world of certainty rational economic expectations are defined as equivalent to the realized economic events. In a world of uncertainty it is necessary to introduce specific propositions about the formation of expectations. One widely accepted proposition suggests that rational expectations "are essentially the same as the predictions of the relevant economic theory."[66] A related proposition implies that information is sufficiently widely dispersed and that there is sufficient economic power and incentive available so that market equilibrium prevails. As a first order condition the equilibrium is in the "local" market so that the same or an equivalent good will not sell for two different prices. As a weaker condition the equilibrium proposition implies that unit prices of all financial goods, adjusted for real differences (returns, risks, other attributes), will be simply related given stable preference functions.

For a great many financial instruments the general theory and its associated propositions give an excellent framework within which to develop detailed models of valuation. Where the uncertainty is low (expectations are closely related to expected values of the real events) we can develop accurate valuation models that meet the desired criteria discussed in Section 4. Thus the domestic price of foreign money,[67] the value of government securities,[68] the value of corporate bonds,[69] the price of convertible debentures,[70] the price of warrants,[71] and the prices of many other financial instruments can be explained in model frameworks where the causation variables are known and parameters remain stable or change in an explicable fashion. Most of these instruments have two things in common that help make uncertainty low: (a) the claim to future flows is explicitly specified (e.g., interest payments); (b) the claim to a future principal amount is specified (e.g., money, a real asset, another financial instrument). So long as there is no difficulty in estimating the current market value of this future principal, uncertainty will be relatively low.[72]

5.1.2 For common stock equities there are no explicitly specified future flows or principal amounts, either in monetary units or alternative financial instruments. Does the failure of existing models of equity valuation mean that the expectations paradigm should be rejected for this instrument? We think not. We do not believe that there is sufficient evidence to suggest that: (a) most existing models fundamentally mis-

[66] See the discussion by Muth [58], pp. 315–17 and a related paper by Modigliani and Bossons [52].

[67] For example the dollar value of English pounds can be closely approximated by knowing the exchange rate parameter.

[68] There has been intensive interest in forward expectations as revealed by the term structure of interest rates; see Meiselman [80] and Kessel [79].

[69] See the study by Fisher [81] which seems to meet all the "good" criteria specified in Section 3.

[70] See for example the Brigham study [84].

[71] Two interesting studies in this area have been done by Chen [83] and Shelton [82].

[72] Note that we are referring here to uncertainty about the relevant explanatory variables and not about value forecasting problems.

specify the process by which investor expectations about future states are formulated; (b) the "local" market for equivalent stocks may be in a constant state of disequilibrium.[73]

In a world of uncertainty it is an unnecessarily strong proposition to assert that the best measure variables for investor expectations are current and historical firm financial variables. First, we know that such measure variables, or even the theoretical constructs that the empirical measures are surrogates for, are not likely to be the combination of variables used by any behavioral unit.[74] Second, we have little evidence to suggest that existing or historical balance sheet and income data constitute elements in the "relevant economic theory" necessary to forecast future states. We do a rather poor job of forecasting earnings for example.[75] Third, for most of the anomalies discussed in Section 4.3, there are no relevant financial statements. Fourth, even when existing financial data are relevant, many models do not specify these data in the adaptive, smoothed form learning theory would suggest as being most appropriate.[76] If it is science and not prescription that researchers are interested in, then investor expectations models must be developed by studying the process by which expectations are formed.[77]

5.2 Areas for research

It has been the thesis of this paper that methodology—the availability of historical financial data, computers, and standardized regression procedures—has led to a significant distortion of the expectations proposition associated with the theory of financial instrument valuation. For those willing to go beyond existing methodological constraints, there would seem to be a number of exciting possibilities for research on equity models in the forthcoming decade. We can only allude to a few of the questions here.

[73] There could be several reasons for such disequilibrium. For example price changes may lead to a reformulation of investor expectations for a security thus increasing differences between securities whose real flows are the same. There may be investor concentrations in particular securities, unwarranted halo effects, etc.

[74] See the discussion by Clarkson [20].

[75] There has been some interesting research in this area recently. See for example studies by Little [47], Murphy [57], Green and Segall [33], Brown and Niederhoffer [15], Cragg and Malkiel [21]. Discussions relating these forecasts to stock prices can be found in Beaver [7] and Benston [9]. In a paper discussing the relation of earnings to stock prices which draws conclusions parallel to this work Baumol [6] is quite pessimistic about the *ad hoc* nature of most empirical models.

[76] See for example the studies by Kolin [41] and Pogue [61].

[77] It is not clear in every case that researchers are interested in science. Many models are really normative specifications dictating how prices should behave in the world of their creators. For those interested in the world of the Creator we do not dictate behavior, we observe it.

(A) Formation of investor expectations

1. A shift to a research focus on the process generating investor expectations would yield immediate benefits in forcing researchers to study real valuation processes for financial institutions and other behavioral units. Portfolio theory for financial institutions has already benefited from such a research methodology and valuation theory may also benefit from a study of the types of information and analytic procedures used by the different behavioral units.

2. It may be possible to learn something about how expectations change over time or from firm to firm by studying those financial instruments that represent a futures contract for corporate equity. With the increase in puts and calls, convertible debentures, warrants, and other options researchers can now study relative differentials between current spot prices and prices for options to receive the stock at some other point in time.

3. If measure variables of investor expectations are to be developed we may have to engage in survey sampling of transactors. Although there has been some classroom experimentation on economic perception, decoding of data masses, and wealth directed decision making, there has been relatively little field work done. It does not seem likely that in this uncertainty situation we will be able to sharply specify investor expectations without having some data inputs from investors.

4. A study of investor expectations processes should reveal how these expectations relate to real phenomena. In such studies anomalies of the type enumerated in Section 4.3 could be particularly useful. What real phenomena are used in formulating expectations? How do expectations relate to subsequent actualities? What is the adjustment process operating when reality and expectations diverge?[78]

(B) Capital structure questions

1. Existing theory and research focus on finding "the correct" cost of capital or "the optimal" capital structure of a firm. In a dynamic, uncertain environment do such questions have any meaning or importance? In equilibrium capital budgeting and the cost of capital (capital structure decisions) are interrelated. In dis-equilibrium the relations are far more complex. What is the appropriate strategy when investor expectations and actuality (relevant economic theory) expectations diverge?

---

[78] This is to be distinguished from (A-1) where we were talking about how expectations are formed. Those processes may or may not relate closely to real firm activity.

2. Does financial risk exist? Is it possible this theoretical construct does not operate in the real world because its magnitude is below the minimum threshold necessary to distinguish it from data noise? Is it possible that individual project selection and financing are so interrelated that measuring both operating risk and financial risk amounts to double counting?

3. Is capital structure a function of firm (industry) maturity as well as current investment opportunities? Some have suggested the possibility of a financial life cycle comparable to product life cycles for the firm.[79] Do financial life cycles exist? How does financing in a period of rapid innovation differ from financing in normal periods? What do such episodic decisions do to the price of equity capital?

4. What is the capital structure of a holding company, conglomerate, or other form of joint operation? Does the price of equity capital of a multinational firm reflect variables not incorporated into prices of uninational firms? When major international (or national) projects are jointly financed by several groups setting up a new subsidiary what should determine the cost of capital and capital structure of the subsidiary?

(C) *Public policy questions*

1. A study of how expectations are formed by different behavioral units should provide data on the types of information needed, the types of information used, the types of information that are superfluous or redundant. How can existing information statements (particularly accounting statements) be reformulated to provide better data? Do we need additional information disclosure?[80]

2. We know something about the impact of tax policy on capital budgeting, but the differential effects of tax policy on the prices of equity shares are not clear. Are there such tax effects? How do interest rate level changes affect the price of equity capital? Do structural interest rate changes have any impact on common stock prices?

3. How does the price of a firm's common stock relate to the aggregate market value of that firm? It is increasingly clear that it is inappropriate to consider demand functions for equity type securities as being perfectly elastic. If the market value of the firm's equity is not equal to the number of shares outstand-

---

[79] For some interesting and mostly untested hypotheses on financial life cycles see Weston and Brigham [72], Carter [18], and Evans [26].

[80] For one opinion see Benston [10].

ing times current share price, how does this affect our measures of capital structure?

4. What role does the price of equity capital play in redistributing real resources to the most productive industries? There is suggestive evidence that current tax policies, legal prohibitions against conglomerate forms, legal prohibitions against public tender offers, and other factors tend to restrict corporate take-overs by outside groups. What are the costs of such restrictions to equity shareholders?

There are many other possibilities. The decade of the 1960's ended with an obvious sterility in much of the empirical research on share price models. Leading researchers in finance meeting in late 1969 to arrange a conference briefly discussed the possibility of a paper on equity price models. The consensus was reported to be, "Oh no, not another model of equity valuation. Who can stand it?" By switching our methodology, so that we are studying real processes in the world, there may be some hope of making share price research an area of virility in the 1970's. The opportunities are there, for despite a vast expenditure of man-hours our empirical knowledge of the determinants of equity share prices has increased very little this past decade.

VI. CONCLUSIONS

In this paper we have been concerned with the methodology used to validate models of equity valuation. We have argued that after two decades of empirical research only the crudest sort of generalizations can be made about those factors explaining share price. This is an area that has benefited from thousands of man-hours of research time, thousands of hours of computer time, and tens of thousands of dollars for related support activity. Few research fields in economics have been so well funded. In view of this continuing outlay of resources it seems prudent to consider strategies that may improve research findings this coming decade relative to the meager results of the past.

Economics as a science must deal with the world as it is, not as we hope it is. We hoped that investor expectations for the uncertain flows accruing to equity shares could be described by simply defined, surrogate firm financial variables. We hoped that relative share price relations could be specified in a simple functional form with independent variables and constant parameters. But these things have not come to pass, and so we must look for new solutions. That we have not looked sooner can be attributed to the power of entrenched methodology. This methodology excludes from its test domain those pieces of evidence, those anomalies, that could be most important in understanding the formation of investor expectations. This methodology biases against those nonlinear, interrelated network type processes that may describe the way value is determined under uncertainty. This methodology, by making one data domain (firm financial variables) readily available, biases against a consideration of alternate measure spaces.

In recent years there has been a recurring and often bitter debate in finance about whether it is more important in financial research to focus on descriptively accurate constructs or quantitatively tractable constructs. The results of empirical research in the area of equity valuation suggest that we do need to observe more carefully the process of expectations formation. But this is hardly likely to be a return to institutionalism, for the constructs necessary to give these observations meaning will probably lead to dynamic feedback-type theories considerably more sophisticated than the naive quantitative (empirical) models currently in use.[81]

REFERENCES

[1] Ahlers, David M. "A Security Evaluation Model," in Kalman J. Cohen and Frederick S. Hammer, *Analytical Methods in Banking*, (Homewood, Ill.: Richard D. Irwin, 1966).

[2] Altman, Edward I. "Bankrupt Firms' Equity Securities as an Investment Alternative," *Financial Analysts Journal* (August, 1969), pp. 1–5.

[3] Archer, S., and L. Faerber. "Firm Size and the Cost of Equity Capital," *Journal of Finance*, Vol. 21 (March, 1966), pp. 69–83.

[4] Arditti, Fred. "Risk and the Required Return on Equity," *Journal of Finance*, Vol. 22 (March, 1967), pp. 19–36.

[5] Barges, Alexander. *The Effect of Capital Structure on the Cost of Capital* (Englewood Cliffs, N. J.: Prentice Hall, 1963).

[6] Baumol, William J. "Performance of the Firm and Performance of its Stocks," in Henry G. Manne, (ed.), *Economic Policy and the Regulation of Corporate Securities* (Washington, D. C.: American Enterprise Institute, 1969).

[7] Beaver, William H. "The Information Content of Annual Earnings Announcements," *Journal of Accounting Research: Selected Studies* 1968, pp. 67–100.

[8] Benishay, Haskel. "Variability in Earnings-Price Ratios of Corporate Equities," *American Economic Review*, Vol. 51 (1961), pp. 81–94.

[9] Benston, George. "Published Corporate Accounting Data and Stock Prices," *Journal of Accounting Research: Selected Studies* 1967, pp. 1–54.

[10] ——. "The Effectiveness and Effects of the SEC's Accounting Disclosure Requirements," in the Manne book [6].

[11] Beranek, William. *The Effect of Leverage on the Market Value of Common Stocks* (Madison, Wis.: University of Wisconsin Institute of Business Research, 1964).

[81] And finally, those "SERM" are of course single equation regression models.

[12] Bosworth, R., K. Kuhlman, and D. Spurdle. "The Decision on Earnings Retention and the Lerner-Carleton Model," *Financial Research and the Computer* (Hanover, N. H.: Amos Tuck School of Business at Dartmouth College, 1967).

[13] Bower, Richard. "Risk and the Valuation of Common Stock" (Tuck School of Business at Dartmouth College: working paper).

[14] Brigham, Eugene F., and Myron J. Gordon. "Leverage, Dividend, Policy and the Cost of Capital," *Journal of Finance*, Vol. 23 (March, 1968), pp. 85–104.

[15] Brown, Philip, and Victor Niederhoffer. "The Predictive Content of Quarterly Earnings," *Journal of Business*, Vol. 41 (October, 1968), pp. 488–98.

[16] Bushow, D. W., and R. W. Clower. "Price Determination in a Stock-Flow Economy," *Econometrica* (1954), pp. 328–43.

[17] Caltagirone, J., Jr. *The Rate of Return on Equity Capital: an Econometric Study*, unpublished doctoral dissertation (New York, N. Y.: New York University, 1969).

[18] Carter, Paul. *Capital Structure Changes over the Life Cycle of Corporations*, unpublished master's thesis (Berkeley, Calif.: University of California, 1967).

[19] Chow, Gregory. "Tests of Equality between Sets of Coefficients in Two Linear Regressions," *Econometrica*, Vol. 28 (July, 1960), pp. 591–605.

[20] Clarkson, Geoffrey P. E. *Portfolio Selection: a Simulation of Trust Investment* (Englewood Cliffs, N. J.: Prentice Hall, 1962).

[21] Cragg, John G., and Burton G. Malkiel. "Consensus and Accuracy of Some Predictions of the Growth of Corporate Earnings," *Journal of Finance*, Vol. 23 (March, 1968), pp. 67–85.

[22] Crockett, J., and I. Friend. "Comment," *American Economic Review*, Vol. 67 (December, 1967), pp. 1258–88.

[23] Durand, David. *Bank Stock Prices and the Bank Capital Problem*, (New York, N. Y.: National Bureau of Economic Research, Occasional Paper 54, 1957).

[24] ———. "Bank Stock Prices and the Analysis of Covariance," *Econometrica*, Vol. 23 (January, 1955), pp. 30–45.

[25] Elton, Edwin J., and Martin J. Gruber. "Marginal Stockholder Tax Rates and the Clientele Effect," *Review of Economics and Statistics* (February, 1970).

[26] Evans, George. "Financial Life Cycle of Corporations" in *Conference in Research in Business Finance* (New York, N. Y.: National Bureau of Economic Research, 1952).

[27] Fama, Eugene. "The Behavior of Stock-Market Prices," *Journal of Business*, Vol. 38 (January, 1965), pp. 34–106.

[28] Fisher, G. R. "Some Factors Influencing Share Prices," *Economic Journal*, Vol. 71 (1961), pp. 121–41.

[29] Friend, Irwin, and Marshall Puckett. "Dividends and Stock Prices," *American Economic Review*, Vol. 54 (September, 1964), pp. 656–82.

[30] Gonedes, N. "A Test of the Equivalent Risk Class Hypothesis," *Journal of Financial and Quantitative Analysis*, Vol. 4 (June, 1969), pp. 159–78.

[31] Gordon, Myron J. "Comment," *American Economic Review*, Vol. 67 (December, 1967), pp. 1258–88.

[32] ———. *The Investment, Financing, and Valuation of the Corporation* (Homewood, Ill.: Richard D. Irwin, 1962).

[33] Green, David, Jr., and Joel Segall. "The Predictive Power of First-Quarter Earnings Reports," *Journal of Business*, Vol. 15 (January, 1967), pp. 44–55.

[34] Gruber, Martin J. *Determinants of Common Stock Prices* (New York, N. Y.: Columbia University, unpublished doctoral dissertation, 1966).

[35] Grunberg, Emile. "The Meaning of Scope and External Boundaries of Economics," pp. 148–65 in the book edited by Sherman Roy Krupp, *The Structure of Economic Science* (Englewood Cliffs, N. J.: Prentice Hall, 1966).

[36] Hawkins, David F. "The Development of Modern Financial Reporting Practices among Manufacturing Corporations," *Business History Review*, Vol. 37 (1963), pp. 135–168.

[37] Jaaskelainen, Veikko. "Optimal Financing and the Tax Policy of the Corporation" (Helsinki, Finland: Helsinki School of Economics, Ph.D. student working paper, 1965).

[38] Johnston, J., *Econometric Methods* (New York, N. Y.: McGraw Hill, 1963).

[39] Keenan, W. Michael, *Toward a Positive Theory of Equity Valuation*, unpublished doctoral dissertation (Pittsburgh, Penn.: Carnegie Mellon University, 1967).

[40] Koestler, Arthur. *The Act of Creation* (New York, N. Y.: Macmillan Co., 1964).

[41] Kolin, Marshall. "The Relative Price of Corporate Equity with Particular Attention to Investor Valuation of Retained Earnings and Dividends" (Cambridge, Mass.: Harvard University student working papers, 1965).

[42] Kuh, Edwin. *Capital Stock Growth: a Micro-econometric Approach* (Amsterdam, Netherlands: North Holland Publishing, 1963).

[43] L'Estrange, Sir Roger. *Fables of Aesop* (New York, N. Y.: Dover Publications, 1967).

[44] Lerner, Eugene M., and Willard T. Carleton. "The Integration of Capital Budgeting and Stock Valuation," *American Economic Review*, Vol. 54 (September, 1964), pp. 683–702.

[45] ———. *A Theory of Financial Analysis* (New York, N. Y.: Harcourt Brace, 1966).

[46] ———. "The Capital Structure Problem of a Regulated Public Utility," *Public Utilities Fortnightly*, Vol. 76 (July 8, 1965), pp. 24–32.

[47] Little, I. M. D. "Higgledy Piggledy Growth," *Oxford Institute of Statistics Bulletin* (November, 1962), pp. 387–412.

[48] Macaulay, F. R. *Interest Rates, Bond Yields, and Stock Prices* (New York, N. Y.: National Bureau of Economic Research, 1938).

[49] Mackay, Charles. *Extraordinary Popular Delusions and the Madness of Crowds* (Wells, Vt.: Fraser Publishing, 1932), pp. 1–45.

[50] Margenau, Henry. *The Nature of Physical Reality* (New York, N. Y.: McGraw Hill, 1950).

[51] Markowitz, Harry. *Portfolio Selection* (New York, N. Y.: John Wiley and Sons, 1959).

[52] Modigliani, F., and J. Bossons. "On the Reasonableness of Regressive Expectations" (Cambridge, Mass.: M.I.T. School of Industrial Management working paper, 1963).

[53] Modigliani, Franco, and Merton Miller. "The Cost of Capital, Corporation Finance, and the Theory of Investment," *American Economic Review*, Vol. 48 (1958), pp. 261–97.

[54] ——. "Reply (to David Durand)," *American Economic Review*, Vol. 49 (1959), pp. 655–69.

[55] ——. "Corporate Income Taxes and the Cost of Capital: a Correction," *American Economic Review*, Vol. 53 (1963), pp. 433–43.

[56] ——. "Some Estimates of the Cost of Capital to the Electric Utility Industry, 1954–57," *American Economic Review*, Vol. 56 (1966), pp. 333–91.

[57] Murphy, J., Jr. "Relative Growth of Earnings per Share," *Financial Analysts Journal*, Vol. 22 (November, 1966), pp. 73–76.

[58] Muth, John F. "Rational Expectations and the Theory of Price Movements," *Econometrica*, Vol. 29 (July, 1961), pp. 315–35.

[59] Myers, Stewart C. "A Time-State-Preference Model of Security Valuation," *Journal of Financial and Quantitative Analysis*, Vol. 3 (June, 1968), pp. 171–203.

[60] Peterson, David E. *Corporate Investment Decisions and Financial Planning*, unpublished doctoral dissertation (Urbana, Ill.: University of Illinois, 1963).

[61] Pogue, Jerry A. *An Adaptive Model for Investment Management*, unpublished doctoral dissertation (Pittsburgh, Penn.: Carnegie Mellon University, 1967).

[62] Robichek, A., J. McDonald, and R. Higgins. "Comment," *American Economic Review*, Vol. 67 (December, 1967), pp. 1258–88.

[63] Samuelson, Paul. "General Proof that Diversification Pays," *Journal of Financial and Quantitative Analysis*, Vol. 2 (March, 1967), pp. 1–13.

[64] Sarma, L., and K. Rao. "Leverage and the Value of the Firm," *Journal of Finance*, Vol. 24 (September, 1969), pp. 673–77.

[65] Sharpe, William F. "Capital Asset Prices: a Theory of Market Equilibrium under Conditions of Risk," *Journal of Finance*, Vol. 19 (September, 1964), pp. 425–42.

[66] Simkowitz, Michael. "A Simultaneous Equation Approach to Security Analysis" (Bloomington, Ind.: Indiana University, School of Business working paper).

[67] Sloane, William R., and Arnold Reisman. "Stock Evaluation Theory: Classification, Reconciliation, and General Model," *Journal of Financial and Quantitative Analysis*, Vol. 3 (June, 1968), pp. 171–203.

[68] Tinbergen, J. "The Dynamics of Share Price Formation," *Review of Economics and Statistics*, Vol. 21 (1938), pp. 153–60.

[69] Watson, James D. *The Double Helix* (New York, N. Y.: Signet Books, 1968).

[70] Weingartner, H. Martin. *Mathematical Programming and the Analysis of Capital Budgeting Problems* (Englewood Cliffs, N. J.: Prentice Hall, 1963).

[71] Weston, J. Fred. "A Test of Cost of Capital Propositions," *Southern Economic Journal*, Vol. 30 (1963), pp. 105–12.

[72] Weston, J. Fred, and Eugene F. Brigham. *Managerial Finance* (New York, N. Y.: Holt Rinehart, 1966), pp. 477–85, 761–803.

[73] White, W. *The Debt-Equity Ratio, the Dividend Payment Ratio, Growth, and the Rate at which Earnings are Capitalized*, unpublished doctoral dissertation (Boston, Mass.: Massachusetts Institute of Technology, 1963).

[74] Williams, John B. *The Theory of Investment Value* (Cambridge, Mass.: Harvard U. P., 1938).

[75] Wippern, Ronald F. "Financial Structure and the Value of the Firm," *Journal of Finance*, Vol. 21 (December, 1966), pp. 615–34.

[76] Kuhn, Thomas S. *The Structure of Scientific Revolutions* (Chicago, Ill.: University of Chicago Press, 1962).

[77] Ijiri, Yuji. *Management Goals and Accounting for Control* (Amsterdam, Holland: North Holland Publishing, 1965).

[78] Theil, Henri. "The Use of Information Theory Concepts in the Analysis of Financial Statements," *Management Science*, Vol. 15 (May, 1969), pp. 459–81.

[79] Kessel, Reuben A. *The Cyclical Behavior of the Term Structure of Interest Rates* (New York, N. Y.: National Bureau of Economic Research, occasional paper 91, 1965).

[80] Meiselman, David. *The Term Structure of Interest Rates* (Englewood Cliffs, N. J.: Prentice Hall, 1962).

[81] Fisher, Lawrence. "Determinants of Risk Premiums on Corporate Bonds," *Journal of Political Economy* (June, 1959), pp. 217–37.

[82] Shelton, John P. "The Relation of the Price of a Warrant to the Price of its Associated Stock," *Financial Analysts Journal*, Vol. 23 (May–June and July–August, 1967), pp. 143–51, 88–99.

[83] Chen, Houng-Yhi. *A Dynamic Programming Approach to the Valuation of Warrants*, unpublished doctoral dissertation (Berkeley, Calif.: University of California, 1968).

[84] Brigham, Eugene F. "An Analysis of Convertible Debentures: Theory and Some Empirical Evidence," *Journal of Finance*, Vol. 21 (March, 1966), pp. 35–54.

[85] Douglas, George W. "Risk in the Equity Markets: an Empirical Appraisal of Market Efficiency," *Yale Economic Essays*, Vol. 9 (Spring, 1969), pp. 3–45.

APPENDIX

SUMMARY OF SYMBOLS

P = price of a stock at the end of period t

DV = dividends for the period t

dv = dividends per share

NI = net income after taxes

ni = NI per share

NW = book value of the net worth of the corporation

nw = net worth per share

S = market value of common stock equity = $(P \cdot N)$

LL = long term debt for the firm, including any preferred stock, at book value

DT = total balance sheet liabilities for the firm

IY = inventory at the end of period t

NP = net plant and equipment

CH = cash at the end of period t

CL = current liabilities

AR = accounts receivable

TA = total assets at book value

N = number of shares outstanding

The Benishay Model

$$Y = a \cdot \exp\left[b\left(x_1\right) + c\left(x_2\right) + h\left(x_7\right)\right] \cdot \left(x_3\right)^d \cdot \left(x_4\right)^e \cdot \left(x_5\right)^f \cdot \left(x_6\right)^g$$

$$(Y) = NI^*/\bar{S}$$

$$NI^* = \left[NI\left(t\right) + \sum_{t-9}^{t-1} NI\left(t\right)/9\right]/2$$

$$\bar{S} = N[P_H + P_L]/2$$

$$= N \cdot \bar{P}$$

$$(x_1) = \text{a growth in earnings factor}$$

$$= b_1/\overline{NI}$$

where b_1 is the coefficient from the regression

$$NI\left(t\right) = a_1 + b_1\left(t\right) \qquad t = t - 8, \ldots, t$$

and

$$\overline{NI} = \sum_{t-8}^{t} NI\left(t\right)/9$$

$$(x_2) = \text{growth in equity value}$$

$$= b_2/P^*$$

where b_2 is the coefficient from the regression

$$P\left(t\right) = a_2 + b_2\left(t\right) \qquad t = t - 8, \ldots, t$$

and

$$P^* = \sum_{t-8}^{t} P\left(t\right)/9$$

$$(x_3) = \text{payout ratio}$$

$$= \left[\sum_{t-2}^{t} DV\left(t\right)/NI\left(t\right)\right] \cdot \left[100/3\right]$$

$$(x_4) = \text{stability of income measure}$$

$$= \overline{NI}/\sigma_{x1}$$

$$(x_5) = \text{stability of equity value}$$

$$= P^*/\sigma_{x2}$$

$$(x_6) = \text{a measure of size}$$

$$= \bar{S}$$

$$(x_7) = \text{a debt-equity ratio}$$

$$= DT/\bar{S}$$

The Gordon Model

$$P = a \cdot (x_1)^b \cdot (x_2)^c \cdot (x_3)^d \cdot (x_4)^e \cdot (x_5)^f \cdot (x_6)^g$$

$$(x_1) = \text{dividends per share}$$

$$= (dv) \text{ or } (.02)(nw), \text{ whichever is greater}$$

$$(x_2) = \text{dividend growth rate}$$

$$= [1 + b'i']$$

$$b'i' = \left(\frac{\bar{y}(t) - dv}{\bar{y}(t)} \right) \cdot \left(\frac{\bar{y}(t)}{nw} \right)$$

$$\bar{y}(t) = [.3NI(t) + .7\tilde{y}(t-1)(1 + G[t])]/N$$

$$\tilde{y}(t-1) = .3NI(t-1) + .7\tilde{y}(t-2)$$

$$G(t) = .3[\tilde{y}(t) - \tilde{y}(t-1)]/\tilde{y}(t-1) + .7G(t-1)$$

$$\tilde{y}(1950) = NI(1950); G(1950) = .03$$

$$(x_3) = \text{earnings instability index}$$

$$= (1 + \hat{\sigma}/NW)$$

$$\hat{y}(t) = \bar{y}(t-1)[1 + G(t-1)]$$

$$\Delta(t) = [\,|\,\hat{y}(t) - NI(t)\,|\,]/NW$$

$$\left(\frac{\sigma}{NW} \right)_t = .3\Delta(t) + .7 \left(\frac{\sigma}{NW} \right)_{t-1}$$

$$L(t) = CL + LL - CH - AR - \widetilde{IY}(t)$$

$$\widehat{IY}(t) = \frac{.4IY}{NW} + .6I\hat{Y}(t-1)$$

$$\overline{IY}(t) = \widehat{IY}(t) \cdot NW$$

$$\widetilde{IY}(t) = IY - \overline{IY}(t)$$

$$\left(\frac{\hat{\sigma}}{NW} \right) = \left(\frac{\sigma}{NW} \right) \left(\frac{NW}{NW + L(t)} \right)$$

$$\left(\frac{\sigma}{NW} \right)_{1951} = \frac{NI(1951) - NI(1950)}{NW(1950)}$$

$$\overline{IY}(1950) = IY(1950)$$

$$(x_4) = \text{leverage index}$$

$$= 1 + h' - rh'/k$$

$$h' = L(t)/NW(t)$$

$$k = \frac{(1 - b')NI}{P} \cdot (1 + h')^{-.3} + (b'i')$$

$$r = .045$$

(x_5) = operating asset liquidity index

$$= \frac{7\overline{IY} + 3NP}{5\overline{IY} + 5NP}$$

(x_6) = firm size index

$$= [TA - CL]/1,000,000$$

The Investor Model

$$P = a \cdot E(dv) + b \cdot E(cg)$$

$E(dv)$ = the greater of (dv) or 40 cents

$E(cg)$ = the greater of (ΔP^*) or \$2.00

$$\Delta P^* = \sum_{-4}^{0} W(t)[P(t) - P(t-1)]$$

$$W(t) = H \cdot B(1-B)^t$$

$$H = 1/[B \cdot \sum_{-4}^{0} (1-B)^t]$$

$$B = .40$$

BENISHAY EQUATION

$$Y = a \cdot \exp\left[(bx_1 + cx_2 + hx_7)\right] \cdot (x_3)^d \cdot (x_4)^e \cdot (x_5)^f \cdot (x_6)^g$$

Group I

	1956	1957	1958	1959
ln a	-1.247	-1.059	-1.006	-1.510
a	.287	.347	.366	.221
b	-1.902^*	-1.587^*	$-.614$	$-.320$
	(.400)	(.438)	(.606)	(.799)
c	.754	$-.048$	$-.521$	$-.263$
	(.429)	(.608)	(.825)	(.867)
d	$-.224^*$	$-.275^*$	$-.347^*$	$-.306^*$
	(.057)	(.089)	(.124)	(.138)
e	$-.044$	.061	.034	$-.048$
	(.056)	(.061)	(.067)	(.048)
f	.100	.028	.066	$.202^*$
	(.058)	(.065)	(.086)	(.086)
g	$-.107^*$	$-.084^*$	$-.075^*$	$-.054^*$
	(.019)	(.019)	(.022)	(.023)
h	$.272^*$	$.242^*$	$.357^*$	$.373^*$
	(.068)	(.079)	(.120)	(.124)
R^2	.755	.692	.622	.616
F	24.8	18.3	13.7	13.4

Estimates for Groups II, III, IV will be supplied by the author upon request.
Note: * = parameter significantly different from zero, assuming standard Normal regression assumptions hold. Standard errors are in parentheses.

GORDON EQUATION

$$P = a \cdot (x_1)^b \cdot (x_2)^c \cdot (x_3)^d \cdot (x_4)^e \cdot (x_5)^f \cdot (x_6)^g$$

Group I

	1956	1957	1958	1959
ln a	2.472	2.343	2.672	2.575
a	11.843	10.409	14.467	13.133
b	.837*	.974*	.832*	.756*
	(.053)	(.059)	(.050)	(.055)
c	6.884*	8.865*	5.029*	7.043*
	(1.857)	(1.905)	(1.988)	(2.442)
d	−2.772	−6.287	1.296	−1.339
	(3.005)	(3.330)	(3.296)	(4.465)
e	−.709*	−.734*	−.502*	−.883*
	(.214)	(.216)	(.197)	(.257)
f	.548*	.485*	.437*	.356*
	(.166)	(.175)	(.164)	(.170)
g	.080*	.071*	.084*	.116*
	(.030)	(.029)	(.027)	(.031)
R^2	.895	.909	.898	.872
F	77.9	91.2	80.3	62.5

Note: * = parameter significantly different from zero, assuming standard Normal regression assumptions hold. Standard errors are in parentheses.

Group II

	1956	1957	1958	1959
ln a	2.248	1.840	2.669	2.959
a	9.472	6.294	14.431	19.276
b	.690*	.838*	.670*	.563*
	(.075)	(.086)	(.058)	(.093)
c	15.524*	10.420*	12.464*	10.255*
	(2.072)	(1.997)	(2.093)	(2.818)
d	−.383	1.251	−.597	.392
	(2.756)	(3.066)	(1.767)	(2.429)
e	−.321	.547*	−.150	.156
	(.352)	(.254)	(.148)	(.458)
f	.812*	.540	−.012	−.036
	(.335)	(.342)	(.263)	(.408)
g	.068	.091	.044	.018
	(.043)	(.052)	(.040)	(.054)
R^2	.751	.706	.793	.498
F	31.7	25.4	40.0	11.1

Note: * = parameter significantly different from zero, assuming standard Normal regression assumptions hold. Standard errors are in parentheses.

Group III

	1956	1957	1958	1959
ln a	2.427	2.407	2.965	2.808
a	11.330	11.097	19.388	16.583
b	.724*	.656*	.702*	.787*
	(.130)	(.136)	(.094)	(.124)
c	5.865	8.616*	8.695*	8.636*
	(3.020)	(2.875)	(2.637)	(3.456)
d	2.242	−2.606	−3.262	3.166
	(2.768)	(2.967)	(2.859)	(3.792)
e	−.482	−1.131*	−.941*	−.614
	(.293)	(.310)	(.294)	(.358)
f	−.306	.738	.537	.374
	(.453)	(.520)	(.458)	(.526)
g	.119*	.141*	.090*	.071
	(.048)	(.054)	(.044)	(.057)
R^2	.624	.662	.734	.651
F	14.5	17.0	23.5	16.3

Note: * = parameter significantly different from zero, assuming standard Normal regression assumptions hold. Standard errors are in parentheses.

Group IV

	1956	1957	1958	1959
ln a	2.351	2.261	2.803	2.627
a	10.499	9.595	16.489	13.828
b	.856*	.938*	.826*	.858*
	(.099)	(.120)	(.108)	(.121)
c	9.357*	6.524*	4.000	6.770*
	(2.555)	(3.021)	(2.285)	(2.859)
d	−.127	.174	.548	.453
	(.817)	(.814)	(.764)	(.990)
e	.394*	.092	−.182	−.163*
	(.174)	(.194)	(.172)	(.073)
f	−.441	−.373	−.288	.046
	(.260)	(.291)	(.285)	(.296)
g	.078*	.075	.074	.092*
	(.039)	(.043)	(.043)	(.045)
R^2	.672	.613	.621	.557
F	19.4	15.3	15.8	12.3

Note: * = parameter significantly different from zero, assuming standard Normal regression assumptions hold. Standard errors are in parentheses.

REGRESSION ESTIMATES FOR THE INVESTOR MODEL

$$P = a\,(dv) + b\,(\Delta P^*)$$

		1956	1957	1958	1959
	a	13.592* (.782)	14.681* (.759)	14.788* (.866)	13.630* (.720)
I	b	2.645* (.501)	1.897* (.543)	2.383* (.248)	3.122* (.207)
	R^2	.911	.916	.942	.956
	F	277.1	295.9	435.7	592.4
	a	10.298* (.654)	8.082* (.937)	7.139* (1.431)	12.997* (.990)
II	b	2.947* (.186)	2.386* (.371)	3.462* (.305)	2.781* (.202)
	R^2	.870	.669	.806	.804
	F	204.3	60.1	127.3	125.8
	a	13.906* (1.804)	12.423* (1.942)	17.737* (1.798)	16.624* (1.406)
III	b	3.620* (.416)	4.075* (.628)	2.944* (.303)	3.661* (.231)
	R^2	.905	.866	.903	.939
	F	233.0	158.4	229.8	374.8
	a	11.756* (.722)	10.119* (1.086)	11.595* (1.031)	10.489* (1.078)
IV	b	3.730* (.179)	4.579* (.355)	3.659* (.147)	4.456* (.159)
	R^2	.929	.844	.937	.949
	F	357.3	146.0	399.6	508.0

Note: * = parameter significantly different from zero, assuming standard Normal regression assumptions hold. Standard errors are in parentheses.

William J. Baumol
Burton G. Malkiel
*Richard E. Quandt**

34. The Valuation of Convertible Securities

Reprinted from the **Quarterly Journal of Economics,** Vol. LXXX, No. 1 (February, 1966), pp. 48–59, by permission of the authors and publisher.

I. INTRODUCTION

This paper addresses itself to the valuation of convertible securities, those issues which may be exchanged at the option of the holder for other securities of the issuing company. We shall focus on convertible bonds, although the techniques developed here are also applicable to other convertible instruments, such as convertible preferred stock, etc. The convertible bonds treated are debenture bonds convertible into the common stock of the issuing company at a specified rate of exchange and within a limited time period. As is well known, convertible debentures normally sell at a premium over the value of otherwise equivalent bonds that are divested of the convertibility feature. They also often sell at a price higher than the debenture's conversion value, the value of the common stocks into which the bond is convertible. The former premium we shall call the premium over the issue's bond value, the latter, the premium over the issue's stock value. The purpose of this analysis is to describe the determination of these premiums as a function of the characteristics of the common stock of the issuing company.

The model we present asserts that the value of a convertible can be divided into two parts. The first is the present worth of the security itself, representing the discounted stream of future coupon payments and the expected value of the security at the end of a specified horizon period. The second is the insurance value of the convertibility feature which enables the holder of the security to treat it either as a stock or a bond.

* Each author is Professor of Economics, Princeton University. The authors are indebted to Professors Charles C. Holt and Donald E. Farrar for very valuable comments and to the National Science Foundation and the Ford Foundation whose grants helped in the completion of this paper. Our work on this subject was begun under the auspices of MATHEMATICA.

Suppose an investor had bought the convertible on a certain date and planned to sell it three years later, expecting, because there was a rising trend in the market value of the shares of company X, that he would finally sell it at a value governed largely by its stock equivalent. This privilege is worth something to him in and of itself as that value will essentially be based on the anticipated (higher) price of the stock at the date of the sale. But our security holder also knows (assuming he has not actually converted his security in the interim) that if it turns out that his forecast was mistaken in that the stock price has in fact fallen sharply, he has the option of disposing of a security whose market price will be largely governed by its value as a bond rather than a stock. Thus the "bond value" of the convertible may provide a cushion limiting the risk assumed by the convertible holder vis-à-vis the outright owner of common shares. Consequently, the determination of the value of a convertible comes down to the analysis of the values of these two components—the expected value of the security and the insurance value of the convertibility feature.

We shall proceed as follows: We begin by presenting a first approximation of a convertible valuation model. In the preliminary application of the model we assert that investors' subjective probability distributions of future common stock prices can be treated as being wholly determined by past distributions of stock prices. Moreover, we abstract from interest payments, dividends, risk factors, and we do not employ a discounting procedure. We then test the preliminary model statistically. We offer sample calculations for seven convertible bonds and compare the normative valuations with actual market prices. Next, the implications of altering several of the assumptions of the analysis are examined. Finally, we indicate how such modifications might be incorporated into the basic model and we offer suggestions for further work.

II. PRELIMINARY MODEL FOR THE VALUATION OF CONVERTIBLE BONDS

Consider an investor who is contemplating the purchase of a convertible security. Let us see how much he should be willing to pay for it in terms of the value of the common stock into which it can be converted and in terms of its value as an ordinary bond. Let

C = the value of the convertible;

B = the convertible's bond equivalent value (its bond value);

S = the number of shares of common stock into which the convertible can be exchanged;

$P(t)$ = the price per common share at date t so that $P(t)S$ represents the convertible's stock equivalent value (its stock value);

$i(t)$ = a price-relative of a share at date t and let t_0 be the date on which the convertible is being evaluated.

Therefore, by definition,

$$P(t) = i(t)P(t_0) \qquad \text{for any date } t \tag{1}$$

Now, suppose our investor expects to sell his convertible at the end of an as yet unspecified horizon period.

We assume for any future date t that there exists a subjective probability distribution of the price-relative $i(t)$ which expresses the purchaser's views on the likelihood of different stock values. This distribution is given by the density function $f(i, t_0)$ where the presence of the t_0 in the function indicates that the shape of the distribution may be affected by the date at which the convertible is valued.

As has been stated, the convertible is going to be worth at least as much as the contract equivalent stock [which sells for $P(t_0)S$] plus the insurance value, V, of having the option of selling the security at its bond value rather than stock value, should the stock value be below the bond value when the security is sold. Thus we have [where for the sake of simplicity we use the abbreviation P for $P(t_0)$]

$$C \geq P(t_0)S + V = PS + V \tag{2}$$

But V refers to the possibility that the bond value, B, will in the future exceed the value of the equivalent stock, $P(t)S = i(t)PS$. For any value of $i(t)$ the difference between the bond and stock values will be $B - i(t)PS$, and this will occur with probability $f(i, t_0)di(t)$. Hence the expected value, V, of all circumstances in which the bond value will be worth more than the stock value will be the sum (integral) of the excesses of the bond over the stock values, each multiplied by its probability of occurring, i.e., we have, assuming B to be a constant, $\bar{B}$,

$$V = \int_0^{\bar{B}/PS} f(i, t_0)[\bar{B} - i(t)PS]di(t) \tag{3}$$

Here the limits of integration, $i(t) = 0$ and $i(t) = \bar{B}/PS$, are arrived at as follows: The maximum value of i for which the stock value is no greater than the bond value is that i which makes the stocks and the bonds equal in value so that $\bar{B} = i(t)PS$ or $i(t) = \bar{B}/PS$. This, then, is the upper limit of integration. And, since stock prices will not fall below zero, $i(t) = 0$ is the lower limit of integration.

Now, substituting from Eq. (3) into Eq. (2) and writing C_s for the right-hand expression Eq. (2) we obtain

$$C \geq C_s = PS + \int_0^{\bar{B}/PS} f(i, t_0)[\bar{B} - i(t)PS]di(t) \tag{4}$$

In exactly the same way we obtain the analogous relationship between the value of the convertible and its bond value, $\bar{B}$

$$C \geq C_b = \bar{B} + \int_{\bar{B}/PS}^{\infty} f(i, t_0)[i(t)PS - \bar{B}]di(t) \tag{5}$$

where the expression involving the integral represents the value of the option of having a call on the common stock of the company.

Moreover, as already explained, the value of the convertible will be equal to the greater of the values of the two expressions given on the right-hand side of Eqs. (4) and (5), that is

$$C = max \ (C_s, C_b) \tag{6}$$

Our final relationships Eqs. (4), (5) and (6) can now be used to evaluate a convertible security in terms of the expected performance of the values of the bond and stock equivalents.[1]

It should be noted that the behavior of our model is in agreement with the observation that the difference between the value of the convertible and the value of the equivalent stocks, $C - PS$ [given by V in Eq. (3)], will tend to disappear when stock prices increase. Since the date t_0 is the date at which our convertible is being evaluated, the price of the stock $P(t_0) = P$ will vary with the date chosen for evaluation. Suppose that the stock price P is high at t_0; then, other things being equal, the upper limit of integration, $i(t) = \bar{B}/PS$ will be low; thus the probability of an $i(t)$ less than this value will be very small. Moreover, if we choose evaluation dates involving higher and higher values of P the upper limit of integration will approach zero and, therefore, V will also approach zero. Hence the difference between C and PS will approach zero, i.e., the premium over stock value will disappear.

III. STATISTICAL IMPLEMENTATION OF THE MODEL

The basic problem in applying the model statistically was the derivation of a distribution of price relatives for stock prices. As a preliminary step we may assume that investors form a subjective probability distribution of future stock prices wholly on the basis of the past behavior of stock

---

[1] It has been argued that certain economic quantities such as speculative prices have the Pareto distribution which, for appropriate values of its parameters, does not even possess a finite first moment. See B. Mandelbrot, "The Variation of Certain Speculative Prices," *Journal of Business*, Vol. XXXVI (October, 1963), pp. 394–419. If that were the case any approach based on expected values would be invalid. The evidence, however, that stock prices have a Pareto distribution with Pareto α less than unity is inconclusive, at least so far.

prices. Specifically, assuming that the bond values remain (relatively) fixed, we may proceed by choosing an earlier date, t_b, and fitting an empirical distribution of price relatives $f(i, t_b)$ which can then be substituted into our relationships.

The choice of the base date, t_b, will affect the resulting empirical distribution in two major ways: (1) through factors peculiar to the security under consideration; and (2) through factors relevant to the entire market. On the assumption that the past distribution of stock prices offers an indication of what may be expected in the future, we may use historical distributions except insofar as the sequence of price relatives contains strong cyclical elements. It was our hope that the period of seven years prior to the date of valuation from which we derived empirical distributions was long enough to wash out the effect of cycles.[2] The price relatives would then reflect only the general trend of the market and factors peculiar to the security in question, both of which are relevant for purposes of extrapolation.

We further assume that investors anticipate selling their convertible securities at the end of a fixed horizon period. Specifically, we posit that these investors are concerned only with making predictions for a period two or three years from now and that their subjective probability distribution of price relatives is based on an empirical distribution of relative prices over intervals two and three years apart. Our incorporation of a fixed horizon into the model naturally leads to a floating base date for the purposes of calculating the price relatives. Monthly closing prices for seven years were taken for each security and price relatives were derived by taking each price and dividing it by the price at some specified earlier time. In accordance with our specific assumption concerning investors' horizon periods, two approaches were used:

$$i(t) = \frac{P_t}{P_{t-24}} \tag{a}$$

and

$$i(t) = \frac{P_t}{P_{t-36}} \tag{b}$$

where t measures time in months. Arbitrarily, the observations were then grouped into seven or six intervals respectively, depending on whether (a) or (b) was used. The frequency of observations in each interval was used to estimate the required probabilities. Equations (4) and (5) were

---

[2] If, for example, the period over which we calculate price relatives encompassed one half of a cycle and began at the cyclical trough, obviously all the calculated i values would tend to be high.

then applied in straightforward manner, except as indicated:

(a) Since we do not have continuous probability distributions, summations appear in the formulas actually used instead of integrals.

(b) The estimated probabilities corresponding to each interval on the $i(t)$ axis were multiplied by the *midpoint* of that interval.

(c) The value $\bar{B}$ used in the formulas was the most recent value of B.

(d) The value P used in the formulas was the most recent value of P.

(e) Whenever the quantity $\bar{B}/PS$ falls within an interval on the $i(t)$ scale (rather than on the boundary of such an interval) the associated frequency of observations in it are deemed to have been divided in the same proportion as the interval itself, with the left-hand part of this divided interval contributing to Eq. (4) and the right-hand part to Eq. (5).

Seven bonds were chosen to test the model. The criteria used in selecting the bonds were that: (1) the bonds be of homogeneous (medium) quality as evidenced by the appraisal of professional rating agencies; (2) they be convertible at a fixed price for a period of at least seven years; (3) the quantity of bonds outstanding be sufficiently large to insure that the quotations for the bonds are good estimates of true market prices; and (4) the common stock of the issuing company have been traded publicly for at least seven years to permit the calculation of a distribution of price relatives over a long period. Table I below presents the market prices predicted by the valuation model on the basis of two- and three-year horizons. They are compared with actual market prices as of mid-1962, the date for which the calculation was made.

TABLE 1

Issue	Actual Market Price* 6/18/62	Rank	Predicted Market Price* (2-yr. Horizon)	Rank	Predicted Market Price* (3-yr. Horizon)	Rank
Homestake Mining	$136\frac{3}{4}$	1	$160\frac{7}{8}$	1	$167\frac{3}{8}$	2
Northrop Aircraft	$120\frac{1}{4}$	2	$150\frac{1}{4}$	2	$176\frac{1}{8}$	1
Burroughs	115	3	$101\frac{5}{8}$	4	$102\frac{3}{8}$	3
Smith Corona Marchant	108	4	$93\frac{5}{8}$	5	$94\frac{5}{8}$	5
Rohr Aircraft	106	5	$103\frac{5}{8}$	3	$101\frac{1}{2}$	4
Allegheny Ludlum	$99\frac{1}{4}$	6	$90\frac{3}{4}$	7	$89\frac{1}{4}$	7
Food Fair	$98\frac{7}{8}$	7	$92\frac{1}{8}$	6	$90\frac{1}{8}$	6

* All market prices expressed as a percent of par value.

Needless to say, the version of the model tested is only a very crude and overly simplified representation of the basic apparatus. We shall indicate in the next section some of the more glaring deficiencies and how they may be rectified. Nevertheless, the results are, in some respects, fairly encouraging. The model has at least been able to do a reasonably good job of ranking the issues. The rank correlation coefficients turn out to be .86 for the two-year horizon and .89 for the three-year horizon. We notice that, for the higher-priced issues, our normative valuations tend to be higher than actual market prices, whereas for the lower-priced issues our valuations tend systematically to understate market prices. We shall note below how our computational shortcuts have contributed to such a result.

IV. ALTERING THE ASSUMPTIONS

We turn now to an examination of the more important assumptions implicit and explicit in the model. We shall indicate as we proceed what modifications seem necessary to our first approximation and the direction in which they will tend to alter our results.

A. Utilizing expected rather than current stock prices

In Eq. (2) we suggested that the convertible should be worth at least as much as the (current) stock equivalent plus the insurance value V of the security's bond value which sets a floor under an investor's possible losses. An alternative formulation utilizing the expected value of the stock equivalent at the end of the horizon period would appear at least equally plausible. In this formulation the current price of the convertible is determined by its expected future stock value plus the actuarial insurance value of having the option of disposing of the security at its bond value rather than its stock value, should the latter fall below the former. Such a formulation has an important computational advantage inasmuch as Eqs. (4) and (5) then become identical.[3] Thus Eq. (5) alone can be used to determine the value of a convertible.

[3] Proof: Substituting the expected value of PS for PS in the right-hand side of Eq. (4) we have

$$C_s = \int_0^\infty i(t)PSf(i, t_0)di(t) + \int_0^{\bar{B}/PS} f(i, t_0)[\bar{B} - i(t)PS]di(t) \tag{4a}$$

or, rearranging terms,

$$C_s = \int_{\bar{B}/PS}^\infty i(t)PSf(i, t_0)di(t) + \bar{B}\int_0^{\bar{B}/PS} f(i, t_0)di(t)$$

But, rewriting the right-hand side of Eq. (5), we have

$$C_b = \int_{\bar{B}/PS}^\infty i(t)PSf(i, t_0)di(t) + \bar{B}\int_0^{\bar{B}/PS} f(i, t_0)di(t) \tag{5a}$$

which is identical to Eq. (4a).

There is one difficulty with this alternative formulation, however, which must be dealt with. We have no assurance that the calculated convertible value will exceed the *current* stock equivalent value PS. Such a possibility must be ruled out since, if any differential existed, an arbitrageur could always make the convertible equal its stock equivalent by simultaneously buying the convertible and selling short S shares of common. The arbitrageur would then convert his bond into common and deliver these shares to cover his short contract. Consequently, the alternative formulation of the model must become

$$C = max \ (C_b, PS) \tag{7}$$

Utilizing the alternative formulation for the seven bonds in Table I we find only slight differences in calculated market prices and insignificant differences in rankings.

B. Modifications for interest payments and appropriate discounting

Recall that in the basic model we neglected the interest payments received by the bondholder. Moreover, we did not discount our final convertible value to present worth despite the fact that the value was found by calculating the actuarial value of the security two and three years hence. To remedy matters we may write instead of Eq. (7)

$$C \geq \frac{R}{\left(1 + \dfrac{\rho}{2}\right)} + \frac{R}{\left(1 + \dfrac{\rho}{2}\right)^2} + \cdots + \frac{R}{\left(1 + \dfrac{\rho}{2}\right)^{2N}} + \frac{C_b}{\left(1 + \dfrac{\rho}{2}\right)^{2N}} \tag{8}$$

and $C \geq PS$, where R represents the periodic coupon payment of the bond (made semi-annually), ρ is the appropriate (annual) discount rate, N is the number of years in the investor's horizon, and C_b represents the actuarial value of the security at the end of the horizon period. Summing the geometric progression we have

$$C \geq \frac{2R}{\rho} \left[1 - \frac{1}{\left(1 + \dfrac{\rho}{2}\right)^{2N}} \right] + \frac{C_b}{\left(1 + \dfrac{\rho}{2}\right)^{2N}} \tag{9}$$

An obvious choice of an appropriate discount rate presents itself in at least two cases. When the convertible sells at zero premium over its bond value (i.e., the expected value of the call privilege on the common stock is nil), the appropriate discount rate is clearly the yield of the bond itself (the capitalization rate for a debt stream of that risk class). If, on the other hand, the convertible sells at a zero premium over its stock equivalent, it would appear that for a good approximation we could employ the discount rate applicable to an equity in that risk class. Presumably for a convertible selling at a premium above both its stock and bond values we would be justified in interpolating between the two discount rates in proportion to the magnitudes of these premiums.

The employment of a discounting technique such as that just described would have brought our convertible value estimates closer to those actually observed as existing market prices. In particular, discounting tends to reduce our calculated valuations of convertibles selling at relatively high prices while leaving low-priced convertibles unaffected. This is so because high-priced convertibles tend to have a low current yield (annual coupon payment divided by market price) relative to the appropriate discount rate. Thus the addition of interest payments and discounting tends to reduce the value of the convertible. For low-priced convertibles the two factors tend nearly to cancel out.[4] To illustrate the effect of discounting we have calculated the discounted present worth for Homestake Mining on the basis of a three-year horizon. The discounted present worth of the stream of interest payments plus the present worth of the calculated convertible price ($167\frac{3}{8}$) is found to be $156\frac{5}{8}$. The discount rate employed was the bond-value yield obtained from the rating services. Were an appropriately higher rate used (i.e., the interpolated stock-bond rate suggested by the argument above) the present worth would have been even lower.

C. Altering the horizon period

In the statistical test of the model we assumed that investors would hold the convertible bond for a period of exactly two or three years. Such a procedure is arbitrary and lacks any theoretical justification. This is so because the price was calculated on the basis of probabilities assigned to a series of possible stock values without allowing for the possibility of any premiums over these values. But is it not reasonable to suppose that two years hence a convertible whose conversion feature has not expired may still command a premium over the value of otherwise equivalent bonds and stocks? Our fixed-horizon method ignores the fact that the market may take into account the probable longer-run behavior of the stock.

This difficulty is easily remedied in theory by extending the horizon period until the conversion feature expires. In this case the bond will be converted into common stock if $P(t)S > B$ and will remain outstanding as a straight debt instrument if $B > P(t)S$. We might then say that the convertible is worth the maximum value over every horizon period from the date of valuation up to the date of the expiration of the conversion

---

[4] When the convertible sells at its bond value, the two factors would exactly cancel by definition.

privilege. It would be possible that some convertibles attain a maximum value when valued on the basis of a short horizon period. This would be the case, for example, if the stock price were expected to rise in the near future (and the convertible would be expected to rise to its stock value) but where the long-term trend was unfavorable. On the other hand, if the long-term trend of the stock price was favorable, presumably the convertible would attain its maximum value when the horizon was extended until the expiration of the option privilege.

D. The nature of the subjective probability distribution of stock prices

We suggested earlier a simple method by which investors' subjective probability distributions of future stock prices could be quantified. We hypothesized that investors formed expectations of future price changes as if they believed that past distributions could be extrapolated into the future directly. Thus, if the common stock in question had enjoyed a rising trend over the period during which the index values were calculated, we assumed that investors would, in effect, project this trend into the future. It was this assumption that contributed to the high valuations obtained for Homestake Mining and Northrop Aircraft, since the common stocks of both companies rose sharply over the period used in calculating the price relatives.

This assumption leaves much to be desired as a theoretical basis for equity valuation. Surely, if investors actually expected a continuation of rising earnings and dividends for the equity in question, such expectations would be reflected in the current price of the issue. If any sense is to be made of the structure of equity prices existing at any moment in time, it must be assumed that such diverse expectations for the prospects of different companies are already incorporated in present market prices. A stock-valuation model accounting for such expectations has been developed by one of us.[5] In that model, all equities of the same risk class are assumed to sell at prices that equalize their net yields. The net yield (discount rate) turns out to be the sum of the dividend yield of the security and the anticipated growth rate of the shares. For standard industrial securities as a group it was asserted that a good empirical approximation to the appropriate discount rate can be obtained by adding the dividend rate of the standard market averages to the long-term growth rate of earnings. Thus, at any moment of time we could calculate an "apparent marginal efficiency" for equities in general. If we assume that the seven sample companies belong (roughly) to the same risk class as the representative

[5] Burton G. Malkiel, "Equity Yields, Growth, and the Structure of Share Prices," *American Economic Review*, Vol. LIII (December, 1963), 1004–31.

standard share, we can actually calculate the expected growth rate of the shares over the horizon period. This will equal the total apparent marginal efficiency less the dividend yield on the shares.[6]

This line of argument leads to an interesting conclusion. It asserts that if a company pays no dividend, it can be assumed that the market expects the growth rate of the price of the shares to equal the appropriate discount rate. On the other hand, if the shares are expected to provide a dividend yield equal to the discount rate, then no growth in the price of the shares is expected.

Given the discount rate and the dividend yield, we can always determine the expected growth rate of the price of the shares. Consequently, the valuation model gives an alternative method of projecting the expected value of the shares into the future. It appears that if our techniques were modified to account for this extra information, our predicted market prices would be closer to the prevailing prices. In particular, we note that our largest underestimation of the market worth of the convertible occurred in the case of Smith Corona Marchant. Our low estimate of the issue's investment value resulted from the downward trend of the stock price over the period used in constructing the price relatives. Had we taken into account the observation that, at the time of our valuation, investors apparently expected a rising trend in the price of the common (the dividend yield on the shares was zero) our calculated valuation would have been raised. On the other hand, the dividend yield on Northrop Aircraft and Homestake Mining (where we overestimated the convertible's value) tended to be relatively high, suggesting that investors anticipated a slower growth rate in the price of the shares (according to the model). In this case the appropriate adjustment would have been to reduce our calculated valuations. Thus we conjecture that an adjustment of our probability distribution of future stock prices, in the manner required by the stock valuation model just discussed, would have tended to improve our results.

This suggests a method of procedure to guide us in further work in the valuation of convertibles. We could attempt to project the mean of the subjective probability distribution of common stock prices on the basis of the equity valuation model referred to above. To determine the variance of the distribution, we could simply extrapolate this information from our record of price relatives over a period in the past. Thus we would be arguing that the past behavior of the common stock indicates its future prospects only with respect to the volatility of the shares, not their expected value.

[6] *Ibid.*, p. 1014 n.

V. SUMMARY COMMENT

Our analytic model for the valuation of convertible securities seems to promise to be serviceable in two respects. It may help us to understand the logic of the security valuation process, and it may enable us to offer some reasonable predictions of security prices. This may be particularly useful to firms involved in the flotation of new issues who must set prices on these issues before they have been evaluated by the market. We, at least, were somewhat surprised by the relative success of the predictions undertaken with the aid of our crude model. The fact that the most obvious and apparently most appropriate modifications of the model all increase its success as a predictor is perhaps even more encouraging.

*James C. Van Horne**

35. Warrant Valuation in Relation to Volatility and Opportunity Cost

Reprinted from the **Industrial Management Review**, Vol. 10, No. 3 (Spring, 1969), pp. 19–32, by permission of the author and publisher. Copyright 1969 by the Industrial Management Review Association.

INTRODUCTION

The purpose of this study is to investigate the valuation of warrants from both theoretical and empirical standpoints. In particular, we explore the relationship between the market price of a warrant and the value of funds to investors, as well as the relationship between warrant prices and the volatility of the common stock. The former represents an opportunity cost, inasmuch as investors must pay more to invest in the associated common stock than they pay to invest in the warrant. We hypothesize that the greater the value of funds to investors, the greater their incentive to invest in warrants relative to the common. Heretofore, this factor has not been investigated in the literature.

In addition to studying the impact of these variables on warrant prices, we analyze the effect of the market price of the associated common stock, the length of time to expiration of the warrant, and the dividend paid on the common. The factors above were tested using cross-sectional and time-series data; and the results were found to be consistent with warrants varying positively with the amount of recent dispersion in common-stock prices as well as with the value of funds to investors. As expected, warrant prices were found to be influenced most strongly by the market price of the stock. Other hypothesized relationships were also supported.

VALUATION OF WARRANTS

It commonly is acknowledged that the market price of a warrant is related primarily to the price of its associated common stock. The value of a

* Associate Professor of Finance, Stanford University.

warrant to an individual investor can be thought of as the expected value of all possible outcomes, discounted by the investor's required rate of return.[1] If the investor intends to hold the warrant until a specific future date, its value P_w might be expressed as

$$P_w = \int_\alpha^\infty (x - \alpha)e^{-kt}f(x)dx \qquad (1)$$

where the x represent possible market prices of the stock expected to prevail at the future date, $f(x)$ is the subjective probability distribution of possible future prices, α is the option price, or exercise price, of the warrant, and k is the investor's required rate of return.

Before proceeding, we first must clarify the meaning of the exercise price α. By way of definition, a warrant is an option to purchase a specified number of shares of common stock of a company at a stated price. For example, TWA warrants are exercisable at $22 a share, meaning that the warrant holder can purchase one share of TWA common stock for $22. Thus, $\alpha = \$22$. In the case of Braniff Airways, however, the warrant holder is entitled to purchase three shares of common stock at a total of $73 for each warrant held. For consistency in comparison, x in Eq. (1) for Braniff should not be expressed as the market price per share of common, but rather as the market price per share multiplied by three. This gives us the market price of the stock associated with a warrant having an exercise price, α, of $73. It is necessary, then, to express the market price per share of the stock and the option price of the warrant in terms of equivalent units.

When we remove the assumption in Eq. (1) of price expectations only for a specific future date, the problem of valuation is complicated considerably. The investor now is able to hold the warrant for any length of time up to the warrant's expiration. Not only do we have the familiar wine-aging problem, but also one of estimating possible stock prices in a number of future periods.[2] Rather than become embroiled in this issue, we will proceed directly to the problem at hand by examining the relationship between the current market price of a warrant and that of its associated stock. If transaction costs are ignored, Samuelson has shown that arbitrage conditions assure that a warrant will sell for no less than its theoretical value and no more than the market value of the associated common stock.[3] The theoretical value of a warrant is simply

$$T_w = x - \alpha \qquad (2)$$

[1] This formulation traces back to Bachelier [1], around 1900, and to the recent work (1961) of Sprenkle [8].
[2] See Poensgen [5].
[3] Samuelson [6], pp. 18–19.

where, as before, x is the market price per share of common, multiplied by the number of shares into which the warrant is exercisable, and α is the warrant's exercise price. Many warrants sell at market prices above their theoretical values. One of the reasons for this occurrence is the dispersion in the probability distribution of possible stock prices.

It has been demonstrated by Sprenkle, Kassouf, and others that the value of a warrant depends upon not only the expected value of possible market prices of the stock but also the dispersion and shape of the probability distribution.[4] To illustrate, suppose an investor were considering a warrant which permitted the purchase of one share of common at $20 a share. Suppose further that he expected the market price per share of common one period hence to be the following

Probability	Price
.20	$ 5
.30	15
.30	25
.20	35

The expected value, or mean, of the probability distribution of possible stock prices one period hence is $20. This price suggests a theoretical value of the warrant of zero. However, because a warrant cannot sell at a negative price, its expected value of theoretical value one period hence is not zero but

$$.20(0) + .30(0) + .30(25 - 20) + .20(35 - 20) = \$4.50 \qquad (3)$$

Thus, the expected value of a warrant increases with the dispersion of the probability distribution above the exercise price. The greater the variance in market price for the stock, the greater the expected value of the warrant, all other things the same.

The value of a warrant also depends upon the length of time to its expiration. For a warrant with a very short time to expiration, arbitrage ensures that the actual market price of the warrant will approximate closely its theoretical value. Samuelson shows that the rational price of a warrant with t periods to expiration is at least as great as, if not greater than, a similar one with $t - 1$ periods to expiration. At the extreme end of the time horizon, he suggests that ownership of a common stock is equivalent to holding a perpetual warrant to buy the stock.[5] Therefore, a warrant cannot sell for more than the price of its associated common.

The fact that a warrant cannot sell at a price below its theoretical value and a price greater than the price of its associated common defines

---

[4] Sprenkle [8], pp. 424–25; and Kassouf [4].
[5] Samuelson [6], p. 18.

the boundaries for its valuation. These boundaries are shown in Figure 1.[6] One line represents the theoretical value of the warrant, which is zero until the exercise price, increasing thereafter. The other line represents a one-to-one relationship of the associated common price with the warrant price.

FIGURE 1

BOUNDARIES OF WARRANT VALUATION

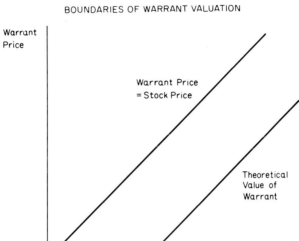

The functional relationship between a warrant and its associated stock is considered by all to be convex.[7] Figure 2 illustrates such a relationship for various periods of time to expiration of the warrant. When the market price of the stock is high in relation to the exercise price, the market price of the warrant approaches its theoretical value. However, the shape of the curve is influenced by the time to expiration. The shorter the period to expiration, the more convex the relationship, and the more it approaches the theoretical value line. As the expiration date increases, the curve should become flatter and higher. This occurrence also is illustrated in Figure 2. Samuelson demonstrates that, even for a perpetual warrant, the relationship between warrant and stock prices must be con-

[6] We assume an adjusted common stock price that corresponds to the number of shares to which the warrant entitles purchase.

[7] For a review of various methods of warrant valuation as well as an empirical investigation, see Shelton [7].

FIGURE 2

WARRANT VALUATION AS FUNCTION OF EXPIRATION DATE

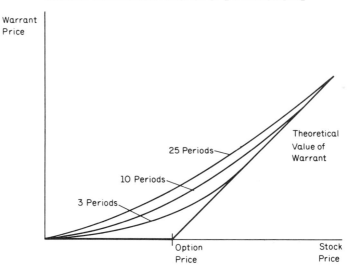

vex, if we assume that the mean expected return from the warrant is greater than that for the stock.[8]

OPPORTUNITY COSTS

We have postulated that the price of a warrant is a function of the price of its associated common stock, the expiration date of the option, and the variance of the probability distribution of possible future stock prices. These variables are considered by most writers to be important in the valuation of warrants. A factor which has been considered only partially is the opportunity cost to the investor of an investment in warrants as opposed to that in the common stock. This factor has two aspects: the value of funds to the investor and the dividend paid on the common stock.

To illustrate the first aspect, consider a stock selling for $40 a share and a warrant to purchase this stock having an exercise price of $20. If the warrant has a market price of $23 and allows the investor to purchase one share of common for each warrant, the differential in price is $17. Our hypothesis is that this differential will vary inversely with the value of funds to investors, all other things the same. If an investor feels that the market place is undervaluing the common stock of a company with warrants outstanding, he has a choice of purchasing either the warrant or

[8] See Samuelson [6], pp. 21–31.

its associated common stock. The greater the value of funds to him, the more likely he is to prefer the warrant to the stock, because the warrant involves a lesser investment. For example, suppose an investor has to borrow the differential in price between the warrant and the stock in order to invest in the stock. When interest rates rise and money becomes tight, leverage through buying warrants would be cheaper in relation to leverage through borrowing to purchase stock. As a result, the investor would be more inclined to invest in the warrant than in the associated common stock. A similar argument can be made when the value of funds to the investor represents an external lending rate.

An increase in the value of funds will therefore exert upward pressure on the price of the warrant relative to that for the stock. As a result, the differential in price between the associated common stock and the warrant would narrow. The opposite would be the case if the value of funds declined; then the differential would widen. If market-determined interest rates are a good proxy for the value of funds to investors, the differential would be expected to vary inversely with interest rates. When interest rates were high, we would expect there to be upward pressure on warrant prices relative to their associated common stock prices, resulting in a narrower differential. When interest rates were low, there would be less incentive to purchase the warrants relative to the stock. As a result, the differential would widen.

The second opportunity cost involved when the investment is in warrants as opposed to the common stock is the dividend foregone on the stock. Because the investor in a warrant does not participate in dividends paid on the common, the greater the dividend on the common, the less attractive the warrant in relation to its associated stock. Thus, the market price of a warrant should vary inversely with the amount of the dividend. This aspect of opportunity costs, unlike the first, has been considered previously in the literature.

EMPIRICAL TESTING

With the inclusion of these opportunity costs, the market price of a warrant can be expressed as a function of the following variables

$$P_w = f(\alpha, x, t, v, i, d) \tag{4}$$

where α is the exercise price, x is the price of the associated common stock, t is the length of time to expiration of the warrant, v is the volatility of the stock price, i is the value of funds to investors, and d is the dividend paid on the common. As discussed, we would expect the following relationships between warrant prices and these factors to hold, all other things the same:

Independent Variable	Relationship with P_w
α	Negative
x	Positive
t	Positive
v	Positive
i	Positive
d	Negative

Two sets of regression studies were undertaken to test these hypothesized relationships. One involved a cross-sectional sample of warrants listed on the American Stock Exchange; the other involved a time-series analysis of the three perpetual warrants—Alleghany Corporation, Atlas Corporation, and Tri-Continental Corporation. The cross-sectional regression study did little more than substantiate the results found by others, with a more recent sample. The second study, however, cast light on the importance of volatility of price and the value of funds to investors.

For comparative purposes, the market prices of both the warrant and the stock were normalized in relation to the exercise price. For the stock, P_s/α_s represents the market price per share over the exercise price for the purchase of one share. If a warrant allowed the purchase of three shares of common stock for a total exercise price of $60, α_s would be $20. For the warrant, P_w/α_w represents the market price of the warrant over the total exercise price associated with the warrant. In the case above, $\alpha_w = \$60$. The normalization of prices, of course, eliminates the exercise price as an explanatory variable.

Beginning with the cross-sectional regression study, the length of time to final expiration is expressed as $1/t$, where t is the number of months to final expiration of the warrant. This formulation, although arbitrary, is based upon the a priori notion of a nonlinear relationship between the length of time to expiration and warrant prices. The difference in value between a warrant with one month to expiration and one with 24 months to expiration is likely to be far more pronounced than that between warrants with 101 and 124 months, respectively. Moreover, the use of $1/t$ allows us to include perpetual warrants in our analysis.[9] For the cross-sectional regression study, a rather crude measure of volatility is employed. It is simply the difference between the high and low market prices per share of common stock in the preceding year over the average price of the common during that year. Finally, the dividend variable is expressed as the ratio of the current indicated dividend per share on the common to the total exercise price necessary to purchase one share, α_s.

[9] Kassouf [4], p. 48, also used $1/t$ as the variable for time expiration.

TABLE 1. REGRESSION RESULTS OF CROSS-SECTIONAL SAMPLE

	Constant Term	Explanatory Variable			
		P_s/α_s	$1/t$	Volatility	Dividend/α_s
Regression Coefficient	− .601	.900	− .941	.184	− .011
Standard Error	.070	.016	.459	.062	.009
T-Ratio	8.56	55.55	2.05	2.95	1.16
$R^2 = .994$					

The sample for the cross-sectional regression study consisted of all warrants listed on the American Stock Exchange in June 1968, with the exception of Hilton Hotels. As that warrant represents an option to purchase several securities in addition to Hilton common, it was not included. The specific warrants, 21 in all, are listed in the Appendix. Closing market prices were collected for the warrant and the common stock for June 14 and June 28. The data were pooled for these two dates, giving 42 observations in total.

While theoretically the relationship between P_w/α_w and P_s/α_s should be convex, tests for linearity showed a linear one to be the best description of the relationship for the specific sample studied.[10] This is not to suggest that the true relationship is linear, but only that, for our limited range of observations, a linear relationship gives the best fit. As our concern is with factors other than the effect of the price of the common on warrant prices, the employment of a linear relationship was deemed appropriate:

$$P_w/\alpha_w = a + b_1(P_s/\alpha_s) + b_2(1/t) + b_3(v) + b_4(Div/\alpha_s) + \mu \qquad (5)$$

where v is the volatility measure, and μ is the error term.

The regression results are shown in Table 1. As expected, by far the most significant explainer of a warrant's price is the price of its associated common stock. It is noteworthy, however, that both the length of time to expiration and the volatility variable are significant and have the right sign. The greater the time to expiration, the lower $1/t$, and the higher P_w/α_w. Similarly, the greater the volatility of stock price, the higher P_w/α_w. The dividend variable is not significant; however, it has the right sign. We hypothesized that the higher the dividend, the greater the relative

[10] Variance analysis employing an F-ratio was used to test for linearity, and several curvilinear functions were fitted. In all cases, a linear relationship was found to result in the highest R^2. The observations were also ordered according to the magnitude of P_s/α_s, and regression Eq. (5) was employed. The Durbin-Watson statistic was sufficiently high so that the hypothesis of a linear relationship could not be rejected. The same tests for linearity were used for the time-series analyses, and identical conclusions were reached.

attraction of the stock and the lower the warrant price, all other things the same.

In general, the results of this cross-sectional regression study support the hypotheses formulated earlier. By and large, they are in agreement with the theoretical and empirical work of others.[11] One factor was missing from our analysis—the value of funds to investors. In order to analyze this factor and volatility in greater depth, we must evaluate the market prices of warrants over time. To study the effect of these factors on warrant prices, perpetual warrants were used.

ANALYSIS OF PERPETUAL WARRANTS

One of the reasons for using perpetual warrants was to hold directly constant the effect of the length of time to expiration. Because the expiration date of a warrant grows shorter and shorter as time unfolds, a warrant's price at the beginning of a sample period cannot be compared objectively with its price at the end. The use of perpetual warrants avoids this problem. Other reasons for their use are the lengthy time span for which existing perpetual warrants have been outstanding and the absence of step-ups in their exercise prices.

Alleghany Corporation, Atlas Corporation, and Tri-Continental Corporation represent the universe of perpetual warrants outstanding which are listed on the American Stock Exchange. The common stocks of all three are listed on the New York Exchange. For each of these warrants and their associated common stocks, end-of-the-month closing prices from January 1961 to December 1967 were collected—84 observations in all.[12] From these data, the ratios P_w/α_w and P_s/α_s were computed. Explanatory variables in addition to P_s/α_s in the regression model include a measure of volatility and the value of funds to investors.

The volatility measure employed is a coefficient of variation, based upon previous stock prices. More specifically,

$$CV = \frac{\sigma}{\bar{P}_s} \tag{6}$$

where $\bar{P}_s$ is the average market price per share of the stock over the previous 18 months, and σ is the standard deviation about that average price. For example, at January 1965, the coefficient of variation would be computed with monthly share-price data from July 1963 to December 1964. Implied in the use of this measure is that the market changes its view of a

---

[11] For empirical testing, see Kassouf [4], and Shelton [7].
[12] Prices for Tri-Continental were adjusted for a stock split that occurred during the sample period.

TABLE 2. AVERAGE OF MONTH-END STOCK PRICES: 1961–67

	Alleghany	Atlas	Tri-Continental*
1961	$11.49	$3.40	$23.03
1962	9.35	2.38	21.27
1963	10.30	2.77	23.11
1964	11.38	2.44	24.05
1965	10.48	2.28	24.86
1966	11.03	3.23	23.00
1967	11.56	4.75	27.24

* Prices adjusted for stock split in December 1965.

stock's volatility over time. The hypothesis to be tested is that the more volatile recent stock prices are, the greater the value of the warrant to investors. The use of the coefficient of variation is based upon the absence of significant trend over time for the three stocks studied. The average prices of the stocks for each of the eight years in the sample period are shown in Table 2. We see that there is little trend involved in any of the three. Only in the case of Atlas Corporation is there a marked shift, and that occurred in the last six months of 1967.

There may be, however, a problem of spurious correlation, for P_w/α_w is a function of the coefficient of variation variable, $\sigma/\bar{P}_s$. As we know, P_w is highly correlated with P_s. If P_s appeared directly in the CV variable, there would be negative correlation between P_w/α_w and CV. While P_s does not appear directly in CV, it may be positively correlated with $\bar{P}_s$, the average market price of the stock over the previous 18 months. However, correlation coefficients for the relationship between $\sigma/\bar{P}_s$ and P_s/α_s were $-.14$, $.71$, and $-.05$ for Alleghany, Atlas, and Tri-Continental, respectively. Thus, the expected negative correlation was slight for Alleghany and Tri-Continental while for Atlas, the correlation was positive. Therefore, spurious correlation would not appear to be a serious problem.

As a proxy for the value of funds to investors, we use the current yield on 180-day Treasury bills. This rate was employed to reflect prevailing yields in the money market. Given the historical perspective of 1959 and 1960, interest rates during most of the sample period did not exceed yields that prevailed earlier. While yields increased more or less steadily from 1961 to 1966, this increase was by and large within the boundaries of previous experience. Only in the latter half of 1966 and of 1967 did yields exceed those prevailing during the latter part of 1959. Most would agree that yields during 1966 and 1967 were high by any previous standard. Thus, the current yield on 180-day Treasury bills may be a reasonably consistent measure of the value of funds to investors over the sample period.

TABLE 3.   REGRESSION RESULTS OF TIME-SERIES
ANALYSIS OF WARRANTS

Warrant	*Constant Term*	Explanatory Variable			*R²*	*DW*
		Pₛ/αₛ	*CV*	*T*		
Alleghany Corporation						
Regression Coefficient	− .363	.794	.260	.026	.945	1.61
Standard Error	(.075)	(.022)	(.222)	(.012)		
T-Ratio	4.84	35.34	1.18	2.17		
Atlas Corporation						
Regression Coefficient	− .138	.526	.325	.0162	.946	1.14
Standard Error	(.013)	(.026)	(.066)	(.0035)		
T-Ratio	10.50	20.61	4.96	4.56		
Tri-Continental						
Regression Coefficient	− .689	.869	.323	.0085	.971	1.09
Standard Error	(.048)	(.019)	(.142)	(.0065)		
T-Ratio	14.43	44.89	2.28	1.29		

As was the case for the cross-sectional sample, tests of linearity revealed that a linear fit was the best description of the relationship between P_w/α_w and P_s/α_s for the three perpetual warrants studied. This occurrence does not suggest that the true relationship over a full range of observations is linear. It is only for the rather limited range of observations that the linear fit is appropriate. With a linear relationship, the regression model becomes:

$$P_w/\alpha_w = a + b_1(P_s/\alpha_s) + b_2(CV) + b_3(T) + u \qquad (7)$$

where CV is the coefficient of variation, T is the yield on 180-day Treasury bills, and u is the error term.

The results of this regression study are shown in Table 3. As before, the price of the associated stock, expressed as P_s/α_s, is highly significant and the chief explainer of the market price of warrants. This, of course, was expected. We see in Table 3, however, that the signs of the other two variables are correct in all cases and significant in the majority of cases. The coefficient of variation is significant for Atlas Corporation and Tri-Continental, but not for Alleghany. The evidence, however, does lend support to the notion that investors value warrants more or less highly depending upon the recent volatility of the stock. The greater this volatility, the greater the value of the warrant; and the less the volatility, the less the value.

For the Treasury-bill variable, the regression coefficients are significant in the case of Alleghany Corporation and Atlas Corporation, but not in the case of Tri-Continental.[13] Overall, the evidence is consistent with the idea that the value of a warrant varies directly with interest rates in the money market. When interest rates are high, funds have greater value to the investor, and he has incentive to invest in the warrant relative to the stock. Contrarily, when the value of funds to investors is low, the incentive to invest in warrants relative to the stock is lower. Thus, the relative incentive for investment in warrants appears to vary directly with the value of funds to investors, as depicted by an external money-market rate.

The last column in Table 3 presents the Durbin-Watson statistic, which is a measure of serial correlation.[14] The figures reported indicate that significant serial correlation exists among the residuals for Atlas Corporation and Tri-Continental Corporation. For Alleghany Corporation, the Durbin-Watson statistic lies in the indeterminate zone between the two limits, d_L and d_U. Therefore the statistic is inconclusive with respect to significant serial correlation. With serial correlation, the least-square estimates of parameters are unbiased but are no longer efficient. The result of this inefficiency is an under-estimation of the sampling variances of the regression coefficients—i.e., the standard errors are too small.[15] If we assume a first-order autoregressive process, we can deal with the problem by transforming the data.[16] We do so by first undertaking a least-squares regression of the residuals:

$$\hat{u}_t = r\hat{u}_{t-1} + e_t \tag{8}$$

where $\hat{u}_t$ is the residual for period t, $\hat{u}_{t-1}$ is the residual for period $t - 1$, e_t is the error term, and r is the coefficient of autocorrelation. Having calculated r, the variables in our regression model are transformed as follows:

$$\left(\frac{P_w}{\alpha_w}\right)_t - r\left(\frac{P_w}{\alpha_w}\right)_{t-1} = a + b_1\left[\left(\frac{P_s}{\alpha_s}\right)_t - r\left(\frac{P_s}{\alpha_s}\right)_{t-1}\right]$$
$$+ b_2[(CV)_t - r(CV)_{t-1}] + b_3[(T)_t - r(T)_{t-1}] + \mu \tag{9}$$

The results, when using the transformed variables for Atlas Corporation and Tri-Continental, are shown in Table 4. The Durbin-Watson statistics in the last column indicate that we cannot reject the hypothesis

[13] Tri-Continental increased its dividend steadily on its common stock over the sample period. To account for this, dummy variables were used to reflect the five different dividend levels. These produced no material change in the results. The coefficient of variation and the Treasury-bill variable continued to have positive signs; only the former was significant. All four dummy variables were positive; three were significant.

[14] See Durbin and Watson [2].

[15] See Johnston [3], Chapter 7.

[16] Johnston [3], p. 194.

TABLE 4.   REGRESSION RESULTS OF TIME-SERIES
ANALYSIS USING TRANSFORMED DATA

Warrant	Constant Term	Explanatory Variable			R^2	DW
		P_s/α_s	CV	T		
Atlas Corporation						
Regression Coefficient	−.076	.510	.342	.0159	.898	1.99
Standard Error	(.012)	(.034)	(.095)	(.0056)		
T-Ratio	6.59	15.05	3.60	2.83		
Tri-Continental						
Regression Coefficient	−.368	.855	.370	.0120	.945	2.04
Standard Error	(.037)	(.026)	(.217)	.0098		
T-Ratio	9.83	32.79	1.70	1.23		

of independence of the errors. The first-order autocorrelation has been removed. As expected in such a transformation, the degree of explanatory power of the model, as indicated by the R^2's, declines for each of the two cases. However, the R^2's still are very high.

All of the regression coefficients continue to have the right sign, but in almost all cases the degree of significance is lower. As expected, the normalized market price of the stock remains highly significant. For the coefficient of variation, the regression coefficient is significant at the 5 percent level for Atlas and at the 10 percent level for Tri-Continental. For the Treasury-bill variable, the regression coefficient again is significant at the 5 percent level for Atlas. As before, it is not significant for Tri-Continental. Obviously, the transformed data do not allow us to make as strong a generalization as before. Nevertheless, the evidence does give indication of the hypothesized relationships—those of warrant prices varying positively with both the volatility of recent stock prices and the value of funds to investors.

CONCLUSIONS

The results of this study suggest that market prices of warrants are influenced by several factors in addition to the price of the associated common stock. The latter, however, still is the principal determinant of warrant prices. Cross-sectional regression studies showed warrant prices to vary positively with the length of time to expiration of the option and negatively with the dividend paid on the common. These relationships were in keeping with those hypothesized and with the empirical findings of others.

Of particular importance was the insight gained into the relationship between warrant prices and the value of funds to investors. Empirical evidence, using perpetual warrants, tended to support the idea that the market price of a warrant varies directly with the value of funds. The higher the interest rates in the money market (our proxy for the value of funds to investors), the greater the opportunity cost for investment in the stock as opposed to the warrant. Therefore, the greater the relative incentive to invest in the warrant and the higher the price of the warrant in relation to that of the common stock. In addition, the evidence was consistent with a positive relationship between warrant prices and the volatility of the stock. Investors appear to value a warrant more highly, the more volatile the recent price behavior of the stock.

APPENDIX

List of Warrants in Cross-Sectional Sample

Alleghany Corporation	Ling Tempco Vought
Alleghany Airlines	Martin Marietta
Atlas Corporation	McCrory Corporation
Braniff Airways	National General
First National Realty and Construction	Realty Equities
Frontier Airlines	Textron
General Acceptance	Trans World Airlines
Gulf and Western Industries	Tri-Continental
Indian Head Incorporated	United Industries
Jefferson Lake Petroleum	Uris Building
Lerner Stores	

REFERENCES

[1] Bachelier, L. "Theory of Speculation." Reprinted in: P. H. Cootner (ed.), *The Random Character of Stock Market Prices* (Cambridge, Mass., MIT Press, 1964), pp. 17–78.

[2] Durbin, J., and G. S. Watson. "Testing for Serial Correlation in Least Squares Regression, I and II," *Biometrika*, Vols. 37 and 38 (1950 and 1951), pp. 409–28 and 159–78.

[3] Johnston, J. *Econometric Methods* (New York, N. Y.: McGraw-Hill, 1963).

[4] Kassouf, S. T. "A Theory and an Econometric Model for Common Stock Purchase Warrants," unpublished Ph.D. dissertation (Columbia University, 1965).

[5] Poensgen, O. H. "The Valuation of Convertible Bonds," *Industrial Management Review*, Vol. 7, No. 1 (Fall 1965), pp. 77–92.

[6] Samuelson, P. A. "Rational Theory of Warrant Pricing," *Industrial Management Review*, Vol. 6, No. 2 (Spring, 1965), pp. 13–31.

[7] Shelton, J. P. "The Relation of the Price of a Warrant to the Price of its Associated Stock," *Financial Analysts Journal*, Vol. 23, Nos. 3 and 4 (May–June and July–August 1967), pp. 143–51 and 88–99.

[8] Sprenkle, C. M. "Warrant Prices as Indicators of Expectations and Preferences." Reprinted in: P. H. Cootner (ed.), *The Random Character of Stock Market Prices* (Cambridge, Mass., MIT Press, 1964), pp. 412–74.

*Charles C. Holt**
John P. Shelton[†]

36. The Implications of the Capital Gains Tax for Investment Decisions[1]

Reprinted from **The Journal of Finance,** Vol. XVI, No. 4 (December, 1961), pp. 559–580, by permission of the publisher.

The major purpose of this paper is to provide investors with a basis for considering the question: To what extent, if any, should the investor be "locked in" because of the capital gains tax? In an effort to communicate the ideas in this paper as clearly as possible, the following dialogue between an investor, age 50, and one of the authors is offered as a prologue.

Investor: "Sure, I think the market is high now and my stocks are priced at a level which is rather hard to justify in view of their prospective earnings or dividends. But I hate to sell them when it means I'm going to lose 15 percent of their value in capital gains tax. I don't see why I should do that unless I expect the market to drop 15 percent."

Author: "Are you willing at this time to commit yourself to hold your present stocks for the rest of your life?"

Investor: "I don't know exactly how long I'll hold them, nor how long I'll live, but probably I won't keep the present holdings for the rest of my life. At least I prefer to keep my investment decisions fairly flexible."

Author: "Then you probably aren't avoiding the capital gains tax by refusing to sell now, you are only postponing it, and the extra annual return you get from postponing the capital gains tax is probably about one and eight-tenths of 1 percent (15 percent $\times$ 12 percent). Isn't it likely that your stocks could fall eonugh in value in the next year to more than offset the benefit of postponing the tax?"

Investor: "Well, that's true if I intended to sell by next year anyway,

* Professor of Economics, University of Wisconsin.
† Professor of Finance, University of California, Los Angeles.
[1] The authors wish to take this opportunity to acknowledge the receipt of financial support from the Carnegie Institute of Technology, where Professor Holt formerly taught, and the Western Management Science Institute.

but what if I hold for a longer period? Or what if I should die unexpectedly while I am holding my stocks and avoid the capital gains tax altogether?"

Author: "Your questions begin to introduce some of the aspects which make the problem complicated. First, let's begin by saying that the best way to consider any investment decision, whether capital gains tax is involved or not, is by comparing the expected future rate of return from one investment against an alternative. If, to simplify matters, we assume that the risk element is the same in each choice, then we can compare the alternatives simply by comparing their expected annual yields. This means that if you ignore, as a first approximation, the possibility of escaping the capital gains tax by death, then the length of time you will hold the security is unimportant except as an element in converting your total expected future return into an annual rate of return. How long you expect to hold the security becomes important only as it increases your probability of dying and thus avoiding the tax altogether. And actually it develops that there are compensating factors that make it not very critical to estimate accurately how long you will hold your present security."

Investor: "Well, how should I evaluate the effect of the capital gains tax on my decisions to sell, hold, or switch? Should I just ignore it completely, or what?"

Author: "No, the capital gains tax shouldn't be completely ignored. Its impact differs, depending on three or four elements, but for many investors it is slight, so slight that it may well be subsidiary to other factors in the decision. Let me state the case in its simplest form. Assume as a first approximation that there is no possibility of death occurring and thus eliminating the tax; then the proportion of your investment that would go to pay the tax can be looked on as an interest-free loan from the government and the annual benefit of staying locked in is merely the rate of return you get on that loan. The problem gets more complicated when you consider the fact that every investor has some probability of dying each year and that probability increases with age. How an investor should consider this possibility of avoiding the tax altogether is too complex to explain fully in a brief sentence, but one way of handling the problem is to consider that any alternative security must return enough more to compensate, on the average, for the probability of having incurred the capital gains tax needlessly."

Investor: "Do you think it is possible to calculate with any precision how an investor should adjust for the capital gains tax?"

Author: "If an investor will take the trouble to read and understand the following analysis he can gain at least two things from it. In the first place he will have acquired a useful way of thinking about the impact of the capital gains tax. He will be able to focus on the important variables: the investor's age, the size of the capital gains tax bite, and the prospective return from the alternative securities. Second, if he wishes to be more precise, he can study how to use the tables in this article and can determine for each case how much extra yield he must expect from an alternative investment in order to overcome the disadvantage of incurring the capital gains tax."

I. INTRODUCTION

With the Dow-Jones Industrials close to 700, as of this writing, with price/earnings ratios averaging approximately 20, and with the dividend yields on common stocks continuing for the third consecutive year to be lower than the yields of AAA bonds, many investors must be considering the advisability of shifting from securities they now own, which may seem to have generously discounted future earnings, into bonds or other less price-inflated stocks. However, some investors will be concerned with incurring the capital gains tax. The purpose of this article is to consider the question: Should the capital gains tax influence investor decisions and, if so, to what extent?

Since this article is intended to help investors evaluate the impact of the capital gains tax on their investment decisions, it will make the treatment complete if some of the major regulations of the capital gains tax and the more obvious implications are briefly mentioned at the outset. [Some important changes have been made in the Internal Revenue Code since the material below was written—Ed.]

If an individual holds an asset (not connected with business inventory) for more than six months, then sells it at a profit, capital gains income is incurred, which is generally taxed at a favorable rate. In most cases a tax saving is effected by postponement of sale until the 6-month period is past. Loss from sale of assets is first offset against any gains. Any loss not thus offset may be subtracted from ordinary income up to $1000 in the year during which the loss was incurred. If a portion of the loss is still unused, it may be charged against capital gains for the next five years or, if that does not absorb the loss, charged against ordinary income up to $1000 for each of the five years. In general, the excess of capital gains over losses is taxed at a 25 percent rate, unless the taxpayer would prefer to apply his regular tax rate to only 50 percent of the gain. This latter, treat-the-gain-as-only-half-taxable, treatment is generally favorable if taxable income on a joint return is less than $32,000. Because losses in excess of $6000 may not gain any tax benefit, it is often wise to take capital gains within five years of incurring large losses. Because losses under $6000 are chargeable against current income, it may not be advisable from a tax viewpoint to offset losses of this smaller magnitude with gains.

If an investor has decided to sell a security near the end of the calendar year, he would be wise, if the asset is selling for less than he paid for it, to establish his loss during the current calendar year and get the tax benefit almost immediately. The converse of the rule that the end of the year is a good time to establish tax losses is that the beginning of a calendar year is the best time to take capital gains, since this postpones the tax payment for one year. If an investor wishes to record a capital loss but not permanently withdraw as a stockholder of the company, he may repurchase the same securities after 30 days from the date of sale. If he chooses to invest in similar securities of comparable firms, he can make such a switch at the same time that he establishes his capital loss. If an investor who owned securities more than six months believes that his stock is quite likely to fall in price before the end of the calendar year, but he wishes to defer the capital gains liability until the following year, he can protect himself by selling short an amount of shares equal to those he holds and thus freeze his profit. This is referred to as "selling against the box." After the end of the year he can cover his short sale by delivering his original shares. The gain is reported when the short position is closed out by delivery of shares to cover it.

One final aspect of the capital gains regulations is important to mention. The capital gains tax liability is eliminated if the investor dies: the asset becomes part of the estate, taken at market value at the time of death. Likewise, no tax is incurred if an asset is donated to a legally recognized charitable organization or school. But the taxpayer is given credit, within the limitation for charitable donations, for the full market value of the asset contributed. Thus investors owning assets with substantial unrealized appreciation may get full value for them as a deduction for charitable purposes and avoid the capital gains tax.

The foregoing is background for analyzing more deeply the "lock-in" implications of this tax for investors.

II. AUTHORITIES DIFFER ON INFLUENCE OF CAPITAL GAINS TAX

An important choice faces the investor who has an asset that has risen in price since he purchased it and is wondering whether to switch to a more promising asset. If he does so, he will incur a capital gains tax, and this may make him reluctant to sell. Should he ignore the tax effects of the decision to change assets, or should he give it considerable weight and, as the saying goes, "be locked into the asset because of the capital gains tax"?

The answer to this question as supplied by professionals in the investment market has been diverse. For example, Standard and Poor's in their publication, the *Outlook*, once said:

> Standard and Poor's organization is one of the largest, if not the largest, in the investment advisory field. . . . Through continuous per-

sonal contact with clients we know beyond question why they are so reluctant to take profits; and, therefore, what the principal reason is for imbalance in the stock market as between supply and demand.

It is the restrictive influence of the capital gains tax. Emphasizing its effect, we estimate that of the funds directly under our supervision, somewhere between 70 percent and 80 percent could not be dislodged from stocks even were we to advise profit-taking sales.

The age of wealthy investors ranges principally from 50 to 75 years. Selling advices to such clients must give full consideration to the tax factor. The combination of a current 25 percent capital gains tax liability and an ultimate estate tax liability is too great a penalty on profit taking, as viewed by most well-to-do investors.

We know from first hand experience that there are many hundreds of investment accounts under our supervision in which a shift of funds from stocks to tax-exempt bonds would be justifiable ... were it not for the deterrent of capital gains tax liability. ... we find that often it would take five to ten years of tax-free income on a 2.5 percent to 3.0 percent basis to make up for the capital gains tax that would be incurred by sale of stocks.[2]

A similar view was advanced in 1955 by the publishers of *Value Line,* an investment advisory service:

[Some investors] now have enormous paper profits over their book costs. To sell now would be to invite the government to confiscate 15 percent to 20 percent of their capital. ...

... many hardheaded investors find that they would come off just about as well today sitting tight even if the stock market should drop 35 percent ... as they would by selling and buying back ... very few get out within 5 percent of the top or get in within 5 percent of the bottom. Therefore, even a 35 percent crack might not be worth trying to avoid.

They state further:

The objection to converting from stocks to cash or bonds or even preferreds, of course, is the capital gains tax. Once a sale is made at a profit, 25 percent of the profit must be surrendered to the government. At this high level of stock prices, the capital confiscation incidental to sale becomes very substantial. Assume, by way of easy example, that the investor owns the Dow-Jones Industrial average at 162 (its low in 1949). Sale at 482 in 1955 would establish a profit of 320 points. The tax would be 80 points, or a 17 percent confiscation of the capital. This certain loss acts as a powerful deterrent, even to the investor who might accept the thesis that stocks are high. If the risk is that of a 10 percent or a 15 percent reaction (in the stock prices), nothing would be gained by selling "good" stocks with long-term growth prospects, paying the tax and getting back in again.[3]

[2] *Outlook* (Standard and Poor's Corporation), Vol. XXVII, No. 3 (January 17, 1955), p. 180.

[3] *Value Line Investment Survey* (March 14, 1955, and September 26, 1955).

It is interesting to note that even in 1928 and 1929, when the maximum capital gains tax was $12\frac{1}{2}$ percent, the capital gains tax was widely blamed for obstructing liquidation of securities, thereby creating a scarcity of stocks for sale and artificially boosting prices.[4]

Walter Maynard, senior partner of Shearson, Hammill and Company, says:

> With capital gains you're betting the certainty of a 25 percent loss versus a problematical gain. And with that certainty of a loss investors will refrain from making a sale even while admitting the price of a security is high enough for him to get out.[5]

An unidentified trustee of a large Boston banking concern is quoted in a recent issue of *Business Week* as follows:

> The money in Boston is mostly in duPont, I.B.M. and other quality issues. If you sell them now it's in expectation of buying them back later. But the price has to go down more than 30 percent to offset what you have to pay in Federal and State Taxes.[6]

The opinion that the capital gains tax may be an important determinant in investment decisions is not shared by all investment authorities. For example, the Twentieth Century Fund, in its study entitled *The Security Markets*, contended that the capital gains tax should have absolutely no effect on investors' decisions:

> The price of a given share must move upward or downward, or remain stationary. From the stockholder's point of view, to sell when one expects the price to go up even if there were no capital gains tax to be paid would be foolish; to hold when the price is expected to decline merely to escape payment of a tax would be equally foolish. If the price is expected to remain stationary, no incentive for selling exists. In none of these three alternatives does the existence of a capital gains tax operate to make the wisest course of action other than it would be were there no such tax....[7]

Mr. J. A. Livingston, a financial columnist with considerable readership, has indicated that he shares the belief that the capital gains tax should not influence investment decisions:

> Taxes are beside the point. The sophisticated investor doesn't allow the tax collector to make his market decisions.... If you no longer like a company..., if you think the stock is overpriced, then you ought to get out, taxes or no.[8]

[4] L. H. Seltzer, *The Nature and Tax Treatment of Capital Gains and Losses* (New York, N.Y.: National Bureau of Economic Research, 1951), p. 176.

[5] Quoted in *Time Magazine* (December 8, 1958), p. 100.

[6] Quoted in *Business Week* (June 6, 1959), p. 74.

[7] *The Security Markets* (New York, N.Y.: Twentieth Century Fund, 1935), p. 346.

[8] Livingston's syndicated column appeared, among other places, in the *Washington Post* and *Times-Herald* (October 12, 1954).

Mr. Harry D. Comer, partner in charge of research for Paine, Webber, Jackson and Curtis, has said in a recent company bulletin:

> The analysis that follows in this letter demonstrates the fallacy of believing that an investor should not accept profits and pay the capital gains tax unless he is really certain that the price will decline enough to permit him to retrieve the tax payment. In fact, *repurchase on any decline works out to the advantage of the investor.*[9]

The conflicting views above indicate the wide range of opinion that may be found among investors regarding the impact of the capital gains tax on their decisions to hold or sell a security. The thesis of this article is that neither of the extreme positions is correct. The impact of the capital gains tax depends on the investor's situation, but only under extreme circumstances should the investor assume that it is unwise to incur a capital gains tax unless the security he is selling is likely to fall by an amount greater than the tax. In fact, a decline of much less than the amount of the tax will justify the selling of the security in most cases. But also it is incorrect to say that sale and repurchase on any decline benefits the investor.

III. IN MOST CASES THE TAX CAN ONLY BE POSTPONED, NOT AVOIDED

The usually accepted economic criterion for answering the question whether or not an investor should switch to an alternate security, regardless of whether he has a capital gains tax, is to compare the present value of the future stream of earnings from his present asset (including the net sale price of the asset at some future date) versus the present value of the income from an alternative asset. While this approach has much to recommend it, the analysis tends to become unwieldy, and hence a more pragmatic, operational guide for decision is sought for the present capital gains study.

To isolate the influence of the capital gains tax, it is assumed that shifts are considered between securities of comparable risk.[10] This means that a similar discount rate can be applied to the future earnings and capital gains of the alternative securities. Consequently, the present value will be maximized if the average annual income is maximized. Average annual income is defined to include both dividends and capital gains or losses that may be incurred in the future. Thus, in many cases, the investor who is considering selling a stock—whether or not he has a capital

---

[9] H. D. Comer, "How to Profit while Paying Capital Gains Taxes," *Research Bulletin* of Paine, Webber, Jackson and Curtis (March, 1960).

[10] The suppression of risk considerations is a limitation of the following analysis. Much more work on this problem is needed.

gain—need ask only the question: "What is the anticipated average annual income from the alternative securities into which I might switch, compared with the anticipated average annual income from the security I'm holding?" Although a forecast of average annual income is an exceedingly simple type of forecast, its simplicity is a virtue when it is used as a basis for an investor to evaluate the impact of the capital gains tax. Furthermore, annual income forecasts are not an unreasonable basis for decisions, since high discount rates significantly diminish the importance of forecasts beyond relatively short horizons.

The major error in the investment analysis of the capital gains tax is the incorrect, though understandable, assumption that the tax on a security showing a paper profit can be *avoided* simply by a decision not to sell. Actually, the only ways that the capital gains tax can be avoided are by holding the security until death; giving the security to a charity; making sufficient capital losses fully to offset the gains; or repeal of the law which established the tax on the capital gains. Aside from these perhaps unpleasant or unlikely alternatives, the capital gains tax is not avoided but merely *postponed*.

Presumably, most investors do not contemplate avoiding the tax by any of the above means; for most people the tax *will be paid*—sooner or later. Hence it is clear that, for most people and institutions, decisions involving the capital gains tax should not focus on this issue: should the tax be *avoided*, but should focus on the issue: should the tax be *postponed*. Usually there is advantage in postponing a tax liability, but, as will be stressed below, the advantage of *postponing* the tax is much less than the benefit that would result if the tax could be *avoided*.

Postponing the sale of a security on which he has a paper profit has the same effect as if the investor obtained an interest-free "loan" from the government of that portion of the security's current value which corresponds to the capital gains tax. The tax payer "owes" the tax, but its due date is postponable. This "loan" from the government becomes due when the investor finally sells the security. How much is this "loan" worth to the investor? Its value depends on its size (i.e., the amount of capital gains tax he would have to pay if he sold now) multiplied by the after-tax yield that he will get from the "investment of the loan" in the security. Thus the investor's choice is between (1) the future dividend and capital gain return on the present investment, including the part that "belongs to the government," and (2) the corresponding return on a smaller investment in an alternative "switch security" that offers a higher yield—the relevant comparison, of course, being after taxes.

A numerical example will illustrate the point. Assume that a share of stock was purchased for $10.00 and its value has risen (more than 6 months later) to $50.00. Further assume that, because of high income, the investor is in the maximum capital gains tax bracket of 25 percent. Note that such a situation makes the penalty of incurring the capital gains tax especially severe; not only is the tax rate maximum, but the stock has shown an unusually large gain. Not many investments attain a capital appreciation of 400 percent. Assume that the investor believes that in the future this stock will, on the average, yield (including both capital gains and dividend income) 4 percent per annum after taxes. If any alternate security can be found that is expected to yield over 5 percent on the average in the future, then the investor should not be deterred from switching because of the capital gains tax. On his present stock he expects to net annually 4 percent × $50.00 or $2.00 per share. If he switches to another stock, he will incur a capital gains tax of $10.00 (25 percent × $40.00 capital gain), which will leave him $40.00 per share to invest in the alternative stock. If this yields over 5 percent, it will give the investor more net income than the $2.00 that he expects to receive annually from continuing to hold his original stock. Thus in this extreme case a yield

FIGURE 1

CAPITAL GAINS TAX ANALYSIS: POSTPONE OR PAY NOW

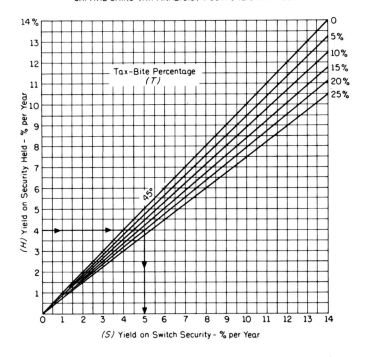

differential in favor of the alternate stock of 1 percent would be enough, as far as current income is concerned, to offset the capital gains tax.

The yield required to justify switching from a stock with a potential capital gains tax liability can be indicated diagrammatically for a wide range of yields and tax liabilities (see Figure 1). The expected future yield of the stock currently owned is charted on the vertical axis labeled H, *Yield on Security Held*. The corresponding yield on the security to which the investor may switch is measured on the horizontal axis, labeled S, *Yield on Switch Security*.

It should be recalled that the yields H and S, as defined in this paper, mean expected future average annual dividend income and capital gains net of taxes divided by the current market value of the respective securities and expressed as a percentage per year. An easy procedure for computing these yields is presented at the end of this section.

Assume for the moment that no tax or other costs were involved in switching; then the investor would sell the stock yielding H and buy the stock yielding S, if S were only slightly greater than H. (This situation is indicated by any point below the 45° line.) If switching stocks requires the investor to incur a capital gains tax, then the yield S must be greater than H to compensate for the tax payment. How much greater S must be than H to warrant a switch depends on the proportion of the presently owned stock investment that would be paid in taxes. Let this "tax-bite percentage" be labeled T.[11]

In Figure 1 the differential between the yields H and S required to neutralize the capital gains tax is indicated by the lines below the 45° line corresponding to different tax-bite percentages. The above numerical example can now be illustrated by drawing a horizontal line from the 4 percent H yield to the 20 percent tax-bite line. Dropping vertically shows that an S yield of 5 percent or better is required to justify switching.

A few other examples will illustrate the use of this graph for estimating the yield differentials that are needed to make switching profitable. If T is 10 percent (which would occur if an investor held a stock that had doubled in value and his income put him in the 40 percent marginal tax bracket so that his capital gains tax was 20 percent), then the second line below the 45° angle indicates that if H is expected to be 4 percent, then a switch will not be profitable unless S exceeds 4.44 percent; for an H of 6 percent, S must be 6.66 percent. If T is 15 percent (this would apply if an investor in the maximum capital gains tax bracket held a stock whose price had risen say from 40 to 100), then S will have to be greater

---

[11] T is equal to $g\ (P_1 - P_0/P_1)$, where g is the percentage rate of tax on capital gains, P_1 is the selling price, and P_0 is the basis price of the security. T is simply the proportion that the "tax bite" is of the market value of an asset.

than 4.65 percent to justify a switch when H is 4 percent; when H is 6 percent, S must be at least 7.05 percent. If T is 20 percent (arising, e.g., from a 400 percent price increase for an investor in the maximum capital gains tax bracket), then if H is 4 percent, S must be 5 percent or greater; if H is 6 percent, S must be 7.5 percent. In short, each line indicates, for its particular tax bite, the alternate yields that are required to justify a switch despite the payment of the capital gains tax. As can be observed it takes *both* a large price appreciation and a high tax rate to generate a relatively large yield differential in favor of holding the current security.

If the investor prefers formulas to graphs, he can calculate the yield that would be required of the switch security from the formula

$$S > \frac{H}{1 - T}$$

If an alternative security has been found with a sufficiently high yield S to justify a switch, then it is possible to calculate the yield increase that is obtained by the switch. The yield increase (which we shall call "switch advantage") is the difference between the yield on the new security after allowance for taxes and the yield on the original security. Thus the switch advantage may be calculated from the expression $(1 - T)S - H$. This may be read from Figure 1 by drawing a vertical line from S until it intersects the T line and then drawing a line left horizontally to the H axis. The difference between this point and the value of H for the security held is the switch advantage.

Thus far in this paper it has been shown that, unless the investor contemplates avoiding the capital gains tax by dying or giving away the stock or incurring a capital loss, he only postpones the capital gains tax by choosing to remain "locked in" securities he holds. The advantage of postponing the tax can be calculated, and the investor can determine how much greater the yield must be from some alternative investment to justify switching. Although precise data are unavailable, it would appear that for most investors the yield differential that is necessary to justify switching is smaller than the uncertainty that attaches to forecasts of future yields of securities and often is smaller than the yield differentials that are forecast between alternate securities.

The principal benefits that a security holder expects to accrue as a result of holding a security are the dividends and capital gains that he obtains after the necessary taxes are paid. To obtain a single yield figure that accurately reflects these benefits involves the consideration of two kinds of income and the tax rates applicable to each.

A tabular presentation that illustrates how the anticipated, after-tax, combined (i.e., dividend plus capital gains) yield for a security might be calculated is shown below for a taxpayer whose marginal tax rate is 30 percent.[12]

Estimated annual dividend yield.....................	4%	
Less: Income tax (30% × 4%).....................	−1.2%	
		2.8%
Estimated annual capital gain yield..................	3%	
Less capital gains tax (15% × 3%)................	−0.45%	
		2.55%
Estimated, after-tax, combined yield (i.e., S or H)...................		5.35%

IV. THE POSSIBILITY OF AVOIDING THE TAX BY DEATH

The analysis up to this point has dealt with the problem: How much influence should the capital gains tax have when an investor is considering switching from a stock with a paper profit to an alternative asset, assuming that sooner or later the capital gain will be realized and the tax paid? This is a suitable assumption for corporations which need not die (by the nature of their legal organization), taxable trusts, and probably most investors under age 50, since they are *likely* to live long enough to have a fairly complete turnover in their security portfolios during their remaining years of life. Even if the investor is elderly with a short life-expectancy, the same analysis applies, assuming that he wants to maximize his income (including future capital gains) during the remainder of his lifetime without consideration of his heirs.

However, the investor may be concerned not only with maximizing his income but also with the value of his estate. There is always the possibility that the capital gains tax on a security will be avoided by dying, unexpected though it is. In this case, a switch that gives the investor greater dollar yield than his present stock, which is the basis of the decision above, may leave him with a smaller estate. To illustrate, if a stock with a current market value of $10,000 yields 3½ percent and an alternative stock promises a yield of 4 percent, the investor would, on the basis of the yield, be indifferent which he holds if the capital gains tax liability incurred by the switch is $1250. However, should he die soon after switching, his estate would have stocks with a market value of only $8750 instead of $10,000.

If an investor wishes to maximize some combination of the value of his estate after death as well as income before death, he must look for an even higher yield on the stock into which he will switch than is required simply to improve expected income. How much larger must the yield be to justify a switch when one includes the possibility of death providing avoidance of the tax? The answer is not simple: it depends on several

---

[12] The marginal income tax rate is the percentage of an additional dollar of regular income that would have to be paid in taxes.

things in addition to the size of the tax bite: How long would the investor keep the stock he is holding if he did not switch now? How likely is he to die before selling? More specifically, what is the probability that the tax will be avoided by death during the period in which he would normally hold the stock? Some examples are illuminating. For an 80-year-old male investor who normally holds a security five years, there is a probability of 50 per cent that death will occur before the stock is sold; for a 45-year-old investor who would be selling his stock in any event within three years, the probability of capital gains tax avoidance through death during the next three years is 1.6 percent.

It is difficult to measure the cost of incurring the capital gains tax when there is a possibility of death canceling the tax liability, because it is not clear what an investor is trying to maximize.

The authors have assumed that a switch would not be warranted unless income was increased *and* the amount of the capital gains tax was expected to be recovered. This criterion enables us to provide the investor a basis for gauging the effect that his mortality prospects have on his investment decisions—a basis that can be related closely to the general, income-maximizing decision rule stated earlier.

The analysis used when estate values are considered requires three assumptions: (1) The investor can estimate how long he will, in all likelihood, continue to hold the present security if he does not switch now. For example, he may think, "I plan to keep this stock four years and then will sell it to pay for my child's college expenses." Or he may simply say, "I find I hold a security about 10 years before I sell it." (2) If he switches from his present security, he will save any additional income and thereby tend to offset the reduction in estate value arising from paying the capital gains tax. (3) Lacking the ability to predict the time of his death, the investor can do no better than to make use of probability data calculated from mortality tables.

How much more needs to be earned on the switch security to expect recapture of the capital gains tax that was paid? The answer depends on these factors: (1) the amount of the capital gains tax; (2) the age of the investor (the older he is, the greater the chance of avoiding the capital gains tax by death); and (3) the length of time the investor plans to hold the security if he does not switch now. If he is going to sell the security fairly soon anyway, his chances of avoiding the tax through death are extremely slight, and he should think of the capital gains tax as postponable, not avoidable—in which case the first analysis suffices.

The two formulas that follow indicate the difference that results if the investor takes the viewpoint that he wants not only to increase his income but also to obtain enough extra income so that he can compensate for incurring the capital gains tax. As was discussed above, the criterion for deciding whether to hold or switch when the investor is focusing only on income is

$$S(1 - T) \geq H$$

When the investor is looking not only at the expected income flowing from the asset but also at the value of the asset, then S needs to be even larger:

$$S(1 - T) \geq H + T \times P$$

In this case S, after being reduced by multiplying by $(1 - T)$, must equal or exceed H *plus* the tax bite multiplied by a probability factor, designated as P (a number whose calculation is rather complex). The letter P stands for the weighted, annual probability that an investor at a given age will die during the period he expects to continue holding the security (if he does not switch).[13]

When the tax bite (stated as a percentage of the asset now being held) is multiplied by P, it gives the extra annual yield that needs to be achieved to replace, on the average, the tax incurred if the asset is sold.

Table 1 indicates the value of P at various ages and for various "continue-to-hold" periods. As would be anticipated, the value of P increases the older the investor gets and the longer the investor expects to hold the present security. But the magnitude of the extra annual yield required warrants consideration. Until the investor reaches 55 and decides to hold the present asset for the rest of his life (if he does not switch at this time), P is less than 5 percent. Furthermore, it should be remembered that P is multiplied by T, which for many investors is less than 10 percent. (An investor whose stock had risen from \$60 to \$100 and was in the maximum tax bracket would pay a capital gains tax of \$10, which is an example of how steep the tax and gain needs to be before $T = 10$ percent.) Thus, for many investors, the increase in yield required to justify a switch if the investor desires not only to maintain his income but also to rebuild his estate is about one-half of 1 percent (10 percent $\times$ 5 percent) per annum.

---

[13] The precise formulation used for calculating the values in Table 1 is

$$P = \left[\sum_{n=1}^{N} P(A, n) \right] \div \left\{ \sum_{n=1}^{N} (n - 0.5) P(A, n) + N \left[1 - \sum_{n=1}^{N} P(A, n) \right] \right\}$$

where N is the number of years in the expected "continue-holding" period, and $P(A, n)$ is the probability that an investor who is now A years of age will die in the nth year from now, where $1 \leq n \leq N$.

For the detailed theory see "The Lock-In Effect of the Capital Gains Tax" by the authors of this paper (manuscript).

Probability data are from Mortality Table X-17, a fairly recent mortality table prepared by a committee of the Society of Actuaries, which probably represents as accurate a current mortality forecast for investors as is available.

TABLE 1.*   THE VALUES OF P: EXPECTED CAPITAL GAINS TAX SAVING BY DEATH PER YEAR OF POTENTIAL TAX LIABILITY

Investor's Age	Years That Investor Will Continue Holding the Security								
	1	2	3	4	5	8	10	15	Life
25	0.159	0.161	0.162	0.164	0.167	0.175	0.182	0.208	2.18
30	0.182	0.186	0.189	0.193	0.197	0.213	0.228	0.283	2.41
35	0.225	0.232	0.240	0.249	0.265	0.298	0.327	0.418	2.71
40	0.330	0.346	0.362	0.378	0.396	0.454	0.500	0.647	3.09
45	0.507	0.530	0.554	0.579	0.607	0.702	0.778	1.02	3.62
50	0.787	0.825	0.866	0.909	0.956	1.12	1.24	1.61	4.20
55	1.26	1.33	1.40	1.47	1.56	1.81	2.00	2.55	5.08
60	2.04	2.14	2.24	2.35	2.46	2.83	3.12	3.89	6.21
65	3.23	3.38	3.54	3.71	3.88	4.44	4.81	5.77	7.82
70	5.11	5.33	5.56	5.81	6.03	6.72	7.30	8.42	9.99
75	7.62	7.92	8.24	8.57	8.91	11.54	12.07	13.28	14.25
80	11.64	12.12	12.58	13.08	13.51	14.73	15.41	16.51	17.14
85	17.52	18.21	18.96	19.39	19.94	21.39	22.12	23.42	23.42

* The figures in this table are percentages. This means that they range from 23.42 percent (highest) to 0.159 percent (lowest). In using the table, it should be remembered that the decimal points need to be shifted two places to the left, e.g., 0.2342 and 0.00159.

The analysis can be further explained by a numerical example. Assume an investor aged 60 and in the top tax bracket owns a security now selling at $50 which he bought at $30. He is considering switching to another security, but he thinks that if he does not make the switch now, he will probably hold the present asset at least 10 years. As best he can estimate, the stock he now holds will, on an annual basis, return him 4 percent after taxes (including both dividends and change in value). If he disregards the size of his estate and is concerned only with the income, he can switch to another security of equal risk if he thinks it will yield more than 4.44 per cent. [This is calculated from the formula $S(1 - T) \geq H$ as follows: $0.0444(1 - 0.10) = 0.04$.] But if he not only wants to maintain his income but add enough each year to compensate—on the average—for tax loss, he must find a security to switch into that yields at least 4.791 percent. [The formula is $S(1 - T) \geq H + T(P)$, which in this case has numerical equivalents of $0.04791(1 - 0.1) = 0.04 + 0.1(0.0312)$.]

Assume that the investor described above owns 200 shares of stock with a market value of $10,000 and an expected after-tax income (inclusive of dividends and change in value) of $400. If he switches to a security that yields 4.44 percent, he will be able to reinvest only $9,000 but will get the same income. If he switches to a security that yields 4.791 percent, he will receive $431.20. By saving the extra $31.20 per year, he will, in a probabilistic sense, leave the same estate as if he held his present security.

The phrase "in a probabilistic sense" needs more explanation. Based on current mortality tables, 27 percent of the American people of age 60 will have died by age 70. Since the capital gains tax in this illustration was $1000, it is clear that $31.20 per year for 10 years would roughly compensate for a 27 percent chance of death nullifying the tax. The reason the actual figure is $31.20 instead of $27 is because the number cited in "Probability" Table 1 is an annual rate of return that has to be weighted by the fact that the probability of death in each year of the assumed investor's next decade is not constant. Clearly, any particular investor will either live through the anticipated 10-year "continue-holding" period and then sell his stock, so he finally incurs the capital gains tax, or he will die during the period and the tax will be nullified. But at the time of his decision, when he is 60, he has no way of knowing whether or not he will live to 70, so he should make his decision by "playing the averages," i.e., by making probability calculations.

Admittedly, the concept of the continue-holding period is a bit awkward and its length difficult to estimate. Fortunately, Table 1 indicates that the estimate is not critical. That is to say, large changes in the length of the continue-holding period do not make large changes in P, and hence errors in estimating the holding period will have little influence on the hold-switch decisions that are made.

V. SALE AND REPURCHASE OF A SECURITY

The capital gains lock-in question also arises in the situation in which a security is held that has attained capital gains in the past and optimistic forecasts are made for gains in the long-term future but price declines are anticipated for the near future. Should the investor sell out now and buy back later at a lower price, or should he ride through the temporary decline and hold for the long-run potential?

TABLE 2

Assumptions

1. Purchase price of 100 shares was $30 each.
2. Current market price is $70.
3. Investor is in the maximum tax bracket, so the capital gains tax is $10 per share.
4. Price is expected to drop in the near future to $65.

Results

If Investor Continues to Hold until Prices Reaches $130	*If Investor Sells, Repurchases at $65, then Resells at $130*
1. Eventual sale price (100 shares × $130)............ $13,000	1. First sale (100 × $70).... $ 7,000
2. Less base price........... 3,000	2. Less base price.......... 3,000
3. Profit before tax.......... $10,000	3. Profit before tax......... $ 4,000
4. Less capital gains tax...... $ 2,500	4. Less capital gains tax..... $ 1,000
5. Net profit................ $ 7,500	5. Net profit.............. $ 3,000
6. Plus original investment.... 3,000	6. Plus original investment................... 3,000
7. Total value of assets at end..................... $10,500	7. Available for reinvestment................... $ 6,000
	8. Number of shares repurchased ($6,000 ÷ $65 = 92.3077).................
	9. Second sale (92.3077 × $130)................. $12,000
	10. Less base price.......... 6,000
	11. Profit before tax......... $ 6,000
	12. Less capital gains tax..... 1,500
	13. Net profit on second sale.. $ 4,500
	14. Plus base investment of repurchase............. 6,000
	15. Total value of assets at end................... $10,500

It would seem to be unusually difficult to justify incurring a capital gains tax when the investor expects to repurchase the same security if the fall in price is likely to be less than the capital gains tax incurred. In this circumstance, the yield on the alternative security is going to be very close to the yield on the security he is now holding, since the "hold" and the "switch" security are one and the same. Analysis shows that the decision here depends on the amount of capital gains tax to be incurred, the amount of prospective decline in the security that can be avoided by selling out and buying later, and the potential future growth of the security price.[14]

The results of this analysis can be illustrated by means of a numerical example, which for simplicity's sake assumes dividends are not being paid. Since it is obvious that any foreseeable decline in price that exceeds the amount of the capital gains tax would clearly justify selling the security, the illustration in Table 2 will assume that the drop foreseen by the investor is less than the capital gains tax. Also we assume, as we did in Section III, that the capital gains tax *will* be paid before death.

Consider the implications of this illustration. The stock ultimately had to rise to $130 before the investor who chose to hold on to his stock and avoid the capital gains tax (despite the foreseeable drop from $70 to $65) did as well as the investor who sold and then repurchased at the lower price. Yet this illustration uses figures that present an extreme case of being locked in: the original increase is large, the investor's tax bracket is maximum, and the drop is only half the tax. If the stock subsequently rises from the low of $65 to less than $130, the investor who sold and repurchased does better than the one who chose to be locked in by the capital gains tax when the expected decline was only $5.00 and the tax liability was $10.00.[15]

VI. IN CONCLUSION

As the analysis has shown, the effect of the capital gains tax will depend on several factors: the investor's tax bracket, the portion of the present asset that represents capital gains, and the expected future income from the asset he holds. If the investor not only is concerned with maximizing

[14] This situation is analyzed in more detail in "A note on R. F. Gemmill's article 'The Effect of the Capital Gains Tax on Asset Prices,' " by Charles C. Holt, *National Tax Journal* (June, 1957), and in Gemmill's article, *National Tax Journal* (December, 1956).

[15] The numerical illustration above can be explained in terms of an analysis of the sell-and-repurchase case. But it can also be understood in terms of the rule $S(1 - T) \geq H$. In this case the yield included in S relates to the growth from $65, and yield H is based on growth from $70. Clearly, S exceeds H. However, the person who held throughout the drop owns more shares, and, when the subsequent gain becomes great enough, the differential between S and H becomes sufficiently small that the value of the extra shares for the "hold" alternative offsets the yield differential that exists for S.

the income that he or his estate will receive but is also seeking to maximize the market value of the estate, then he must also consider his age and the length of time he will probably continue to hold the present asset.

Some idea of the magnitude of the difference in yield necessary to justify a switch when the capital gains tax is involved can be obtained from analyzing the situation of a typical investor. Based on recent surveys, the typical (median) American common-stock owner's annual income is about $7500, he is about 50 years old, and he has held his stock about five years. If we assume his stock has shown about the same price appreciation as the average, he will have nearly a 50 percent gain, which means that about 33 percent of the current market value of his security is subject to capital gains tax. For example, if he bought a stock at $40, it is probably selling at about $60 now. Since the extra tax he would have to pay would be 15 percent (half his marginal tax rate of 30 percent) of the capital gain T (the percentage of the asset going to taxes) would be 5 percent (0.33 × 0.15). If he expects the present stock to yield from the combination of dividends and appreciation approximately 6 percent per year after taxes, he will suffer a decline in income if he cannot find another investment that will have an expected yield (calculated as above) of at least 6.32 percent. In short, the typical American investor may find that the capital gains tax requires him to seek one-third of 1 percent extra annual yield to justify switching. If he not only wants his income to remain undiminished but also wants his estate to have no reduction in market value, he finds, by including information from Table 1, that he should not switch unless the alternative security promises a yield of 6.37 percent, assuming that he thinks he will continue to hold the present security another five years if he does not sell now.

Consider an extreme case: the investor is in a maximum tax bracket; he is 70 years old; he has an asset that has tripled in value; he thinks that he will hold this asset, which he expects will provide an after-tax annual return of 6 percent, for life. He should not switch unless an alternative asset yields 7.2 percent if he is not concerned with the market value of his estate. If he also wants to leave an undiminished estate, he will need to find an asset with annual expected yield of 8.87 percent (details of the calculations for these two cases are shown in Case 1 and Case 2, respectively, in Table 3).

What does this analysis mean for the investor who, understandably, may feel bemused by the theoretical overtones of the formulas and graphs? Unfortunately, some complexity is necessary if the conclusions are to be supported. Even for an investor who finds little practical value in the details, the analysis gives insight into the essential aspects of how the capital gains tax can influence investment decisions. For one thing, to ignore completely the capital gains tax, as some advisers have recommended, is seen to be in error. On the other hand, it is equally misleading

TABLE 3. EXAMPLES OF THE CALCULATION PROCESS

	Case 1	Case 2
1. Present market price of stock...............	$60	$60
2. Base price for tax purposes................	40	20
3. Taxable gain............................	$20	$40
4. Capital gains tax rate ($\frac{1}{2}$ marginal tax rate, but not greater than 25%).....................	15%	25%
5. Amount of capital gains tax (Row 3 × Row 4).	$ 3	$10
6. Tax as a percent of market value—denoted as T in this paper (Row 5 ÷ Row 1)...........	0.05	0.167
7. Expected, annual, after-tax rate of return from dividends and change in market value for security now held—denoted as H in this article.	0.06	0.06
8. Minimum rate of return (calculated on same basis) required from alternative security to maintain income—denoted as S in this article [Row 7 ÷ (1 − Row 6)]..................	$\dfrac{0.06}{0.95} = 0.0632$	$\dfrac{0.06}{0.833} = 0.072$

If the investor not only wishes to maintain or increase his income, but also will not shift unless, in all probability, he will get enough income to recapture the amount of the tax that he has to pay, then he must first estimate his "continue-holding" period. This is the length of time that he will be likely to continue to hold the present asset if he does not sell it now. At the end of this period, if he is still living, he will sell the asset anyway and the tax will have to be paid. Thus the probability of death nullifying the tax is applicable only for the duration of the continue-holding period. In this case assume that the investor in the left-hand column is 50 and expects to hold his security for five years; the other investor is 70 and expects to hold for the rest of his life if he does not sell now. Then turn to Table 1 and find the appropriate cell, given age, and continue-holding period.

9. Value of P considering age of investor and length of continue-holding period (from Table 1)................................	0.00956	0.0999
10. Extra yield required from alternate security to replace, on the average, the amount of the tax (Row 9 × Row 6)........................	0.00478	0.01666
11. New value for S, considering estate value as well as income flow (Row 8 × Row 10).......	0.063678 (i.e., 6.37%)	0.08866 (i.e., 8.87%)

to feel that the investor must anticipate a drop of 20 or 30 percent in the price of the stock he is holding before he can justify selling out. In fact, it is clear that in most cases an anticipated decline in the particular stock held by the investor can be considerably less than the amount of the tax to justify selling, even if he plans, at a later date, to rebuy the same security.

But the investor may still feel that the analysis is too theoretical for his purposes, since it requires him to make a forecast of the annual rate of return that he will expect from the security which he is holding and from an alternate security into which he might switch. "This," the investor might say, "is the counsel of perfection." The ability to forecast rates of return accurately would make most investors willing to forget the small burden of the capital gains tax. Furthermore, the investor, if he wishes to use the second approach above, needs to estimate how long he plans to continue to hold his existing security.

However, the fact that these elements are difficult to estimate does not negate the value of the analysis. It still can help the investor to focus on the issues that are important and thus enable him to place the important factors in the decision in perspective rather than being misled, e.g., by identifying the maximum capital gains tax rate of 25 percent with the necessary potential price decline.

In sum, the virtue of the analysis for most investors is that it will enable them to concentrate on the relevant factors that should be associated with making a decision to hold or switch when a capital gains tax is involved instead of being possibly misled by largely irrelevant considerations. For those who wish more precision, the formulas, charts, and tables are available.

Since security prices typically fluctuate as much as 3 percent per month and since the investor forecasts of the rates of return that can be expected from dividends and changes in asset value are hazy, one may conclude from this analysis that the capital gains tax usually makes such a slight difference in the magnitude of the yields required to justify switching that it can easily be subsumed in the larger aspect of uncertainty regarding future yields. Or, to put it another way, if switching is considered at all, it is usually because the expected difference in combined yield between a stock currently owned and an alternative is sufficiently great that the impediment resulting from the capital gains tax will be more than overcome.

On the other hand, an investor may feel that, since he faces considerable uncertainty in forecasting the yields whenever he shifts from one asset to another, the definite fact that a yield differential—even a slight one—must be found to justify a switch will discourage him from selling one asset and buying another. This paper does not draw conclusions on the extent to which the capital gains tax actually locks investors into the stock market. It has presented an approach by means of which investors can evaluate approximately how much extra yield must be provided by an alternate security to justify selling an asset on which the investor has a capital gain.

part Five

STUDIES IN STOCK MARKET
BEHAVIOR

$\mathcal{S}eymour\ \mathcal{S}midt^{*}$

37. A New Look at the Random-
Walk Hypothesis

Reprinted from the **Journal of Financial and Quantitative Analysis,**
Vol. III, No. 3 (September, 1968), pp. 235–261, by permission of
the author and the publisher.

I. INTRODUCTION

The basic idea behind the random-walk hypothesis is that in a free competitive market the price currently quoted for a particular good or service should reflect all of the information available to participants in the market that influence its present price. To the extent that future conditions of the demand or supply are currently known, their effect on the current price should be properly taken into account.

A statistical process which has the property that the expected future value of a random variable is independent of past values of the variables is said to be a Martingale process. What is generally referred to as the random walk hypothesis requires that in a perfectly competitive market, price changes should be outcomes of a Martingale process. In the last decade considerable effort has been devoted to testing hypotheses of this nature. The data most commonly used have been obtained from security markets and from commodity futures markets.

There are many different probability distributions of price changes that would be consistent with the random-walk hypothesis. Similarly, there are many alternatives to randomness that would violate the hypothesis. Statistically, testing the random-walk hypothesis involves testing a composite null hypothesis against a composite alternative hypothesis. The fact that a particular test fails to contradict the null hypothesis does not guarantee that another test, possibly using the same data, might not lead to a contradiction. Most tests that were used in the early stages of investigation of this hypothesis have been interpreted as being consistent with the null hypothesis. However, the first tests used were very general. That is, they were not designed to test against specific alternative hypotheses. There is

* Cornell University.

always the danger that the null hypothesis will be accepted, even though it is false, because the test being used is insufficiently powerful with respect to a correct but unknown alternative hypothesis. One would have more confidence in the validity of the random walk hypothesis if it had been tested more extensively using procedures that are known to be statistically powerful against the specific alternatives that are *a priori* most likely.

Price changes that are consistent with the random walk hypothesis could occur under at least three distinct sets of circumstances. One possibility is that information that becomes available to market participants is itself random in its effect on market price. (cf. Samuelson, 1965, p. 42) This is possible but it seems most unlikely. A second possibility is that all the market participants are thoroughly informed about all new information as soon as it is publicly available, and about any statistical dependencies in the information generating process. Under these conditions, for example, if an event that had a bullish influence occurred, and if it were known that future events also having a bullish influence are more likely to occur given that this event has occurred, then the price would respond both to the event that had occurred and to the increased probability of future events tending in the same direction. In this case price changes would tend to be random even though the effects of news are not random. This set of circumstances is only slightly less unlikely than the first for most markets in which empirical tests have actually been conducted. For example, in most markets, there are important groups of participants who are not as fully informed as others, or who learn about relevant new information only after a significant time lag compared to some well-informed participants. In this third set of circumstances it might still be true that the price changes would follow a random walk very closely. This requires that the well-informed market participants anticipate how lags in the information available to less well-informed participants will affect the latter's trading.

However, well-informed traders have an incentive to eliminate price dependencies only if there is sufficient nonrandomness so that they can earn a competitive return by using their superior knowledge. This modified random-walk hypothesis requires that the profits that can be achieved from eliminating strong systematic dependencies in price changes be sufficient to attract just enough people into this activity. Thus this set of circumstances is the one which advocates of the random-walk hypothesis seem mainly to have had in mind.[1]

Two significant implications of this third version of the random-walk hypothesis have been given insufficient attention in the literature to date. According to this version of the hypothesis, *one should expect to find some*

---

[1] For a clear statement of this point of view see Fama (1965). Although the text emphasizes lack of information, and lags in responding to information as the source of dependencies in price changes, the argument is more general. Any systematic tendencies in price changes that create opportunities for superior profits should be eliminated by traders who become aware of these systematic tendencies.

systematic dependencies in price changes. These dependencies may result from dependencies in the underlying information generating process, the cost of transactions, the cost of acquiring and processing information and, in general, all of the frictions and lags that tend to be ignored in abstract discussions of perfectly competitive markets. Persons accepting this third version of the random-walk hypothesis should be wary of interpreting a test that uncovered no dependencies as strong evidence supporting the random-walk hypothesis. Rather such test results can often be interpreted more properly as indicating that the test was insufficiently powerful against relevant alternative hypothesis.

The second implication of this version of the hypothesis is that the profits that can be generated by taking advantage of the systematic dependencies in the price changes should be at most those necessary to attract and hold resources in the activity of eliminating them. It is a violation of this requirement that would contradict the random-walk hypothesis.

In practice, even when systematic dependencies in price changes have been detected, determining whether their magnitude and frequency is sufficient to constitute a violation of the random-walk hypothesis is extremely difficult. The problem would be relatively simple if each type of systematic dependency could be eliminated only by a firm that must necessarily specialize in providing the service of reducing the magnitude of that type of dependency. Even then the problem is not easy, since it would involve a careful estimate of all of the costs involved, and of the return on capital required to justify the risks involved. Often, however, the relevant firms are not specialized. A firm may act in such a way that it tends to reduce the magnitude of several kinds of systematic price dependencies. The firm as a whole may earn a return that exceeds the competitive rate even though the excess return cannot be attributed to any one type of activity. To complicate matters even further, firms that act in such a way as to reduce the magnitude of some types of price dependencies may at the same time contribute to the magnitude of other types of price discrepancies.

The true significance of the random walk hypothesis is that it suggests a fruitful and sensitive though indirect means of studying aspects of economic behavior that are extraordinarily difficult to study directly. For example it is difficult to estimate from direct observations of the behavior of various categories of investors whether lags in investor response to new information have a significant impact on security prices. The random-walk hypothesis provides a means of looking for the effects of such lags, because it tells us what to expect if the lags exert no effect.

Most empirical tests of the random-walk hypothesis have dealt solely with sequences of price changes. However, the random-walk hypothesis is more general. Since the basic idea is that the current price should reflect all relevant available information, the expected future price change should be statistically independent of such things as the volume of activity in the stock, the size of the last transaction, and the percentage change in the firm's earnings during the last quarter, provided only that this information is publicly available. If the random walk hypothesis is significant because it provides a powerful tool to help us understand how organized markets really work, then characteristics like volume and size of transactions ought to be incorporated into the analysis more frequently than they have been in the past, since they are produced by the same market process that produces price changes.

In summary, this section has suggested that the empirical investigations of the random-walk hypothesis would be most fruitful if they were conducted in the spirit of attempting to determine the size and extent of systematic tendencies that may exist in price series. Even if the largest part of a sequence of price changes may be described as following a Martingale process, it is the remaining systematic components that are the most interesting. It was also suggested that a search for systematic tendencies is likely to be more fruitful if it is guided by specific hypotheses about the characteristics of the systematic tendencies that are believed to be present. The rest of the article will consider the kinds of behavior that seem most likely to produce some residual systematic tendencies in sequences of price change. Three main sources of systematic tendencies will be considered. These result from the demand for liquidity, lags in response to new information, and inappropriate responses to new information. The empirical evidence currently available will also be evaluated. In some instances, suggestions for further research will be made.

II. THE SUPPLY SCHEDULE OF LIQUIDITY

In conducting economic affairs there is often a considerable advantage in being able quickly to exchange one asset for another. In a monetary society one of the two assets in the exchange is nearly always money. The facilities and institutions that make quick exchange possible can be thought of as producing a service. The production of this service is costly, and buyers are frequently willing to pay to have the service provided to them. Amazingly, there is no generally accepted term in economics that refers precisely to this service. In this paper, the term liquidity is used to refer to this service.[2]

---

[2] Other writers have used other terms to refer to what in this paper is called liquidity service. Demsetz (1968) states that "On the NYSE two elements comprise almost all of transaction cost—brokerage fees and ask-bid spreads . . .. The ask-bid spread is the markup that is paid for predictable immediacy of exchange in organized markets; in other markets, it is the inventory markup of retailer or wholesaler." (pp. 35–36). "Immediacy of exchange" is a good synonym for liquidity service. The cost of obtaining "immediacy of exchange" is, in our view, not the bid-ask spread, but half that amount

If liquidity is thought of as a service, a quantitative measure of it is needed so that the quantity of liquidity demanded and its supply price can be estimated. Since liquidity is ordinarily supplied when property is exchanged for cash, it seems appropriate to measure the amount of liquidity supplied in terms of the number of units of property exchanged.

In the absence of an actual transaction, the state of the market is represented by quoted bid and asked prices. Assuming that these quoted prices represent real commitments to buy or sell at least the smallest unit traded, it is a reasonable first approximation to define the market price as the average of the quoted bid and asked prices. If a transaction takes place because a seller is anxious to conclude his transaction immediately, the price paid for liquidity can then be defined as the market price less the price at which the transaction takes place. In this case a positive quality of liquidity is supplied, and the price of liquidity is positive. If a transaction takes place because a buyer is anxious to conclude his transaction immediately (that is, because he is anxious to reduce his liquidity by exchanging cash for some other asset), then the price paid to become illiquid can be defined as the transaction price less the market price.

If illiquidity is thought of as negative liquidity, a supply schedule of liquidity can be defined for which the amounts supplied can be either positive or negative; the price of liquidity, in this general sense, is the market price less the actual transaction price. Negative quantities of liquidity are supplied at negative prices.

A justification for treating the average of the bid and asked prices as the market price, and the difference between the market price and the transaction price as a payment for liquidity is that the initiator of the transaction can avoid buying liquidity if he so desires.[3] To do so he need

---

(for the smallest unit traded). The inventory markup of most retailers and wholesalers includes payments for other services in addition to liquidity.

Holbrook Working uses the term "execution cost" to refer to the cost, in the form of price concessions, that traders must incur when they use market orders to insure prompt execution. We prefer the term, "costs of liquidity," because it is more general. Execution costs are the form in which the costs of liquidity are incurred in some, but not all markets.

[3] This discussion assumes the market price is the same before and after the transaction. However, it may happen that as a result of the transaction, or simultaneously with the transaction, there is a change in the market price. In this case, it will be convenient to define the price of liquidity in terms of the market price that prevails after the transaction, rather than before.

Liquidity, as defined above, is a noun, referring to a particular service. However, the term liquidity is often used as an adjective to describe an attribute of a particular type of property. A convenient index of liquidity for an asset is the ratio of the price that could be obtained by selling the asset to its market price. (Another way of describing this index is that it is one minus the ratio of supply price of liquidity for the asset over the market price of the asset.) A perfectly liquid asset, one that can be sold at its market price, would have an index of liquidity of one. A perfectly illiquid asset is one that has a sale price of zero. Some assets may have a negative index of liquidity. One must pay removal costs to dispose of them.

only place his order as a limit order rather than as a market order. If he does so and is lucky, he may receive a payment for liquidity. If he is unlucky, his order may be executed only after a long delay, or never.

Having defined liquidity as a service, consider the means by which the demand and supply for liquidity is expressed in the market.

One indication of the demand for liquidity in a market is the percentage of orders to buy or sell "at the market." If there is a low level of demand for liquidity (or for illiquidity) a small fraction of the sell (or buy) orders received will be market orders. Most of the orders received in such markets will be limit orders. A market with a high ratio of limit orders should tend to exhibit a narrow spread between the bid and asked prices.

By contrast, if the demand for liquidity is high, most orders arriving in the market will be orders to buy or sell "at the market." If liquidity were supplied only through buyers and sellers willing to place limit orders, the spread between bid and asked prices would tend to be large. Whether the demand for liquidity were high or low, if liquidity were supplied only by those willing to place limit orders there would be a systematic tendency for the price at which actual transactions take place to fluctuate between the bid and asked prices of the unfilled limit orders.

Depending on the gap between the bid and asked prices, the rate at which transactions took place, and other factors, the systematic tendency for transaction prices to fluctuate between the bid and asked prices might create opportunities for traders to make money by specializing in supplying liquidity.

Limit orders appear to be used as a means of supplying liquidity mostly by traders who view supplying liquidity as only a supplementary source of income. Traders who are mainly interested in supplying liquidity are characterized by their willingness to be either buyers or sellers of the asset in question provided they can make the transaction at a price sufficiently below (or above) what they consider to be the market price. Such traders might utilize limit orders, if they were not located at the point of sale. Alternatively they might wait at the point of sale and attempt to offer more favorable terms than the existing limit orders when a market order arrived for execution.

The mechanism by which liquidity is supplied by traders who specialize in supplying it depends in part on the amounts of liquidity demanded. In most organized markets there is some unit quantity, such as a 100-share lot, or a 5,000-bushel contract. All regular trades take place in terms of integral multiples of this unit. Most transactions are for the unit quantity, or a small multiple of this basic unit. In so far as the quantity for which an individual decision-making unit wants prompt execution is the unit quantity, or a small multiple of that unit, one can say that the discrete amount of liquidity demanded is small. The price effects of demands for small units of liquidity, the mechanism by which these price effects are produced, and the role of professional traders in supplying these demands for small units of liquidity are relatively well-understood. The systematic departures from randomness produced by such small demands for liquidity have been documented for both stock exchanges and commodity futures markets. This evidence will be summarized first.

Some decision making units desire prompt execution of orders whose total amounts are many times as large as the unit of trading. The demands for large blocks of liquidity are also capable of producing systematic patterns of price movements. However, the possibility that such movements may exist has been recognized only recently. The evidence for such movements is still quite fragmentary. The price effects of the demand for such large quantities of liquidity will be discussed separately.

III. THE DEMAND FOR SMALL QUANTITIES OF LIQUIDITY

The demand for small quantities of liquidity produces a systematic tendency for transactions in which the price change is in one direction to be followed by transactions in which the price change is in the opposite direction. This characteristic of price changes from one transaction to the next has been well documented for both commodity futures markets and stock exchanges. The evidence for commodity futures is due to H. Working (1954, p. 124); for the New York Stock Exchange, the evidence is due to Niederhoffer and Osborne (1966). Working's data are based on 143 series consisting of 100 consecutive price changes in wheat futures. In more than half of the price series, the proportion of price changes that were reversals exceeded .75. In all but two percent of the price series, the proportion of reversals exceeded .65. The Niederhoffer and Osborne results are based on a sample of over 10,000 transactions. Ignoring consecutive transactions in which there was no change in price, they found, for example, that the conditional probability of a price increase, given that the previous change was a decrease, was .76; by contrast the marginal probability of an increase, given only that the previous transaction was not at the same price, was .4984.

Broadly speaking the mechanism that produces these reversal tendencies is well known. The tendencies result from the fact that as orders for immediate execution arrive at that market, they tend to be executed at either the bid or asked price. Presumably there is a tendency for buy and sell orders to arrive in a random order, though this has not been documented directly, and the actual pattern may be much more complex. Demsetz (1968) also presents evidence that the bid-asked spread tends to decline as the volume of transactions increase. Working (1967, p. 22) notes that it tends to increase if rapid price level movements take place.

With respect to the random-walk hypothesis, the relevant question is not whether systematic patterns exist, but whether they provide unexploited opportunities to make above normal profits. To the author's knowledge, no direct evidence on this question is available for any organized market; nor do we know of any study that has attempted to obtain such evidence. Indirect evidence is available based on a knowledge of the institutional barriers to entry that might prohibit traders from taking advantage of opportunities for unusual profits, if they existed. Based on this indirect evidence one can be fairly confident that no such unexploited profit opportunities exist on the active commodity futures markets. However, it is not possible to make a confident judgment about either the relatively inactive futures markets, or the United States stock exchanges.

IV. THE DEMAND FOR LARGE QUANTITIES OF LIQUIDITY

In both the commodity futures and common stock markets, some participants have holdings that are many times larger than the minimum transaction size. Liquidity demands from such participants should also produce patterns of systematic changes in transaction prices. The systematic patterns produced by the acquisition or liquidation of a large position may be different from those produced when small positions are acquired or liquidated. However, the failure to detect systematic price patterns that could be attributed to demands for large quantities of liquidity would raise a question as to the sensitivity of the tests used for the random-walk hypotheses.

A better understanding of the mechanisms involved in supplying liquidity in large quantities to anxious buyers and sellers under various institutional arrangements is particularly important at present. Both the increasing concentration of stock in institutional hands, and the emphasis on short-run performance have led to rapid increases in the number of large blocks traded. The possible effects of these trends on the market institutions are not well understood.

Evidence that systematic patterns of price movements are produced by attempts to acquire or liquidate a large position has only recently become available. In every case, the evidence that some systematic (nonrandom) patterns of price movements existed was recognized before it was realized that the pattern could be most easily interpreted as a price effect of attempts rapidly to acquire or liquidate a large position.

For a number of reasons, it is convenient to begin by discussing the evidence that pertains to commodity futures markets. Historically, the systematic price effects of attempts to acquire or dispose of large positions were first observed on such markets, and their interpretation as being due to liquidity demands is better substantiated for such markets. In addition, the exposition is simpler, because the alternatives available to the anxious buyer or seller of a large quantity of commodity futures contracts are more limited. Legally, all transactions in commodity futures must be conducted in public on the floor of the exchange during the regular trading period. Furthermore, the ticker services of such exchanges report price changes, but not volume. Thus traders not present on the trading floor can become quickly aware of the existence of a large liquidity demand (positive or negative) only through the price changes it produces.

The only alternatives available to the anxious seller (or buyer) of a large quantity of commodity futures are either to attempt to obtain execution on the entire quantity in one brief interval, or to submit a sequence of orders, thus spreading the demand over a period of time. In practice, the latter alternative seems to predominate, since it is the only alternative that can attract buying (or selling) support from traders not physically present on the trading floor.

Large liquidity demands, spread over a period of days should produce a reversal pattern similar to that observed in transaction data, except that the price moves should be larger, and should be spread over a longer period of time. In a recent paper, Holbrook Working (1967) has made another signal contribution to our knowledge of organized markets. First, he has called attention to the fact that previous observations, that had not been satisfactorily explained, could be interpreted as the result of dips and bulges due to concentrated demands for large quantities of liquidity. (On commodity futures markets, such demands arise when large merchandising corporations attempt to place or to lift their hedges). Second, he has presented significant new evidence to support his interpretation.

The previous observations, that had not been satisfactorily explained were due to Larson (1960) and Smidt (1965). Larson showed that there are small negative autocorrelations, at lags of up to three or four days, in corn futures prices. Smidt showed that a trader who used a one cent filter on day-to-day closing prices in soybean futures could make significant profits. The rule required selling after a price advance of one cent or more and buying after a close-to-close decline of the same magnitude. Both of these observations can be explained if one assumes that there is a systematic tendency for small day-to-day price changes in one direction to be followed by price changes in the opposite direction, spread over the next three or four days.

Working confirmed this observation by analyzing the trading record of a professional floor trader. The hypothesis that this trader profited mainly from the systematic patterns described above provided a satisfactory explanation of the trading record. Previous hypotheses, applied to the same data, had not been satisfactory. The analysis of the trading record is too complicated to summarize here.

The organized securities markets differ from commodity futures markets in some important institutional details. All the differences relevant here give the anxious buyer or seller of a large quantity of stock a wider range of means of completing his transactions. The options available involve different combinations of price concessions versus marketing effort. The initiator of a large transaction can contact interested parties to arrange a transaction that need not occur on the floor of the exchange. He can advertise his willingness to buy or sell; he can obtain the use of a sales force to contact potential buyers or sellers. To the extent that extra marketing costs of arranging a quick transaction are substitutes for price concessions, the cost of liquidity may not appear in the pattern of recorded prices.

Nevertheless, liquidity demands may produce dips and bulges in the prices on organized stock exchanges just as they do on commodity exchanges. Relevant evidence is contained in a study by Fama and Blume (1966). In this study filter trading rules were applied to the daily closing prices of the 30 stocks in the Dow-Jones average. The number of consecutive trading days per individual stock averaged approximately 1,400. The filter used was expressed as the percentage change from the previous peak or trough. Price data were corrected for dividend payments. The filter sizes used ranged from 0.5 percent to 50 percent. The trading rule used in this study requires taking a long position in a stock when its closing price exceeds a reference trough by the size of the filter. The long position is then held until the closing price is less than a reference peak by the amount of the filter. At this point the position is switched from long to short. Short or long positions are continued until a signal to change them is reached. The reference peak (trough) is the highest (lowest) preceding closing price from the day the position was opened.

A simple buy and hold policy applied to this data yielded an annual rate of return of approximately .10. If there were no systematic patterns in this price series other than the upward drift, one would expect to earn a return of .10 during the period when long positions were open and a return of minus that amount during the period when short positions were open. The actual results for the range of filters of interest here are summarized in Table 1.

The filter rule used in this study requires a trader to be long as many times as he is short. However, it is not necessary that the number of days that long positions are held be the same as the number of days short positions are held. For this reason, as well as because of other sources of sampling error, even if the data followed the random-walk hypothesis, the observed returns from long and short positions might not be identical to the expected returns.

There are four filter levels whose observed returns for both long and

TABLE 1. NOMINAL ANNUAL RATES OF RETURN BEFORE
COMMISSIONS BY FILTER: AVERAGED OVER ALL COMPANIES

Filter	Total Transactions	Long Positions Only (Rounded)	Short Positions Only (Rounded)
.005	12,514	.21	.01
.010	8,660	.14	− .05
.015	6,270	.11	− .08
.020	4,784	.09	− .11
.025	3,750	.07	− .14
.030	2,994	.07	− .14
.035	2,438	.07	− .13
.040	2,013	.08	− .13
.045	1,720	.06	− .15
.050	1,484	.06	− .16
.060	1,071	.08	− .12
.070	828	.07	− .13
.080	653	.08	− .13
.090	539	.08	− .12
.100	435	.08	− .10
.120	289	.10	− .09

short positions differ in absolute magnitude by .04 or more from their expected levels. For two of these, .005 and .01, the observed returns from both long and short positions exceed the expected return. For two other filters, .045 and .050, the observed returns from both long and short positions are less than the expected returns. Deviations as large as this cannot reasonably be attributed to chance.

It is true that a trader who had to pay the regular NYSE commissions could not earn normal profits if his trading was based solely on these systematic tendencies. The possibility that a member of the exchange could profitably take advantage of them will be examined later.

Whether or not this data should be interpreted as a violation of the random-walk hypothesis, that is, as evidence of significant market imperfections, it would be interesting to know the source of these systematic tendencies. The hypothesis suggested here is that they represent price concessions by purchasers or sellers anxious to quickly exchange a large volume of stock. This hypothesis would be a priori reasonable if it could be shown that both the positive dependency indicated by the small filters, and the negative dependency indicated by the large filters could result from the occurrence of dips and bulges of the type that seem to be associated with liquidity demands on commodity markets.

To see why this suggestion is reasonable, first note that for every filter size in Table 1, the actual returns earned by the long and short positions are displaced from their expected returns by approximately the same absolute magnitude. This strongly suggests that whatever systematic pattern exists in the stock price sequence is a highly symmetric pattern. The simplest pattern that could account for this characteristic in the data is a wave-like motion around the long-term upward trend in the data. If the waves were all of the same amplitude, then any filter size greater than the amplitude of the wave would produce no transactions. In fact, the data show that the number of transactions decreases as the filter size increases. This suggests a mixture of waves of different amplitudes. For example, the number of wave-like price movements that produce transactions with a 5 percent filter is about one-tenth the number that produce transactions with a 0.5 percent filter.

The profits produced by the trading rule studied by Fama and Blume depend on the amplitude of the wave and the size of the filter. If the amplitude of the wave is less than the filter size it produces no transactions. Such waves are filtered out, and ignored. Suppose that the trough of a wave occurs when the stock is priced at $100 dollars per share and the peak when the stock rises to $100 + A$ dollars. The amplitude of the wave is A percent. With an I percent filter (assuming $A > I$), a buy signal will be given when the price reaches $100 + I$ dollars. A sell signal will occur when the price passes the peak and declines to $100 + A - I$ dollars. Thus the profits on this long open position will be $A - 2I$ dollars or $A - 2I$ percent before commissions. In general, the trading rule will produce gains (losses) if the average amplitude of waves that exceed the filter size is greater than (less than) twice the filter size. The data in Table 1 suggest that for the stocks in the Dow-Jones average the average amplitude of the waves detected by a one percent filter is greater than 2 percent. On the other hand, the average amplitude of the waves detected by a 5 percent filter is less than 10 percent.

If these wave-like patterns are due to the demands for relatively large amounts of liquidity, the amplitude of the waves presumably results from the number of shares of stock which the anxious buyer or seller has available for exchange, and the intensity of his desire to complete the transaction rapidly. The term wave is used in a metaphorical sense. It is not suggested that if the price series were plotted that one would necessarily be able to observe a persistent wave-like pattern. The waves must be defined statistically in terms of the conditional probabilities of price changes given that the price is already in a certain relation to the previous peak or trough.

Fama and Blume argue that the statistical dependencies indicated by their data do not constitute a contradiction to the random-walk hypothesis because it is not possible to profit by taking account of these dependencies.

Even if this is true, it is important to identify the dependencies that exist and determine the source of deviation from strict statistical randomness.

Although Fama and Blume believe that the statistical dependencies they have uncovered are not large enough to be a potential source of trading profits, I find their logic unconvincing. A trader who was not a member of the New York Stock Exchange could not earn a normal rate of profit on his funds by trading in such a way as to take advantage solely of these systematic price patterns. However, if knowledge of these patterns were more widely publicized among such traders, it is possible they would modify their trading patterns in such a way as to increase their profits and reduce even further the degree of statistical dependence that Fama and Blume observe. An example of a situation where this seems to have occurred will be presented later.

Fama and Blume base their analysis on the 0.5 percent filter, which is appropriate, since it is apparently the most attractive for a trader who is a member of the NYSE. The average return before commissions from following this rule is 11.5 percent, assuming the trader takes both long and short positions. The clearinghouse fees from following this rule would amount to about 8.4 percent per year. (The rule requires an average of 84 transactions per security per year.) Taking only clearinghouse fees into account, the annual return is reduced to about 3 percent. Fama and Blume conclude that clearinghouse fees alone are "more than sufficient to push the returns from the simple filter rule below those of a buy and hold policy." (p. 238)

This calculation assumes the trader follows the rule literally. That is, he is long when the rule gives a long signal and short when the rule gives a short signal. However, a trader who wished to take advantage of the 0.5 percent filter rule might also wish to take advantage of the fact that the expected return from a long position in a security was about 10 percent. He could take advantage of the expected return from a buy and hold policy by buying, say, 100 shares of stock in a given security. If in addition he wished to take advantage of the filter rule he could "trade around" this average long position. When the filter rule signalled a long position he would increase his holding to 200 shares. When the filter rule signalled a short position, he would decrease his position to zero shares. On the average his investment would be the amount required to carry 100 shares. (His investment might average slightly more or less if the filter rule requires that a long position be open for slightly more or less than half the time.) The return on the average investment would be the sum of the return from the buy and hold policy and the return from the filter rule, or about 13 percent.

The reader may object, and with some justice, that the return should be calculated not on the average capital employed but on the total capital employed. In the example just given this is the amount required to carry 200 shares of the stock. From this point of view the pure buy and hold and the pure filter trading policies give the same results as before, 10 percent and 3 percent, respectively. In considering the policy of trading around the trend we must ask what the trader does with the funds at his disposal when they are not invested in stock. Presumably they will be invested in some short-term money instrument. Five percent is a rough indication of what can be earned this way. On the average half of his capital will be so invested. His return from trading around the trend will be $(10 + 5 + 3)/2$ or about 9 percent. Admittedly this return is less than the expected return from a simple buy and hold policy. But a comparison of the two policies must also take risk into account. With the buy and hold policy the return is entirely from one source, and is likely to be quite variable. With the policy of trading around the trend the return comes from three sources, the long position in stock, the short-term money market, and the filter trading rule. There is likely to be much less variation in return from a policy of trading around the trend. A member of the NYSE might well find it attractive to take advantage of the statistical dependencies that Fama and Blume have so well documented.

Although the above argument is highly simplified, it does indicate the difficulties involved in estimating whether a statistically significant deviation from independence of price changes represents an economically significant deviation from the random-walk hypothesis. The model of a trader as a single product firm is inadequate and misleading. The hypothetical trader described in the previous paragraph is analogous to a multi-product firm. His profits are derived from three distinct, though complementary activities, investing in common stocks, lending short-term money and filter trading. In practice, professional traders frequently engage in more than three distinct activities. Presumably during the period covered by the data it was not profitable for traders to act so as to further reduce the magnitude of the statistical dependencies discovered by Fama and Blume. Whether or not this was due to conditions of imperfect competition (such as barriers to entry) cannot be determined from the presently available data.

V. LAGS IN RESPONSE TO NEW INFORMATION

In a frictionless market, prices would respond instantaneously to new information. Furthermore, the response would, on the average, be correct and take into account any dependencies in the information generating process.[4] If frictions exist, as they undoubtedly do in the real world, then there should be some lags in the response of prices to new information (see Working, 1958, p. 195). The challenge in this instance, as in others, is to identify the lags in response to new information, and to estimate whether their magnitude is justified by the cost of reducing them even further.

The frictionless model would be violated if prices failed to respond to relevant new information, or if they responded, but not immediately. A delay in the response to new information might take the form of a rapid adjustment that occurred some time after the new information became available.[5] A delay could also take the form of a gradual adjustment of prices to the new information. In the latter case there should be a systematic tendency for price movements in one direction to be followed by additional movements in the same direction, a pattern that could be called a price trend. Of these alternatives, only the price trend would be detectable from an analysis of price changes alone.

In a model that allows for the fact that it is costly to obtain and evaluate data to determine if it contains any relevant new information, one would not expect that, on the average, prices would respond immediately to new information that was potentially available. One would expect a relatively long lag in cases where it is relatively costly to obtain and process data, and where the expected value of the information contained in the data is low; a relatively short lag would be expected if it is relatively easy to obtain and process new data, and if the expected value of the informa-

---

[4] For an elaboration of this point of view see Fama (1965), pp. 36–39.

[5] A striking example of a rapid, but lagged response to new information is contained in the following quotation from the column by Robert Metz in the *New York Times*, Friday, August 23, 1968. Referring to the market activity in Control Data on the previous day, the column states:

> The news for the current quarter is not regarded as good. Lost in the shuffle of the stockholders' meeting last Thursday called (to approve) the merger with Commercial Credit, was a remark that earnings in the September quarter would be significantly lower than the year-earlier quarter. *Analysts who follow the stock and heard the comment* estimated that Control Data would earn 35 to 40 cents in this quarter compared with 50 cents a share a year ago.
>   *It seemed that the word did not reach Wall Street's performance funds until yesterday.* The stock held steady on Monday and eased $3\frac{7}{8}$, to 152 on Tuesday. But yesterday was a different story.
>   Big stockholders banged out without regard to price yesterday in an effort to clean house before the earnings outlook became generally known. (Parenthetical phrase and italics added.)

The story then proceeds to describe why the mutual funds now thought the earnings prospects were below what they had been expecting, and to summarize the market action in the stock on the previous day. The price dropped $16.75 in one day on a volume of over 900,000 shares. Nearly two-thirds of the volume was accounted for by six large blocks (each in excess of 19,000 shares), including one block that was the largest in terms of dollar volume ever recorded in common stock in the history of the NYSE. The closing price of Control Data on the day of the stockholder meeting was $154\frac{1}{2}$. On successive trading days after that meeting the closing prices were $154\frac{1}{2}$, $155\frac{7}{8}$, 152, $135\frac{1}{4}$, and 128.

tion contained in the data is high.[6] The available evidence is fragmentary, but it is generally consistent with this interpretation of the random walk hypothesis.

It is apparently extraordinarily difficult to detect the existence of price trends by observing only price movements. Some evidence that price trends may exist has been reported by Brinegar (1954) and Larson (1960) based on commodity futures prices, and by Cowles (1960) based on common stock price indices. However, the evidence is fragmentary and the interpretation of the evidence as being due to lagged responses to new information is open to question.

The most fruitful means of identifying price trends involves identifying specific items of new information whose date of publication can be reasonably estimated, and studying the pattern of price change on or around that date of publication. An interesting example of this approach is contained in a study by Davis (1967) which estimated the response of stock prices to the publication of sales and production data for the auto and steel industries. The example of automobile sales is most clearcut, since sales data contain more relevant information than production data, and because the data are reported separately by company. These data are reported regularly in *The Wall Street Journal* and are therefore easily and promptly available to the general public. Each report covers a recent 10-day period. Although sales are an important determinant of earnings, sales during any 10-day period are a small part of the total sales and they contain significant random variation. There is also considerable dependency in the data, since a company's market shares tend to shift when new models are introduced, and to remain relatively stable for the remainder of the marketing year. For this reason, the new information in a sales report for a 10-day period usually leads to a very small shift in stock values. These shifts are not large enough to warrant a purchase or sale solely on that account. Nevertheless, Davis was able to detect a definite though small correlation between the movement of stock prices and the information content of the sales data. The most striking conclusion of the study is that the adjustment of stock prices to the new information tends to be "concentrated in the two days prior to the data of publication and the three days following publication." (Davis, p. 38) Davis' study tends to support strongly the viewpoint that stock prices will respond promptly to even

---

[6] The Control Data incident described in the previous footnote contradicts the frictionless version of the random-walk hypothesis. If one assumes, as seems likely, that the expected value of the new information an analyst could obtain from attending a stockholders meeting is low, then most interested analysts may have correctly concluded that it is not worthwhile for them to attend stockholder meetings. Only with the benefit of hindsight is it apparent that it would have been worthwhile to attend this particular meeting. Thus it is not necessarily the case that the Control Data incident contradicts a version of the random-walk hypothesis that makes allowance for the costs of overcoming frictions.

relatively trivial bits of new information, provided the information is easily available at low cost to a wide number of persons.

A study being conducted by Myron Scholes has developed evidence that the occurrence of secondary distributions is treated by the market as conveying information that leads to a reduction in the price of the stock. Again, the information is easily available to interested parties, and the market response to the new information is relatively prompt.

Ferber (1958) attempted to estimate the effect on stock market prices of buy and sell recommendations by four widely distributed market services. Ferber concluded that there is a small but statistically significant shift in the price of the stocks in the direction that would be expected. (That is, an increase for buy recommendations and a decrease for sell recommendations.) Most of the price change took place in the first few days immediately following the publication of the recommendations. The change apparently persisted; there was no evidence of a movement in the opposite direction for at least four weeks.

Ferber's study is consistent with the results reported by Davis and Scholes in that it indicates a very prompt market response to events that are widely publicized and therefore available to many persons at low cost.[7] Unfortunately, Ferber's study was not specifically designed to test the random walk hypothesis. It does not distinguish between recommendations based on information contained in recent data, and other recommendations based on an analysis of data that was potentially available for some time before the recommendation was published. The random walk hypothesis would suggest that the first type of recommendation would lead to greater price effects than the second.

The studies by Davis, Scholes, and Ferber all deal with situations in which information, or at least data, is available at low cost to large numbers of persons. There is a need to construct more powerful tests of the random-walk hypothesis by attempting to determine the speed and adequacy of response of prices to relevant data that is more costly to obtain or to process.[8]

---

[7] Ferber reports that the price response to the publication of a recommendation took place very promptly. By contrast publication of a recommendation about a company apparently stimulates an increase in the volume of transactions in that company's shares that continues for several weeks. J. Hass has suggested to me that this observation is consistent with the idea that only a small number of knowledgeable traders, acting promptly, are sufficient to bring about a price response to new information. A much larger group of investors may eventually wish to make some shifts in their portfolios as an eventual result of obtaining this information. It is these shifts that apparently produce the increased volume. The traders who respond quickly are presumably the "sophisticated traders" postulated by Fama (1965, pp. 37–40).

[8] Two examples of the kind of study we have in mind might be mentioned. Larson (1967) attempted to determine the extent to which speculators in egg futures were able to predict cyclical changes in egg prices. The period studied was one in which the relevant cycles were very regular. His results were inconclusive. One test indicated some forecasting ability, but another test did not. An unpublished study by Smidt and Johnson (1962) suggests that meat packers responded systematically to anticipated shifts in the supply of pork, but not to anticipated shifts in demand.

When information is expensive to obtain and process, the speed with which prices can be expected to respond should depend on the economic incentives that could lead someone to devote resources to acquiring the information. The means by which one could profit from new information can be conveniently classified into three groups. First, obtaining the new information could be profitable because it is used directly by the persons who acquire it as a basis for their own investments. The securities research done by institutions managing their own portfolios is a clear example. When information is acquired for this purpose, the persons acquiring the information have an incentive to restrict its distribution, at least until they have completed whatever transactions they consider appropriate.

A second type of incentive for acquiring new information is the possibility of selling the information directly to an interested party who can make profitable use of it. Usually, but not always, the buyer will plan to use the information as a basis for his own trading. Investment counselors, and publishers of subscription market letters, are examples of firms that have an economic incentive to acquire information, with the idea of re-selling it. Normally, in this case, the producer of the information has an incentive to restrict its availability to those who have agreed to pay him for it.

A third type of incentive for acquiring new information occurs if the person who acquires the new information believes he will profit by the way other people react to the new information. One example of this situation is the brokerage firm that acquires new information and passes it along to its customers in the expectation that the brokerage firm will earn commissions when customers decide to trade on the basis of the new information. Another example is contained in the following quotation:

> One of the publisher's two regular subscription services, which regularly recommended purchases of securities, had a paid circulation of 5,000 and in addition was distributed free on some occasions to as many as 100,000 nonsubscribers. During a 9-month period in 1960 the publisher traded in securities which it recommended, purchasing shortly before the recommendation and selling shortly after the publication of the recommendation, without disclosing the facts to its subscribers. . . . In one instance the publication compared two companies in the same industry. As to one where the publisher had a short position, it suggested the stock had reached its peak, while in the other, where it held call options, it recommended purchase.[9]

A more comprehensive analysis of the costs and incentives of acquiring information might reasonably be expected to suggest fruitful new approaches to testing and refining the random walk hypothesis. For example,

[9] U.S. Congress, House Committee on Interstate and Foreign Commerce, *Report of the Special Study of Securities Markets of the Securities and Exchange Commission*, House Document No. 95, Part 1, 88th Congress, 1st Session (Washington, D.C.: Government Printing Office, 1963), p. 382.

the incentive to acquire new information about a company may vary systematically with the size of the company, the characteristics of its stockholders, the characteristics of its capital structure, etc. To what extent are there corresponding systematic differences in the speed with which the company's share prices respond to new information?

VI. SPECULATIVE BUBBLES

Speculative bubbles are produced by an inappropriate response to new information. Since the response is inappropriate it is eventually followed by a corrective price movement.

Superficially the price pattern produced by a speculative bubble resembles the dips or bulges produced by liquidity demands, except that speculative bubbles are likely to produce larger price fluctuations and to extend over much longer periods of time. The price fluctuations caused by demands for liquidity are normally caused by the action of a single decision-making unit. Speculative bubbles, like trends, are the result of the actions of large numbers of decision-making units responding to the same information. In the case of a trend, the price reaction is appropriate in magnitude, while in the case of a speculative bubble, the price reaction is exaggerated, and eventually produces a corrective reaction in the opposite direction.

One type of speculative bubble is the result of an exaggerated response to new information. Presumably it is most often the result of exaggerated optimism, but in principle it could also be the result of exaggerated pessimism. Speculative bubbles can also result if prices responded to false or misleading information.

In a sense, the existence of speculative bubbles is hypothetical. The available information on speculative bubbles is based wholly on historical studies and similar case histories of apparent examples of this phenomenon. The South Sea Bubble, the Tulip Craze, and the bull market of the late 1920's are examples of episodes that some, at least, would classify as speculative bubbles. Of more relevance to the present paper are similar episodes that may affect the stock of a single company or industry. The danger in attempting to identify speculative bubbles solely from historical studies is that price sequences having the required characteristics can be expected to occur occasionally by chance in a time series whose changes follow precisely a random walk. The historian, examining such an episode *ex post*, may easily exaggerate the causal significance of certain events. Evidence that prices responded inappropriately to new information in particular instances is not necessarily a violation of the random-walk hypothesis. In its simple version, this hypothesis requires only that the expected response should be appropriate. The random-walk hypothesis would be violated if it could be shown that there is a systematic tendency for prices to respond inappropriately. For example, it would be a violation of the random-walk hypothesis if it could be shown that there was a systematic tendency for security prices to rise temporarily during periods when dealers had a greater than normal incentive to sell such securities.

The fact that existing studies of the random-walk hypothesis have not uncovered evidence of the existence of speculative bubbles is far from convincing. Such price patterns, if they exist, probably extend over a period of months or years. The sample sizes and the statistical techniques used in existing studies would be inadequate to detect the existence of such speculative bubbles, even if they did exist.

VII. SUMMARY

The significance of the random walk hypothesis is that it provides a fruitful null hypothesis to use in statistical studies of price behavior in organized markets. Proponents of the hypothesis should not expect to find a complete absence of systematic elements in their empirical studies. Rather, the failure to detect some degree of nonrandomness sometimes can be interpreted more properly as evidence that the statistical tests used were insufficiently powerful. On the other hand, the detection of some nonrandom components is not evidence against the random-walk hypothesis unless it can be shown that the systematic tendencies present unexploited opportunities to make above normal profits.

Statistical studies employing the random-walk hypothesis as a null hypothesis are more likely to be fruitful if they utilize tests specifically designed to detect categories of nonrandomness that are *a priori* most likely. Three sources of systematic price tendencies are considered in this paper. They are demands for liquidity, lags in response to new information, and exaggerated responses to new information. The main part of the article is devoted to describing the price patterns that could be expected from each of these sources, and to summarizing some of the most significant evidence currently available with respect to each type of systematic tendency.

REFERENCES

Alexander, S. S. "Price Movements in Speculative Markets: Trends or Random Walks," *Industrial Management Review*, Vol. 2 (May 1961), pp. 7–26.

——. "Price Movements in Speculative Markets: Trends or Random Walks, No. 2," *The Random Character of Stock Market Prices*, Revised Edition, P. A. Cootner (ed.) (Cambridge, Mass.: M.I.T. Press, 1964), pp. 338–72.

Brinegar, C. S. "Statistical Analysis of Speculative Price Behavior," unpublished Ph.D. dissertation (Stanford University, 1954).

Cowles, A. "A Revision of Previous Conclusions Regarding Stock Price Behavior," *Econometrica*, Vol. 28 (October 1960), pp. 909–15.

Davis, J. V. "The Adjustment of Stock Prices to New Information," unpublished Ph.D. dissertation (Cornell University, 1967).

Demsetz, H. "The Cost of Transacting," *Quarterly Journal of Economics*, Vol. 82 (February 1968), pp. 33–53.

Fama, E. F. "The Behavior of Stock Market Prices," *Journal of Business*, Vol. 38 (January 1965), pp. 34–105.

——, and M. E. Blume. "Filter Rules and Stock Market Trading," *Journal of Business: Special Supplement*, Vol. 39 (January 1966), pp. 226–41.

Ferber, R. "Short-Run Effects of Stock Market Services on Stock Prices," *Journal of Finance*, Vol. 13 (March 1958), pp. 80–95.

Larson, A. B. "Measurement of a Random Process in Futures Prices," *Food Research Institute Studies*, Vol. 1 (November 1960).

——. "Price Prediction on the Egg Futures Market," *Food Research Institute Studies, Special Supplement*, Vol. 7 (1967), pp. 49–64.

Levy, R. A. "The Theory of Random Walks: A Survey of Findings," *The American Economist*, Vol. 11 (Fall 1967), pp. 34–48.

Mandelbrot, B. "Forecasts of Future Prices, Unbiased Markets, and 'Martingale' Models," *Journal of Business: Special Supplement*, Vol. 39 (January 1966), pp. 242–55.

Niederhoffer, V. "Clustering of Stock Prices," *Operations Research*, Vol. 13 (March–April 1965), pp. 258–65.

——, and M. F. M. Osborne. "Market Making and Reversal on the Stock Exchange," *Journal of the American Statistical Association*, Vol. 61 (December 1966), pp. 897–916.

Osborne, M. F. M. "Brownian Motion in the Stock Market," *Operations Research*, Vol. 7 (March–April 1959), pp. 145–73.

——. "Periodic Structure in the Brownian Motion of Stock Prices," *Operations Research*, Vol. 10 (May–June 1962), pp. 345–79.

——. "Some Quantitative Tests for Stock Price Generating Models and Trading Folklore," *Journal of the American Statistical Association*, Vol. 62 (June 1967), pp. 321–40.

Samuelson, P. A. "Proof that Properly Anticipated Prices Fluctuate Randomly," *Industrial Management Review*, Vol. 6 (Spring 1965), pp. 41–50.

Smidt, S. "A Test of the Serial Independence of Price Changes in Soybean Futures," *Food Research Institute Studies*, Vol. 5 (1965), pp. 117–36.

—— and A. Johnson. "Expectations and Information: A Study of Pork Inventory Behavior" (Graduate School of Business and Public Administration, Cornell University, 1962). (Mimeo)

Stigler, G. J. "Public Regulation of the Securities Market," *Journal of Business*, Vol. 36 (April 1964), pp. 117–42.

Working, H. "Price Effects of Scalping and Day Trading," *Proceedings of the Chicago Board of Trade Annual Symposium* (1954), pp. 114–139.

——. "A Theory of Anticipatory Prices," *American Economic Review*, Vol. 48 (May 1958), pp. 188–99.

——. "Tests of a Theory Concerning Floor Trading on Commodity Exchanges," *Food Research Institute Studies, Special Supplement*, Vol. 7 (1967), pp. 5–48.

Ying, C. C. "Stock Market Prices and Volumes of Sales," *Econometrica*, Vol. 34 (July 1966), pp. 676–85.

*Paul H. Cootner**

38. Stock Prices: Random vs. Systematic Changes

Reprinted from the **Industrial Management Review**, Vol. 3, No. 2 (Spring, 1962), pp. 24–45, by permission of the author and the publisher.

The subject matter of this paper is bound to be considered heresy. I can say that without equivocation, because whatever views anyone expresses on this subject are sure to conflict with someone else's deeply-held beliefs.[1]

For the purpose of exposition, I can characterize these beliefs as falling into two classes. Apparently there are, or were, a substantial group of economists who believe(d) that common stock prices tended to move in a deterministic, cyclical manner, where the term "cyclical" is taken, not in the sense that the National Bureau uses it, but in the mechanical sense of a movement perfectly predictable in timing and extent. These cycles might be quite complex, but diligent effort, and perhaps Fourier analysis, would eventually solve the riddle and bring a pot of gold to the persevering.

Except for a small fringe of opinion largely confined to stock market

---

* Professor of Finance, Massachusetts Institute of Technology.

[1] There have been a considerable number of articles dealing with the subject of independence in price changes in speculative markets over the last two decades. The earliest work on this subject was by a French mathematician statistician, M. L. Bachelier [2]. H. Working investigated the subject [21]. A. Cowles and H. Jones did further work in 1937 [6]. H. Working followed [23], and M. G. Kendall examined the subject [13]. More recent investigations have been made by M. F. M. Osborne [17]; H. Houthakker [10]; S. Alexander [1]; A. Larsen [15]; H. Working [22]; A. Cowles [5]; and H. Roberts [18].

Related to this question is the recent extensive controversy about risk premiums for which a bibliography is available in P. H. Cootner [4]; see also P. H. Cootner, "Risk Premiums: Seek and Ye Shall Find" (forthcoming).

There are also a number of unpublished sources on the subject: a paper by Paul A. Samuelson on Brownian motion in the stock market; a Ph.D. thesis by Arnold Moore at the University of Chicago; a bachelor's thesis by R. Cryer at M.I.T.; and related work in Ph.D. theses on put, call, and warrant markets by Richard Kruizenga at M.I.T., Case Sprenkle at Yale, and James Boness at Chicago. Other work is in progress on commodity markets at the Food Research Institute of Stanford University, principally by H. Working, and at Cornell University under the direction of S. Smidt and M. DeChazeau.

professionals, this point of view is moribund today, but its refutation has bred an important and intellectually intriguing countertheory.[2] The stock exchange is a well-organized, highly-competitive market. Assume that, in fact, it is a perfect market. While individual buyers or sellers may act in ignorance, taken as a whole, the prices set in the marketplace thoroughly reflect the best evaluation of currently available knowledge. If any substantial group of buyers thought prices were too low, their buying would force up the prices. The reverse would be true for sellers. Except for appreciation due to earnings retention, the conditional expectation of tomorrow's price, given today's price, is today's price.

In such a world, the only price changes that would occur are those which result from new information. Since there is no reason to expect that information to be nonrandom in its appearance, the period-to-period price changes of a stock should be random movements, statistically independent of one another. The level of stock prices will, under these conditions, describe what statisticians call a random walk, and physicists call Brownian motion. In the normal course of events, the level of prices, i.e., the summation of these random movements, will show movements that look like cycles but in fact are not.[3] Nothing can be learned about the future from looking at these price series. Buying a stock based on signals from such a chart will produce results no better than those from repeated flipping of a fair coin. The time might just as well be spent on analyzing the results of a fair roulette wheel.

You can see why the idea is intriguing. Where else can the economist find that ideal of his—the perfect market? Here is a place to take a stand, if there is such a place.

Unfortunately, it is not the right place. The stock market is not a random walk. A growing number of investigators have begun to suspect it,[4] and I think I have enough evidence to demonstrate the nature of the imperfections. On the other hand, I do *not* believe that the market is grossly imperfect. In fact, I do not know why the process I see going on in the market is not worthy of the name perfection too. It strays from "perfection" only to the extent that it defines the Frank Knight-Milton Friedman assumption of profitless speculation. Even more interesting, perhaps, is that my model is perfectly compatible with much of what I interpret Wall Street chart reading to be all about. Like the Indian folk doctors who discovered tranquilizers, the Wall Street witch doctors, without the benefit of scientific method, have produced something with their magic, even if they can't tell you what it is or how it works.

[2] A more complete exposition can be found in H. Roberts [18], or H. Working [23].
[3] For discussions of this phenomenon, see W. Feller [8], and J. E. Kerrich [14].
[4] Principally Houthakker, Alexander, Moore, and Larsen, though it should be pointed out that Moore and Larsen prefer to stress the randomness rather than the imperfections.

In this paper I will present a hypothesis which fits the data much better, and which has implications substantially different from that of the random walk hypothesis. There is a certain tentativeness about these results, however, because the testing is not quite complete. For one thing, although the basic outlines of the hypothesis I will present here were formulated in advance of the testing, some modifications were made in the course of the testing, so it is not truly appropriate to consider the results to be a proof of the theory. Secondly, while the hypothesis was tested against a wide variety of stock prices, the stock sample was not randomly drawn. Both of these deficiencies will be eliminated in further testing now under way, but for the time being these results are only tentative.

I. THE MODEL

First, I will present my own model of stock market behavior along with its statistical implications. After that I will compare the results of some statistical analysis with the implications of the two competing models. Finally, I will outline the further work contemplated along these lines and their implications for tests of randomness.

Let us start with the concept of a perfect market held by random walk theorists, but let us achieve this perfection without assuming a high degree of knowledgeability of the participants. They are all engaged in other occupations in which they have a comparative advantage so it is very costly, at least in terms of opportunity cost per unit of relevant information uncovered, for them to devote time to the relevant kind of stock market research. (In Stiglerian terms, their cost of search is very high.)[5] As a result, they tend to accept present prices as roughly representing true differences in value and they choose between stocks largely on the grounds of their attitudes toward risk. Those of them that do choose among stocks on the basis of information about future prospects are just as likely to be wrong as not. Demand for stocks will mostly depend upon changes in the level of income and its distribution among stockholders with different preferences. As the present moves into the future, the stockholders will face all kinds of surprises, but most of the surprises which come this week will not be related, in any systematic manner, to the surprises which will come next week.

Now let me introduce another group of investors and speculators who specialize in the stock market. As professionals, their opportunity cost of research is much less than that of the uninformed (largely because they know *what* to look for and where), but it is, nevertheless, nonnegative.

[5] G. Stigler [20]. In R. Nelson's terms, they have a prediction equation with a larger R^2 (correlation coefficient) and so the value of a piece of information is greater [16].

They do have an idea of what is going to happen in the future, but they cannot profit from it unless the current price deviates enough from the expected price to cover their opportunity costs. Their profits will come from observing the random walk of the stock market prices produced by the nonprofessionals until the price wanders sufficiently far from the expected price to warrant the prospect of an adequate return. In other words, when prices have deviated enough from the expected price that they can expect future surprises to force prices toward their mean more often than not. Competition among these professionals will tend to restrict the potential profit to the opportunity costs. Furthermore, they must recognize the possibility of error in their own forecasts and must recognize that even if they buy the stock at a favorable price the actual rate at which the stock appreciates or depreciates will be governed in fact by the random rate of approach to the expected price.

Let me illustrate. For simplicity, assume that every professional has the same expectations, and the same opportunity costs. Then prices will behave as a random walk with reflecting barriers. In something like the manner once suggested by Taussig, prices within those upper and lower limits will tend to move like a random walk. If prices fell to the lower limit, however, the rate at which the price moves back to the expected price is governed by the random process which operates within the barriers, so that even if their expectations are correct, their profit rate is still a stochastic variable. In addition, the individual buyer is unlikely to know for certain that his estimate of the price is correct or that other professionals share his estimate.

Furthermore, within this class of professionals, another sort of random walk environment operates. There is no reason to expect that changes in the price expectations of professionals should occur in other than a random manner. As a result, there probably would also be random changes in the trends around which the random walk takes place. That is, the path of stock prices over any substantial period of time would be composed of a random number of trends, each of which is a random walk with reflecting barriers. There is much random behavior in such a series, but it is substantially different from a random walk, and while it has some implications which are quite similar to that of a random walk, it has others which are strikingly different, as we shall see before long.

Note, for example, the customary distribution of weekly changes in the logarithms of stock prices. The mean of such weekly changes is very likely to be less than 0.005; the standard deviation, on the other hand, is likely to be much larger, usually between 0.02 and 0.03. (For these purposes, we will accept this fact as given, although it could be developed from the general theory.) (Table 1.) One implication of this, of course, is that it would be very difficult to detect the significance of any weekly

TABLE 1

Company Number	Company	Dates Covered	Mean	Standard Deviation
1	Socony Mobil	56–60	−0.0001	0.0298
2	Westinghouse	56–60	0.0025	0.0249
3	Chrysler	56–60	−0.0020	0.0297
4	Procter and Gamble	56–60	0.0042	0.0226
5	General Motors	56–60	0.0004	0.0208
6	RCA	56–60	0.0011	0.0310
7	Goodyear	56–60	0.0026	0.0257
8	General Foods	56–60	0.0046	0.0258
9	Commercial Solvents	56–60	0.0013	0.0355
10	B.F. Goodrich	56–60	−0.0008	0.0300
11	Du Pont	56–60	−0.0001	0.0195
12	May Department Stores	56–60	0.0010	0.0206
13	Standard of New Jersey	56–60	0.0000	0.0215
14	Brunswick Corporation	56–60	0.0130	0.0452
15	Ford Motors	56–60	0.0011	0.0257
16	Douglas Aircraft	56–60	−0.0025	0.0281
17	North American Aviation	56–60	0.0013	0.0382
18	Boeing Aircraft	56–60	0.0012	0.0392
19	International Paper	56–60	0.0003	0.0230
20	American Can	56–60	0.0000	0.0190
21	Allegheny Steel	56–60	0.0013	0.0372
22	Bethlehem Steel	56–60	0.0008	0.0226
23	Byers Corporation	56–60	−0.0006	0.0618
24	Carpenter Steel	56–60	0.0030	0.0383
25	Colorado Fuel and Iron	56–60	−0.0014	0.0334
26	Continental Steel	56–60	0.0033	0.0465
27	Granite City Steel	56–60	0.0033	0.0355
28	Inland Steel	56–60	0.0020	0.0269
29	Interlake Iron	56–60	−0.0002	0.0386
30	Jones and Laughlin	56–60	0.0014	0.0320
31	Pittsburgh Steel	56–60	−0.0025	0.0665
32	Republic Steel	56–60	0.0013	0.0274
33	U.S. Steel	56–60	0.0019	0.0242
34	Wheeling Steel	56–60	0.0005	0.0288
35	Continental Oil	51–55	0.0041	0.0207
36	Studebaker-Packard	54–60	−0.0017	0.0648
37	Dow Chemical	55–60	0.0022	0.0264
38	Coca Cola	56–60	0.0028	0.0221
39	Nabisco	50–60	0.0015	0.0164
40	IBM	50–60	0.0049	0.0277
41	Reynolds Metals	50–60	0.0056	0.0406
42	Int'l. Telephone and Telegraph	50–60	0.0004	0.0349
43	Brown and Bigelow	56–60	0.0022	0.0204
44	Interstate Department Stores	56–60	0.0025	0.0282
45	National Dairy Products	50–60	0.0031	0.0234

mean price change if the series were truly a random walk. But the high variance also means that any professional who did feel knowledgeable about the mean price would still want to set his buying price considerably away from the mean to protect against risks. If the lower edge of the barrier were to average several weekly standard deviations away from the mean, by far the greater portion of the successive weekly price changes would be totally uncorrelated with each other. On the other hand, when prices neared the barrier there would be a tendency for some negative autocorrelation, since movements to the barrier would be more likely to be followed by movements in the opposite direction. The net effect would be a moderate negative correlation near the boundary which would be heavily diluted by the number of cases when the price was near the mean, which would show no such negative autocorrelation.[6]

In addition to this negative correlation, the effect of the barriers would be to produce more small price changes than would be expected from a normal distribution of price changes. When unencumbered by the barrier, the central limit theorem would tend to ensure that the total weekly effect of a large number of individual transaction price changes would be approximately normal. The existence of the barrier, however, would cut short some of the price movements toward the barriers without restricting as much the very large price movements which could still occur in the direction away from the barriers. We would expect the distribution of price changes over short periods of time to be more leptokurtic under such conditions then the normal distribution.

As we look at changes over longer periods of time, however, other factors, which are relatively unimportant in the case of weekly changes, become much more significant. I have spoken of stock price series as composed of several trends of different slopes. As we lengthen the period over which we take differences the mean becomes more important relative to the standard deviation. (In a random walk this would be true because the increase in the mean of the price changes is directly proportional to the interval over which the price change is measured, while the standard deviation increases only as the square root of the interval. If there are reflecting barriers, the standard deviation will increase less rapidly than in a random walk so this effect will be even more pronounced.) Furthermore, the mean of each of the component trends becomes more distinguishable from the group mean. This will result in an increasing element of positive autocorrelation as long as the time interval of the differencing is less than the length of the trends. That is, the successive changes in an uptrend will all tend to be higher than the overall mean and the successive

---

[6] These, and similar results discussed later in the paper can readily be derived from basic texts in Markov chain theory. On this point, e.g., see Kemeny and Snell, [11].

changes in a downtrend will all tend to be lower.[7] As the differencing interval exceeds the length of some of the trends, this positive autocorrelation will begin to disappear.

The positive autocorrelation is also present in changes over one-week periods, but over such short periods the absolute magnitude of the differences in the means is so small relative to the standard deviation that the effect is negligible. It simply becomes increasingly prominent particularly when measured against the negative serial correlation induced by the barriers as the time interval increases.

In addition, the kurtosis of the distribution over longer differencing intervals will also change if the reflecting barrier hypothesis is true. If there were only a single trend, the distribution of price changes over successively longer time intervals will approach that of a rectangular distribution: i.e., it will be equally likely to get any value for the price change equal to or less than the width of the barriers. If the series were a single random walk, the distribution of price changes over successively longer intervals should become more and more normal as the central limit theorem becomes more and more applicable. So, if the random walk hypothesis is correct, kurtosis should be near 3 at weekly intervals and get closer to 3 as time goes on. If the reflecting barrier or trend hypothesis is correct, kurtosis should be greater than 3 to begin with and should approach the kurtosis of the rectangular distribution in the limit if a single trend is involved.

Where trends change over time, the predicted pattern is not completely clear, but the average value of the stock price *trend* over any substantial period of time is likely to be severely limited by the possibility of transferring funds among different investment outlets. Thus it is likely, under the reflecting barrier hypothesis, that kurtosis of the price changes will be somewhat larger than that of a rectangular distribution.

The primary element underlying all of these implications is that the stock price series will simply not be free to wander as much as they would if the series were a random walk. This tendency can be tested directly by utilizing the distributions of the range of a random walk developed by W. Feller.[8] Given these distributions it is possible simply to calculate the probability that a segment of the series is drawn from a random walk. If my hypothesis is correct, it should be possible to break each series up into

[7] This would be true even if each series was composed of several random walks each with a different mean. In this latter case, however, the positive autocorrelation would be much slower to appear.

[8] W. Feller [9], M. Solari and A. Anis [19], have shown that the mean of the actual distribution converges very slowly to the asymptotic distribution. It can be shown, however, that this slow convergence of the mean is due to the (small) probability of very large ranges under asymptotic conditions. Actually, the left-hand tail is a very close approximation to the exact distribution and it is this tail in which we will be interested.

(a relatively few, long) segments each of which is significantly different from a random walk. The results of this test are discussed below.

I have drawn this hypothesis in fairly abstract terms for the sake of clarity,[9] but it is possible to relax many of the assumptions without substantially altering the conclusions. Instead of breaking investors into two categories, one almost completely uninformed, the other almost completely knowledgeable, all I need is that there should be a considerable gulf in knowledge between the two substantial groups of investors and that there are relatively few people in the penumbra. I think the principle of comparative advantage insures this division to the necessary degree.

Similarly, it is not necessary to assume that all professionals share exactly the same expectations or have the same search costs, so that the barriers to price change may be soft and rubberlike rather than rigid. Some professionals will be willing to buy before others, but as the price falls, the cumulative percentage of professionals willing to sell will also rise. We can investigate the nature of this phenomenon by constructing a transition matrix of probabilities of rise or decline. That is, once we detect a trend by use of the distribution of the range, we can construct a frequency

---

[9] Statistically, the difference between this hypothesis and the simple random walk can be stated as follows. The general first-order autoregressive structure is of the form

$$X_{n+1} = \alpha_n X_n + \beta + \sigma Y$$

where Y is a random variable from a normal density function with zero mean and unit variance. If the process is a random walk, β is the mean price change per period and α_n equals unity for all n. This reduces to

$$(X_{n+1} - X_n) = \beta + \sigma Y_n$$

i.e., the changes are distributed normally with mean β and standard deviation σ. One possible deviation from randomness might be $\alpha_n \neq 1$. In that case

$$X_{n+1} - X_n = (\alpha_n - 1)X_n + \beta + \sigma Y$$

in which case the distribution of the changes would be autocorrelated. If $\alpha_n > 1$, an increase in X_n would raise the expectation that the next change would also be an increase. If $\alpha_n < 1$, the changes would show negative autocorrelation. My hypothesis is closer to the argument

$$\alpha_n = 1 - \frac{(X_n - X_0 - \beta_n)}{X_n} \epsilon \qquad (\epsilon > 0)$$

so that when $X_n > X_0 + \beta_n$, $\alpha_n < 1$, a rise is more likely to be followed by a fall, and when $X_n < X_0 + \beta_n$, a rise is more likely to be followed by a rise. If this were strictly true, a conventional attempt to estimate α_n as a constant should be expected to result in an estimate equal to 1, and indicate zero autocorrelation despite substantial nonrandomness.

My hypothesis differs from this one because I do not assume Y_n to be a normal variable for all n. In my formulation Y_n would be normally distributed for values of X_n close to $X_0 + \beta_n$ but would be skewed for much larger or smaller values of X_n. It is this skewness which accounts for the predicted (and observed) negative correlation.

distribution of the price changes conditional upon the price being a certain distance from the mean of the trend. For example, we can discover the number of times the price was 5 weekly standard deviations from the mean of the trend and the frequency distribution of its price change during the following week.

II. THE STATISTICAL RESULTS

The statistical results I will present here are based on a sample of 45 stocks all drawn from the New York Stock Exchange. Of these 45 stocks, 26 were selected by students from a list of 50 major companies with stock option plans which was drawn up for another purpose; 13 other stocks were drawn from the steel industry[10] so as to cover as wide a range of sizes of companies as possible; 3 stocks were chosen because a stock market advisory service had referred to them as offering evidence of long trends in prices; 3 others were chosen because they exhibited strong seasonality of sales and earnings. Five of the 45 series covered a 10-year period; 40 were weekly observations for 5 years; except for one series, all of the 40 5-year stocks covered the 1956–60 period.

All of the series were corrected for dividends by adding back all dividends, both cash and stock. As a result, the means of the price changes all include the average dividend yield on a weekly basis. Because earlier investigation had indicated that stock price changes were distributed more in accord with the log-normal distribution than the normal, all prices were converted to natural logarithms for the following computations. After all these computations had been completed, it was realized that the combination of correcting for dividends and *then* taking logarithms tends to bias downwards the variability of observations toward the end of the period of observation. It seems unlikely that this effect was large enough to be of importance, but I cannot be sure. Computations are now under way to verify the results under different methods of computation. In addition, further work is about to go forward on a random sample of 70 companies with data covering 10 years.

All the tests of the autocorrelation of weekly stock price changes published so far have consistently shown deviations from random behavior, though these deviations have been uniformly small, and there is some difference in the behavior of British stock price indexes and data based on prices of individual American stocks. Kendall's data for 29 British stock indexes,[11] Arnold Moore's data for 33 American companies[12] and

---

[10] One additional steel company, U.S. Steel, was part of the 26-company sample drawn from the stock option group.

[11] M. Kendall [13].

[12] A. Moore, unpublished Ph.D. thesis, University of Chicago.

my own data for 45 other American companies all indicate autocorrelations which are generally small in magnitude. In each case, however, some are significantly different from zero, and what is more important is that all tend to have the same sign. In the American data for *individual companies*, the one- and two-week price changes show negative autocorrelation much more frequently than would be expected from a population which was truly nonautocorrelated. For the British *indexes*, the first three weekly price changes exhibit the same pattern except that the overwhelming proportion are positive. For slightly longer differencing intervals, Kendall's series revert to the American pattern, but it is not easy to say whether the differences are due to the fact that the British data are indexes or whether they are due to such institutional differences between the markets as the British institution of settling transactions only every two weeks.

To test this tendency toward excessive reversals, I applied the mean-square successive-differences test, which is very sensitive to this kind of nonrandomness. Basically, the test is a comparison of the variance of the *difference* between successive one-week price changes and the variance of the price changes themselves.[13] Fourteen of the 45 series showed a significant tendency (at the 5 percent level) toward excessive reversals in the one-week price changes and 11 showed the same tendency in two-week price changes. Only one in the 45 price series showed a significant tendency toward positive autocorrelation at that differencing interval (Table 2).

At the 14-week interval, the situation was almost reversed. Nine of the 45 series now showed a significant tendency for price changes to follow one another (at the 5 percent level), and 35 of the 45 series showed at least some tendency toward positive autocorrelation. The odds are more than 100 to 1 against such a preponderance of trends occurring if there were no such tendency in the population. Furthermore, the shift from an excessive tendency for reversals to an excessive tendency for trends takes place relatively uniformly as the interval increases.

As several writers have already noted, the distribution of price changes in speculative markets tends to be significantly leptokurtic. The data of my sample bear this out. Of the 45 price series tested (Table 3) only two had a kurtosis less than 3—which is the kurtosis of a normal distribution— and those two values were 2.95 and 2.98. The average kurtosis (Table 4)

---

[13] The statistic used is $1 - \dfrac{E}{2}$, where $E = \dfrac{\sum\limits_{i=1}^{n-1} (X_{i+1} - X_i)^2}{\sigma_x^2}$ and where the X_i are the *price changes*. If the changes are independent, E should equal 2. The statistic is distributed normally with mean zero and standard deviation $\dfrac{n-2}{(n-1)(n+1)}$. See C. A. Bennett and N. L. Franklin [3].

TABLE 2. MEAN-SQUARE SUCCESSIVE DIFFERENCE TEST, $1-E/2$

Company Number	1-Week Changes	14-Week Changes
1	−0.276*	−0.171
2	−0.027	0.116
3	0.019	0.070
4	0.007	0.214
5	0.005	0.155
6	0.091‡	0.172
7	0.168*	0.256
8	−0.086‡	−0.236
9	−0.108†	0.068
10	0.015	0.071
11	0.033	0.390†
12	−0.170*	−0.613*
13	−0.086‡	0.065
14	−0.026	−0.179
15	0.051	0.384†
16	0.021	−0.243
17	−0.080‡	0.051
18	−0.071	−0.010
19	0.043	0.403†
20	−0.040	−0.316
21	0.038	0.373†
22	−0.077	0.289
23	−0.333	0.180
24	0.032	0.490*
25	−0.084	0.220
26	−0.233	0.496*
27	−0.084	0.346†
28	0.013	0.025
29	−0.162*	0.328
30	0.010	0.068
31	−0.337*	0.236
32	0.039	0.187
33	0.037	0.116
34	0.038	0.428†
35	0.011	0.177
36	0.076	0.254
37	0.061	0.145
38	−0.112†	0.215
39	−0.092	−0.035
40	−0.125*	−0.410†
41	0.076	0.440†
42	−0.131*	0.325‡
43	0.011	0.111
44	−0.137*	0.176
45	−0.154*	0.072

* Significant at 1 percent level.
† Significant at 5 percent level.
‡ Significant at 10 percent level.

TABLE 3. KURTOSIS

Company Number	1-Week Changes	14-Week Changes
1	11.30	2.99
2	3.19	1.59†
3	3.15	1.56†
4	4.43	1.81†
5	3.20	1.96†
6	3.39	1.61†
7	3.04	1.99†
8	6.45	1.81†
9	3.63	3.50
10	3.08	2.07*
11	3.32	1.90†
12	3.46	2.04*
13	3.73	3.34
14	3.10	2.18*
15	3.27	1.99†
16	3.55	1.78†
17	4.54	1.86†
18	4.43	1.56†
19	3.28	1.96†
20	3.43	2.48
21 (Steel Companies)	3.42	2.22*
22	3.73	2.76
23	21.34	2.34*
24	4.13	2.41
25	3.11	3.41
26	5.65	2.21*
27	3.17	2.10*
28	2.95	2.59
29	15.01	1.85†
30	3.30	2.28*
31	4.75	2.63
32	3.09	2.29*
33	3.21	2.45
34	3.11	2.70
35	2.98	2.00*
36	5.89	1.46†
37	3.83	2.02*
38	5.71	3.70
39	4.11	2.25*
40	16.11	2.35*
41	3.45	2.05*
42	10.45	1.80†
43	5.31	2.39
44	5.30	3.06
45	3.10	2.18*

* Values less than 2.36 but greater than 2.00.
† Values under 2.00.

TABLE 4. AVERAGE KURTOSIS

Number of Weeks Over Which Differences Are Taken	Expected Value	Average (including No. 35)
1	2.96	4.90
2	2.91	3.63
3	2.86	3.15
4	2.81	3.47
5	2.77	3.04
6	2.73	2.56
7	2.69	2.60
8	2.65	2.30
9	2.61	2.46
10	2.57	2.53
11	2.52	2.40
12	2.47	2.36
13	2.43	2.16
14	2.36	2.26

This calculation includes all stocks for a five-year period. For all companies except No. 35 (Continental Oil) for which it is 1951–55, the five-year period is 1956–60.

was 4.90, with three values greater than 10, and 15 others between 4 and 10. If the successive changes were independent, we would expect that price changes over longer intervals would more closely approach the average kurtosis of a normal distribution. In fact, however, the kurtosis decreases so rapidly that it very soon falls *below* that of a normal distribution. At the 14-week interval only 14 of the 45 series have a kurtosis greater than 2.363 which is the expected kurtosis of the small samples I have had to use. Sixteen of the series show a kurtosis less than 2.0.[14]

[14] The expected kurtosis of a sample from the normal distribution is $3\left(\dfrac{n-1}{n+1}\right)$, where n is the sample size. In the computations in this paper, we computed $\dfrac{m^4}{\sigma^4}$ instead of $\dfrac{m^4}{s^4}$, and as a result the expected value is $\dfrac{(n-1)^2}{n}$ times the indicated value. For the 14-week kurtosis figures, $n = 17$. M. Kendall [12].

It is particularly interesting to note the way that the 14 steel companies stand out in the sample in a negative way. Only 7 out of those 14 have a lower kurtosis than the random hypothesis would suggest. The sample of steel companies is much more cyclical in its behavior than the other stocks in the sample; and, as we would expect, if a series were composed of a large number of different "trends," the resultant kurtosis would be more like that of a normal distribution. As I indicate below, the more sensitive "range test" for trends, suggests this is the case.

A complete analysis of the data on the basis of the range of a random walk[15] has not yet been possible because of certain conceptual problems. Only two companies have a trend which is significant over the entire period of observation at the 5 percent level. But in most cases this is because of several long segments each of which is in itself very unlikely to have come from a random sample. For example, the price of National Dairy Products in the 300 weeks beginning in January, 1950, moved in a range which was significantly too small to be random at less than the 1 percent level. Furthermore, from that time to the end of 1960 (209 weeks) it moved within a range around another trend which was similarly too small to be random. International Telephone and Telegraph has successive consecutive intervals (i.e., each begins where the prior one left off) of 100, 50, 125, 100, and 60, all of which are significant at the 1 percent level (only the first 60 weeks out of a 530-week period of observation fail to show any such significant trends.) The entire I. T. and T. series would be significantly nonrandom at the 12 percent level. General Foods shows two consecutive trends, each of which covers half of a 5-year period of observation. National Biscuit, Continental Oil, Procter and Gamble, and Coca Cola all behave similarly. That is, each of these companies has only one or two trends covering all of the periods studied. Each of the 45 companies studied has at least one trend of more than a year in length and most have at least one longer trend and very few long stretches *without* a trend. The more stable investment grade companies tend to have only two or three consecutive, nonoverlapping trends covering all of a 5- or 10-year period. The more "cyclical" companies like the steels can similarly be broken down into consecutive, nonoverlapping trends, but these "trends" tend to be shorter and are sometimes separated by short intervals which do not fit into any "trend."

The conceptual problem is one of *significance*. Almost *any* series of any length has some segment which is unusual in some way. If the segments are not chosen at random, the significance of finding them is not at all clear. On the other hand, the longer (and fewer) the segments, the more significant each must be and this conclusion is strengthened if we require that the trends be consecutive, i.e., that the next one start where the last one ended. It would seem as if the lengths of the trends involved in the price series studied, especially in conjunction with the other evidence

[15] Feller, *op. cit.*, Feller finds two asymptotic distributions for the range: one which is appropriate if the mean of the random walk is known, another if it is unknown. The latter has the smaller sampling variance, and is the one used. In that procedure, the range is computed around the trend line found by using the observed mean price change to be the true mean. The distribution is skewed and was computed especially for this purpose. A smaller distribution for the maximum deviation is derived in Doob [7].

The distributions derived by Feller depend upon the population standard deviation. I have derived the related distributions which use the sample standard deviation in the statistic and which are independent of the population statistics. A paper deriving and computing these distributions will be published separately.

presented, are significant indications of nonrandomness, but the analysis in this direction has much further to go.

Although my relatively limited investigations into commodity price behavior along these lines suggest a much closer approach to randomness, I should also point out that these results seem largely compatible with the results of Arnold Larsen's more extensive investigations into those markets. Larsen finds a tendency for shocks to be followed by reversals over short periods of time and then by weak trend effects over longer periods. His path of research, using somewhat different methods developed in collaboration with Holbrook Working, shows great promise for research in this area.

It should also be noted that evidence of trends presented here is quite compatible with a similar kind of evidence presented by Sidney Alexander and Hendrick Houthakker. These researchers found little evidence of useful short-run autocorrelations, but did find strategies which suggested that stock and commodity prices did move in trends.

Both Alexander and Houthakker attacked the problem this way. If it is true that stock prices are a random walk, there is no strategy which will, in fact, make money. If there is such a strategy, price changes cannot be random. Houthakker's strategy (used on commodity futures) was: buy a security and hold it for a fixed period with a stop-loss order x percent below the market. Alexander's related but more complicated strategy was: select a stock and watch it. If it goes up x percent, buy it and hold on to it until it falls x percent from a subsequent high in which case sell the stock you own and go short an equivalent amount. Stay short until it rises x percent from a subsequent low. In this case the x percent is conceived of as a filter for small, "unimportant," price changes.

Houthakker tested his rule against the behavior of actual commodity futures prices. Alexander tested his rule against movements in the Dow-Jones and Standard and Poor's indexes. Unfortunately, Alexander's rule is not nearly as effective when used on individual common stocks. Used with the indexes, gains in excess of simple strategies are achieved with "filters" as small as 5 percent even after allowing for commissions. For individual stocks, the filter has to be of the order of 25 percent. For a random sample of 76 stocks from the New York Stock Exchange in the period 1950–59, *gross* gains (omitting commission charges) ran about 50 percent of that which could be achieved from a simple investment strategy.[16] This is, of course, an unfavorable period for testing any alter-

---

[16] Allen Shiner, "An Analysis of Price Movements in the Stock Market by the Filter Technique," unpublished Bachelor's thesis, M.I.T. (1962).

Actually, Shiner's results are not a literal reproduction of the Alexander hypothesis, since Shiner uses only weekly closing prices to establish highs and lows. The intraweek highs and lows would have to be more extreme, but there is no *a priori* way to measure the bias, since errors in both directions are possible. However, they are very unlikely to be important enough to affect these results.

As in Alexander's original paper, the gains referred to are geometric gains; i.e., they assume pyramiding of all profits.

native to simple buying and holding, but these results are quite dismal, and indeed are intrinsically so. With a filter of 25 percent, declines must be very sharp indeed to permit profits on short sales.[17] Since a gain of 25 percent of the price of the stock must be sacrificed on a long position if the price indeed rises, substantial profits on short positions are essential if the filter technique is to be superior to simple investment. Clearly only periods including very substantial market declines would make this possible.

On the other hand, it is easy to improve upon Alexander's original and imaginative beginnings, if a model like mine proves to be true. Alexander's rule requires that the company's stock prices actually fall substantially before the stock can be sold. A rule based on a fall *relative* to some trend would permit much more rapid response to changes of direction. One such procedure involving the use of the probability of the range of fluctuation around the trend seems extremely promising. This involves buying (selling) the stock when its recent behavior has a low probability of arising from a random walk and selling (buying) it when that probability rises above a previously specified level. This particular strategy is very difficult to implement computationally, but short-cuts are being developed and may soon prove feasible. It has the advantage of being conceptually similar to the methods actually suggested by stock market "technicians" and thus is a fairer test of their hypotheses. From a practical point of view, it would have several advantages over the "filter" rule. First, it would enable a follower to sell (buy) a stock when it stopped rising (falling) along the previously defined trend, rather than waiting for a substantial reversal. Second, it would permit an investor the alternative of holding cash rather than adopting a position in either direction—as the filter rule (though not Houthakker's stop-loss) requires.

While the rule I have suggested is difficult to implement, there are other simpler rules which also possess the properties I have described. One such simple decision rule is a modification of a rule actually suggested by some investment services. The rule is usually stated as follows: Compare the price today with an average of the price in the last 200 days. If the current price is higher than the moving average, buy the stock; if it is less than the moving average, sell short. If the current price rises above the moving average, cover short positions. If the price falls below the moving average, eliminate long positions.

Since the data in this study are weekly closing prices, I substituted a

---

[17] Actually, for large filters Alexander uses "logarithmic filters" rather than percentages; i.e., the percentage difference from the high (low) is always measured on the low price. Thus, with a "25 percent filter," the price need only fall 36 percent to enable a short sale to make money. The short sale would take place when the price dropped to 80 percent of the previous high. If the price fell to 64 percent of the high, a repurchase would be effected when the price rose to 125 percent of the lower price.

40-week average for the suggested 200-day average, and compared the result of this strategy with the results of buying each stock on the 40th observed week,[18] and holding it to the end of the period of observation. The indicated strategy is much superior to simple buying and holding if only gross profits are considered. While this is strongly suggestive of non-randomness, it is *not* necessarily indicative of a nonrandomness noticeable enough to lead to a remunerative strategy, since the moving average procedures lead to much more frequent trading than simple investment. In fact, after allowing for commissions, the moving average strategy is much inferior.

Most of the excessive transactions occur when the actual stock price remains in a narrow range. As a crude rule-of-thumb to reduce the number of transactions, the decision rule was modified to allow for transactions only when the moving average and the current price diverged by more than a certain percentage. Under this new strategy, the stock was to be bought only when the price rose above the moving average by more than 5 percent and would be sold whenever the price fell below the moving average by any amount: short sales would only be undertaken when the moving average rose above the price by more than 5 percent but would be covered whenever the price moves above the moving average by any amount. The results (Table 5) show that the gross gain from this strategy is 17 percent greater than simple investment but the *net* gain is still smaller. More important, however , is the fact the average *net weekly* gain is substantially higher for several alternative strategies. This is because the 5 percent rule now leaves the investor free to divert his funds to other uses whenever the stock price shows no particular trend. For example, the *net* weekly gain from the moving average strategy is 9.5 percent greater than from simple investment. The weekly gain from the moving average strategy ignoring the short positions is 76 percent greater. In addition, the risk-averting speculator may be attracted by the fact that the variance of these strategies is some 30 percent less than a simple investment alternative.

The significance of these calculations is not altogether clear. If individual stock prices were independent of one another, they would indicate very worthwhile advantages for nonrandom strategies. If, as is true, individual stock prices are not independent, the attractiveness of these particular

---

[18] This is the appropriate comparison for this strategy since, unlike the filter, this moving average rule can be implemented at any point of time by simple reference to the past 40 weeks of observed data. That is, no lag from the commencement of the application of the rule is necessary.

All comparisons indicated here are between sums of the logarithms of the price changes; i.e., we refer to geometric (or pyramiding) profits. These are necessarily smaller than the corresponding arithmetic sums.

TABLE 5.   RESULTS OF MOVING AVERAGE DECISION RULE*

5 Percent Threshold

	Average Return per Stock (Percent)		Average Return per Stock per Week (Percent)		Average Return per Stock per Week (Percent) (annualized)		Average Transactions per Stock
	Gross	Net	Gross	Net	Gross	Net	
Buy and hold	63	60	0.19	0.18	10	10	2
Moving average strategy (long and short)	79	54	0.26	0.20	14	11	15.2
Moving average strategy (long only)†	68	56	0.38	0.32	22	18	8.0

Zero Threshold

	Average Return per Stock (Percent)		Average Return per Stock per Week (Percent)		Average Return per Stock per Week (Percent) (annualized)		Average Transactions per Stock
	Gross	Net	Gross	Net	Gross	Net	
Buy and hold	63	60	0.19	0.18	10	10	2
Moving average strategy (long and short)	74	32	0.22	0.11	12	6	82.8
Moving average strategy (long only)†	68	48	0.33	0.25	19	14	40.6

All profits figures are geometric means: averages of the logarithms of profits reconverted to arithmetic values. Net profits are computed by assuming 1 percent commissions per transaction.

* The Decision Rule is as follows: buy the stock when the price exceeds a 40-week moving average by more than the threshold amount and sell the stock whenever the price dips below the moving average by any amount. Sell the stock short whenever it falls below the moving average by more than the threshold amount and cover the short sale whenever the price rises above the moving average by any amount.

† Same rule as in footnote *, except that only long positions are included.

strategies depends upon the alternative uses of the funds when they are not employed in common stock investment. On the other hand, these strategies are hardly exhaustive and, indeed, we have indicated some that look more promising. In addition to tests based on the range, we have not investigated moving averages of varying lengths or rules involving different thresholds. Furthermore, the period of investigation has been one which has been peculiarly satisfactory for simple investment policies, and the sample of stocks chosen is one in which the markets are much more likely to be perfect that would be the case if smaller companies were involved.

Finally, I turn to a study of the transition matrices of price changes within the trends.

For some of the periods marked off by the trends I have detected, I have computed transition matrices for the price changes. Some of these are indicated in Figures 1 through 4. The N rows of the matrix represent N classes of prices, each of which is equal in width to $1/N$th of the range of the series around a trend line computed from a least-squares time trend. The minimum of the deviations from the trend is in the uppermost row; the maximum is in the lowest row. The columns are identically defined, with the lowest price class on the left and the highest on the right. The transitions are from the class denoted by row to the one denoted by the column. The diagonal entries represent movement within the same class. The entries to the right of the diagonal represent price rises. The entries to the left, price declines.

The matrices shown are typical of all those computed. There is apparently a mild tendency, especially near the maximum and minimum, for price changes to move toward the mean. This is shown by the righthand marginal totals. There is no *clear* similar tendency as far as the direction from which a class is entered. The lower marginal totals indicate the average move *into* a given class. If the random walk hypothesis were correct, there would be the same (zero) expectation of price change in each row and each column.

The Houthakker-Alexander approaches, as well as my own tests based on the range of moving averages, all suffer from lack of a good statistical test of significance; on the other hand, they come closer to testing for the kind of nonrandomness which stock market traders claim exists. It is a foolish sort of statistical reasoning which would suggest we limit our investigations to those hypotheses which are easy to investigate. The way in which actual markets operate is one of the more fascinating of current economic questions. If their behavior is more complicated than the random walk models suggest, it will take more sophisticated statistical testing to discover it.

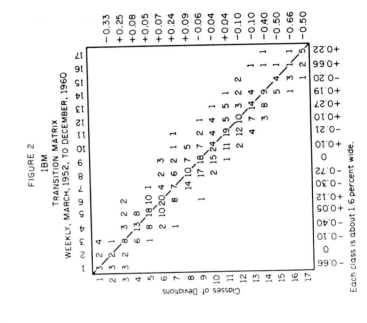

FIGURE 2
IBM
TRANSITION MATRIX
WEEKLY, MARCH, 1952, TO DECEMBER, 1960

Each class is about 1.6 percent wide.

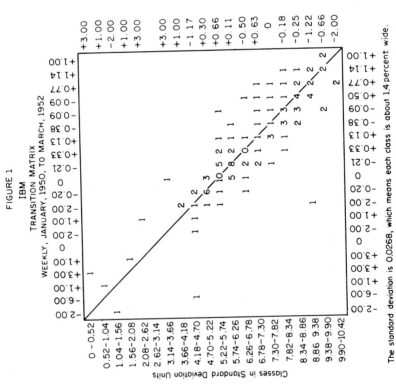

FIGURE 1
IBM
TRANSITION MATRIX
WEEKLY, JANUARY, 1950, TO MARCH, 1952

The standard deviation is 0.0268, which means each class is about 1.4 percent wide.

The classes are numbered starting from the minimum deviation, so the topmost row is the lowest price class and the lowest row contains the maximum.

The outlying points are the aftermath of the Korean War outbreak.

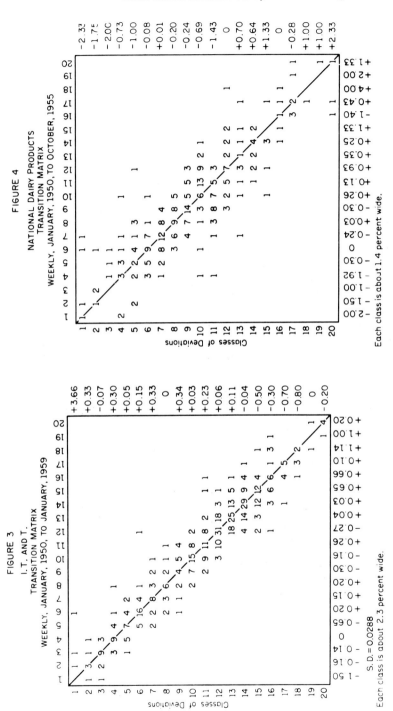

FIGURE 4
NATIONAL DAIRY PRODUCTS
TRANSITION MATRIX
WEEKLY, JANUARY, 1950, TO OCTOBER, 1955

Each class is about 1.4 percent wide.

FIGURE 3
I.T. AND T.
TRANSITION MATRIX
WEEKLY, JANUARY, 1950, TO JANUARY, 1959

S.D. = 0.0288
Each class is about 2.3 percent wide.

REFERENCES

[1] Alexander, S. "Price Movements in Speculative Markets: Trends or Random Walks," *Industrial Management Review*, Vol. 2, No. 2 (May, 1961), pp. 7–26.

[2] Bachelier, M. L. *Theorie de la Speculation* (Paris, France: Gauthier-Villars, 1900).

[3] Bennett, C. A., and N. L. Franklin. *Statistical Analysis in Chemistry and the Chemical Industry* (New York, N. Y.: John Wiley and Sons, 1954).

[4] Cootner, P. H. "Returns to Speculators: Telser vs. Keynes," *Journal of Political Economy*, Vol. 68, No. 4 (August, 1960), pp. 396–403. (Also, comment and reply, pp. 404–18.)

[5] Cowles, A. "Revision of Previous Conclusions Regarding Stock Price Behavior," *Econometrica*, Vol. 28, No. 4 (October, 1960), pp. 909–15.

[6] ——, and H. Jones. "Some A Posteriori Probabilities in Stock Market Action," *Econometrica*, Vol. 5, No. 280 (July, 1937).

[7] Doob, J. L. "A Heuristic Approach to the Kolmogorov-Smirnov Theorems," *Annals of Mathematical Statistics*, Vol. 20 (1949).

[8] Feller, W. *An Introduction to the Theory of Probability and its Applications*, Vol. I (New York, N. Y.: John Wiley and Sons, 1957).

[9] ——. "The Asymptotic Distribution of the Range of the Sums of Random Variables," *Annals of Mathematical Statistics*, Vol. 22 (1951).

[10] Houthakker, H. "Systematic and Random Elements in Short-Term Price Movements," *American Economic Review*, Vol. 51 (May, 1961), pp. 164–72.

[11] Kemeny, J. G., and J. L. Snell. *Finite Markov Chains* (Englewood Cliffs, N. J.: Prentice-Hall, 1959).

[12] Kendall, M. G. *The Advanced Theory of Statistics*, Vol. I (London, England: Griffin, 1943).

[13] ——. "The Analysis of Economic Time Series—Part I: Prices," *Journal of the Royal Statistical Society* (Series A), Vol. 96 (1953), pp. 11–25.

[14] Kerrich, J. E. "Random Remarks," *The American Statistician*, Vol. 15 (June, 1961), pp. 16–21.

[15] Larsen, A. "Measurement of a Random Process in Futures Prices," *Food Research Institute Studies*, Vol. 1, No. 3 (November, 1960).

[16] Nelson, R. "Uncertainty, Prediction and Competitive Equilibrium," *Quarterly Journal of Economics*, Vol. 75, No. 1 (February, 1961), pp. 41-62.

[17] Osborne, M. F. M. "Brownian Motion in the Stock Market," *Operations Research*, Vol. 7, No. 2 (March-April, 1959), pp. 145–73. [Also, comment and reply in Vol. 7, No. 6 (November-December, 1959).]

[18] Roberts, H. "Stock Market 'Patterns' and Financial Analysis," *Journal of Finance*, Vol. 14 (March, 1959), pp. 1–10.

[19] Solari, M. E., and A. A. Anis. "The Mean and Variance of the Maximum of the Adjusted Partial Sums of a Finite Number of Independent Normal Variables," *Annals of Mathematical Statistics*, Vol. 28 (1957), pp. 706–16.

[20] Stigler, G. "The Economics of Information," *Journal of Political Economy* (July, 1961).

[21] Working, H. "A Random-Difference Series for Use in the Analysis of Time Series," *Journal of the American Statistical Association* (March, 1934), pp. 11–24.

[22] ———. "Note on the Correlation of First Differences of Averages in a Random Chain," *Econometrica*, Vol. 28, No. 4 (October, 1960), pp. 916–18.

[23] ———. "The Theory and Measurement of Price Expectations," *American Economic Review*, Vol. 34, No. 3 (May, 1949) p. 150–66.

Michael D. Godfrey
Clive W. J. Granger
Oskar Morgenstern*

39. The Random-Walk Hypothesis of Stock Market Behavior[1]

Reprinted by permission of the authors and publisher from **Kyklos,**
Vol. XVII (1964), pp. 1–29.

I. INTRODUCTION

In a previous paper by Granger and Morgenstern [4][2] spectral methods of analysis were applied to weekly and monthly price and volume series from the New York stock market. The results of this work were frequently surprising and generally controversial, as the large number of letters and comments received by the authors indicate. As is usual the results suggested numerous other interesting phenomena deserving investigation. It is the object of the present paper to study the market in further detail by the use of not only weekly data but also daily and individual-transaction data.

The first important result obtained in [4] was the confirmation of the random-walk hypothesis for weekly and monthly price data from the New York market. Because of the restriction on the resolution of the spectral estimates imposed by the length of data available, the random-walk hypothesis could not be tested at very low frequencies. However there was some indication that at these frequencies the hypothesis could not fully explain the spectral estimates. The series examined were the Dow-Jones, Standard and Poor, and various SEC indices as well as the price series of certain individual companies.

* All, Princeton University. Further research by the same authors is included in *The Predictability of Stock Market Prices* (Heath & Co., Lexington Books, 1970), by Oskar Morgenstern and Clive W. J. Granger.

[1] The research described in this paper, performed in the Econometric Research Program at Princeton University, was supported by National Science Foundation Grant NSF-GS30. The computer facilities used are supported by National Science Foundation Grant NSF-GP579. This paper was originally presented at the Summer Meeting of the Econometric Society in Cleveland, Ohio, September 4–7, 1963. The authors would particularly like to acknowledge the helpful comments and criticisms of an earlier draft made by John W. Tukey.

[2] Numbers in brackets refer to References, page 735.

The second main result of [4] was that no connection could be found between the price series and the corresponding volume of transactions series. This result cast doubt on the belief that the application of conventional demand and supply theory would prove useful in the study of stock market behavior. Other results indicated in [4] were that no annual cycle could be found in the data (although certain harmonics of the annual were just recognizable), nor—far more significant—was there any indication of any important business cycle frequency. Using weekly data no pattern could be found in the interconnection between sub-sections of the market. It was evident that no one sub-section was consistently leading the others.

II. THE RANDOM-WALK HYPOTHESIS

The initial idea that the fluctuations in stock market prices could be explained by a random-walk model was made by Bachelier [2] in 1900. This work has been little noticed by economists but influenced physicists concerned with the theory of Brownian motion. In recent years this proposal has been further explored by various authors, for example Alexander [1] and Osborne [6]. The random-walk process is defined by

$$x_t - x_{t-1} = \epsilon_t \tag{2.1}$$

where x_t is the variable generated by the random-walk and where ϵ_t forms, for successive values of t, a sequence of random, independent numbers. These numbers need not be drawn from identical distributions, however all of the distributions must have zero mean values. From Eq. (2.1) it is clear that

$$x_t - x_{t-u} = \sum_{j=t-u+1}^{t} \epsilon_j \tag{2.2}$$

Thus differences of the form $x_{t_1} - x_{t_2}$ and $x_{t_3} - x_{t_4}$ are independent random variables if $t_1 > t_2 > t_3 > t_4$. If $t_1 > t_2 > t_3 > t_4$ then the two sequences are independent of each other. If $E[(\epsilon_t)^2]$ is independent of t, then differences of the form $x_t - x_{t-u}$ possess variances which are also independent of time. On the other hand the variance of x_t is given by:

$$E[(x_t)^2] = E[(x_{t-1})^2] + \sigma_{\epsilon_t}^2 \tag{2.3}$$

where

$$\sigma_{\epsilon_t}^2 = E[(\epsilon_t)^2]$$

If the process is assumed to have started at $-T$ then

$$E[(x_t)^2] = (T + t)\sigma_{\epsilon_t}^2 + E[(x_{-T})^2] \tag{2.4}$$

However if we take two sequences of the form

$$x_{t1}, \ x_{t_2+u_1}, \ x_{t_2+2u_1}, \ \ldots \tag{2.5}$$

$$x_{t_2}, \ x_{t_2+u_1}, \ x_{t_2+2u_1}, \ \ldots$$

where

$$t_2 = t_1 - u_2$$

and form, by taking first differences, series of the form

$$x_t - x_{t-u_1} \tag{2.6}$$

$$x_{t'} - x_{t'-u_1}$$

where

$$t' = t - u_2$$

then these two series (Eq. 2.6) will have second order stationarity under the assumption that ϵ_t is stationary. Each will also be a sequence of independent random variables. However, for $u_2 < u_1$ they will be correlated with each other.

As this is the form of the first differences of the series of daily opening prices and the series of daily closing prices it is relevant to derive the expected correlation between the series. First [defining the auto-covariance function of the first and second series by $R_{1,1}(s)$ and $R_{2,2}(s)$ respectively], the expected auto-covariance functions for the two sequences are given by

$$R_{1,1}(s) = E[(x_t - x_{t-u_1})(x_{t+u_{1s}} - x_{t-u_1+u_{1s}})] \tag{2.7}$$

$$= E[(x_t - x_{t-u_1})^2] \qquad s = 0$$

$$= 0 \qquad s \neq 0$$

and similarly

$$R_{2,2}(s) = E[(x_{t-u_2} - x_{t-(u_1+u_2)})^2] \qquad s = 0 \tag{2.8}$$

$$= 0 \qquad s \neq 0$$

The cross-covariance function $[R_{1,2}(s)]$ is given by

$$R_{1,2}(s) = E[(x_t - x_{t-u_1})(x_{t-u_2+u_{1s}} - x_{t-(u_1+u_2+u_{1s})})] \tag{2.9}$$

$$= E[(x_{t-u_2} - x_{t-u_1})^2] \qquad s = 0$$

$$= E[(x_t - x_{t-u_2})^2] \qquad s = -1$$

$$= 0 \qquad -1 > s > 0$$

As a notational convenience we introduce

$$E_{u_i, u_j} = E[(x_{t-u_i} - x_{t-u_j})^2] \tag{2.10}$$

Then, taking the Fourier transform of Eq. (2.9) the cross-spectrum is

$$Q(\omega) = E_{u_2,u_1} + E_{0,u_2} \cos \omega + iE_{0,u_2} \sin \omega \tag{2.11}$$

The coherence is then

$$S^2(\omega) = \frac{(E_{u_2,u_1} + E_{0,u_2} \cos \omega)^2 + (E_{0,u_2} \sin \omega)^2}{E_{0,u_1}E_{u_1,u_1+u_2}} \tag{2.12}$$

The phase is similarly

$$\Phi(\omega) = \tan^{-1} \frac{E_{0,u_2} \sin \omega}{E_{u_2,u_1} + E_{0,u_2} \cos \omega} \tag{2.13}$$

The "speed" of the process may be defined as

$$M = \frac{E[(x_{t_2} - x_{t_1})^2]}{t_2 - t_1} \tag{2.14}$$

for observations at time t_1 and t_2 such that $t_2 > t_1$. In terms of the process these two observations may be thought of as separated by u units. Thus

$$E[(x_{t_2} - x_{t_1})^2] = E[(x_t - x_{t-u})^2]$$

Then, making the assumption that

$$E[\epsilon_t^2] = \sigma_\epsilon^2 \tag{2.15}$$

we have

$$M = \frac{u\sigma_\epsilon^2}{t_2 - t_1} \tag{2.16}$$

Then u gives the number of new values of x_t which appear to have been generated between the observation at time t_1 and that at t_2. In this case M is directly proportional to u. A change in the variance of the difference $x_{t_2} - x_{t_1}$ would indicate that, while the variance term σ_ϵ^2 was unchanged, the value of u had changed. It is, of course, also possible to take the view that u remains constant and σ_ϵ^2 changes. M is then proportional to the variance of the disturbance term ϵ_t, however Eq. (2.14) still measures the "speed" of the process. It is not possible from the available data to distinguish between these two possible interpretations of "speed". The random-walk hypothesis, as stated here, is consistent with either view.

We will assume for notational and conceptual convenience in describing the relationship between the first differences of the opening price series and the closing price series that the residual terms, ϵ_t, have a common variance σ_ϵ^2. Equation (2.10) may now be written as

$$E_{u_i,u_j} = (u_i - u_j)\sigma_\epsilon^2 \tag{2.17}$$

Substituting this expression for E_{u_i,u_j} into Eqs. (2.12) and (2.13) we have

$$S^2(\omega) = \frac{[(u_1 - u_2) + u_2 \cos \omega]^2 + [u_2 \sin \omega]^2}{u_1 u_2} \tag{2.18}$$

and

$$\Phi(\omega) = \tan^{-1} \frac{u_2 \sin \omega}{u_1 - u_2 + u_2 \cos \omega} \tag{2.19}$$

These considerations of the random-walk process are important in terms of the treatment of a particular realization. If a realization of the x_t series is analyzed directly, then one is involved in the analysis of a nonstationary series and the expected values of the covariance functions and spectral estimates will be dependent upon the initial conditions of the process. In the context of the properties of the stock market, it does not seem reasonable to assume that T is large. However, it is also not clear exactly what assumptions should be made about T and what value should be assigned to it. One might postulate that, for the purposes of the market representation, the random-walk process started at a fixed time in history. Then the value assigned to T would be dependent on the separation between the realization and the assumed historical starting point, T. Another postulate would be that, for each realization, the process will appear to have started at a fixed length of time before the realization. While it may be of interest to investigate problems of this kind, assumptions concerning the way in which the process started have been avoided in this paper by analyzing first differences of the observed series.

The purpose of the present paper is to give an explicit description of the random-walk hypothesis, and to examine this hypothesis through the application of spectral analysis to the relevant data. Spectral methods were initially applied in this field by Granger and Morgenstern [4]. In this paper data are analyzed which have not previously been examined by spectral methods.

As speculative prices of the kind investigated cannot become negative, a theoretically superior, but in practice very similar, statement of the random-walk hypothesis is that the logarithms of the price series are generated by a random-walk. Although calculations were in some cases performed both before and after taking logarithms, the results presented were computed without taking logarithms except where specifically noted. The most important implication of the random-walk hypothesis is that the past values of the random-walk contain no information useful for prediction of future values. It is clear that the (unbiased) estimate of x_{t+1} which has the minimum mean square error is simply

$$\hat{x}_{t+1} = x_t \tag{2.20}$$

The mean square error of the estimate is of course $E[(\epsilon_{t+1})^2]$. If, as is necessary for speculation, one tries to forecast the quantity $x_t - x_{t-u}$ the "best" estimate is a random number from a distribution with zero mean and variance given by

$$E[(\sum_{j=t-u+1}^{t} \epsilon_j)^2]$$

The analogy of this forecasting problem to that encountered in roulette is obvious.[3]

The random-walk hypothesis is put forward as an explanation of speculative price changes. It is clearly not intended to explain long-term trends in price series. Long trends and very slow cyclical variations in price series are outside the scope of the random-walk hypothesis if, given the time horizon of the speculators in the market, they do not represent potential opportunities for profit. In addition, a practical limitation is placed on the testing of the random-walk hypothesis for very slow variations due to the limited length of the time series available.

Finally, it should be emphasized that the testing of the random-walk hypothesis is confined to the linear aspects of the time series. Thus, for example, moments of order three and greater are not considered in the analysis.

III. DESCRIPTION OF DATA

Table 1 lists the data used in this paper together with the data sources and time periods taken. Brief mention should be made here of the accuracy of these series. For the most part the accuracy is felt to be extremely high by economic standards. However there are two specific known sources of error. The first concerns the series of "bargains marked" on the London market. The London market does not operate under so extensive a set of formal rules as are applied to the New York market. In London there is a considerable amount of actual trading when the market is officially closed. Furthermore it is not compulsory there to record the volume—or price—of all transactions even during normal market hours. The "bargains marked" are those transactions, during normal market hours, which are officially recorded. Since recording is not compulsory there is a tendency for the percentage of transactions that are recorded as "bargains marked" to decrease as trading becomes heavy. The second specific source of error concerns the transactions data for the New York market. While the volume

---

[3] This point has been mentioned in [4] and is only repeated here for completeness. However, the analogy may be extended slightly by making an analogy between the roulette wheel's bias in favor of the 'bank' and the bias in the speculative game introduced by transactions costs. Presumably both biases are adjusted on the basis of profit maximization on the part of the "operators" of the respective games.

TABLE 1

Series	Description	Time Period	Source
1. Financial Times Industrial Index	Weekly series of Wednesday values of index of prices of shares traded on London market	January 1959 to December 1962	Economist, London
2. Economist Indicator	Weekly series of Wednesday values of index of prices of shares traded on London market	January 1959 to December 1962	Economist, London
3. 'Bargains Marked'	Weekly series of total volume of shares traded and recorded on London market each Wednesday	January 1959 to December 1962	Economist, London
4. Standard and Poor Industrial Index	Weekly series of Wednesday values of the index of New York stocks	January 1959 to December 1962	Economist, London
5. Standard and Poor Government Bond Index	Weekly series of Wednesday values of index of Government Bonds traded on the New York market	January 1959 to December 1962	Economist, London
6. International Telephone and Telegraph (ITT) daily series	1. Daily opening price 2. Daily closing price 3. Daily high price 4. Daily low price 5. Daily volume of shares transacted	January 2, 1951 to June 27, 1952	New York Times
7. Eastman Kodak (EK) daily series	1. Daily opening price 2. Daily closing price 3. Daily high price 4. Daily low price 5. Daily volume of shares transacted	January 2, 1952 to May 31, 1953	New York Times
8. International Telephone and Telegraph (ITT) individual-transaction data	1. The price of each transaction on the New York market 2. The volume of shares of each transaction	April 1963	*Stock Sales on the New York Stock Exchange* Francis Emory Fitch, Inc., New York
9. Bell and Howell individual-transaction data	1. The price of each transaction on the New York market 2. The volume of shares of each transaction	April 1963	*Stock Sales on the New York Stock Exchange* Francis Emory Fitch, Inc., New York

of transactions series from these data provides a very nearly complete list of the total volume of transactions, the authors understand that the data are prone to one rather odd kind of error. If the volume of transactions has been exceptionally large the linotype setting of the data sheets may fall behind schedule, in which case two or more successive transactions at the same price may be grouped as one single transaction with a volume which is the total of the several actual volumes. It was not possible to discover any effects which could be attributed to this source of error in the analysis of the data. In terms of the more conventional errors of typography and transcription the data appeared to be of uniformly high quality. The daily ITT series was found to have, on only one day, a "low" which was higher than the "high", and higher than the opening and closing. No other typographical errors were found.

IV. THE LONDON AND NEW YORK MARKETS

The data used were the three weekly price series, two from London and one from New York, and the "bargains marked" series from the London market. Before the histogram and spectral computations were performed the logarithms of the data were taken and a linear trend was removed by regression. The spectra of the first differences of each of the logarithmic price series were flat. Thus, the random-walk hypothesis appears to provide a reasonable model for the logarithmic series—from both New York and London—over the frequency range from one cycle every two weeks to one cycle per year. The cross-spectrum between the two price series for the London market (series 1 and 2, Table 1) gave a very high coherence at nearly all frequencies. There was no evidence of one series lagging the other. This suggests that, for a weekly time interval, the two series provide practically the same information. The harmonics of the annual cycle were not significant and the series were too short to provide an estimate of the annual frequency with reasonable reliability. The cross-spectrum between the price series and the bargains marked (i.e. volume) series gave a generally small coherence, as did the cross-spectrum between the absolute value of first differences of the prices and the bargains marked.

To test for any short-run correlation between the London and New York markets the cross-spectrum between the Economist Indicator and the Standard and Poor Index of Industrials was estimated. The coherence was generally quite low, exceeding a value of 0.35 only at frequencies corresponding to 13 weeks and 6.5 weeks, both of which are harmonics of the annual frequency. Using the Financial Times Index instead of the Economist Indicator gave nearly identical results. We thus conclude that the price movements in the two markets are practically independent over the frequency range of one cycle every two weeks to one cycle per year.[4] This lack of correlation between the two markets seems to disagree with market "folklore."

V. MANDELBROT'S HYPOTHESIS

In several monographs Mandelbrot [5] has suggested that the variance of speculative prices is infinite. His model is that if x_t is the price at time t then:

$$\log x_t - \log x_{t-1} = \gamma_t \qquad (5.1)$$

where γ_t is a random, independent sequence from a stable Pareto-Lévy distribution with infinite variance.[5] If such a model were correct spectral methods would not be appropriate, as they are quite sensitive to a few very extreme values. In order to investigate the Mandelbrot hypothesis

FIGURE 1

HISTOGRAM OF THE FIRST DIFFERENCES OF THE LOGARITHMS OF THE FINANCIAL TIMES INDUSTRIAL INDEX AFTER REMOVAL OF A LOG-LINEAR TREND *

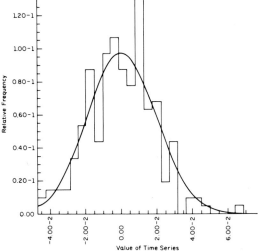

* As the form of numerical scales on these figures may be unfamiliar to many readers an explanatory note is in order. The numbers on the scales have the form: a minus sign if the number is negative, one digit before the decimal point, two digits following the decimal point, and then another digit which may be preceded by a minus sign. This last digit is the exponent of ten which determines the actual value of the number. For example, the number 1.23−4 should be read as 1.23 × 10⁻⁴ or 0.000123.

[4] The cross-spectrum for the Standard and Poor Industrial Index and the Government Bonds Index was also estimated. The coherence in this case never exceeded a value of 0.25.

[5] For the original discussion of this family of distributions see Chapter VI of Paul Lévy, *Calcul des Probabilités* (Paris, France: Gauthier-Villars, 1925).

the histograms of the residual terms ϵ_t of Eq. (2.1) (i.e. the first differences of the observed data) were computed for all of the price series.

For the weekly indices the histograms generally take the form shown in Figure 1 with the mode slightly greater than the mean. There is no evidence of the long tails which Mandelbrot's hypothesis would predict. For the daily ITT and EK price series the histograms of the four series for each company are all well approximated by a normal distribution. However in each case there is a tendency for the histogram to be slightly skewed to the right so that again the median is somewhat greater than the mean. There is some evidence that certain integer prices near the median occurred more frequently than would be expected on the basis of the approximated normal distribution.

FIGURE 2

HISTOGRAM OF THE FIRST DIFFERENCES OF THE DAILY 'HIGH' OF THE PRICE
SERIES OF INTERNATIONAL TEL AND TEL (ITT)*

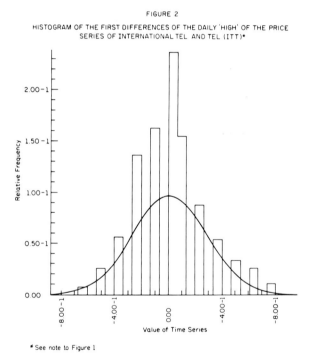

* See note to Figure 1

Figure 2 is typical of these histograms. The histograms of the first differences of the individual-transaction price series gave similar, nearly normal, shapes. However, because the range of the price differences was relatively small, the effect of the discreteness of the price series was particularly noticeable in these series. No evidence was found in any of these series that the process by which they were generated behaved as if it possessed an infinite variance.

VI. MARKET TIME AND REAL TIME

In this section we investigate the effect upon the daily price series of the nightly and weekend closing of the market. If the market behaved like a formal system in which price changes are generated only by the actual operation of the market, the opening price on each day would have to be the same as the closing price on the previous trading day. An alternative hypothesis is that the price generating mechanism is entirely independent of whether the market is open or closed. A third hypothesis, for which we will present evidence, is that the price generating mechanism (i.e., the random-walk) continues to operate while the market is closed, but at a lower "speed." The "speed" of the market is measured, as described in Section II, by the variance per unit time of the first differences of the price series.

A variety of reasons could be suggested to explain the change in speed; the currently available data do not, however, allow us to discriminate between alternate hypotheses. The speed of the process can be determined in two ways: by considering the variance of the change in the price during a trading day, over night, and over weekends; and by examining the phase estimates provided by the cross-spectrum between the first differences of the opening prices and closing prices respectively for the same day. The significance of these computations in terms of the random-walk model was discussed in Section II.

In order to investigate the above mentioned three alternate hypotheses concerning the price determining mechanism the histograms of the following series were computed:

1. Series of differences between each Tuesday's opening and the preceding Monday's closing price.
2. Series of differences between each Wednesday's opening and Tuesday's closing price.
3. Series of differences between each Thursday's opening and Wednesday's closing price.
4. Series of differences between each Friday's opening and Thursday's closing price.
5. Series of differences between each Monday's opening and Friday's closing price.
6. Series of differences between opening and closing on the same weekday.

During part of the year the market was, through the period covered by these data, open on Saturday. However it was not practical to attempt to discriminate between periods of Saturday openings and the rest of the series. The data for Saturdays, when available, were not included in any of the analysis. Thus the spectrum analyses were made as if Friday were immediately followed by Monday.

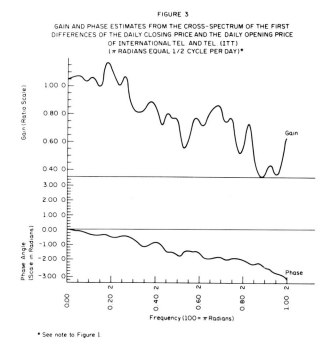

FIGURE 3

GAIN AND PHASE ESTIMATES FROM THE CROSS-SPECTRUM OF THE FIRST
DIFFERENCES OF THE DAILY CLOSING PRICE AND THE DAILY OPENING PRICE
OF INTERNATIONAL TEL. AND TEL. (ITT)
(π RADIANS EQUAL 1/2 CYCLE PER DAY)*

* See note to Figure 1.

The histograms were usually dominated by the bars corresponding
to changes of zero, or of plus or minus one eighth of a dollar, and they
displayed no tendency toward long tails. For the ITT data it is interesting
to note that, although there was a slight upward trend in the data, the
mean of each histogram was negative. While the means were all small
(under a half of one eighth of a dollar) this does suggest that the opening
price of ITT was systematically below its previous close. No similar phenomenon was observable for the EK price series.

The overnight variances for Monday through Thursday night were
nearly equal and therefore only their average is shown. The variances are
as follows:

	ITT	*Eastman Kodak*
1. Variance of price change from opening to closing of market each day..............................	0.0325	0.0357
2. Average variance of price change overnight (Monday–Thursday night)...........................	0.0206	0.0420
3. Variance of price change over weekends...........	0.0474	0.0438

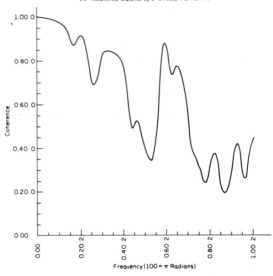

FIGURE 4

COHERENCE ESTIMATE FROM THE CROSS-SPECTRUM OF THE FIRST
DIFFERENCES OF THE DAILY CLOSING PRICE AND THE DAILY OPENING PRICE
OF INTERNATIONAL TEL. AND TEL. (ITT)*
(π RADIANS EQUAL 1/2 CYCLE PER DAY)

* See note to Figure 1

The cross-spectra between the first differences of opening and closing prices give coherences and phase-diagrams which accord well with
the expected results given in Eqs. (2.18) and (2.19).

Figures 3 and 4 show the gain, phase and coherence diagrams between the first differences of the series of openings and closings on the
same day. The phase-diagrams relationship between market open and
market closed can be computed from Eqs. (2.7) and (2.8). This information may also be computed directly from the variance estimates. The phase
and variance estimates indicate the following fractions of a full day (i.e.,
market opening to market opening on two consecutive weekdays):

FRACTIONS OF DAY

	ITT		EK	
	Phase	*Variance*	*Phase*	*Variance*
1. Market open during day.........	0.66	0.61	0.50	0.46
2. Market closed over week-night...	0.34	0.39	0.50	0.54
3. Weekend.....................		0.89		0.56

These estimates, which seem generally consistent, indicate that a significant proportion of the price determining activity goes on while the market is closed. The variance of the price series over the weekend causes the daily observations to be nonequispaced in terms of the random-walk model. This fact does not prevent spectral analysis of the price series. However, it does present fundamental problems in terms of the postulation of theoretical relationships between price series and other variables such as volumes traded.

The price series seems to exist at all points in time, whether a transaction is possible or not, and the series seems to be generated by the same process independent of the possibility of transactions. However, the existence of the price at times when transactions are not possible is clearly dependent on the expectation in the "market" that it will sometime again be possible to make transactions. This expectation need not be held with certainty and it seems reasonable to suggest that the confidence that speculators place in the expectation of future trading and the length of time before trading may be resumed both influence the price. A model which is expected to provide useful information concerning the relationship of speculative price series to other variables must consider basic problems such as this.

VII. SPECTRAL ANALYSIS OF DAILY DATA

In the previous section the results of spectral analysis of the daily opening and closing prices, in conjunction with the analysis of the variance of these series, were shown to provide interesting information concerning the way in which the price determining mechanism operates over time. In this section further results of the application of spectral and cross-spectral methods to several pairs of series which are derived from the daily data will be discussed.

The spectral and cross-spectral estimates of the following six pairs of series were computed for both the International Tel. and Tel. (ITT) and Eastman Kodak (EK) series.

Estimate Number	*Series A*	*Series B*
1	First difference of closing price	First difference of opening price
2	Absolute value of the opening on each day minus the previous close	Volume of shares transacted
3	First difference of 'highs'	First difference of 'lows'
4	Volume transacted	High minus low
5	Volume transacted	Highs
6	Volume transacted	Lows

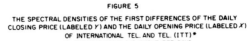

FIGURE 5

THE SPECTRAL DENSITIES OF THE FIRST DIFFERENCES OF THE DAILY
CLOSING PRICE (LABELED *Y*) AND THE DAILY OPENING PRICE (LABELED *X*)
OF INTERNATIONAL TEL. AND TEL. (ITT)*
(π RADIANS EQUAL 1/2 CYCLE PER DAY)

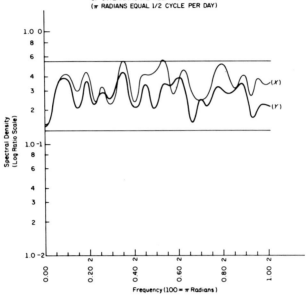

* See note to Figure 1.

[These estimates will be identified by the estimate number given on the left above, then the series identification A or B if the spectral estimate of one of the series is referred to separately, and then the letters ITT or EK, i.e. 1A (ITT) refers to the spectral estimate of the first difference of closing price of the ITT series.] None of the spectra of the first differences of the opening, closing, high, and low series is significantly different from the spectrum of a random, independent variable. These spectra all support the random-walk hypothesis as specified in Section II.

Figure 5 shows the first differences of the opening and closing prices of ITT (1-ITT). A 95 percent confidence band is shown for the hypothesis that the observed spectra are sample estimates from a purely random process.

In addition Figure 6 shows the spectral densities of these two series before taking first differences. The daily data permit the testing of the random-walk hypothesis with a sampling time of one day. Thus the daily data correspond to a Nyquist frequency of 1/2 cycle per day (i.e. the range of the frequency axis for all of the spectral estimates of daily series is zero to 1/2 cycle per day).

The coherence between the series of opening prices and the series of closing prices is high. The same is true for the coherence between the

FIGURE 6

THE SPECTRAL DENSITIES OF THE DAILY CLOSING PRICE (LABELED Y)
AND THE DAILY OPENING PRICE (LABELED X)
OF INTERNATIONAL TEL. AND TEL. (ITT)*
(π RADIANS EQUAL 1/2 CYCLE PER DAY)

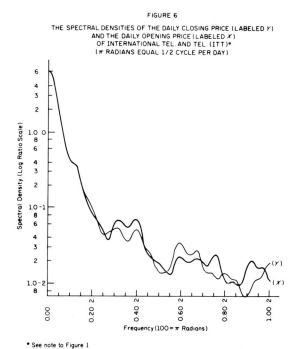

* See note to Figure 1

series of highs and the series of lows. However, when a relationship between prices and volume is looked for it is found that the coherence is
almost uniformly low. It has been pointed out by Osborne[6] that a high
correlation between absolute values of first differences of prices and the
volume series should be expected. Neither of the two cross-spectra using
absolute values [2A(ITT) and 2A(EK)] yielded significant coherences.
In addition the coherences between the volume series and either the series
of lows or the series of highs [5(ITT), 5(EK), 6(ITT), 6(EK)] were quite
small. There was very little area under any of the coherence curves for
values of coherence above 0.30, although some sharp peaks exceeded this
value. This result agrees with the earlier results in [4] for weekly and
monthly data. However, the coherence between the volume series and the
difference between high and low for the day [4(ITT) and 4(EK)] had
values in the range 0.4 to 0.6. The values were relatively larger at the lower
frequencies. The phase diagram in this case indicates an unlagged relationship.

Another interesting result in this set of spectral estimates is that
the phase derived from the cross-spectrum between the volume series and
the series of daily lows varies consistently around $\pi/2$ over the entire

[6] M. F. M. Osborne, private communication.

frequency range. While the corresponding coherence was fairly low, thus reducing the significance of the phase estimate, this result does suggest a "fixed phase lag" between the series. This kind of lag can be very nicely explained by the prevalent use of stop-loss orders. When the series of successive lows is falling the volume of transactions will tend to increase as more "stop-loss" orders are executed. Thus, regardless of the frequency of variation, the volume series will tend to be a quarter cycle (or $\pi/2$ radians) out of phase with the series of lows. The fact that this relationship is asymmetric with respect to the sign of the change in the series of lows, and thus nonlinear, may in part be responsible for the low coherence.

The most interesting result of this analysis is that it is only the volume and the difference between high and low series which are at all strongly correlated. This is added evidence in support of the idea, put forward in Section II, that the determination of price goes on in a hypothetical sense during the time when the market is formally closed. The fact that the opening and closing prices are not correlated with volume indicates that they are not, at least in this respect, different from other prices during the day. The opening and closing may be looked upon as simply two more realizations of the random-walk process. The day's high and low on the other hand are not periodic samplings of the process, instead their difference measures the range of the process during the daily time interval. The structure of the market in terms of stop-loss and buy-above-market orders clearly suggests that the volume of transactions should increase as the price diverges from its current mean. In our concluding remarks more will be said about the relevance of this information to the applicability of conventional demand analysis to market situations.

VIII. ANALYSIS OF INDIVIDUAL-TRANSACTION DATA

The form of these data is a listing of the price and the volume of each transaction taking place during each half day on the New York market. The transactions are listed separately for the morning period, 10:00 A.M. to 1:00 P.M., and the afternoon period, 1:00 P.M. to close. The major purpose of the analysis of these data was to test the random-walk hypothesis on the series of actual price realizations, and to test for correlation between price and volume. In the analysis of these series the "time" used was the serial number of the transaction beginning with the first transaction of the month-long sample.

The spectra of the first differences of the individual-transaction price series are not significantly different from the expected spectrum of a random, independent variable with the same discrete nature as the price series.

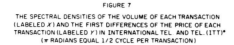

FIGURE 7

THE SPECTRAL DENSITIES OF THE VOLUME OF EACH TRANSACTION
(LABELED X) AND THE FIRST DIFFERENCES OF THE PRICE OF EACH
TRANSACTION (LABELED Y) IN INTERNATIONAL TEL AND TEL. (ITT)*
(π RADIANS EQUAL 1/2 CYCLE PER TRANSACTION)

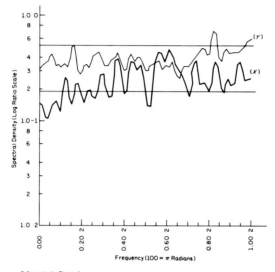

* See note to Figure 1

Figure 7[7] shows the spectral density of the first differences of the individual-transaction price series for ITT. As the number of transactions during each half daily period, and the times at which they occur, are random variables it is not possible to relate the spectrum of the series to chronological time. However it is particularly interesting to note that the price series continues to follow the random-walk hypothesis when sampled at the shortest intervals for which data are available.

The other major result of this analysis is that the coherence between the price and volume series is rarely greater than 0.1. A typical value is 0.02.[8] This lack of correlation may be taken to be a tribute to the "orderly" character of the market in the face of changing demand conditions.

Two other computations were made on these data. The first was an attempt to test the "folklore" hypothesis that prices which end in certain numbers of eighths of a point are more likely to occur than other prices. The preferred endings are usually held to be the whole numbers, halves, and quarters. However from our data no significant differences in the frequency of occurrence of eighths was observed. A valid test of

[7] The spectral density of the volume series is also shown in this figure. The 95 percent confidence band refers to the spectral density of the price series only.

[8] These values of coherence are consistent with the null hypothesis of zero correlation. As a matter of passing interest they are the lowest estimates of coherence from actual observations of economic processes known to any of the authors.

this curious hypothesis would require many more observations and more samples than were used here.

In addition a transition matrix of price changes was computed. This matrix gave the frequency of occurrence of all possible price changes between successive time periods. While definite conclusions were difficult to draw from these matrices—a very large sample size would be required to establish statistical significance—there was some evidence to support the hypothesis that the price is "sticky" at round numbers. The probability of remaining in a round number was often two to three times the probability of remaining in prices adjacent to the round number price. There was also some evidence that entering a round number price was somewhat less probable than would be expected.

IX. CONCLUSION

Our fundamental conclusion may be stated in the form of a law: *The price-determining mechanism described in Section II is the only mechanism which is consistent with the unrestrained pursuit of the profit motive by the participants in the market.*

The logical validity of this law may be established by an investigation of the adaptive nature of the market. If the mechanism were such that the mathematically expected value of the price at future times differed from the current price then an investor could establish a predictive decision rule which would result in a net profit when exercised in the market. However since all investors operate on the basis of a profit motive, the realization that an opportunity for profit exists, will result in a change of the mechanism which will remove this opportunity. This is clear since if all investors in the market use the same decision rule, which—when not used by anyone—had been a profitable rule, then the realized profit of all cannot be positive.

If this law is viewed in terms of the frequency range over which it would be expected to be valid, the low end of the frequency spectrum will clearly be limited by the time horizon of the investors. If no investor is interested in profits which cannot be realized until, say, 5 or 10 years have passed, a cyclical variation with a period much longer than this would not—even if it could be predicted—be viewed as an opportunity for profit. As regards the high frequency end there is opportunity for profit, on the basis of the ability to predict price changes, down to a matter of fractions of a minute. Thus there is a band of frequencies at the low end, including the zero frequency, to which the law does not apply, while the upper end is limited only by the speed of the market mechanism.

In addition, as previously mentioned in [4], the law does not preclude the possible value of "inside information." "Inside information" is defined as information held by only a small segment of the market which if generally known would produce a predictable price change. The profitable use of "inside information," then, consists of acting on the basis of the prediction and then announcing, or awaiting the general realization of, the "inside information." Thus each bit of this information is self-destroying; a continuing flow of new "inside information" is required for continuing profits.

Although individual stock prices appear to be generated by a random-walk process, it is not suggested that all stocks vary independently. It would be of interest to investigate a covariance matrix, the i, jth element of which would be given by

$$C_{i,j}(s) = \frac{1}{N} \sum_{t=1}^{N-s} (x_{i,t} - x_{i,t-1})(x_{j,t+s} - x_{j,t+s-1})$$

where $x_{i,t}$ = price of stock i at time t.

For s equal to zero, one would expect mainly positive off diagonal terms. Computation of the off diagonal terms of the matrix for increasing values of s will test the market hypothesis that certain stocks, or groups of stocks, lead or lag others. While, as shown in [4], there is no evidence of lags between the indices of weekly prices which were investigated, it would be of interest to investigate the behavior of individual stocks, and to extend the analysis through the use of daily data.

A basic problem[9] which this analysis points out clearly is the lack of a useful theoretical framework in economics for the analysis of speculative markets. The three points brought out in this paper which are relevant are

1. There is a weak correlation of the difference between the daily high and the daily low of the price series on the one hand, and the daily volume transacted on the other.

2. There is no other correlation between observed prices (or absolute values of price differences) and observed volumes transacted.

3. New prices are generated, and one may suppose that a hypothetical price exists, during times when actual transactions are impossible.

Thus it is clear that no simple functional relationship between the observed variables is likely to be of value. The common sense view of the price as being adjusted to provide an equilibrium between supply and demand cannot be refuted. However it is clear that in the situation described here the volume of shares transacted bears no discernable relationship to any conventional concept of supply or demand. (While it is not commonly suggested that a simple direct supply or demand relationship could be

---

[9] An early discussion of this problem occurs in "Demand Theory Reconsidered" by O. Morgenstern, *Quarterly Journal of Economics*, Vol. 62 (February, 1948), pp. 165–201.

applied to this situation there have been various suggestions of a connection between price and "activity" such as Osborne's suggestion referred to in Section VII.) Observed changes in the price of a stock are not correlated with the observed volume of transactions.

Since from our analysis the price and volume transacted are two nearly independent stochastic variables we are left with the question: what does determine the price and what determines the volume? The specialists on the floor of the exchange contribute to the price determination, as do the brokers. It is in the profit interests of both of these groups, within limits, to increase the variance and rate of change of the price. However they are not solely responsible for the variance as is indicated by the sizable variance during the periods when the market is closed. Nor is there any evidence that they determine the price. The specialist attempts to equilibrate, and also to influence, hypothetical demand and supply relationships which apparently are neither derived from, nor result in, any observable data. It must certainly be considered as a weakness of the present demand theory that this theory—widely accepted and often applied though it is—cannot provide even an operational framework within which to analyze the problem of speculative prices, much less a valid predictive theory for this price mechanism.

APPENDIX

A. Description of Computations

All of the computations for this paper were performed on the Princeton University IBM 7090 computer. Extensive use was made of the spectral output facilities provided on the computer for producing, directly from the computer, a graphical display which is recorded on 35 mm microfilm.[1] With this facility it was possible, in a total time of 3 to 4 minutes per pair of series of 1000 observations each, to compute the histograms, auto and cross-correlation coefficients, spectral densities, and cross-spectral estimates of pairs of series and record the results in the form of graphs. Thus the use of spectral methods has been made much more efficient in terms of presentation of computed information. A great many curves may be produced without the great delays and considerable costs of manual or mechanical curve plotting. (It is also possible to view the curves on a display screen as the computer is running and, for instance, to alter the number of lags used or initiate another computation on the basis of results currently being displayed.) The efficiency and speed of obtaining results in the exact form required for analysis has been so much increased that a greater proportion of the total time spent may be

---

[1] The authors would like to give special acknowledgement to Professor P. J. Warter of the Princeton University Electrical Engineering Department who, as author of the computer subroutine which operates the microfilm output equipment, provided the programming information and other assistance which made possible the use of this equipment. As the computations for this paper represent one of the first extensive uses of this valuable new facility acknowledgement is also due to the Computer Center staff for their extensive help in overcoming various technical problems.

devoted to analysis of results. The graphs shown in Figures 1 through 7 are reproduced from the computer generated microfilm.

A basic program was written by M. D. Godfrey which accepts two time series and computes the following quantities:

1. The histogram of each series, upon which is superimposed a normal curve with the same mean and variance. In addition the mean and variance of the series are printed across the botton of the display.

2. The auto and cross-correlation coefficients are computed from the following equations

$$R_{xy}(s) = \frac{1}{N} \sum_{t=1}^{N-s} (x_t - \bar{x})(y_{t+s} - \bar{y})$$

where

$$\bar{y} = \frac{1}{N} \sum_{t=1}^{N} y_t$$

$$\bar{x} = \frac{1}{N} \sum_{t=1}^{N} x_t$$

These equations are explicitly stated because there is more than one definition of the auto and cross-correlation coefficients in use in spectral analysis. An important reason for using this form was that it provides, even in the presence of nonstationarity, a positive definite estimate of the spectral density and an estimate of the cross-spectrum for which the square of the magnitude must be equal to, or greater than, the product of the spectral densities of the two series. Some of the properties of this form, for a zero mean series, are discussed by Parzen.[2]

3. The spectral densities of the two series using the Parzen form of the weighting function.[3]

4. The cross-spectrum and derived quantities consisting of the co-spectrum, the quadrature-spectrum, the cross-amplitude, the gain, the phase, the coherence, and the residual spectrum.

Table 1 below gives the numbers of lags and the numbers of observations used for each of the types of data.

TABLE 1

Series	Duration	Number of Observations	Number of Lags
Weekly data of London and New York Markets.......................	4 years	208	40
Daily New York market data:			
ITT.............................	18 months	389	60
Eastman Kodak..................	17 months	369	60
Transaction data:			
Bell and Howell..................	1 month	1108	100
ITT.............................	1 month	896	100

[2] E. Parzen, "Mathematical Considerations in the Estimation of Spectra," *Technometrics*, Vol. 3 (May, 1961), p. 174.

[3] *Ibid.*, p. 176, e.g. (5.10).

B. Glossary of Spectral Analytic Terms

As it is thought that many readers may be unfamiliar with certain of the statistical techniques used in this paper it is hoped that the following glossary may aid comprehension. The basic idea of a spectrum has been discussed in Granger and Morgenstern [4].[4]

Spectrum. A power spectrum decomposes a series into a set of frequency bands and measures the relative importance of each of the bands in terms of the contribution of that band to the total variance of the series.

Frequency. A frequency is the number of times a periodic function of time repeats itself in a specified time period. If a particular frequency has the period k, it has the frequency $2 \pi/k$. Thus a 'low frequency' corresponds to a long period, a 'high frequency' to a short period.

Random-walk. A random-walk process has been discussed in Section II. The power spectrum of a random-walk is

$$f(\omega) = \frac{\sigma_\epsilon^2}{4 \pi(1 - \cos \omega)}$$

where ω is the frequency in radians per unit time. The power spectrum of the first difference of a random-walk series is a constant over the whole frequency range $(0, \pi)$.

Cross-spectrum. The cross-spectrum measures the relationship between two series. It is a complex-valued function and from it are derived the coherence, gain and phase estimates.

Coherence. Coherence measures the degree of relationship between the corresponding frequency components of the two series. It is similar to the square of the correlation coefficient between components of the same frequency.

Gain. The gain may be thought of as the absolute value of a complex-valued regression coefficient computed for each frequency band.

Phase. The phase measures the phase difference between corresponding frequencies in the two series. If the coherence is not significantly different from zero the phase estimate has no meaning. If one series has a constant time-lag to the other, the phase estimate lies about a straight line the slope of which measures the time-lag. If the phase estimate lies about a nonzero horizontal line the series are said to have fixed-angle lag. A case of such a lag, which occurred in this paper, is the case in which the estimate lies about the value $\pi/2$. This occurs when each frequency component of one series is $\pi/2$ radians out of phase with the respective frequency component of the other series, i.e., a peak in one series corresponds to the midpoint between a peak and a trough in the other series.

----

[4] A full description of the technique used in this paper is given in: *Spectral Analysis of Economic Time Series* by C. W. J. Granger with M. Hatanaka, Princeton U.P., 1964.

REFERENCES

[1] Alexander, Sidney S. "Price Movements in Speculative Markets: Trends or Random-Walks," *Industrial Managements Review*, Vol. 2 (1961), pp. 7–26.

[2] Bachelier, L. *Théorie de la Spéculation* (Paris, France: Gauthier Villars, 1900).

[3] Cootner, P. H. "Stock Prices: Random vs. Systematic Changes," *Industrial Management Review*, Vol. 3 (1962), pp. 24–45.

[4] Granger, C., and O. Morgenstern. "Spectral Analysis of New York Stock Market Prices," *Kyklos*, Vol. XVI (1963), pp. 1–27.

[5] Mandelbrot, B. "The Variation of Certain Speculative Prices," IBM Research Note NC-87. Thomas J. Watson Research Center, Yorktown Heights, N. Y.

[6] Osborne, M. F. M. "Brownian Motion in the Stock Market," *Operations Research*, Vol. 7, No. 2 (March–April 1959), pp. 145–173.

SUMMARY

A model of the form

$$x_t - x_{t-1} = e_t$$

where x_t is the price of a share at time t and e_t forms a sequence of independent random variates is postulated as a model of the price determining mechanism of stock markets.

The form of the distribution function of the e_t's is investigated. In opposition to suggestions that have been made in connection with other speculative price mechanisms it is found that the distribution function appears to be well approximated by a normal distribution. There is no evidence that the data treated are samples from a stable process with an infinite variance.

It is found that the model mentioned above, termed the random-walk model, provides a good explanation of the variation of stock market prices for daily observations of the price, and for the series formed by the price of every transaction taking place in the market. In the context of this model it is noted that it appears that the price determining mechanism continues to operate at a reduced "speed" during times when the actual market is closed.

While it has been suggested that a correlation between the volume of shares transacted and the absolute value of the first differences of the price series should be expected, no such correlation was observed.

Two questions which the paper leaves open are the question of cross-sectional correlation between different shares, and the question of the possibility of information in moments of order greater than two.

In conclusion the following law is stated: "The price determining mechanism described in Section II (i.e. the random-walk indicated above) is the only mechanism which is consistent with the unrestrained pursuit of the profit motive by the participants in the market."

$\mathcal{G}eoffrey\ \mathcal{P}.\ \mathcal{E}.\ \mathcal{C}larkson$*

40. A Theory of Stock Price Behavior

Reprinted from the **Industrial Management Review**, Vol. 6, No. 2 (Spring, 1965), pp. 93–103, by permission of the author and publisher. Copyright 1965 by the Industrial Management Review Association.

INTRODUCTION

The behavior of stock prices has attracted the attention of laymen and economists for years. Many attempts have been made to discover whether the movements in prices follow some discernible pattern, for, if anyone could establish a rule, his monetary reward would more than compensate for the time and effort he spent determining it. It is presumed, however, that stock price behavior is not examined solely for pecuniary motives, and that the fundamental objective is to be able to explain and predict the behavior of such time series.

In order to explain the behavior of a given phenomenon we require a theory from which the requisite events may be deduced. Economic literature uses three main types of theory for market behavior—classical, statistical, and behavioral. While the first two have been employed in a number of investigations this paper is concerned with an application of the third type of theory to stock market behavior.

Under classical economic theory market behavior is analyzed in terms of demand and supply schedules and the stability of their intersection at equilibrium. The procedure by which equilibrium is reached is customarily represented by some form of Walrasian tâtonnment process—a process that permits prices to respond to excess demand through a recontracting device which allows exchanges to take place only when equilibrium is reached.[1] One consequence of this theory is that all changes in price are a result of shifts in either the demand or supply schedules. Concurrently, once such movements in price are stated as a time series of actual prices these prices represent a sequence of equilibrium positions. To understand

* Professor of Business Finance, University of Manchester. This research is supported by funds provided by the Sloan School of Management, M.I.T., for research in decision behavior.

[1] An excellent review article devoted in part to the properties of this recontracting procedure is provided by Negishi [15].

the behavior of a specific market it is necessary to be able to account for such price changes. If one employs classical theory one is led to search for the processes which govern the behavior of the demand and supply schedules as well as the process or processes that represent the equilibrating mechanism.

The second approach is represented by investigations into the statistical characteristics of the behavior of stock price time series. The object of this research is to determine for particular series whether price changes follow some recognizable pattern or whether such price behavior is indistinguishable from that of Brownian motion, i.e. that of a pure random walk.[2] Recently, results have been published which suggest that although stock price behavior does not in general fit a pure random walk hypothesis, prices *do* move in a random fashion between certain limits or reflecting barriers. Since these barriers do not remain constant, it is their shifts that indicate the existence of a trend, while price movement within such limits is that of a random walk.[3] One result of this approach is that the market processes which generate price series can be represented by the same mechanisms that produce a random walk. In short, stock price movement is governed by certain stochastic processes that do not take into consideration the determinants of market behavior as contained in classic theory. One corollary of this theory is that one cannot explain or predict specific price changes; for under a random walk hypothesis, price is a random variable whose value at a given time is determined by a random draw from the variable's density function. Hence, all price values are independent of each other and none can be explained from a knowledge of the others.

Alternatively, there is a third and somewhat different theoretical scheme for interpreting market phenomena called behavioral theory which seeks to explain and predict observable decision-making behavior.[4] A basic assumption of the theory is that there are certain empirical regularities in the decision processes of economic actors. (Such hypothesized regularities can be investigated as the decision behavior of individuals and groups.[5]) Decision makers are represented by a set of decision processes which act on as well as react to information which is already available in memory or which may be procured from the environment. Hence, all behavior is a response of some describable decision processes to an ascertainable body of

---

[2] Some recent examples of this endeavor are to be found in Osborne [16], Working [18], and Houthakker [12]. (The Osborne and Working papers are reprinted in Cootner [8].)

[3] See the results and analysis cited in Alexander [1] and Cootner [7]. (Both articles are reprinted in Cootner [8].)

[4] The empirical foundations of behavioral theory are examined in detail in Part IV of Clarkson [4]. For an application of same to firm behavior see Cyert and March [9].

[5] See for example the research presented in Part II of Feigenbaum and Feldman [10].

information. Whether one is dealing with one or many individuals acting by themselves or in groups, the resulting decision behavior can be described in these terms.[6] Since both individuals and firms frequently buy and sell commodities through a market, it is a reasonable extension of this theory to say that market behavior is a direct consequence of the interaction of a collection of such individual decision processes.

Little attention has been given to the problem of explaining a market's behavior by accounting for the interactions which take place among the actual decision processes of its participants. The research reported in the main body of this paper, while only in its initial stages, is directed toward this specific task. Indeed, the purpose of this research is to demonstrate that the behavior of prices in a particular market—the Over-the-Counter security market—can be explained by a knowledge of the decision behavior of the individuals concerned. Furthermore, the possible existence of a testable theory of stock price behavior raises a number of questions, for once a price setting mechanism is known one would want to assess the relative merits of alternative mechanisms.

GENERAL CONSIDERATIONS

One reason for the lack of empirical research on market decision processes may be that in many market situations price is a part of the information which determines the quantity to buy or sell. Price is often set prior to making a decision. While prices may change over a period of time, the price at a given moment is that with which the decision-maker operates. In such an instance price itself is not subject to negotiation. The buyer (seller) can decide to buy (sell) more or less of a particular commodity at the stated price but he does not have the opportunity to revise the price by a tâtonnment or other recontracting process at the time that he is making his decision.

A consumer in a department store, supermarket, or other retail establishment is in such a situation since all items have stated prices and his problem is to decide how much of each, if any, to purchase. To explain a consumer's behavior, all one needs to know are the prevailing prices and his decision processes. It is not necessary to know anything about the mechanism which sets these particular prices. In some situations it may be necessary to know something about the recent history of certain prices, for example whether they are special sale prices. However, even in this event, it is unnecessary for the explanation of the consumer's behavior to know why the prices have changed.[7]

[6] For further detail see Clarkson and Pounds [5].
[7] A theory of consumer behavior based upon this approach is described in Clarkson [3].

An example on the seller's side is provided by decision processes which account for the setting of prices in a department store. Again, at any given time only one price is attached to each item in the store, and it is up to the price setter to decide whether to alter these prices or not. Such alterations, however, do not occur from instant to instant; they are based on a set of rules activated by certain events, notably, the recent history of sales, the level of inventories, the change in seasons, the approach of holidays, etc. All this information constitutes part of the conditions for the price setting decision process. Although, prices do change over a period of time, prevailing prices at a given time can be explained solely by means of the price setting decision process and not by the customer's immediate reaction to these prices.[8]

Under these conditions a classical market, with its own mechanisms for setting and adjusting prices, does not appear to exist. Prices are set by one set of decision processes and purchases are determined by another. At no one point in time do these processes directly interact. That is to say, the department store or supermarket is perhaps a convenient place for consumers to examine the available goods and for merchants to display their wares but within these shops all purchases and sales are conducted at set prices and there is no opportunity for the classic balancing of price and quantity to be carried on from one moment to the next. To understand the behavior of the buyer or seller it is sufficient to know their respective decision processes and, consequently, it is not necessary to develop a further set or body of theory for this situation.

There are other kinds of markets, however, where the interaction of buyer and seller directly establishes price and quantity. One such case is provided by the various security markets. In this instance the commodity in question, whether it be a bond, a stock, or a future, is known to both buyer and seller, and through their interaction purchase and sales agreements are made. Since fluctuation in prices is one of the chief characteristics of these markets, it is here, if anywhere, that a classical theory of market behavior might be required. Indeed, if it is a function of a theory of market behavior to explain price movements, then the price changes of security markets are prime candidates for such a theory.

However, it appears that a theory of market behavior, as such, is not required to explain the behavior of security prices. For even in this situation price is a direct consequence of the decision processes of the individuals concerned, and no additional mechanism or theory is required. Although classical theory employs a supply-equal-to-demand relation to establish an equilibrium market price, it is questionable whether such a mechanism is necessary. Behavioral theory suggests that prices can be

---

[8] For a detailed model of the price setting decision process in a department store, which has survived empirical tests, see Cyert and March [9].

explained without explicit reference to a separate equilibrating process, and further, that market behavior is strictly determined by the decision processes of its participants.

While this is hardly a novel conclusion, it implies that for any specific market one needs to know in detail the decision processes of all participants. If the behavior of certain commodity prices is under examination the number of participants could be very large indeed, and if one must describe each individual decision process, the explanation will be a formidable and wearisome task. Security markets, however, like other types of markets are not composed of a collection of individuals indiscriminately competing for the opportunity to buy and sell. On the contrary, the process by which orders to buy and sell are executed is governed by certain institutional constraints, and the participants in the market can be classified into different categories. For example, in a security market actual transactions are usually conducted through official agents, such as brokers and traders, and the participants can be categorized as to whether they represent investment societies, banks, insurance companies, pension funds, or private individuals.[9] If the traders in a given market behave according to a specific set of decision rules, and this is clearly a testable proposition, it is possible to describe the decision processes which determine their behavior. If each category of investors behaves in recognizably different ways, such discrepancies must be a result of differences in their decision processes; and if, within each category, decision behavior is sufficiently similar, a set of decision rules can be described which will represent the decision-making procedures of each class of investors. Under these assumptions, the problem of explaining price behavior becomes relatively simple and straightforward, for the prevailing price at any given moment will be a direct consequence of the interaction of the relevant classes of decision processes.

PRICE BEHAVIOR IN A SECURITY MARKET

According to the previous discussion, by determining the decision processes of the relevant classes of participants, a theory can be constructed to account for the Over-the-Counter security market's behavior. Clearly, it has yet to be demonstrated that each class of investors, traders, and brokers can be adequately represented by one type of decision process but let us assume that it is so.

The theory consists of a set of decision processes where market behavior—fluctuations in the prices of particular securities—responds to specific sequences of interactions among the processes. It is hypothesized that there are three main classes of decision processes—those of investors,

[9] While this is hardly an exhaustive set of categories, the participants in any market can be categorized into a finite number of classes.

brokers, and traders. This is not to say that all investors, for example, have the same portfolio selection process. Rather, it is postulated that there is a describable class of decision procedures which represent investor decision behavior and that differences among investors can be accounted for by alterations in certain parameters within this class of decision mechanisms.

To illustrate the general structure of the theory of stock price behavior and to describe in some detail the particular decision processes, let us consider the decision behavior of the three classes of market participants.

The trader

In the Over-the-Counter market a trader deals only with stockbrokers or other traders. Under no circumstances is it possible for a private individual or institution to deal directly with a trader. The stockbroker takes orders from private or institutional investors and then telephones a trader to ascertain price. Since brokers charge a fee for this service, the cost per share to the ultimate purchaser differs somewhat from the price set by the trader. A trader usually maintains an interest in between 15 and 20 stocks, and in response to an inquiry will quote either a selling (asked) or a buying (bid) price on any one of these securities.[10]

A trader is undoubtedly influenced by many different items of information. He has access to a number of sources, the Dow-Jones ticker, the Dow-Jones broad tape, the daily publication of the National Quotation Bureau which gives for each security the traders concerned and the respective prices at the middle of the preceding day, and telephone conversations with other traders and stockbrokers. Nonetheless, all trading activity is carried on over a telephone in very brief intervals of time, and at any moment a trader can be asked over the telephone for the price on a particular security. He responds, as a rule, with the bid and asked prices on a 100-share lot. Whether there will be an immediate transaction or not depends entirely upon the broker's reaction to the trader's quoted price. Since the broker can telephone any of the traders who are known to have an interest in this particular security, he is not dependent upon a single quote from one trader. However, as soon as the broker accepts a price, the transaction is made at that price and it becomes the market price at that moment.

Before examining a trader's pricing decision process in detail it is pertinent to consider his possible alternative strategies. One alternative is for the trader to deliberately maintain either a net long or net short position in a particular security. In a rising market the value of his inventory will increase, and he would want to have a net long position. Conversely, in a falling market a profit can be made by buying back stock at a lower value

[10] The difference between asked and bid prices is what is known as the spread.

FIGURE 1

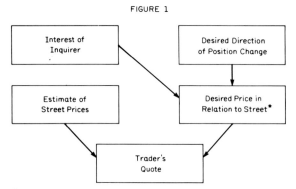

* "Street" is the name given by traders and brokers to the market as a whole.

than that which he sold it for, and he would want to maintain a net short position. During certain periods of time traders may actively seek to maintain long or short positions.[11] Currently the strategy is to make a profit by trading on the difference between the bid and asked prices. Though traders may make a certain amount of profit by taking advantage of a position they find themselves in, their principal return comes from buying at the bid and selling at the asked price. As a result, to be successful the trader must maintain a spread between prices which assures him adequate compensation when combined with the volume of trading.

THE PRICING DECISION. As to the pricing or quoting decision process itself, a decision is required of a trader each time a broker telephones to ask for a price. Since a trader must reply at once, one would not expect the pricing process to be unduly complex. According to a recent study[12] the basic components of the pricing process can be represented by Figure 1. While each of these components is influenced by a number of other factors,[13] the decision process which takes place during the telephone conversation can be represented by the interaction of these four items. For example, a trader alters his quote depending upon the characteristics of the inquirer. Such factors as whether the inquirer is a buyer or seller, whether the orders from this person are usually large or small, and whether he is a friendly[14] competitor or not, affect the quote in the manner outlined below. Moreover, a trader knows whether he wants to increase or decrease his current long or short position in a particular stock. For, at all times the trader is aware of his current position as well as his estimate of the position he would like to have. A trader normally has a maximum amount of money

---

[11] The most notable period when these strategies were actively pursued was in the latter part of the 1920's; see Friend [11].

[12] Jenkins [13].

[13] For a full description of the decision process see *ibid.*, Chapter 3.

[14] A friendly competitor is one who does not take advantage of a bargain or poor quote.

that he can invest in any one security; his general impressions of and attitudes toward the market, constrained by this limit, define his desired position and any discrepancy between his desired and actual position provides what has been labelled the "desired direction of position change."

The estimate of the current market price is normally derived from the broker's reply on the telephone. If a trader's quote is accepted, he is either right on or a little below (on asked price), right on or a little above (on bid price) the current market. Conversely, if no transaction is effected, his asked price is a bit high and his bid price is a bit low. If, for some reason, the stock has not been traded for a while, a trader can obtain an estimate of the current price by telephoning a competitor; but if the stock is being actively traded, each trader will have a fairly accurate estimate of the street price. Given this estimate and any desired change in position, the quoted price can be directly determined.

While the actual increments, $\frac{1}{8}, \frac{1}{4}, \frac{3}{8}$, etc. may vary with different securities[15] the price setting decision process can be represented by Table 1. Table 1 describes the components of the price quoting decision process in sufficient detail to permit some of them to be subjected to test. Furthermore, from the evidence presented in the study, these decision processes

TABLE 1. COMPONENTS OF THE DECISION PROCESS

Inquirer and His Interest	Desired Direction of Position Change	Desired Price Relation to Street	
		Bid Price	Asked Price
Retail buyer	longer indifferent shorter	$\frac{1}{8}$ above street equal street $\frac{1}{4}$ below street	$\frac{1}{4}$ to $\frac{1}{2}$ above street $\frac{1}{8}$ above street equal street
Retail seller	longer indifferent shorter	equal street $\frac{1}{8}$ below street $\frac{1}{4}$ to $\frac{1}{2}$ below street	$\frac{1}{4}$ above street equal street $\frac{1}{8}$ below street
Friendly competitor (interest unknown)	longer indifferent shorter	equal street equal street $\frac{1}{8}$ below street	$\frac{1}{8}$ above street equal street equal street
Enemy competitor (interest unknown)	longer indifferent shorter	much lower than street	much higher than street

[15] See *ibid.*, Chapters 3 and 4 for a detailed discussion of the variation in spread—in particular the relation of the size of the spread to volume and price.

are sufficient to account for a substantial proportion of the observed changes in traders' prices for a number of securities.[16] Consequently, it can be accepted, for the moment, as a detailed representation of the price setting decision process.

Of particular interest in this decision procedure is the mechanism by which a price is changed. If a trader quotes a price which does *not* result in a transaction, no change is made in the price. But, if a transaction is effected— the broker accepts the trader's price—then the trader's price will change in the direction specified by the process outlined above. As a result, price changes are, for the most part, a consequence of a transaction being consummated and are seldom altered to secure a transaction.

Lest the reader feel that somehow the price setting process could not be as simple as it has been portrayed, or that it would be more likely for the trader to change his price in order to get transactions, it is worth noting that the process outlined above apparently reflects a decision procedure which is used by many people when placed in roughly the same situation. That is to say, when faced with the task of bidding for contracts in an experimental market situation most subjects employ decision procedures which are strikingly similar to those used by the Over-the-Counter trader. This observation is one result of a series of experimental investigations of individual and group decision processes.[17] The experiment consists of placing a subject in a situation where he has to announce bids in two markets simultaneously. The subject states his bids in monetary terms, and the experimenter by consulting a specific list of random numbers determines whether these bids "win" or "lose." A bid "wins" when it is below the experimenter's number, and "loses" when it is equal to or above it. In some cases there is a fixed cost associated with each trial, but in all variations examined so far the subject is restricted to making at most one new bid on each trial. Hence, on each trial the subject has to decide which market to leave alone and which bid to alter, if at all. A subject's earnings are a direct function of the contracts he wins in a given number of trials.

In this experiment, a subject's behavior is a record of prices on two markets. These prices change over a period of time. Consequently, an explanation of this behavior consists of an explanation of the changes in the respective prices. Since subjects have no direct knowledge about the list of numbers employed by the experimenter, their behavior is determined by how they decide to respond to their record of wins and losses as it unfolds. While many subjects who participate in this experiment employ slightly different decision procedures, there is one set of processes that

---

[16] See *ibid.*, Chapters 4 and 5.
[17] See Pounds [17] and Clarkson and Tuggle [6].

TABLE 2

	Win	*Lose*
Win	Raise the lower of the two bids	Lower the losing bid
Lose	Lower the losing bid	Lower the higher of the two bids

characterizes and accounts for a large proportion of the observed behavior. This process is expressed in Table 2. The table does not include a process which determines the amount by which to alter the price, nor does it contain a procedure for deciding what to do in the event that both markets have won or lost and both bids are the same; but it does show the principal components of most subjects' price setting procedures. The primary characteristic of such a decision process, aside from its simplicity and symmetry, is that new bids are made in response to contracts made or lost. Prices are lowered when losses occur and are raised or held the same when contracts are won.

It is significant to note that it would be perfectly simple for a subject to choose prices according to some sampling or other statistical procedure. One could note the frequency of wins and losses at various prices in each of the markets and choose that price which appeared to yield the desired earnings. In fact, despite the statistical training of many of the experimental subjects, very few chose to behave in this fashion. Thus, it appears that when little or nothing is directly known about the environment, processes are frequently employed which *respond to rather than anticipate* the occurrence of the relevant events. This is not to suggest that the subjects in this experiment are all fledgling traders, nor that the two situations are the same. It is the similarity of characteristics between traders' and subjects' decision processes that is too striking to ignore. And since the simplicity of a trader's pricing decision process is reflected in a subject's bidding process, the validity of the trader's price setting process can be considered to have received a certain measure of independent, empirical support.

The broker

In the Over-the-Counter market the broker's function is to accept orders from customers and, by talking directly with traders, to negotiate the transactions. Clearly, a broker does not have to accept the first price he receives over the telephone, but if he frequently deals with a particular set of traders, he will have an estimate of the relation between their prices and the prices of other traders, that is, the street. What the broker does not know is the trader's desired direction of position change, and hence whether his price is deliberately slightly above or below the street price. A broker's task is to find a favorable price for his customer, and if he believes he can do better by trying another trader all he has to do is pick up the telephone and find out.

One of the factors which influences the trader's price, not noted above, is the volume of purchases or sales in a particular security. Each trader has a ceiling on the amount of money he can commit to a single stock which, given the prevailing price, places a limit on the number of shares of this stock that he can hold. If traders in Stock A are known to be holding approximately 500 shares each, and a broker receives an order to buy (sell) 4,000 shares, he is placed in a bit of a dilemma. Since no one trader can fill his order, he must buy (or sell) from a number of traders. News of this activity in Stock A spreads to competing traders fairly rapidly, and consequently the broker can expect the price to rise (fall) as he proceeds from one trader to the next. Thus, a broker faced with a large order for a particular security is unlikely to be able to negotiate the entire transaction at a single price.[18]

To account for a broker's behavior the theory makes a number of simplifying assumptions about his decision behavior. First, it does not allow for an inventory of securities in a broker's own account. Second, no provision is made for the possibility of a broker advising an investor on what securities to buy or sell. In short, a broker is represented as an agent whose task is to transact a client's orders at a favorable price, where the term "favorable price" is defined in terms of the broker's estimate of the street price. Thus, while the theory contains a brokerage process that permits transactions to take place it cannot be reported upon in detail as it has not yet been subjected to empirical investigation.

The investor

While each investor may feel that he analyzes the market by an unique method, there appear to be a number of similarities among such methods of approach. It is posited that investors can be placed in a modest number of categories defined in terms of the methods of analysis and selection employed. To identify these categories it is necessary to examine the portfolio selection processes of a number of types of investors.

For example, the portfolio selection process of investors of trust funds for banks consists of a set of decision processes which are described in terms of specific discrimination nets. These nets contain a collection of individual tests which refer to those attributes of securities considered

---

[18] The possibility of a broker carrying an inventory of securities is currently ignored.

important for trust investment purposes. While the theory of trust investment[19] cannot as yet claim to represent the portfolio selection process of all trust investors, it would not be a difficult task to conduct the requisite tests.[20] If such tests were successful, this particular set of decision processes would represent in detail the procedures by which investors of trust funds select securities for their portfolios. Once these procedures are known the only other information required is the amount of funds available for investment classified by the types of portfolios desired—growth, income, income and growth, etc. By an application of the decision process to current market data, specific portfolios of securities are generated. These portfolios represent the orders which are given to the broker by the investor.

It is worth noting that portfolio decisions are relatively insensitive to the exact prices prevailing in the market at the time the portfolios are selected. The actual price for a particular order is only determined after the broker has received it and has contracted with a trader. Hence, the investor must select his portfolios on the basis of some previous prices. These prices may closely approximate the actual prices paid after the broker has completed his transaction; nevertheless, portfolio decisions are clearly made without an exact knowledge of the price per security that will be paid.

Due to various legal constraints investors of trust funds are not allowed to purchase securities on the Over-the-Counter market. However, since it is possible to describe the portfolio procedures of trust investors there is no reason to suppose that the investment behavior of other institutional investors who do participate in the Over-the-Counter market cannot be described in a similar manner. Consequently, since a theory of each class of investors can be constructed and tested, it is possible to describe the processes by which brokers' orders are generated.

TESTING THE MARKET PROCESSES

In a current model of the theory of stock price behavior, price movements are generated by interactions among brokers and traders. That is to say, if one is not concerned with explaining the flow of buy and sell orders to the broker, and orders are considered as a part of the model's given conditions, the behavior of prices is a result of the interaction of the broker's transaction process and the trader's price setting process.

[19] Clarkson [2].
[20] Indeed, part of this testing process has been carried out with quite favorable results on the trust investment process within a bank in Massachusetts; see Mihaltse [14].

In order to subject the theory to empirical test two types of market situations are considered. The first is the simple case where one trader holds an inventory in a particular stock. Since this condition is likely to occur only when there is little interest and activity in a security, the number of brokers who receive orders for this stock will also be quite limited. Given such a situation, one can specify the relevant parameters of the decision processes employed by each of the participants. Once these processes are described, with the brokers' orders forming a part of the initial conditions, the price behavior of this particular security can be immediately explained. For the interaction of these decision processes will generate a sequence of price movements which should be identical to the observed.

To test the accuracy with which such a model reproduces observed price movements in the selected security, it is only necessary to set up a criterion of success and failure and compare the two time series. Such a comparison can be conducted upon the actual prices themselves, as well as on whether the model produces a set of prices that move at each decision point in the same direction as the observed. Once measures of success and failure are defined—that is, the conditions under which the model's movements in price are to be considered the same as the actual—the model's level of success can be measured by the frequency with which it accounts for observed changes. Since each of the individual decision processes can be independently subjected to test, the model as a whole can be satisfactorily tested on its ability to reproduce the observed time series.

A second and more general test would require considering a situation where more than one trader holds an inventory in a particular security. Under this condition the model becomes correspondingly more complex, for once there are several traders as well as a number of brokers there may be more than one price prevailing at any given time. Each broker agrees to a transaction when he thinks he has secured a favorable price, but each broker does not canvass all traders before making a decision. In addition, more than one broker may be interested in a certain security at a given time; therefore, it is possible for there to be slightly different prices prevailing over any given period.

In order to reproduce these detailed events the model has to include the individual decision processes of each participant. To determine these separate processes is a time-consuming task, but if a complete explanation of a particular stream of price behavior is desired the separate decision processes must be taken into account. However, if an explanation of each movement in price is not required and if one is only concerned with some of the more general characteristics of price behavior over a given period, such as the direction of change from beginning to end of interval, the size of increment, etc., a simplified model would suffice. Such a model would consist of a generalized broker's decision process interaction with a generalized price quoting process. Whether such a model would produce the desired behavior is open to investigation, but since each of the individual processes can be independently subjected to test, the validity of the entire model is not solely dependent upon the characteristics of the generated time series being similar to the observed. Consequently, it would appear that it is quite possible to develop a general model of price behavior without too much difficulty.

The point to note is that none of these models requires a special equilibrating mechanism. Each is based solely upon the interaction of independent decision processes. Thus, although their empirical validity has yet to be demonstrated, the research completed so far is, in my opinion, sufficient to indicate the theoretical and empirical merit of this approach.

SOME IMPLICATIONS FOR FUTURE RESEARCH

In Section I it was noted that a number of statistical investigations have been conducted on stock price time series and that the results indicate that such price movements are consistent with the hypothesis of a random walk between reflecting barriers. Changes in price over a period of time, however, are a consequence of the interactions between broker and trader; consequently, it would appear that more could be learned about the relevance of the statistical characteristics of these time series by an experimental examination of the behavioral processes by which they are generated. For, by an analysis of the price setting mechanism, it may well be possible to identify the principal factors which affect the movement of prices over time.

Consider, for example, the simple case mentioned in the previous section. Here the time series of price for one security is a direct result of the interaction between one trader and one or more brokers. All of these decision procedures can be described in detail and it is clearly possible to construct a specific model of this market behavior. If the model is provided with the requisite information the final result will be a series of prices. This sequence of prices will, if the model is properly constructed, correspond to an actual, observable time series; and, since the sequence is an orthodox time series, it can be submitted to the same statistical analyses as are employed in the previously noted researches on stock prices. But, and this is the important point, whatever inferences are drawn from such statistical analyses, the model provides the mechanism by which these statistical characteristics are produced. Indeed, if it can be shown that certain decision processes on the part of both broker and trader, lead invariably to the generation of time series with particular statistical characteristics, then a basis would have been established from which inferences could be made to the underlying decision procedures. If different sets of decision processes lead to time series with significantly different characteristics, they could be grouped into separate classes.

While these suppositions may appear idealistic, and may be rejected as requiring far too much effort to investigate, it should be remembered that they can readily be subjected to empirical analysis. A theory of the price setting process can be assessed under a variety of initial conditions and environments. If the time series produced vary significantly in their characteristics, it would follow that these properties can be classified by decision procedures as well as by environmental conditions. At the same time, by examining different price setting decision processes it would also be possible to identify the effect these differences have on the behavior of prices over a period of time. In short, such research would lead to a more detailed understanding of market behavior as well as an explication of the origins of specific time series and their statistical characteristics.

One consequence of such investigations would be the ability to discover, on empirical grounds, answers to such questions as: (1) How should trading in the securities markets be managed? (2) How should traders behave in order to improve their performance?

Consider the problem posed by Question (1). First one has to establish the criteria by which a market is to be defined. A possible criterion is that under all possible environmental conditions the trading process must be such as to achieve an orderly market. One way of describing an orderly market is in terms of the properties of its time series. If certain classes of time series are considered to satisfy the relevant criteria, it would be necessary to prescribe a set of decision mechanisms which would produce the requisite series. These mechanisms would, no doubt, have to include some safety devices to accommodate the occurrence of a large run on the system, but a solution can be discovered by an experimental analysis of the properties of alternative decision processes.

Question (2) can be resolved in a similar manner. For, if the primary concern is to ensure that the security markets serve investors and not just traders and brokers, one is searching for improvements in trader performance that will enhance the behavior of the market as a whole. Once again specific criteria must be introduced and accepted before proposed improvements can be critically examined. However, as soon as appropriate standards are devised, better procedures can be discovered, evaluated, and adopted. Consequently, once a tested theory of the price setting process exists, questions such as these can be answered by the application of a set of procedures that are common to all branches of applied science.

REFERENCES

[1] Alexander, S. "Price Movements in Speculative Markets: Trends or Random Walks," *Industrial Management Review*, Vol. 2 (May, 1961).

[2] Clarkson, G. P. E. *Portfolio Selection: A Simulation of Trust Investment* (Englewood Cliffs, N. J.: Prentice-Hall, 1962).

[3] Clarkson, G. P. E. *The Theory of Consumer Demand: A Critical Appraisal* (Englewood Cliffs, N. J.: Prentice-Hall, 1963).

[4] Clarkson, G. P. E. *Empirical Foundations of Economic Analysis*, Sloan School of Management, Working Paper No. 83-64, Massachusetts Institute of Technology, 1964.

[5] Clarkson, G. P. E., and W. F. Pounds. "Theory and Method in the Exploration of Human Decision Behavior," *Industrial Management Review*, Vol. 5 (December, 1963).

[6] Clarkson, G. P. E., and F. D. Tuggle. *A Theory of Group Decision Behavior*, Sloan School of Management, Working Paper No. 92-64, Massachusetts Institute of Technology, 1964.

[7] Cootner, P. H. "Stock Prices: Random vs. Systematic Changes," *Industrial Management Review*, Vol. 3 (May 1962).

[8] Cootner, P. H. (ed.). *The Random Character of Stock Market Prices* (Cambridge, Mass.: M.I.T. Press, 1964).

[9] Cyert, R. M., and J. G. March. *A Behavioral Theory of the Firm* (Englewood Cliffs, N. J.: Prentice-Hall, 1963).

[10] Feigenbaum, E. A., and J. Feldman. *Computers and Thought* (New York, N. Y.: McGraw-Hill, 1963).

[11] Friend, I., *et al. The Over-the-Counter Securities Market* (New York, N. Y.: McGraw-Hill, 1958).

[12] Houthakker, H. "Systematic and Random Elements in Short Term Price Movements," *American Economic Review*, Vol. 51 (May 1961).

[13] Jenkins, R. A. *Professional Trader Price Quoting in the Over-the-Counter Stock Market*, unpublished Master's thesis (Sloan School of Management, Massachusetts Institute of Technology, 1964).

[14] Mihaltse, W. *A Model of an Institutional Investor*, unpublished Master's thesis (Sloan School of Management, Massachusetts Institute of Technology, 1965).

[15] Negishi, T. "The Stability of Competitive Economy: A Survey Article," *Econometrica*, Vol. 30 (October 1962).

[16] Osborne, M. F. M. "Brownian Motion in the Stock Market," *Operations Research*, Vol. 7 (April 1959).

[17] Pounds, W. F. *A Study of Problem Solving Control*, unpublished Ph.D. thesis (Carnegie Institute of Technology, 1964).

[18] Working, H., "Note on the Correlation of First Differences of Averages in a Random Chain," *Econometrica*, Vol. 28 (October 1960).

Alfred Cowles

41. Stock Market Forecasting[1]

Reprinted from **Econometrica**, Vol. 12, Nos. 3-4 (July, October, 1944), pp. 206–214, by permission of the publisher.

The analysis reported here is a continuation of a study begun at the end of 1927 and originally published in 1933.[2] At that time were reported the results achieved by 24 financial publications in forecasting the course of the stock market during the period from January, 1928, to June, 1932. This earlier investigation disclosed no evidence of skill in forecasting. The present study extends the records of 11 of the forecasters. In the case of 7 of these the record now covers the $15\frac{1}{2}$ years from January, 1928, to July, 1943, and, for the remaining 4, periods of about 11 years ending in 1938 or 1939. The forecasters include 4 financial periodicals and 7 financial services. These organizations are well known. Names are omitted here because their publication might precipitate controversy over interpretation of the records. The wording of many of the forecasts is indefinite, and it would frequently be possible for the forecaster after the event to present a plausible argument in favor of an interpretation other than the one made by a reader.

The method used in this analysis was for each of two readers[3] to grade the forecasts independently according to the degree of bullishness or bearishness which he thought they contained. The average of the two interpretations was used as the basis for computing the record. It was assumed that the reader, if the forecast was 100 percent bullish, would invest all of his funds in the stock market; if the forecast was 50 percent bullish, he would put three-quarters of his funds in stocks; if the forecast was doubtful, he would put half of his funds in stocks; if 50 percent bearish, one-quarter in stocks; and if 100 percent bearish, nothing in stocks. The forecasts thus tabulated have been tested in the light of the fluctuations of the stock market as reflected by the Standard and Poor's average of 90

[1] Cowles Commission Papers, New Series, No. 6.

[2] Alfred Cowles, "Can Stock Market Forecasters Forecast?" *Econometrica*, Vol. 1 (July, 1933), pp. 309–24.

[3] The author is indebted to Dickson H. Leavens, Forrest Danson, and Miss Emma Manning of the Cowles Commission for Research in Economics, The University of Chicago, for assistance in tabulating the forecasts and computing the records.

representative common stocks. If the forecast is 100 percent bullish and the market rises 10 percent, the forecasting score is 1.10. If the forecaster is doubtful, the score is 1.05, reflecting one-half of the market advance, on the assumption that the investor, being doubtful, would place one-half of his funds in stocks and hold one-half in reserve. If the forecast is 100 percent bearish, the score is 1.0, regardless of the subsequent action of the market, on the assumption that the investor would have withdrawn all of his funds from the market. If the forecast is 100 percent bullish, and the market drops 10 percent, the score is 0.90, and if the forecast is doubtful and the market drops 10 percent, the score is 0.95. The compounding of the weekly scores for each agency gives its forecasting record for the whole period. These results are compared with a figure representing the average of all possible forecasting results, arrived at by compounding one-half of the percentage change in the level of the stock market for each period, which hereafter for convenience will be referred to as the "random forecasting record." The results presented, hereafter called the "index of performance," are derived by dividing the actual compounded record of each forecaster by the random forecasting record referred to above and subtracting 1. The results have also been decompounded so as to represent an effective annual rate. If a forecaster's record is plus it is better, and if minus it is worse, than the random forecasting record. Most of the agencies published forecasts every week and these were tabulated on a weekly basis. In other cases the latest forecast was assumed to be in effect until the next one appeared.

The process described above may be expressed in algebraic terms as follows; let

$$t = \text{date, measured in weeks;}$$

$$p_t = \text{actual market (Standard \& Poor's index of 90 stocks) at date } t;$$

$$\frac{p_{t+1}}{p_{t+1}} - 1 = \text{increase or decrease (rate) in actual market from date } t \text{ to date } t + 1;$$

$$\frac{1}{2}\left(\frac{p_{t+1}}{p_t} - 1\right) = \text{increase or decrease (rate) in "random forecasting record," that is, one-half increase or decrease in actual market;}$$

$$r_t = \frac{1}{2}\left(\frac{p_{t+1}}{p_t} - 1\right) + 1 = \text{ratio of random forecasting record at date } t + 1 \text{ to random forecasting record at date } t;$$

$$\prod_1^t r_i = r_1 r_2 \ldots r_t = \text{compounded random forecasting record at date } t + 1;$$

q_t = fraction of funds kept in market on advice of forecaster from date t to date $t + 1$;

$$f_t = q_t \left(\frac{p_{t+1}}{p_t} - 1 \right) + 1 = \text{ratio of value of above investment (including idle cash) at date } t + 1 \text{ to value at date } t;$$

$$\prod_1^t f_i = f_1 f_2 \ldots f_t = \text{compounded value of investment at date } t + 1;$$

$$I_1{}^t = \frac{\displaystyle\prod_1^t f_i}{\displaystyle\prod_1^t r_i} - 1 = \text{``index of performance'' of forecaster from date 1 to date } t + 1, \text{ that is, ratio of compounded value of investment to compounded random forecasting record.}$$

Work sheets for the computation have the form shown in Table 1 (using hypothetical values and working to only 2 decimals as compared with 4 used in the actual study).

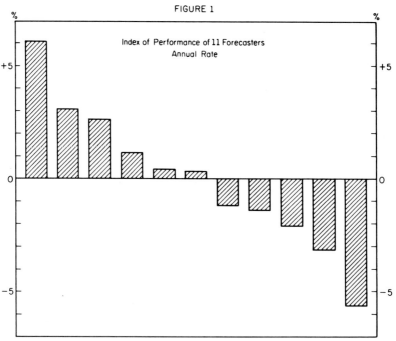

FIGURE 1

Index of Performance of 11 Forecasters
Annual Rate

The index of performance is the percent by which the compounded record of each forecaster is better or worse than the random forecasting record.

TABLE 1

1	2	3	4	5	6	7	8	9
					Forecaster A			
Weeks	Actual Market	Rate of Increase or Decrease in Actual Market	Ratio of Random Forecasting Record at $t+1$ to That at t	Compounded Random Forecasting Record	Fraction of Funds in Market	Ratio of Value at $t+1$ to That at t	Compounded Value	Index of Performance
t	p_t	$\frac{p_{t+1}}{p_t} - 1$	r_t	$\prod_1^t r_i$	q_t	f_t	$\prod_1^t f_i$	I_1^t
1	50	+0.20	1.10	1.10	1.00	1.20	1.20	+0.09
2	60	+0.25	1.12	1.23	0	1.00	1.20	-0.02
3	75	0	1.00	1.23	0.50	1.00	1.20	-0.02
4	75	-0.20	0.90	1.11	1.00	0.80	0.96	-0.14
5	60	-0.10	0.95	1.05	0.50	0.95	0.91	-0.14
6	54							

Thus the hypothetical forecaster was better than the random fore-casting record in the first week because he had 100 percent of his funds in the market instead of only 50 percent; in the second week he lost by staying out of a rising market; in the third week the market did not move and he just held his own (which he would have done regardless of his position in the market); in the fourth week he lost by being bullish in a bear market; and in the fifth week he lost but maintained the same relation to the random forecasting record as the week before.

Figure 1 indicates that 6 of the 11 forecasters met with some degree of success and that 5 were unsuccessful in their forecasts. The 11 fore-casters were on the average only 0.2 percent a year better than the random forecasting record. That one of the forecasters had an average annual rate 6.02 percent better than the random forecasting record is to be discounted by the fact that it is the best of the 11 records examined. Assuming a complete lack of ability, if one had the opportunity to make 11 attempts, the best of these by chance might show a considerable degree of success. In this analysis, the least successful of the forecasters, with an average annual rate 5.62 percent worse than the random forecasting record, was wrong almost as much as the most successful one was right.

Figure 2 depicts the result of dividing the $15\frac{1}{2}$-year period into 17 major swings and for each of these computing the average index of per-formance; that is, the average result of the 11 forecasters[4] as a percent-age of the random forecasting record. Any rise exceeding 33 percent, or decline of more than 25 percent, was designated as a major swing, the daily highs or lows being considered rather than weekly or monthly aver-ages. The last swing was arbitrarily terminated in July, 1943, because when the analysis was made the market in that month had reached its highest point since the low of 1942, and subsequent to July, 1943, it had not declined as much as the 25 percent necessary to establish a major down-swing. It appears that the consensus of opinion was always right in the case of bull markets, and wrong in the bear markets. Of the 6904 forecasts recorded, 4712 were bullish, 1107 doubtful, and 1085 bearish. Yet only 88 months of the period are occupied by bull markets and 98 by bear markets, and in July, 1943, the end of the $15\frac{1}{2}$-year period, the market was at only about two-thirds of its level at the beginning of this period in January, 1928. In the case of every one of the 11 forecasters the number of bullish predictions far exceeded the number of bearish ones. The per-sistent and unwarranted record of optimism can possibly be explained on the ground that readers prefer good news to bad, and that a forecaster who presents a cheerful point of view thereby attracts a following without which he would probably be unable to remain long in the business of

---

[4] For the period subsequent to 1939 only 7 of the 11 forecasting records were available.

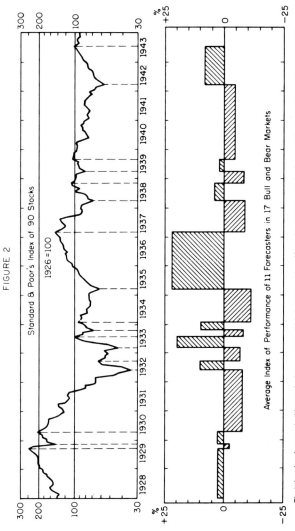

FIGURE 2

Standard & Poor's Index of 90 Stocks

1926 = 100

Average Index of Performance of 11 Forecasters in 17 Bull and Bear Markets

The index of performance in this case is the per cent by which the average of the compounded records of all forecasters is better or worse than the random forecasting record for each of the 17 major swings. The curve in the upper half of the chart shows the monthly averages of Standard & Poor's Index of 90 stocks except at terminations of bull markets where the highest of the daily averages are shown, and at terminations of bear markets where the lowest of the daily averages are given.

forecasting. In extenuation, however, it may be said that the last 15 years is the longest period on record in which the industrial stock averages failed to move into new high ground. During the 57 years from 1871 to 1927, the average rate of gain for industrial common stocks in the United States was 3.8 percent a year in addition to dividend income, and the longest period in which a previous all-time high was not exceeded was $9\frac{3}{4}$ years from June, 1889, to March, 1899. This background may have exerted a strong influence during the last 15 years on the minds of the forecasters.

It was found possible to extend back to 1903 the published record of the forecasting agency with the most successful record for the period from 1928 to 1943. While three individuals were for different periods responsible for the forecasts throughout those 40 years, the general principles followed by them all were similar and the succeeding forecasters were avowed disciples of their predecessors. It therefore seems justifiable to treat the combined record as a continuous one for the 40 years in question. In analyzing this record, the same method was used as in the case of the 11 forecasters previously reported except that corrections were made to include cash dividends, brokerage charges, and interest which could have been earned on idle funds. Also, the Dow-Jones Industrial Average[5] was used in computing the market gain or loss on each forecast instead of the Standard and Poor's average of 90 stocks since the latter is not available prior to 1926. The resulting figure was reduced to the actual effective annual rate of gain instead of to the index of performance. The rate of gain computed as above indicated is 14.2 percent a year, of which about 4.2 percent is dividend and interest income. In the same period a continuous investment in the stocks composing the Dow-Jones Industrial Average would have shown a return, including dividends, of 10.9 percent a year. Following the forecasts, therefore, would have resulted in a gain of 3.3 percent a year over the result secured by a continuous investment in the common stocks composing the Dow-Jones Industrial Average.

Breaking the record down into four periods of 10 years each, we find that following the forecasts would have shown an average annual capital gain of about 13 percent from 1904 to 1913, 7 percent from 1914 to 1923, 13 percent from 1924 to 1933, and 7 percent from 1934 to 1943. This is without including the cash dividends and interest earned on idle funds which would have averaged around 4.2 percent a year. There were two fairly long periods in which following the forecasts would not have resulted in profits. One of these was the $5\frac{1}{2}$ years from the fall of 1909 to the spring of 1915 when losses averaging about 3 percent a year would have been incurred. The other was the last 6 years of the record from June, 1937, to June, 1943, when little if any profit would have been secured. Both of these

---

[5] Where needed in order to preserve the continuity of this average, corrections were made to offset the effect of stock dividends and changes in the list of stocks included.

were, however, periods in which stock prices were lower at the end than at the beginning, so that following the forecasts would not have been less successful than a continuous investment in common stocks.

In view of this moderately but consistently successful result over such a long period it may be of interest to consider the forecasting method used and some statistical evidence as to the soundness of the principles involved. The theory of these forecasters was that there was a prevalence of sequences over reversals in the movements of stock prices[6] and that it was, therefore, desirable to swim with the tide. They evolved various devices for recognizing when the tide had turned, no attempt being made to anticipate such an event. The magnitude of the cycles to be identified apparently was of several years' duration and particular significance generally was not attached to developments requiring less than a few weeks to materialize. A detailed discussion of the statistical devices employed in the forecasts will not be attempted here because the forecasters never reduced their method to terms which could be defined precisely in a mathematical sense or which made possible its application by two independent operators with any assurance of securing identical, or at least similar, results. It will suffice to say that they tried to recognize when the long-term trend of the market had reversed itself simply by the superficial appearance of the general pattern presented rather than by any precise statistical test.

What statistical evidence is there as to why such an apparently naïve procedure should be successful? The author and the late Herbert E. Jones once made an investigation of the evidence as to the element of inertia in stock prices as follows:[7] In a penny-tossing series there is a probability of one-half that a reversal will occur. If the stock market rises for one hour, day, week, month, or year, is there a probability of one-half that it will decline in the succeeding comparable unit of time? In an attempt to answer this question, sequences and reversals, as defined in footnote 6, were counted.

A study of the ratio of sequences to reversals will probably disclose structure as previously defined, if it exists within the series, and the significance of this structure can be investigated by ordinary statistical methods. For instance, the probability can be determined that any ratio occurred by chance, from a random population of possible price series. Also, from the frequency distribution of these ratios one can estimate the probabilities of success in forecasting a rise or decline in stock prices. Samples of adequate length, where available, were examined, the intervals between observations being successively 20 minutes, 1 hour, 1 day, 1, 2, and 3 weeks,

---

[6] The word "sequence" is used here to denote when a rise follows a rise, or a decline a decline. A "reversal" is when a decline follows a rise, or a rise a decline.

[7] Alfred Cowles and Herbert E. Jones, "Some A Posteriori Probabilities in Stock Market Action," *Econometrica*, Vol. 5 (July, 1937), pp. 280–94.

1, 2, 3, ..., 11 months, and 1, 2, 3, ..., 10 years. It was found that for every series with intervals between observations of from 20 minutes up to and including 3 years, the sequences outnumbered the reversals. As a result of various considerations it appeared that a unit of 1 month was the most promising from a forecasting viewpoint. In the case of the 100-year monthly series of common stock prices from 1836 to 1935, a total of 1200 observations, there were 748 sequences and 450 reversals. That is, the estimated probability was 0.625 that, if the market had risen in any given month, it would rise in the succeeding month or, if it had fallen, that it would continue to decline for another month. The standard deviation for such a long series constructed by random penny tossing would be 17.3; therefore the deviation of 149 from the expected value 599 is in excess of 8 times the standard deviation. The probability of obtaining such a result in a penny-tossing series is infinitesimal.

An investigation of the average amount the stock market moved in each month, a consideration of brokerage costs, and determination of the degree of consistency revealed by the data, were used to supplement the information as to the ratio of sequences to reversals. This further analysis indicated an average net gain of 6.7 percent a year with a probability of a net loss in 1 year out of 3. To this should be added the expected dividend and interest income which for the period analyzed would have been about 5 percent a year. The anticipated degree of success in forecasting should be modified by a consideration of the fact that the unit of time employed, 1 month, was selected by hindsight after investigation of various other possible units of time. The investigation, however, discloses evidence of structure in stock prices sufficient to account in large measure for the success of the 40-year forecasting record herewith reported.

CONCLUSION

1. The records of 11 leading financial periodicals and services since 1927, over periods varying from 10 to $15\frac{1}{2}$ years, fail to disclose evidence of ability to predict successfully the future course of the stock market.

2. Of the 6904 forecasts recorded during the $15\frac{1}{2}$-year period, more than four times as many were bullish as bearish, although more than half of the period was occupied by bear markets, and stocks at the end were at only about two-thirds of their level at the beginning.

3. The record of the forecasting agency with the best results for the $15\frac{1}{2}$ years since 1927, when tabulated back to 1903, for the 40 years showed results 3.3 percent a year better than would have been secured by a continuous investment in the stocks composing the Dow-Jones Industrial Average. Under present laws the capital gains tax might wipe out most

of this advantage. While prospects for the speculator are, therefore, not particularly alluring, statistical tests disclose positive evidence of structure in stock prices which indicates a likelihood that whatever success may be claimed for the very consistent 40-year record is not entirely accidental. A simple application of the "inertia" principle, such as buying at turning points in the market after prices for a month averaged higher, and selling after they averaged lower, than for the previous month, would have resulted in substantial gains for the period under consideration.

Editor's Note:

In a recent paper, "A Revision of Previous Conclusions Regarding Stock Price Behavior," *Econometrica*, Vol. 28, No. 4 (October, 1960), pp. 909–15, Cowles acknowledges a statistical deficiency in his 1937 results. "Where each unit of a time series is an average of points within that unit, the effect of such averaging will be to introduce a positive first-order serial correlation in the first differences of such a series even where the original series is a random chain" (p. 909). Since at least a part of the 1200-month series analyzed previously reflected averaged observations, the nonrandom structure found is largely attributable to the averaging bias. In the 1960 paper a deviation of 32 from the expected value of 498 sequences (as opposed to 149 from 599, above) is reported.

Despite these results, Cowles retains the conclusion that price movements persist: "A positive first-order serial correlation in the first differences has been disclosed for every stock-price series analyzed in which the intervals between successive observations are less than four years" (p. 914). However, he fails, as Alexander has noted, to take account of the higher relative frequency of rises than declines to be expected in a market exhibiting an upward trend. See Sidney S. Alexander, "Price Movements in Speculative Markets: Trends or Random Walks," *Industrial Management Review*, Vol. 2, No. 2 (May, 1961), pp. 21–22.

4 2. The Market Break of May, 1962

Shortly after the market break of May 28–31, the Special Study was asked to add to its agenda an examination of that important occurrence. Some of the results of its inquiry are reflected in other chapters (especially VI and VII) and a general summary is contained in this chapter. In view of the fact that the NYSE has published its own study[1] containing relevant aggregated data for the three particular days, the Special Study has sought to avoid duplication of that analysis. Instead it has attempted to take a somewhat wider look, by examining trading on 16 additional days, and at the same time a closer look, by studying specific stocks and disaggregated data.

In its analysis of the disaggregated data, the study found that while there were general patterns of behavior, there were also striking departures from the overall picture. For example, odd-lot customers in the aggregate were net sellers on May 28, but they had a purchase balance in AT&T. The open-end investment companies studied, on the other hand, were overall net buyers of stocks on that day but were sellers on balance in General Motors and U.S. Steel and had no transactions in Avco or Brunswick. Similarly, although specialists as a group had a purchase balance, they were relatively large net sellers of Korvette and had modest sale balances in IBM and U.S. Steel. These variations in the practices of the participants in individual issues reveal the inadequacy of aggregated data alone to portray realistically the diversity of members' and nonmembers' transactions in individual stocks.

Neither this study nor that of the New York Stock Exchange was able to isolate and identify the "causes" of the market events of May 28, 29, and 31. There was some speculation at the time that these events might be the result of some conspiracy or deliberate misconduct. Upon the basis

---

* *Report of Special Study of Securities Markets of the Securities and Exchange Commission*, Part 5 (88th Congress, 1st Session, House Document No. 95, Pt. 5; Washington: U.S. Government Printing Office, 1963), Ch. XIII. Part 5 of the *Special Study* includes the summaries, conclusions, and recommendations of Parts 1, 2, 3, and 4 of the study. For a more detailed treatment of the market break see Part 4, Ch. XIII, which also includes this selection.

[1] NYSE, "The Stock Market Under Stress" (1963).

of the study's inquiry, there is no evidence whatsoever that the break was deliberately precipitated by any person or group or that there was any manipulation or illegal conduct in the functioning of the market.

The avalanche of orders which came into the market during this period subjected the market mechanisms to extraordinary strain, and in many respects they did not function in a normal way. Particularly significant were the lateness of the tape and the consequent inability of investors to predict accurately the prices at which market orders would be executed. Further indicative of the disruption of the trading mechanisms, some odd-lot orders on May 28 were not executed at the first round-lot sale following receipt as required, but at the day's closing price, in most instances considerably lower, plus or minus the odd-lot differential.

On the 3 days of the market break the percentage distribution for purchases and sales by types of orders[2] on the NYSE was as shown in Table 1.

TABLE 1. DISTRIBUTION OF TYPES OF ORDERS ON THE NEW YORK STOCK EXCHANGE, MAY 28, 29, AND 31, 1962
(Percent)

	Market	Limit	Stop
May 28, total............................	53.1	42.4	4.5
Purchases............................	35.4	64.1	.5
Sales.................................	70.1	21.5	8.4
May 29, total............................	69.3	29.1	1.6
Purchases............................	64.5	34.6	.9
Sales.................................	74.1	23.5	2.4
May 31, total............................	60.5	38.5	1.0
Purchases............................	68.2	31.3	.5
Sales.................................	51.3	47.2	1.5

Source: NYSE, "The Stock Market Under Stress," (1963), p. 37.

It is noteworthy that on May 28, 70.1 percent of public sell orders were market orders and another 8.4 percent were stop orders, whereas 21.5 percent were limit orders. On the buy side, on the other hand, 64.1 percent were limit orders, and 35.9 percent market and stop orders. Since May 29 was

[2] Three main types of orders are used to buy or sell securities in the auction market of the NYSE: market orders, limit orders, and stop orders. Briefly, a market order is one to buy or sell at the best price available. A limit order is one to buy or sell at a specific price or better; on the sell side the specified price would be above the prevailing market, and on the buy side, below the prevailing market. A stop order, sometimes called a "stoploss" order, specifies a price at which, if the market moves adversely, the customer desires an execution. If the order is on the sell side, it specifies a price below that prevailing; on the buy side, a price above that prevailing—the reverse of the situation in limit orders. It does not, however, guarantee execution at the specified price, but merely becomes a market order if and when that price is reached. It is to be expected that the volume of sell-stop orders would ordinarily exceed that of buy-stop orders.

characterized by a continuation of the sharp decline during the earlier part of the day and a very sharp recovery in the later part of the day, and since it was not possible to allocate orders between these two phases, significant relationship in terms of types of orders could not be established. On May 31, however, when prices moved sharply upward, there was a distinct reversal of the pattern from that of Monday: on the purchase side 68.7 percent of orders were market and stop orders, whereas on the sell side only 52.8 percent were market and stop orders.

The relatively large volume of sell-stop orders on May 28 is also worthy of note. As already mentioned, such an order is used as a protective measure to assure a prompt sale if the market price reaches or falls below a previously specified figure, and it becomes a market order when that price is reached. Thus, a sharp decline such as that of May 28, already involving a heavy preponderance of market sell orders as compared with buy orders, produces a separate source of market orders as stop orders are triggered by the decline. The sell-stop orders held by specialists on May 28 may not have been entered on that day; some may well have been placed at any time previously and have come into play as prices fell.

The "snowballing" effect of stop orders on May 28 was pointed out by a specialist who testified:

> ... the book was heavy with stop orders, and they, as much as anything, were responsible for the decline, with an overhanging volume of market short orders. The bid had to be dropped considerably to take care of the new stop orders that were put into effect . . . .

The volume of short selling in the aggregate, and for certain individual stocks, by classes of participants, is shown elsewhere in the report,[3] but these figures do not necessarily reveal the full impact of short selling. In testimony taken by the study, specialists indicated that there was a significant amount of potential short selling (brokers in the "crowd" waiting for an uptick) which was never realized in transactions. This potential short selling overhanging the market may well have prompted some specialists to moderate their stabilizing activities, since they would know that any rally would be met by short-sale orders in the "crowd." As one specialist put it, short selling during the break acted to "lengthen the time that it took a stock to go up because there had to be substantially more buyers to move the stock up. . . ."

The Exchange Act makes it clear that there is an important public interest in the effects of rapid price fluctuations both up and down. The Act states as one of the reasons for its passage the fact that "national emergencies . . . are precipitated, intensified, and prolonged by . . . sudden

[3] Part 2, Chapter VI.H.5.b.

and unreasonable fluctuations of security prices and by excessive speculation. . . ."[4] Accordingly, the Commission is given the authority and responsibility—

> if in its opinion the public interest so requires, summarily to suspend trading in any registered security on any national securities exchange for a period not exceeding 10 days, or with the approval of the President, summarily to suspend all trading on any national securities exchange for a period not exceeding 90 days.

The power to suspend all trading on an exchange is indeed an awesome one, as indicated by the requirement of Presidential approval, and the Commission has never invoked it. Once market changes became so chaotic as to warrant halting all trading on the exchanges, it is possible that investor tensions would be so acute that unexpected and severe reactions might follow from the suspension itself.

On the other hand, assuming that any intermediate, technical measures—i.e., measures short of suspension of all trading—would be feasible and desirable, it obviously is not practicable to wait until a severe break is in progress to determine what they may be. The uncertainties and pressures existing under such conditions militate against the development of a sound course of action. Nor is it possible at the time of a market break, unless arrangements for gathering information have been worked out in advance, to obtain speedily the kind of current and meaningful trading data which the Commission and other government agencies might consider useful in discharging their responsibilities. Yet, once a break has passed, there is a tendency to forget the concerns existing at the time and the apprehensions as to what might happen should it continue.

The history of the May 28 market break reveals that a complex interaction of causes and effects—including rational and emotional motivations as well as a variety of mechanisms and pressures—may suddenly create a downward spiral of great velocity and force. This, in turn, may change the impact of various normal market mechanisms, and thus temporarily impair the market's fair and orderly character. Where the latter situation prevails, a public interest in orderly markets, quite distinguishable from any public intervention in the setting of price levels, may come into play.

The question thus arises whether it would be desirable and feasible for the Commission and the industry jointly to formulate programs for exchanging information and/or for the taking of intermediate, technical steps—short of suspension of trading—that would be designed to provide market conditions as orderly as possible in a period of stress, even though they could not, of course, be expected to alter major market trends. The

[4] Exchange Act, Sec. 2(4).

Special Study is of the view that, whether or not such programs would ultimately be found practicable or desirable, the question is one deserving further exploration.[5] Any program of intermediate measures that might be evolved would presumably contemplate action to be taken primarily by the industry as distinguished from the Commission, which would remain essentially in the role of overseer of self-regulatory action.

It would be unrealistic and indeed illusory to believe that the narrow and technical powers possessed by the Commission itself could ever prevent basic price changes. The Commission's role is primarily regulatory, not economic. Traditionally and consistently, it has exercised its powers in such manner as to avoid dealing with price levels or permitting any misconception that it was dealing with price levels. Nothing in this chapter is intended to suggest a change in this role in the direction of "managing" price movements or purposefully affecting prices.

The NYSE is already endeavoring to develop improved equipment which should greatly ameliorate the problems arising from tape lateness. The implementation of various specific recommendations made elsewhere in the report, in part upon the basis of data relating to the market break, with respect to such matters as short selling, the capital position of specialists, floor trading and odd-lot transactions, should also tend to improve the ability of Exchange mechanisms to function more effectively in times of stress. The study being made by the division of trading and exchanges with respect to stop orders should contribute to this effort.

The Special Study concludes and recommends:

Neither the Study nor the NYSE has been able to ascertain the precipitating "causes" of the May, 1962, market break. However, analysis of disaggregated market data has permitted identification of certain specific factors in the operation of market mechanisms that may have accentuated its severity. At most, any measures that might be taken with reference to

---

[5] After war was declared in September, 1939, lines of direct communication to important sources of information in the financial community were established and liaison with the national securities exchanges was developed:

"Through its machinery for gathering as much information as possible, it kept constant scrutiny over the volume and trend of orders as they came into the leading brokerage offices before those orders reached the floor. Each morning before the markets opened the Commission and its experts were in contact with its sources of information to find out the character and size of the brokerage orders which had accumulated overnight. It kept track of the effect of market changes upon margin accounts. It received current reports on the size of short positions and the condition of the books of the specialists in various leading stocks on the floors of the various exchanges. It was able, in cooperation with the New York Stock Exchange, the Treasury, and certain houses specializing in foreign dealings, to judge the trend and volume of foreign transactions." S.E.C., *6th Annual Report* (1940), p. 89.

Similar steps were taken on later occasions such as at the time of President Eisenhower's heart attack.

such factors could only be addressed to ameliorating their impact. The Commission's role is to promote an orderly market and not to affect fundamental economic forces or price trends. The following recommendation must be viewed in this context.

The Commission and representatives of the industry, particularly the exchanges, should make a joint study of possible intermediate measures, short of suspending trading, that might be invoked to assure minimum disruption of the fair and orderly functioning of the securities markets in times of severe market stress. While the Special Study has not undertaken to evaluate the possibilities, the types of intermediate measures to be considered might include such things as limitations on short selling (see Ch. VI.H, recommendation (3), special provisions in respect of the handling of stop-sell orders or market-sell orders, and temporary interruption of trading in individual securities under predefined circumstances. It is possible that the implications of such actions could be tested in advance through the use of simulation techniques on a computer. There should also be Commission-industry consultation with a view to collecting certain crucial types of trading information that might be helpful in connection with possible application of any of such intermediate measures or that might be useful in times of market stress to other governmental agencies having wider economic responsibilities.

Index of Authors*

*Page numbers in boldface indicate cross-references to articles included in the book.